A LONGMAN PAPERBACK

CRISIS AND COMPROMISE

By Philip Williams
Politics in Post-War France
The French Parliament 1958-67
Wars, Plots and Scandals in Post-War France

By Philip Williams and Martin Harrison
De Gaulle's Republic

CRISIS AND COMPROMISE

Politics in the Fourth Republic

by

PHILIP M. WILLIAMS

LONGMAN

Longman Group Limited
London

Associated companies, branches and
representatives throughout the world

First published 1954 under the title
Politics in Post-War France

Third edition 1964 under the title
Crisis and Compromise

This paperback edition first published 1972

ISBN 0 582 11102 1

PRINTED AND BOUND IN ENGLAND BY
HAZELL WATSON AND VINEY LTD
AYLESBURY, BUCKS

PREFACE

This book has a large but limited theme: the political machinery of the Fourth Republic and the combinations of men who operated or obstructed it. It describes each of the principal parties and political institutions of the regime, and analyses its working as a system. But it does not attempt to recount the history of the period, or to discuss problems of policy except where this is necessary to explain their impact on institutions or parties. As it stops in 1958, the old title, *Politics in Post-War France*, is no longer appropriate.

To deal with the sweeping changes of the Fourth Republic's last five years, the book has been entirely recast. Of the thirty-one chapters eleven are quite new, and all but three of the rest have been completely rewritten. For when the first edition was completed ten years ago, France was at war in Indo-China and at peace in Algeria. Tunisia, Morocco, Madagascar and much of Western and Equatorial Africa were still ruled from Paris. The future of western European union seemed to depend on the fate of the European Defence Community, and most Frenchmen bitterly regretted Britain's absence from that project. At home, industrial production lagged at the 1929 level: the French economic miracle lay ahead. With Gaullism in ruins and Poujadism not yet born, the political system seemed secure. Neither Pierre Mendès-France nor Guy Mollet had attained the premiership. The Algerian war had not begun its stealthy encroachment on the freedom of minorities: opposition newspapers were not yet confiscated by the government, meetings were not broken up, internment camps for suspected terrorists had not been established, and though the officer corps might grumble at its political masters it did not dream of challenging their authority.

Some old material has been omitted to make room for the new developments, and in some respects I have changed my mind. In 1953 I seriously overestimated the stability of a regime which had yet to face a political and emotional challenge as grave as the Irish question in Britain, or the problem of the South in the United States. It may be that different governmental actions and policies could have saved the Fourth Republic, and an attentive reader of both editions would find my views on some leaders, groups and practices more severe than they used to be. But I am inclined to doubt whether France could have accomplished her disengagement from North Africa without the sacrifice of at least one Republic at home (in the end it very nearly cost her two). General de Gaulle, who had the immense advantage of coming to power as the nation's last resort, used it skilfully to settle a problem before which his predecessors had been impotent – yet, with far greater prestige and a far freer hand than they, he often had to employ similar expedients. The frequency with which undesirable practices of the old regime were taken over by the new shows that they often arose from the difficulties of the situation as well as weaknesses of the leaders' characters or faults in the constitution. In pointing this out from time to time I do not necessarily condemn the Fifth Republic, which has had even more difficult situations to confront.

To keep this work within manageable dimensions, many important and interesting subjects have had to be omitted. Administration, justice and 'France overseas' fall within its scope only where they impinged on domestic politics. The social and philosophical background is not treated; revealing episodes such as the worker-priest movement, or the protest against the Rosenberg executions, find no place; and even the influence of press and army, trade unions and universities is touched on only briefly. In my approach, though I have tried to appreciate all points of view about French affairs, I have found it neither possible nor desirable to avoid acquiring preferences and prejudices. While the British academic tradition in writing about politics is one of complete detachment, the French (even in their state-controlled universities) are less concerned to avoid the appearance of taking sides. There is much to be said for both approaches; there is nothing to be said for professing one and practising the other. Bias is dangerous only when it is concealed – or unconscious. The reader is therefore entitled to know my political standpoint, which is that of the moderate wing of the Labour party.

The title, part of Chapter 28 and much of Chapter 29 are adapted from an article of mine which appeared in the *Political Science Quarterly* in 1957. I am grateful to the publishers for permission to use this material.

My principal debt of gratitude is to the Warden and Fellows of Nuffield College, Oxford, for making it possible for this book to be written and later rewritten, and for much stimulus and encouragement in the process. I am grateful for valuable advice and comment to Saul Rose and Francis de Tarr, who read Chapter 7 and Chapter 9; to those who read all or large parts of the manuscript: Malcolm Anderson, Ian Campbell, Bernard Donoughue, François Goguel, Martin Harrison, Serge Hurtig, David Shapiro and Nicholas Wahl; and especially to David Goldey and Anthony King, who read the proofs as well. Jean Brotherhood was not merely a paragon among secretaries (not least in patience) but helped invaluably with the index. It is impossible to name all, and would be invidious to mention only a few of the academic, political, official and journalistic friends in France without whom this book would never have been written; but I must particularly thank Jean Touchard and his colleagues of the *Fondation nationale des sciences politiques* for their help and friendship over many years. None of these, of course, has any responsibility for the views I have expressed or the errors I have committed.

CONTENTS

CONTENTS

MAPS

BIBLIOGRAPHY

APPENDIX

DIAGRAMS

ABBREVIATIONS

I. *French Parties*

(*with a separate group in the National Assembly; III – Third Republic only; V – Fifth Republic only.)

*ARS	Action républicaine et sociale
*CNI, CNIP	Centre national des indépendants (et paysans)
*IOM	Indépendants d'outre-mer
JR	Jeune République
MLP	Mouvement pour la libération du peuple
*MRP	Mouvement républicain populaire
*MTLD	Mouvement du triomphe des libertés démocratiques (Algerian)
PDP	Parti démocrate populaire (III)
PPF	Parti populaire français (III)
*PRA	Parti du regroupement africain
*PRL	Parti républicain de la Liberté
PSA	Parti socialiste autonome (V)
PSF	Parti social français (III)
PSU	Parti socialiste unifié (V)
*RDA	Rassemblement démocratique africain
*RGR	Rassemblement des Gauches républicaines
RGRIF	Rassemblement des groupes républicains et indépendants français (1951 and 1956 elections)
RN	Rassemblement national (1956 election)
*RPF	Rassemblement du peuple français (Gaullists)
*RS	Républicains sociaux (Gaullists)
*SFIO	Section française de l'Internationale ouvrière (official title of the Socialist party)
*UDI	Union démocratique des indépendants
*UDMA	Union démocratique du Manifeste algérien
*UDSR	Union democratique et socialiste de la Résistance
UDT	Union démocratique du travail (V)
UFD	Union des forces démocratiques (V)
*UFF	Union et fraternité française (Poujadist deputies)
UGS	Union de la Gauche socialiste
UNIR	Union des nationaux et des indépendants républicains (1951 election)
*UNR	Union pour la nouvelle République (V)

II. *Other Organizations*

ACJF	Association catholique de la jeunesse française
APEL	Association des parents des élèves de l'enseignement libre
APLE	Association parlementaire pour la liberté de l'enseignement
CFTC	Confédération française des travailleurs chrétiens
CGA	Confédération générale de l'agriculture
CGC	Confédération générale des cadres
CGSI	Confédération générale des syndicats indépendants
CGT	Confédération générale du travail
CGT-FO	Confédération générale du travail – Force ouvrière
CGPME	Confédération générale des petites et moyennes entreprises
CGV	Confédération générale des viticulteurs
CNPF	Conseil national du patronat français
DST	Direction de la surveillance du territoire
EDC	European Defence Community
ENA	École nationale d'administration

II. *Other Organizations* (*continued*)

FLN	Front de Libération nationale (Algerian)
FNSEA	Fédération nationale des syndicats d'exploitants agricoles
FO	Force ouvrière
IGAME	Inspecteurs-généraux de l'administration en mission extraordinaire ('super-prefects')
INSEE	(see Publications)
JAC	Jeunesse agricole chrétienne
JOC	Jeunesse ouvrière chrétienne
NATO	North Atlantic Treaty Organization
OAS	Organisation de l'armée secrète (V)
PME	Petites et moyennes entreprises
SDECE	Section de documentation extérieure et de contre-espionnage
SEATO	South-East Asia Treaty Organization
UDCA	Union de défense des commerçants et des artisans (Poujadists)

III. *Publications*

AN, Doc. no. ...	Documents published by the National Assembly
AP	*L'Année politique*, published annually from 1944–45 by Éditions du grand siècle, from 1957 by Presses universitaires françaises
APSR	*American Political Science Review*
BC	*Bulletin des Commissions* (published by the National Assembly)
BCE	*Bulletin du Conseil économique*
INSEE	Institut national de statistiques et d'études économiques
JO	*Journal Officiel de la République française*. Unless otherwise stated the series referred to is that of *Débats parlementaires* either of the Constituent or of the National Assembly according to the date. The date shown is that of the debate, not that of publication.
JO(ACE)	*Journal Officiel ... Avis et rapports du Conseil économique.*
JO(AUF)	*Journal Officiel ... Débats de l'Assemblée de l'Union française*
JO(CR)	*Journal Officiel ... Débats parlementaires, Conseil de la République*
JP	*Journal of Politics*
P. Adm.	*Public Administration*
P. Aff.	*Parliamentary Affairs*
PS	*Political Studies*
RDP	*Revue du droit public et de la science politique*
RFSP	*Revue française de science politique*
RPP	*Revue politique et parlementaire*
SCC I	*Séances de la commission de la constitution, comptes rendus analytiques* (First Constituent Assembly)
SCC II	*Séances* ..., etc. (Second Constituent Assembly)
TM	*Temps modernes*
WPQ	*Western Political Quarterly*

PRINCIPAL DATES

	GOVERNMENT	DOMESTIC
'44	*June* De Gaulle: Bidault, Foreign	*Aug.* Paris liberated
		Oct. Resistance militia dissolved
'45		
	Apr. Mendès-F. resigns	
		Oct. referendum; *election*; 3 big parties
'46	*Jan.* Gouin, Soc.: *Tripartisme*	*Mar.–May* nationalizations, social security
		May referendum, 53 % *non*
		June *election*, Socs. lose
	June Bidault, MRP: Socs. lose Finance	*June* De Gaulle's Bayeux speech
		Sep. Mollet leader of Soc. Party
		Oct. referendum, 53 % *oui*
		Nov. *election*, Socs. lose
	Dec. Blum: all-Soc. government	*Nov.* Monnet Plan agreed to
'47	*Jan.* Ramadier, Soc.	*Jan.* Auriol (Soc.) elected President
	May Communists out	*Apr.* De Gaulle founds RPF
		Oct. RPF win municipal elections
	Nov. Schuman, MRP: Moch, Interior	*Nov.* Communist-led strikes;
		Nov. CGT split
'48		
		May Poinso-Chapuis decree
	July Marie, Rad.: Schuman, Foreign	*July* Duchet founds CNIP
		Oct.–Nov. Communist coal strike
		Nov. New upper house: no RPF maj.
'49		
	Oct. Bidault, MRP	
'50	*Feb.* Socs. out, lose Interior	*Jan.* 'Scandal of the Generals'
	July Pleven, UDSR; Socs. back	
'51	*Mar.* Queuille, Rad.	*June* *election*, 120 RPF
	Aug. Pleven; Socs. out	*Sep.* *Loi Barangé* (church schools)
'52	*Jan.* Faure, Rad.	*Mar.* RPF splits in NA on Pinay
	Mar. Pinay, Cons.	*May* last big Comm. demonstrations
'53	*Jan.* Mayer, Rad. Bidault, Foreign	
	May 5-week crisis	*May* De Gaulle ends RPF (as party)
	July Laniel, Cons.: Gaullists in	*July* 1st Pouj. agitation; *Aug.*, big strikes
		Dec. Coty (Cons.) elected President
'54		
	June Mendès-F.: MRP out, lose Foreign	
		Sep. 'Scandal of the leakages'
		Nov. Constitution amended
'55	*Feb.* Faure, Rad.: MRP back	*Mar.* Poujadist pressure on NA
		May Mendès-F. leads Rad. Party
		Dec. NA dissolved, *election* Jan. 2
'56	*Jan.* Mollet, Soc.: MRP out	*Jan.* Left gains, but 50 Poujadists
	Feb. Lacoste M. for Algeria	*Spring* 11 Poujadists unseated
	May Mendès-F. resigns	*Spring* 'leakages trial'
		Oct. Rad. Party split
'57		
	May Govt. falls	*May* Mendès-F. loses Rad. Party
	June Bourgès-M, Rad.	*July* NA accepts internment camps
	Oct. 5-week crisis	
	Nov. Gaillard, Rad.: MRP, Cons. back	*Nov.* Gaullist propaganda campaign
'58		*Mar.* Constitutional reform fails
	Apr. 3rd crisis in a year	
	May 14th Pflimlin, MRP; Socs. join	
		May 24th Gaullists seize Corsica
	June De Gaulle; all but Comms. in	*June* NA allows govt. to draft const.
		Sep. referendum, 85 % *oui; Nov. election*

PRINCIPAL DATES

Imperial		Foreign		
				'44
		Dec.	Franco-Soviet treaty	
		Feb.	Yalta conference ends	'45
May	Algerian outbreak repressed	*May*	European war ends	
				'46
Nov.	Haiphong bombarded			
Dec.	Indo-China war begins			
Mar.	Madagascar revolt			'47
		Apr.	Moscow conference fails	
Aug.	Algerian government bill	*June*	Marshall Aid offered	
		Feb.	Communist coup in Prague	'48
Apr.	Algerian 'elections'	*Mar.*	Berlin blockade begins	
		July	NA ratifies Atlantic Pact	'49
		Dec.	Communists win in China	
		May	Schuman Plan (Coal and Steel)	'50
June	Tunis negotiations open	*June*	Korean war begins	
Oct.	Indo-China frontier posts lost			
				'51
Dec.	Tunis talks broken off	*Dec.*	NA ratifies Schuman Plan	
				'52
Mar.	Tunis repression, ministers arrested	*May*	EDC treaty signed	
				'53
Aug.	Sultan of Morocco deposed			
May	Dien-Bien-Phu falls			'54
July	Indo-China peace			
July 31st	Tunis negotiations	*Aug.*	NA defeats EDC	
Nov.	Algerian war begins	*Dec.*	NA accepts German rearmament	
Jan.	Soustelle Gov-Gen. Algeria			'55
July	NA ratifies Tunisian treaty			
Aug.	Outbreaks in Morocco, Algeria			
Nov.	Sultan returns to Morocco			
	ALGERIA, ETC.			'56
Feb. 6th	Europeans riot			
June	Bombs in Algiers. *Loi-cadre* for Black Africa			
Oct.	Ben Bella 'kidnapped'	*Nov.*	Suez war; Budapest repression	
Jan.	Massu i/c police; bazooka fired at Salan			'57
		July	NA ratifies Common Market	
Sep.	NA defeats Algerian *loi-cadre*			
Nov.	GB, US sell arms to Tunisia			
Feb.	Sakiet (Tunisia) bombed	*Feb.*	GB, US offer 'good offices'	'58
Apr.	NA rejects 'good offices'			
May 13th	European riot, C. of Pub. Safety			
May	Parachutist threat to Paris			
July	De Gaulle appeases Tunisia			

PART I

THE BACKGROUND

Chapter 1

THE BASIS OF FRENCH POLITICS

1. FRANCE AND BRITAIN: THE BACKGROUND

The British have never had much respect for the political capacity of their nearest neighbour. Official and ministerial circles too often share the general impression that the French are incapable of governing themselves properly, or even of managing a democratic system at all. There is little understanding of the deep differences between the British and the French outlook on politics, or of the fundamental reasons for these differences. The faults in the political structure of France are the result of her historical and geographical background. No country can rid itself of its past.

In the first place the Reformation failed on the other side of the Channel. The Catholic Church is active and powerful, retains the allegiance of a substantial proportion of the population, and is therefore, as in all Catholic countries, a focus of political controversy. Education remained an explosive problem for half a century longer than in Britain; and the conflict was always more bitter because the issues were more clear-cut. As Bodley once put it, the group structure characteristic of French politics was reproduced in Britain in the religious sphere – and the clear and straightforward British party system was paralleled in France by the struggle between clericals and anticlericals.[1]

Secondly, the form of the state is still open to attack. Frenchmen are used to changes not merely of government but of the whole political regime. In 170 years they have had fifteen new constitutions. The British practice of revolutionizing the reality while retaining the name and the façade was reversed in France: there the fundamentals of life continued with comparatively little change over large regions of the country, while the political surface was always turbulent. The stability and resilience of French life below that surface were unfortunately less striking than the apparent chaos at the top. The well-known story of the Paris bookseller regretting that he could not supply a copy of the constitution 'because we do not deal in periodical literature' dates from 1848; its modern counterpart could be seen in the huge posters in the Metro just a century later – 'Republics pass: Soudée paint lasts'. The Fourth Republic was then two years old and had ten more to live.

Thirdly, though the political form of the state may be open to question and change, its administrative structure has stood without fundamental alteration since the reforms of Napoleon. It is a tightly centralized system, based on a uniform pattern and closely controlled from Paris. The police, who enjoy much more power than in Britain, are directly subject to the ministry of the interior. A centralized administrative and police system is reinforced by a centralized judicial organization under the ministry of justice, and protected

1. Bodley, *France*, i. 138; ii. 457. Information on the date and place of publication of books is given at the first reference when the author is cited in one chapter only, in the bibliography on p. 465 when he is cited in more than one. Articles are cited in the footnotes by number only, as listed on pp. 470–7.

by an army much stronger than the British – for France has three land frontiers. The seizure of power is greatly simplified where in the words of Deschanel, 'We have the Republic on top and the Empire underneath.'[2]

The Frenchman's approach to the problem of authority is consequently shaped by three crucial experiences: a political struggle waged with sectarian bitterness and sparing few sectors of the country's organized life; a recent memory of governments abusing their authority to maintain their position; and an immensely powerful administrative machine providing a standing temptation to abuse. There is a latent totalitarianism in the French attitude to politics which makes French democrats fear the power of government, and expect from it more danger than advantage.

These historical factors were reinforced by geographic, demographic and economic ones. Uncertainty about the future was engendered by a stationary population and an invasion in every generation; it provided fertile soil for defeatism and disillusionment. Above all, France remained until 1940 a country of small enterprise. Agriculture was far more important than in Britain: in 1946 France still had one industrial worker for every agricultural worker, while Britain had nine. Small towns and small industry predominated: there were sixty-one towns with a population of 100,000 in Britain, only twenty-two in France. Almost half the population still lived in agricultural communities. Where in Britain the small farm was destroyed by enclosures and the small business subjected to the full force of competition, in France they not only survived but were protected economically, courted politically and glorified ideologically.[3]

France was not naturally a wealthy country. Her early efforts at industrialization failed, prejudicing Frenchmen for generations against capitalist progress and its consequence, the ruin of the unsuccessful. Business families often valued security and stability far more than risky expansion on borrowed money which might endanger their control of their firms. Until the Fourth Republic the ruling economic outlook was 'Malthusian': a conviction that the market was fixed and one trader's gain meant another's loss, a preference for high profit on a low turnover, and a willingness to mitigate competition sufficiently to keep the weaker firms afloat. Almost everyone worshipped the cult of the 'little man'; no adjective was more favoured in election speeches and newspaper titles than *petit*.[4] Social stability was prized above economic progress, and the politician who sought votes in good times or feared revolution in bad ones used laws, taxes and tariffs to protect the weak – and so hamper the strong. In Britain free trade was a Liberal policy and almost a Liberal

2. See Index for brief biographical notes on persons named. The Vichy regime has indeed been called 'nothing but this sovereign state apparatus ... deprived of its democratic and republican façade': Lüthy, *The State of France*, p. 38.

3. Of a working population of 20,500,000, there were 9,100,000 who lived in rural communes where over 20% worked in agriculture: *Bulletin mensuel de statistique*, October 1952, p. 44. Britain, the United States, Germany, Italy and the Netherlands had all become urbanized far sooner and more thoroughly: see the striking diagram in Morazé, *Les Français et la République*, p. 217; and for later figures, below, n. 32. Cf. Goguel in *Aspects de la société française* (henceforth cited as *Aspects*), pp. 248–50.

4. Lüthy, pp. 287, 332; Siegfried, *Tableau des partis en France*, p. 90 – translated as *France: A Study in Nationality*, pp. 42–3; Siegfried, *De la IIIe à la IVe République*, p. 25; Thibaudet, *La République des professeurs*, pp. 259–60.

religion, but in France it was the work of an autocrat, Napoleon III, and it did not long survive the advent of the Third Republic.[5]

The principle that the state should not interfere with the economy was thus accepted in theory by both countries but applied very differently in practice. One result was that in France business success was suspect, since it was assumed (not always wrongly) to be due to political favours.[6] From the state, it was thought, came improper privileges for the powerful and very proper protection for the weak. 'A subject rather than a citizen, the rural Frenchman continues to expect his sustenance from his suzerain.'[7] Progress was resisted because it meant sacrifices for some; and the resistance was effective enough to bring about long periods of decline – until these in turn provoked discontent and revolution. France had achieved her economic and social (and therefore political) equilibrium not by integrating the conflicting forces into a society which all accepted but by bringing them into a condition of mutual stalemate.[8]

2. FRANCE AND BRITAIN: POLITICAL ATTITUDES

Differences so deep-rooted explain why few of the political terms and axioms of British politics applied across the Channel. Words like 'Right' and 'Left' had quite different connotations in the two countries. For in France three issues were fought out simultaneously: the eighteenth-century conflict between rationalism and Catholicism, the nineteenth-century struggle of democracy against authoritarian government, and the twentieth-century dispute between employer and employed. On the Continent, Right and Left defined positions in relation to the philosophical and political struggles, which turned in normal times on educational policy and in crises on the structure of the regime; the social contest over the distribution of the national income provided a new topic of division, already foreshadowed in the Revolution, which after 1848 cut the political Left in two.

Thus, where Britain had two major political attitudes, France never had fewer than three. The clerical and conservative Right was opposed by a socialist Left (itself, since the rise of the Communist party, internally divided by the deepest fissure of all). But between these rivals was a great amorphous mass of peasants and small businessmen, who were social and economic conservatives yet ardent Republicans and anticlericals. As they owed their position to the Revolution it was indeed the heritage of revolution that they

5. On these two paragraphs and the next see Morazé, pp. 46–7, 56–61, 69–72, 116–18, 199–206; Siegfried, *France*, pp. 15–17, 21–3, 113–14, and *Tableau*, pp. 32–7, 44–8, 232–4; Lüthy, pp. 179–180, 286–334 (especially 311–13, 320–3); Maillaud, *France*, Chapter 6; Tannenbaum, *The New France*, Chapter 3; Fauvet, *La France déchirée*, pp. 29–30, translated as *The Cockpit of France*, pp. 33–5; Earle, ed., *Modern France*, particularly Chapters 4 (by J. B. Christopher), 17 (by J. E. Sawyer) and 19 (by D. S. Landes); Landes, article no. 135 (see Bibliography on pp. 470–7), pp. 329–50. For an instance of opposition to modernization, Chevallier, *Les Paysans*, pp. 141–56, 169–79; for the political preponderance of the small independent business and professional man, Priouret, *La République des députés*, pp. 180–7, 215–18; for qualifications to the thesis of French economic stagnation, Raymond Aron, *France Steadfast and Changing*, pp. 45–8, 53–64, 141–3.

6. Lüthy, pp. 25–6; Priouret, *Députés*, pp. 138–42; Morazé, p. 73; E. Beau de Loménie, *Les responsabilités des dynasties bourgeoises* (4 v., 1943, 1947, 1954, 1963), *passim*.

7. Morazé, p. 202 (cf. p. 61 on other classes).

8. The Third Republic has been called 'the stalemate society'; Hoffmann in *France: Change and Tradition* (henceforth cited as *Change*), p. 3, and in no. 126, p. 29. Cf. Aron, *Steadfast*, p. 135.

were determined to conserve. This was the basic source of the curious contradiction between their words and their deeds: revolutionary language in the political field, conservative actions in the social. Best represented by the Radical party, they dominated French politics between 1900 and 1940.[9]

Since Left and Right divided on issues other than those predominant in Britain, it is not surprising that they had a different electoral basis. The equation between industry and the Left, agriculture and the Right was largely invalid in France. The agrarian Midi was the stronghold of the Left, industrial Lorraine voted Right. When the Socialists first became an important party in the election of 1893, their highest percentage of votes in the provinces was in the agricultural Cher department.[10] In June 1951 the Communist vote exceeded 40% in three constituencies – one in the Paris suburbs and two in the rural centre, Creuse and Corrèze. The reputation of the Right as more nationalist and more concerned with defence than the Left, even if undeserved, helped it to win the allegiance of the industrial departments on the eastern frontier.

This persistence of old issues reflected the failure of the industrial workers to impose their own demands on politicians and the public. They failed partly through sheer lack of numbers, partly because the small scale of French industry and the individualism of its employees hampered their organization, and partly because governments were more responsive to the rural vote. The dominant groups of the Third Republic, the Radicals and their allies, drew their strength from the countryside and small towns where individualism flourished; they had little following in the urbanized regions where the economy was changing, the division between proletariat and bourgeoisie was sharpening, and a new and more highly organized type of politics was developing.

British and French attitudes towards government differed as profoundly as political behaviour or political terminology. Habits which remained powerful in France had been formed in an age when politics were a luxury remote from the realities of day-to-day life. There was no nineteenth-century tradition of independent local government to breed an attitude of responsibility. The country's governing personnel was recruited far more than in Britain from the professions and the intellectuals, and far less from businessmen, farmers, or workers; the more theoretical and unreal character of the issues was both cause and consequence of this situation.[11] For there was (and is) a curious blend of idealism and cynicism in the characteristic French attitude to political programmes – an idealism which attaches more importance to the symbolic value of a proposal than to its practical effect, a cynicism which

9. The Radicals have been called 'les conservateurs du musée révolutionnaire': **Hoffmann,** *Le Mouvement Poujade*, p. 384. The 'three-party' interpretation is also proposed by **Dupeux,** no. 80, pp. 332–4.

10. Bodley, ii. 465. Names of departments are shown in Map 21 on p. 461.

11. In France 'politics are the hobby of individuals, not the condition of their lives': R. de Jouvenel, *La République des camarades*, p. 4. At the turn of the century more than half the deputies were drawn from the professional classes, while only a fifth were dependent upon agriculture, industry or commerce – the occupations of five-sixths of the electorate: Bodley, ii. 157–63. Cf. Priouret, *Députés*, pp. 123–5, 145–6, 180–7; Lüthy, p. 24. For the Fourth Republic see below, p. 332.

remains unshakably confident that nothing will ever really be done. According to the influential Radical philosopher Alain, 'The true power of the voters should be defined, I believe, rather by resistance to the authorities than by reformist action. . . . The important thing is to construct every day a little barricade or, if you like, to bring each day some king before the court of the people.'[12]

This outlook could flourish in a country whose atomized, small-scale economy helped for decades to breed individualism, strong local loyalties, sharp regional differences, and a political psychology better adapted to resistance than to construction: and whose history was a source not of shared experiences but of bitter conflicts, in which each side had its own memories, its own anniversaries, its own symbols and its own martyrs. Marianne, who personified the regime, was to one vigorous group of enemies merely the hireling of the capitalists, to another the kept woman of the freemasons.[13] It was precisely because the centrifugal forces were so strong that the heirs of Rousseau uncompromisingly defended the Republic one and indivisible; they feared any geographical decentralization, any recognition of *corps intermédiaires* between state and individual which might allow their enemies on the Right or the Left to build up a La Rochelle, a Vendée or a Paris Commune as a bastion of separatism.

In a naturally fragmented and individualist society their doctrinaire antagonism to organized social groups helped powerfully to reinforce the peculiar French style of authority, which was characterized by a 'horror of face-to-face discussion'. Instead, problems were referred for settlement to a superior authority, the state, supposedly above the battle but inevitably remote, impersonal, arbitrary and suspect: *Them.* And many Frenchmen in turn reacted like 'draftees in a modern army, where the goals are to preserve one's individuality, evade the regulations wherever possible, and obtain special privileges, preferably on a permanent basis'. Here were the roots of the *incivisme* or lack of civic responsibility which made them regard the state as an enemy personified in the tax-collector and recruiting sergeant.[14]

Yet those two agents of the hostile state were regarded very differently. When conscription was politically unthinkable in Washington or Westminster, Frenchmen bore a crushing burden of military service. Thus *incivisme* was not exactly bad citizenship, but rather civic indiscipline (or individualism) in domestic affairs: where the British response to government was instinctively co-operative, the French was traditionally negative. This outlook was least attractive in economic matters, where reluctance to pay taxes was reinforced by suspicious peasant tight-fistedness. But the same contrariness protected the individual against oppression, inspired resistance to an occupying enemy, and produced movements of indignation and protest whenever authority was

12. Alain (Émile Chartier), *Élements d'une doctrine radicale* (4th ed., 1933, first pub. 1925), pp. 123–4. 'It is a good idea to talk of reforms, but imprudent to carry them out': quoted Siegfried, *Tableau,* p. 76 (*France*, p. 36).

13. The first act of the rioters who stormed Government House at Algiers on 13 May 1958 was to carry off her bust.

14. Crozier, no. 64, pp. 779–97 ('face-to-face'); Wylie, *Village in the Vaucluse*, pp. 206–10. 330–3 ('Them'); Tannenbaum, pp. 6–7 ('draftees'). Cf. Siegfried, *De la IIIe*, p. 254.

gravely abused. It gave rise to the conception of democracy summed up by Alain as *Le Citoyen contre les Pouvoirs*: 'the title of one of his books and the substance of all of them'.[15]

France, then, was a country without consensus. Internal divisions went deeper and the feeling of community was less widespread than in Britain. It was assumed that governments could never be trusted and must always be checked, since their aims were as questionable as their methods. Against a state regarded as 'not a referee but a player – and probably a dirty player', the Frenchman used his 'ancient secret weapon of anarchy' or the improved modern model, democratic institutions. It was not surprising that democracy, worked in this spirit, seemed to many Frenchmen incompatible with effective government. But the spirit itself was 'a reflex to political disorder' as well as a cause of its persistence.[16]

The constitution of the Fourth Republic was thus a characteristic symptom rather than a basic cause of the weakness of the French democratic state. Its imperfections of detail mattered not in themselves but because of the absence of a will to govern and accept government. Nor is it sufficient to complain that the French are too intellectual or too narrow-minded, too selfish or too utopian, too intransigent or too fond of *combinazioni*, to be capable of managing democratic institutions. The French, like the rest of us, are the prisoners of their past; and the outside observer must endeavour to follow Spinoza: 'Do not laugh, do not weep – try to understand.'

3. THE THIRD REPUBLIC

The Third Republic was established in 1875 by a majority of one vote in an Assembly dominated by monarchists who could not agree on a king. It never won the genuine allegiance of its opponents. In the *Ralliement* of the 1890's, the Catholic Church made its peace with the regime. But the Dreyfus case soon vividly showed that most Frenchmen of the Right still instinctively sympathized with the violent attacks on democracy launched by men like Charles Maurras. Maurras himself lived to become an outspoken apologist for the Vichy regime and to describe his sentence of life imprisonment at the Liberation as 'the revenge of Dreyfus'.

For though Great Britain has many conservatives (in all parties) who prefer to make progress slowly, it is happily free of real reactionaries. France is not. Men who condemned all that was done in the years following 1789 could not simply be dismissed as harmless cranks. Sixty years ago an English commentator observed that 'France is the land of political surprises, where lost causes come to life again.' Thirty years later the most acute of French political writers pointed out that every regime of the past retained its partisans, awaiting the opportunity to reassert their claims to power.[17] In 1940 the chance

15. Fauvet, *Cockpit*, p. 26. Cf. *ibid.*, p. 29, and *Déchirée*, pp. 22, 24–5; Siegfried, *De la IIIe*, p. 118; D. Thomson, *Democracy in France* (1st ed., 1946), pp. 14, 17; N. Wahl's analysis of the clash between the representative and the administrative traditions of government in *The Fifth Republic* (1959), pp. 24–30, and in Beer and Ulam, *Patterns of Government*, Part III.

16. I take the 'reflex' phrase from Professor H. W. Ehrmann's stimulating essay (no. 86), p. 11; the 'dirty player' from a broadcast by Professor D. W. Brogan; the 'secret weapon' from Lüthy, p. 128.

17. Bodley, ii. 352. Siegfried, *France*, pp. 96–7; *Tableau*, pp. 199–200; cf. *De la IIIe*, pp. 81, 85.

came, and a vast body of opinion rallied joyfully to the men of Vichy – not indeed to the Lavals and Déats, but to the men who felt, as Pétain allegedly once said, that 'France will never be great again until the wolves are howling round the doors of her villages.'

What was at stake in the French political struggle was thus more than specific issues of economic or educational or foreign policy. It was the framework within which these specific issues should be tackled. To Republicans the heritage of the Revolution meant political freedom, the responsibility of the rulers to the ruled; freedom of opportunity, the chance to rise to the top – and in practice a preference for rulers drawn from the under-privileged; freedom from clerical domination; freedom to own one's own land. The Right stood for authoritarian government, for the rule of the wealthy and respectable, for clericalism and landlordism. It is understandable that for electoral purposes it was essential to look and sound Left; indeed it became almost a recognized rule of French politics that a party added the word *Gauche* to its title at the moment when it contracted an alliance with the Right. In some areas candidates of the Right called themselves Independent Socialists. Just before the war the most conservative group in the Senate was named *Gauche républicaine*. Usually when a new parliamentary assembly was elected there was a noisy quarrel over the seating arrangements, the party allocated the benches on the right denouncing this monstrous misrepresentation of its position – as the Gaullists did in 1951 and the Poujadists in 1956.

In electoral campaigning the danger from the Right played the principal part, but in parliamentary conflict the Socialist pressure, which split the Republican majority, became more and more important during the present century. French politics came to focus on these two threats, from the Right against the Republic and from the Left against property. Their tone was therefore overwhelmingly defensive.[18] Moreover, as we have seen, the dominant section of opinion remained intensely suspicious of the power of the government even after capturing it. Two Napoleons had overthrown the Republic, two other generals (MacMahon and Boulanger) had threatened it; so Alain's ideal politician was Camille Pelletan, minister of marine from 1902 to 1905, who systematically disregarded his professional advisers. The results were unfortunate for the navy but (in Alain's view) advantageous for the regime: the leading Republican intellectual might have echoed the slogan of his great enemy Maurras – *Politique d'abord!* In 1906 this strange philosopher of a governmental party wrote:

> In France there are a great many radical electors, a certain number of radical deputies and a very small number of radical ministers: as for the heads of the civil service, they are all reactionaries. He who properly understands this has the key to our politics.[19]

Familiarity with office did not change the Radicals' outlook fundamentally. They continued to use their position to weaken the institutions of government and to thwart the progress of powerful personalities. In 1900 it had been observed that the Republicans 'use all the force of governmental machinery to

18. D. Thomson, *The Democratic Ideal in France and England* (1940), p. 59.
19. *Op. cit.*, p. 25. But cf. below, pp. 337, 343.

crush men of parts who seem apt to win popular favour'. In 1940 this attitude had not altered. The Left, alarmed at having produced Clemenceau in 1917, had made certain that he should have no successor. Promotion went to safe men of the type who had formed the Tiger's cabinet, and whom he had described as 'the geese who saved the Capitol'.[20]

The weakness of government was only partly due to this hostility to strong personalities. It was also the result of many institutional barriers which had been set up in the cabinet's path. The electoral system promoted political individualism. The constitution allowed the President with the consent of the Senate to dissolve the Chamber; but President MacMahon's dissolution for partisan purposes in 1877 so discredited this weapon that no successor ever dared make the attempt. Consequently the deputies knew they could count on four years before they would have to face the electors again, and felt free to overthrow ministries with impunity. Parliament's work was organized by committees of specialists which developed a point of view and a prestige of their own, and whose views the Chamber tended to follow. Since the leaders of the committees were almost *ex officio* potential ministers with an interest in replacing the incumbents, they tended to behave as critics rather than as allies. The President of the Chamber had far less authority than the Speaker of the House of Commons, and procedural rules left the ministry much weaker than in Britain: it had no control of parliamentary time, and devices like the interpellation seemed to have (and had) been invented for the express purpose of keeping the government subject to the domination of the deputies. Above all the Senate, a powerful and sober second chamber carefully insulated from the dangerous control of universal suffrage, stood guard to check any 'hasty' legislation or any over-presumptuous cabinet with which the Chamber failed to deal. The governmental system of the Third Republic was 'a machine so well provided with brakes and safety-valves that it comes slowly to a state of immobility'.[21]

Yet even these institutional devices were not the main difficulty. For the weakness of French government was due less to the number and potency of the brakes than to a deficiency of motive power. It was because there was no majority for action in the country that there was no pressure strong enough to overcome a resistance which found so many points of advantage in the constitutional framework. This became apparent at the turn of the century when the Radicals and their allies, including most of the Socialists, had an anticlerical programme to enact. They organized a steering committee, the *Délégation des Gauches*, which dominated the Chamber. Since a majority was ready to support its instructions, it could overcome the hostility of committees or interpellators without difficulty. For three years their leaders wielded an authority as great as that of a British government because there was for once a real political objective, capable of rallying a real majority.

20. Bodley, i. 328 ('men of parts'); Brogan's introduction to Werth, *The Twilight of France*, p. xvi (Clemenceau); J. Hampden Jackson, *Clemenceau and the Third Republic* (1946), p. 170 ('geese'). 'Only mediocrity was reassuring ... of all possible perils genius was the one from which the nation soon found itself most thoroughly preserved': H. de Jouvenel, *Pourquoi je suis syndicaliste* (1928), p. 20; cf. R. Binion, *Defeated Leaders* (New York, 1960), p. 137

21. Brogan, *loc. cit.*, p. vi.

But such a programme had to be political in the narrow sense. The industrial workers were neither numerous nor organized enough to attract similar support for their own demands. The small farmers and small businessmen feared and suspected the working class: they resisted reforms for its benefit at their own expense, they cherished an individualist type of society which powerful trade unions might threaten, and they valued economic efficiency less than social stability which enabled the least fortunate of them to maintain his independent existence and escape the ultimate disaster of proletarianization. The political pattern of the Third Republic was therefore clearly marked: at election times the two wings of the political Left united to defend the Republic, but once in power they divided over social and economic policy.[22] So Chambers as well as individual politicians regularly began their careers strongly inclined to the Left and ended them strongly inclined to the Right. It was even made a complaint against the Fourth Republic that this traditional evolution occurred less smoothly than in the past.

The basic reason for the weakness of French government was thus the contentedness of the dominant section of opinion. This middle block, Centre or even Right in British terminology but Left in the Continental sense, was wholly negative in outlook, equally opposed to clerical reaction and to socialist experiment, neither wanting nor expecting advantage from positive governmental policies. Its aim was to prevent action, of which it was almost sure to disapprove; its method was to keep the government too weak to embark on dangerous courses; and its principal instrument was the Senate, controlled by moderate Radicals – older men and less subject to electoral pressure than their colleagues in the Chamber – who ejected any ministry which leant too far towards either clericalism or socialism. This situation explained why governments changed so frequently and policies so little; as early as 1875, indeed, Laboulaye had described France as 'a tranquil country with agitated legislators'.[23]

For it was only in major crises that Right and Left confronted one another in battle array. Normally political decisions were taken not after a clear and intelligible clash between opposing sides, but as a result of quite minor shifts of view or emphasis within the centre groups which permanently predominated in power. The cautious, uncommitted, unstable floating vote, which in Britain was usually polarized by the two-party system, in France provided the leadership for almost every government. Since small changes at the fulcrum might upset the balance of power and bring great policy decisions, they were sometimes bitterly fought over and provoked big displacements of votes elsewhere.[24] But the legislators were equally agitated over shifts which had no such significance for policy, yet still raised some men up on the seesaw and cast others down. For superimposed on the battles over policy was another

22. See Siegfried, *France*, pp. 60–1 (*Tableau*, pp. 125–6), for one of many descriptions of this process. Cf. Priouret, *Députés*, pp. 177–8, 208–11, 219–20 (he points out that the first Republican social measure was the abolition of the Sunday rest day as a clerical survival).

23. Bodley, i. 57.

24. So of three Radical premiers elected in 1953, 1954 and 1955, one obtained 200 more left-wing votes in the Assembly than the other two. Morazé, p. 149; cf. pp. 23, 123, 132, 152, 218, 252–4.

contest for careers, office and power, which, as in eighteenth-century Britain, often seemed to approximate to the pure-game theory of politics.[25] Conducted according to elaborate unwritten rules in the 'house without windows' where the Chamber of Deputies sat, the game fascinated the closed circle of players but repelled their uncomprehending constituents. The people felt little more sense of participation in the government when it was representative than when it was authoritarian.

The gap between citizens and politicians had no grave immediate consequences before the 1930's. A comfortable majority of the electorate remained loyal to the regime and the centre politicians who defended it. In a fairly self-sufficient small-scale economy, politics had no day-to-day effect on the life of the ordinary voter, who could judge his deputy's behaviour by theoretical and doctrinaire standards. The type of question which excited politicians was whether the navy ought to celebrate Good Friday, or whether the army should supply guards of honour for civil as well as religious funerals.[26]

Below the parliamentary surface the country's need for government was met, as under the monarchy and empire, by the permanent bureaucracy (for the Radical distrust of the administration had the strange result that by constantly upsetting cabinets it allowed few ministers the time or authority to acquire real control of their departments, and so ensured that a long-term policy in any sector of government could normally originate only with the feared and suspected officials).[27] In times of great crisis the politicians suspended their game and the ideologists their crusade, and the country conferred on some respected leader – a Clemenceau or a Poincaré – an authority which was almost unlimited for a time. The needs of efficient government reasserted themselves briefly against those of representative control – to be thrust back into their subordinate place as soon as the emergency was over.

The Third Republic maintained this equilibrium for three generations, far longer than any previous regime since 1789. Politically the powers of government were concentrated in Paris, but its functions were narrowly limited and its abuses checked by a close parliamentary control in which, however, between elections the ordinary voter had no part to play. Socially, like that other stalemate society the Habsburg Empire, the regime contrived to keep the contending groups in a 'balanced state of mild dissatisfaction' which most of them found preferable to any serious alternative, even if in the Burkean partnership of the dead, the living and the yet unborn the French state seemed over-committed to those who were dead.[28]

But the structure was ill-adapted to shocks from outside, and it broke down when confronted with the economic and international crises of the thirties. When the financial and economic difficulties of the inter-war years called for measures that were electorally unpopular, no majority for them could be

25. Hoffmann in *Change*, p. 16, and no. 126, p. 31; Aron, *Steadfast*, p. 5.

26. Even in May 1951 urgent parliamentary business was delayed by the Socialists' insistence that since the Assembly was not to sit on Ascension Day it must not sit on Labour Day either.

27. Maillaud, p. 39; J. Barthélemy, *Le Gouvernement de la France* (1939 ed.), pp. 142–3; M. Augé-Laribé, *La politique agricole de la France* (1950), pp. 386–91 – referring respectively to foreign, educational and agricultural policy. Cf. Lüthy, p. 39.

28. Ehrmann, no. 86, p. 7.

found; the only solution that the deputies could devise was to hand over to the government special powers to legislate by decree. If democracy meant paralysis the capacity for action had to be restored by suspending democracy. The return to normal only underlined the lesson. From February 1930 to February 1934 the country had fourteen ministries. When the Germans entered the Rhineland France had a caretaker government awaiting a general election, and therefore too timid to call up reservists. When they marched into Austria, France was in a ministerial crisis. During the Munich episode there was a government but no parliament; Daladier, having been granted special powers, had sent the Chamber off on holiday. The defeat of 1940 did not kill the Third Republic, it merely drew attention to the fact that it was dead. 'The constitutional crisis that opened in the thirties is still awaiting its solution.'[29]

4. SOCIAL TRANSFORMATION

The changes which matured in the next generation have been described as the most far-reaching since 1789.[30] For the first time for over a century the birth-rate began to rise; the coming decade will see the impact of an abnormally large generation of impatient young adults upon the psychological, social and political outlook of their countrymen. The economy expanded far faster than the British or American. Both the changing age-structure and the economic advance brought problems as well as benefits, for large sectors and regions were still excluded from or even harmed by the process of modernization. But for the first time the predominant economic outlook was forward-looking and expansionist; 'the market is at last seen as growing instead of frozen'.[31] Progress, prosperity and rejuvenation cracked the crust of the old society at many points; horizons broadened and some barriers to communication and comprehension between Frenchmen were lowered if not eliminated. The new influence of youth weakened the hold of the old tightly-closed authoritarian family. Unprecedented numbers of students started to force a breach in that fortress of political radicalism and academic conservatism, the teaching profession – *l' Université*.

Though small businesses flourished for a time after the war, their numbers soon began to fall off. The proportion of the population engaged in agriculture dropped sharply.[32] Everywhere the family farm was in decline; everywhere the isolation of the village was diminishing, and indeed in some regions it was ceasing to be the main economic or even social centre as a result of the steady drift to the towns and the demand for better conditions and facilities in the countryside. Progress and expansion after a generation of inflation transformed the attitude to savings: there was less determination to hoard and more willingness to invest and risk. Even the tenacious class divisions were somewhat less bitter. The traditional owner gave way to the professional manager; much of the business community at last accepted the welfare state;

29. *Ibid.*, p. 10.
30. Hoffmann in *Change*, p. 60.
31. Hoffmann, no. 126, p. 62; cf. *Change*, pp. 63–4.
32. From 44% in 1906 to 36% in 1936, 27% in 1954 and under 25% in 1960: Tannenbaum, p. 12. Cf. Wahl, p. 25; Aron, *Steadfast*, pp. 52–3; Siegfried, *De la IIIe*, pp. 259–60. (Figures from INSEE.)

workers, though still feeling alienated from society in many ways, grew less savagely rebellious as they drew away from the poverty line; and between the sides in the class war the new technical and administrative cadres formed a buffer growing in size and importance.[33] The defeatism and depression of the pre-war years were replaced by a new vitality and self-confidence. At the same time, however, the country's relative power in the world had declined sharply: the more sharply because it had been artificially prolonged between the wars. Simultaneous progress at home and retreat abroad set up acute psychological strains.[34] In some areas adjustment was remarkably rapid, in others remarkably slow, but the price in both cases was a tension with explosive potentialities.

This new France which began to show itself in the middle 1950's was the result of changes which had begun twenty years before as dissatisfaction with the old 'stalemate society' became widespread. Greatly accelerated by the second world war, these changes were often encouraged and promoted – in fact if not always in intention – by Vichy and the Resistance alike.[35] Many representatives of groups which had been excluded from positions of influence in the Third Republic rose to power in the economy, society and government of post-war France. The newcomers were younger and more progressive than their predecessors, and the society they meant to modernize was less fragmented, less individualist, more willing for and responsive to organization than pre-war France had been. Yet the impulse for change came from above rather than from below, as it had done ever since the first Napoleon.

The new climate was visible first of all in the willingness to allow authority to men in their prime. Resistance organizations, writes Hoffmann, were 'dominated by young men who acceded to responsibilities which French youth had been deprived of since the days of the Revolution'.[36] No longer could the gibe be repeated that France was ruled by men of seventy-five because the octogenarians were dead: in 1952 she had her youngest prime minister for seventy years, and in the next six the new record was again broken twice. Five of the last ten governments of the Fourth Republic were led by men in their forties. Yet it was precisely in politics that the new generation made least impression. As one critic cruelly asked, 'What's the good of being young if you carry out the old men's policies?'[37]

The technocratic elements in business management and public administration (which in France are closely linked) composed another group which vastly improved its position, firstly through Vichy's industrial 'organization committees' which gave great power to the managers of the big firms, and later through the post-war planning machinery, nationalized industries, and

33. Priouret, *Députés*, pp. 240–52; Aron, *Steadfast*, pp. 57–60, 64–5; Tannenbaum, pp. 10–23; Fauvet, *Cockpit*, pp. 150–5, *Déchirée*, pp. 147–52. From 1953 to 1957 industrial production increased by 10% a year, and (1949 = 100) real wages rose from 118 to 145, production of household appliances from 202 to 562, of radios, television sets and gramophones from 166 to 513: INSEE figures quoted Wahl, p. 21, cf. Aron, p. 65. Farm tractors were 56,000 in 1946, 211,000 in 1953 and 628,000 in 1959: INSEE figures, more fully in *Change*, p. 418.

34. Wahl, pp. 20–3; Aron, *Steadfast*, pp. 146–50.

35. This is one theme of Professor Hoffmann's chapter in *Change*, to which this section owes a great deal. Cf. also Priouret, *Députés*, pp. 229–31.

36. *Change*, p. 36; no. 126, p. 46.

37. Pierre Cot, *JO* 5 November 1957, p. 1350.

expanding private businesses.[38] Thibaudet had listed the Saint-Simonian devotion to industrial progress as one of the half-dozen important political attitudes in France; now 'the Saint-Simonian tradition was no longer underground'.[39] The ascendancy of Jean Monnet and his planning staff, says Professor Ehrmann, 'provides an excellent example of a highly intense minority which overrode, at the price of ceaseless efforts, the traditional values and preferences of a relatively indifferent majority'.[40]

The Liberation gave them an exceptional opportunity of which they took full advantage: business was unpopular, scared, and anxious to redeem by co-operation its rather murky wartime record, while under Communist leadership the working class, sharing briefly in power almost for the first time, was also willing to co-operate in laying economic foundations for the overdue social reforms it demanded. After that first favourable moment, however, the planners could not have maintained the momentum without exploiting other assets: Marshall Aid; effective planning instruments for influencing the supply of credit and the direction of investment; a large nationalized sector; above all, despite the 'relatively indifferent majority', the goodwill of their contemporaries in business and the administration and of most of the holders of political power.[41] Their success was to widen still further the gap between those economic sectors and geographic regions which were willing and able to adapt and those which refused and revolted: between 'modern France' and the 'static France' which uttered in Poujadism its strident protest against the incomprehensible injustices of the new world.[42]

The devout Catholics, who had normally been excluded from power in the Third Republic, formed another group which was promoted by both Vichy and the Resistance. Their party, the *Mouvement républicain populaire* (MRP), belonged to the majority for all but seven and to the government for all but thirty months of the fourteen-year period from the Liberation to the fall of the Fourth Republic. They were convinced if cautious advocates of social reform, economic modernization and accommodation to France's new position in Europe (though over colonial matters they were less enlightened). In post-war journalism, in administration, in party politics and in the public life of rural France, active Catholics played a far more prominent part in the Fourth Republic than under its predecessor. No longer, therefore, was it unquestioned republican orthodoxy to condemn social pluralism and group organization

38. Hoffmann in *Change*, pp. 39–42, 53–4; in n. 30 he points out that de Gaulle's first finance minister had been chairman of Vichy's organization committee for coal-mines; cf. no. 126, pp. 40–43, 48–9; no. 127, pp. 47, 56–7, 63–4, 68–9; Priouret, *Députés*, pp. 229–30. On the organization committees see also Ehrmann, *Organized Business in France*, Chapter 2; Pickles, *France Between the Republics*, pp. 37–8, 210.

39. Hoffmann in *Change*, p. 40; Thibaudet, *Les idées politiques de la France*, Chapter 3. Even Vichy contributed to the Saint-Simonian revival, for Pétain's own pastoral ideology was by no means shared by ministers like Pucheu and Bichelonne: Hoffmann in *Change*, p. 42, nos. 126–7, *loc. cit.*; Ehrmann, *Business*, pp. 63, 68–76.

40. Ehrmann, no. 86, p. 16; cf. Lüthy, pp. 288–97.

41. See below, pp. 337, 343; on the machinery, Wilson, *French Banking Structure and Credit Policy*.

42. Goguel, *France under the Fourth Republic*, pp. 141–6; Lüthy, pp. 287–91, 301–15, 430–1, 453–4; Priouret, *Députés*, pp. 249–58; Fauvet, *Cockpit*, pp. 97–100, *Déchirée*, pp. 90–3; Hamon, no. 120, pp. 841–5; and below, Chapter 12.

and to oppose any *corps intermédiaires* screening the state from the individual citizen.

The proliferation of new organizations in a once atomized and individualist society was indeed among the most significant of the new developments. Again the war played an important part. Vichy with its corporative state doctrine threw up new bodies from which grew the main post-war organizations of business (the *Conseil national du patronat français*, CNPF), of the peasantry (the *Fédération nationale des syndicats d'exploitants agricoles*, FNSEA), and of several leading professions – and in some cases also discovered their post-war leadership.[43] The fragmentation of the country into several sealed-off zones concentrated attention on the interdependence of different parts of France, and stimulated willingness to plan on a national rather than a local or regional scale;[44] before long the planners and the progressive businessmen were to find France itself too small a unit for the developments they wanted to encourage. The reforms of the Liberation marked an irreversible expansion of the state's economic and social activities, by nationalization, planning and social welfare measures[45] (though generous family allowances and retirement pensions – and subsidies for church schools – all date back to 1939 and 1940). Politically, the large constituencies adopted at the Liberation as a framework for proportional representation did, despite the many drawbacks of that system, help to widen the limited horizon of the local politician. And the personnel of Parliament was a little less cut off from the country's economic life than before. The Gaullists recruited many managers, engineers and industrialists, and the Socialists (and even MRP) allowed more influence to trade unionists than the governing parties of the Third Republic had ever given them.

These changes, however, did little or nothing to solve the problem of a political authority which still appeared as remote, as impersonal and as arbitrary as ever. There were a number of useful and important administrative measures taken to strengthen the machinery of the state, but the changes designed to harness popular political energies proved a total disappointment. The Fourth Republic did no more than the Third (or the Fifth) to encourage genuine political participation. Assiduously though the deputy might cultivate his constituents, they continued to regard him not as an agent for the enactment of policies they had had a hand in deciding but as a local ambassador, or rather consul, performing services and seeking benefits from a foreign body over whose inexplicable whims they had no control. How could it be otherwise when the result of general elections bore no visible relationship to the composition of governments, which still seemed to be arbitrarily made

43. Hoffmann in *Change*, pp. 38–9, no. 126, pp. 40–1; Ehrmann, *Business*, pp. 67, 79, 81n., 115, etc.; Lüthy, p. 288; Fauvet and Mendras, eds., *Les paysans et la politique* (henceforth cited as *Paysans*), pp. 235, 289–90. The trend had begun earlier: cf. Tannenbaum, p. 9; Sharp, *The Government of the French Republic*, pp. 88–9. These bodies were of course always centres of pressure-group activity and sometimes of resistance to modernization; but even the arch-conservative *Petites et moyennes entreprises* (PME) proved such a two-way transmitter between the government and the membership that the latter revolted to follow Poujade.

44. Hoffmann in *Change*, p. 40; no. 126, p. 43.

45. Priouret, *Députés*, pp. 230–1, 238–9; Aron, *Steadfast*, pp. 61–2: social security and welfare payments made up over 40% of the total of wages and salaries in 1947. Cf. Lüthy, pp. 326–8.

and unmade by the politicians in the course of their endless private game? But this game, 'the System' as General de Gaulle called it, and the *immobilisme* which it protected received shorter shrift from the citizens of the Fourth Republic than from those of the Third. Until 1934 the System and the stalemate society held the allegiance of a safe majority of the electorate and an overwhelming majority in Parliament. But in the post-war years society was no longer in stalemate and the enemies of the System could sometimes command a third of the seats and nearly half the votes. In their insistence that representative government must mean their own dominance over the cabinet, the deputies did not merely degrade government: they themselves ceased to represent.[46]

In these conditions a weak regime was dangerously vulnerable to shocks from abroad. The resurgence of Germany had fatally weakened the Third Republic before the *Wehrmacht* crushed it in the battle of France. The sense of national humiliation which resulted was to influence the outlook of French political leaders from Georges Bidault, first foreign minister of the Fourth Republic, to Michel Debré, first prime minister of the Fifth, and to determine that of one important social group, the officer corps. And where the Third Republic had enjoyed the credit for winning an empire, the Fourth suffered the odium of losing it. The new regime was inherently no stronger than the old, and it succumbed when confronted with the French equivalent of the Irish question or America's problem of the South: the war in Algeria.

46. Hoffmann in *Change*, p. 51; no. 126, p. 56. In 1957 an inquiry among 3,500 conscripts found that 97% knew the winner of the Tour de France (the annual bicycle race) and 15% the prime minister: Georgel, *Critiques et réforme des constitutions de la République*, i. 177. An inquiry late in 1958 asked how many parties were desirable: 97% said there were too many; the average member of a splinter group wanted only 3·5 parties, members of a major party 3, and others 2·8: Converse and Dupeux, no. 59, p. 10.

Chapter 2

THE WAR AND ITS AFTERMATH, 1936–1947

World war shook France from the economic stagnation and political paralysis which had marked the last years of the Third Republic. Defeat provided the opportunity for a counter-revolution directed against both the working-class movement and the democratic regime itself. The Resistance was a revolutionary response to this challenge, and its triumph revolutionized the political situation. But the apparent national unity was quickly dissipated. The Communist drive for power forced all groups to take sides. During 1945 and 1946 there proceeded simultaneously a national effort at indispensable economic reconstruction, a struggle over the framing of the new constitution, and a bitter political 'cold war' between the ruling parties. When the Communists went out of office in May 1947 the regime gradually returned to normal and the political practices of the past slowly revived.

1. POLITICAL FORCES, 1936–45

Before the second world war the Radicals were politically dominant, appealing to all those who 'wore their hearts on the left and their wallets on the right'. The party was so loose in its organization and discipline that members with very different opinions could join; the Radicals in the Senate (such as Caillaux) were far more conservative than those in the Chamber (like the rising young leader Daladier). At elections the latter could usually impose an alliance with the Socialists, but during the course of each parliament's life the moderate wing gradually encouraged their colleagues into coalition with the Right. Its pivotal position gave the party a permanent hold on power; the premiership and ministry of the interior were generally in its hands, and it was able to train many skilful and experienced politicians both in Paris and through its extensive hold on local government.

But the Radicals had the defects of their qualities. The body of opinion represented by them was broad but shallow. This negative, unconstructive and timid following handicapped the party in a period of crisis. Loose discipline allowed it to attract such wide support that it became less a party in the British sense than a social club attached to an electioneering machine. Its hold on power meant that it attracted the careerist politician and the unscrupulous henchman: few were the political and financial scandals in which Radicals were not involved. And in training its young men it sought not to promote strong personalities but to suppress them. Many Radicals positively preferred mediocrity to ability.

Until 1936 the Socialist party sat on the far Left in Parliament. Once revolutionary and anti-militarist, the Socialists had settled down as orthodox defenders of the regime – although they long refused to take office. When they changed their minds in 1936, on becoming the strongest party in the Popular Front majority, they were already feeling the breath of competition on their Left. For at that election the Communist party was accepted as an ally by the

Socialists and Radicals. Hitherto badly under-represented by the electoral system, it suddenly leapt from a dozen parliamentary seats to seventy, but in its turn refused office and gave Blum's government only the cold comfort of 'support without participation'.

The Right, like the Socialists, was too weak to win an electoral majority. Much of its strength lay in the support of influential figures like Pétain in the army, Chiappe in the police, Coty in business, Maurras among intellectuals. During the thirties such men became more and more sympathetic towards fascism. At home strong fascist leagues grew up of which *Croix de feu* was the largest (and least extreme). Abroad the entire Right demanded a policy favourable to Mussolini's Italy and to Franco's cause in Spain, and many of its supporters came to see the predominance of Nazi Germany as a lesser evil than the rule of a Jewish Socialist prime minister in Paris.

Fascism did not attract the Right alone. Among its most extreme exponents were the former Communist leader Doriot and the 'Neo-Socialist' Déat. It gained indirectly, too, as Hitler's successive victories sapped the determination and paralysed the will of French leaders – including most Radicals and half the Socialists as well as the Right. Since at first the Communists stood for resistance to Germany, by the time of Munich anti-Communism had become the main bond between the forces of appeasement and the main motive of governmental policy. Then when the Nazi-Soviet pact was signed the Communists turned defeatist, playing into the hands of those of their enemies for whom the class war at home was more important than the fight against Hitler.

So where the first world war had brought national unity, the second destroyed it. The regime had long been opposed by an extreme Right which felt excluded from government and an extreme Left which felt alienated from society. For some years it had also been losing former supporters who believed it could no longer fulfil its task. The defeat seemed to prove them right. An overwhelming majority conferred full powers upon Marshal Pétain as chief of the French State: the very name of Republic was abandoned. His regime was based primarily on right-wing opinion, which found at Vichy (not of course among the German puppets in Paris) the political leadership it really sought. But the Marshal's first cabinet also included two prominent Socialists, a Radical ex-premier, and an assistant secretary of CGT, the trade union federation. Conversely when General de Gaulle issued his appeal on 18 June 1940 he found followers in all political camps from Socialists to *Croix de feu*, but his support from the Right came from individuals only.[1] In the Resistance inside France the pioneers were usually Socialists, Catholic democrats or army officers. Only after Germany's invasion of Russia did the Communist party play its active part.

Though directed against a foreign occupier, the Resistance was potentially a revolutionary movement; and the Liberation was potentially a revolutionary change. For a few months indeed the new Gaullist authorities shared precarious power with the largely Communist-controlled militia and

1. The Communists denounced him as a hireling of the City of London: cf. Rossi, *La physiologie di Parti communiste français*, pp. 86–7, 90–3, 220, and his other books cited in the bibliography.

insurrectionary committees which dominated most of southern France.[2] But at the end of 1944 Thorez allowed his supporters to be disarmed and the Liberation Committees disbanded without resistance. The war was still raging and the party had decided to bid for power by legal means. It knew that the old political leaders as a group (and often as individuals) had suffered a disastrous loss of prestige. The Right was discredited by Vichy; the Radicals were blamed for the events leading up to the war, for their weakness and lack of responsibility in power, and for their rather unheroic part under the occupation. Thus two of the three main forces on the pre-war scene were under a heavy cloud. New men rose to the top who, as in any revolution, included both inexperienced idealists and more or less scrupulous and patriotic adventurers. Welded into a strong Resistance party they might form a buffer against the Communists; dispersed and divided, they would easily be outmanœuvred by the largest and best-disciplined party.

The Resistance party was never formed. The Communists were bent on hampering any organization they did not control. Some Resisters from the old parties, especially Socialists, were unwilling to lose their former political identity. Christian Democrats who could hope at last to found a major party would not renounce this opportunity for an uncertain fusion with rather reluctant anticlerical partners. Above all General de Gaulle, who in 1943 had revived the discredited old parties by bringing them into the National Resistance Council to strengthen his hand in Washington and London, was in 1944–45 still unwilling to forfeit his position as a national hero by stooping to lead a political party.[3] The attempt to transform the non-Communist Resistance into a political movement was thus stillborn, and instead three parties succeeded in canalizing the new enthusiasm.

The Communists reaped in votes the reward of their Resistance record after 1941, becoming the largest single party; and they contrived through their dynamism, their organizing capacity and their ruthless use of slander and violence to capture control of CGT.[4] Equally spectacular was the sudden emergence of a new party, the *Mouvement républicain populaire* (MRP), based on an old tradition of Catholic democracy which had never before found effective political expression and on a new generation of progressive Christians who had come to maturity in the Resistance. Between these two the old Socialist leaders hoped to rejuvenate their party and make it the link and leader of all the new forces.

In these forgotten years of 1944–45 General de Gaulle was earning distinction at home as the first French premier to bring Communists into his administration, and abroad as the chief advocate of the middle way between

2. Robert Aron, *Histoire de la Libération de la France* (1959), pp. 573–637; Lüthy, pp. 100–4; Rieber, *Stalin and the French Communist Party*, pp. 150–8, 168–74.

3. Wright, *Reshaping of French Democracy*, pp. 32–6, 64–78; Matthews, *Death of the Fourth Republic*, pp. 107–11; Fauvet, *La IVe République*, pp. 24–7; H. Michel, *Histoire de la Résistance* (1950), pp. 47–8, 51; M. Granet and H. Michel, *Combat* (1957), pp. 297–306; R. Hostache, *Le Conseil National de la Résistance* (1958), Chapters 2 and 3; Bourdet, no. 27, pp. 1837–62; Frenay, no. 95, pp. 43–8.

4. Lorwin, *French Labor Movement*, pp. 107–11 (and in Earle, pp. 202–4); Rioux, *Le Syndicalisme*, pp. 75–6; Lefranc, *Les expériences syndicales en France*, pp. 140–1, 151–68; Rossi, pp. 444–5; Rieber, pp. 179–82, 220–4.

Washington and Moscow. Vincent Auriol, later President of the Republic and champion of 'the System' against Gaullism, was the General's chief constitutional adviser and his agent in dealing with the politicians. The Communists were seeking fusion of their party with the Socialists; the voters of the Right could find an electoral home only with MRP; the General was on intimate terms with both Socialists and MRP but sharply divided from the Radicals and Conservatives.[5] And the style of government, in which a national hero of authoritarian temper carried out the revolutionary policies of an insurrectionary committee subject to the criticism of a parliamentary assembly, was one which combined features cherished by the extreme Right, the extreme Left and the moderate Centre.[6]

2. POLITICS AND CONSTITUTIONAL REFORM, 1945–47

The Third Republic formally committed suicide on 10 July 1940 when the Chamber and Senate, sitting together as a National Assembly empowered to revise the constitution, voted full powers to Marshal Pétain. The rival government of General de Gaulle established itself at Algiers in 1943. It gradually obtained Allied recognition, and took control in France in 1944. But until 21 October 1945 its authority was based on no formal or legal title.

On that day the French electorate had three decisions to take. They had to choose their parliamentary representatives. They had to decide by referendum whether the new assembly should draft a new constitution: if not, it would simply become a Chamber of Deputies, a senatorial election would take place according to the pre-war procedure, and the new parliament might or might not proceed to revise the constitution in the manner prescribed in 1875. But if the voters gave the new assembly constituent powers (as they did), they would also have to accept or reject a governmental proposal limiting its authority to seven months and requiring its draft constitution to be approved by another referendum. For General de Gaulle was unwilling to confer unlimited power on a single assembly checked by no rival institution.

The referendum produced an overwhelming vote of no confidence in the Third Republic. Only the Radicals advocated returning to the system of which they had been the principal beneficiaries (and only one in three of their two million surviving voters followed them). The Assembly was given constituent status by 18,600,000 votes to 700,000.[7] But this enormous majority divided over the Assembly's powers. Socialists and MRP supported General de Gaulle and called on their followers to vote *OUI – OUI*. The Communists, against whom the restrictions on the Assembly's powers were directed, campaigned vigorously for *OUI – NON*. On the second question they were joined by the Radicals, who disliked plebiscites in principle and General de Gaulle in

5. The term 'Conservative' is used to denote the small and shifting right-wing groups like PRL (*Parti républicain de la Liberté*), the Peasant party, the Independent Republicans, and the dissident Gaullists: see below, Chapter 11. Without a capital letter, 'conservative' refers to a social and economic outlook which some anticlericals share.

6. Morazé, p. 141.

7. Voting figures from Husson, *Les Élections et Référendums* (1945–6, two volumes, cited henceforth as Husson i and ii).

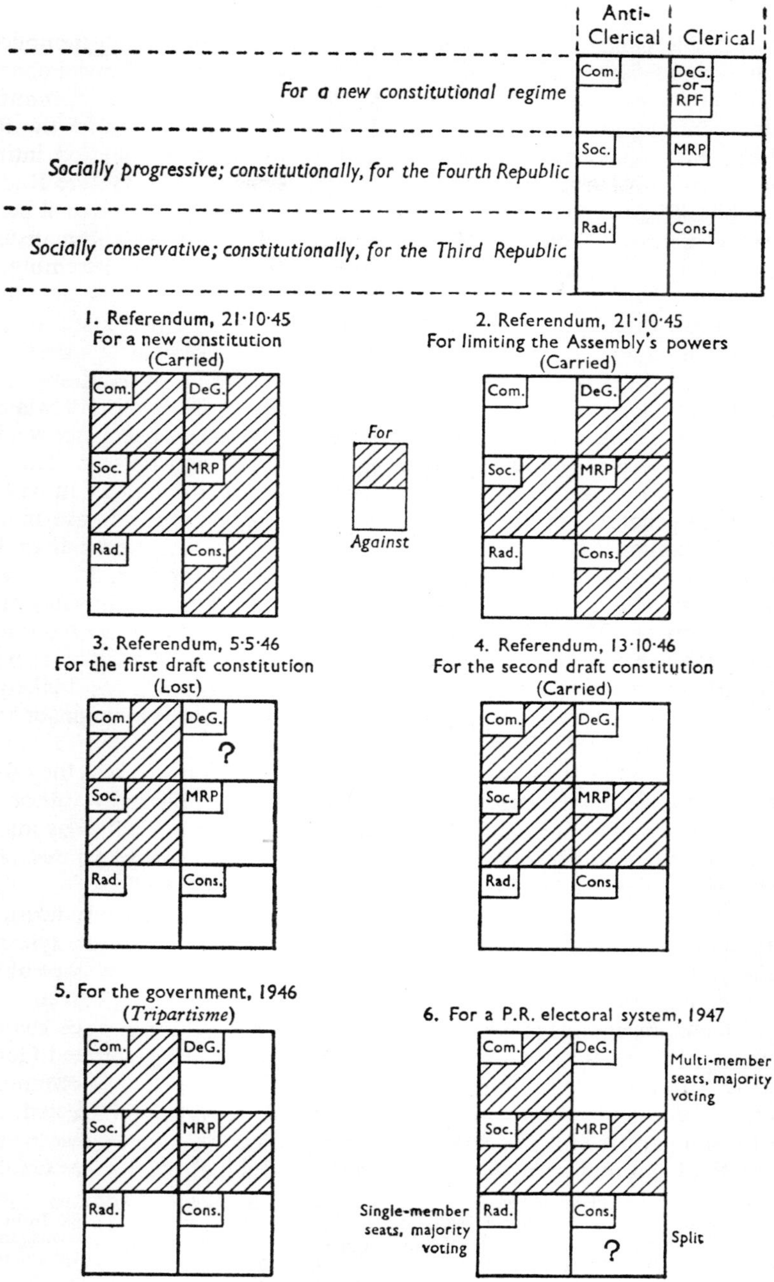
Anti-Clerical
Clerical
For a new constitutional regime
Com.
DeG. or RPF
Socially progressive; constitutionally, for the Fourth Republic
Soc.
MRP
Socially conservative; constitutionally, for the Third Republic
Rad.
Cons.
1. Referendum, 21·10·45
For a new constitution
(Carried)
2. Referendum, 21·10·45
For limiting the Assembly's powers
(Carried)
For
Against
3. Referendum, 5·5·46
For the first draft constitution
(Lost)
?
4. Referendum, 13·10·46
For the second draft constitution
(Carried)
5. For the government, 1946
(*Tripartisme*)
6. For a P.R. electoral system, 1947
Multi-member seats, majority voting
Single-member seats, majority voting
Split
?

Fig. 1. Party Alignments 1945–7

practice. The General won this vote by nearly 13 million to 6½ million. For the first time France had a Constituent Assembly with limited powers.

The election produced an Assembly unlike any of its predecessors. The three large organized parties, Communists, MRP and Socialists, polled 5, 4¾ and 4½ million votes respectively. These three disciplined groups shared between them in roughly equal numbers nearly four-fifths of the 586 seats in the Assembly. The Radicals were routed; they and their allies polled 2 million votes, but the party held only 24 seats in metropolitan France and many of its leaders were beaten. The different varieties of Conservative did a little better with about 2½ million votes and 64 seats.

For nearly three years after the Liberation the Communists held office and their pressure on the government dominated the political struggle. They pinned their hopes on completing the revolution legally, by electoral victory and infiltration of the state machine. The basis of their strategy was a close alliance with the other great Marxist party; and the reluctance of the Socialist leaders was to be overcome by arousing their followers who still recognized 'no enemies on the Left'. The Radicals were also potential allies, for distrust of political generals had led them to co-operate with the Communists in the 1945 referendum. MRP was to be discredited as the standard-bearer of reaction; in particular the clerical dispute, which many hoped had been buried in the Resistance struggle, was resuscitated in order to prevent any close combination between MRP and the Socialists.[8] But proportional representation, in many ways a help to the Communists, hindered them here: for it allowed each party to fight the electoral battle alone, and so enabled the Socialists to escape being forced into a Marxist coalition which might have alienated them irrevocably from MRP.[9]

Immediately after the election General de Gaulle reconstituted his government and based it on the support of all the main parties. But a few weeks later, on 20 January 1946, he suddenly resigned in exasperation with the quarrels and demands of the parties. Like some other war leaders, he was more interested and knowledgeable in military than in economic affairs; reconstruction of the army was his most cherished objective, and the interference of party politics in this sphere precipitated his departure.[10] He rejected any idea of carrying out a *coup d'état*, and Blum and Auriol advised him against appealing by radio to the public.[11]

His departure inaugurated a year of *tripartisme*, a coalition government of the three main parties, headed at first by the Socialist President of the Constituent Assembly, Félix Gouin. The three parties associated in the government (allied would be too strong a word) could reach no agreement on the constitutional problem. The Socialists, having failed to arrange a compromise, joined the Communists against all the other principal parties in voting the

8. See Hamon, no. 119, pp. 103–5.

9. Goguel, *Fourth Republic*, pp. 61–2.

10. The last straw was a large cut in the military budget, moved by the Socialists in order to embarrass the Communist minister responsible but promptly taken up and carried by the Communists themselves. But see below, p. 386; and Fauvet, *IVe*, pp. 64–5.

11. Wright, *Reshaping*, p. 131; Chapters 4 and 5 give the fullest account of the General's relations with the cabinet and parties. For his rejection of a *coup*, see *La France sera la France* (a collection of his pronouncements published by RPF), pp. 31–3; *Monde*, 13 March 1951; *Rassemblement*, 11 July 1952 – but cf. his memoirs: *Le Salut*, pp. 286–7.

draft constitution on 19 April 1946 and campaigning for it in the referendum. Its opponents attacked the draft itself (which conferred virtually unchecked power on a single chamber); the electoral law associated with it; and the controversial preamble – especially the omission of the right to 'freedom of education', the guarantee of the Catholic schools. But they were even more hostile to the sponsors than to the provisions of the draft. They feared that acceptance would constitute a triumph for the Communists, consolidating both their alliance with the Socialists and their domination of that alliance.

The referendum of 5 May 1946 checked the steady Communist advance. For the first time in French history the electorate answered *NON* in a plebiscite. The draft constitution was rejected by a majority of just over one million votes in a poll of twenty million. Some Socialists had evidently voted against their leaders – who tried to recover the lost ground by a sharp reversal of policy and violent denunciation of the Communists. Nevertheless, in the general election on 2 June the Socialists were the principal losers. The Communists gained a little, MRP gained more. As it emerged as the largest party, its leader Georges Bidault succeeded Gouin at the head of the tripartite government. An equally important shift of power was the replacement of André Philip, the Socialist minister of finance who favoured a controlled economy, by Robert Schuman, on economic matters one of the most conservative members of MRP.

During the referendum campaign General de Gaulle maintained complete silence and did not even vote.[12] But after the election he emerged from his reserve. At Bayeux on 16 June he denounced the working of the regime, attacked the power of the parties, and expounded his own remedy of strong presidential rule – the so-called Bayeux constitution.[13] His open opposition presented a challenge to MRP, which claimed to be the *parti de la fidélité*. But the MRP leaders believed that an unsatisfactory compromise was better than another controversial draft constitution, another rejection by referendum, and another seven months of provisional government. Until a constitution had been adopted there could be neither relief from the paralysing pressure of imminent elections nor hope of upsetting the coalition with the Communists.

MRP therefore accepted the last-minute concessions offered by the chastened Communists and worried Socialists. But to their vast embarrassment General de Gaulle, in another speech at Épinal, denounced the new proposals.[14] The October referendum proved MRP's fears well-founded. The constitution was adopted by a majority of only 9 million against 8 million; a third of the electorate, 8½ million people, did not trouble to vote. Plainly it was accepted not on its merits but as an escape from provisional government.

The Socialist and Communist parties alone had polled on 2 June half a million more votes than were cast in favour of the constitution on 13 October. Yet since June MRP with its 5½ million voters had joined the *OUI* camp. There was therefore a gap of 6 million between the earlier vote for the three parties and the subsequent vote for the constitution they had framed. General de Gaulle had shown his power. But he was not yet ready to re-enter the

12. *L'Année politique* (henceforth cited as *AP*), 1946, p. 161.
13. Text of the speech in *ibid.*, pp. 534–9; cf. *La France sera la France*, pp. 36, 51, 167.
14. Extracts in *ibid.*, pp. 16, 44, 169; text in *AP* 1946, p. 245.

political arena, and the general election of 10 November again gave nearly three-quarters of the seats to the three main parties. MRP lost the half-million votes which they had gained in June, and the Socialist decline continued. The Communists slightly increased their vote, again becoming the strongest party; but their real power diminished, for the Socialist defeat deprived the Marxist parties of their (theoretical) majority. The groups opposed to *tripartisme* adapted their tactics to the electoral system and divided the constituencies between them; this particularly helped RGR (Radicals and allies) who won 70 seats. The Assembly contained 183 Communists, 166 MRP, 103 Socialists, and 74 Conservatives. It lasted until 1951.

Tripartisme was dying. MRP wanted to demonstrate its anti-Communism to the voters who had deserted it in the referendum; the Communists feared to lose their hold on the working class by staying in office. Since neither party would vote for the other's candidate, Thorez and Bidault in turn failed to secure the absolute majority of the Assembly which they needed to be elected prime minister. The immediate problem was solved by the formation on 16 December of a one-party Socialist government under the veteran Léon Blum. The general public was delighted to find a ministry which knew its own mind; the rival parties were less pleased. In January the constitution was officially inaugurated by the election as President of the Republic of Vincent Auriol, who had succeeded Gouin as President of the Assembly a year before. Blum resigned (as was customary on the election of a new President) and the big parties renewed the coalition under another Socialist, Paul Ramadier. The Radical party, after a year in opposition, now returned to office and began its climb back to power; but its influence was as yet small and the Ramadier ministry rested on the alliance of Socialists and MRP.

The Communists were increasingly uneasy partners. They were opposed to the other parties both on domestic issues, especially wages policy, and on colonial questions (Madagascar and Indo-China were both in revolt). In March their deputies – other than ministers – abstained in a vote of confidence on Indo-China, though the party stayed in office in the hope of influencing French policy during the foreign ministers' conference in Moscow. By May France had aligned herself with the West, and a strike at the Renault works warned the Communists that their trade union influence was threatened: the whole party (including ministers) voted against the government on wages policy. The ministers refused to resign, and were dismissed on 5 May 1947, the most important date in the history of the Fourth Republic.

The Republic had won its 'battle of Prague'. It had taken the risk of admitting Communists into the government, but had escaped the fate of most countries which tried that gamble. The Socialists had not been enticed into an alliance controlled by their rivals. The Communists had neither gained control of the key ministries nor penetrated the governmental machine sufficiently to paralyse it. They were not strong enough either to win a free election or to create a revolutionary situation. Their one great asset was their grip on the trade unions; and France had now to be ruled against the opposition of the largest party and the industrial working class.

A month earlier General de Gaulle had re-entered politics. At Strasbourg on

7 April 1947 he appealed to all Frenchmen to rally to his *Rassemblement du peuple français* (RPF), a new non-party movement to reform the constitution, combat the Communist 'separatists' and regenerate national life. His appeal met with a large response in the country. In the autumn RPF extended its activity to Parliament, setting up an 'inter-group' which all deputies (except Communists) were invited to join while still remaining members of their former parties. But Socialists and MRP forbade their members to adhere, so that the new body consisted of old opponents of *tripartisme* reinforced by a few MRP dissidents who preferred the leadership of the General to that of the party. Gaullists and Communists, whose alliance in 1944 had laid the foundations of the Fourth Republic, were now both bent on its destruction.[15]

3. SOCIAL CONFLICTS

The events of 1947 transformed French politics. Domestically, imperially and internationally there were adjustments and reversals of policy (not all for the better). The working of the regime changed completely. Party cohesion declined as soon as it ceased to be indispensable in defence against Communist pressure. Old individualist habits revived and profoundly affected both political behaviour and constitutional practice.

In the autumn of 1947 the creation of the RPF inter-group and the beginning of active Communist opposition opened a new phase of parliamentary life. The problem of the political regime emerged again into the forefront of controversy. There was massive support in the country for both the drastic solutions, 'people's democracy' leading to Communism, and presidential democracy leading perhaps to authoritarian rule from the Right. Their advocates in the Assembly combined in a negative coalition to make all government impossible, hoping afterwards to fight out their own battle over the ruins of the parliamentary republic. Only by the alliance of all the middle parties, loyal to the classic forms of parliamentary rule, could a system of the familiar type be preserved.

Union of the centre groups was indispensable to the regime's survival and perhaps to their own. But even on the constitution itself they disagreed: Socialists and MRP had created the Fourth Republic, Radicals and many Conservatives still preferred the Third. A graver weakness arose from the clash of party ambitions. The middle parties had a common interest in standing together against the oppositions. But this could neither suppress their rivalries nor prevent the weaker Radical and Conservative groups from pressing continually for a larger share in power as their parliamentary bargaining position improved. Nor was this merely a matter of jobs, for the majority was deeply divided on all questions of policy.

The main cause of division was the economic problem: the distribution of the national income and of the burdens and benefits of government expenditure among different social groups. In the post-Liberation inflation, fixed-income groups suffered but small businesses flourished, paying their debts and taxes in depreciated francs. The wage- and salary-earner could not escape direct taxation; but the self-employed defrauded the treasury on a massive

15. Lüthy, p. 137.

scale. Peasants, because of their electoral influence, had always paid far less than their share of taxation.[16] Radical and Conservative politicians passionately advocated a free economy – but insisted on guaranteed agricultural prices and government-supported markets.[17] Moreover, wartime and post-war food shortages meant a golden age for the peasantry. In August 1947 – the peak year for farm prices – the average town worker was spending almost three-quarters of his wages on food.[18] Since the supply nearly all came from small farmers, rationing was far less effective than in Britain (where half of it entered through the ports). And the German occupation had reinforced and strengthened old habits of obstruction by making resistance and sabotage a national duty.

For a generation before the war, opposition to taxation had prevented France from balancing her budget. Deputies would not risk electoral disaster by voting adequate taxes; governments would not court parliamentary defeat by proposing them. They paid their way by inflation. Between the wars the monetary problem dominated French politics as unemployment dominated British – largely because of the determination of the better-off to evade their share of the national burdens. Frenchmen were always more reluctant to give their money than their blood.

The remark that 'France is a land of excessive taxation, fortunately tempered by fraud' was as true of the Fourth Republic as of the Third. In 1948 the ministry of finance raised £10,000,000 from Parisians owning American cars, three-quarters of whom had been paying no income tax at all. Officials estimated evasion of one tax at 20%, of another at 30 to 50%.[19] Governments had to rely on indirect taxation which fell most heavily on the poor. This increasing burden on those least able to bear it was the main cause of the recurring political crises; and it could never be tackled effectively because of the conflicting electoral interests of the governing parties.

In 1945 Mendès-France, as de Gaulle's minister of economic affairs, had urged an austere policy of controlling the economy, reforming the currency and limiting governmental commitments in order to avoid inflation. He was opposed by bankers and businessmen, peasants and profiteers, conservatives

16. Wright, *Reshaping*, p. 254: 19% of national income, 1·3% of taxes. For other estimates see Pickles, *French Politics*, pp. 247–8; Goguel, *Fourth Republic*, p. 191; Duverger, *Institutions financières*, pp. 130, 154–6, 168–75; Raymond Aron, *Le Grand Schisme*, pp. 220–1; Meynaud, *Groupes de pression en France*, p. 203 and n.; *Statistiques et études financières, Supplément finances françaises*, no. 18, 1953, p. 202, summarized in *Monde*, 6 to 9 June 1953, and by B. de Jouvenel in *Manchester Guardian*, 6 and 7 July 1953; Shoup, no. 199, pp. 341–2.

17. See for instance Aron, *Schisme*, pp. 215–16; Siegfried in *AP* 1952, p. xi.

18. Agricultural prices in relation to the general price level reached 121 in 1947 (1913 parity 100). In the thirties and forties they were nearly always over 100, but they dropped below 90 during the fifties: *Paysans*, p. xxv.

19. Cars: René Pleven, *rapporteur* of the finance committee, to a committee on fiscal reform (*Figaro*, 9 December 1948); Jules Moch, minister of the interior, to a Socialist conference (*Bulletin intérieur SFIO*, no. 39, February 1949, p. 69). Percentages: *Figaro*, 12–13 August 1950; Edgar Faure, minister of state for the budget, *JO* 23 May 1950, p. 3814, who quoted an estimate of 3–400 milliards (£3–400 million) for loss through fraud. Ehrmann, *Business*, p. 314, puts it 50% higher. Among small businesses investigated in 1950, the fraud rate was 80%: Duverger, *op. cit.*, p. 168. In 1949 even tax-exempt government bonds proved unsaleable as long as purchasers' names were recorded: M. Wolfe, *The French Franc between the Wars* (New York, 1951), p. 21n. (I owe this reference to Dr. D. Goldey.) For some important qualifications see Aron, *Steadfast*, pp. 49–51; and on the whole subject Shoup, no. 199, pp. 325–44.

and Communists. The General preferred the more comfortable advice of his finance minister, René Pleven; Mendès-France resigned and the inflation promptly followed. As prime minister in 1946, Georges Bidault called a conference of business, peasant and trade union representatives at the Palais Royal; but they merely agreed to support one another's demands for price and wage increases and so gave the inflation a further impetus.[20] In December Léon Blum formed an all-Socialist government which could at last formulate an agreed economic policy; the other parties allowed it to survive for a month. Significantly, a public opinion poll found that 62% thought it the most successful cabinet since the Liberation.[21]

At the root of the long-term economic problem was the technical inadequacy of France's agriculture and small-scale industry. The Monnet Plan was a bold attempt to lay foundations for modernization. But since the necessary investments were financed mainly through the budget (and Marshall Aid) this policy entailed real sacrifices, which provoked stubborn political resistance and persistent efforts to shift the burden. In one form or another the economic problem destroyed most governments in the first seven years of the Fourth Republic.[22] In November 1947 Ramadier was swept out of office by the repercussions of the month's great strikes. Schuman's first ministry was beaten in July 1948 over the military budget, Marie's broke up in August over price policy, Schuman's second fell in September because the Conservatives objected to the appointment of a Socialist minister of finance. Wages policy split Queuille's cabinet in October 1949 and Bidault's in February 1950; the latter was finally defeated in June over civil service pay. Throughout 1951 economic policy was in constant dispute within the successive governments; in January 1952 the second Pleven ministry was beaten when it tried to economize on the railways, in February the Faure cabinet fell when it proposed increased taxes, in December Antoine Pinay was ousted over his proposals to meet the social security deficit, and in May 1953 René Mayer was overthrown on demanding special powers to economize by decree.

Until 1948 prices rose steadily; either wages rose correspondingly, giving a further twist to the inflationary spiral, or wage stabilization led to strikes and a reinforcement of the Communist party. But in 1949 and 1950 the heavy investments of the post-war years at length began to produce results. The national income rose while prices remained stable – until the Korean war destroyed the equilibrium once again. At the same time some post-war governments made a real if insufficient effort to finance their expenditure by taxes instead of inflation: the proportion of the national income taken by the government rose substantially after the war.[23] The ministries of the Fourth Republic lasted no longer than those of the Third, but they did try to tackle problems that their predecessors had shelved.

Gratitude is not a political sentiment. The modernization programme imposed burdens which were fiercely resented by men on the margin, terrified of

20. See below, p. 394 and n. 21. *Sondages* 1947, p. 38; also Aron, *Schisme*, p. 189.
22. 'The movement of the *American* wholesale price index seems to mark the rhythm of French politics': Morazé, p. 146 (cf. p. 139; his italics).
23. See below, p. 267n.

proletarianization and unable easily to carry extra liabilities. After 1952 the small businessman lost the advantages of inflation; his customers migrated to the booming industrial areas; and stricter checks on fraud made the high nominal rates of taxation seem intolerable. The peasantry were embittered by the fall in agricultural prices which ended their 'golden age'. For these small men in town and country were often poor; they were a burden on the economy because of their excessive numbers, not their undue individual wealth.[24] Many indeed were barely kept alive by 'that barbed-wire entanglement of protective devices which enables the marginal producer to survive without really enjoying it'.[25] Modernization, however indispensable, threatened their cherished (if unreal) economic independence – and an 'inhuman technocracy' added insult to injury by maintaining that their disappearance would benefit themselves and their country. The exasperation and resentment of 'static France' was the political price paid for Monnet's economic miracle.[26]

4. THE LINES OF POLITICAL DIVISION

The economic problem tended to unite the parties which competed for working-class votes, the Socialists and Communists, against those with no working-class following, Radicals and Conservatives. MRP at first stood with the parties of the Right in the hope of retaining the vast mass of conservative support which it had acquired at the Liberation. But the foundation of RPF won away right-wing supporters of MRP, which was thus thrown back on the Catholic trade unions and from 1948 normally aligned itself in economic controversies with the Socialists. A few years later RPF in turn lost these right-wing supporters to the old-fashioned Conservatives, and from 1950 a tendency developed for some Gaullists to seek working-class votes and join with the Left in support of working-class claims.

The economic problem was not the only cause of division between those centre parties whose union alone kept governments in being. Colonial and military questions often produced a similar alignment of forces, with first Socialists and then members of MRP advocating conciliation of Indo-Chinese or North African nationalism, while most Radicals and Conservatives demanded firm government and the maintenance of French rule. On such issues the Gaullists for years sided with the Right, and within the majority a 'Fourth Force' of Conservatives and Radicals found themselves more often in agreement on policy with the Gaullist opposition than with their 'Third Force' Socialist and MRP partners.

But this simple division into four groups, authoritarian and democratic conservatives, totalitarian and democratic socialists, omits a major historical factor, the clerical question. To most foreign observers the problem of the church schools seemed trivial, but to many Frenchmen education was as vital an issue as it is to American Catholics, or was to Englishmen half a century ago. It symbolized the attempt to mould the nation's life in either a Catholic or

24. *Statistiques*, pp. 208–9, 215–16, and summaries (see n. 16).
25. Wright, no. 227, p. 7.
26. See below, pp. 167–9.

a secular spirit. And even the least ideologically-minded politician knew that in some regions *laïcité* was still the real electoral dividing line.[27]

This cleavage cut right across the social and political divisions, splitting the 'Fourth Force' as well as (though less deeply than) the Third, and uniting most Radicals and all Socialists with the Communists in a common hostility to the claims pressed alike by Conservatives, MRP and RPF. This was the weapon used by the Communists in 1945 to keep Socialists and MRP apart. It split the first Schuman government in 1948, led the Socialists to ally with Radicals instead of MRP in the subsequent local and senatorial elections, and so provoked bitterness which gravely weakened the majority up to the 1951 election. It was by exploiting the church schools question in the new Parliament that RPF alienated the Socialists from their former partners and finally broke the old majority.

Since politics turned on several different conflicts instead of one, there was a coherent majority neither in the country for a single party nor in Parliament for a lasting coalition. Associates on one issue were bitter opponents on others.[28] MRP for example worked with Socialists, Radicals and most Conservatives in defending the regime against Communists and Gaullists. On matters involving working-class interests and sometimes on colonial questions it sympathized with the Socialists and Communists; Radicals, Conservatives and (until 1951) RPF were hostile to its views. But over church schools MRP found its friends (or competitors) among Gaullists and Conservatives, while all Socialists and most Radicals joined the Communists against it. And on Europe it agreed with most Conservatives and Socialists and opposed Communists and RPF, with the Radicals split. So complicated a situation put a high premium on the arts of manœuvre and facilitated other, temporary combinations. Electoral tactics united MRP with the Communists against all the other parties in defence of proportional representation; Socialists and RPF often held very similar views on the problem of Germany.

Most of the peculiarities of French government were thus caused by the country's history. The battle against the Church and the struggle for political freedom were still political issues in the middle of the twentieth century, and they split public opinion on lines different from those imposed by the contemporary social and economic conflict. This persistence of several major political dividing lines was the basic cause of the instability of government, as the bitterness of the conflicts and the recent memories of power abused were the fundamental reasons for its weakness. Strong organizations like the Labour or Conservative parties, each seeking to form a (fairly) homogeneous government to put into practice a (fairly) coherent policy, were impossible in France. The young and dynamic on each side, impatient with the compromise and weakness of coalition government, were consequently tempted into extremist organizations which alarmed more prudent sympathizers and enraged opponents. The democratic parties could not compete effectively because they were at loggerheads over the clerical question, which lay

27. It was the only political problem on which voters' views corresponded closely with their party sympathies: Converse and Dupeux, no. 59, p. 19.

28. See Figures 1, 3 and 4 (above, p. 21, and below, pp. 43, 52).

between Socialists and MRP, preventing the development of a Labour party, and between Radicals and Conservatives, weakening still further the rudimentary links between the political representatives of the bourgeoisie. No French party could hope to attract a majority of voters or deputies. No French government could be based on a single party which put its policy into practice and then submitted it to the judgment of the electorate. Every ministry was a coalition. Responsibilities were never clearly apportioned; the government parties devoted as much energy to mutual recrimination as to fighting the opposition. The clash of political principles became obscured in the complexity of parliamentary manœuvring. The public grew apathetic and cynical; divided ministries, lacking effective support in the country, were too weak to impose necessary sacrifices on any powerful private interest or organized social group. But these undoubted evils had causes deeper than the structure of political institutions.

Chapter 3

THE SEARCH FOR A MAJORITY, 1947–1953

Between 1947 and 1953 the orientation of French policy changed slowly but drastically. While they remained in alliance the three 'social' parties, Communists, Socialists and MRP, had dominated the Assembly and the government. But with the Communist withdrawal into impotent isolation the French proletariat found itself virtually disfranchised, at least for constructive purposes. Socialists and MRP were not strong enough to govern without Radical and Conservative support, and within the new coalition the struggle to dominate policy was, though less desperate, as active as in the period of *tripartisme*. In the 1946 Assembly a precarious equilibrium was maintained. But at the 1951 election the isolation of the Communists enabled the conservative groups to improve their parliamentary position and secure temporary control of power and policy.

1. SOCIALIST DISCONTENT

The tripartite coalition had great difficulty in holding together. But while it did so governments had no need to worry about their parliamentary strength. The breach with the Communists at once restored the 'problem of the majority' to its former predominance. During the Third Republic the main source of parliamentary instability had been the contradiction between the Radical attitudes on political (especially clerical) and on economic questions; most Chambers began with a period of uncertainty in which the initial left-wing majority, elected on traditional political grounds, fell apart when governments had to deal with financial matters. In the Fourth Republic the difficulty was aggravated since the extreme groups were much stronger. The 1946 election returned 180 Communists, and RPF at first rallied 80 Gaullists. Together they slightly exceeded the combined strength of MRP and the Socialists. A centre combination therefore needed to attract the votes of most members of the loosely-organized Radical and Conservative groups, without alienating the two big disciplined parties.

Coalitions with no bond but fear of the extremists could have no common policy, and the division and impotence of governments gave an immense electoral advantage to their opponents. So the self-interested but useful motives which attach men and parties to power were counteracted by powerful pressures in the opposite direction. Deputies were tempted to vote against the government to ensure their own re-election, and parties felt that they could recover lost ground by a spell out of office. The Socialists could not constantly compromise on trade union claims without forfeiting support to the Communists, while MRP, unless they could produce benefits for the Catholic schools, risked the defection of the Church to General de Gaulle.

These pressures were not remote but immediate. The French people cast their votes twelve times in four years: in three referendums and three general elections between October 1945 and November 1946, second chamber elections at the end of 1946 and 1948, municipal elections in spring 1945 and autumn 1947, departmental council elections in autumn 1945 and spring 1949. No politician, party or government could plan ahead, for all were preoccupied with averting imminent disaster at the polls. The compulsion to take short views was irresistible. Feeling the tide was with them, the Radicals and Conservatives made demands to which the Socialists had to sacrifice more and more of their policy.

Some Socialist leaders, more influential in the country than in Parliament, urged the party to resign and repudiate responsibility for a policy which it disliked. They feared that continual concessions for the sake of governmental unity were losing votes and weakening the non-Communists in the trade unions. Others were more afraid that by going into opposition the Socialists would precipitate the breakdown of parliamentary government and the triumph of General de Gaulle. But even these rarely advocated unconditional participation in government – in August 1948, when the Socialists broke up the Marie cabinet, only five deputies (mainly ex-ministers) at first favoured joining its successor. The great majority of the party were for conditional participation, and the battle raged around the stringency of the conditions. When rank and file pressure became too great or their partners in office too exacting, the Socialists would revolt: during the 1946–51 Parliament they brought down six governments in a vain attempt to check the drift to the Right. When they finally escaped into opposition exactly the same dilemma faced MRP, which was now on the exposed flank of the majority.

2. RADICAL REVIVAL

The first reaction to the collapse of *tripartisme* was an attempt to constitute a new coherent majority around the Third Force formula. This depended on a close alliance of Socialists and MRP, reinforced by any Radicals or Conservatives who accepted its fundamental premises: social reform to win back the allegiance of the proletariat, and defence of the regime against both RPF and Communists.

By the autumn of 1947 the Ramadier ministry was breaking up. The Socialists disliked its unprogressive proposals for the government of Algeria, MRP resented its municipal election law tampering with proportional representation, and Radicals and Conservatives criticized its economic policy. The majority fell from 182 in May to only 49 in September; the prime minister was persuaded not to resign by the President of the Republic. At the October municipal elections RPF won control of the thirteen biggest cities in France, and had 40% of the votes against only 25% for Socialists and MRP together. With far more support in the country than the government, General de Gaulle demanded the immediate dissolution of Parliament, and his followers in the Assembly tried to impose it by voting systematically with the Communists.

In November 1947 Ramadier fell. The new Communist policy of intransigent opposition was launched by great strikes which reached revolutionary temper in Marseilles and other southern towns. Before the complicated negotiations for a ministerial reshuffle had been completed, the cabinet resigned and Léon Blum was put forward as a Third Force premier. But he

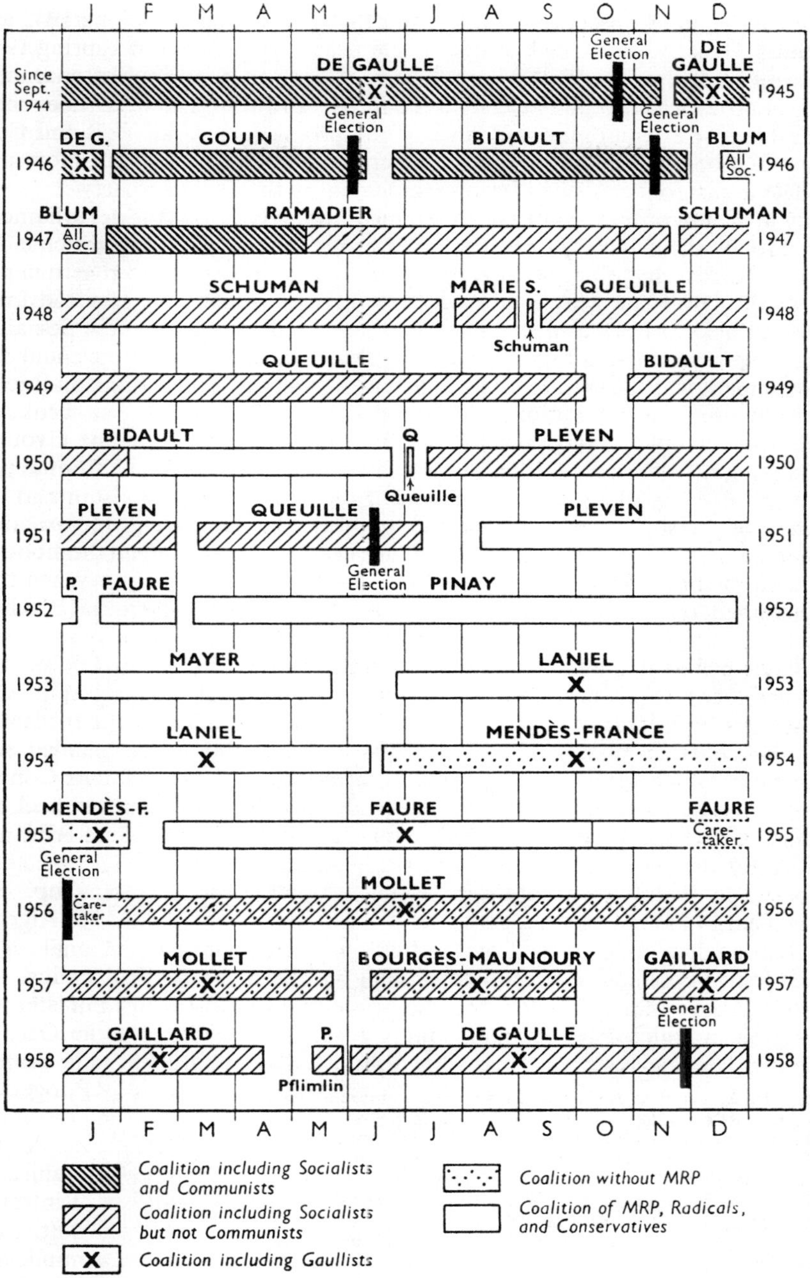

Fig. 2. Duration and Composition of Governments 1945–58

alienated many Conservatives and Radicals by attacking Gaullists and Communists equally, and failed to obtain the necessary absolute majority of the Assembly. Plainly the Third Force was too weak to govern without support from parties which repudiated its basic ideas. All future cabinets were therefore based on temporary and uneasy compromises, and all parliamentary combinations had a shifting and incoherent character.

The ministerial crisis had been precipitated by the Socialist party secretary Guy Mollet in order to shift the government to the Left. But the demonstrable need for Radical and Conservative votes brought about instead a move to the Right. Robert Schuman became prime minister and was replaced as minister of finance by René Mayer, a Radical with big-business and administrative connections. As in December 1946 the leadership of the government passed to a party just repudiated by the electorate.[1] More important than the change of government was the split in CGT. The anti-Communist minority broke away to form a separate federation, *CGT-Force ouvrière* (FO), which was politically independent but friendly towards the Socialist party. FO and the Catholic trade union federation, CFTC, now provided a counterpoise to Communist control of the working-class movement. Moreover, internal division and the failure of the strikes so weakened the unions that after the end of 1947 they could neither challenge the government nor even effectively defend the interests of their members against the employers.[2]

Schuman once described his government's life as an obstacle race. In March 1948 General de Gaulle's former minister René Pleven tried to remove one obstacle by reconciling his old leader with the parties of the Third Force, but his advances were rejected by both sides. The nominal majority split over Mayer's stiff fiscal levy at the end of 1947, over devaluation at the beginning of 1948, over dismissals of civil servants in June, and above all over two questions which revived the clerical controversy: the fate of twenty-eight Catholic schools belonging to the nationalized colliery companies, and the Poinso-Chapuis decree (named for the minister of health who issued it) which indirectly allowed local authorities to subsidize church schools. The Socialists decided on 19 July to bring the government down, proposing as a pretext a trivial cut in the military budget.

Once again a crisis opened by the Left ended in a move to the Right. The most active conciliator in the late cabinet had been the Radical minister of justice, André Marie. He now became prime minister at the head of a broad coalition in which Paul Reynaud, the Conservative leader, was minister of finance. The Socialists, who had vetoed Reynaud's appointment nine months

1. Parties in decline are less dangerous and so more acceptable to a people who prefer weak government: Aron, *Schisme*, pp. 188–9. See below, p. 452.

2. On the crisis of 1947 and its sequel, the coal strike of 1948, see Lüthy, pp. 139–57; Fauvet, *IVe*, pp. 135–8; Matthews, Chapter 12; Lorwin, Chapter 8; Earle, Chapter 12; Pickles, *French Politics*, pp. 82–5, 97–9, 102–6; Werth, *France 1940–1955*, pp. 368–86, 402–5; Lefranc, pp. 184–93, 210–22; and below, p. 74n. The FO split was imposed on reluctant leaders by a rank and file exasperated at Communist violence: Lorwin, p. 126; Earle, pp. 206–7; Lefranc, pp. 191–3; Rioux, pp. 69, 79; Lüthy, p. 150; Ehrmann, no. 82, pp. 155–6; Godfrey, *The Fate of the French Non-Communist Left*, pp. 48, 51–3; but Werth (pp. 385–6) thinks that since American trade unions helped with money, it must have been a political plot. (In his view French workers are tainted by taking dollars from American workers but Tunisian workers are not: cf. pp. 570ff.) On FO see below, p. 359.

before, now accepted him reluctantly. As a condition of taking office he insisted on emergency powers to reorganize by decree the civil service, the taxation system, the nationalized industries and the social security organization. On securing these powers from Parliament he used them to raise food prices; the trade unions protested violently and the Socialists broke up the government.

Significantly, MRP supported the Socialists. In 1947 they had shown their determination to remain politically on the Left by resisting the appeal of General de Gaulle. This decision cost them most of their conservative following and gave greater weight to their working-class rank and file. In 1948 they emerged as a party of the social and economic Left too. Robert Schuman, narrowly elected to a second premiership, chose the only Socialist minister of finance between 1946 and 1956, Christian Pineau. His tenure lasted just two days; on 7 September 1948 the cabinet met the Assembly and the Conservatives overthrew it by six votes. Three days later Henri Queuille, a Radical leader from pre-war days, was elected prime minister.

The significance of this long ministerial crisis was great though negative. In terms of measures it proved the impracticability of any clear-cut orientation of policy, whether Right or Left; and in terms both of men and of constitutional methods it seemed for a time to mark the triumph of the defunct Third Republic over the upstart Fourth. At the Liberation new leaders had replaced the discredited seniors; but soon the old politicians were recalled. None of the first three premiers had held office before the war; four of the next five had done so.[3] The Marie administration, with the first Radical prime minister and the first Conservative minister of finance, marked a stage in this revival of the old regime.[4] The reversion was equally apparent in constitutional practice; the Marie cabinet was mostly and the Queuille cabinet wholly selected before the respective prime ministers had been chosen by the Assembly. Marie developed his predecessor's method of evading the constitution by making matters unofficially questions of confidence, and defied the spirit of the new regime both by demanding special powers and by staking the existence of his government on the second chamber's consent to them.[5]

The events of August and September 1948 defined an equilibrium of forces which was to last for three years. The older leaders and groups regained a share in power but not a monopoly or even a preponderance; the constitutional pendulum swung half-way back to the Third Republic. The failures of Reynaud and Pineau showed that no wholehearted policy, Conservative or Socialist, could command the support of the Assembly. The centre parties

3. Of the first three, Gouin had been a deputy, de Gaulle and Bidault not. The next five (Blum, Ramadier, Schuman, Marie and Queuille) had all spent twelve years or more in the Chamber, though Schuman's first office was under Pétain. Governments from 1949 to 1954 were formed by three pre-war office-holders (Queuille, Laniel, Mendès-France), one pre-war parliamentarian (Pinay) and four 'new men' (Bidault, Pleven, Faure, Mayer). After 1954 Pinay was the only pre-war deputy nominated for the premiership.

4. Reynaud was assisted at the ministry of finance by Joseph Laniel and Maurice Petsche, so that the three Conservative groups (Republican Independents, PRL and Peasants) were all represented. Queuille was at first his own minister of finance, but soon transferred the post to his junior minister (*secrétaire d'état*) Petsche, who retained it until 1951.

5. See Prélot, no. 184, pp. 720–30; and below, pp. 226, 232–3, 270–1, 281.

were 'condemned to live together' in compromise and frustration. Therefore the government was too weak to challenge any of the great organized interests, employers, workers or peasants.[6]

3. DOCTOR QUEUILLE

Henri Queuille proved surprisingly well suited to this difficult situation. He was a characteristic figure of Third Republican politics. A country doctor by origin, he had served in twenty pre-war cabinets, in a dozen of them as minister of agriculture. His skill in the despised arts of parliamentary manœuvre was to stand him in good stead. Competent observers gave his ministry three weeks; it lasted thirteen months and reversed the steady drift of opinion away from the parties of the Centre.

Queuille believed, like Stanley Baldwin, that 'the art of statesmanship is to postpone issues until they are no longer relevant'. His first expedient was to lower the political temperature by deferring for six months the imminent departmental council elections. General de Gaulle protested in angry speeches hinting at insurrection. But after an ugly clash between Gaullists and Communists at Grenoble in September, and a bitter and violent miners' strike in October, public opinion rallied to the government in alarm at the spectre of civil war.

In Parliament, however, the ministry faced a new obstacle. It had been agreed in 1946 that after two years the upper house, the Council of the Republic, should be wholly re-elected and its method of election reconsidered. To weaken the Communists the new law greatly restricted proportional representation, which had made the first Council almost a replica of the Assembly, and reverted to a system very like that used to elect the old Senate. MRP also suffered from this change; both parties fell to a score of members out of a total of 320. Almost half the new senators (a title they forthwith bestowed upon themselves) had sought RPF support at the election. In the end only 58 of them accepted the Gaullist whip, so that RPF could not, as it had hoped, use the new Council to block all legislation and force the government to hold new elections. But the Radical and Conservative senators found the upper house a useful weapon, and the new 'second thoughts chamber' celebrated its appearance by rejecting the budget.[7]

At the beginning of 1949 the government's prestige stood high. Queuille had started with a modest aim: to ensure that ministerial crises could occur without endangering the regime. His very success made it safe to overthrow him. Previous ministerial crises had been affairs of desperation, provoked by parties which felt their support slipping away and their very existence at stake. The impending ones were crises of hope, the work of groups or leaders gaining ground in the country who felt entitled to exert more influence on policy. In May Reynaud began a vigorous drive to remove the Socialists from office;

6. Prélot points out that the Radical recovery meant a victory for the peasants and that Reynaud's policy involved an agreement with CGA (*Confédération générale de l'agriculture*) and a breach with the trade unions. He adds, 'as the trade unions ejected M. Paul Reynaud, the employers' unions executed M. Christian Pineau' (*ibid.*, pp. 729–30). 'Condemned': Queuille, *JO*, 24 May 1949, p. 2871.

7. See below, pp. 279–80 (electoral), 286–7 (political).

some MRP leaders (notably Bidault) contemplated abandoning them for an alliance with RPF, but the rank and file firmly refused. At the end of July the Conservatives attacked Daniel Mayer, the Socialist minister of labour, for a minor infringement of the wage freeze and the majority fell to three. Only the parliamentary recess saved the government, and before the reassembly in October it had broken up. British devaluation forced France to follow suit, and Mayer seized the opportunity to demand a return to free collective bargaining (suspended since before the war). This proposal split the government; attempts at compromise failed and Queuille resigned on 5 October 1949.

The rules of the parliamentary game required that the Socialists, who had brought down the last government, be invited to form the next. President Auriol called on Jules Moch, who as minister of the interior had broken the great strikes, helped devise the new electoral law for the Council of the Republic, and produced several compromise proposals before the Queuille government fell. But he was too strong a personality to be popular. The bitter hatred of the Communists was indeed an asset to him, but many MRP deputies and some even of his own party were also unfriendly. He was elected prime minister with only one (disputed) vote to spare, failed to form a government and had to resign. The same fate befell the next nominee, René Mayer, who had a comfortable majority of 158 but was unable to reconcile the demand of his own Radical party that Daniel Mayer should leave the ministry of labour with the Socialists' insistence that he should remain there.

It was now MRP's turn. The bickerings of the politicians had exasperated the public, and Bidault took advantage of this impatience, refusing to confront the Assembly until the parties had accepted his cabinet. This enabled him to form a government but did nothing to resolve the conflict. Radical attacks on the budget nearly destroyed his ministry in December, in February the Socialists resigned over wages policy, and four months later they turned him out over the salaries of civil servants – many of whom were Socialist voters.

The crisis of June–July 1950 showed that the political balance had changed little in the previous two years. The Socialists would not give up their new freedom without compensation. They helped elect Queuille to the premiership, but refused to join his government and overthrew him (with the aid of the left wing of MRP) when he formed a conservative cabinet. The Socialist leader Guy Mollet then drew up a programme including constitutional and electoral reform, to please the Radicals and Conservatives, and a halt to deflation, to satisfy his own party and MRP. On this basis the Socialists returned to office; but they were not strong enough to claim the premiership, which fell to the leader of the smallest of the majority parties, René Pleven of UDSR.

The approaching general election made the coalition even harder to maintain. Mistrust between the Socialists and MRP had persisted since the former left the Bidault government, and worsened in November when several MRP deputies voted to impeach Moch (Pleven's minister of defence and principal colleague).[8] Moreover the conflict over economic policy broke out again,

8. See below, p. 299.

Socialists and MRP advocating industrial subsidies, Radicals and Conservatives attacking them. Most serious of all was the disagreement on electoral reform. The Radicals demanded a return to the pre-war double ballot which MRP bitterly opposed. The Conservatives were divided. The 100 Socialists were comparatively indifferent and voted in turn for each solution proposed; the 180 Communists voted equally regularly against each and so the Assembly rejected them all. For a time the government maintained a precarious neutrality, but at the end of February it at last broke up.

As the Socialists were now the party of conciliation on the crucial issue, Guy Mollet was nominated for the premiership. When he failed to obtain an absolute majority, Queuille contrived to solve the crisis by simply reconstituting his predecessor's cabinet. To minimize the ravages of electoral fever he resolved to hold the elections in June, four months early. As no electoral reform could pass without the consent of MRP, he persuaded his Radical friends to give way, and the new law and the budget were passed just in time for elections on 17 June.

4. THE NEW ASSEMBLY

The results showed a severe defeat for the two parties most responsible for creating and governing the Fourth Republic. MRP lost half their 5 million voters of 1945, and of the 4½ million Socialist votes only 3 million were left. Communist strength at 5 million was almost unimpaired; Conservatives and RGR – Radicals and allies – retained nearly all their supporters, 2½ million and 2 million respectively.[9] RPF (which had not existed in 1945) won 4 million votes. Some came from conservative-minded electors who had switched from MRP to General de Gaulle when the former made too many compromises with the Communists. Others were voters for the older parties whose candidates had thought it advantageous to climb on the Gaullist bandwagon; these 'political hitch-hikers' were mainly Conservatives who soon jumped off, as many Radicals had already done.

For RPF had passed its peak. It still had over 20% of the vote, second only to the Communists with their 25%; but in the municipal elections of 1947 some 67% had voted for these two parties. Together the Socialists with nearly 15%, Conservatives (13%), MRP (12½%), and RGR (11%) held a narrow popular majority. But these four parties of the regime were divided over the social reforms of the Liberation, which were still approved by a majority of voters (Communists, Socialists, MRP and some RPF), and over church schools (where the balance in the electorate was now very close).[10]

Changes in the Assembly were greater owing to the new electoral law (see Chapter 22). This modified proportional representation by allowing parties to form alliances, and discarded it entirely where an alliance (or single party)

9. These 2½ million exclude 300,000 who voted Gaullist in 1946: Goguel, *Fourth Republic*, pp. 90, 102. Both RGR and Conservatives claimed great gains; they did win seats but they lost votes.

10. On these results see Goguel, *op. cit.*, Part III; Pickles, *French Politics*, Chapter 9; Williams, no. 219. Some RGR voters favoured the Catholic cause in education.

won a majority of votes. Radicals, Conservatives and MRP gained most from the new system; the Socialists gained less as they were often excluded from the centre combinations. RPF could have made alliances, but its leader nearly everywhere preferred independence even though it cost him a few seats. The Communists were isolated throughout the country and lost heavily by the new law. The two opposition parties had just under half the votes; the old system would have given them over half the seats, the new one gave them a third.

The six major parties were approximately equal in the Assembly but the three strongest were those least able to combine: 121 Gaullists, 107 Socialists and 101 Communists out of 627. With the Communists in unrelenting opposition there was no majority for a government unless either RPF or Socialists could be won over or split. As the Socialists were eager to escape taking responsibility for the policies of others, RPF could achieve a commanding position by widening the breach between them and their former partners. It did so by using the clerical question to divide the centre parties as the Communists had done six years before.[11]

In accordance with custom Queuille resigned after the election. A Radical, René Mayer, was nominated for premier; MRP thought him too anticlerical. A Conservative, Maurice Petsche, failed for lack of Socialist support. René Pleven's last government had pleased the Socialists; he won their votes and was elected premier but they would not join his cabinet. RPF pressed its advantage. A powerful pressure-group, the Association for Educational Freedom, had enrolled a majority of the Assembly, and in mid-September its bill (called the *loi Barangé* after its sponsor) was voted by the combined clerical groups, the government remaining neutral since most Radicals opposed the bill. The Socialists could now claim that the old partnership had been broken by others.

In December the Pleven ministry won its solitary triumph when the Assembly ratified by a large and unexpected majority the Schuman plan for a European coal and steel community. But its own supporters were no longer reliable. MRP joined the three oppositions in passing the sliding-scale bill (a Socialist measure tying wage rates to the cost of living, which the upper house delayed and drastically amended). Radicals and Conservatives attacked Robert Schuman for attempting to conciliate the Tunisian nationalists. René Mayer, minister of finance, was a target for the Peasant group of right-wing Conservatives. Finally the budget, which called for special powers to reorganize the social services and nationalized railways, drove the Socialists into opposition and they defeated the cabinet in January 1952. The new premier was Edgar Faure, a young Radical leader, who tried hard to win them back by concessions over Europe and Tunisia, the budget and the sliding-scale bill; the Conservatives and many of his own party revolted, and on proposing higher taxes he was beaten at the end of February. A Conservative, Antoine Pinay, was nominated; his failure was meant to show these rebels that there was no right-wing alternative to the old majority and they must therefore make the necessary concessions. But to the general astonishment he achieved the impossible:

11. See above, p. 22.

twenty-seven Gaullist deputies defied their whip to vote him into the premiership at the head of the most conservative majority France had known for twenty years.

Aided by a world-wide fall in prices Pinay succeeded in checking inflation (and expansion), restoring confidence and winning a great popular reputation. Inevitably this provoked parliamentary jealousy. But not until the end of 1952 did Radicals and MRP feel it safe to overthrow him, the former with their usual skill manœuvring the latter into taking the blame. By then external questions had come to overshadow domestic ones. For it was under Pinay that the new resident in Tunis took it upon himself to arrest the local ministers; and it was his foreign minister, Robert Schuman, who signed the treaty establishing a European defence community. MRP's main aim thenceforth was to get the EDC treaty ratified; to stop it, the Gaullists were ready to work with the Communists as well as the 'anti-Europeans' in the traditional parties. In January 1953 René Mayer purchased precarious RPF support for his new cabinet by sacrificing Schuman and equivocating on the European army. But in May the Gaullists turned him out when he demanded special powers to effect economies; the next premier, Joseph Laniel, gave them office and obtained the special powers. His election, however, was preceded by the longest ministerial crisis on record, which for the first time brought into parliamentary discussion the basic choices facing the country.

For this President Auriol was largely responsible. In sending first for Paul Reynaud and then for Pierre Mendès-France, he gave a platform to two leaders who had consistently refused office without power. Reynaud announced that he would form no ministry until the constitution had been revised to allow governments to dissolve the Assembly at will; Mendès-France proposed to choose his ministers without regard to party claims, and to make them promise not to join the next cabinet. His appeal for clear choices and general sacrifices brought a remarkable public response, and won him support from many – but not enough – younger deputies in revolt against their leaders. Georges Bidault, the next nominee, also declined to consult the parties and affirmed that he would use his full constitutional powers; he was beaten by a single vote. André Marie adopted the more traditional tactics of equivocating on policy and appealing to men of tried experience; he received the lowest vote of the four. But the long crisis was now discrediting the parties, especially MRP (who, after blocking Marie, deterred Pinay from standing). When Laniel was nominated they thought it prudent to support him, and he was comfortably elected.

The new cabinet was paralysed by its internal divisions. It omitted the Conservatives closest to Pinay, and included friends of Mendès-France such as Edgar Faure and François Mitterrand, as well as Gaullist members (soon renamed Social Republicans) who were no longer recognized by the General. The ministry's economy decrees, drafted in August under the new special powers, attacked many vested interests; but the first to become known affected workers and state employees, who seemed once again to bear the burdens which others would evade. Their wrath provoked a strike movement on a scale unknown since 1936, and – unlike the Communist-led strikes of

1947–48 – remarkable for its spontaneity and orderliness.[12] MRP pressure obtained a few concessions for the strikers, whose movement was followed in October by widespread demonstrations of peasant discontent.

Still more important developments were occurring in the French Union. Public opinion, as Mendès-France's candidature had shown, was weary of the Indo-China war and uneasy about events in North Africa. This mood grew stronger in June, when the King of Cambodia fled to Siam, and in October, when the Vietnam national congress resolved against remaining in the French Union in its existing form – although, too late, a new doctrine of the Union's constitutional status was slowly being evolved in Paris. Even men of the Right began to ask why France should divert her forces from Europe to a Far Eastern war where victory could bring no benefit.

Thus over Indo-China the failure of 'association' to satisfy nationalist aspirations tended to bring part of the Right into agreement with the Left. But in North Africa it merely stiffened the diehards. In August 1953 the resident in Morocco deposed the Sultan, who was the nationalist leader as well as the monarch and the religious chief. Faure protested and Mitterrand resigned; but the responsible minister, Bidault, justified an action he had previously forbidden. For the first time serious observers began to hint that the enemies of liberal policies abroad might one day endanger democracy at home.[13]

Even these problems were far overshadowed by that of the European army. Gaullists and Communists were willing to accept any alliance in order to defeat the treaty, and its principal sponsors played into their hands. For it was primarily to save EDC that MRP had accepted unpopular conservative policies at home and in the empire. Instead the consequence was a hardening of opposition to the treaty on the Left. When the two houses met at Versailles in December 1953 to elect a President of the Republic, the Communists, Socialists and Radicals sometimes acted and cheered together as in the days of the Popular Front.[14] When Herriot retired a month later the Socialist André Le Troquer was elected President of the Assembly, with Gaullist as well as left-wing support, against the strongly 'European' Pierre Pflimlin of MRP. Several new committee chairmen owed their elevation to Communist votes, and it no longer seemed unthinkable that a premier might be installed in the same way.

The presidential election harmed the regime. Hitherto one day and two ballots had always sufficed to find the clear majority required. But this time the old conflict of Left and Right, already complicated by the EDC quarrel, was still further embroiled by a prolonged contest of wills between Laniel, who maintained that as premier he had a quasi-constitutional right to the presidency, and the Radicals, who hoped Queuille would ultimately emerge victorious from the general exhaustion. On the seventh day and thirteenth ballot the

12. Rioux, pp. 119–21; Godfrey, pp. 66–7. Because of a leakage, it began before the decrees were published: see Delouvrier in *Crise du pouvoir et crise du civisme* (henceforth cited as *Crise*), p. 83.

13. Fauvet, no. 90, p. 107; cf. his *IVe*, pp. 293–4.

14. On EDC see Aron and Lerner, eds., *France Defeats EDC* and Grosser, *La IVe République et sa politique extérieure*, pp. 234–46, 312–20. The presidential election is minutely dissected in Melnik and Leites, *The House without Windows*,

electors chose René Coty, a highly respected Conservative senator of seasoned, Third Republican presidential timber (he was vice-president of the upper house). He had voted for Pétain in 1940 but had never compromised with the Germans; illness had kept him from taking sides over EDC; Gaullists and MRP both voted solidly for him; and with his election the ideals of the Resistance and Liberation seemed to have been peacefully laid to rest.

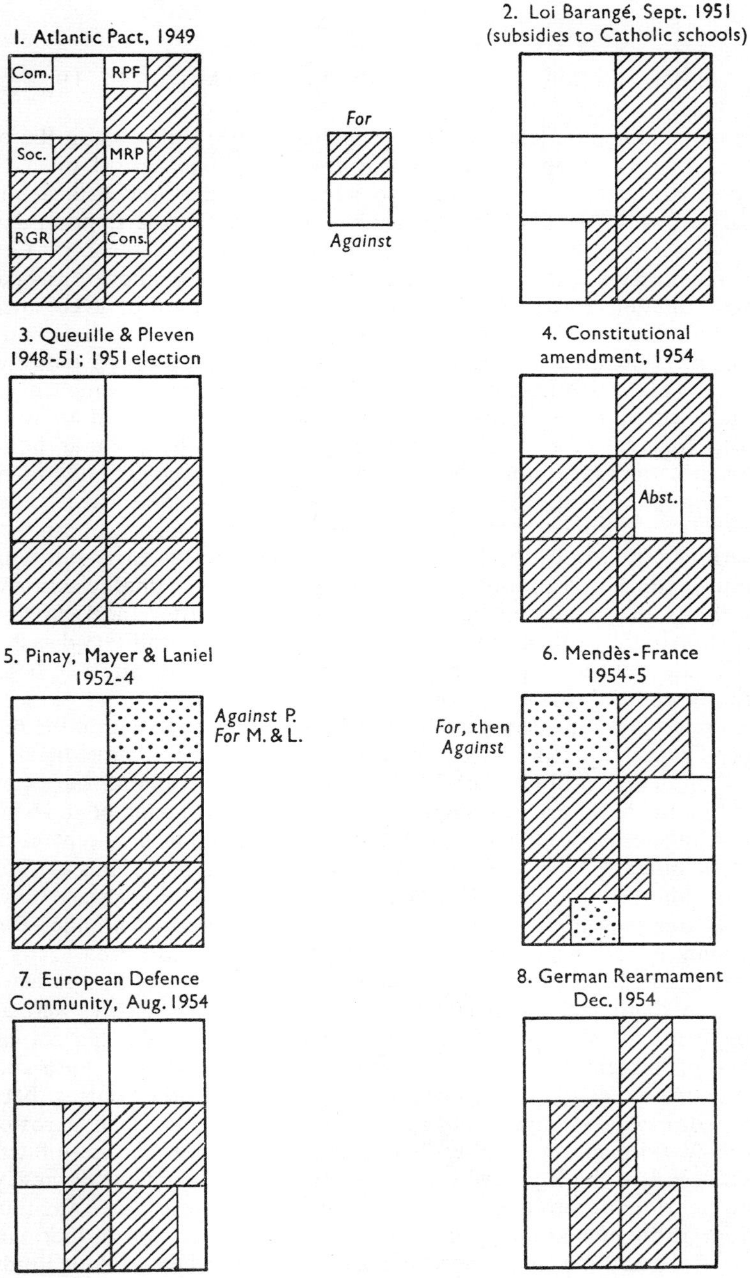
1. Atlantic Pact, 1949
Com.
RPF
Soc.
MRP
RGR
Cons.
For
Against
2. Loi Barangé, Sept. 1951
(subsidies to Catholic schools)
3. Queuille & Pleven
1948-51; 1951 election
4. Constitutional
amendment, 1954
Abst.
5. Pinay, Mayer & Laniel
1952-4
Against P.
For M. & L.
6. Mendès-France
1954-5
For, then
Against
7. European Defence
Community, Aug. 1954
8. German Rearmament
Dec. 1954

Fig. 3. Party Alignments 1947–4

Chapter 4

REVOLTS AGAINST THE 'SYSTEM', 1954–1958

In the early years after the war foreign policy played little part in the parliamentary struggle. Communists, MRP and de Gaulle agreed on a 'hard' policy of dismembering Germany to which only the Socialists demurred. France had to retreat from this untenable position, and the London declaration of June 1948, by which the Allies decided to restore a central German government, marked the collapse of her policy; the political price was paid by Georges Bidault, foreign minister (except for one month) ever since the Liberation. His successor Robert Schuman, after the Atlantic pact had been ratified overwhelmingly in July 1949, set French policy on an entirely new course. His plan for a European coal and steel authority was launched in May 1950 and voted by Parliament in December 1951. It helped to hold the majority together, for the centre parties welcomed the popular policy of European economic union; their cohesion was endangered only when the highly unpopular cause of German rearmament was linked to it. The first proposal for a European army came in late 1950, and coincided both with the first serious criticism of the Indo-China war and with the early rumblings of the coming storm in the North African protectorates. The final rejection of the EDC treaty in the summer of 1954 followed soon after the turn towards conciliation in the protectorates and the peace – sequel to military disaster – in Indo-China. Only a hundred days after that war ended, another began in Algeria. It was to destroy the Fourth Republic.

The same year, 1954, saw the one real attempt at change within the regime. Mendès-France enjoyed a success that was spectacular but short-lived. In so right-wing an Assembly a liberal leader had little chance, and that little was denied him by the Allies' insistent demand for German rearmament. He hoped for a stronger position in the next Parliament, but his apparent electoral victory of January 1956 was soon followed by total defeat. Thus in 1956 the System triumphed over its various enemies: first the Gaullists were routed at the polls and then the new challengers (Poujade as well as Mendès-France) each found his following melt away as swiftly as it had appeared.

The tragedy of these last years of the Fourth Republic was that catastrophe abroad overshadowed its real success at home. Post-war sacrifices were at last bearing fruit in rising production and rapidly improving living standards. Relieved of immediate economic pressures many voters lapsed into apathy; but an active minority neither understood nor accepted the contrast between growing domestic strength and self-confidence and the steady erosion of France's world position. The result was an assertive nationalism, influencing the Left as well as the Right, which focused the political conflicts of these years on external rather than internal affairs. The revolt against EDC was the first symptom of the new mood, and its outcome – the admission of Germany to NATO – did nothing to assuage the widespread bitterness at Allied indifference to French views and interests. Such resentments strengthened the repeated right-wing protests against any withdrawal overseas: Tunisia was the occasion for Mendès-France's defeat early in 1955 and Morocco ruined Edgar Faure's credit later in the year. When the Algiers settler riots of February 1956 led Mollet to reverse his conciliatory policy, he was followed by most of his Socialist and Radical supporters as well as by his conservative opponents, but was soon condemned by both extremes: the few advocates of timely concessions to Algerian nationalism, and the settlers, soldiers and right-wing 'ultras' who were resolved to prevent such concessions and eager to silence those who favoured them.

Once again France was fighting to hold an untenable position. In office, most politicians soon found this out, and almost every government after 1953 was overthrown for truckling to Arabs or foreigners. When the crisis came in the spring of 1958 it showed the weakness of the ultras in the National Assembly, where they could destroy cabinets (with Communist help) but not replace them. But it also showed the precariousness of the regime, for on failing in Parliament the ultras turned to direct action. And against the threat of civil war the Fourth Republic found itself helpless: its citizens apathetic, and its professional defenders disloyal. For too long weak governments had allowed generals and proconsuls to defy them with impunity, and by May 1958 disobedience was universal.

When faced with a major crisis French politicians, even those of the Left, turn by instinct to a national saviour. The Chamber of the *Cartel des Gauches* elected Poincaré in 1926, the left-wing victors of 1932 chose Doumergue in 1934, the Parliament of the Popular Front voted for Pétain in 1940. In 1958 the National Assembly of the Republican Front averted an open military revolt by installing General de Gaulle.

1. 'SUPERMAN'

The first signs of revolt appeared in the spring of 1954. Laniel's government was intensely unpopular; the Left's dislike of him was feeble compared with the army's hatred. EDC was condemned by a chorus of generals headed by Marshal Juin, who quarrelled publicly with Pleven, the minister of defence. During the battle for Dien-Bien-Phu Pleven and Laniel were assaulted by ex-soldiers and serving officers in mufti at a war memorial ceremony, the police showing little enthusiasm in their defence. Soon, however, the military zealots of the Right were to acquire a new target for their hatred.

In May Dien-Bien-Phu fell. Five weeks and three votes of confidence later the Laniel government was beaten by thirteen. President Coty summoned Mendès-France, the unofficial leader of the opposition, who promised to resign either if he owed his election to Communist support or if he failed to make peace in Indo-China within a month.[1] He needed 314 non-Communist votes. To everyone's surprise he received 320.

The seven months of his premiership saw a series of spectacular policy decisions, bewildering cabinet reshuffles, and complex shifts of party allegiance. He began by choosing his own colleagues, defying the usual rules (only four

1. But before resigning he promised he would bring in a bill to authorize sending conscripts to Indo-China – a measure none of his predecessors had ventured to propose.

had served in the last government and only one was an ex-premier) and ignoring the parties (though he carefully balanced supporters and opponents of EDC). The cabinet was based on Radicals and Gaullists; the Socialists and Communists were in the majority but not in the ministry, a few MRP and Conservative dissidents took office although their parties were reserved or hostile. The deputies were sufficiently impressed by the premier's sudden popularity in the country to give him massive majorities for his settlement in Indo-China, his conciliatory policy in Tunisia, and his demand for sweeping special powers over the economy.

This brief honeymoon was ended by EDC. No decision on that subject could have left the cabinet or the majority intact. When Mendès-France tried (in vain) to induce France's partners to modify the terms of the treaty, three 'anti-European' ministers resigned; when the government decided to bring the unchanged text before Parliament while itself staying neutral, three 'pro-Europeans' left it. On a procedural vote, with half the Socialist deputies defying their whip, ratification was defeated by 319 to 264. This outcome was neither a victory of parliamentarians over the public (who were indifferent), nor of extremists over democrats (who were divided), nor of *immobilistes* over reformers (both camps included supporters as well as opponents of change). It was no accident which could have been altered by a different stand on the premier's part: the deputies' minds were made up. Yet it surprised the 'Europeans' in Paris and Washington who had so rashly helped to wreck any compromise, and it earned the prime minister the unrelenting enmity of MRP. To save the Atlantic alliance Mendès-France then sponsored the London and Paris agreements rearming Germany. Dulles called him 'Superman' when he forced these through the Assembly in the face of bitter Communist hostility, reluctant opposition from many of his own staunch supporters, and a most discreditable attempt by the leading 'Europeans' (other than Schuman and Pflimlin) to stir up the nationalist and anti-German passions they had been deploring for years.[2]

Meanwhile on 1 November the Algerian war had begun. François Mitterrand, minister of the interior, dissolved the main nationalist party; Mendès-France appointed Jacques Soustelle as a reforming governor-general; both reaffirmed that Algeria was for ever part of France. The rising strengthened conservative hostility to the premier, which was further aggravated when he attacked the alcohol interest. In February 1955 he was overthrown by the votes of Communists and Conservatives reinforced by twenty right-wing dissidents from his own Radical party – and by MRP, despite their approval of his North African policy on which the vote was taken.

Late in 1954 the constitution had been amended: would-be premiers now formed their governments before the vote, in which a clear majority of the Assembly was no longer required. Antoine Pinay (Conservative) declined nomination; Pierre Pflimlin (MRP) failed to form a ministry; Christian

2. Some of them even spread rumours that ministers were betraying defence secrets to the Communist party: see Williams, no. 222; Wright, no. 229; Théolleyre, *Le procès des fuites*; Fauvet, *IVe*, pp. 280–3. The prefect of police, Jean Baylot, and Superintendent Dides were dismissed; on them see pp. 52, 98n, 130n., 146n., 165n., 347–8.

Pineau (Socialist) tried to revive the European programme and the MRP alliance but was beaten in the Assembly. Success went at last to a Radical, Edgar Faure, finance minister in the last two cabinets and foreign minister for the last two weeks. A talented conciliator, he carried by a huge majority the Tunisian agreements which had destroyed his predecessor. But the storm-centre had now moved to Morocco, where French right-wing extremists (in the police force) murdered a leading liberal newspaper-owner.[3] The premier sent out a new resident, Gilbert Grandval, a progressive Gaullist whose long period of authority in the Saar had won him a reputation as a forceful pro-consul.[4] But the Right would not allow concessions to nationalism in a second North African territory. Grandval's mission was wrecked by blatant military and administrative sabotage, openly encouraged by some Gaullist ministers and Conservative parliamentarians. On 20 August 1955, the anniversary of the Sultan's deposition, there were outbreaks and massacres both in Morocco – as the resident had warned – and in Algeria. Grandval resigned and with him vanished the last chance of compromise. The obstructionists (among them the new resident, General Boyer de la Tour) soon brought about the very result they feared. Within three months the Moroccan nationalists were able to impose the triumphant return of the exiled Sultan.[5]

The National Assembly faced an election in June 1956 and would approve no drastic step, forcible or conciliatory, to halt the spreading Algerian war. Faure therefore resolved to go to the country, escaping months of electioneering, permitting an earlier decision on Algerian policy – and also retaining an advantageous electoral law and denying his opponents time to develop their campaigns. His coalition was under heavy fire both from Poujade whose demagogic tax-resistance movement was sweeping the south, and from Mendès-France who had captured the Radical machine. The latter demanded a return to the pre-war electoral system of single-member constituencies and two ballots; as it was favoured by the countryside, the proposal of the leader of the Left was voted by the conservative (but rural-minded) upper house. With Communist help Faure resisted this demand, but on 29 November 1955 he was beaten by an absolute majority in a vote of confidence. This defeat enabled him to take the bold (but unexpectedly popular) decision to dissolve the Assembly for the first time for nearly eighty years.

The election offered the voter his clearest choice since the war – although over the predominant North African issue every leader except Bidault and Poujade professed liberal intentions. In 1951 a broad centre majority had straddled every question. Now the centre was broken. On the moderate Right Faure's parliamentary coalition formed the basis of constituency alliances embracing MRP, the Conservatives, and the premier's Radical associates (who were expelled by their party). On the Left a rival Republican Front was called for by Guy Mollet (Socialist), Mendès-France (Radical), Mitterrand

3. See below, p. 350n. The victim, Lemaigre-Dubreuil, had himself been a right-wing extremist in the thirties, and later helped to plan the Allied landing at Algiers in 1942.

4. Later in the year the Saar voted heavily to rejoin Germany.

5. He formed a cabinet identical with that proposed to Paris eight years earlier by the liberal resident Labonne – except that then foreign affairs and defence were to be in French hands. Labonne had of course promptly been recalled: Bloch-Morhange, *Les Politiciens*, pp. 57–8.

(UDSR) and Chaban-Delmas (Social Republican).[6] These opposing democratic combinations were harassed on their flanks by Communists and Poujadists – who left one another severely alone. The slogan of the former was *Front populaire !*, that of the latter, *Sortez les Sortants !* (roughly, 'Throw the rascals out!'). Vulgar and violent, these political newcomers used rowdyism and occasionally physical force on a scale unheard of in French electioneering. Though these tactics did them more harm than good, they appealed successfully to nationalist and racialist feelings about North Africa, to the discontents of peasants and small shopkeepers, and above all to the widespread distrust of all politicians as a class.[7]

2. FROM SOCIALISM TO 'IMMOBILISME'

On 2 January 1956 France recorded her highest vote since the war. The strength of the traditional parties was little altered: Communists, Socialists and right-wing Radicals maintained their percentage share of the poll, MRP fell back slightly, the Conservatives gained 2½%. But among the various groups of critics there were sweeping changes. The Gaullists, divided and absorbed into the System they had been elected to oppose, lost nearly four-fifths of their four million votes. Mendès-France's Radical supporters doubled their vote, from one to two million, and raised their share of the poll from 5 to nearly 10%; they gained most around Paris and in the booming industrial north-east. But in the rural south, which was losing population to the expanding areas, it was the Poujadists who crystallized the demand for change. To everyone's surprise (even their own) they polled 2½ million votes or nearly 13%. In a few areas these came largely from the Gaullists, but in the south they gained from every party including the Communists.

The conservative coalition thus suffered a double disappointment. First, despite the Gaullist collapse they added only 800,000 to their vote and 1% to their share of the electorate, while the Left – Communists, Socialists and Mendès-France Radicals together – gained two million (5%). Secondly, the electoral system failed to help them. They had hoped in conservative departments to win a clear majority of votes (and therefore all the seats), while in left-wing areas neither Communists nor democratic Left would command a clear majority and so proportional representation (PR) would continue to apply.[8] Poujade frustrated these calculations by making heavy inroads both on their own former votes and on those they had expected to acquire from the Gaullists. Consequently it was hard for anyone to win a clear majority. In 1951 it had been done in forty constituencies, usually by an alliance of the centre parties, but in 1956 in only eleven (one Left, ten Right). Everywhere else PR applied. The Poujadist surge thus benefited not only their own candidates but also the Communists, who regained fifty seats of which the

6. The Social Republican (Gaullist) ministers were dismissed by Faure in October 1955; the party's candidates were divided, most choosing conservative rather than left-wing allies (see below, p. 136n.).

7. Cf. below, p. 325n. For this election see Nicholas *et al.*, nos. 167–70; Pierce, no. 180; *Les élections du 2 janvier 1956* (1957, henceforth cited as *Élections 1956*). For the Poujadists see below, Chapter 12; and for the dissolution, below, p. 239.

8. See pp. 315–6 below.

electoral law – rather than the electorate – had deprived them in the last Parliament. To hamper Mendès-France, Faure's cabinet had risked strengthening Thorez; and their tactical ingenuity had produced an Assembly with only 200 of their own supporters, 150 of the Republican Front, 40 Radical and Gaullist doubtfuls, 150 Communists and 50 Poujadists.[9] It seemed, and was, even more ungovernable than its predecessor. Yet Guy Mollet's new cabinet was to prove the longest-lived of the Fourth Republic.

The country's swing Left had changed the parliamentary balance. Mollet was the master of the legislature, for without the hundred Socialist votes no government could survive, and Communists and Conservatives alike feared to drive him into the arms of their rivals. Mendès-France's leadership in the election campaign therefore availed him little.[10] He refused the ministry of finance, fearing the inflationary consequences of Socialist domestic policies; was vetoed for the foreign ministry by MRP; and was finally relegated to an uneasy office without portfolio. Worse was to follow. On 6 February 1956 (anniversary of the Paris riots of 1934) the new prime minister visited Algiers to inaugurate his policy and install his liberal minister for Algeria, General Catroux. A mob of the poorer Europeans greeted him with rotten tomatoes and he sacrificed his minister as Faure had thrown over Grandval.

In Catroux's place Mollet appointed Robert Lacoste, who of all the Socialist leaders had been the most favourable to General de Gaulle ten years before and to Mendès-France in 1954. Refusing to fight simultaneously against both settlers and Moslems, the new minister firmly postponed political concessions until the day of military victory. The national pride which Mendès-France had tried so hard to rekindle was now mobilized against him by his former allies, Soustelle and Lacoste. The ex-premier resigned in May after delaying his departure so as not to seem to disavow the sending of conscripts to Algeria; his fellow-Radicals stayed in office as he (quite superfluously) advised them. Few of his colleagues came to his defence against the outrageous treason charges of 1954 which the crypto-fascist Right now revived, ably exploiting a long and sordid official secrets trial to reveal many police intrigues and rivalries and further discredit the regime.[11]

The liberal mood of the election campaign and the protests of the first conscripts sent to Algeria were soon forgotten as public opinion reacted against long years of humiliation and defeat. The Suez expedition was acclaimed by most Frenchmen and supported by a united cabinet, including the most liberal ministers, François Mitterrand and Gaston Defferre; many conservative politicians privately thought it unwise, but Mendès-France found little

9. The majority unseated eleven of the Poujadists and declared their rivals elected. Though probably legally correct, this was politically inept and injured Parliament in general and the Republican Front in particular.

10. In polls during the campaign, 27% had said they would like Mendès-France as premier and 2% that they would like Mollet: cited Duverger, *La VIe République et le régime présidentiel*, p. 133, cf. his *Demain la République*, pp. 51, 82. But looser institutional ties with Algeria were rejected by almost two to one: *Élections 1956*, p. 122.

11. On the secrets trial see n. 2. Bloch-Morhange, p. 195 (cf. p. 200) claims that Lacoste's appointment was imposed by an inter-party 'shadow cabinet' which had managed the campaign against EDC, of which he himself was secretary and Lacoste a member. This claim is not supported by Fauvet, *IVe*, pp. 316–17, or by *AP* 1956, p. 24.

backing for his cautious public disapproval.[12] The repression of the Hungarian revolt disillusioned the allies of the Communist party, incensed its enemies and completed its isolation. In January 1957 a by-election in south Paris showed how opinion had moved: the Conservative won, the Socialist did well, the Communist receded, the Mendesist lost three-quarters of his predecessor's vote, and Pierre Poujade in person kept only half that of his candidate a year before.

This much-maligned ministry introduced some overdue reforms at home (higher old-age pensions and longer paid holidays) and in Black Africa and Madagascar, where Defferre's *loi-cadre* for once enabled France to keep pace with the demands of local nationalism and retain the goodwill of its leaders.[13] For, if the Right was happy to see a Socialist-led government take responsibility for waging the war in Algeria, Mollet was skilful at extracting advantage from his opponents' reluctance to turn him out. It was under his ministry, however, that the ravages of the Algerian conflict began to afflict France itself. First, a war superimposed upon a boom rapidly dissipated the record reserves of foreign exchange built up by Edgar Faure, and once again subjected France's economy to inflation and her policy to the need for foreign aid. Secondly, this government began the legal harrying of minorities, manipulation of opinion and petty interference with the freedom of the press; its successors went so much further that before long a colonel in the defence ministry could have all copies of a newspaper illegally seized without even seeking the formality of ministerial approval. And, thirdly, the Mollet cabinet presided over a further decline of the civil power across the Mediterranean.

Though the 6 February riots had installed a new minister and a new policy in Algiers, the government continued secret talks with the rebel FLN and in October serious negotiations seemed possible for the first time. But as Ben Bella and four other FLN leaders were flying to a preliminary conference at Tunis (in a Moroccan plane with a French crew) they were diverted and arrested at Algiers by French military intelligence. One junior minister knew in advance and another resigned in protest, but Guy Mollet, like Georges Bidault before him, covered and justified a *fait accompli* he had disapproved or forbidden.[14] Then as murderous and indiscriminate FLN terrorism sowed chaos in Algiers, Lacoste handed over complete power in the city to General Massu's parachutists. They broke the terrorists, but their methods alienated Moslem opinion and in France itself aroused vociferous criticism.

Without the army Algeria could no longer be administered; and within it officers were increasingly angered by the government's hesitations and the attacks of a part of French opinion. In December 1956 General Jacques Faure was found plotting to seize power in Algiers; the government gave him

12. Among the doubters were Faure, Reynaud, Pinay, Pflimlin, and every speaker at the Conservative party meeting: Fauvet, *IVe*, pp. 321–2; Isorni, *Le silence est d'or*, pp. 173–6. But only eleven Radicals abstained with Mendès-France; seventeen Socialists later condemned the expedition. The only avowed opponents were the Communists – and M. Poujade, who opposed 'fighting for the Queen of England'. On the Communists see below, p. 172.

13. See Robinson, no. 192.

14. See above, p. 41. Max Lejeune, minister of state (*secrétaire d'État*) for the army, knew beforehand; Alain Savary, minister of state for Tunisian and Moroccan affairs, resigned and so did the ambassador at Tunis.

sixty days' fortress arrest and posted him to Germany.[15] Next month French extremists killed an ADC with a bazooka shell fired into the office of the commander-in-chief, General Salan, who was then considered a loyal republican; the perpetrators were arrested and their leader Kovacs implicated leading Gaullist politicians in the plot. His charges, even if false, served their purpose and investigation of the bazooka plot was hushed up.

In May 1957 the Mollet government was at last overthrown by the Right. They approved of the war but not of higher taxes, accused the cabinet of extravagant spending, and suspected its intentions in Algeria. But though the Socialists had lost the premiership they still controlled the Assembly. Because of their lukewarmness and Radical hostility, Pierre Pflimlin (the new chairman of MRP, who held mildly liberal views about Algeria) withdrew his candidature without a vote; the Socialists then gave their willing support to Maurice Bourgès-Maunoury, the Radical minister of defence who had been mainly responsible for the infringements of civil liberties under the Mollet government. He formed a Socialist and Radical cabinet without those ministers who had been critical of Lacoste's Algerian policy, and obtained from the Assembly the narrowest vote of confidence (240 to 194) ever given an incoming premier.

The deputies promptly granted to the new ministry the tax increases they had refused to the old one. In July they voted by a large majority to ratify the treaties setting up the Common Market and 'Euratom'; Mendès-France joined the Gaullists, Poujadists and Communists in opposition. Algerian terrorism was met by setting up internment camps in France, but Lacoste's *loi-cadre*, a mild measure of Algerian political reform, divided the cabinet. A 'round table' of parliamentary leaders patched up a compromise. But the Right revolted and brought the government down.

Ten years earlier the Assembly of 1946 had been chosen by a system of proportional representation which guaranteed a third of the seats to the various enemies of the regime. Now the 1956 election had produced a similar result, and a similar dilemma. Unless all the other parties stood together no government could be formed or survive; yet these parties could agree only on a standstill policy (*immobilisme*) which in turn provoked discontent within their own ranks. When Pinay was nominated the Socialists showed that he could not command a majority; when Mollet stood the Conservatives returned the compliment (both of course were assisted in their demonstration by the votes of their common enemies). After five weeks a young Radical, Félix Gaillard, emerged to form a combination as broad and shallow as Queuille's nearly a decade before. For the first time since the 1956 election MRP and Conservative leaders sat in cabinet alongside not only the Radicals, but also the Socialists to whom they had been opposed for six years. But the Socialists could not concede too much without losing control of their party, nor the Conservatives without seeing their rural followers go over to Poujade.

15. The same penalty was inflicted on General Paris de la Bollardière for resigning and publicly denouncing military brutality in the countryside. Paul Teitgen, the senior police official who exposed General Faure's plot, also soon resigned in protest against the tortures and 'disappearances' of Moslems in Algiers. On the army's mood see Planchais, *Le malaise de l'armée*, Chapter 5; and Girardet in *Military Politics*, Chapter 5, and no. 99b.

Though the Gaillard government introduced some necessary economies, its energies were mainly occupied in avoiding its own disintegration.

These domestic strains were accompanied by an endless colonial war. Over Algeria as over Indo-China, there was a majority neither for victory at any price nor for peace by negotiation, but only for ineffective compromise solutions; when Gaillard reintroduced and passed the Lacoste *loi-cadre* it had to be so whittled down in order to attract the votes of the Right that few remembered it had once been meant to win over the Moslems. North Africa, however, was nearer home than Indo-China, and the tensions it generated were much more serious. They were to destroy not merely a government but a regime.

3. THE DELIQUESCENT STATE

Across the Mediterranean the authority of the Republic had been flouted for years. Generals and residents, prefects and riot leaders had imposed their own disastrous policies at Tunis in 1952, Rabat in 1953, Algiers in 1956. More recently the disease had spread to France. Left-wing officials gave military secrets to the press; right-wing police officers falsely accused their political superiors of treason and found respectable politicians to purvey their slanders. Military judges showed gross political bias. General Faure was not punished for sedition; Kovacs was not tried for murder;[16] Bourgès-Maunoury, minister of the interior, did not even resign when in March 1958 the Paris police (organized by ex-superintendent Dides) staged an ugly anti-parliamentary and anti-semitic demonstration outside the Assembly. Socialist and Radical ministers were too busy denouncing left-wing critics of the Algerian war, seizing their papers and banning their meetings, to recognize the real threat to French democracy.

The Fourth Republic was crumbling both at the top and at the base. The long ministerial crises of 1957 exacerbated public opinion and sapped the self-confidence of the political leaders themselves. Dr. Queuille's medicine was too insipid when the political temperature, raised by Indo-China and Tunisia, Morocco and Suez, was kept at fever pitch by the Algerian war. This was the year of two bitter emotional agitations, one by the Right over Captain Moureau, an officer who was seized and doubtless murdered by Moroccan guerrillas, the other by the Left over Djamila Bouhired, a Moslem girl accused of terrorism who was tortured and sentenced to death in Algiers after a scandalous trial.

The democratic politicians could not agree on the measures to be taken either at home or overseas. The conflicts between the parties were complicated by bitter divisions within each of them, especially among the Radicals who had traditionally specialized in managing political transitions. A solution through the normal political process seemed unattainable, and the familiar remedy of constitutional reform again came into fashion. In press and intellectual circles a campaign in favour of a presidential system obtained support in unexpected quarters. While the parliamentary leaders preferred less drastic

16. After de Gaulle came to power Kovacs was brought to trial but given bail on medical grounds and escaped from the country. On the leakages and slanders see above, pp. 46n., 49.

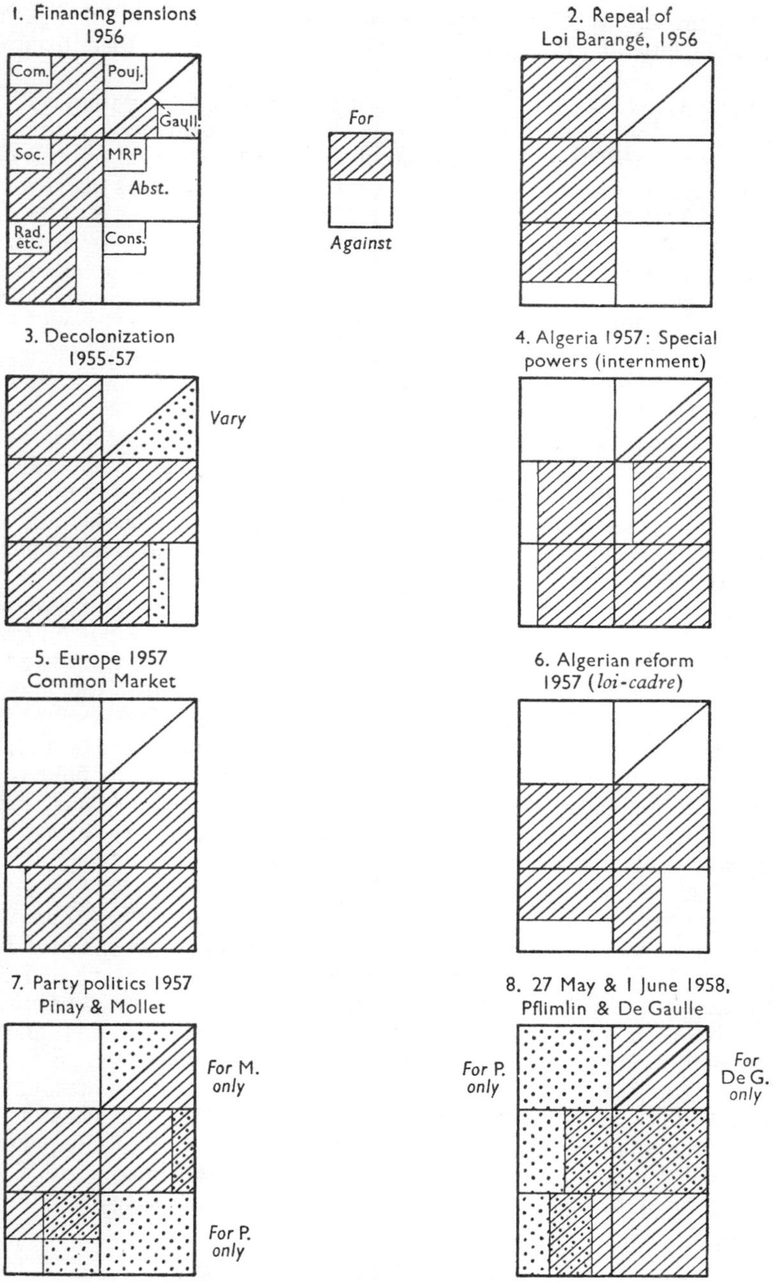
1. Financing pensions 1956
Com.
Pouj.
Gaull.
Soc.
MRP
Abst.
Rad. etc.
Cons.
For
Against
2. Repeal of Loi Barangé, 1956
3. Decolonization 1955-57
Vary
4. Algeria 1957: Special powers (internment)
5. Europe 1957 Common Market
6. Algerian reform 1957 (loi-cadre)
7. Party politics 1957 Pinay & Mollet
For M. only
For P. only
8. 27 May & 1 June 1958, Pflimlin & De Gaulle
For P. only
For De G. only

Fig. 4. Party Alignments 1955–8

and more ingenious schemes, more and more of them felt that changes must come soon, either by their own initiative or else imposed on them from without.

Yet they knew also that the chance of agreed reform from within was small indeed. Therefore, from President Coty downwards, some were turning as a last resort to a towering figure outside the regime. In the final months of the Fourth Republic General de Gaulle was receiving more visitors than for many years past, and they ranged from the far Right to the very fringes of the Communist party. The left-wing weeklies *L'Express* and *France-Observateur*, the bitterest critics of Guy Mollet and his younger protégés and successors, gave space and encouragement to the Gaullist alternative. Meanwhile the Gaullist leaders were multiplying their activities. They appealed to public opinion with new journals like Michel Debré's *Courrier de la Colère* and Jacques Soustelle's *Voici Pourquoi* (both started in November 1957). Behind the scenes they organized for illegal action, reviving the old wartime and Resistance networks and penetrating into the heart of the state machine. They had a foothold in the *Conseil d'État* and a stronghold in the ministry of defence under a Gaullist minister, Jacques Chaban-Delmas; they enjoyed the sympathy of the chief of the general staff and of a number of senior officers in Algeria; and Léon Delbecque, a Gaullist on the minister's personal staff, provided a link between the discontented military chiefs and the revolutionary Europeans of Algiers.

The Gaullists were not the only plotters; the crypto-fascist Right were also active in Algiers and vigilant in Paris. They had no public support in France. Up to the very moment of crisis, by-elections and local elections showed little change in opinion; Communism was standing still, Poujadism was in decline and the other extreme Right groups were utterly negligible.[17] But if an explosion occurred they could count on public indifference, for no one (not even the Communists, as the Gaullists rightly foresaw) was willing to fight for the regime. The detonator for the explosion – every explosion – was ready in Algiers. But it could not be touched off without the assent of the army.

The soldiers had little love for the Algiers Europeans, whose demonstration against Lacoste's *loi-cadre* had been stopped in September 1957 by General Massu. But they deeply distrusted the politicians in Paris and were determined never to permit a 'government of scuttle' to hand Algeria over to the FLN. They were furious when at the end of 1957 Britain and the United States delivered arms, after France had refused, to Tunisia – which had become the FLN's base. Then in February 1958 the air force caused an international outcry by bombarding the Tunisian village of Sakiet; as usual the government had not been informed beforehand. The Left (including some ministers) wanted to defy the army and punish those responsible, the Right to defy world opinion and reoccupy Tunisia. The Centre feared the consequences of either challenge, and Gaillard accepted Anglo-American mediation. But the Right resented his minor concessions to Tunisia and suspected that the

17. At Marseilles in February 1958 an extreme-Right candidate won 2 % of the vote; in north-west Paris in March another won 3 % on the first ballot and under 1 % on the second, 2,500 votes out of 580,000 electors. (In both cases the official Conservative was very right-wing.) The Gaullists were recovering slightly from their low point of 1956.

Algerian problem also would be internationalized. In April they overthrew the cabinet – the third they had defeated in twelve months. So opened the last and longest interregnum of the Fourth Republic.

It soon became clear that those who had caused the crisis were unlikely to gain by it. Soustelle had no more chance of forming a cabinet than Mendès-France. Bidault was sent for; he was frustrated by his own party and in particular by its chairman Pflimlin. Pleven, a specialist in reconciling opposites, was prevented from forming a cabinet by the refusal of orthodox Radicals to sit with a right-wing ex-Radical, André Morice. The Socialists decided to stay out of office altogether so as to remove Lacoste from Algiers without directly disavowing him. The crisis provoked by the Europeans of Algeria was leading to the progressive elimination of all their political friends. And to crown the process the premiership was offered to Pflimlin, leader of the liberal wing of MRP.

In the hothouse atmosphere of Algiers his nomination seemed a prelude to capitulation to the FLN. The army leaders officially warned President Coty that the election of a 'government of scuttle' would have incalculable consequences; the mob, stimulated by the rival plotters and remembering their success of 6 February 1956, rioted against Pflimlin's candidature. On 13 May 1958, with the connivance of a section of the army, they occupied Government House in Algiers a few hours before the Assembly was due to vote, and set up a Committee of Public Safety under General Massu. But the news rallied support to Pflimlin and induced the Communists to abstain; instead of failing as expected, he was comfortably elected. Hoping to win the army back to its allegiance he delegated civil power in Algiers to General Salan. But the commander-in-chief, after a day's hesitation, publicly appealed to a third general: de Gaulle.[18]

4. 'RESURRECTION'

General de Gaulle's name had been canvassed on the Left as well as the Right; but a candidate for the premiership had to appear before the National Assembly, and when sounded privately by President Coty ten days earlier, de Gaulle had refused to do so. Now he seized the chance presented by Salan: that evening (15 May) he publicly announced his readiness 'to assume the powers of the Republic'. The brief trial of strength had begun.

Although the cabinet was reinforced by the entry of the Socialists and by repeated and massive majorities in the Assembly, the isolation and discredit of Parliament and the politicians now became painfully clear. Against the threat (or bluff) of insurrection in France and invasion from Algeria the government found itself defenceless. The army and air force were openly mutinous; the police had shown their feelings in their demonstration in March; the civil administration disregarded orders. Nor was the defection of the state machine offset by any mobilization of popular forces. Hardly any Frenchmen believed that the former leader of the Resistance now intended to destroy democratic

18. For a fuller account of the 13 May crisis and its background see Williams and Harrison, *De Gaulle's Republic*, Chapters 3 and 4; Werth, *The De Gaulle Revolution*, Parts I and II; Macridis and Brown, *The De Gaulle Republic*, Part I; Williams, no. 220.

liberties, and few would run risks or make sacrifices for the Fourth Republic – or even for the proletarian revolution.

On Saturday 24 May Corsica was taken over by supporters of de Gaulle. Convinced at last of their own impotence, ministers secretly opened negotiations with the General. But he feared the army would launch the planned invasion from Algeria, Operation Resurrection, and tried to rush matters. He only stiffened resistance in the Assembly, where a majority still preferred even a Popular Front to the Algiers Committees of Public Safety; for once the deputies were desperately trying to keep in office a premier who wanted only to escape from it. The resignation of the Conservative ministers gave Pflimlin the pretext he needed, and despite his enormous majority of 408 to 165 he resigned in the early morning of 28 May. Later that day in eastern Paris some 200,000 people demonstrated for the parliamentary Republic.

In a special message next afternoon President Coty threatened to resign his own office unless the deputies elected de Gaulle premier.[19] It took the Socialist leaders three more days to bring round enough of their followers. The General's moderate language won over some members, the composition of his ministry (which included Mollet and Pflimlin but not as yet Soustelle) reassured many more. On Sunday 1 June he appeared in the Assembly he had once said he would never enter again, and delivered the shortest investiture speech of the Fourth Republic. With nearly half the Socialists voting for him, he was elected with a majority of more than a hundred.

The deputies had not yet said their final word. General de Gaulle asked Parliament to vote bills continuing the government's special powers in Algeria, giving it full authority in France for six months, and allowing it to draft a new constitution to be ratified by referendum. The deputies wanted Parliament to vote the draft, but gave way when de Gaulle threatened to resign; after exacting a promise that he would not alter the electoral law they departed, reassured, into an exile which they still could not believe would be permanent.[20] But they were not to meet again, and fewer than a quarter of them would reappear in the first National Assembly of the Fifth Republic.

During the summer the government hastily drafted its constitutional proposals, submitted them to a mainly parliamentary consultative committee whose objections were mostly ignored, and presented them with an immense publicity campaign for ratification by the electorate. Most of the Fourth Republican parties approved, the Socialists by a large and the Radicals by a fairly narrow majority. The non-Communist Left opposition refused to defend the Fourth Republic and insisted that their *NON* vote implied the election of a Constituent Assembly to draft a new constitution in the proper democratic way. The Communist party, after denouncing them for hair-splitting when the Republic was in danger, discovered the unpopularity of the old regime in its own ranks and itself came out for a Constituent Assembly. On 28 September, in a record 85% poll, four-fifths of those voting approved

19. Coty's resignation would have opened the way to a Popular Front government; cf. below, pp. 202–3.

20. The government sought and obtained the right to change this law from a higher authority, the people themselves, in the referendum of 28 September 1958.

the new constitution. As all the *OUIs* and nearly all the *NONs* were voting against the defunct republic, the electorate's condemnation of it was quite as overwhelming as their repudiation of its predecessor thirteen years earlier.[21]

21. For a fuller account of the interregnum period and the referendum campaign see Williams and Harrison, *De Gaulle's Republic*, Chapter 5, and 'France 1958' in Butler, ed., *Elections Abroad*; Macridis and Brown, Part II; Werth, *op. cit.*, Chapters 20–25.

PART II

THE PARTIES

Chapter 5

POLITICAL COMMUNICATION AND PARTY STRUCTURE

The Third Republic had found its democratic base in the provinces rather than Paris. Its six hundred small constituencies were remarkably self-contained, and the deputy who entrenched himself in his fief by conscientious local services had little to fear from pressure-groups or prefects, party whips or national swings. Party and professional organization was very weak; few prefects cared to offend a powerful politician; and the floating vote was small. The opinions of the electorate remained stable over long periods, changing their labels but rarely their proportions. The focus of political organization on the Right was often the château or the Church; on the Left, an *ad hoc* committee of lawyers, doctors or schoolteachers, influential in local government and sometimes linked by freemasonry; and everywhere the small local newspapers, which were born for, lived on, and sometimes died of electioneering. Occasionally a daily in a provincial metropolis became a great power in its region, like *Le Progrès* at Lyons, but there was no national press and broadcasting was used politically only in the last few years. The capital was a remote and suspect world: its ministers, writers, bureaucrats, salons, journalists and proletarians might influence the policy-makers at times, but they had little if any impact on the voters.

After 1945 the rapid changes in French society outpaced the slow evolution of political methods. Parties were better organized than in the Third Republic, though (except in 1945–47) worse than in most democratic countries. Pressure-groups grew in number, scale and power.[1] The press, temporarily reorganized at the Liberation, never quite resumed its old role. Radio and television developed in the Fourth Republic, but their full impact on politics was reserved for the Fifth.

1. THE MEDIA OF COMMUNICATION

Before 1939 the smaller local newspapers were already declining as transport improved, and in the Fourth Republic many of them disappeared. The great regional journals were more widely read: Toulouse kept its militant *Dépêche*, a mighty force within the Radical party, and Marseilles had an old-style newspaper war between the Socialist *Provençal* and the reactionary *Méridional*. But these were exceptional, for most of the regionals were reluctant to offend potential readers by violent polemics. The largest, *Ouest-France*, was Catholic and moderate but gave little space to politics. Some provincial papers took no clear line at all.

Another sign of the reader's distaste for polemical politics (or for politics) was the rapid decline of the official party publications after a momentary post-war expansion. The Liberation brought a revolution in the journalistic balance

1. Parties are discussed in the following chapters, and in Chapter 23; pressure-groups in Chapters 25 and 26.

of power, for the presses of papers which had appeared under German censorship were provisionally allotted to new party or Resistance organs. In 1939 journals supporting the Radicals and Conservatives had had 5,000,000 readers and Socialist and Communist ones 1,300,000; in 1944 these figures were reversed. MRP had a new press with 1,300,000 readers, and many 'non-party' conservative papers passed to Resisters of the Left. These sweeping changes helped to cripple the old parties and strengthen the new in the early post-war elections, and a law of 1946 sought to perpetuate them. But it was thwarted first by political opponents and then by the readers themselves. In ten years the Communist papers lost two-thirds of their circulation and many had to close. MRP's national daily, *L'Aube*, ceased publication in 1951. The Socialist *Populaire* survived precariously, thanks to the British Labour party and other sympathizers, as a bulletin for party members rather than a newspaper.[2]

Resistance journals like *Combat* soon suffered a similar fate. At the Liberation there had been great hopes that a new, purified and independent press would replace the notoriously venal Parisian papers (which were often on sale both to foreign governments and to French bankers and industrialists). But financial weakness and inexperience soon forced many of the newcomers into merger or liquidation. Business recovered much of its power, though its new organs were more discreet and less corrupt than the old ones. But one exception stood out: *Le Monde* preserved that 'financial and intellectual independence [which] in some quarters seems astonishing if not almost scandalous'.[3] Financiers tried to buy it or wreck it; a Socialist government abused price-control powers to force it into bankruptcy; but its circulation rose steadily and by 1958 was nearly 200,000, over three times that of the old *Temps*. Arousing strong admiration and intense hatred, it became the indispensable paper of a serious generation of students and of the entire political class. At times it was more effective as a critical forum than Parliament itself.

The other Paris dailies also had more readers than before, and their standards were not quite as abysmal as those of their predecessors (or some of their popular counterparts in other countries). Usually they were more anxious to increase circulation than to influence opinion: *Le Figaro* was a weathercock of respectable bourgeois opinion, *France-Soir* ran no risks but had a mild preference for progress, and *Le Parisien Libéré* attracted many Communist readers by giving little emphasis to its extreme reactionary politics. The place of the old *journaux d'opinion* was taken by the weeklies. On the Left, the satirical but well-informed *Canard Enchaîné* was joined by several newcomers. When Claude Bourdet was evicted from *Combat* he founded *L'Observateur*, later *France-Observateur*, to appeal to the neutralist intellectuals. *L'Express* rallied the progressive bourgeoisie to Mendès-France; *Témoignage Chrétien* wrote for the Catholic Left, a new group who also influenced the tone of other Catholic papers like the daily *La Croix*. The right-wing weeklies were not much

2. On the Communist press see below, p. 77; on the 1946 law, below, p. 392. By 1950, 109 dailies had closed; by 1957, 27 more: list in *AP* 1957, pp. 552–3. In 1958 the ten main regionals had 45 % of the total provincial circulation: Grosser, p. 162 (the best short account of the press).

3. Delouvrier in *Crise*, p. 82. See also A. Chatelain, Le Monde *et ses lecteurs* (1962), Chapter 2, p. 183, n. 53.

read: *Aspects de la France* was a pale shadow of the pre-war daily *L'Action française*, and *Rivarol* poisoned far fewer minds than *Gringoire*. Also in sharp contrast to the 1930's, the leading monthlies were the Left Catholic *Esprit* and the neutralist *Temps Modernes*, with the Vichyite *Écrits de Paris* far behind. But all these journals gave focus to currents of opinion whose influence was out of proportion to their numbers. Among the individualist extremists on both political wings there were parties around a newspaper rather than newspapers belonging to a party.

Sound radio played less part in France than in other great democracies. As elsewhere, political broadcasting mattered less than 'non-political' daily programmes (though Mendès-France's fireside chats helped consolidate his brief popularity). Every government abused its control of the radio, but only the Socialists approached the degree of partisanship which became commonplace in the Fifth Republic. To escape manipulated information, listeners turned increasingly to the independent stations, Radio Luxembourg and Europe No. 1. In television the state network had no competitor, but it still covered only a limited area when the Fourth Republic fell; it was not used in an election until 1956, and then with conspicuous ineptitude by everyone except Pierre Poujade.

Thus means of communication were slow to adapt to the growing 'nationalization' of political issues and moods. With television in its infancy, radio not much used, the Paris press influential only close to the capital, and few political leaders making electioneering tours, there was hardly more national political campaigning in the Fourth Republic than in the Third.[4] Nor did the forms of party organization change much more rapidly, although all the many parties of the Fourth Republic were twentieth-century foundations.

2. THE PARTIES: MEMBERS AND OUTLOOK

The Radical party has enjoyed a continuous existence since 1901, the Socialist party in its present form since 1905 and the Communists since 1920. For in France political parties are a left-wing innovation: the Radicals established a very loose formal framework, the Socialists introduced disciplined voting, and the Communists extended that discipline to all spheres of party activity. Conservative forces, relying on the influence of powerful individuals, were long reluctant to organize politically except in very loose formations which avoided both the name and the habits of party (Democratic Alliance, Republican Federation), or in anti-parliamentary leagues dedicated to the violent overthrow of the democratic system (*Action française*).

The second world war gave a great impetus to party organization. MRP, born of the Resistance and founded in 1944, was intended to be a 'movement' with a purpose broader than mere electioneering. Two small Conservative parties, the Peasants and the *Parti républicain de la Liberté* (PRL) were also formed at the Liberation; but only after the foundation in 1948 of the *Centre national des indépendants et paysans* (CNIP) did the moderate Right for the first time in its history gradually build a headquarters recognized by most of

4. On propaganda in the 1956 campaign see *Élections 1956*, pp. 67–195, especially pp. 88, 110, 161, 182, 195; and Nicholas *et al.*, nos. 168–70, pp. 147, 160–1, 257–60, 280–1.

its troops. Two very different leaders, General de Gaulle and Pierre Poujade, were successively to evoke the latent anti-parliamentary sentiments of many of their compatriots. Although their followings also differed greatly, both men attracted support predominantly from the Right and marginally from the Left. The Gaullist RPF, founded in 1947, was already withering when the General withdrew his patronage in 1953; the Poujadist *Union et fraternité française* (UFF), formed to fight the 1956 election, had perished within a few months – except in the Assembly against which it so vigorously vituperated. One of the smaller groups, *Union démocratique et socialiste de la Résistance* (UDSR) emerged from the Resistance movement. The rest arose from splits within other parties: *Action républicaine et sociale* (ARS) were conservative Gaullists on their way into CNIP, the Dissident Radicals were opponents of the progressive policies and strong leadership of Mendès-France, and one wing of the Peasant party refused to submerge its identity in a wider Conservative coalition.

French parties bore little resemblance to one another and still less to political parties as they are conceived of in Britain. First, they were much smaller. At their peak just after the war the Communists and RPF each claimed about a million members, the Socialists a third and MRP a fifth of that number; but within five years most of these had deserted. The Conservative groups never attempted, and the Radicals tried only under Mendès-France, to organize their rank and file supporters; instead these parties contented themselves with a network of notables scattered through the small towns and the countryside, who sprang into sudden activity at election times. Pierre Poujade claimed 350,000 for his Shopkeepers' and Artisans' Defence Union (UDCA), which started with a professional purpose but later developed into the political UFF; Mendès-France brought the Radicals above the 100,000 mark; both successes were short-lived. By the end of the Republic the Communists were probably the only party with over 100,000 members and the Socialists their only rival with over 50,000. Thus if most of the main groups could rely on influential supporters in the localities, only the Communists could boast of anything like the constituency structure of a big British party.

Discipline differed immensely from one group to another. For a short period at the Liberation it seemed that the pressure of the more rigid parties would react on the looser ones. Until 1935 the Radicals and Conservatives together with the smaller intermediate groups had controlled four-fifths of the seats in the lower house, but ten years later they held little more than a quarter. The rest were divided between two old well-organized parties, Communists and Socialists, and a new one, MRP, which also despised and condemned the personal and parochial politics of pre-war days and aspired to become a powerful and disciplined unit. Like the Communists it owed much of its force and cohesion to a base of support deeper than simple electoral loyalty.

While these three strong parties were agreed they dominated Parliament. But once the Communists were relegated to the opposition, the fate of governments again came to depend on a handful of marginal votes – and life and uncertainty returned to the parliamentary scene. In day-to-day business every party could still count on the votes of the enormous majority of its members;

but on the major questions where discipline was worst, party authority was soon little stronger than in pre-war days. It was most effective on the Left, which had always hoped by mass organization to offset the personal prestige of its conservative adversaries. It was weakest in the Centre: for there politicians were often torn between their conflicting views on social and economic questions and on political and religious problems; and were particularly likely, because of their pivotal position, to be tempted by the sweets of office into personal decisions of which their colleagues disapproved.[5]

At bottom the differences in behaviour reflected differences in purpose. The ordinary Communist deputy obeyed his party because he believed it was a force dedicated to constructing a new society. The Poujadists at first seemed a solid group when they arrived in Parliament in 1956 to make their inarticulate but vehement protest against the existing political order; in 1951 the Gaullists had created the same impression, though it soon became plain that many of them were making the protest only in order to arrive in Parliament. And if those parties of revolt could not keep their ranks unbroken once they were subjected to the temptations of power, their governmental rivals were naturally even more vulnerable.

All the democratic politicians of the Fourth Republic were under intermittent pressure from a new political generation, impatient with the System and insistent on more positive and progressive government. Though the reforming zeal of the Liberation did not last, there remained a pent-up demand for change which sought expression at different times through MRP and the Socialist party, Mendès-France and de Gaulle. But when Mendès-France sought to impose discipline as well as reforming policies on the Radical party, he soon found that the members of that electoral co-operative would not renounce the right to vote as conscience, career or constituency dictated. MRP soon lost most of its initial missionary fervour and its leaders accommodated themselves all too readily to what de Gaulle called 'the games, the poisons and the delights of the System'. Among the parties of piecemeal reform only the Socialists retained the strict parliamentary voting discipline of which they were traditionally proud; in compensation (or in consequence) a decision committing the party's vote caused them more acute internal dissension than any of their rivals suffered. Ultimately, exasperation with the Republican politicians was to give another chance to the General whom they had ousted in 1946 and thwarted in 1951.

3. MONEY AND POWER

In organization, too, the same terms covered different realities. But since all parties existed largely and some exclusively for electoral purposes, an apparent similarity was imposed by the local government system. France has ninety departments very roughly corresponding to English counties, and 38,000 communes varying from tiny hamlets to great cities like Lyons or Marseilles. The Socialists, a relatively well-organized party, had a 'federation' in each department, and should have had a 'section' in each commune (or each ward of a big town), though in practice this ideal was only partly realized. The

5. See below, pp. 397–400, 418–9.

sections met monthly or fortnightly, and collected members' subscriptions, keeping most of them. At the national level there were an executive committee for current business, an annual conference which was the party's supreme authority, and between the two a national council or 'little conference' consisting of a representative from each federation and meeting quarterly (more often in emergencies). There were also special committees to regulate disputes over discipline and check the party's accounts.[6]

All the parties were poor. Subscriptions were low, members were few, and loyalties tended to be local: for instance in the Socialist party the sections decided the rate of subscription and the central organization received only a fixed sum per member. The better-organized parties tried to raise funds and strengthen cohesion by levies on the salaries of their members of parliament. All charged something for the services of the group's office, and members sometimes voluntarily offered more. The Communists went much further, collecting most of these salaries and repaying only the equivalent of a skilled worker's wage. Poujade in his heyday tried to imitate their system by housing his troop of 'non-political' provincials in a single hotel, drawing their deputies' salaries in common, and retaining much of them for the party (but his attempt to increase its share late in 1956 seems to have helped to undermine his authority over his followers). It was believed that the lucrative if illegal profits of trading in over-valued Indo-Chinese piastres were used for years to replenish the funds of several parties, though only one – RPF, scourge of the corrupt System – was exposed in public. But the main source of party finance seems to have been business. Senator Boutemy, a former Vichy prefect who was made minister of health in 1953 but had to resign after violent Communist attacks, was alleged without contradiction to be the political paymaster for CNPF and in 1951 to have financed members of all parties except the Communists; any Radical deputy could have £500 from his funds and ex-ministers (including the then premier) £1,000.[7]

6. Socialists and RPF called their national council the *conseil national*; MRP, *comité national*; Radicals, *comité exécutif*; Communists, *comité central*. Those of Communists and MRP were supposed to meet every two months; the Radicals' and (till 1956) the Socialists', every three months; RPF's met less often and was used more for long-term policy-making. The executives were called *bureau politique* (Communist), *comité directeur* (Socialist), *commission exécutive* (MRP and, till 1955, Radical), *conseil de direction* (RPF); members of parliament were generally kept in a minority on them (except by the Communists) but usually managed to dominate them. MRP and RPF gave representation to 'corporative' organizations of youth, women, workers, etc. For these large parties, conferences mustered from a thousand to four thousand delegates (Communists rather fewer). They were generally held in summer, though the Radicals preferred autumn; in most parties they were annual, but the Communists held theirs every two years in principle and less frequently in practice (between 1947 and 1959 only three instead of the statutory five). Special conferences were called as occasion arose. CNIP, the least structured of the big parties, held no full conference until 1954. See Campbell, no. 47, pp. 412–23.

7. *JO* 17 February 1953, p. 1067, M. Pronteau – a Communist who was informed by some of the beneficiaries: Bloch-Morhange, p. 43. See also *ibid.*, pp. 118–23; Isorni, *Ainsi passent les Républiques*, pp. 9–10 (who says no promises were required in return for the money); *JO* 24 November 1948, p. 7196, letter of M. Macouin (PRL) read by M. Duclos; Ehrmann, *Business*, pp. 223–7; below, p. 371 and n. Allegedly the amounts were doubled in 1956: Fauvet, *Cockpit*, p. 142, *Déchirée*, p. 135. On RPF and the piastres scandal, *Monde*, 1, 22, 23, 30 and 31 October 1953; all parties except CNIP and the Communists were implicated, according to a biased source, Faucher, *L'agonie d'un régime*, p. 26. On Communist and Poujadist levies see also below, pp. 80, 165; Socialist members contributed about one-sixteenth of their salaries to the party and provided from 20 to 25% of its budget. On electioneering costs and on particular party funds, below, pp. 371–2.

These central contributions were spent mainly in the constituencies. This both reflected and reinforced the individual deputy's remarkable independence of his party headquarters. Nowhere was the contrast with Britain more striking than in the capital. Paris could neither offer the facilities nor perform the functions that a British party expects from head office at Westminster. Apart from the Communists only the Socialists had an organization comparable even with the British Liberals. Most French parties had no more than six or ten headquarters officials, with even fewer typists and doormen.[8] Some like CNIP, with hardly any full-time staff, had to recruit outside sympathizers for an election campaign; others like MRP, normally better organized, found half their regular officials disappearing to contest seats in the provinces. However, parties could manage with these tiny staffs because campaigns were so localized – some headquarters did not even know the names of the candidates they were nominally sponsoring.

Thus the politician could not expect much help (or hindrance) from his party. He had to rely on his own reputation, activity, financial resources and friends for his campaign; the party label helped, especially in the towns and especially on the Left, but except in 1945–46 the deputy was more often an asset to the party than the party was to him. Moreover, when so many organizations were competing, expulsion from his original party need not terminate a parliamentarian's career.[9] Therefore members were independent enough to defy the machine when its instructions ran counter to their own views or ambitions or the needs of their constituents. In every party (except possibly the Communist) there were conflicts between the members of parliament and those who sought to give them orders – whether these were the delegates of the active rank and file or an authoritarian party leader. As in the Third Republic, the militants or the external leadership suspected the deputies of an excessive willingness to compromise at the expense of principle, while the parliamentarians upbraided their critics for narrow sectarianism and flagrant irresponsibility.

Power was centralized in two parties other than the Communist. RPF's national organs were not elected but nominated by the Founder-President, and at first all key posts were filled and major policies decided by him. But the strict discipline, which proletarian Communists had accepted only with reluctance after fifteen years of pressure, could not suddenly be clamped down upon a bourgeois movement whose members were far less prepared by their personal lives for organized collective activity. Central office interference in elections produced a constant stream of resignations in the constituencies; and

8. In Britain in 1951 Conservative headquarters numbered 220, Labour 100, Liberals 50; a fifth of the Liberals and a third of the other two were policy staff: D. E. Butler, *The British General Election of 1951* (1952), pp. 25–7. The French Socialists had to cut staff from 102 to 37 in 1948–49; Ligou, *Histoire du Socialisme en France 1871–1961*, p. 589. They had 60 permanent employees in 1958: Laponce, *Government of the Fifth Republic*, p. 62 (a useful source for party organization). Robert Buron claims that only half a dozen party officials in all counted politically: *Le plus beau des métiers*, p. 20.

9. See below, pp. 324–8. In a poll in November 1944, 72% favoured voting for a programme and 16 % for a man; by January 1958, 52 % wished to vote for a man and only 27 % for a party: cited *Le référendum de septembre et les élections de novembre 1958* (henceforth cited as *Élections 1958*), p. 278.

when in 1951 RPF acquired a strong parliamentary group, the deputies proved so recalcitrant over policy and tactics that within two years General de Gaulle had repudiated all connection with them. Nor had Poujade any better fortune, though the inadequacy of his followers' educational background and their total lack of political experience should have made them easier to manipulate – even if they did not take too seriously his warning that whoever betrayed the movement would be hanged. Within ten months of entering the Assembly a third of his deputies had disobeyed his order to vote against the Suez expedition, and in 1958 the whole group defied its leader and supported General de Gaulle for the premiership.

Another pair of formations was at the opposite extreme of decentralization. The Radicals and Conservatives were hardly more than federations of parliamentary personalities who enjoyed strong influence in their own constituencies. They made little attempt to impose common tactics or policies. So far from the parliamentary parties being affiliates of organizations in the country, the latter existed (if at all) merely as constituency appendages to individual deputies. In 1951 about a third of the seats were contested by more than one Conservative list, and about a sixth by rival lists each claiming allegiance to the Radicals or one of their allies in RGR (*Rassemblement des Gauches Républicaines*, a combination including Radicals, UDSR and some smaller groups); in 1956 the former were rather better co-ordinated but the latter much worse. Deputies elected against one another might join the same parliamentary group, or members returned on the same list profess different loyalties in the Assembly. Thus when dissensions appeared in these organizations they normally reflected not revolt at the grass roots but struggles between rival parliamentary chieftains: Daladier and Herriot among the Radicals, Pleven and Mitterrand in UDSR, Antier and Laurens in the Peasant party. And when Mendès-France tried to bring order out of the Radical anarchy by imposing a common policy and disciplined voting, he soon found that the new recruits he won for the party in the country did not compensate for the alienation of its parliamentary stalwarts. Within less than a year the Radicals had split, and six months later even the extra-parliamentary organization turned against its turbulent leader.

If three of the seven parties were more or less disciplined despotisms and two more or less quarrelsome oligarchies, the other two could make fairly plausible claims to be 'democratically' organized bodies. Socialist candidates were chosen locally; the executive committee was annually elected by the conference and most of its members had to be outside Parliament; between conferences it was the executive which settled policy, imposed discipline, and even in a ministerial crisis had greater authority over tactics than the parliamentary group. But Guy Mollet gradually established a tight grip on the machine which, with the firm support of the two largest federations (Nord and Pas-de-Calais) sufficed to ensure him effective control of the party. MRP's constitution was deliberately designed to reduce the weight of the large federations;[10] it gave the parliamentarians virtual control of the executive and substantial representation on the national council – though dissensions did

10. See below, pp. 106–7.

appear both there and at annual conference. In neither party, however, was there normally a clear-cut division between those in and those out of Parliament. Usually at both levels there were representatives, if in different proportions, of both wings: MRP conservatives and progressives, Socialist supporters and opponents of the leadership.

No party was really ruled by its rank and file. In those that were despotically organized the conference itself was controlled from above. In the oligarchies it was usually easily manipulated, and could always be defied with impunity. And even in the more democratic parties the leadership had sufficient influence to get its way, though occasionally at the price of tactical concessions. Only in 1946 among the Socialists and (irregularly, as usual) in 1955 among the Radicals did a conference succeed in replacing an incumbent leadership.

4. PRINCIPLE AND PRACTICE

Parties in the Fourth Republic – even more than elsewhere – were characterized in theory by lofty aspirations to universality and in practice by a humbler concentration on representing particular groups and interests. In Parliament the democratic parties all chose their representatives mainly from the professional classes; there were very few workers, except on the Communist benches, and peasants were rare except on those of the Conservatives (and in later years of MRP).[11] Some parties had a special attraction (or repulsion) for particular occupational groups. Priests tended to favour MRP; the many engineers and army officers in RPF both gave it and responded to its technocratic and military tone; lawyers were most numerous in the loose traditional parties, Radicals and Conservatives; commercial travellers and shopkeepers in the food trades predominated among the Poujadists; minor civil servants like postmen and railwaymen were often Socialists (though police officers might equally be Radical and rural schoolteachers Communist).

Each party found it profitable to work on specific sections of the electorate and futile to try to cultivate others. In 1956 68% of practising Catholics voted MRP or CNIP, 68% of Protestants were Radical or Socialist, and 79% of the irreligious cast Socialist or Communist ballots.[12] Communists and Socialists naturally found little welcome among businessmen, or Radicals and Conservatives among industrial workers. The state tended to take its employees from its own schools, while private industry often recruited them from the Catholic educational system: so in 1951 among white-collar workers in private business 52% voted MRP or RPF and only 13% Socialist or Radical, while among those employed by the state the proportions were nearly reversed (17% and 48%).[13]

11. For details see tables by M. Dogan in *Partis politiques et Classes sociales en France* (henceforth cited as *Partis et Classes*), p. 298, and *Élections 1956*, p. 456. See also below, pp. 80n., 95n., 109 n. 14, 110 n. 21, 123, 140, 156.

12. Lipset, *Political Man*, p. 245. On Protestant voting in 1946 and 1951 see Schram, *Protestantism and Politics in France*, Chapter 15; for 1956, *Paysans*, pp. 377–85.

13. M. Crozier in *Partis et Classes*, pp. 89, 95–8. A poll in the 1956 election (taken from a very small sample in southern Paris) found that shopkeepers and artisans provided only 10% of the CNIP voters but 54% of the Poujadists, while retired people, rentiers and women without occupation were respectively 48% and 19% – although by income-groups the composition of the two parties was very similar: Stoetzel and Hassner in *Élections 1956* (from Table III *bis* on p. 249).

There was geographical as well as social differentiation. Parties were concentrated in particular areas, and because of the diversity of the country and the multiplicity of political issues they might represent different interests and groups in different regions. Even the tightly disciplined Communists needed to make very dissimilar appeals in the coalfields and factories of the north and in the prosperous Protestant vineyards near the Mediterranean coast. Around Toulouse the Right was so weak that the political struggle was fought out between the traditionally dominant Radicals and the Socialists who were threatening to replace them. In the west MRP and RPF competed for the favour of the Catholic Church; in Alsace the former was the Catholic and the latter the Protestant party; in the third main Catholic area, the Massif Central, the Peasants replaced both. The Socialists in Limoges both kept a strong working-class following and rallied all opponents of the Communists, who dominated the region through their hold on the peasantry. Around Nantes and St. Nazaire Catholic trade unionists supported MRP while anticlerical businessmen voted Radical. Thus the outlook and interests of members of the same party might differ according to their region of origin.

Nor were these the only factors of division within political groups. Numerous as they were, the parties only imperfectly represented the real tendencies of opinion even on domestic questions, and in the later years of the regime, when external affairs became crucial, the gap between organizational façade and political reality grew wider still. Every question that raised passions – Indo-China, the European army, the Algerian war, the advent of de Gaulle – caused dissension within all the parties of the majority and often those of the opposition as well. For example, in 1958 the extreme *Algérie française* champions were in Parliament a Gaullist, a Conservative, an MRP and a Radical leader, and in the cabinet a Socialist; yet each of their parties contained both a minority which favoured sweeping concessions to Moslem nationalism and many supporters of a middle course. So policy disputes added to and cut across geographical divisions and personal quarrels, destroying the cohesion and paralysing the effectiveness of every party and group.

French parties, excepting the special case of the Communists, thus differed from British ones in being very much smaller, much less well organized, far poorer and far more decentralized. Their frequent and notorious internal divisions took place within organizations supported by only a small fraction of the voters and numbering their members at best in tens of thousands. No party had the slightest hope of ever attaining power and applying a programme; their only object was to win a marginal increase in the bargaining power they could wield in the inevitable deals with other minority groups. To achieve this limited aim they had to appeal to sectional interests – social, geographical or religious – and to express a sectional outlook more forcibly and intransigently than their rivals who were tilling the same electoral field. But on arriving in the legislature they discovered that to put any of their principles into practice, achieve any short-term gains for their clients, or use any such successes to assure their own re-election, they had to compromise. A continued refusal to join in the parliamentary game spelt only political impotence and the sacrifice of the interests of the sections they represented. (French industrial workers would have obtained many more immediate concessions from governments had they not 'sterilized' their votes by bestowing them on a party in root and branch opposition to the regime.)

Some groups – the Communists, the Poujadists at first, a section of the Gaullists – preferred to remain as protest parties reflecting and profiting politically from the latent revolt of many Frenchmen against a regime from which these politicians usually tried to dissociate themselves completely. Others enjoyed or endured a central position which made them indispensable to almost any conceivable governing coalition. In the Third Republic this had been the role of the Radicals, who shared it in the Fourth with a sometimes reluctant MRP; there were always minor collections of 'king's friends' such as the pre-war Republican Socialists and the post-war UDSR; and at one time a fourth group, the ex-Gaullist Social Republicans, discovered an unexpected vocation as a pivot-party.[14] Intermediate between protesters and compromisers were the parties of policy, Socialists and various brands of Conservative, who were willing to join governments whose general attitude satisfied their (not always exacting) requirements; their bargaining position varied with their own strength, with the stability of the regime, and with the pliability or stubbornness of their leaders. But all parties which tried to work the system had to adopt between elections a posture of bargaining in defence of particular interests, which contrasted sharply with the high-principled intransigence they expressed at the polls. Repeated over several elections, this contrast reinforced the unjust conviction of the ordinary citizen that politicians (even those of his own party) were beings from a different world, untrustworthy in their promises, greedy and corrupt in their motives, erratic and absurd in their behaviour, disastrous for the nation because of their factionalism and ineptitude. Perhaps even more than specific discontents this attitude provided an inexhaustible source of recruits for the parties of revolt, of which the largest, longest-lived and most feared was the Communist party.

14. Morazé, pp. 148f.

Chapter 6

THE COMMUNIST PARTY

1. HISTORY

The French Communist party, like its opposite numbers elsewhere, has used varying tactics to attain unchanging objectives. Moscow often embarrassed its faithful followers by sharp and sudden turns of policy which required them to contradict themselves overnight. But the embarrassment was only a matter of public relations; the hardened Communist knew that the party line of the moment was merely a device to acquire governmental power in his own country and to promote (as he supposed) the world revolution by serving the interests of the USSR.

The French party was founded in December 1920 when the Tours conference of the Socialist party split over affiliation to the Third International. A large majority of the party's members (though only a small minority of its deputies) accepted the twenty-one conditions imposed by Moscow, which included the expulsion of the dissentients and the adoption of the name of Communist party. But the initial success was not followed up. The repercussions of the struggle for power in Russia, the internal feuds within the party, and the resentment of revolutionary Frenchmen at receiving instruction from novices in backward Moscow all contributed to a sharp Communist decline and a recovery of the old Socialist party and its associates in the trade unions. Between 1924 and 1928 Communist membership fell from 88,000 to 52,000; and though the party gained votes, these came largely from the traditional Left. The decision in 1928 to treat the Socialists as the main enemy to be destroyed, and to maintain Communist candidates against them on the second ballot, cost the party 40% of its votes between the two ballots and reduced its membership in the Chamber to a dozen.[1]

Nor did its situation improve for some years. The party was divided by bitter personal and political rivalries. Maurice Thorez, arrested in 1929, believed that he had been betrayed by colleagues who had seized the opportunity to be rid of him. When he came out of prison a year later, he described the party as weak and declining in numbers, full of mutual suspicion, lacking any sense of reality, and ruled by an arbitrary leadership which demanded from its followers uncritical obedience.[2] The separate Communist trade unions had proved a complete failure. In the 1932 election the party lost 300,000 of its former million votes, and on the second ballot little more than half its remaining supporters continued to vote for it against better-placed candidates of the Left. If the Socialists had retaliated where a Communist was in the lead, the latter would have lost eight of the ten seats which they retained.[3] In the Chamber and in the provinces (though not in the capital) their

1. The fullest account of its development (to 1940) is Walter, *Histoire du Parti communiste français*; he is a sympathizer. *Crapouillot*, no. 55 (January 1962), is hostile but useful. On 1936–45 see Rossi; Ehrmann, *French Labor from Popular Front to Liberation* (1947); and *Esprit*, no. 80 (May 1939), pp. 157–70. The 1928 figures come from Walter, p. 191, and Rossi, p. 331.

2. M. Thorez, *Fils du Peuple* (1st ed., 1937), pp. 63, 72–3.

3. Walter, pp. 240–1.

political influence was negligible. But the party itself was not primarily concerned with immediate electoral success. Expulsions, reorganizations, and changes of line were gradually building it into a disciplined movement available to promote whatever policy seemed likeliest to bring it to power.

The Popular Front gave the Communists their chance. As late as the beginning of 1934 the party line still insisted that social democracy, not fascism, was the real enemy of the working class. On 6 February 1934 Communist ex-servicemen marched beside the fascists against the Chamber of Deputies. But on the 12th, after an abrupt change of line, Communist and Socialist trade unionists joined in huge anti-fascist demonstrations in defence of the despised bourgeois Republic. Next year Laval signed the Franco-Soviet pact, and Stalin's commendation of the French rearmament programme put an immediate end to Communist anti-militarism. At the 1936 election the Radical, Socialist and Communist parties made an official alliance for the second ballot, and the electoral system no longer harmed the Communists so severely. They won 1½ million votes and returned seventy members to the new Chamber.

The new line was decided from above without prior discussion by the rank and file.[4] But it was certainly more popular than the old one among party members and voters alike. An even greater advantage was that Blum and Daladier, by accepting Communist co-operation, seemed to testify to non-Communists that the outstretched hand had really replaced the knife between the teeth. But the Communists had changed their 'image', not their nature. They refused office in the Blum government, keeping their hands free to exploit domestic discontent and attack its foreign policy. Their real sentiments towards their partners of the Popular Front were shown when the Vichy regime put the leaders of the pre-war governments on trial, and prominent Communists wrote to Marshal Pétain offering to give evidence for the prosecution. *L'Humanité* protested when Vichy released Socialist leaders from jail and even when they were treated as political prisoners instead of as ordinary criminals.[5]

The Popular Front had come to power at the worst possible moment. As the German menace came more and more to determine the course of politics, the government drifted further to the Right. By 1938 the Radicals again dominated the ministry; and Daladier, three years earlier the chief Radical advocate of the Popular Front, became the man of Munich. The Socialists, hopelessly split between pacifists and resisters, went out of office and saw their political influence disappear. Only the Communist party stood solidly for opposition to Germany, and this alone discredited the resistance policy with much of the French bourgeoisie. After the general strike of November 1938 the Daladier ministry was primarily an anti-Communist administration, and many conservatives allowed their support for appeasement to turn into sympathy for fascism.

4. See *Esprit*, *loc. cit.*, p. 167.

5. Rossi, pp. 83, 431–2; he quotes Billoux's letter, the first published. During the 1951 election campaign the former president of the high court of justice published several others in *Le Populaire*. (Ironically, one ex-minister against whom the Communists offered 'evidence' was Pierre Cot, later a leading fellow-traveller.) Cf. *Crapouillot*, pp. 46–7; *Histoire du Parti communiste français* (by an opposition group of party members, henceforth cited as *Histoire*), ii. 42–7.

The signature of the Nazi-Soviet pact led to another complete change of party line. After violently denouncing the appeasers of Germany, the Communists turned overnight into demagogic pacifists and anti-patriotic defeatists. Their enemies seized the opportunity to suppress the party and its satellite organizations and expel its deputies from the Chamber. But resentment at the 'phoney war' and the government's anti-working-class policy enabled the Communists to survive their somersault without disastrous damage. After the German victory they continued their defeatist policy, claiming that the war was an imperialist one, that the main enemy was at home, and that the downfall of the French bourgeoisie gave the party its opportunity. The leaders hoped to carry out their revolution with German connivance and the backing of Germany's partner, Russia, just as the men of Vichy hoped to carry out theirs with Italian support and German acquiescence. The first Communist reaction to the German entry into Paris was to apply to the occupation authorities for permission to publish *L'Humanité* legally.

In May 1941 tension between Germany and Russia produced the first signs of change, and in June the Nazi attack on the USSR led to another violent reversal.[6] Now that the Soviet Union was in danger the 'mercenaries of the City of London' became overnight 'our gallant British allies', the Gaullists suddenly changed from traitors to comrades, and the Communists took the lead in Resistance activity, showing a zeal and a heroism which their own rank and file and many non-Communists equated with patriotic enthusiasm for the French cause. But the temporary coincidence of French and Russian interests led to no relaxation in the struggle for power.

The Resistance movement helped Communist penetration into circles previously impervious to it. In agricultural areas their influence in the *maquis* offered a useful basis for the extension of their hold on the peasantry. A body like the *Front national*, safely controlled by the party behind a respectable façade of Marins and Mauriacs, enabled them to appeal to groups which they could not normally reach; the Right was unused to working with the Communists and willing to accept them as patriotic Frenchmen – though the experienced Socialists were much more suspicious.[7] Above all the war permitted the Communist capture of the trade unions. Under the Popular Front their penetration was already well advanced. In 1940 many anti-Communist union leaders went over to Vichy, and the rest had neither the numbers nor the organization to resist effectively.[8]

No doubt the sharp changes of party line destroyed the Communists' reputation for consistency and cost them some peripheral support. But they strengthened the cohesion and discipline of the solid core of militants. Those who survived these repeated switches were reliable followers, available for any purpose for which the leadership wished to use them. The Resistance movement gave the party new advantages to exploit when, in 1944, victory over

6. Some individual party members were, however, already engaged in Resistance activities. See Domenach in Einaudi *et al.*, *Communism in Western Europe*, p. 74; Michel, p. 38; *Histoire*, ii. 30, 33–5, 50–4, 70–5; Rieber, p. 84; A. Lecœur, *Le Partisan* (1963), pp. 141–66, 172–7.

7. Debû-Bridel, *Les Partis contre de Gaulle*, pp. 36, 52; cf. Bourdet, no. 27, pp. 1844–5, 1849, 1857. (Marin was a Conservative leader, Mauriac a famous Catholic writer.)

8. See above, p. 19 and n.

Germany appeared imminent and power seemed within its grasp. At the Liberation the Communists tried to discredit experienced political adversaries, use the purge of collaborators to rid themselves of potential opponents, and pay off old scores by murdering ex-Communists who had left the party in protest against the Nazi-Soviet pact – whether they had subsequently collaborated or resisted.[9] But even more important than this revolutionary violence was another consequence of the Liberation: thanks to General de Gaulle they became for the first time a government party, with greater prestige, power, and opportunity to infiltrate part of the machinery of the bourgeois state.

Though the Communists escaped being outflanked on the Left by leaving office in May 1947, they continued for months afterwards to proclaim themselves a party of government. Indeed, André Marty and the extreme wing of the party thought with some cause that the leadership had wasted a revolutionary opportunity and become corrupted by this period of respectability.[10] Later in the year, however, the Cominform was set up, Zhdanov 'exposed their errors', and a new revolutionary phase opened. The strike weapon was ruthlessly used for political purposes until it broke in the party's hands.[11] They found less and less response to their violent agitations: the general strike against Jules Moch's candidature for the premiership in 1949 failed, and so did the attempts in 1950 to stop arms arriving from America or troops leaving for Indo-China, the campaigns against Generals Eisenhower and Ridgway in 1951–52, and the protest strikes against the arrest of Jacques Duclos in 1952. For a moment it even seemed that these successive defeats might give an opposition within the party the upper hand.[12]

In the end the old leaders were able to survive and to insist on continued doctrinal rigidity and verbal intransigence. But they had to modify their political tactics. During the honeymoon period of 'peaceful co-existence' after Stalin's death, the Communists tried hard to re-enter the normal political arena and had some success with nationalists like Daladier, Gaullists like Soustelle, and especially neutralists like Bourdet. In 1954 they offered their

9. Rieber, pp. 178–80, and Rossi, pp. 442–5 give details. Ex-members killed at the front or in concentration camps were omitted by Communist papers and spokesmen from lists of fallen deputies. Almost half the leaders who had resigned were assassinated or had narrow escapes: Micaud, no. 162, p. 347. Cf. *Histoire*, ii. 89–90.

10. A. Marty, *L'Affaire Marty* (1955), pp. 240–51, 257–8; he denies that he ever favoured armed insurrection. At the meeting which set up the Cominform in 1947 Duclos admitted that some Communists had opposed leaving office in May; other delegates then denounced Thorez's 'nostalgia for government', and Duclos promptly confessed to 'opportunism, legalitarianism, parliamentary illusions': E. Reale, *Avec Jacques Duclos au banc des accusés* (1958), pp. 84, 136, 163. Cf. Dumaine, *Quai d'Orsay*, p. 180; *Histoire*, ii. 253, 256–9; and sources below, p. 401 n. 17.

11. In the 1948 coal strike no decision was taken without prior reference to Thorez: A. Lecœur, *L'autocritique attendue* (1955), p. 37; on 1947 strikes see references above, p. 34n.; in both there were serious economic grievances for the party to exploit. At the 1947 Cominform meeting Duclos at first called the Communists 'the party of order' who would not play into de Gaulle's hands by violence; but in his self-criticism after being denounced, he promised to mobilize the people for extra-parliamentary action against American imperialism: Reale, pp. 87, 160, 163. Cf. Lecœur, *Partisan*, pp. 225–30 (Cominform), 230–41 (strikes).

12. For the internal disputes (especially the repudiation and reaffirmation of Billoux's 'ultra-Left' article in 1952), see P. Hervé, *Lettre à Sartre* (1956), pp. 22–35. In *Crapouillot*, Hervé (who wrote the post-war section, pp. 54ff.) suggests that the ultra-Left wing, with Chinese support, wanted to concentrate on opposing the Indo-China war rather than German rearmament: no. 124, pp. 67–70. See also Lecœur, *Partisan*, pp. 256–8. On Duclos' arrest see below, p. 211n. *Histoire*, ii. 259–61 accuses Thorez of systematically purging Resisters.

support to the opponents of EDC, and voted for Mendès-France as premier; in 1955 they temporarily saved Edgar Faure's government and averted a change of electoral law; in 1956 they gave prolonged backing to Guy Mollet, and voted the special powers which were to make General Massu the master of Algiers.

Fluctuations of policy were accompanied by changes in leadership. At the 1950 congress Léon Mauvais (said to belong to the extremist wing) was dropped from the secretariat and Arthur Ramette, leader of the Nord federation, lost his seat on the *bureau politique*. Two years later André Marty, the party's *vieillard terrible*, and Charles Tillon, its chief Resistance leader, were removed from all their offices; the former was subsequently expelled. In 1954 Auguste Lecœur, who had replaced Mauvais and led the attack on Marty, was in turn disgraced and then ejected. Many local leaders were also purged. And in 1956 the most prominent of the younger intellectuals, Pierre Hervé, was hastily and irregularly expelled for prematurely demanding the 'destalinization' which the Twentieth Congress of the Soviet Communist party was about to approve. For the French *bonzen* had been proud of their exceptionally fulsome adulation of Stalin, and may well have feared that repudiation of the 'genial leader' would affect their own power.[13] Certainly they were conspicuously reluctant to destalinize: Raymond Guyot publicly upbraided the Italian, Polish and Hungarian Communists and praised only the Albanians.[14] The Budapest repression disturbed many of the party's intellectual adherents (including Picasso) and all its fellow-travellers (notably Sartre) and completed its political isolation. Its working-class followers, too – as the party discovered in May 1958 – were silently losing confidence.[15] And the advent of the Fifth Republic was to aggravate rather than to diminish dissensions within the ranks.[16]

2. ORGANIZATION AND FOLLOWING

The party's formal structure was unique in two ways. First, below the section level was a basic unit, the cell, which was supposed to comprise all party members working in the same establishment. Secondly, all party executive bodies were responsible upwards to their superiors as well as downwards to their constituents (thus the central leadership often appointed and removed officials of departmental federations). All links were vertical through the hierarchy, and it

13. For their ultra-Stalinism see Duclos' speech on Thorez quoted by Jean Baby, *Critique de base* (1960), pp. 140–1; *ibid.*, p. 215; Hervé, no. 124, p. 65. For the leaders' motives, cf. Baby, pp. 15–16; Hervé, *Lettre*, pp. 44–5, 152–3, 155. Baby (who defends the Hungarian intervention, pp. 28–32) was expelled for writing his book.

14. *France-Observateur*, 22 November 1956. Cf. Hervé, *Lettre*, pp. 44–61, and no. 124, p. 75; and the quotations by Macridis, no. 152, pp. 620–1. Early in 1956 some local units apparently enjoyed greater freedom, and in June the deputies and central committee genuinely debated (for five hours) the decision to abstain on an Algerian vote in the Assembly; but this case was unique in the Fourth Republic. See R. Barrillon's articles in *Le Monde* between 15 and 24 July 1956, especially those of the 17th and 18th.

15. Baby, p. 179, cf. also pp. 35, 37, 211, 218; D. Mothé, *Journal d'un ouvrier 1956–58* (1959), pp. 82–95 and *passim*; Hervé, no. 124, pp. 73, 74.

16. MM. Servin and Casanova, disgraced in 1961 for crypto-Gaullist heresies which had lasted for three years, seem to have attracted more support (especially from younger members) than any previous dissidents. Characteristically, they had formerly been the most rigorous defenders of orthodoxy.

was a grave violation of discipline to try to create horizontal links which might interfere with the chain of command.[17] The cells were not allowed to criticize the party's political line. But discussion was encouraged, for it informed the leaders of the reception given to their policies and enabled heresy to be exposed and smothered at birth. The isolation of each unit prevented any dissentient from contaminating its neighbours. If a cell showed signs of deviation a senior party member was assigned to bring it back into line; if his ability and prestige failed to retrieve the situation, it was dissolved. Thus dissension could rarely reach the section, still less the federation or central committee.

The workplace cell was a good instrument, in normal times for agitation and direct action (far more important for a revolutionary party than electioneering), and in an emergency for clandestine work. But the leadership had continually to combat the members' preference for organization based on residence; in 1946 there were 28,000 rural and local cells and only 8,000 workplace ones, and in 1954 only 5,000 out of 19,000 were workplace cells (perhaps no more than 2,000 in industrial plants).[18] Moreover, in later years reports of cell meetings no longer emphasized the vigour and freedom of discussion. '. . . The life of a great many cells . . . has been profoundly transformed. They are more or less cut in two: on one side those who approve blindly . . ., who tolerate no criticism; on the other those, workers or intellectuals, who want to say why they are disturbed or discontented.'[19]

For the party's formally democratic constitution was a sham. Often the rules were flatly violated. Expulsions were carried out unconstitutionally.[20] Party conferences, national councils (due in years with no conference) and central committee meetings were held much less frequently than the constitution required. Conferences and councils were so carefully prepared in advance that no post-war expulsion or purge aroused the least whisper of dissent.[21] The central committee never really debated policy, and far from it electing the national executive bodies, its own composition was settled by a few leaders who used their power to reward the orthodox, punish the hesitant, and so reinforce their own authority.[22] But in the end control from the top stifled enthusiasm at the base. 'In periods of crisis, the dissenters, who know it is useless to vote "against" something with their hands, prefer to "vote with their feet": they leave the party.' And, when the crisis period ended, 'everything

17. For fuller details of the formal organization see *Politics in Post-war France*, pp. 48ff. (henceforth cited as Williams).

18. On the initial resistance to workplace cells see Walter, pp. 121ff. On post-war developments, Domenach, p. 84, and Naville, no. 164, p. 1914. On the whole subject, Duverger, *Political Parties*, pp. 27–36; *Partis et Classes*, pp. 181–3 (anonymous article written by Pierre Fougeyrollas).

19. Baby, p. 27; also pp. 35, 74, 101, 134, 149, 152, 154, 205, 217; cf. *Histoire*, ii. 266–7. Contrast earlier accounts in Domenach, pp. 84–5; Micaud, no. 162, p. 338; Brayance, *Anatomie du Parti communiste français*, p. 38.

20. See for instance Hervé, *Lettre*, pp. 240–50.

21. Baby, pp. 35, 152–4; Domenach, pp. 89–90.

22. Baby, pp. 150–1; Lecœur, *Partisan*, pp. 249–50; Brayance, pp. 98–9. Baby, p. 137: '. . . in practice, an authoritarian centralism [which] paralyses any genuine democracy . . .'; cf. pp. 134, 135, 154, 202, 217. Hervé, *Lettre*, p. 44: 'What has poisoned the internal life . . . of international communism is the extension of the police regime, of the police spirit, of the police type of manœuvre . . . '; cf. pp. 47, 115, and also his *Dieu et César sont-ils communistes?*, pp. 66–8. One report claimed that four-fifths of the central committee members never opened their mouths: see Godfrey, no. 100, p. 329. Also see Lecœur, *Autocritique*, pp. 21, 31–2, 71.

returned to normal – that is to the routine of declarations nobody reads, protests nobody hears, meetings nobody attends'. The party might retain a substantial membership and a vast electoral following, for there was no acceptable alternative. But behind the impressive façade its strength was slowly crumbling away.[23]

The great increases in Communist membership came in the two periods of ostentatious patriotism, the Popular Front and the Liberation. Between 1934 and 1937 the number of adherents rose from 45,000 to 340,000; below 400,000 in 1944, it was soon alleged to have reached the million. Subsequently it dropped steadily until 1956, when a membership of 430,000 was claimed; it then levelled off, and the figure given in 1959 was only 5,000 fewer. These claims were certainly inflated, perhaps by 50%.[24] Nevertheless, in 1958 Communist membership probably equalled that of all other parties combined – and it demanded more of the individual than did the others. The demands, however, were not always met. Even in the early fifties only a minority of members (between a third and a fifth) seem to have attended cell meetings, and half of these were otherwise inactive.[25] And in later years their zeal continued to decline.

One sympton of disaffection was the collapse of the party press. In 1954 *L'Humanité*'s circulation in the Paris area was only half the pre-war figure (77,000 against 144,000 in 1937) while in the provinces it had dropped still further.[26] In 1949 the party admitted that only a third of its voters in the Paris region read *L'Humanité*, and five years later that only a quarter did; the proportion fell to 2% in some rural areas. The circulation of the Communist press dropped by two-thirds in the ten years after 1947, and few of the 900,000 remaining readers still believed what they read.[27]

Another failure was in a sphere to which the party attached great importance: the recruitment of youth. Here centralization of party authority made it

23. 'Crisis', Domenach, p. 90 (cf. Baby, pp. 27, 35, 154); 'normal', Baby, p. 115, cf. Hervé, no. 124, p. 70. And see below, pp. 85–7.

24. The official 1954 figure was 506,000; Lecœur, ex-organizing secretary, says (*Autocritique*, p. 24) that the real figure was below the 340,000 of 1937 (and that the decline was worst in the working-class areas). Since he also claims (p. 62) that the apparent half-million drop since 1946 was 'false', the real peak figure must have been 800,000 or (probably) less. In 1945 there were 545,000 paid-up members and 825,000 claimed: *Histoire*, ii. 285. Figures in text from Fauvet, *Les forces politiques en France*, p. 36; Domenach, pp. 71–2; Duverger, *Parties*, pp. 87–8, 317; Brayance, pp. 205–7; Hervé, no. 124, p. 70n. (he suggests there were about 700,000 card-holders in 1945 and 300,000 in 1961). In *Partisan*, p. 280, Lecœur says that the peak figure of cards distributed was 800,000, but that the real membership was far lower.

25. Brayance, p. 207; cf. Lecœur, *Autocritique*, pp. 23, 24, 64; Naville, no. 164, p. 1915; Domenach, p. 101. Micaud (no. 162, p. 334) was told the real militants were usually under 5%. Meynaud and Lancelot, *La participation des français à la politique*, p. 31, suggest that the party in 1961 may have had about 150,000 active members (plainly their definition of 'active' differs from Micaud's).

26. Partly because of the party's new provincial papers, though these too were in decline and many were soon to close; at the beginning of the fifties they had only 40% of their 1945 daily circulation: Bauchard, no. 9b, p. 600.

27. Mothé, pp. 83–4, 123; Wylie, p. 214. The last two figures are from Fauvet, *Déchirée*, p. 133n., *Cockpit*, p. 140n.; those for 1949 from Domenach, p. 118; the rest from *Humanité*, 13 November 1954. Cf. Godfrey, no. 100, p. 328. *Humanité* printed 600,000 copies in 1945 and 192,000 in 1960: Hervé, no. 124, p. 70n. All party papers have lost readers and every party has lost members.

easy for the leaders to insist on early promotion. In 1946 the Communist parliamentary group had the lowest average age (forty) of any important party. At the 1950 conference the delegates averaged only 31 and hardly any were over 45. Half the *bureau politique* of 1952 were in their forties, and party spokesmen proudly pointed out that Maurice Thorez had entered it at twenty-five and Benoît Frachon (general secretary of CGT) at thirty. A generation later, however, they were still in place. The Communists were indeed the only Fourth Republican party to retain their pre-war leadership; and, in spite of the changes lower down in the hierarchy, they found it increasingly hard to attract young recruits. At the 1954 conference their failure was blamed on Marty, who had recently been expelled – yet in the next five years the number of members under 25 was halved.[28]

The leadership also tried to encourage the industrial working-class element in the party; petty-bourgeois origins were considered as dangerous as middle age for a revolutionary movement. The great extension of its appeal at the Liberation had diluted its working-class character.[29] In 1950 there were official complaints that only 44% of federal secretaries and 37% of federal committees were workers, and insistent demands that the proportions be greatly increased.[30] But at the congresses of 1954 and 1959 the proportion of working-class delegates was still only 40%, and dissident Communists indeed claimed that the party's crisis was worst in the great factories round Paris which had once been the strongholds of militancy.[31]

Ironically, the party did best in the sphere to which it should have attached least importance. Throughout the Fourth Republic its electoral influence remained intact. From just under 1½ million votes in 1936, or 15% of the votes cast, the Communists jumped to 5 million in October 1945, over 26% (of a total doubled by the admission of women). By November 1946 they had gained another 500,000; at the general election of June 1951 their vote fell back almost to 5 million. Nearly half the loss of 450,000 votes occurred in the areas where the Church is strong and the main issue was often that of the Catholic schools – twenty-nine north-western, eastern frontier and Cevennes departments which contained altogether only 27% of the electorate. But the industrial departments, the scene of the main Communist progress in November

28. For the pressure in favour of youth, Brayance, pp. 70, 214–15 and *Humanité*, 6 April 1950; for the 1954 criticisms, *ibid.*, 5 and 7 June 1954; for the under-25s, Marcel Servin's report in *Monde*, 27 June 1959 and Baby, pp. 88–9 (10·2% in 1954 and 5·6% of almost the same total in 1959). The youth organization in 1956 had only 30,000 members, a tenth of its post-war and a third of its pre-war strength: Baby, p. 87 (Domenach, p. 90, gives the 1936 figure of 100,000). Among conference delegates the average age rose to 32 in 1954, 35 in 1956 and 38 in 1959, and pre-war party members were 35, 41 and 37% of the respective totals: *Humanité*, 8 June 1954 and 21 July 1956, *Monde* same dates and 27 June 1959. Membership among *École normale* students dropped from 25 to 5%: *ibid.*, 17 November 1956. But inconclusive figures suggest some Communist success among young voters in 1956: *Élections 1956*, p. 408 and Williams, no. 168, p. 174n.

29. Between 1937 and 1945 party membership rose 50% in industrial, doubled in semi-industrial and more than trebled in agricultural regions: Duverger, *Parties*, p. 34. The latter had the highest membership in proportion to population in 1945 (*ibid.*) but also the largest drop subsequently, by 1954 the number of rural cells was halved: see C. Ezratty in *Paysans*, p. 78 (but cf. *ibid.*, p. 439).

30. *Monde*, 13 February 1950; cf. Duverger, *Parties*, pp. 158–9.

31. Lecœur, *Autocritique*, p. 23; Baby, pp. 9, 156, 179; cf. Mothé, *passim*; contrast Micaud, no. 162, writing of an earlier date.

1946, also contributed more than their share of the losses five years later.[32] In 1956, however, the party recovered there: over the whole country its vote increased to 5,600,000 (though as the total poll also rose, its percentage share remained the same). Gains in the industrial north were offset by losses in the rural south, where part of the perennial protest vote was attracted by the novelty and violence of another enemy of the System, Pierre Poujade.[33] No major nation-wide decline in Communist electoral support occurred until the advent of General de Gaulle.[34]

The party was strongest in the industrial zone between Paris and Belgium, on the northern and western edge of the Massif Central, and along the Mediterranean coast (with parts of the hinterland). In the rural areas its influence derived less from its championship of the proletariat than from its annexation of the traditions of 1789. In the south and centre almost all the departments where Communism was strongest had been on the Left since the beginning of the Third Republic; only in the towns and in the industrial north did the party make a specifically working-class appeal.[35] Its influence on the peasantry was not confined to the poor sharecroppers of the centre, but extended to prosperous southern farmers and winegrowers who voted to express a political rather than a social choice; in Gard most Protestant peasants (who own their land) probably voted Communist.[36] In some rural areas Communist leadership in the *maquis* gave the party a foothold which improved its political position both directly, and also indirectly through giving its members the opportunity to take over official positions.[37] But the crucial

32. From the 15 most industrial departments (see Map 21), which include some 35% of the electorate, came 45% of the Communist gains in November 1946, 51% of their losses in 1951, and nearly 70% of their net gains in 1956. (Four eastern departments are both industrial and Catholic.)

33. The Communist share of the poll fell most where the Poujadists did best, and rose most where no Poujadist stood:

In constituencies where Poujadist vote was:	Communist share of poll was down 2½%	stable	up 2½%
over 15%	16	18	–
10–15%	5	22	2
under 10%	3	24	4
(no candidate)	–	5	4

See also Pierce, no. 180, p. 412 and n.; Werth, *The Strange History of Mendès-France* ..., pp. xvii, 271 (who claims that even party members voted for Poujade and a more ruthless policy in Algeria); *Paysans*, pp. 60, 203, 249; below, pp. 87n., 167n.

34. Even then fewer than half the defectors voted for any other party, at least in the Marseilles area: Olivesi and Roncayolo, *Géographie électorale des Bouches-du-Rhône* (cited as Olivesi), pp. 124, 130, 224–5, 238.

35. Goguel, *Géographie des élections françaises*, pp. 105, 117; also Fauvet, *Forces*, p. 39, *Cockpit*, pp. 95–9, *Déchirée*, pp. 88–91; and Maps 2 and 9. In the 1947 municipal elections their percentage varied directly with the size of communes: Cotteret *et al*, *Lois électorales et inégalités de représentation* (henceforth cited as *Inégalités*), p. 121.

36. Schram, p. 201. On peasant Communism see Wright, nos. 224, 228, Chapter 13 in Earle; Ehrmann, no. 83; Klatzmann, no. 132; *Paysans*, pp. 51–2, 65–6, 69–83, 307, 380, 439; Fauvet, *Cockpit*, pp. 93–6, *Déchirée*, pp. 86–9, and in *Partis et Classes*, pp. 172–7; Siegfried, *De la III*[e], pp. 209, 261–4; Morazé, pp. 194, 218–19; Lüthy, pp. 435–6; Wylie, pp. 212, 218–21. Rural party membership was often small (only 1,000 of its 54,000 voters in Corrèze in 1951: Brayance, p. 69).

37. Duclos in Reale, p. 86; Duverger, *Parties*, p. 317; Goguel in *Aspects*, pp. 259–60, and no. 102b, p. 951; Derruau-Boniol, no. 69, pp. 61–2; *Partis et Classes*, p. 191. For example in Haute-Vienne a Communist prefect and a mayor of Limoges enabled the party to appeal to the peasantry as a 'serious' instead of a 'wild' movement. (But the mayor's defection in 1952 did not correspondingly reduce the party's popular support.)

facts remain that (outside Alsace-Lorraine) most industrial workers voted Communist and that the party depended overwhelmingly on their support.[38]

To the Communists, however, elections were a test of efficiency rather than a road to power. They considered Parliament a minor field of operations. In 1924 the International insisted that the French party must apply strictly the rules drawn up at the Second World Congress. The Communist deputy was 'responsible not to the anonymous mass of electors, but to the Communist Party'. He was to make use of his parliamentary immunity to facilitate the illegal as well as the legal work of the party, subordinate his parliamentary to his party work, and introduce 'purely propagandist proposals, drafted not with a view to their adoption but for publicity and agitation', as the party leaders might require. The parliamentary group was dominated by the party executive, which had to approve its choice of officers, had a representative with a right of veto at all its meetings, and gave instructions in advance on all matters of importance (including the right to choose who should speak for the party and to approve the text of their speeches). Every Communist candidate had to give a written undertaking in advance to resign if called upon to do so by the party.[39]

Party leaders and officials were usually found seats in Parliament; in 1950 the fourteen members of the *bureau politique* were all deputies except Léon Mauvais, who had been a senator (though of the seventeen members nominated at the 1956 conference, six were not in Parliament). The party thus arranged for its corps of professional revolutionaries to be maintained by the state they were subverting, for it drew the salaries of Communist parliamentarians and paid them only the equivalent of a skilled worker's wage.[40] This practice brought into the central party funds nearly twice as much as the ordinary members' subscriptions even when membership was at its peak.[41] It kept the ordinary deputy's outlook close to that of the class from which he had usually sprung.[42] It enabled the party to exploit the ordinary Frenchman's prejudice against politicians; and it helped to avoid the internal disputes between rank and file and parliamentarians which plagued all left-wing movements,

38. It was estimated in 1956 that 70% of manual workers voted Communist in Paris and almost as many in Marseilles, and that from 75 to 80% of Communist voters in these cities were working class: Paris, J. Klatzmann in *Élections 1956*, p. 273; Marseilles, Olivesi, pp. 246, 253, 268, 271. For the five elections of 1945–56 over all France M. Dogan estimated the first proportion at 50 and the second at 70%: in Hamon, ed., *Les nouveaux comportements politiques de la classe ouvrière* (1962), pp. 113–14; cf. *Partis et Classes*, p. 33, and Fauvet, *Cockpit*, p. 93n., *Déchirée*, p. 86n. (but see below, p. 95n.). For estimates in two Paris suburbs in 1946, P. George in Morazé *et al.*, *Études de sociologie électorale*, pp. 82–5, and L. A. Lavandeyra in P. George *et al.*, *Études sur la banlieue de Paris*, pp. 131–2.

39. Theses of the Second World Congress, quoted Walter, pp. 143–4.

40. In 1958 each deputy kept £15 a week and the party took £70: G. Gosnat at the 15th party conference, *Monde*, 28–29 June 1959 and *Humanité*, 29 June 1959.

41. In 1946: Priouret, *La République des partis*, p. 177. The *élus*' contribution rose each year from 1952 (262 million francs) to 1958 (492 million): Marrane's report to 14th conference (*Cahiers du Communisme*, special number 1956, p. 409) and Gosnat's to 15th, *loc. cit.* But so few Communist deputies were returned in the 1958 elections (under de Gaulle) that the party's finances were hard hit and it had to reduce staff and suspend several local dailies: *ibid.*, and *AP* 1958, p. 155.

42. In 1951 38% of the Communist deputies had been manual workers and another 20% white-collar workers (including minor civil servants); in 1956, 42% and 17%. These social categories were next strongest in MRP, where they had fewer than 20% of the deputies between them. See Dogan's tables (above, p. 68n.).

especially the Socialists. To the militant, the deputy was less suspect when his origins and standard of living plainly cut him off from the parliamentary fraternity, the *République des camarades*. To the deputy, the militant was no threat when both formed part of a tightly-disciplined army whose commanders were themselves members of parliament.[43] Nor could he easily forget his own subordinate role, for the party staff prepared his bills, resolutions and even speeches.[44]

The low rating given to parliamentary activity resulted in a low level of ability. Often the educational background of the Communist deputies made them less articulate than others, and at times their truculent approach inhibited mutual understanding – which indeed was rarely their object.[45] Apart from a few skilful procedural specialists the rank and file made little impression in debate, although their leader Duclos and their brilliant fellow-traveller Pierre Cot showed that the handicaps could be overcome. As assiduous workers they were sometimes effective in committee.[46] But, as the International had instructed in 1924, the Communist deputy had always to 'remember that he is not a "legislator" trying to find a common language with other legislators, but a Party agitator sent into enemy territory to carry out the decisions of the Party'.[39]

3. CHARACTERISTICS

The characteristics of the party were essentially military. The high command was in theory elected but in reality self-perpetuating; it appointed and dismissed subordinates, settled the party line and conveyed detailed directives down to the lower levels. Although all the troops had volunteered, many of them – like some regular soldiers – in time found it hard to imagine existence outside the ranks in which their friendships had been made and their life organized.[47] For the party expected much of its members: it sought to dominate their whole mental outlook, claimed most of their leisure time, assigned and withdrew duties from them as it saw fit.[48] It aimed indeed to be far more than an ordinary legal political party, more than a massive conspiracy for the seizure of power, more even than a state within the state. 'It is a discipline opposing a discipline, a university opposing a university, a police opposing a

43. It was not always realized that the commanders – the members of the *bureau politique* and secretariat – in effect kept their full parliamentary salary: Lecœur, *Autocritique*, pp. 57–8. This may have contributed to their isolation from the rank and file, on which see Baby, pp. 214–16; Micaud, no. 162, pp. 348–9; cf. *Histoire*, ii. 290.

44. Buron, p. 155.

45. But cf. Fauvet, *Cockpit*, p. 87, *Déchirée*, p. 80; Noël, *Notre Dernière Chance*, p. 110; and Christian Pineau's novel *Mon cher député*, pp. 56–8. Lecœur says that some deputies, and particularly the leaders, were on familiar terms with 'reactionary' colleagues though hostile to the Socialists: *Nation Socialiste*, no. 9 (March 1957), p. 36. Marty claimed (*op. cit.*, p. 85) that Jacques Duclos called in two RPF doctors (one a former deputy) to get him out of prison on health grounds in 1952. Resistance friendships were sometimes tenacious, and some of the fellow-travelling Progressives maintained wide contacts.

46. Isorni, *Ainsi*, p. 55, and *Silence*, pp. 132–3 (cf. p. 57). But some, especially the leaders, were conspicuous absentees: Noël, pp. 63, 109; and see below, p. 244 n. 9, 246 n. 21.

47. Cf. Micaud, no. 162, pp. 338–41; E. Morin, *Autocritique* (1959), pp. 159–60, 174.

48. In 1952 the paper edited by Pierre Hervé was suppressed without his being consulted, and he was formally ordered to undertake other propagandist work which he did not want: Hervé, *Lettre*, pp. 20–2, 27, 245, cf. *Dieu et César*, pp. 25–32, 41–2, 54–6.

police, an organization of workers, women, children, old men, cripples, tenants, tradesmen, housewives, sportsmen, motion picture stars. It is a complete society which, in embryonic form, already exists inside the society it aims to replace.'[49]

The Communist appeal was wide.[50] The largest and least regionalized French party, it had support throughout the country. Satellite organizations – from the Tenants' League to the Federation of Ciné-Clubs – spread its influence in a dozen subsidiary fields.[51] Just after the war the Communists won many supporters, from Picasso to Joliot-Curie, among the intellectuals who enjoy such exceptional prestige in France. Generosity, social conscience, revolt against the existing order and (for persons compromised in the war) personal prudence brought some bourgeois Frenchmen to join or support the party. But it forfeited much of this sympathy by its rigid Stalinism and its defence of the repression in eastern Europe; in 1956 Budapest finally alienated most of the remaining intellectuals and nearly all the fellow-travellers.[52]

This heterogeneous army was recruited and maintained by uninhibited tactical opportunism. In office the Communists allowed no considerations of cabinet solidarity to blunt their attacks on ministers of other parties, and abandoned their own policy of wage restraint as soon as it seemed likely to weaken their position in the trade unions. Out of office they promoted every demagogic cause with a robust contempt for cost, consistency or practicability.[53] In 1945 they displayed – and exploited – the crudest chauvinism against Germany and over the disputed Italian frontier, and in Algeria they denounced rebellious Moslem nationalists as instruments of Nazism.[54] They 'have long since taken over practically all the slogans and subject matter of the former Fascist movements, including the systematic exploitation of national hatred, economic nationalism and protection of the middle class, and chauvinism and conservatism in the arts'.[55] Hunting peasant and small-shopkeeping votes, in

49. Domenach, p. 67.

50. Rossi, Chapters 27–29, discusses the Communist appeal to different sections of the population; cf. Micaud, no. 162.

51. Duverger, *Parties*, pp. 107–8; Brayance, pp. 129–50; Coston, *Partis, journaux et hommes politiques*, p. 487. Control of the Tenants' League was incomplete: Brayance, pp. 143–4.

52. Even some Progressive deputies (see below, pp. 171–2) publicly differed from the party line. (But though the Hungarian crisis was the party's worst since 1939 – when a third of its deputies had resigned – in 1956 only one out of 150 did so.) On the intellectuals see Macridis, no. 152, pp. 629–32; Hervé, *Lettre*, pp. 108–24, *Dieu et César*, p. 220; Morin, *passim*; Baby, pp. 9, 177–81. *Ibid.*, pp. 157, on front organizations, 117–18, 193–201, on hostility to the non-Communist extreme Left ('for the Party leadership . . . the principal enemy', p. 199). Morin was expelled for writing in *France-Observateur*; the party spokesman told his cell that it was 'the journal of the Intelligence Service': Morin, pp. 167–71.

53. Just before the 1951 election the prime minister (Queuille) estimated the cost of the party's bills and amendments at £2,000 million: see below, p. 261n.

54. 'Finally I was unaware that the party allowed the Algerian nationalist movement to be persecuted or even took part in the persecution. Besides, I had completely forgotten the colonial problem. The salvoes of victory had deafened our ears to the massacres of Sétif . . . it was a crazy outburst of patriotic flag-waving': Morin, pp. 68–9, cf. pp. 72–3, 79, 87. On Algeria, 'It is necessary to mete out the punishment they deserve to the Hitlerite killers who took part in the events of the 8th of May, and to the pseudo-nationalist leaders . . .': *Humanité*, 19 May 1945, quoted (with many other damaging citations) in *Voie communiste*, March–April 1962; and in G. Mollet, *13 mai 1958–13 mai 1962* (1962), pp. 140–1; cf. C. H. Favrod, *La révolution algérienne* (1959), p. 76. Generally, Grosser, pp. 104–5, 144, 206, 215; Rieber, pp. 313–28.

55. Lüthy, pp. 437–8 (cf. pp. 134, 433–6). In 1947 they exploited anti-Semitic hostility against Léon Blum: Ehrmann, no. 82, p. 150.

1946–47 they joined the Right in condemning food rationing and economic controls, and a few years later they were active in fostering the Poujadist movement – until it became a dangerous competitor in demagogy.[56] Their political activity had but one objective: the acquisition of power. About methods they had few scruples and about policies little concern – save as means to this one end. (Yet when their strategy dictated a policy of co-operation, their single-minded devotion could produce results which none of their rivals could match; witness the admirable restraint of the trade unions during the Liberation period.[57])

The experiences of 1936–38 and 1945–47 showed the difficulty of working with the Communists in government. In opposition, their bitter hostility to the regime drove their opponents together and the unmeasured fury of their attacks saved more than one cabinet. By defying the ordinary parliamentary rules they sterilized their votes for constructive (though not for obstructive) purposes, and so falsified the political balance by removing most of the weight from the left-hand scale. Yet these self-inflicted wounds were the price of homogeneity and discipline. And every parliamentary display of common hostility to the Communists reinforced the workers' sense of isolation from the community which gave the party its hold on their imagination.

Here was the secret of the Communists' power. The best young working-class leaders were naturally attracted to a force which claimed to express the aspirations and defend the interests of their own people – especially when so few other organizations in French society offered scope for a poor youth's abilities. But the party could not turn to Moscow's ends the strength it could command as the champion of the proletariat. Hardened party members might favour alliances with the nationalist Right for reasons of foreign policy, and regard the Socialists as their real enemies. But to the working-class Communist voter his Socialist neighbour was also a man of the Left and a potential ally in a new Popular Front.[58] Thus workers who adhered to Communist-controlled unions often remained suspicious of the party itself, as the elections of social security administrators in April 1947 showed: CGT candidates polled only half their claimed membership while CFTC (Catholic trade union) candidates nearly doubled theirs, and many workers deliberately voted against individual Communist leaders.[59] Six months later CGT split; it no longer commanded a majority of trade union votes, and after 1948 it proved useless to the party as an instrument of direct action.[60] In 1956 CGT refused to approve the Soviet intervention in Hungary.[61]

56. *Ibid.*, p. 154; *AP* 1946, p. 191, 1947, pp. 97, 139, 245, 1948, p. 42; cf. Domenach, p. 128. Later, Lavau in *Partis et Classes*, pp. 63, 72–3; Macridis, no. 152, p. 626n.; *Paysans*, p. 307; below, pp. 87n., 163n.

57. 'The communists have recreated in their ranks the sense of responsibility which Frenchmen of recent Republics have totally lost': Brayance, p. 13. This severe but pseudonymous author is really Alain Griotteray, later a right-wing conspirator against the Fourth Republic.

58. *Partis et Classes*, pp. 186–7.

59. *AP* 1947, p. 77; Beaulieu, no. 10, pp. 557ff.; Lorwin, p. 116; Lefranc, p. 147; Galant, *Histoire politique de la Securité sociale*, pp. 126–7. Even so CGT had 60% of the vote and CFTC only 26%.

60. See above, pp. 34, 74. In the social security elections of 1950 *Force Ouvrière* took 15% of the vote from CGT; CFTC lost 5% to minor groups which often sympathized with FO. In 1955 CGT with 43% held its narrow lead over the combined forces of CFTC (21) and FO (16). See *AP* 1956, pp. 171–3.

61. It was condemned publicly by some CGT unions and locals, and by Pierre Le Brun's

[*over*

The party's organizational basis was a weakness here. The cell unit was supposed to help identify party work with the member's daily life. But this identification itself concealed a danger: the member might neglect aspects of party work which did not concern him intimately. Trade union demands might arouse the rank and file much more than the political campaigns imposed by the leadership. Nor was this heresy of 'economism' confined to the lower levels. Leaders in the unions, who knew their followers' wishes, resented the dissipation of their own strength and credit in futile demonstrations which often bore no relation to the interests of the French working class. This deviation caused the downfall of Marcel Paul, ex-minister and leader of the electricity workers, and even Benoît Frachon himself was suspected of sympathy for it.

The unsuccessful political strikes of 1947–48 shattered the power of the unions. In the 1950 social security elections CGT polled fewer than half the votes – and a third of those eligible did not vote at all. For years even strictly economic strikes were doomed to failure; in 1950 the combined pressure of the unions backed by open governmental and newspaper sympathy could not overcome Michelin's resistance at Clermont-Ferrand. And so successfully did the Communists combat 'economism' that the great strikes of 1953 and 1955, provoked by purely economic grievances, owed nothing whatever to CGT leadership. A weak and divided trade union movement, determined not to allow its remaining strength to be dissipated in political adventures, was of very little use to a revolutionary party.

Nor did the Communists' other assets compensate for this major disappointment. Even in votes they soon seemed to reach saturation point; in the Paris 'red belt', their pre-war stronghold, they made no progress at the Liberation and polled less well in 1951 than in 1936. Their infiltration of key positions was limited even when they held office and soon reversed when they left it. And 1947 showed that a Communist threat would provoke a stronger counter-revolutionary riposte. That October in the municipal elections de Gaulle's RPF led the field in the thirteen largest cities in France.[62]

This rallying to the strongest anti-Communist movement at a moment of crisis was no accident. The party deliberately set out to draw a sharp line between itself and all its political rivals. 'We are not a party like the others.' All opponents were confounded together. Thereby the Communists provided their divided enemies with a bond of union. But they also went far to establish among the masses the impression they most wished to create: that their own determined, energetic and youthful movement, able to offer solutions for the day-to-day problems which beset the ordinary Frenchman, confronted quarrelling cliques of tired old men interested only in cynical bargaining to prolong, probably for corrupt purposes, their stay in office.

small but active non-Communist opposition in CGT: see *ibid.*; *France-Observateur*, 15, 22 and 29 November 1956; Rioux, p. 66; Grosser, pp. 145–6. Contrast CGT's approval in 1949 of Thorez's statement that French workers would support the Red Army if it crossed France's border 'in pursuit of an aggressor': *AP* 1949, p. 25; Lorwin, p. 283. On CGT and Communism generally, Lorwin, pp. 279–91; Godfrey, no. 100, pp. 323–7.

62. Red belt: cf. Goguel, no. 102b, p. 956, and in *Fourth Republic*, p. 98. Infiltration: see below, pp. 391–2. On Communist strength in 1947, Van Dyke, no. 212.

Political disillusionment provided fertile soil for this Communist campaign. After the elections of June 1946 the French Gallup poll found 58% of Communist voters completely satisfied with their party: their nearest rivals were MRP with 31%. Only 9% of Communists were not reasonably satisfied: the corresponding percentages were double for Socialists and MRP, and higher still for Radicals and Conservatives.[63] The psychology of the French Communist militant was very different from that of other politically-minded Frenchmen. Party members displayed none of the individualism which so often frustrated rival parties. In a crisis like the war the Communists could count on exceptional discipline and devotion for the advancement of their creed; in humdrum matters like running a municipality they were sometimes able to develop among their constituents a quite unusual sense of civic responsibility. Their dynamism, certainty and conviction offered an attractive contrast to the disputes and hesitations of their old-fashioned, self-doubting and internally-divided competitors.

Yet the Communist achievement of changing the mental outlook of their militants (for it was nothing less) was bought at a high price. Rigid discipline required complete suspension of individual judgment.[64] Men convinced of the triumph of their cause proved willing to accept any crime to 'shorten history's birth-pangs'. The party was a state within the state, warring against its legal rival; the genuine qualities of citizenship which it sometimes evoked were deformed for destructive and disastrous ends. In the last resort its most important psychological achievement was to kill the intellectual honesty and pervert the moral integrity which inspired its best recruits.

As the fifties progressed, however, the Communists' revolutionary fervour diminished. The destalinization and Hungarian crises provoked growing criticism of the party's bureaucratic structure among both members and sympathizers. The leadership was attacked for conservatism, dogmatism, incorrect analyses and false priorities; for losing touch with the workers, checking them when they wanted to fight, using the most backward and lethargic to break the militancy of their more active fellows;[65] above all for prolonged equivocation over the Algerian war (no doubt partly due to the growing racial feeling of the French working class).[66]

The party's failing dynamism seems hard to reconcile with its stable voting base. Yet they may have a common cause. The narrower but more revolutionary organization of the inter-war years was dominated by the industrial

63. *Sondages* 1948, p. 225. In 1952, 62% of Communist voters professed full confidence in their party; again MRP with 51% came second: *ibid.*, 1952, no. 2, p. 6.

64. When Laurent Casanova wrote to Maurice Thorez in 1960, 'I attach more importance to my self-respect and human dignity as a communist than to my membership of the *bureau politique*', the leader commented: 'This is unheard of. I must say I have never heard such a remark.' *Monde*, 2 March 1961.

65. J. Simon in *Socialisme ou Barbarie* 3.18 (January 1956) on the 1955 provincial strikes, especially pp. 4–6, 13–16, 26–8, 31; Lecœur, *Autocritique*, p. 74; Mothé, pp. 108–9, 127–30, 146–7; Baby, pp. 35, 37, 70, 122, 211. Cf. n. 72.

66. Mothé, pp. 107–9, shows that workers no less than intellectuals condemned the party for discouraging the spontaneous opposition to the war which arose in 1956; cf. Baby, p. 115; Morin, p. 192; *Voie communiste*, *loc. cit.* On the later growth of working-class racialism, *ibid.*; Mothé, p. 172; Rioux, pp. 87–8; Tillion, no. 208, p. 10; cf. above, n. 33; Morin, p. 223. The party lost its hold on many of the young Communists conscripted for the Algerian war.

workers. After the war, expanding into new fields, the party presented itself as all things to all men: 'a Radical party' operating as a pressure-group on specific bills and governments.[67] It was the class party of the workers yet it lobbied for the shopkeepers and the *bouilleurs de cru*. The champion of *laïcité*, it extended the outstretched hand to the Catholics. Internationalist, it went through a 'crisis of chauvinism'.[68] In revolt against existing society, it controlled much patronage – important more for status than for cash – in Parliament, local government, the social security system and the nationalized industries. 'It is in favor of modernization but also supports all the marginal groups that impede it; it is for socialization and for private property ... it is slowly becoming a captive of the many and diverse forces whose support it has cultivated. It has reached a dead center of compromise and synthesis beyond which there can be no movement in one direction or another without serious electoral, and perhaps organizational and ideological, dislocations.' Only a centralized and ruthless bureaucratic machine could hold together so heterogeneous a party.[69]

The consequences were not surprising. As in Russia, those who rose to power in the party were the natural bureaucrats rather than the natural revolutionaries. Inevitably their policy tended to preserve the balance of forces in which they flourished, and their disciplinary authority was used to crush critics who threatened their position. 'Fossilized' in their refusal to confront new ideas or recognize new circumstances – which contrasted so sharply with the flexibility of their Italian comrades – the French Communist leaders displayed over the years a narrow and obstinate conservatism reminiscent of their own bourgeoisie at its worst.[70] Yet from their standpoint the alternative was no more satisfactory. If the workers participated actively in the industrial transformation of the country, their revolutionary *élan* would be weakened: better to keep them in their ideological ghetto, even through absurd propaganda campaigns like that of 1955 asserting that the masses were becoming poorer. By allowing revisionist discussion and criticism, Togliatti was risking the erosion of his party's unity and discipline in the hope of broadening its appeal; Thorez preferred to maintain the monolithic authority of the organization over a smaller membership and a narrower sphere of influence.[71]

By this strategy he preserved a disciplined striking force for use in a revolutionary situation which he became less and less capable of exploiting. Politically, the French party behaved so cautiously and equivocally over Algeria that it avoided immediate unpopularity and repression, but also forfeited the long-term credit it might have earned by an early and courageous

67. Hervé, no. 124, p. 73.

68. Grosser, p. 104 (and see above, n. 54).

69. Macridis, no. 152, pp. 626–8, 633–4 (he points out that in 1956 there were 1,300 Communist mayors and 25,000 municipal councillors). Cf. also *France-Observateur*, 15 February 1957; Naville, no. 164, pp. 1909–20 (especially 1911–12); Godfrey, no. 100, pp. 321–38; Mothé, p. 166. In the 1952 poll, 41% of Communist voters thought the party most useful in office (31% even in a coalition) while only 47% preferred it to remain in opposition; 32% considered it 'the strongest bulwark of parliamentary institutions', and only 40% favoured forcible seizure of power in any circumstances: *Sondages*, 1952, no. 3, pp. 56–8.

70. Crozier, no. 64, p. 791. 'Fossilized': Hervé, no. 124, p. 79. 'They have become part of the familiar furniture of the do-nothing Fourth Republic, like old clocks that have gone slow, and which no one notices as they strike midday at two in the afternoon': Hervé, *Dieu et César*, p. 242.

71. Fougeyrollas, no. 94, pp. 121–31.

campaign for Algerian independence. Socially, in championing all the backward groups which were suffering from the country's modernization, it gradually lost touch with those who were benefiting.[72] Thus towards the end of the Fourth Republic it disqualified itself for leadership either in the hypothetical social revolution which was plainly receding, or in the real political crisis which was fast approaching. Its hope could lie only in a transformation of the international balance of power to the advantage of the USSR; and only in Moscow's accounting could Thorez's policy conceivably yield any returns.

The French working class, and the many devoted and self-sacrificing party militants, deserved better leadership than the Communist party gave them. But where else were they to turn?

72. Hervé thought the party was in danger of coming to represent the most backward sections of the working class, like Bonapartism in an earlier generation, and was mobilizing the revolt of the parasitic elements in society like 'a "Poujadism" of the extreme Left': *Dieu et César*, pp. 235, 239.

Chapter 7

THE SOCIALIST PARTY

1. HISTORY

The Socialist party – officially the *Section française de l'Internationale ouvrière*, SFIO – was formed in 1905 by the junction of two smaller groups. The French working-class movement was weak in numbers and organization, and torn between the demands of its revolutionary ideology and those of parliamentary strategy. The Dreyfus case posed its dilemma starkly: when reactionary forces tried to reverse the verdict of 1789, should Socialists continue to agitate for a new revolution and so endanger the conquests of the old one? Jean Jaurès and most Socialist deputies advocated an electoral and parliamentary alliance with the Radicals to save the Republic, while another wing under Jules Guesde adhered to the orthodox Marxist doctrine of opposition to all bourgeois governments.[1] The struggle came to centre on Alexandre Millerand, the Third Republic's first Socialist minister. In 1904 the Amsterdam congress of the Socialist International, under German leadership, demanded the expulsion of Millerand and the unification of the French movement. Jaurès accepted its decision and a year later the united party was established. The affair demonstrated both the profound internationalism and the abiding mistrust of leaders which were for years to characterize SFIO.

Nevertheless, Jaurès soon established his ascendancy as the great tribune of Socialism and indeed of the whole Left. The genuine revolutionaries deserted politics for anti-political syndicalist agitation in the trade unions, and the Socialist politicians finally became 'herbivorous rather than carnivorous Marxists', still uttering revolutionary rhetoric at banquets but no longer organizing disorder in the streets. Despite Jaurès' assassination on the eve of war, revolutionaries and reformists alike rallied to the defence of the nation in 1914; and the parliamentary leaders – including the orthodox Marxist Guesde – entered the government of national unity. But the endless carnage aroused growing dismay among the militants, and when the Russian Revolution provided a new focus for extremist loyalties the latent conflict between reformist leadership and revolutionary rank and file burst forth irrepressibly. At the Tours conference in 1920 the Bolsheviks used it to split the party with their twenty-one conditions. 'They are at once', said Guesde, 'everything I have recommended all my life and what all my life I have condemned.'[2]

In 1924 SFIO revived its old electoral pact with the Radicals and formed the left wing of Herriot's parliamentary majority. The associates in this *Cartel des Gauches* shared a common republican and anticlerical outlook, but they differed too deeply over economic policy for the alliance to be lasting; Radicals preferred to govern (though not to face the voters) in combination

1. As late as May 1956 SFIO delegates visiting Moscow heard a Soviet leader condemn Jaurès for his support of Dreyfus. '"No," said Kaganovitch, "this was not a matter for the working class, and there was no need to mingle in this affair"': D. J. Dallin, *Soviet Foreign Policy after Stalin* (Philadelphia, 1961), p. 240. (I owe this reference to Dr. Anthony King.)

2. Quoted by Natanson, no. 163, p. 94.

with Conservatives rather than Socialists. In any case this choice was imposed on them by the intransigence of the SFIO rank and file, who in 1929 overruled the deputies when they wished to join a Radical government, and in 1933 again shattered the alliance, which had been restored for the 1932 election. The most moderate deputies resigned to form a new group led by Pierre Renaudel; one wing of these 'neo-Socialists', headed by Marcel Déat and Adrien Marquet, fell increasingly under Nazi influence. In 1936 the alliance of the Left parties was reconstituted and extended to include the Communists, and won another electoral victory. As the largest group in the new majority, SFIO took over the premiership. This first experience of office in peacetime lasted for only two years.

The short-lived success did not end Socialist dissensions. As Nazi power increased Léon Blum and most of the leaders officially (though somewhat half-heartedly) advocated resistance to Germany; but nearly half the party, led by the general secretary Paul Faure, clung to its traditional pacifism and accepted first appeasement and then Vichy. In 1940, 36 out of 80 votes against full powers for Marshal Pétain were cast by Socialists; but three-quarters of the SFIO members of parliament were on the other side. Paul Faure's chief trade union ally, René Belin, became the Marshal's minister of labour.

During the occupation many Socialists played an active and creditable part; some Resistance movements, like *Libération-Nord*, were predominantly controlled by them. Their contribution was perhaps less spectacular than that of the Communists or the Catholics, who had more solid organizations behind them; but as individuals the Socialists had nothing to be ashamed of. Their position at the Liberation seemed very favourable: parliamentary democracy and political freedom had regained prestige; drastic social reforms were considered inevitable and indeed overdue; many pre-war parties were discredited; and SFIO seemed to have an obvious role in reconciling the new claimants to power, Communists and Catholics, with the Republic from which they had hitherto been virtually excluded. Revisionist leaders like Blum hoped to rejuvenate their movement as a French Labour party, emancipated from a Marxist creed which they had long ceased to take seriously, and to open it to new blood from the Resistance organizations for which it could provide the most natural political channel.

This opportunity was lost. The rank and file remained attached to the old doctrines, the old prejudices, and the old faces: they would not grant rapid promotion to newcomers with no record of party service. Potential new members, and above all potential new leaders, occasionally joined other groups but more frequently abandoned politics.[3] On the other hand, an exceptionally drastic purge of the members who had supported Pétain sacrificed practical experience to presumed ideological purity.

The election of October 1945 found the Socialists only the third largest party. Like the British Liberals between the wars, they were ground between stronger rivals on either flank. Whether they worked with the Communists against MRP in defending the first draft constitution, or with MRP against the Communists as in subsequent months, they still alienated support. A

3. See below, pp. 97, 174.

second electoral defeat in June 1946 brought their internal differences to a head. At the Lyons conference of that year the old leadership was repudiated and the left wing won a narrow majority on the executive committee. Daniel Mayer, a revisionist protégé of Léon Blum, was replaced as general secretary by the doctrinaire Marxist Guy Mollet, who extended the authority of the executive over the deputies and sought to take the party into opposition. Upon the expulsion of the Communist ministers in May 1947 he nearly persuaded SFIO to withdraw too, and six months later he brought down the Ramadier government.

But the Socialists were virtual prisoners of their conservative partners. They dared not repudiate responsibility for policy by going into opposition, for without their votes no majority could be found: in 1947 or 1948 their resignation would have brought General de Gaulle to power. But they were too isolated to impose their own views, and could only, with MRP's help, try to prevent the dismantling of their post-war reforms. They had to retain office in governments they disliked, alienating most of their followers by continual compromises. The resentment of the militants was expressed by three ex-ministers – André Philip, Daniel Mayer and Édouard Depreux – who had taken the revisionist side in 1945–46; but Guy Mollet, as party leader, became an advocate of participation in government.

As these reversals of position suggest, the division was more tactical than fundamental. It reflected differences about the best means of competing with the Communists and not about the desirability of an alliance with them – which both sides rejected. One wing preferred opposition in order to advocate the policies of the party and repudiate responsibility for the actions of its rivals; the other relied on office to win practical reforms to benefit their followers or to prevent injury to them. In France as elsewhere it was usually the middle-class Socialists, those who were in a small minority in their own areas, who showed most devotion to doctrinaire principle and least interest in the responsibilities of power; and in 1951 the smaller federations carried a motion empowering the executive committee, rather than the parliamentary group, to take decisions in a governmental crisis.[4] The large working-class federations like Nord and Haute-Vienne regularly supported the leadership. But there were many cross-currents, for each SFIO federation enjoyed a good deal of autonomy and played its own different electoral role: the focus of anticlericalism at Rennes and of anti-Communism at Limoges; the chief rival of Radicalism in the south-west, but a proletarian party in the northern industrial area. Their tactics depended on particular circumstances more than on general principle. Before the 1956 election the chief advocate of local alliances with the Communists was Robert Lacoste.

The quarrel over participation was settled when SFIO returned to opposition, first for a few months in 1950 and then for five years in 1951. But instead the problem of EDC and German rearmament soon came to dominate Socialist politics. Here the factional lines differed from previous and subsequent struggles: many governmental-minded or nationalistic leaders were opposed to EDC (e.g. MM. Auriol, Moch, Naegelen, Lacoste, Lejeune)

4. For details see Williams, p. 73, n. 27. Also cf. below, pp. 403–4.

while Guy Mollet defended it in association with his bitterest critic, André Philip. The militants favoured the treaty and so did the executive which they chose. But a majority among the deputies turned against it and finally defied party discipline to ensure its defeat.

The bitterness of the EDC fight was carried over into the dispute on Algerian policy which racked SFIO after its return to office in 1956. Robert Lacoste and Max Lejeune, who were mainly responsible for the policy, were attacked not only by the old opponents of participation but also by those 'governmental' Socialists who had been their allies against EDC.[5] But their critics found little support in the party, least of all in the big federations (of which only Bouches-du-Rhône, led by Gaston Defferre the mayor of Marseilles, inclined to their side). By now not much trace remained of the comradely feelings which had held the party together through earlier internal battles, and by 1958 many of the Algerian opposition were on the brink of secession. In the May crisis they won the support of some of Mollet's closest associates (such as Albert Gazier and Christian Pineau) and carried a majority of both deputies and executive against de Gaulle's candidature, which the general secretary favoured. But though this reinforcement of the opposition threatened Mollet's position, at the September 1958 conference he was saved by Defferre – who credited de Gaulle with liberal intentions in Algeria. The conference therefore approved the proposed constitution of the Fifth Republic, and the old critics, still led by Depreux, Mayer and Philip, withdrew to form a new party.[6]

2. ORGANIZATION AND FOLLOWING

SFIO was democratically organized. The basic unit, the section, corresponded to the lowest local government area, the commune (or in large towns to the *arrondissement* or ward, Lyons for instance having eight sections); but while there are 38,000 communes in France there were in 1959 only 8,000 SFIO sections. A departmental federation had to have at least five sections and a hundred members. These units elected their own officers and conference delegates and controlled their own finances, settling the amount of the subscription and paying over a fixed sum to the centre; prosperous members paid more than the minimum, but local branches were prone to keep the balance.

5. None of the 17 deputies who protested against the Algerian and Suez policies in December 1956 had supported EDC, although outside Parliament André Philip had.

6. On it see below, pp. 173–4; and on SFIO divisions, MacRae, no. 149, pp. 203–9. Leaders' positions for Mollet (F) and against him (A) can be tabulated:

	Traditionalism 1945–47	Participation 1949	EDC 1954	Algeria 1956–57	de Gaulle Sept. 1958
Majority (Mollet)	F	F	F	F	F
Gazier	A, then F	F	F	?F	A
Pineau	A	F	F	?F	A
Lacoste	A	F	A	F	F
Lejeune	A	F	A	F	F
Defferre	A	F	F	A	F
Auriol	A	F	A	A	F
Moch	A	F	A	A	F
Philip	A	A	F	A	A
Mayer	A	A	A	A	A
Depreux	A	A	A	A	A

The Socialists were the poorest of the big parties, and in the 1951 election probably spent no more than £100,000.[7] Only about ten wealthy federations could afford a full-time secretary. But after the party took office in 1956 SFIO headquarters employed 'federal assistants' resident in the provinces and travelling 'national delegates'.[8]

At conference the smaller federations had more than their share of delegates (who voted as individuals in electing the executive) but hardly more than their share of 'mandates' for other votes. In 1951, for instance, there were fifty-five federations with fewer than 500 members and six with more than 3,000; the former with 16% of the total membership had 112 delegates out of 374 and 649 mandates out of 3,937; the latter with 40% of the membership had no more delegates (113) but many more mandates (1,606).[9] Delegates were usually mandated to vote for one or another of the long policy motions proposed – as a rule – by deputies and party leaders. Many federations split their votes proportionately between the different motions. But the large working-class federations (like a British trade union at a Labour party conference) carried habits of industrial solidarity into politics and usually voted as a block; since the smaller federations were always divided, the big federations were unbeatable if they stood together.

Before the war the executive was elected by proportional representation from the different factions (*tendances*) which each had its own local following, its own journal and sometimes even its own subscription.[10] In 1944, in an attempt to make SFIO more than a mere federation of parties, the executive's powers were extended, and its cohesion reinforced by abolishing PR. This change made possible the internal revolution of 1946. In future, members of any minority wing sat on the executive by grace of a majority which might always withdraw its favours.[11] In 1951 Jules Moch was ejected for suggesting with his usual unforgivable clarity that, as the traditional proletariat was declining in numbers and the party's main appeal was now to other social groups, it ought to adapt its programme and vocabulary accordingly. In 1956

7. Fusilier, no. 96, p. 261 (the Communists spent ten times as much on posters alone). Cf. above, p. 66n. For the local branches see *Report* to the 45th Conference, pp. 15–16. (The party authorities sometimes in practice appointed a section secretary when no member appeared suitable.)

8. Critics charged that these organizers influenced the federations to which they were sent by their services, money and pressure: A. Philip, *Le Socialisme trahi* (1957), p. 200. It seems that they did, for at the 1957 conference the share of the total opposition vote cast by the 14 federations to which a federal assistant had been assigned dropped from 18% to under 10% (including Seine – see below, p. 99 – it fell from 34% to 18%). The opposition increased elsewhere in the provinces but carried only 5 of these 14 federations (9 previously), and only 39% of their votes (58% previously). But the numbers involved were too small to affect the result. (From *Report* to the 50th Conference; cf. pp. 32, 146–7, 159–60.) In 1960 federal assistants were abolished and more national delegates appointed. It may be no coincidence that SFIO increased staff on entering the government and reduced staff soon after leaving it.

9. *Report* to the 44th Conference, pp. 219–20. Each federation had one mandate plus another for every 25 members, and two delegates plus another for every 15 mandates (or fraction over 7). The mandate system of voting was also used at the national council (*conseil national*); this body was largely attended by party officials who were responsive to the leadership: Grosser, pp. 114–15. Rich federations like Pas-de-Calais or Sénégal inflated their voting strength within the party by buying more cards than they could dispose of: Duverger, *Parties*, p. 81.

10. *Ibid.*, p. 120.

11. The minimum vote needed for election in a given year has often been as high as 60% of the total: Laponce, p. 59. Cf. Ligou, pp. 588, 620–1, 632.

two opponents of Guy Mollet's Algerian policy lost their seats on an enlarged executive. In 1960 all the minority members resigned when one, Georges Dardel, was thrown off by the majority for accepting Communist votes in his election as chairman of the Seine departmental council.

As the organ of the rank and file, the executive frequently clashed with the parliamentarians. Suspicion of their integrity had marked the very foundation of the party, and was kept alive by the tendency of French politicians to start a career on the Left and conclude it on the Right. At first no parliamentarian could belong to the executive (or represent his federation at a national council); but in 1913 ten members of parliament were allowed on the executive of 31, and in 1956 the number was raised to 20 out of 45. Moreover, through successive conflicts and compromises the deputies gradually increased their influence in ministerial crises.[12]

Control over discipline, however, remained with the representatives of the rank and file. The executive could dissolve and reconstitute a rebellious federation such as Seine in 1939, or Pyrénées-Orientales in 1950.[13] Recalcitrant party leaders were often subjected to mild penalties by the executive or severe ones by the national council. In 1954 half the parliamentary party successfully defied the executive in their revolt over EDC; next year seventeen deputies (including Mayer, Moch and Lejeune) were expelled for repeating the offence over German rearmament, though they were soon readmitted because of the imminent general election. Isolated rebels were less fortunate: Philip was expelled in 1957 for his denunciation of the leadership, and Mayer driven to resign his seat soon afterwards for opposing internment camps for Algerians in France.[14] By this time the party machinery had become subordinated to the government; in 1956–57, with the general secretary as prime minister, the executive met less frequently and rarely discussed politics.[15] The anathemas once hurled by a militant rank and file at leaders who compromised themselves with the ruling class were now reserved by ministers for their inconveniently intransigent critics.

The split at Tours in 1920 had divided the parliamentarians from the rank and file. Membership fell from 180,000 to 52,000 in 1921.[16] By 1936 it had regained the former level, and a year later the record figure of 285,000 was attained (though nearly a third of these had fallen away by the outbreak of war). At the Liberation came another influx, and in 1946 a new record of

12. See below, pp. 403–4. On their financial contribution see above, p. 65n.

13. On it see below, p. 328. Seine was led before the war by a perennial rebel, Marceau Pivert.

14. In June 1957 Mayer and 25 other deputies refused to vote the special powers allowing the government to set up camps, and in November he alone voted against them; for this he was 'suspended' by the party for the whole Parliament (i.e. he lost his committee seat – he was chairman of the foreign affairs committee – and was supposed not to speak without party leave). In March 1958 he became president of the League for the Rights of Man, and chose to resign his seat rather than face expulsion for his next offence against discipline. (Philip was expelled, technically, for publishing his criticisms in non-Socialist papers – Socialist ones being closed to him.)

15. In 1951–56 it had averaged 39 meetings between July and March. But from July 1956 to March 1957 it met only 18 times: *Report* to the 49th Conference, p. 150. It had no opportunity to discuss Suez: Philip, p. 200. Of its 45 members, 9 were ministers.

16. Rimbert, no. 190, p. 125. The Communists attracted 130–140,000 members but only 13 deputies; SFIO kept 53 deputies but only 30,000 members: Walter, pp. 45, 50, 53.

354,000 was reached. For the next eight years membership – as in other parties – steadily declined; for the Socialists this was the first drop lasting more than two years and also the first to include a general election year, 1951. At the end of 1954 they claimed only 113,000 – almost the lowest figure since 1928.[17] But in the pre-election year of 1955 there was a slight increase, and at the end of 1957 they claimed 118,000.

The party's voting strength fell sharply, from 4½ million in October 1945 to 2¾ million in June 1951. From 20% of those voting in 1932, and 19% in 1936 (before woman suffrage) the Socialist share increased to 23% in 1945, only to fall back in three successive general elections to 14% six years later. But the decline slowed after 1946 and was reversed in 1956, when SFIO recovered a little to 3¼ million votes (14½% of the poll). It retained this total in the Fifth Republic's first election in 1958.

Before this revival many observers claimed that the Socialists were taking over the Radical party's old electoral following. The 1952 poll found that they had fewer supporters than any other major party in the big cities with over 100,000 inhabitants, and drew 42% of their votes from the rural communes with under 2,000. (This strength in the provinces was both cause and effect of a provincial press far more flourishing than that of the Communists.[18]) It was rarely based on the industrial proletariat, for in most areas working-class Socialist support came from small plants, secondary industries, and state or public employees – the fields where *Force ouvrière* also found recruitment easiest.[19]

In 1956 the limited Socialist electoral revival occurred in the industrial departments, which were little affected by the ravages of Poujadism, and it was offset by losses in the rural south.[20] In Nord and Pas-de-Calais the Socialist vote exceeded the Communist for the first time for a decade. SFIO's 'Radicalization' had plainly been exaggerated, for though the party attracted only 15–20% of the manual workers, even this limited proletarian following made up more than 40% of the total Socialist vote. Moreover the remainder came from white-collar workers rather than from the small businessmen, artisans

17. In 1934 it was only 110,000. See Rimbert, no. 190, p. 125 for figures up to 1950; Fauvet, *Forces*, p. 87, for those of 1945–50; *Reports* to next year's conference for those of later years; Duverger, *Parties*, pp. 81ff., for a discussion of their significance. The membership claimed is the number of party cards sold; it is inflated, e.g. in 1954 (113,000 claimed) monthly subscriptions paid were only twelve times 88,000. Moreover some subscriptions were bogus: see above, n. 9. Coston, p. 392, estimates the real figure for 1958 at only 60,000, barely half the number claimed.

18. Its circulation was half as great again in 1952: Bauchard, no. 9b, p. 601. It was well over twice as great in 1958: J. Kayser in *Élections 1958*, p. 82. But in Paris *Le Populaire* clung to life with the utmost difficulty.

19. Rimbert in *Partis et Classes*, pp. 204–7. At Lyons in 1958 75% of salaried or wage-earning members of SFIO were in FO unions, 10% in CGT unions (mainly those like the printers who had no alternative) and 15% in no union: Grawitz, no. 115, p. 463 – she confirms Rimbert throughout. On FO and SFIO see Lorwin, especially pp. 186–7, 291–4; Rioux, pp. 81–2, 130–1; Godfrey, pp. 54–6; Williams, p. 71; Ehrmann, no. 82, pp. 158–9.

20. The 15 most industrial departments (see Map 21) with 35% of the electorate contributed 30% of SFIO's losses in 1951 but 80% of its net gains in 1956. These gains were greatest in the most industrial areas; at Nantes, after the 1955 strikes, the Socialist vote more than doubled (a much bigger gain than that of the Communists) while elsewhere in Loire-Inférieure it rose only by 50%; in the Lille and Arras constituencies it rose by nearly half, but in the rest of Nord and Pas-de-Calais only by a quarter; at Marseilles SFIO's share was 3% up, in the rest of Bouches-du-Rhône 1% down. And see Pierce, no. 180, p. 414; and Map 10.

and professional men on whom the Radicals had relied. Civil servants were particularly attracted to SFIO, and in 1951 it was estimated that with their wives and retired colleagues they made up 30% of its vote.[21]

Though the civil servants played the leading part in the life of the party, more workers belonged to it than was often supposed. In 1951 an inquiry covering 14,000 members found that a third were workers (25% in private and 9% in nationalized industry). Another 15% were civil servants (including postmen and teachers); almost a quarter of the membership thus enjoyed the status and security of state employees. In the leadership, both local and national, the workers were under- and the civil servants over-represented. In 1951 the latter provided 37% of the federal committees, and among the hundred-odd Socialist deputies who sat in the Assemblies of the Fourth Republic there were never more than four industrial workers or fewer than thirty teachers.[22]

Young men were almost as rare as industrial workers in the Socialist leadership. The party youth organization was suspect; in 1947 it was deprived of its autonomy for Trotskyist heresies. Ten years later it existed in only forty-eight of France's ninety departments.[23] In 1951 only 30% of party members were under 40; they were in a majority only on one federal committee in eight. In 1946 SFIO had fewer deputies aged 35 or less than any rival party; in 1956, none at all. This situation in part reflected the influence of the civil servants, whose long professional struggles against favouritism had given them an ingrained preference for 'advancement in order of stupidity'. But their pressure only reinforced the traditional insistence of the militants on long service as a condition of promotion. Five years' membership was a minimum for almost any important function in the party. Even in all the turbulence of Liberation – with a new generation emerging from the Resistance and the old one thinned by wartime losses and a drastic purge – SFIO still chose far more pre-war politicians as candidates than any other party.[24]

Moreover in practice, though not in theory, the Socialists seemed to share the Radicals' traditional antipathy to females in politics. Anticlerical parties were handicapped in appealing to women, among whom religious observance was much commoner than among men. But, the Communists apart, they were

21. Proletarians 40%: Dogan in Hamon, pp. 113–14. In Paris the proportions were about 10% and 33% (Klatzmann, *Élections 1956*, p. 273) and at Marseilles 17% and 30% (Olivesi, pp. 251, 261, 268, 271). Fauvet's estimates of 15% and 21% in all France (*Cockpit*, p. 93n., *Déchirée*, p. 86n.) omit wives and agricultural workers. Civil servants 30%: R. Catherine in *Partis et Classes*, pp. 140–1 (roughly confirmed by the 1952 poll). In 1956 Klatzmann thought that one white-collar worker in six voted Socialist in Paris (*loc. cit.*); and at Marseilles SFIO got a third of the white-collar vote and drew 43% of its own vote from this group (Olivesi, pp. 259–61, 271). Long before the war Herriot had quoted an inn-sign which he applied to SFIO: 'Restaurant ouvrier. Cuisine bourgeoise.'

22. Rimbert in *Partis et Classes*, p. 197, for the 1951 inquiry, and no. 191, p. 297 for federal committees. For candidates and deputies before 1956, Williams, p. 70 (civil servants regularly outnumbered workers by ten to one); for the 1956 Assembly, Dogan in *Élections 1956*, p. 456. In 1951 14% and in 1956 17% of SFIO deputies were manual or white-collar workers (see above, p. 68n.).

23. *Report* to the 50th Conference, pp. 54–7 (but in 1950 it had existed in only 30 departments). The Socialist students had to be reorganized again at this time (1957).

24. Under-forties: Rimbert in *Partis et Classes*, p. 196, and no. 191, p. 292. Deputies: Duverger, *Parties*, p. 168, and no. 81, p. 1880. 'L'avancement au tour de bête', *ibid.*, p. 1882. On candidates in 1945 see p. 111n.; on SFIO and young voters in 1956 see final references above, p. 78, n.28.

not particularly hospitable to those they did recruit. In 1951 only 12% of SFIO members were women; there were only a hundred among the 1,800 members of federal committees and never more than one out of thirty-one on the executive (at one time even the women's committee had a male chairman). The family associations and similar organizations were almost all in clerical or Communist hands.[25]

Not surprisingly, recruitment dried up. Young people were discouraged by the party's stress on seniority, and women by its indifference to the newly enfranchized half of the electorate. Some potential supporters were antagonized by its faded Marxist vocabulary, others alienated by its narrow anticlericalism, and yet others offended by its repeated – if sometimes reluctant – compromising of the principles it still professed. Whereas before 1939 the proportion of new members to old ones in any given year had never fallen below 15%, for years after 1945 it was under 4%.[26]

The Socialists were thus a predominantly lower-middle-class and white-collar party which kept some local support from industrial workers. They acted as democratic reformists while still talking the language of Marxist revolutionaries. Their practice bore no relation to their professions; but in 1945–46 they refused to adapt their professions to their practice. This reaffirmation of a radical creed was a profoundly conservative gesture.[27] But the gesture inhibited an effective reformist appeal.

3. CHARACTERISTICS

The option of 1945–46 affected the party's internal character as well as its capacity for expansion. It strengthened the influence of conservative forces within SFIO by giving them a cloak of militancy, and it sharpened the contrast between brave revolutionary words and cautious reformist actions. But while impeding Socialist recruitment among white-collar workers and Catholics, it did not win back workers in industry.

SFIO had always suffered from the anti-political tradition of French trade unionism. This semi-anarchist heritage had deprived it of any organic connection with the industrial labour movement. French unionism was always based on the civil servants and other employees of the state;[28] strong co-operatives or mass unions in private industry, so familiar in Britain or Scandinavia, were unknown in France. Indeed when industrial workers

25. Fauvet, *Forces*, p. 8. The 1952 poll found that 41% of Socialist voters were women. For members, Rimbert in *Partis et Classes*, p. 195, and for committees, no. 191, p. 292. When the executive was enlarged to 45 in 1956, a second woman won a seat.

26. Duverger, *Parties*, p. 89.

27. Blum told the conference after Mayer's defeat: 'You are nostalgic for everything that might recall this Party as you knew it in other days . . . you are afraid of what is new.' Mollet's successful motion proclaimed '. . . that all attempts at revisionism must be condemned, particularly those inspired by a false humanism whose real purpose is to mask that fundamental reality, the class struggle. . . . It is these deviations and errors which tomorrow would lead [us] down the same path as the Radical party. . . . To enrich Marxism . . . and in no way dilute it . . . to combat all forms of imperialist exploitation, to help the overseas peoples in their struggle for emancipation . . .': Ligou, pp. 544–7 (cf. Grosser, p. 114). After the 1962 election SFIO reaffirmed its 1945 programme professing its revolutionary aims.

28. Martinet, no. 156, especially p. 776; Ehrmann, *Labor*, p. 25; Lorwin, pp. 60–1; Rioux, pp. 37–8; Godfrey, pp. 24–5. State employees were naturally predisposed to emphasize electoral and parliamentary rather than industrial or revolutionary action.

without organizational experience did come flooding into the unions in 1919, 1936 and 1944–45, they were organized mainly by the Communists or their revolutionary forerunners.[29] In the Fourth Republic, therefore, there were only a few departments where the Socialist party retained its hold on important sections of the industrial working class. But these few, where the real political struggle was between the two proletarian parties, had both the largest and the most anti-Communist federations in SFIO.

If the Socialists could not satisfy the revolutionary workers, their appeal to the reformists was hampered by the religious quarrel.[30] They could never attract the Christian proletariat because of the fervour with which they clung to the anticlerical tradition. *Laïcité* was the hidden reef that wrecked the proposal for a French Labour party which Blum and his friends vainly launched at the Liberation. Many Resisters then held that only by combining Socialists and progressive Catholics in one solid organization could the democratic Left carry weight in coalition politics and impose reforms which might loosen the Communist hold on the French workers. When the Resistance had challenged the assumption that no Catholic could be a good republican, there appeared a chance—probably slender and certainly fleeting—to build a party which could reconcile devout Catholic citizens with the Republic and Catholic workers with socialism.

The first reconciliation was achieved by others and the second was not achieved at all. The foresight of a few Resisters and SFIO leaders could not overcome the determination of the militants to stand by their old creed and flag. The Socialist rank and file would not welcome the Resistance generation, which broke away with UDSR or retired into disillusionment.[31] And though they gradually learned to work with the new party of progressive Catholics they never trusted, understood or sympathized with it: they preferred to vote Radical or even sometimes Gaullist rather than MRP.

In the Fourth Republic anticlericalism came to centre in SFIO; in 1955 Guy Mollet was still describing MRP as a party which had no right to exist because it was not based on a class.[32] In many rural areas *laïcité* was the real electoral watershed – and the few places where SFIO maintained its vote in the disastrous election of 1951 were almost all among those where it fought unencumbered by clerical allies.[33] Parliamentary co-operation between

29. Lorwin, pp. 52–7, 74–5, 108–9; Ehrmann, *Labor*, pp. 20–3, 51–2; Godfrey, pp. 33, 46; Rioux, pp. 22–6, 49–50, 54, 75–6.

30. See Derczansky, no. 68, p. 677.

31. The price the party paid could be clearly seen in Bouches-du-Rhône. In the first constituency (Marseilles) its new young leaders – Gaston Defferre, a pre-war Socialist who rose through the Resistance, and Francis Leenhardt, one of the few who came over from UDSR – defeated a traditionalist revolt in 1945 (below, p. 388n.). From November 1946 SFIO made steady progress, even at the 1951 and 1958 elections when it lost ground nationally, gaining especially among white-collar but also among industrial workers. But in the second constituency it had an elderly, discredited and traditionalist standard-bearer, Félix Gouin, and it lost steadily until his retirement in 1958 – when under new and younger leadership it made striking advances. See Olivesi, especially pp. 274–6.

32. *AP* 1955, p. 59. In the Fifth Republic Mollet suggested that a *curé* might well become secretary of a Socialist section. For SFIO's strong appeal to Protestants see Schram, pp. 133, 149, 186, 201; *Paysans*, pp. 378–9.

33. There were SFIO-MRP alliances in 55 of the 103 French constituencies, but in only two of the eight where SFIO held or increased its share of the vote; for details see Williams, p. 74n.

[*over*

Socialists and MRP was buried in 1951 by the Barangé bill subsidizing church schools; five years later it could be resuscitated, ironically enough, only because the Socialist proposal to repeal that law was blocked by the very Mendesist Radicals against whom the revived Socialist-MRP understanding was largely directed. To the teachers who were so numerous in SFIO this was the crucial question; and its electoral importance made it an important link between the rank and file in the country and the compromisers in Parliament.

Indeed many Socialist deputies and would-be deputies were really Radicals in spirit. The most distinguished of these was Paul Ramadier, sometime chairman of the parliamentary freemasons' group, prime minister in 1947, and consistent champion of Socialist participation in government. Freemasonry, once the backbone of Radicalism, had begun to invade SFIO between the wars; and in the Fourth Republic one wing of it evolved rapidly towards the far Right and carried a section of the party along with it.[34] But for years the traditionalists of the Left found a common bond in anticlericalism, and as late as 1957 the Socialist bosses preferred the premiership to go to Radicals as illiberal as Bourgès-Maunoury or as prudently ineffective as Gaillard, rather than to an enlightened MRP leader like Pflimlin.

Comfortably installed in national and local administration, and strategically placed at the political centre of gravity, SFIO grew increasingly reluctant to disturb the workings of the System. No party defended the regime more resolutely against the RPF assault. The Socialists voted for Mendès-France but stayed out of his government, and lest he steal their own (muted) thunder they gave only grudging and short-lived sympathy to his campaign to revitalize French political life. On institutional questions they were staunchly conservative, opposing the stronger executive which their social and economic policies seemed to require, rejecting any suggestion of a presidential system, and even resisting attempts to give fairer representation to the big cities – where there were so few Socialist voters.[35] Over both Indo-China and Algeria they were radicals in opposition but standpatters in office. Only in their consistent support of European economic union did they seriously favour a major change – but one supported by most centre politicians, even the most conservative.

To many voters, therefore, SFIO seemed a timid, old-fashioned, bourgeois party, sadly lacking in dynamic energy and ceaselessly buffeted by stronger rivals. This impression was not always justified. At the Liberation Socialists showed courage and foresight in resisting the anti-German chauvinism of Gaullists, Communists and MRP. The short-lived all-Socialist government of

(One Socialist allied to MRP was the anticlerical zealot Maurice Deixonne, who a few weeks later led a furious attack on the Barangé bill.)

34. Pre-war: Thibaudet, *Idées*, pp. 186–7; Fauvet, *Cockpit*, p. 138, *Déchirée*, p. 132; Bardonnet, *L'évolution de la structure du Parti radical*, pp. 238–42; below, pp. 115, 434–5. Post-war: the 'McCarthyite' prefect of police Jean Baylot (pp. 46n., 347–8) was an active freemason and a member of SFIO until the 1958 election (when he was returned as a Conservative deputy endorsed by Georges Bidault's Christian Democrats). On right-wing freemasonry see Coston, pp. 350–3; on Baylot also *ibid.*, p. 504.

35. On cities see Goguel, no. 112, p. 85, who refers to SFIO without naming it; *JO* (*Sénat*) 11 July 1961, pp. 765, 768–9; above, p. 94.

December 1946 acted with vigour and energy; Moch took over the ministry of the interior when it was the least coveted post in the government and left it the most sought-after; Mollet and Lacoste did not evade responsibility in 1956–1957, however grave the responsibilities they incurred. But all too often the party was obliged by its own indispensability to take office in a coalition which it did not control, and responsibility for policies which it did not approve. In four of the five Assemblies elected between 1945 and 1958 (and in many municipal councils throughout France) it held the pivotal position once occupied by the Radicals: that of the party without whose consent no majority could be found and no administration formed.

Before 1956 it was widely believed that as the Socialists slipped into the Radical party's social and geographical skin they were also acquiring its political habits and temperament. But SFIO's electoral success in 1956 reversed the 'Radicalization' of its voting base while apparently accelerating the 'Radicalization' of its political behaviour. The party's reputation had already suffered from the charge that associates of Socialist ministers were involved in every major scandal from the Algerian wine deals in 1946 to the 'affair of the generals' in 1950. Now, on taking office, SFIO distributed more patronage to its supporters than any party had ventured to disburse for years.[36] Thereby it encouraged what a bitter critic called 'the invasion of certain sections by men devoid of any principle'. The influx was particularly marked in Paris, and perhaps explains the Seine federation's unusual, sudden and short-lived support for the party leadership.[37] But it occurred in the provinces also; in Lyons in 1958 one member in twenty was a police official, and of these two-thirds had joined SFIO only since the party had re-entered the government.[38]

Locally, too, the Socialists were often a party of administration rather than of opposition. In big towns they kept a large membership, wrote an ex-deputy, only as a 'mutual aid society of municipal employees' in places where the mayor 'belonged'. In 1957 they claimed 60,000 municipal councillors, more than half the nominal figure of party members. Like most French parties they had become an organization of local politicians, but one enjoying a pivotal position in many councils; thus they controlled Marseilles in 1945 in alliance with the Communists, and again after 1953 in opposition to them. This strategic situation made them an especially attractive choice for would-be mayors and administrators, and in national elections SFIO's influence depended heavily on the prestige of these local leaders.[39]

36. King, no. 131, pp. 437, 441. See also Coston, pp. 397–8, on colonial appointments; Planchais, pp. 33–4, on military ones; Philip, p. 199, on the radio; Isorni, *Silence*, pp. 45–6; Siegfried in *AP* 1956, p. viii, 1957, p. viii. On scandals see below, pp. 299, 339n.

37. 'Invasion': Philip, p. 203. For similar influences in another party see Bardonnet, pp. 116, 118.

38. Grawitz, no. 115, p. 462. In 1957 this local party had a resident federal assistant and was visited by a national delegate, and nearly doubled its membership (newcomers 45% of the 1958 total, see table on p. 458). Among these recruits far fewer were trade unionists than among the longer-standing members (26% as against 64%, calculated from figures on pp. 458, 463) and the former were not even much younger than the latter (average age 43 as against 49). The newcomers' attitude to policy is not recorded, but the federation switched from opposing to supporting the leadership at the 1957 party conference (cf. n. 8 above).

39. See (e.g.) C. Leleu on Isère in *Élections 1956*, pp. 381–4. On Bouches-du-Rhône in 1956, Olivesi, pp. 30, 92, 161–2, 182; in 1958, *ibid.*, pp. 104–6, 112, 138, 201, 263, 274–6, and Williams

[*over*

The contrast between the party's formal creed and its day-to-day practice became increasingly evident during the life of the Fourth Republic (notably when Mollet cited Marx in his defence of the Suez expedition).[40] Yet the leadership maintained a control over the party which its predecessors would have envied. Hitherto SFIO militants had never been charged with excessive concern for power or indifference to principle, but rather with a doctrinaire intransigence which constantly impeded the compromises without which a system based on party coalitions would become unworkable. In the past the rank and file, having the last word on policy, had repeatedly defied the parliamentary leaders – though almost always with disastrous results: they had chosen Communism in 1920, helped paralyse Parliament and endanger the Republic in the early thirties, favoured appeasement later in the decade, and in 1945–46 prevented any revision of the party's doctrine, any broadening of its base or any introduction of new blood into its leadership.

Yet 1946 was the militants' last revolt. When German rearmament strained SFIO's cohesion and discipline in 1954, it was the parliamentarians who were the rebels. And those of them who had flouted the party's code of conduct over EDC were all the more reluctant to repeat the offence over Algeria – especially when a Socialist premier was pursuing enlightened policies of which they approved both at home and in Black Africa. Despite their internal disputes the Socialists could still regard their party as a community and be proud of the freely accepted discipline which symbolized its solidarity.[41]

But the breakdown of this discipline over EDC affected the leadership also. A major policy endorsed by the majority of the party had been defeated owing to the deliberate and repeated defiance of its representatives in Parliament; were this to happen again, SFIO would be in danger of disintegration. In these conditions discipline was reinforced, and extended to penalize not merely votes cast against party policy but also criticisms levelled against it.[42] This rigidity might have been appropriate to revolutionaries in a revolutionary situation: it was unacceptable to democrats in revolt against policies which, they thought, betrayed the party's principles. The camps and prisons of Algeria finally destroyed the solidarity and comradeship which had survived all previous quarrels, and the minority found family life in the *vieille maison*

and Harrison in *Elections Abroad*, pp. 37n., 83–4. On Somme in 1958, J. Blondel in *ibid.*, pp. 100–2. 'Mutual aid': Conte, *La Succession*, p. 54. In 1951 SFIO was called: 'a party of patronage . . . of ministers and deputies, mayors and county councillors, prefects and police officials, a true coalition of the ambitious and the interested, within which a few old-style militants curiously survive as political small rentiers, sadly living on the capital of their memories'; Martinet, no. 155, p. 55.

40. At the 1957 conference: *Monde*, 2 July 1957.

41. Grosser, p. 113. Yet suppressed resentments might prevail in a secret ballot: see Melnik and Leites, pp. 80–2.

42. No one preached the need for rigour more forcibly than André Philip, who was so soon to suffer from it. But critics who had respected discipline did not escape. Madame Brossolette in 1958 declined (on party instructions) an offer to stand as the only left-wing candidate in an important Paris by-election to the Assembly; a few weeks later the majority denied her re-election to her seat in the upper house. Among those who resigned from the party in 1958 were Édouard Depreux (below, p. 400n.), and Mireille Osmin, another critic who as candidate in a Paris by-election in 1957 had obediently advocated the Algerian policy of the majority.

increasingly intolerable. After their resignations Guy Mollet pronounced their epitaph: 'They have never been real socialists.'[43]

Early in the century Péguy said that 'tout commence en mystique et tout finit en politique'. The remark still applies to the Socialists (as to every Fourth Republican party which ever ventured to claim a *mystique* at all). An extreme right-wing critic lamented SFIO's 'intellectual downfall'. A left-wing observer noted that: 'Its doctrine is an embarrassment. It dare not reject it, or apply it, or renovate it: another aspect of the party's sclerosis. SFIO still calls itself revolutionary, but neither its leaders nor its cadres nor its members nor its voters have any desire to make a revolution.' Yet with all its failings the party obstinately maintained and even slightly improved its position during the Fourth Republic. As Jacques Fauvet put it, 'If today it no longer has the method of Marx nor the faith of Jaurès nor the austerity of Guesde, what has it left? Power, no doubt: which is much – and nothing.'[44]

There were many to accuse SFIO of thinking power was everything. Yet the only serious attempts to reconcile the industrial workers to the Republic were made under Socialist inspiration in 1936 and in 1945–46; their failure should not deprive the party of the credit for tackling a task which most of its rivals preferred to ignore or obstruct. In 1956, with no majority either in Parliament or in the country, the Socialists succeeded in passing some useful reforms at home and in preventing the errors committed in North Africa from being repeated south of the Sahara. And if they failed disastrously to solve the desperately difficult problem of Algeria, progress was not so very much faster under a successor with far greater prestige and freedom of action.

The party's opportunism in these years was violently attacked by Socialists and others at home and abroad. But they were mistaken in thinking that its course was wholly determined by the character of its leader and his skill at manipulating the machine. Over EDC in 1954 and de Gaulle's election as premier in 1958, Guy Mollet failed to convince his party. While his success was normally assured by the support of Nord and Pas-de-Calais, he usually had a majority of the other votes as well; in any case the numerical weight of the two big federations only reflected their unusual achievement in retaining a mass working-class base. And when as prime minister Mollet was denounced for failing to apply party instructions (often by the very same critics who had attacked him ten years before for trying to impose party orders on the Ramadier ministry) he could call in return on the strong loyalties evoked by the first Socialist-led government for nearly a decade.

Still more important than party loyalty was the support of a public opinion to whose moods he was uncannily sensitive. In France as elsewhere, a politician charged by his fellow-partisans with 'putting country before party' tends to find his standing with other citizens enhanced. If Mollet unjustly

43. *Combat*, 19 April 1960. To others the *vieille maison* was still home; even when the Socialists decided to support Lacoste's removal from Algiers, he refused to leave SFIO and lead the settlers. 'You don't throw off a party like an old coat': J. Ferniot, *Les Ides de Mai* (1958), p. 7.

44. Fauvet, *Forces*, p. 67 (from *Monde*, 4 October 1947); Coston, p. 390 ('downfall'); Duverger, no. 81, p. 1871 ('doctrine'). But some observers still found SFIO quite distinctive in professing concern for doctrine and looking beyond Parliament to the country: Melnik and Leites, pp. 53–5.

despised the intellectuals and their criticisms, so did many other Frenchmen. If he was nationalist in 1956, so were his compatriots; if he turned to de Gaulle in 1958, so did they. Again like the Radicals of twenty years before, the Socialists were among the gravediggers of a Republic less because they misrepresented the French people than because they represented them all too well.

Chapter 8

THE CHRISTIAN DEMOCRATS (MRP)

1. HISTORY

The *Mouvement républicain populaire* represented an old tradition in French thought, which before 1940 found no effective political expression. Ever since Lamennais there had been Catholics who were aware of the problems created by the industrial revolution and Catholics (not always the same ones) who were anxious for reintegration in the French political community from which, during much of the Third Republic, they were virtually excluded. In the early years of this century Marc Sangnier's *Sillon* formed a focus for liberal Catholicism as important as that provided for reactionaries by Maurras and *Action française*.[1] A more important electoral influence was *Action libérale populaire*. This party was already in decline by 1914, but it had claimed nearly eighty deputies a decade before.

Between the wars the progressive Catholic tradition was represented by two small groups, the *Parti démocrate populaire* and *Jeune République*. PDP was based on Brittany, Alsace, Lorraine, and one or two mountainous southern departments; commentators found it hard to classify as either Right or Left. *Jeune République*, founded by Sangnier after the ban on *Sillon*, was not a party but an extra-parliamentary 'league'. Less clearly confessional, less electorally oriented and more progressive than PDP, it adhered to the Popular Front of 1936.

MRP had deeper roots than these predecessors, since it could tap the social organizations sponsored by the Church or inspired by its principles: notably the Catholic trade union movement, *Confédération française des travailleurs chrétiens* (CFTC) and the youth organizations like *Jeunesse ouvrière chrétienne*, *Jeunesse agricole chrétienne* and *Association catholique de la jeunesse française*. Some of these were created and others greatly extended between the wars, and in 1932 Thibaudet, describing Christian socialism as one of the six great French political traditions, declared that only leadership was needed to create a powerful new movement.[2] Francisque Gay's paper *L'Aube*, with its contributors from PDP, CFTC, Catholic Action and *Jeune République*, foreshadowed the combination from which MRP emerged.

1. Both movements were condemned by the Vatican. Sangnier ended his life as honorary president of MRP and on his death was officially honoured by the Socialist party. Maurras was sentenced to life imprisonment for collaboration, and just before his death in 1952 he celebrated his compassionate release by demanding the execution of the minister of justice responsible for the post-war purge.

2. 'Il y a une jeunesse, elle attend un guide; des cadres, ils sont prêt pour un tableau; des hommes, il leur faudrait un homme': *Idées*, p. 118. Cf. Priouret, *Partis*, pp. 59–61; L. Biton, *La Démocratie chrétienne dans la politique française* (1954), pp. 49–61; Dansette, *Destin du Catholicisme français 1926–1956*, Chapter 2; Bosworth, *Catholicism and Crisis in Modern France*, Chapters 4 and 5, and especially pp. 24, 37, 241–2, 249, 323. Of MRP's 52 bureau and executive members in 1959, 40 had been active in Catholic Action and similar groups: *ibid.*, pp. 254–5 (full list), cf. Williams, p. 78n. For a full account of MRP see Goguel (with M. Einaudi), *Christian Democracy in Italy and France* (1952); for its relations with the Church, Bosworth, pp. 239–61.

These developments were accelerated by the war and the Resistance. The progressive Catholic groups refused to compromise with fascism either at home or abroad. They opposed Mussolini's attack on Abyssinia, Franco's rising in Spain and the capitulation to Hitler at Munich; and after the defeat their members and leaders could claim a splendid Resistance record. MRP was formed in 1944 at Lyons, a centre of Catholic Resistance. Starting with new men and a clean sheet, it set out to reclaim for the Republic two dangerously alienated groups, the devout Catholics and the industrial workers. It chose to call itself a movement, not a party, in order to emphasize that its purposes went beyond electoral success to the promotion of Catholic principles and doctrines in society. In the purified atmosphere of the new regime it hoped to regenerate French political life.

In pursuing these ambitious objectives it enjoyed important advantages. A solid basis in the Catholic youth and social organizations was reinforced by the clergy's powerful support (which was ardent among the parish priests, more prudent among some of their formerly Vichyite superiors who were now seeking merit by association with authentic Resisters). This strong backing gave it the organization and discipline to compete with the Communist party. The MRP leaders had no responsibility for either the despised inter-war regime, the war itself, or the Vichy counter-revolution. Besides the prestige of novelty and an admirable Resistance record, they enjoyed the tacit blessing of the greatest of Catholic Resisters, General de Gaulle; and millions of French Conservatives, bewildered by the disgrace of their former leaders, rallied to the movement. So MRP achieved an initial success which astounded its own leaders: in August 1945 it had 100,000 members, in October nearly five million votes.[3]

This triumph was artificial. Only a minority of MRP voters shared the progressive views of the party militants; the majority were Conservatives for whom MRP was a temporary barrier against Communism and not a permanent political home. To preserve this swollen electoral following MRP leaders and deputies often adopted a more conservative attitude than the membership would have wished, but they did not move far enough Right to satisfy their voters. During 1946 MRP first acquired new support by leading the opposition to the first draft constitution, then forfeited it again by reluctantly accepting the second. To millions of its voters this was compromising with Communism. They had as yet no alternative party; but they expressed their resentment in the referendum of October 1946 when some two-thirds of the MRP voters, especially in the conservative west and north-east, responded to General de Gaulle's condemnation of the constitution. Given a lead, they would desert a party whose aims they had never shared to follow a more acceptable standard.

In April 1947 de Gaulle gave that lead, and the lost Conservatives went over in droves to RPF. In the October municipal elections MRP kept only 10% of the votes as against 25% the year before (and Gaullists cruelly suggested that *L'Aube*, now the party paper, should change its name to *Le Crépuscule*). But when the decline was halted a smaller but more homogeneous movement

3. Wright, *Reshaping*, p. 76 (membership).

emerged.[4] Although MRP deputies still felt the pressure of right-wing competition, at the Strasbourg conference of 1949 the militants checked Georges Bidault's attempt to flirt with RPF. And at Nantes in the following year a left-wing candidate for general secretary obtained 40% of the vote (224 against 341 for the official nominee, André Colin).

Yet the movement was being driven inexorably towards the Right. A breach with the Socialists over wages policy early in 1950 was healed – temporarily – a few months later. But in the 1951 election a quarter of the MRP deputies held their seats in alliance with the Right or even RPF and in opposition to the Socialists; only RPF intransigence kept even Robert Schuman from allying with these opponents of the government in which he served. Moreover, by halving the party's numbers in the Assembly this election increased the relative weight of its Catholic strongholds; nearly half its deputies now came from the conservative departments of the north-west and north-east. To avoid being outbid by RPF for the favour of the Church, MRP had to vote for the Barangé bill subsidizing Catholic schools and so to reopen the breach with the Socialists.

In the new Assembly the movement supported the conservative Pinay and Laniel cabinets. Its ministers now bore the main responsibility for repression in Tunisia, for crisis in Morocco and for the long war in Indo-China. Its deputies gave no support to the strikes of 1953, although these were largely led by CFTC, and voted steadily for Conservative candidates in the presidential election at the end of that year. Its leaders were the main target of Mendès-France's criticisms, and when he came to power it formed the core of the opposition to him – finally defeating him over North Africa despite its approval of his policy there. In the 1956 election its candidates allied with Conservatives and right-wing Radicals against the Left's Republican Front.

This rightward movement was punctuated by a number of mutinies. In 1950 a third of the MRP deputies frustrated Queuille's attempt to form a conservative ministry. Two years later the same proportion withheld their support from Pinay, whose administration (detested by the militants) was brought down in December 1952 by an MRP revolt. In the long ministerial crisis of the following summer half the deputies opposed Reynaud, three-fifths supported Mendès-France, almost all repudiated Marie, and only with extreme reluctance did they resign themselves to Laniel. At the beginning of Mendès-France's government in 1954 most of them voted him special economic powers, and on his fall they did their best to recover a left-wing reputation by supporting a Socialist, Christian Pineau, for the premiership.

MRP's situation was as uncomfortable as that of the Socialists a few years earlier, and its struggles to escape were as unavailing; at the 1953 congress its president, P. H. Teitgen, argued like Socialist leaders before him that by going into opposition the party would merely paralyse government, discredit the regime, and play into the hands of the Right. MRP also feared that to leave a majority which the Gaullists had just entered would enable the

4. CFTC's strength in the social security elections suggests that working-class voters were more faithful to MRP than bourgeois ones: see Goguel, no. 109, pp. 249–50. But see n. 14.

nationalist forces to halt progress towards European integration, and in particular to prevent the ratification of the European army treaty. It was largely because they blamed Mendès-France for the eventual defeat of EDC that they ended by pursuing him with unrelenting hostility. At odds with the Gaullists about foreign affairs, with the Socialists about educational and colonial policy, and with the Radicals about almost everything, MRP were forced into the embrace of the Conservatives whose political influence they had once hoped to destroy.

Yet the movement did not disintegrate. The extreme left wing, which had always been far to the Left of the Socialists, became finally disillusioned; three deputies broke with the party in 1950, a few parliamentarians were expelled in 1954 – temporarily for supporting Mendès-France or permanently for opposing EDC – and in the 1956 election some Catholic intellectuals campaigned for the Mendesist Radicals and some trade unionists for the Socialists. On the other flank, Bidault, now a diehard colonialist, enjoyed a little support in Parliament but none among the militants; by 1955 he was already isolated within the party (though he stayed in it three more years). In the centre, the great majority of members followed Pierre Pflimlin in cautiously urging progress in Morocco in 1955 and in Algeria in 1956 and 1957;[5] out of power, MRP leaders proved more liberal than most ministers from the Republican Front parties. In the 1956 Assembly MRP's concentration on the European programme, instead of reinforcing conservative coalitions, now supplied a link with the dominant Socialist and Radical leaders. And in the Fourth Republic's final crisis MRP, like most Radicals and half the Socialists, shifted from a stern republican condemnation of the mutinous army of Algiers to support for General de Gaulle as the alternative to civil war and the safeguard against repression and reaction.

2. ORGANIZATION AND FOLLOWING

MRP's organization followed the Socialist model but was modified to strengthen the leadership. At the base were the familiar sections and federations; as in SFIO the subscription rate was fixed by the federations, and there were the customary difficulties over the collection of affiliation fees by the centre. Members of parliament did not have to subscribe part of their salaries to party funds, but generally did so. Federations could choose candidates freely for municipal elections, but those standing for Parliament or a departmental council had to be approved by the national executive. The supreme authority nationally was the annual conference, which was supplemented by the usual national council (*comité national*) of about 200 members, and executive committee (*commission exécutive*) of about fifty.

These bodies differed sharply from their Socialist counterparts. Delegates to the national council, members of parliament and of the Assembly of the French Union had a vote at conference. There the federations were represented not in proportion to membership as in SFIO, but under a sliding scale favouring the smaller units. The object was to prevent the strong Breton and

5. Pflimlin won the party presidency in 1956 by 429 votes to 167 for a rival more progressive on social questions, François de Menthon: *AP* 1956, p. 55.

Alsatian branches gaining an ascendancy which might have hampered the movement's appeal elsewhere; but an indirect consequence was to weaken potential opposition, since in a new and inexperienced party the large federations – which lost votes by the sliding scale – were those likeliest to challenge the leadership.[6]

The annual conference elected the party's president, who was almost always a prominent ex-minister and served for three years, and the general secretary whose tenure was unlimited; André Colin held the latter office from 1945 until 1955 when he was succeeded by René Simonnet. They were assisted by a *bureau* dominated by the leadership.[7] The officers, chairmen of parliamentary groups and ministers (or five ex-ministers when in opposition) sat *ex officio* on both the national council and executive committee and naturally carried great weight. Deputies and senators chose a third of the national council, which elected twelve of them to the executive. The national council further co-opted twenty-four militants and elected five of these to the executive; these were unlikely to be opponents of the leadership and could be members of parliament or party officials. Thus rank and file representation was severely restricted. The federations elected only about half the national council, which in turn chose their eighteen representatives on the executive of fifty-odd (in contrast, Socialist parliamentarians were unrepresented on the former body and limited to a third of the latter).[8] Although *ex-officio* members could not number more than a fourth of the executive or parliamentarians more than half, the rest were likely to include few rebels.

The militants were kept in check by the party's structure, but they also showed more docility (or team spirit) than had been usual among their Socialist counterparts. MRP conferences were dominated by ministers and faithfully supported their policies even when these conflicted with party orthodoxy – or with one another.[9] Given the strains on an inexperienced party which very quickly lost half its following, more internal dissension might have been expected. But there were naturally many defections among the deputies in the 1946 Assembly; and voting discipline in Parliament soon had to be relaxed since any attempt to coerce the Left minority would have split the party. During the Pinay government parliamentary discipline collapsed altogether; although there was some improvement subsequently, the whip was rarely enforced on recalcitrant politicians (except for spectacular offences such as joining Mendès-France's cabinet, and even then the members expelled for

6. Duverger, *Parties*, p. 144; but the big working-class federation of Nord supported the Pinay government. Federations had a delegate for every 50 members up to 200, every further 100 up to 5,000, and every 200 beyond. Thus whereas a Socialist federation with 200 members had 9 delegates and one with 2,000 had 81, MRP allotted them 4 and 22 respectively: Campbell, no. 47, p. 416.

7. Six members sat *ex officio*; in 1951, of the seven elected by the executive all but one were deputies and most were ex-ministers. (The rank and file were given slightly more representation in 1959.) On officers see Grosser, p. 121.

8. Until 1956 (above, p. 93, on SFIO). Federations had a national council delegate for every thousand members or fraction thereof. These could not be M.P.s (but could be party officials); however their alternates might be M.P.s, and in ministerial crises distant federations were often represented by their deputy – or not at all, for attendance was often as low as half the membership: Laponce, p. 375 n. 6.

9. Grosser, pp. 121–4.

this were soon readmitted). For years Bidault was permitted to flout the policy of the party, though it did refuse to support him for the premiership during the Fourth Republic's final crisis in May 1958.[10]

One original feature needs special mention. In accordance with Catholic corporatist ideas MRP required every federation to set up groups (*équipes*) from whose nominees the national council co-opted twelve representatives. These groups were to organize women, youth, workers, professions and management (*cadres*), local councillors, and peasants; the last was much the most effective.[11] The workers' *équipe* was a potential nucleus of opposition; at the 1953 Paris conference it defeated the platform on workers' control in industry, and in 1954 it protested against the expulsion of a left-wing deputy, André Denis. But disillusioned militants in MRP were more likely to leave the party than to remain rebelliously within it. The rank and file's solidarity and devotion to a common cause enabled ministers easily to defeat their critics, but also preserved the movement from the violent internal clashes so common among its rivals.

Like those rivals MRP suffered from the general decline of parties. From over 200,000 members in 1946 it fell to under 100,000 in 1950 and under 40,000 in 1957. *L'Aube* ceased publication in 1951; the total circulation of the party's press was then 600,000, only half the figure at the Liberation. MRP's vote reached a peak of 5,600,000 in June 1946. But this too was an artificially swollen figure, which fell by more than half when General de Gaulle launched his RPF a year later. The remainder proved unexpectedly loyal, and in 1951, 1956 and 1958 alike the movement obtained nearly 2,400,000 votes and about 11% of the poll.[12]

At the Liberation MRP was a youthful party. Its early congresses were dominated by men in their thirties; in 1946 it had the second highest proportion of young deputies (after the Communists) and in 1951 the highest of all. But the gradual disillusionment of many left-wing militants took its toll, and little new blood was brought in. By 1960 a left-wing Catholic journalist could describe MRP as the party of a generation which had come to maturity in the 1930's; its leaders were men of 45 to 55, and their juniors were in groups further to the Left.[13] By the end of the Fourth Republic the movement also seemed to have tempered its early (and relative) enthusiasm for women candidates.

Like other Christian Democratic parties MRP included employers, workers and peasants. Its parliamentary membership was representative of the country's political personnel as a whole, though it included more former

10. On MRP discipline see below, pp. 402–3; MacRae, no. 149, pp. 194–203.

11. Bosworth, pp. 246–7; cf. R. Plantade in *Paysans*, p. 125.

12. For membership, Fauvet, *Forces*, p. 182, *Déchirée*, p. 117n., and *Les partis politiques dans la France actuelle*, p. 99 (where he gives MRP 450,000 members in 1947); Laponce, pp. 105–6. For the press, Bauchard, no. 9b, p. 602; Biton, p. 135; but cf. J. Kayser in *Élections 1956*, p. 85. For votes, 12·3% in 1951, 11% in 1956, 11·8% at the first ballot in 1958 (including 500,000 for Bidault's dissidents): *Monde*, 25 November 1958.

13. Suffert, *Les Catholiques et la Gauche*, pp. 37, 41, 97. This is borne out by the 1956 Assembly in which 55% of MRP deputies (but no more than 45% of any other party) were men in their forties – MRP having fewer old members, as well as fewer young ones, than most of its rivals.

wage-earners (and fewer lawyers) than any party but the Communists. Opinion polls suggest that among industrial workers MRP had less support than Communists, Socialists or RPF, but that among white-collar workers (*employés*) it usually led the field.[14] Of the 100,000 members of MRP in 1950, these groups accounted for 20% and a further 10% were state employees (including railwaymen). Five years later the working-class element was down from 20% to 15%.[15]

The Church backed MRP strongly in the early post-war elections, but became much more reserved after 1951, partly because the hierarchy preferred more conservative parties.[16] Moreover the movement itself (like the German CDU) wished to attract non-Catholics and gladly promoted the few who joined it. In the upper house a Jewish senator was chairman of an important committee, a Protestant presided over the MRP group, and in 1959 two of the four MRP senators from Bas-Rhin (which has many Protestant voters) were practising adherents of that faith. But the electorate continued to regard the party as essentially Catholic. In its north-eastern stronghold MRP did badly wherever the hold of the Catholic Church was weak, and where it had less support its following was concentrated in districts noted for their piety.[17] As religious observance is much more widespread among women than men, MRP was the only party which invariably had more female than male support at the polls.[18]

Once MRP shed its conservative fellow-travellers of the Liberation period, this dependence on Church support confronted it with the risk of becoming a regional party like PDP between the wars. Of the eighteen departments where 15% of the electorate voted for it in 1951, seven were in the west and four more

14. Among its deputies, wage-earners were 19½% in 1951 and 18% in 1956: from Dogan's tables (p. 68n.), cf. Williams, p. 84n. Polls: for 1952 *ibid.*, p. 452, citing *Sondages* 1952, no. 3 (cf. Appendix VII); for 1956 and 1958 Lipset, pp. 225 and 163. They suggest that MRP took at least 8% (more in 1958) of the industrial and about 25% (less in 1958) of the white-collar workers' vote; had 20% of the peasant vote in 1951 and 30% in 1956–8; and drew about 15% of its total support from industrial workers, a little more from peasants and a little less from white-collar workers (wives, who were probably more pro-MRP than their husbands, are not included in these figures; and cf. p. 68 above on the distinction between state and private employees). These polls must be treated cautiously, for when recalculated on a comparable basis they indicate some wildly improbable changes over the years; I cite only figures that seem reasonably consistent. They suggest that some 360,000 industrial workers voted MRP; Bosworth, pp. 273–4, gives an estimate of 150,000 (but points out that this was only a fifth of CFTC membership).

15. For 1950, J. Fonteneau (assistant secretary) at the Lyons conference: *MRP à l'Action* no. 115 (May 1951), p. 4; 22% were engaged in commerce or industry, 15% in agriculture, 8% in the professions or as students; the rest were retired or without occupation, i.e. housewives. For 1955, D. Pépy in *Partis et Classes*, pp. 212–14; his inquiry covered a sample of 5,000 members. Of them 12% were peasants, who formed only 3% of the local and 6% of the national leadership; workers supplied 22% and 14% respectively.

16. Siegfried, *De la IIIe*, p. 191; Grosser, pp. 180–2; Goguel, *Fourth Republic*, p. 89; J. Charlot in *Élections 1956*, pp. 131–41; Noël, pp. 43n., 81–2.

17. Dreyfus, no. 79, pp. 541, 552, on the north-east; Goguel, no. 108, p. 330, and Bodin and Touchard, no. 21, p. 347, both on Paris; Fauvet in *Partis et Classes*, pp. 171–2 on Brittany; Olivesi, pp. 47, 60 on Bouches-du-Rhône; *Élections 1956*, pp. 317–18 on Lyons; *ibid.*, pp. 386–7 on Isère; cf. Wylie, pp. 217–18, and maps in Bosworth, pp. 345–58.

18. Though CNI and RPF often had; see Goguel *et al.*, *Nouvelles études de sociologie électorale*, pp. 188 on Vienne, 195 on Grenoble, 197 on Belfort; *Élections* 1956, pp. 394–5 on Vienne in 1956; opinion polls show similar results. One poll in 1952 showed 54% of all regular churchgoers favouring MRP: Fogarty, *Christian Democracy in Western Europe*, p. 361; cf. Bosworth, pp. 251–2, and below, p. 125n.

on the Franco-German border. Thus, despite its original preference for the Left, MRP found its support coming from the traditionally conservative strongholds of the Church.[19] In 1951, nearly half the MRP deputies (37 out of 83, omitting overseas members) came from the west and north-east; in 1956 the proportion reached three-fifths (44 out of 70) since the movement lost seats in the south but gained in Brittany and Alsace. But this was not the whole story; by increasing its vote outside its traditional strongholds it foreshadowed the resilience it was to show, to its own surprise, in 1958.[20]

The growing influence of young Catholic peasant leaders was reflected in the departmental councils, where MRP made gains at every post-war election. By the end of the Fourth Republic MRP was firmly implanted in those parts of the French countryside where Catholicism was still a living force; it had built up a network of local councillors and rural militants who were both younger and more authentically agricultural than the small-town doctors and lawyers who had manned the pre-war Radical committees. With the help of its new notables MRP survived even the introduction of the single-member constituency which it had always feared.[21] But in the towns it was another story. In 1958 no MRP deputy was returned from any of the seven largest cities in France.[22]

3. CHARACTERISTICS

MRP's founders held high ambitions: to reconcile the workers to the Catholic Church and the Church to the Republic, to end the ancient quarrel over clericalism which was preventing national unity, and to transform the quality of French public life. Believing in a plural society of many independent social groups, they found themselves in head-on opposition to the Jacobin tradition which still inspired most French democrats (from Gaullists to Socialists). They rejected equally the Marxist collectivism professed by the Left and the conservative individualism proclaimed by the Right; and while their ideological originality set them apart from the other parties, they were proud of it precisely because they believed it could transcend the old divisions.[23]

MRP's greatest asset was that its members felt they had a philosophy and a

19. In 1932 the Right won the votes of 45% of the electorate in eight of the 18 departments and fell below 30% in only three; the Radicals reached 30% in only four and the Socialists and Communists (even added together) in only two. Goguel, *Géographie*, pp. 49, 77 and 113; Pickles, no. 177, p. 178 (for Radicals in 1932). In 1945 a conservative Pyrenean peasant claimed he had always voted M R P 'like my father and grandfather': d'Aragon in *Paysans*, pp. 502–3.

20. In 1956 it gained votes in 30 constituencies of which 14 were in the south (Goguel in *Élections 1956*, pp. 486–7) but lost seats there because of the electoral law (see Chapter 22). See also Pierce, no. 180, pp. 416–17; and Maps 5, 6 and 13.

21. For single-member seats, see Chapter 22. In 1951 6% of MRP deputies were peasants. in 1956 12%, in 1958 17%: Dogan's tables (p. 68n. and *Élections 1958*, p. 267). For MRP's success in rural elections, Goguel *et al.* in *ibid.*, pp. 353–9; R. Plantade in *Paysans*, pp. 123–7, For Catholic rural organizations, M. Faure in *ibid.*, pp. 345–60; Fauvet in *Partis et Classes*, p. 175; Suffert, pp. 128–32; Dansette, *Destin*, pp. 384–90; Bosworth, pp. 122–3, 247; Wright, nos. 226, 228; below, p. 365.

22. In 1958 Paris had 31 deputies and the six next largest cities 29. (In 1956 the capital had had a distinctive electoral law which gave MRP seven members where under the ordinary system it would have had none: see below, pp. 313n., 504.)

23. Einaudi and Goguel, pp. 130–2; Biton, especially pp. 83–4; cf. Bosworth, pp. 310–13; Fogarty, Chapters 4–7. But see below, p. 113.

purpose wider than electioneering. Rather like the Communists, they distinguished between formal and real democracy; they believed that political parties should bridge the gap between 'us' and 'them' and restore the broken circuit of confidence between citizen and government, *le peuple* and *le pouvoir*. They had a strong sense of the unity and mission of their movement (like the younger and less hidebound members of SFIO, who in the early years consequently felt far closer to MRP than to their traditional Radical partners). But as a new and overwhelmingly Catholic party MRP had a conception of discipline different from that of the more pragmatic and freethinking Socialists: 'no longer a technique ... but a kind of sacrament'. In the social organizations by which the Church appealed to various categories – youth, women, peasants, workers, students – they had effective channels to approach the masses with a wider and deeper appeal than individualist groups could make. And as individuals they were political newcomers, not long exposed to the contagion of the world's slow stain.[24] Was it wholly accidental that when the Paris parliamentary correspondents voted to choose the most likeable deputy in the 1946 Assembly the first three places went to MRP members?[25]

A public penchant for righteousness in politics has its distasteful features, and MRP morality recalled the failings as well as the virtues of the British Nonconformist conscience a few decades earlier. Its adherents often displayed a real concern for the standards of public life, a political vision not limited to personal careerism, a willingness to allow idealism and imagination to intrude even into foreign affairs, an appreciation of problems, like the scourge of alcoholism, that fell outside the well-worn party grooves. On the other hand their policies were often both restrictive and unrealistic. Some of them betrayed an illiberal desire to impose minority moral standards on their fellow-citizens, and a short-sighted weakness for unenforceable legislation (against, for example, prostitutes and *pastis*) which either drove these social evils underground or was so openly flouted as to bring the law into contempt. On wider issues, too, they were prone to exaggerate the importance of formal structures and to view institutions as ends in themselves irrespective of the forces controlling them. This tendency was particularly marked over the problem of Europe.

MRP's championship of European integration was passionate, if somewhat belated. In 1945 the movement was proud of its 'national' – not to say nationalist – foreign policy and contemptuous of the Socialists' more liberal (and more realistic) attempts to modify French attitudes towards Germany. But in 1950, after years of steady retreat under Allied pressure, the Schuman plan restored initiative to Paris. MRP now gave a warm welcome to European

24. In 1945 62% of MRP candidates had held no previous elective post nationally or locally, compared with 56% of Communists, 48% of Radicals, 43% of Socialists (the Conservatives had to put forward new men since most of the old ones were ineligible, having supported Vichy): calculated from Husson, i. xxii. See also Melnik and Leites, p. 82 (discipline); Fauvet, no. 89, pp. 13–14 (purpose, SFIO), cf. P. Cot in *ibid.*, p. 62n.; Duverger, *Demain*, pp. 24–6, 50–4, 66 (circuit of confidence).

25. *Monde*, 3 May 1951. Or that MRP was the only party to choose its typists for competence rather than beauty?: Isorni, *Silence*, p. 182. Or that it alone tried to meet Poujadist pressure honestly and not demagogically?: Hoffmann, p. 371n., Guy, *Le Cas Poujade*, pp. 128–43 (quoting each party's reply). In Wylie's village only MRP voters trusted their leaders: pp. 217–18, 221.

economic association, and quickly became the chief defender of the European army proposal which soon followed. When EDC was defeated Mendès-France, to satisfy the Allies, accepted the restoration of a German army; MRP leaders denounced 'Mendès-Wehrmacht' with a venom which suggested either an excessive confidence in the formal safeguards provided by EDC or a violent underlying anti-Germanism – or else a tactical unscrupulousness unedifying in a movement so accustomed to parade its superior moral standards. But for many MRP leaders Europe had by this time become a psychological necessity. They could promise themselves that they would now accomplish within a new framework the social and political advances they had once intended to achieve at home and in the empire.[26]

A substitute for lost hopes was the more needed because the failures had so largely been MRP's own fault. In 1946 Georges Bidault, by frustrating the attempt to create a federal French Union, had exasperated nationalists from Casablanca to Hanoi. Then for seven years Paul Coste-Floret and Jean Letourneau presided over Indo-Chinese affairs while incompetence, corruption and political blindness rotted the French position away – and the party supported them throughout from a strong sense of personal loyalty, combined perhaps with concern for the Catholics of Tonkin. In North Africa it was Radicals and right-wingers who obstructed reforms and demanded repression most vociferously. But Maurice Schumann succumbed to their pressure over Tunisia in 1951 and Georges Bidault over Morocco in 1953, and by 1956 the chief critics of these policies within the movement had all been eliminated (for other reasons). Yet, conscious of the purity of their own intentions and confident of those of their leaders, MRP members bitterly resented such criticisms – for, again like Nonconformists, they were naïvely surprised to find that in politics even the most well-meaning men and movements are judged by results.

MRP's success had been too rapid for its own good, and its early illusions were soon shattered. The enormous tail of voters who shared none of the movement's constructive aims had made it the largest party in France and confronted its inexperienced leaders with crushing responsibilities. During the ten years after the Liberation MRP was in office for all but a month. No wonder it was described as having 'the soul of an opponent but the body of a joiner'. With SFIO it occupied the Radicals' old pivotal position in French politics; the Catholic democrats were almost as indispensable to every majority as the conservative anticlericals had once been. But a movement which was constantly exposing its conscience in public, whatever its merits and services, was unlikely to facilitate the smooth working of the political machinery.[27] For politicians concerned with power rather than principles could change allies more easily than men acutely conscious of their mission; an organization manipulated by a few leaders had a freer hand than one influenced, however intermittently, by a militant rank and file; an old party with a tradition of co-operating alternately with Right and Left found willing

26. Cf. Grosser, pp. 124–7, 193; also 206, 214–15, 325–6.

27. '... no possible majority with them or without them': Siegfried, *De la IIIe*, p. 192 (cf. *ibid.*, pp. 163–4). They felt 'persecuted and hoodwinked', 'troubled and anxious', and were prone to 'feverish examinations of conscience': Melnik and Leites, pp. 45–6, 54–5, cf. 172–3.

partners more readily than a new movement which prided itself on its originality of doctrine and outlook.

The traditional parties were slow and reluctant to accept MRP as a political ally or even admit its right to exist at all.[28] The MRP militants who despised and rebelled against the traditional Conservatives were forced into unwilling association with them by the reticence of more desirable partners. For at the Liberation the Resistance dream of co-operation with the Communists was shattered by their denunciation of the *Machine à Ramasser les Pétainistes* and their revival of the old clerical quarrel in order to drive MRP to the Right. The alliance with the Socialists lasted until 1951, when it was destroyed by the Right's exploitation of the same dispute; but the Socialists had never been happy with it, were delighted at the opportunity to break it off, and were adamant in rejecting MRP's attempts to renew it four years later. The old-style Radicals were MRP's antithesis, and though their spokesmen sat with MRP's leaders in many cabinets they could never work together comfortably. The Gaullists blamed MRP for deserting the General in 1946 and frustrating the RPF campaign in later years; MRP members in turn feared Gaullist obstruction of the European integration programme to which they had sacrificed so much. The defeat of EDC was also the decisive count in their indictment against Mendès-France, whose new radicalism MRP denounced as fraudulent and reactionary in social, constitutional, electoral and foreign affairs alike.[29] Yet perhaps they found it hardest of all to forgive him for trying to play the progressive, regenerating role in which they had once cast themselves; for reproducing their former attacks against a 'System' to which they now belonged; for appealing to the very groups – youth, women, progressive Catholics – which they had once hoped to make their own; and for attracting a popular enthusiasm and confidence which their own leaders had failed to arouse.[30]

MRP deputies (and especially potential ministers) were always more impressed than the militants with the advantages of participation in government. Their hold on the party was secured not only by its organizational structure but also by the increasing weight of its conservative-minded electorate in the west and north-east. The left wing suffered repeated frustrations, and in 1956 a million Catholic votes were thought to have gone to the Republican Front. MRP was then widely written off as a party of 'Christian Radicals' who had abandoned their principles for the sake of power. François Mauriac attacked its 'spiritual bankruptcy' and accused it of developing 'a holy patience. It knows how to wait, and while waiting it installs itself . . .'[31]

28. Einaudi and Goguel, pp. 214–18 (and see above, pp. 97–8).

29. For a content analysis of electoral themes and vocabulary showing that MRP and Radicals had few common concerns and no common language, A. Touraine in *Élections 1956*, pp. 298–9, 302. On their instinctive mutual antagonism cf. Melnik and Leites, pp. 96, 162, 250; Einaudi and Goguel, pp. 216–17; and below, p. 437.

30. For a similar view see Grosser, p. 307, and in *Élections 1956*, pp. 116–17.

31. *L'Express*, 14 May 1959; quoted Bosworth, p. 259. 'Bankruptcy': *Terre humaine*, September 1953, pp. 6–10. Cf. Duverger, *Parties*, p. 188; Hoffmann, no. 125, p. 816: '. . . in practice everything that gave MRP its ideological originality has been hidden under a bushel for the last ten years'. Suffert, p. 44, describes the typical MRP outlook more kindly as that of 'a conservative in a changing world'. On 1956 see below, p. 173.

Yet behind the parliamentary façade the movement was slowly acquiring the local roots it had formerly lacked. The new generation of young Catholics was no less civic-minded but much less conservative than its predecessors. Within CFTC, leadership passed in 1957 to the young progressives of the former opposition, the Reconstruction group.[32] Young Catholics rose to local leadership in the peasant organizations. The authorities of the Church in (or, more commonly, outside) France could sometimes hamper and even destroy their organizations – such as ACJF – but they could only check the movement, not reverse it.[33] After the collapse of Mendesism, many of this generation were driven back to MRP because they found the alternatives on the Left even more unsatisfactory. Their conditional support enabled the movement to weather the storm in 1958 more successfully than either its friends or its enemies had ever expected. But the combination of progressive militants and conservative voters remained precarious in the new Republic as in the old.

32. Suffert, pp. 89–91, 95–7; Rioux, pp. 88–96; cf. Barnes, no. 9a; Lorwin, pp. 170, 294–8; Bosworth, pp. 266–78, 323–8.

33. *Ibid.*, *passim*, especially pp. 57–65, 90–3, 106–8, 162–3, 198–9, 323; Dansette, *Destin*, Chapters 6 and 8; Suffert, pp. 38–41, 111–13, 116–20; Grosser, pp. 160, 179–82; Rémond, nos. 187–88 (summarized pp. 819–20); Jussieu, no. 130, pp. 116–25; on peasants, n. 21 above.

Chapter 9

THE RADICAL PARTY

1. HISTORY

The oldest political party in France is a conservative-minded organization 'which still calls itself "Radical-Socialist", in pious memory of its impetuous youth'.[1] Radical politicians had acted as a group from the early days of the Third Republic. Based on Paris and adhering to the Jacobin traditions of the capital, they advocated sweeping constitutional reforms including abolition of the Presidency and Senate and election of judges. In their struggle to democratize French institutions and weaken the power of the Church and the landowners, they saw the few industrial workers and their socialist spokesmen as potential allies.

In the last years of the century, at the time of the Boulanger and Dreyfus crises, the character of Radicalism underwent a rapid change. Industry spread quickly, especially around Paris; the suburban proletariat grew in numbers, power and aggressiveness; and for the first time the capital itself began voting for the Right. In retreat from the cities, the Radicals still found a welcome among the middle class of the small towns and villages: the schoolteachers and shopkeepers, country doctors and lawyers who acted as the spokesmen of the inarticulate peasantry. These rural and small-town notables claimed to defend the little man against the big, the constituencies against the bureaucracy, the provinces against Paris. They distrusted all organized power, whether wielded by governments or landlords, bishops or generals. Their outlook, vocabulary and enmities were derived from the Revolution of 1789, and despite the growing strength of Socialism these traditions bound them to the Left.

In 1901, during the battle over the Dreyfus case, the *Parti républicain radical et radical-socialiste* was officially constituted. In itself this step had no great consequences, for the organization remained highly localized in the country and poorly disciplined in Parliament; there was no one official Radical group until 1910 in the Chamber, or ever in the Senate. Nevertheless Radicalism attained its peak of power and cohesion at this period, for the adherence of freemasonry – hitherto predominantly favourable to the moderate republicans – gave new and solid backing to the isolated election committees of the small towns. Against the priests and soldiers the Radicals joined forces with the Socialists whom Jaurès had rallied to defend the Republic, and moved on to their greatest triumph, the separation of Church and State. Yet this victory was to undermine the foundations of their strength, for by taking much of the bitterness out of the clerical quarrel it weakened the party's main source of ideological vitality. Henceforward the intellectual sterility of Radicalism was to be a commonplace of political commentators.[2]

1. Lüthy, p. 166.

2. On the early period, Kayser, *Les grandes batailles du radicalisme*; on organization, Bardonnet, pp. 141n., 144–8; on freemasonry, *ibid.*, pp. 228–42, and Duverger, *Parties*, p. 149; on the effects of the separation, Thibaudet, *Professeurs*, pp. 182–3, 193–4, and *Idées*, pp. 47, 82–3, 120, 153–5.

This defeat of the Right also loosened the ties between Radicals and Socialists. Comfortably installed within the institutions of the state, the Radicals became less eager for their reform; there was no point crusading for the abolition of a Senate which Radicals dominated. Moreover the revival of working-class militancy confronted them for the first time with an organized power – and therefore an enemy – that threatened them from the Left. In 1906, a year after the foundation of SFIO and the separation of Church and State, the trade unions adopted the revolutionary syndicalist Charter of Amiens. By 1907 Jaurès was bitterly condemning Clemenceau when as prime minister the former *enfant terrible* of the Left used the power of government to deny the right to strike.[3]

The growth of Socialism provoked among the Radicals a conflict between their traditions and their interests which divided the party. The provincial committeemen had no love for Clemenceau. His 'proconsular' brand of Radicalism, energetic, nationalist and authoritarian, derived from an authentic Jacobin strain. But the *comitards* were cautious traditionalists who suspected organized power; their vision was bounded by the horizon of their constituencies, and for many of them politics was an eternal round of petty local jobbery and intrigue which ensured electoral triumph – and so gave new opportunities for jobbery and intrigue. They overthrew Clemenceau in 1909; eight years later he had his revenge. At the crisis of the war he swept the party aside and brought two of its leaders, Caillaux and Malvy, to trial for defeatist activities. But when he stood for the presidency in 1920 the Radicals defeated him through the safe secrecy of the parliamentary ballot, and in the 1924 election Herriot reverted to the old Socialist alliance. The *Cartel des Gauches* was returned to power – and Clemenceau commented scornfully, '0 plus 0 plus 0 equals 0.'[4]

Radical parliamentary strength was swollen by the double ballot electoral system, for the party profited by championing progress against reaction in some regions, moderation against revolution in others. Some Radicals therefore owed their election to Socialist votes at the second ballot and others to Conservative support. By balancing in the middle of the electoral seesaw the party gained seats but lost cohesion; there was permanent tension between the two wings. The Left relied on the militants in the country and predominated at election times. The Right were reinforced by the Radical senators, who were older than their Chamber colleagues and not answerable to a popular electorate; their point of view prevailed on budgetary and financial matters. The Socialist-Radical alliances of 1924, 1932 and 1936 all collapsed within two years, usually over finance (though the last was further strained by the exigencies of a third partner, the Communists).

Acting as a buffer between more positive and dynamic forces, the Radicals facilitated transitions whenever the balance of power shifted. These old enemies of central authority now sought to enter every government; in particular they always coveted and usually controlled the ministry of the interior.

3. Priouret, *Députés*, pp. 204–20; M. Agulhon in George *et al.*, *Banlieue*, pp. 51–5, for the striking suddenness of the change among Radicals in one locality, Bobigny.

4. Thibaudet, *Idées*, pp. 143, 147–51.

Daladier in 1934 led one cabinet which the Socialists supported and the Conservatives opposed, in 1938 another which was favoured by the Right and attacked by the Left; in between, his party had belonged to Conservative governments until the 1936 election approached, then switched to the Popular Front. By joining each combination and moderating each swing of the pendulum the Radicals made government workable in a deeply divided land. But they did not offer strong leadership for a dangerous period.

Although at the top they had become a governmental party, in the country they were still dedicated to protecting the humble citizen against overweening authority and the simple provincial against the wily Parisian. These predilections limited the leaders' breadth of view and reduced their freedom of manœuvre. Radical militants and deputies were devoted to the single-member constituency which restricted the politician's horizon; Radical ministers were often inhibited from vigorous action by the traditions and habits of mind of a party which preferred weak and conformist leaders to strong personalities.

In 1930 Siegfried called the Radicals the true conservatives of France, representative of all the backward elements in her life: the small towns, the regions unaffected by industrialization, the political traditionalists.[5] This party for quiet times was utterly unsuited to the crises of the thirties and the trials of the German occupation. The great majority of Radical parliamentarians supported Munich and voted for Pétain (though 26 of his 80 opponents were Radicals). Herriot and Daladier were deported to Germany and some well-known Radicals were killed by the Germans or the French fascists; but the party's contribution to the Resistance was not very impressive.

In the unfamiliar world of 1945 the Radicals were at a grave disadvantage. Their failure of leadership both before and during the war had cost them the support or confidence of many of their followers (in the 1945 referendum two-thirds of their remaining voters repudiated the constitutional regime under which the party had flourished).[6] To the new groups which had come to political activity through the war and the Resistance – youth, workers, progressive Catholics – their outlook seemed decadent and outmoded. They avowed their preference for the old press, constitution and electoral law at a time when these were condemned by the public as dangerous or demoralizing political influences.

New legal conditions also hampered them. A party based on distrust of organized power was severely handicapped in the new regime of disciplined political units backed by strong social organizations such as the trade unions or the Catholic Church. More than any of their rivals the Radicals had relied on the personal influence of local notables and individual politicians; they could no longer exploit this asset since most parliamentarians who had voted for Pétain – though still in good standing with the party – were (until 1953) barred by law from any public position. Under legislation which the Radicals bitterly criticized, many of their newspapers changed hands. A new electoral

5. *France*, pp. 78–9; *Tableau*, pp. 159–61. On the last few paragraphs also *France*, pp. 36–8, 59–60; D. Halévy, *La République des comités* (1934), pp. 46, 96–7, 165; and on provincialism, Bardonnet, pp. 26–7, and De Tarr, *The French Radical Party*, pp. 18–19.

6. See above, p. 20. Opinion polls showed Radical voters as the least satisfied with their leaders: see *Sondages*, 1948, pp. 225 and 240; 1952, no. 2, p. 6.

law, offering no scope for alliances, prevented them from reaping their usual profit from contradictory combinations in different areas. They could no longer prevent women getting the vote (a change which they had always feared would strengthen the influence of the priests). At local elections early in 1945 the party did so badly that in the autumn its supporters, fearing to waste their votes, turned elsewhere to stop the Communists.[7]

Yet simultaneously the Radical leaders were conducting a strange flirtation with the Communists themselves, which was based on a common dislike of plebiscites and distrust of General de Gaulle. In the referendum campaign of October 1945 the two parties advocated opposite answers to the first question (a new constitution) but the same negative reply to the second (limited powers for the Constituent Assembly). Since the campaign centred on the second question, the Radicals and Communists made an unofficial non-aggression pact for the general election held on the same day.[8]

At that election most of the party leaders were beaten and only two dozen seats were saved. The Radicals belatedly accommodated their tactics to the hated new electoral system which favoured strong parties, especially where smaller competitors multiplied opposing candidatures. In April 1946 a Radical-UDSR alliance was announced, and in November the Radicals negotiated a pact with the new Conservative party (PRL) by which each refrained from contesting a number of departments. Within a year they had switched from friendship with the extreme Left to friendship with the extreme Right.[9] The new combination added very little to their vote but much to their parliamentary strength.

Since electoral success was always their object, the sudden rise of RPF swept most Radicals along with it. In the elections for town councils in 1947 and the second chamber in 1948 most Radical candidates sought Gaullist support by accepting the RPF label – a device, as the sequel showed, for emergency use only. Older leaders like Herriot always remained suspicious of generals in politics, and in 1951 they at last persuaded the party to forbid the 'bigamy' by which its members could simultaneously belong to RPF. But the attractions of Gaullism had already diminished before sentence was pronounced, and most of the 'bigamists' had long since returned to their original hearth; Paul Giacobbi, the first chairman of the RPF inter-group in the Assembly, entered the government in 1950 to draft the electoral reform which was to blight Gaullist hopes. In the 1951 election three-quarters of the Radical deputies won their seats in alliance with Socialists and MRP.[10]

In the new Parliament the party again formed an intermittent part of every majority and a permanent component of every ministry. In 1952–54 three conservative-minded premiers were elected with solid Radical support; the

7. Goguel in *L'influence des systèmes électoraux sur la vie politique* (henceforth cited as *Systèmes électoraux*), pp. 80–1. On the press law see below, p. 392.

8. De Tarr, pp. 43–6.

9. 'They sleep with everybody but no longer reproduce'; quoted Wright, no. 227, p. 6. For the electoral system see below, pp. 309–10; for UDSR, below, pp. 174–6; for the PRL pact, Priouret, *Partis*, p. 106.

10. Of the 78 Radical and allied members for French constituencies 58 were elected in alliance with these Third Force parties, 3 in alliance with RPF, and 17 in opposition to both. On Radicals and RPF see De Tarr, Chapter 6. See also below, p. 121.

last of them, Laniel, was overthrown by the defection of one wing of the party. Earlier and later left-centre cabinets (both led by Radicals) were upset by the revolt of another faction. Of the four Radical premiers in this Parliament, Edgar Faure was elected in 1952 with Socialist votes, René Mayer in 1953 by a conservative majority, Pierre Mendès-France in 1954 with temporary Communist and consistent Socialist support, and Edgar Faure again in 1955 in opposition to the entire Left – even though he had been a leading colleague of Mendès-France. 'In a single month, one Radical leader was thrown out of office by another and replaced by a third. The founder of the party was surely Judas, not Gambetta.'[11] But the Radicals themselves were disconcerted by these speedy acrobatic turns – which always seemed to end on the Right. During 1955 Mendès-France led a growing demand for a more progressive policy, democratic party organization, and rigid discipline. This pressure brought about a revolution and then a reaction within the party which went far to destroy it as an effective political force. These events are discussed in Section 4.

2. ORGANIZATION AND FOLLOWING

The paper structure of the Radical party had some superficial resemblance to that of its rivals but bore even less relation to reality. The lowest territorial unit was the committee (*comité*) based on the commune or canton, and above it were departmental and sometimes regional federations, the strongest being that of south-western France. The committees differed from the sections of other parties in being entirely self-sufficient; indeed the party itself had been formed by bringing existing *comités* together.[12] The federations enjoyed full independence in choosing candidates and election tactics, and could not be used as an instrument of pressure by the centre against the deputy; nevertheless they were suspected and feared by Radical members of parliament lest they interfere with the politician's cherished freedom of action.[13]

Membership was open to individuals, organizations and newspapers supporting the party's nebulous doctrines. (However, in later years few newspapers retained their membership.[14]) Since the rules governing conference membership were very vague, the admission of individual members made it easy for conferences to be packed. Important Radical *élus* (members of parliament and of major local councils) attended *ex officio*. Local parties sent an indeterminate number of delegates (in practice only the well-off). Any paid-up

11. Fauvet, *Cockpit*, p. 27, *Déchirée*, p. 23. Mendès-France was overthrown by Mayer and succeeded by Faure (cf. below, p. 127).

12. Effective committees might have 80 members and 30 or 40 attending monthly meetings; Mendès-France's committee at Louviers numbered 117 and that at nearby Evreux, 300. But many committees were phantom. Allen, no. 2, pp. 449–50; cf. Bardonnet, p. 38.

13. *Ibid.*, pp. 33–42, 53–62, 63 n.141, 67–8. Thibaudet says the committees acted as 'brakes rather than motors' and 'miniature senates' (*sénaticules*): *Idées*, p. 141. On the federations' financial autonomy see Allen, *loc. cit.* Because of it, national headquarters could be small, and in 1929 its budget (not published in the Fourth Republic) was only a tenth of the Socialist figure: Halévy, pp. 191–2.

14. On their former importance, Duverger, *Parties*, p. 150; Bardonnet, pp. 32–3; F. Goguel in *Encyclopédie politique*, i. 323–4. (The late M. Kayser told me that the journals of Patenôtre and Laval did not belong to the party and these politicians owed their influence upon it to other sources.)

member could buy a special card; factions tried to have conferences held in a favourable region so that their supporters could attend, and leaders bought cards for distribution to sympathizers – not always party members – who could shout and demonstrate, though not (in theory) vote. There was wide scope for fraud: 'card-votes, proxies and obscure voting rules . . . allow very small groups to neutralize, if necessary, the wishes of the conference'.[15]

The national council (*comité exécutif*) was supposed to organize conferences and decide electoral and disciplinary matters. On it *élus* outnumbered rank and file representatives by at least three to one. Members of parliament dominated both by personal prestige and because meetings were held in Paris; only if the quorum was not reached (and it was only 150 out of a total varying from 1,200 to 2,000) were decisions referred to another session to which 'the provincial members shall be summoned' (*sic*). Nevertheless from 1946 to 1955 the party leaders preferred to work through the executive committee of seventy (then called the *commission exécutive*, before and since known as the *bureau*), whose weekly meetings were attended on the average by only twenty members – among whom party officials and members of parliament or of ministerial *cabinets* were naturally much more numerous than representatives of the provincial rank and file. Tactics in ministerial crises were decided by a joint sitting of the executive and the deputies called, from the town whose delegate proposed its establishment in 1917, the 'Cadillac committee'; it too was dominated by parliamentarians and very loosely managed (there were sometimes more votes cast than members).[16]

Control from the top was no guarantee of harmony. Dissensions could arise not only between parliamentarians and militants but among the parliamentarians themselves, owing to differences of age, policy, local interest or tactical appreciation. Usually the rank and file had been to the Left of the *élus*, and between the wars Édouard Daladier led them in attacking the cautious policies of his former schoolteacher, Édouard Herriot. But in the lean years after the war the militants were on the Right; older leaders like Herriot might support Third Force governments for fear of de Gaulle, but 'young Turks' and Radicals in the country were convinced that opposition was electorally more fruitful. At the Toulouse conference of 1949 Daladier stood against Herriot in a bitter contest for the party presidency; the leaders arranged a curious deal with the pro-Gaullist faction, and beat off his attack by 759 to 382. Six months later the loser became president of RGR and the quarrel was

15. A. Gourdon in *Partis et Classes*, p. 233, cf. p. 235; Bardonnet, pp. 38, 74–6, 83–7; Duverger, *Parties*, pp. 41–2, 143–4, 145–6; Goguel, *loc. cit.*; De Tarr, p. 23n.; Frédérix, *État des forces en France* (1935), pp. 131–3, 212–3; below, pp. 127, 129. For an estimate (by Goguel in 1951) that 500 men decided party policy, Bardonnet, pp. 71–2. But before the war the rank and file were credited with more influence by Siegfried, *France*, p. 72, *Tableau*, pp. 147–8; Soulier, *L'instabilité ministérielle*, p. 371; Thibaudet, *Idées*, pp. 146–7, 188, and *Professeurs*, pp. 152–6, 244–5 ('any honest Radical deputy will tell you that a year before a general election the pressure of his committees drives him dotty', p. 245).

16. Bardonnet, p. 127; *ibid.*, pp. 125–8 on Cadillac, 114–18 on the executive. On the *comité exécutif*, *ibid.*, pp. 93–110, 138; Gourdon, *loc. cit.*; Goguel, *loc. cit.*; Duverger, *Parties*, pp. 41–2, 143–4; De Tarr, p. 247. The 1951 decision to ban 'bigamy' with RPF was voted by 543 to 128 at a meeting attended by two-thirds of the 1,200 members; at the same meeting 271 out of the 382 present confirmed the expulsion of Chambaretaud (below, pp. 178–9): *L'Information radicale*, 6th year, no. 61: *Monde*, 15 March 1951.

peacefully resolved – for the 'war of the two Édouards' was not fought to make *le grand Charles* king. Herriot was made unassailable as life president, and the machine was entrusted to an administrative president, Léon Martinaud-Déplat, whose policies provoked another revolt of the militants at Marseilles in 1954. Daladier was again their standard-bearer (though this time on the Left of the battlefield) and was very narrowly defeated by 746 to 689.[17]

When the chieftains were agreed the clansmen rarely raised their voices. But the officers would not accept a rigid chain of command, and any attempt to impose centralized control would have foundered on the mutual jealousies of the parliamentarians long before it began to meet resistance in the federations. These cherished their autonomy, though they often prized tactical flexibility more than particular policy preferences, and sometimes even chose their candidate to suit their alliance partners.[18] Protected by the divisions at the top, they retained unrestricted freedom except that from 1947 they were forbidden to ally with the Communists.

Where the party itself was weak this impotence of the centre benefited the local notables. Elsewhere it profited the members of parliament, who individually often dominated their departmental federations and collectively controlled the party's central institutions – if they were united. But since some of them owed their seats to support from the Right and others to the sympathy of the Left, they agreed only in defence of their personal independence of judgment and decision. Thus deputies did not need to fear *discipline de vote* (the equivalent of a three-line whip); and no one ever pretended to expect party loyalty from senators.[19] On the Left Mendès-France flouted every canon of Radical orthodoxy on economic, military and colonial policy. From the Right Daladier and the 'young Turks' actively opposed governments supported or even headed by Radical leaders.[20] Many other Radicals allied with or even joined RPF; there was a clause in the party statutes forbidding members to belong to another political organization, but for four years it was conveniently ignored. The 'bigamists' were not forced to choose between their loyalties until 1951, when Chaban-Delmas – the Radical and Gaullist mayor of Bordeaux – invaded Herriot's own territory at Lyons to speak for his RPF opponent, Soustelle. Bowing to the wrath of the patriarch (and impressed by the ebbing of the Gaullist tide) the *comité exécutif* at last invoked the forgotten clause and banned 'bigamy'.[21] But discipline did not improve. In the second National Assembly three of the four Radical premiers were overthrown mainly by members of their own party.

17. *AP* 1949, pp. 198–9, 1954, pp. 81–3; De Tarr, pp. 130–1; Bardonnet, pp. 76n., 77n., 83n., 121–2 and n. At both the Toulouse and Marseilles conferences irregularities in the voting were alleged. On Daladier and RGR see below, pp. 177–8.

18. On the importance of alliances see below, p. 323. At Bordeaux in 1951 they picked one candidate to stand if RPF agreed to an alliance, and another in case the Conservatives did (but in the end ran no list); in Aube they were refused by RPF, so they allied with the Socialists and changed their candidate in consequence: *Monde*, 22 and 31 May 1951; Bardonnet, p. 155n.

19. *Ibid.*, Chapter 3, for parliamentary control generally; below, p. 398n. for an exceptional case of *discipline de vote*.

20. Like some Pacific tribes, Radical young Turks organized to 'shake the old men out of the coconut-tree and finish them off': Duverger, quoted Bardonnet, p. 177n. Their leaders (Bourgès-Maunoury and Gaillard) were given office, and Daladier was offered it, in 1950–51.

21. *Ibid.*, pp. 154–60; De Tarr, pp. 145–52; *AP* 1951, pp. 34, 71; above, p. 118. For other bigamies see below, pp. 129, 178.

Control by oligarchy thus ensured the independence of the *élus* both at elections and in Parliament. But parliamentary dominance did nothing at all to assist the Radicals to decide on and promote a policy. When Mendès-France became leader and tried to turn the old electoral co-operative into a modern party with a purpose, he shattered both his own career and the organization – and perhaps even the Fourth Republic.

The party had from 80,000 to 100,000 members between the wars, but only 30,000 in 1946; it revived to 62,000 in 1948, but fell back to 51,000 the next year. Votes cast for the Radicals and their allies were two million in 1951, 150,000 fewer than in 1946, and their share of the electorate was down from 8½ to 8%; probably losses to RPF were masked by gains from other parties.[22] But at the same time the party was steadily regaining political influence, returning sixty-eight deputies from metropolitan France in 1951 compared with only twenty-four in 1945.[23] For departmental councils and most senatorial elections majority voting was used, so that the Radicals could once again profit from alliances with Socialists in some departments and Conservatives or Gaullists in others. In Parliament they long presided over both houses, and earned the title *le parti des présidences*. From 1947 they held office in every government, and from 1950 they or their UDSR allies filled at least three of the six chief ministries.[24]

In their following as in their outlook, behaviour and policies the Radicals seemed to be a party of a bygone age.[25] Their votes came from the elderly, and their constitution and conduct showed their profound reverence for seniority. Yet they were no mere collection of greybeards. War and Liberation had removed many older leaders, and rank and file influence did not (as among the Socialists) check the ascent of their juniors or interfere with their independence of judgment. Some able and progressive young political newcomers joined the Radicals, whose parliamentary group in 1946, with an average age higher than any other, still contained proportionately more members under 35 than the Conservatives and twice as many as the Socialists.[26] In 1956, after

22. On members, Bardonnet, pp. 50–1; Fauvet, *Forces*, p. 110; for the 1946 figure I am indebted to Dr. F. De Tarr; see also below, n. 49. On votes, Goguel, *Fourth Republic*, p. 90 (the 1946 figures in Husson i and ii differ slightly, as alliances and joint lists allow different classification). On losses and gains see a 1951 poll quoted by Stoetzel, no. 204, pp. 113–14, Table IV.

23. Radicals and UDSR together in 1945 (when they were not yet allied) had 45 members from France and 59 counting overseas deputies; in November 1946, as allies in RGR, they had 55 and 70, and in 1951, 78 and 95. On UDSR see below, pp. 174–6.

24. Édouard Herriot presided over the Assembly until 1953, Gaston Monnerville over the Council of the Republic throughout its existence, Albert Sarraut over the Assembly of the French Union from 1951 and Émile Roche over the Economic Council from 1954. In the first Assembly the average cabinet had four Radical full ministers and in the second, six.

25. Fauvet, *Forces*, p. 103; De Tarr, p. 14 (who quotes a Christmas cartoon of a small boy pointing at Santa Claus: 'Look, a Radical!'). In 1952 and 1955 two polls (by one organization) found that RGR had fewer voters under 35 and more over 50 than any other party: *Sondages*, 1952, no. 3, p. 81; Stoetzel, no. 204, p. 116, Table XII, for 1955. Under-35s were 11 and 23% respectively of the Radical total, minimum for other parties 30 and 25%; over-50s were 65 and 47%, maximum for other parties 45 and 42%. (Between 1952 and 1955 mortality among Radicals over 50 seems to have been alarmingly high.)

26. Duverger, *Parties*, pp. 165–8; Bardonnet, p. 179; Lavau, no. 138b, pp. 1903–4, on the attractions of Radicalism for a young politician. Thibaudet once maintained that there were no young Radical idealists: *Idées*, p. 258.

the Mendesist revolution, their percentage of members under 40 was double that of any other democratic party and exceeded only by the Poujadists.

In social composition the Radicals were overwhelmingly middle-class. Well over two-thirds of the RGR deputies were always professional men and over a quarter were lawyers; businessmen far outnumbered peasants; there were three ex-wage-earners in 1951 and one in 1956. Radical mayors, usually peasants, administered 5,000 of France's 38,000 communes.[27] The party was strongest in the small country towns; in the industrial regions its share of the electorate in 1951 was only half that attained elsewhere.[28] In 1952 and 1958 polls estimated that 5% or fewer of industrial workers voted Radical (but 11% in 1956 under Mendès-France).

In agricultural areas its influence, once strong, was diminishing: from 18% of the agricultural vote in 1951 it dropped to under 12% in 1956 although its share of the total vote rose – for Poujade was taking away old Radical votes in the countryside while Mendès-France was gaining new ones in the towns. More permanently, the foundations of the party's rural strength had been undermined when it was deprived of much of its provincial press by the purge laws of the Liberation, and subsequently lost its former secure hold on the ministry of agriculture and the powerful professional and co-operative organizations.[29] Without these sources of influence the Radicals were in danger of becoming a rootless group dependent on the personal popularity of individual leaders (which alone had saved their few seats in 1945).[30]

In the Fourth Republic several attempts were made to secure a base for the party. There was some progress in recovering the traditional southern strongholds: of thirty-six departments where 10% of the electorate supported the party in 1951, only a quarter were north of the Loire, and of twenty-one where 15% did so, eleven were in the south-west – still influenced by a great Radical newspaper, the *Dépêche du Midi* of Toulouse. But the newer groups which were trying in different ways to reshape the party sought to penetrate quite new social groups and geographical regions. Mendès-France's modernizing Radicalism won widespread (if short-lived) support in the Paris area and the industrial north-east in 1956. In some provincial towns and in Parisian bourgeois quarters there took root an aggressive right-wing 'neo-Radicalism' closely linked to the wealthy settlers of North Africa. 'Alongside Toulouse and Lyons, Paris and Algiers have become the capitals of a new Radicalism.'[31]

27. Deputies: Dogan's tables, p. 68n. above; only SFIO had as many professional men and only CNIP as many lawyers. Gourdon in *Partis et Classes*, pp. 224–30 (for mayors, candidates and deputies).

28. In the 17 most industrial departments it had 4·9%, in the other 73, 9·8%: Goguel, *Fourth Republic*, p. 113 (cf. Williams, p. 101n.). In the 1947 municipal elections it was strongest in communes with 2,500 to 4,000 inhabitants, weaker in those with fewer (the countryside) and weakest in those with more: *Inégalités*, p. 121. Above, p. 109n. 14, for polls cited next sentence.

29. Below, p. 392, and De Tarr, pp. 55–6 (press); *Paysans*, pp. 18–19, 48, 53, 461 (votes, including RGR), 106–8, 113 and 276–8 (organizations), 112 and 257–64 (ministry). The Radicals had never put forward many peasant candidates but this had not hitherto prevented them garnering rural votes: *ibid.*, pp. 108 (pre-war), 212 (post-war).

30. L. Latty and J. M. Royer in *ibid.*, p. 111. Cf. *ibid.*, pp. 42, 53.

31. Gourdon, *loc. cit.*, pp. 235–8; cf. n. 39 below. For regional varieties, also De Tarr, pp. 82–5; Goguel, no. 108, pp. 329–31 for bourgeois Paris; in *Fourth Republic*, pp. 103–6, and *Géographie*, pp. 110–11, for 1951; in *Élections 1956*, pp. 488–92, for 1956; and cf. Map 11. There were 51

[over

3. CHARACTERISTICS

'Neos' and Mendesists were utterly different in their policies, their standards of political behaviour and their impact on French public life. The former publicly proclaimed their solidarity with right-wing Conservatives;[32] the latter ultimately found an uneasy home among the left-wing Socialists. Yet they had something in common. Each group included a few old party members and many newcomers. Each prospected new fields in its search for support. And each tried to make the party face issues instead of fudging them – though they faced in opposite directions.

This meant attempting a complete change in the party's character. For among French political groups the Radicals had the best lines of communication with all the others: lines which the Neos would have broken on the Left and the Mendesists on the Right. The Radicals had great experience and skill at playing party politics and attracting a wide variety of opinions. North of the Loire they could appear as a party of the Left hostile to clericalism and reaction; around Paris they were (till 1956) the spokesmen of extreme conservatism; in the south they won right-wing votes as the last bulwark against the Marxists.

Expert tacticians though they were, this diversity was not merely tactical. Many different traditions, from Bonapartism to the Paris Commune, stemmed from the great Revolution which all good Radicals venerated. Yet though wide, the tolerance on which the party prided itself was not unlimited: in 1946 the Left Radicals were expelled because they claimed (like Clemenceau) that the Revolution was indivisible and therefore refused to break with the Communists; and in 1951 the Radical Gaullists, proconsular nationalists in the Jacobin tradition (also like Clemenceau), were forced to choose between the party and RPF.[33] The leaders could reasonably maintain that continuing an alliance on grounds of mere principle when it was no longer politically advantageous was an un-Radical activity; and even after the departure of these small groups the party still embraced a great variety of views. But by the beginning of the Fifth Republic it had shed both Neos and Mendesists and retained only the two most traditional species of the genus: the inveterate opponents and the immovable supporters of every cabinet whatever its complexion.[34]

With a core of members who subordinated policy to popularity or power, and fringe groups which advocated every conceivable policy choice, the

Radical deputies from agricultural and 18 from industrial areas in 1951; 32 and 24 in 1956; 21 and 21 after the split (below, p. 128). Western and southern Radicals dropped from 50 to 31 and then 18: Laponce, no. 137, p. 355.

32. De Tarr, p. 129.

33. De Tarr gives the fullest account of how each different group followed and diverged from the central party tradition. Of the Left Radicals, most ended as Communist 'fellow-travellers' (below, pp. 171–2), but Jacques Kayser was readmitted in the Mendesist period, and the strongly anticlerical Albert Bayet became an intransigent defender of *Algérie française*.

34. The party was split both in 1949–50 when the Socialists supported Bidault against attacks by the Right, and in 1953 when the Left opposed the Conservative Laniel; seven Radical deputies took a right-wing and five a left-wing line on each occasion, but twelve supported and eight opposed *both* governments. Sometimes when a Radical obtained office transmutation between the species occurred (above, n. 20). Cf. below, pp. 407–8, 418–19; MacRae, no. 149, pp. 187–94.

Radicals were serious claimants to office in any situation, and therefore a pole of attraction for able young politicians who reinforced their team of elder statesmen. Sometimes, like Queuille in the crisis of 1948–49, they could teach more earnest and less easy-going rivals an object-lesson in experience, patience and guile. Often they were more eager to control the levers of power than to use them for any constructive purpose. Always they were 'compromisers, bargainers, conciliators, administrators and caretakers . . . willing to adapt their policies to the needs and desires of the day' and to echo Queuille in 1951: 'I will do my best, the least harm possible; you can pass judgment afterwards; France must have a government.'[35]

It was a limited conception of leadership for a country whose social structure and world position were rapidly being transformed. The Radicals' prestige suffered from their ineffectiveness in the thirties and their heavy share of responsibility for 1940, and although by tactical skill the leaders brought the party back to power, they could not restore the intellectual identity and sense of purpose which had been waning for years. As the party of the French Revolution Radicals stood for values and fears deeply ingrained in French political psychology: the defence of the weak against the powerful, the cult of the little man, the mistrust of aristocracies of birth and wealth, the demand for equality. But the Socialists were formidable competitors in the same field, and the rise of Communism gave more weight to the conflicts which placed Radicals on the Right than to those which had located them on the Left. To Thibaudet *laïcité* had been at the very centre of the Radical outlook; but it began to seem out-of-date when even rural Radicals feared the Communists more than the Church.[36] To preserve the traditional electoral alliance with the Socialists most provincial deputies opposed the Barangé bill to subsidize the church schools; but they did so half-heartedly, avoiding the subject when they could, voting as constituency interests dictated when they had to, and leaving fervent anticlericalism to their allies.[37] The innovators of both Left and Right, Mendesists as well as Neos, gave vital economic and colonial problems priority over that faded shibboleth.

On these problems Radicals could no longer remain all things to all men: the interests of their voters drew them too strongly to the conservative side. The 'young Turks' of 1930 had been on the Left; those of 1950 were on the Right. In the Fourth Republic 'the supporters of conservative political and economic interests not only had links with the party: they joined it, led it, and

35. Quotations from De Tarr, pp. xvii, 165–6.

36. Thibaudet, *Idées*, pp. 159–61, 165; *Paysans*, pp. 276–7. A 1952 poll found that 40% of Radical voters were practising Catholics: Bosworth, p. 252, Stoetzel, no. 204, p. 117, Table XVI, and *Sondages*, 1952, no. 4, p. 40. This poll omitted all persons not baptized Catholics (20% of the population by its own estimate, 4% by another: *ibid.*, p. 54). For other polls see Fogarty, p. 361; Bosworth, pp. 251–2; Lipset, p. 245.

37. Lavau, no. 138b, pp. 1894–5, 1901 and n.; De Tarr, pp. 125–6; Goguel, *Fourth Republic*, p. 126; Fauvet, *Cockpit*, p. 72, *Déchirée*, p. 66; cf. Siegfried, *De la IIIe*, p. 188. In the key divisions on the Marie bill (4 September 1951), the Barangé bill (10 September 1951) and article 6 of the education budget (9 November 1952), pro-clerical votes were cast by Parisian and Algerian Radicals and those elected in alliance with RPF or Conservatives, and anticlerical votes by members elected against strong Conservative opposition; most members who temporized represented departments where the Conservatives were weak and their votes might be won in future. (My analysis.)

tried to transform it into their own image'.[38] The rich spokesmen of the North African settlers – 'a veritable French "Tamany Hall"' (*sic*) – were 'found at every turn of the party's political life and through their agents controlled its machine'.[39] The new leadership not only subordinated social progress to economic expansion (Mendès-France himself did that) but also threatened the trade unions; defended the interests of farm lessors against the lessees for whom the party had once stood; gave much more support to Conservative than to Socialist candidates for the premiership; opened an anti-Communist campaign which shared many features with McCarthyism; and championed the narrowest interests of colonialism, above all in North Africa.[40] The party which had once expressed provincial mistrust of Paris now represented the most reactionary elements in the capital. In 1930 Siegfried had claimed that its allegiance to the Left was 'its real *raison d'être*'; a quarter of a century later it was said to have no link with the Left at all.[41] On becoming leader, wrote Mendès-France privately, he had found the headquarters 'with no funds and no files' and the party 'with no soul and no modern ideas'.[42]

4. REVOLUTION AND REACTION

The Mendesist revolution was supported by two groups who for quite different reasons were determined to reverse the rightward trend which the Neos had imposed on the party. A few modernizers wanted to substitute an equally clear and permanent leftward orientation which they claimed to be the true vocation of Radicalism. But a far larger number were discontented traditionalists who followed Jean Baylet, controller of the *Dépêche du Midi* and prototype of Alain's provincial Radical.[43] They took a different view of the party's vocation, and wanted no lasting choice of direction. Their eyes always fixed on the next election, they feared that the Neos' liking for discredited conservative governments would lose votes and prevent an alliance with the Socialists, and they hoped that the broad coat-tails of a premier enjoying unrivalled popular prestige would carry them to victory. But their support of Mendès-France wavered when he left office, fell off when his popularity waned, and disappeared altogether when his policies split the party and threatened to reduce each faction to a powerless rump. Their defection broke

38. De Tarr, p. 80; cf. Lavau, no. 138b, p. 1899; Bardonnet, p. 267.

39. Gourdon, *loc. cit.*, pp. 237, 239; cf. De Tarr, pp. 82–4; Lavau, no. 138b, pp. 1899–1900; Bardonnet, pp. 267–8; Hamon, no. 120, p. 840; Grosser, pp. 131–2; Nicolet, *Pierre Mendès-France ou le métier de Cassandre*, pp. 104–5; below, p. 354.

40. Gourdon, *loc. cit.*, p. 223; Fauvet, *Forces*, pp. 111–12; Lavau, no. 138b, pp. 1896–1900; De Tarr, Chapter 5.

41. Siegfried, *Tableau*, p. 160 (and *France*, p. 79) – cf. *De la IIIe*, pp. 192–3. Lavau, no. 138b, p. 1901.

42. Quoted Nicolet, *Cassandre*, p. 149. Yet even under his leadership the party could appeal to the 'little employer or future little employer, little property-owner or future little property-owner ...' (De Tarr, p. 20) as almost fifty years before it had claimed: 'Small bourgeois, small employers, small shopkeepers, small peasant owners, small white-collar workers, small civil servants have discovered that they are closer to the working class than to the great banks, the big capitalists and those specially favoured by wealth ...' (F. Buisson in 1910, quoted Bardonnet, p. 265n.).

43. On the *Dépêche* see *Economist*, 27 January 1962 (friendly) and *Lectures françaises* no. 31, October 1959 (hostile).

the left wing in 1957 as it had broken the right in 1955.[44] By then not much remained of the party which once had dominated French politics.

Pierre Mendès-France was never really a Mendesist.[45] Unlike his young followers of the Jacobin Club or the new recruits he won for the party, he was a lifelong Radical. He went less far than they in anti-colonialism, shared neither the neutralism nor the nostalgia for the Popular Front that many of them professed, was more favourable to traditional Radical causes like *laïcité* and the single-member constituency, more amenable to tactical compromises, and more averse to open quarrels. As prime minister he organized no coherent parliamentary following, but carried each successive policy by a different but always disparate majority like a virtuoso of the System. So far from seeking to impose discipline on his own party, he would not help his friends to oust Martinaud-Déplat from the administrative presidency in 1954.[46] But his neutrality did not appease the Neos: the successful attack on his government four months later was led by René Mayer. Worse still, the new premier who revived the Conservative alliance was Mendès-France's own minister of finance, Edgar Faure.

These developments determined the fallen premier's course. The existing Radical party had proved too unstable a base; the misadventures of General de Gaulle were a warning against attempting to form a new party; the only alternative was to renovate the old one. Already the provincial militants were seething. At the special conference of May 1955 the right-wing leaders used all the dubious practices which had preserved their power for so long, but were defeated by a no less irregular Mendesist *coup d'état*.[47] Martinaud-Déplat's post was abolished and Mendès-France became first vice-president, Herriot remaining titular president. A committee of seven was set up to reorganize the party and give more influence to the rank and file; its half-heartedness contributed to the ultimate failure of the Mendesists.[48]

There had been other internal revolutions in the Radical party. But never before had its membership nearly doubled in a couple of years.[49] Many of the new recruits came from groups hitherto closed to Radicalism: youth, women, technical and managerial staffs, even Catholics.[50] At the annual conference in

44. Nicolet, *Cassandre*, pp. 105–8, cf. pp. 158–62.

45. De Tarr, pp. 191–201, 219–21; Bardonnet, p. 20n. For useful summaries of the whole episode see Allen, no. 2, and Laponce, no. 137; also Brigitte Gros's novel, *Véronique dans l'appareil* (1960).

46. See above, p. 121.

47. *AP* 1955, pp. 46–8; De Tarr, pp. 131–3; Bardonnet, pp. 76n., 151n., 212n.; Nicolet, *Cassandre*, pp. 111–12. One reactionary journalist (never eloquent on abuses of the past) wrote that: 'Nowadays seizing control of a party is like raiding a bank van': Faucher, p. 152.

48. Nicolet, *Le Radicalisme*, pp. 117–18; Allen, no. 2; Bardonnet, pp. 98–9, 100, 118–19, 127–8, 130–1, 273–4. The Mendesists did try to organize in greater depth a party in which membership was 'exclusively political, without effect on professional or family life' (*ibid.*, p. 271) by bringing together Radical civil servants, lawyers, businessmen etc.; the attempt was a total failure and the one successful society (the doctors) distinguished itself only by opposing the social reforms of the Mollet government (*ibid.*, pp. 219–23).

49. From 57,000 in May 1954, just before Mendès-France became premier, to 73,000 soon after (November), 90,000 a year later, and 105,000 at the peak: Bardonnet, p. 51. For previous revolutions (especially after 1927 under Daladier) see *ibid.*, pp. 17–19, 22, 165–6. On membership see also Nicolet, *Radicalisme*, p. 116. In *Cassandre*, p. 114, he suggests that the real increase was from about 35,000 to 75,000.

50. *Ibid.*, pp. 114–18.

November 1955 they consolidated Mendès-France's victory. Partly to check his rival's progress, Faure seized the chance which his opponents rashly gave him to dissolve the Assembly. The traditionalist Radicals were still fervently Mendesist, especially as the dissolution meant an election fought under an electoral law they detested; most Radical minsiters resigned, and the party expelled Faure and several leading Neos – including Mayer, Martinaud-Déplat and Lafay – who were organizing RGR as a stronghold of their faction.[51]

Mendès-France's progressive policies appealed to the Left; his personal vigour and style attracted the Gaullists and evoked echoes of Clemenceau. In the election the vote of his Radical supporters doubled while that of his opponents hardly changed. But the Mendesists had no time to choose reliable candidates, and in most constituencies they endorsed sitting Radical members who included many traditionalists and a few open enemies. Those whose votes had contributed to Mendès-France's fall did conspicuously badly. But the outgoing deputies who had only recently found salvation shared in the boom as well – though not as much – as the truly Mendesist new candidates, and among the fifty-eight Radical members returned wearing their leader's label only a small minority, mostly young newcomers from Paris, went as far or further than he in their zeal for reform.[52]

The old Radical instinct to join every majority and then slow down its progress was soon at work. The first disputes over the ministry's composition showed the weakness of the Radical leader's position and the anxiety of his Socialist allies to conciliate their opponents – both in the Assembly and in Algeria.[53] At first, when the young Mendesists wanted the party to refuse office, their leader sided with his senior colleagues against them. Then after he resigned in May (finding himself impotent to influence policy in Algeria) he continued to discourage his followers from attacking the twelve remaining Radical ministers or their Socialist partners.[54] It made no difference; public opinion in its new nationalist mood was with the government, and even muted criticism cost Mendès-France the popularity which alone had enabled him to impose his outlook and policies upon the parliamentarians of the System.

The old parliamentary hands had defected, but the new recruits remained faithful. At the Lyons conference of October 1956 Faure's expulsion was confirmed and Mendès-France's policy endorsed overwhelmingly. Twenty senators and fourteen deputies, among them Queuille, Morice and Marie, thereupon resigned from the party. A year earlier it had included five ex-premiers of the Fourth Republic; now Mendès-France alone remained. And when, riding the crest of the nationalist wave, the government invaded Egypt, only eleven Radicals abstained with their nominal leader in the Suez vote.[55]

51. See below, p. 178.

52. On these results see Goguel, *Élections* 1956, pp. 488–92; Williams, 2nd. ed., p. xx n., and no. 168, pp. 168–70; Pierce, no. 180, pp. 415–16; above, p. 48 and below, p. 178n.

53. They were given the chance to do so by Mendesists who put principle before tactics and voted to postpone a bill repealing the church schools subsidy – a measure which was anathema to MRP, but which no Socialist could oppose. See above, p. 98.

54. De Tarr, pp. 219–21.

55. See above, pp. 49–50; and Williams, p. xxi n.; another of the few open Suez critics was Edgar Faure. Of the fourteen deputies who resigned at Lyons, nine had voted against Mendès-

over]

The electorate was also turning against Mendès-France. At a by-election in south Paris in January 1957 the Radical vote was only 20,000 (against 80,000 a year earlier and 27,000 even in 1951). He had both split his party and flouted public opinion, and the south-western traditionalists who had joined him in hopes of electoral success and governmental patronage now deserted him just as the Gaullist 'hitch-hikers' had left the General five years before – for fear of immediate exclusion from the corridors of power and subsequent disaster at the polls.[56] Again as with RPF, an attempt to enforce disciplined voting brought the quarrel to a head. In March 1957 Mendès-France, by moderating his stand on Algeria, induced the parliamentary group to agree to vote as the majority decided in important divisions. The new rules were at once broken by the twelve ministers and nine of their supporters, reaffirmed at a special conference in May (at the price of more policy concessions which offended the young Mendesists) and again promptly defied by the ministers and their friends; the *bureau* – the party executive, supposedly a Mendesist stronghold – refused to expel two of the recalcitrants and Mendès-France resigned the leadership.

At the November conference at Strasbourg Jean Baylet, the south-western traditionalist, reappeared as kingmaker. The Mendesists carried their policy motion but lost all their offices – since only *comité exécutif* members could vote to elect the *bureau*.[57] Soon they were subjected to the discipline they had tried to enforce. When the Fourth Republic collapsed a few ex-Gaullists among them returned to their old allegiance, but most of them joined with the opposition Socialists in a new anti-Gaullist group, UFD. In the 1958 election 'bigamy' was forbidden, and by choosing to continue the new liaison they excluded themselves from the original hearth exactly as they had ejected their adversaries during the previous campaign.[58]

If disarray was complete among Radicals of the Left, it was scarcely less among their right-wing opponents, who were split into three groups. The oldest, RGR, had been turned by the leaders expelled in 1955 from an alliance of parties into an independent formation.[59] But the 1956 election gave it only a dozen deputies, and its limited influence was dissipated by personal disputes. Its secretary Jean-Paul David was one of the two bosses of right-wing Radicalism in the Paris area; the other – Bernard Lafay – set up a group

France when his government was overthrown and only three for him (two were new to the Assembly). The split showed how unwisely Mendès-France had allowed his prestige to benefit his opponents in the election.

56. Nicolet, *Cassandre*, p. 161: traditional Radicalism insisted on the need 'for friendly wire-pulling as a check on arbitrary power ... It means the defence of local groups of citizens against dishonest appeals to the general interest. But it is also, and more frequently, a *complete* ignorance, a *total* contempt – whatever the verbiage – for this general interest. Mendès-France wore himself out against this instinctive insistence on office.' (His italics.) No Radical cry was more venerable than 'Justice for all, and jobs for friends!': De Tarr, p. 156. On Gaullists, below, p. 140.

57. On the *comité exécutif* see above, p. 120; on the south-western influence, Nicolet, *Cassandre*, pp. 158–62.

58. On the defeat of Mendesism see Allen, no. 2; Laponce, no. 137; De Tarr, pp. 226–33, 236–8; Bardonnet, pp. 98–9n., 119–20, 169–73, 274n. On the 'bigamies' see *ibid.*, pp. 159–60 and nn., and De Tarr, pp. 134 and n., 238. On UFD see below, p. 174.

59. See above, p. 128, and below, pp. 176–8.

of his own, the Republican Centre, which showed some strength in the by-elections of 1957. While these parties contended for the urban Neos, the Dissident Radicals who split off at Lyons appealed more to conservatives in the countryside.[60] Henri Queuille was their president and André Morice their secretary, and they spread further confusion by calling themselves 'the Radical Socialist party' until restrained by the courts. At their first conference at Asnières in April 1957 the Dissidents piously adopted the constitution of the old party with all the old abuses, and claimed to have attracted a third of its membership (33,000 in over fifty federations). The prosperous commercial atmosphere of their headquarters and the tone of their conference – with few women or young men, no disagreements, and the rank and file firmly relegated to the role of 'innocent and passive shareholders' – stamped them as a party of the Right. Morice joined an *Algerie française* 'quartet' with Bidault, Duchet and Soustelle, and fervently demanded the silencing of journals which criticized the war and its abuses.[61]

During 1957 attempts to unite the splinter groups were frustrated by personal differences, political disputes and internal divisions: Martinaud-Déplat joined the Dissidents; J.P. David controlled RGR and Lafay was not invited to discuss reunion; Queuille wanted to rejoin the Radical party (and did so in 1958) but Morice would not; Mitterrand and most of UDSR still sympathized with the Mendesists; Pleven (also of UDSR) offered Morice a post in May 1958, and so the 'orthodox' Radicals prevented him forming a government.[62] The advent of General de Gaulle split both the 'orthodox' Radicals and UDSR – while the right-wing groups all supported him in hopes of riding the Gaullist wave to a safe electoral haven. But the division had shattered both factions, and though Morice pooled his provincial influence with Lafay's financial and Parisian strength in the Republican Centre, at the November election both men lost their seats.[63]

Even after the departure of the Dissidents, the attenuated Radical party was divided in every important vote. General de Gaulle was an old adversary, and when he stood for the premiership he was opposed by eighteen of the forty-two Radical deputies: most of the Mendesists, their staunch ally Daladier, their faithless friend Baylet, and their illiberal antagonist Bourgès-Maunoury. At the party conference in September 1958 these incongruous associates mustered 40% of the votes against the new constitution; at the November

60. See *Paysans*, pp. 115–16; and note 31 above. Of the fourteen seceding deputies only three were from industrial departments, and only one was from northern or eastern France (though none came from Baylet's south-western stronghold). Reactionary Radicalism in all its forms owed much to one wing of French freemasonry (cf. Coston, pp. 346–53, and also above, p. 98 and n.) which moved Right as the Catholic Church moved Left.

61. The journals retaliated: cf. below, p. 351n. On Asnières see *AP* 1957, pp. 36–7; De Tarr, p. 225; Bardonnet, pp. 28, 73, 107 (organization), 51n. (numbers), 91 and n., 133n., cf. 267–8 (tone).

62. 'Some are departing, others want to return; it's no longer a party but a railroad station': De Tarr, p. 243, quoting a delegate in 1957. Cf. *ibid.*, pp. 134, 225; Bardonnet, pp. 50–2 and nn.; *AP* 1957, p. 119, and 1958, pp. 50–1.

63. The right-wing Radicals polled 1,400,000 and returned twenty members. The Republican Centre (see Coston, pp. 349–50) ran several crypto-fascist candidates who had formerly followed Colonel de la Rocque, Pierre Poujade and Me Tixier-Vignancour (see Chapter 12); also Jean Baylot, ex-prefect of police and Mendès-France's enemy in 1954 (see p. 46n.).

elections the Gaullist tidal wave swept them all away. At a far lower ebb even than in 1945, the Radical party was reduced to 20,000 members, a million votes and thirteen seats. Perhaps the old men had been right to 'prefer effectiveness in a sordid cohabitation to disaster in a healthy split'.[64]

The weaknesses of that traditional Radical doctrine were all too evident. France in the middle of the twentieth century could not afford timid political leadership. Her industrial re-equipment demanded painful sacrifices, her imperial retreat called for uncomfortable reappraisals, her foreign policy required clear-cut choices. The Radical party existed to protect its following from painful sacrifices, uncomfortable reappraisals and clear-cut choices. Its voters were a drag on any constructive and vigorous economic policy. Its financiers used the party to obstruct timely reforms overseas. Its deputies joined every majority and its ministers sat in every cabinet, bewildering and disgusting the voter by ensuring that he was never presented with clear alternatives.

Having neither policy nor discipline nor consistency in its choice of allies it contributed greatly to political confusion – even in its own ranks, where conferences regularly applauded speakers who employed a common vocabulary to advocate opposite policies, and then voted a *nègre-blanc* motion endorsing both points of view. Prudence and guile, not decision and discipline led Radical politicians to success: and when Mendès-France tried to impose a real choice they frustrated him within a month and broke him within a year. But in the end 'wearing their ears out by dragging them along the ground' harmed the politicians themselves, for in 1958 as in 1945 the Radical record was overwhelmingly repudiated by the electorate.

Yet despite its failings the party performed an essential function in French public life. Its chiefs were used to power, and had a *sens de l'État* often lacking in less experienced groups. Its wide embrace enabled it to recruit able men, its lax discipline allowed them freedom to preach their individual views, and it therefore afforded a platform from which unpopular minority views could be put by men of recognized standing. The conviction that 'the main task of a great party is the same as that of a good stomach: not to reject but to assimilate' provided an indispensable element of continuity in a deeply divided country. Inevitable political transitions could occur with the minimum of disturbance when a highly flexible party was available to switch without embarrassment from one coalition to another. Radicalism formed a buffer between more active and constructive but also more ruthless rivals: when the Mendesist demand for decision and clarity broke it into impotent fragments, the buffer was eliminated. Majorities could no longer be assembled nor ministries formed because an indispensable component of both had disappeared. At the end of the Third Republic a hostile critic conceded, 'Perhaps it was a Radical party that Spain lacked in 1936'. By the end of the Fourth, France lacked one too.[65]

64. G. Martinet, *France-Observateur* 14 October 1954. Cf. De Tarr, pp. 233, 235–8; on membership, Laponce, pp. 76, 83.

65. B.S. (Goguel), no. 87, p. 187 ('Spain'); cf. pp. 174, 183, 221; also De Tarr, pp. 9 ('stomach'), 238–45. Verdicts on the Radical party are commonly, and appropriately, *nègre-blanc*.

Chapter 10

THE GAULLISTS

1. HISTORY

In the Fourth Republic the Gaullist movement took three political forms: the short-lived *Union Gaulliste* of 1946, the *Rassemblement du Peuple français* (RPF) founded in 1947, and the party of *Républicains sociaux* (RS) which succeeded it in 1953.[1] But Gaullism was born much earlier, on 18 June 1940 – the 125th anniversary of Waterloo – when the unknown under-secretary for war in the outgoing French government proclaimed over the BBC that the battle of France had not decided the war. Without the slightest organized backing he was setting out upon a revolutionary path. Already he had revealed in his writings his extraordinary self-confidence and self-sufficiency; the resounding vindication of his solitary stand inevitably confirmed his certainty of his own mission. Long before Winston Churchill addressed him as 'the man of destiny', the General had cast himself in that role.[2]

The decision of 1940 and its consequences profoundly influenced the development of Gaullism. They gave the movement the centralized structure which was intended to make it the exclusive instrument of its founder's will. They gave it its leadership, for General de Gaulle never fully extended his confidence to any but his earliest collaborators. They gave it much of its constitutional doctrine, for the General's political prescriptions were deeply affected by the fear of another 1940 and the need to devise remedies in advance against such a catastrophe.[3] They even bequeathed to RPF many of its internal problems. For that revolutionary decision placed the General in opposition to the great majority of the army, to nearly all the Right and to most of the influential men and classes in the country. Ten years later these men and classes formed the bulk of a new Gaullist movement: but neither they nor their leader forgot that at a crucial moment they had taken opposite sides.

Gaullism, more even than MRP, was the movement of a generation. Twenty years later the core of the party was still formed by men who had answered the call as Resisters or Free Frenchmen. Very many original followers became devotees for life who willingly subordinated their own views (and careers) to the General's successive policies and appeals. These true Gaullists were contemptuous of the timid bourgeoisie who applauded Pétain in 1940 and stayed prudently *attentiste* until 1944. For them Conservatism was a slothful or cowardly acquiescence in existing trends and Gaullism a bold

1. For useful accounts of RPF see Pierce, no. 178; Neumann, no. 166; Casalegno, no. 49. On Gaullism in the Fifth Republic see *Élections 1958*, pp. 15–19, 361–71, and sources above, p. 57n.

2. Since he was twelve: Wright, *Reshaping*, p. 42.

3. As he told the press on 17 August 1950:

'The nation remembers how a regime of the same type, though with less glaring vices, literally evaporated when the disaster against which it had been unable to protect us had broken down the country's defences ... It is therefore necessary that in good time another power appear, morally capable of taking in charge the independence and interests of France. This has been accomplished once! The country may rest assured that it would be accomplished again.' *AP* 1950, p. 296; see also *AP* 1946, p. 538, 1948, p. 329; and below, p. 191 and n.

assertion that the course of history could be changed by human will;[4] with the traditional Right there might be occasional co-operation but no trust, esteem or lasting understanding. Dedicated to their charismatic leader and their lofty cause, Gaullists too often attributed attacks on either of them to mere pettiness, corruption or even treason.

Suspicion of Gaullist intentions was fostered by the General's prickly intransigence and arrogance, the character of some of his associates, and the determination with which they waged the political struggle in London and Algiers. But these doubts proved unjustified. De Gaulle established neither a dictatorship nor the quasi-presidential regime he himself desired. His government held free and genuine parliamentary elections only five months after the end of the European war, and allowed the country to make its own constitutional choice. No doubt he influenced the results by allowing women to vote (against Radical protests), by the form of his constitutional proposals, and by his new electoral law. But these were honest attempts to find a democratic solution in a revolutionary situation.

In January 1946, three months after the election, the brief honeymoon between the parties and the General came to an abrupt end. Conciliation and compromise had never been marked features of his character, and no doubt he made too little allowance for the difficulties of partners who had to meet a totalitarian and demagogic rival on the electoral battlefield. But to be a prime minister unable to act without first conciliating three strong and mutually suspicious parties, and leader of a ministry whose solidarity was little more than a mockery, would have frustrated a humbler and more patient man. Making no attempt to seize power, General de Gaulle quietly withdrew into private life.[5]

MRP did not follow him; and a breach was opened between the party of Resistance Catholics and the Catholic leader of Resistance. For a great political movement could not go into silent retirement like a single individual, and MRP dared not withdraw from office and so leave the Socialist lamb in a *tête-à-tête* with the Communist tiger. But the General felt himself betrayed in January, and in May he returned the compliment: he left MRP to bear alone the brunt of opposing the constitution which the Marxist parties had drafted, and did not even cast his own vote against it. Not until the battle was over did he fire his first shot, the Bayeux speech of 16 June 1946 calling for a quasi-presidential constitution. And in the referendum of October 1946 the *parti de la fidélité* clashed with the leader to whom it had proclaimed its faithfulness, and found that two-thirds of its voters preferred to follow his leadership.

Millions of MRP electors were disillusioned with their party and hostile to *tripartisme*. But they would not throw their votes away on a new, weak party lacking the endorsement of the General himself; the Gaullist Union, founded by René Capitant to advocate the 'Bayeux constitution', secured only 300,000 votes in the November election and returned only half a dozen members (who mostly joined UDSR). To mobilize the electoral influence he had demonstrated

4. See for instance Noël, pp. 72–6, 80–1; R. Capitant, preface to Vallon, *L'Histoire s'avance masquée*, pp. 6–11; cf. E. Michelet, *Le Gaullisme passionnante aventure* (1962).

5. See above, p. 22 and n., and below, pp. 386–7.

at the October referendum, de Gaulle personally had to take the lead of all the forces opposed to *tripartisme*, including the Right which had never loved or trusted him, and the Radicals who had so recently allied with the Communists against him. The man who had once hoped to rebuild France with the aid of Socialists and MRP now became the chief of a movement challenging these parties for power.

At Strasbourg on 7 April 1947 General de Gaulle launched his Rally of the French People, RPF. In May the Communists went into opposition, and the government had to try to govern against the hostility of most of the organized workers. The atmosphere of alarm and tension was aggravated by the onset of the cold war; de Gaulle himself feared an imminent Russian attack and another 1940. Amid continuing colonial troubles, grave economic difficulties and violent revolutionary strikes, RPF seemed the one force capable of checking the Communist advance. Before the end of 1947 it was claiming more members than the Communists themselves. And in the municipal elections of October 1947 the Gaullists (with their allies on coalition lists) secured nearly six million votes, almost 40% of the total and far more than MRP and Socialists combined. They united the Conservative and Radical followings, took over the disillusioned from MRP, and in the big cities also ate into the electoral support of the proletarian parties. De Gaulle's triumphant return to power seemed only a matter of time.

At first the General and his supporters earnestly denied that the Rally was a new party. It was meant to attract Frenchmen of all views who were loyal to the state (but not collaborators or Communists). It would form no new parliamentary group, only an 'inter-group' of deputies who would remain members of their original parties. In the event these came mainly from RGR and Conservative groups; yet this was not the wish of the Gaullists but the choice of SFIO and MRP, who both forbade their members to join the inter-group.

The great expectations of November 1947 were never realized. The Marshall Plan averted the expected economic collapse. The inter-group attracted less than eighty deputies; the inevitability of the General's triumph was evidently not appreciated at the Palais Bourbon. The Assembly majority ignored his invitation to them to commit political suicide by voting their own dissolution.[6] Trying to impose discipline on its supporters just as if it were a new party, RPF came up against the refractory individualism of the French deputy of the Right; only two dozen members accepted the strict Gaullist whip.[7] After a great effort to capture control of the upper house, RPF claimed 150 of the 320 senators elected in November 1948. But many candidates, especially Radicals, had welcomed Gaullist support with no intention of accepting Gaullist discipline. When RPF formed within this new inter-group a separate group pledged to obey orders, it recruited only fifty-eight senators.

Queuille's long ministry, from September 1948 to October 1949, ended

6. De Gaulle demonstrated his determination to come to power legally when he demanded that the Assembly dissolve itself by the two-thirds majority required for a constitutional amendment, since the regular conditions for dissolution (see below, pp. 236–7) were not fulfilled in 1947.

7. Pierre Montel (a vice-president) and twelve Conservative deputies resigned from the inter-group in protest against instructions to oppose Paul Reynaud's financial programme in the brief Marie government.

Gaullist hopes of early success. Those who had hoped that RPF would shield France from revolutionary violence were shocked by a clash at Grenoble in which two men were killed. Prices stopped rising, and at the beginning of 1949 a successful loan was floated. Increasingly RPF suffered from clashes between parliamentarians and militants, clericals and anticlericals, just like the parties it despised. When the ministry finally broke up the crisis lasted a month; yet even this unfortunate spectacle did not help RPF.

By 1951 it was evident that the Gaullists would not obtain power by themselves. But if together with the Communists they commanded a clear majority in the new Assembly, they might threaten to paralyse government and thus dictate terms. To avoid this result, an electoral law was voted which encouraged party alliances by discriminating against parties which were too suspect (like the Communists) or too intransigent (like RPF) to contract them. For the General still hoped for a nation-wide response to his appeal, which he would not allow to be tarnished by compromises with the System; besides, he had learned a lesson from the senatorial elections, and refused to swell the ranks of his parliamentary supporters with men whose electoral commitments divided their loyalties. So local RPF branches were allowed to enter into electoral combinations in a handful of departments only.[8] Partly as a result, and partly because the movement obtained rather fewer votes than had been expected (perhaps in consequence of the electoral law), the Gaullists won only 120 seats instead of the 200 for which their optimists had hoped.

Even so, at the beginning of the new legislature they scored an important success. By forcing to the front the question of the church schools they obliged MRP either to oppose them and forfeit the support of the Church, or to follow them and break with the Socialists. When the Barangé bill to subsidize the Catholic schools went through in September 1951, the old majority was broken. If the indignant Socialists began voting with RPF and the Communists on other matters, the opposition would command a majority of the Assembly. Two governments fell, one through Socialist and the other through Radical defections, and RPF's moment seemed to have come.

But the Gaullist manœuvring had unexpected results. Since the centre of gravity of the majority had been shifted far to the Right, a Conservative, Antoine Pinay, was put up for the premiership – and the former Conservatives in RPF insisted upon voting for him. In March 1952 he became prime minister at the head of the most Conservative parliamentary majority for twenty years. Inside the Gaullist movement months of friction followed. The rebellion was soon consolidated when the by-elections showed that in middle-class areas RPF had lost two-thirds of its votes within a year. But left-wing Gaullists in the cities proved equally uncompromising, and in divisions the once monolithic group split three ways like mere Radicals, or saved its unity by undignified but unanimous abstention.[9]

8. Eleven RPF deputies owed their election to alliance with Conservatives; eight of them revolted before or in July 1952; less than a quarter of the other members of the group did so (see below, p. 153n.). On the electoral law see below, pp. 313–14.

9. On a minimum wage bill in April, 26 RPF deputies voted for Pinay, 29 abstained and 28 – mainly from Paris and the industrial areas – voted against him: Williams, p. 136n. On the split see also below, pp. 140, 153, 372.

In July the General and his advisers decided to impose new disciplinary rules, and a quarter of the Gaullist deputies resigned to form a new group, ARS (see Chapter 11). But indiscipline was contagious, and in January 1953 even the 'orthodox' parliamentary group defied the leadership by voting for a new prime minister, René Mayer. In May a heavy Gaullist defeat in the municipal elections convinced the General that he had failed, and he required RPF to abandon all parliamentary and electoral activity. The deputies, re-christened first URAS (*Union des républicains d'action sociale*) and then Social Republicans (RS) were at last free to play the parliamentary game. Two months later their leaders were in office.

In supporting Mayer for the premiership the Gaullist deputies had changed their tactics. By entering the majority they hoped generally to strengthen their influence and specifically to defeat the European army treaty. To achieve this crucial objective intransigent Gaullist leaders were ready to appear on platforms with Communists, while the more opportunist were willing to sit in cabinet with MRP and other pro-European colleagues. Claiming to be a centre party and apparently reconciled to the System, they were learning with the zeal of neophytes how to turn its own weapons against it. All four premiers elected from 1953 to 1955 won a majority of their votes, but only Mendès-France – himself a distinguished rebel against and victim of the System – kept their support to the end. The other three were defeated by defections in which the Social Republicans played a decisive part. André Diethelm, RS chairman in the Assembly, could claim: 'We are still alive, for we can destroy – if not create.'[10]

This conduct did not endear the party to the electorate. From 120 deputies in 1951 the Gaullist numbers dropped to 71 at the dissolution in 1955; in the new house only 21 were returned. The collapse was due to their rather lofty attitude towards their constituency duties, to the conservatism of their original voters (for only four of the ARS dissidents were beaten), and above all to de Gaulle's withdrawal; but also to their attempt to manipulate the System they were pledged to destroy. By entering, leaving and then rejoining the conservative coalition they had given an impression of unreliability which was reinforced by their quarrels with Edgar Faure (and with each other) over Morocco, and then by their conduct in the election campaign. Their leader Chaban-Delmas (a former Radical) joined Mollet and Mendès-France in the Republican Front, but most outgoing RS deputies were allied with the Right. They had won their spurs as a centre party.[11]

In the election Social Republicans of the Left and Right each lost three-quarters of their votes. The few who survived were those who enjoyed strong constituency loyalties.[12] Two of their leaders entered the Mollet cabinet,

10. *JO* 21 May 1953, p. 2816; *AP* 1953, p. 43.

11. Morazé, pp. 147–8, 150–1. Ten candidates made *apparentements* with the Left (of which 8 included and 2 excluded Socialists); but of 49 sitting members who stood again, only one did so (after the Conservatives had rebuffed him) and 26 preferred to ally with the Right – among them even so thorough a Mendesist as Diomède Catroux, nephew of General Catroux.

12. Even these often depended on personal reputation rather than genuine local roots. Thus in Lyons (Soustelle's seat) RS had no real local base and met in the big public halls, while an old party like the Radicals preferred ward meetings in clubs and cafés: *Élections 1956*, p. 320.

which most of the group supported until its fall; thereafter they again began voting for premiers at their first appearance but quickly turning against them. Nor was their opposition now confined to the parliamentary stage; leaders like Soustelle, Chaban-Delmas and Debré were actively working for the overthrow of the regime. The result was seen in May 1958.

2. ORGANIZATION AND FOLLOWING

RPF was built around its leader, constructed according to his ideas, led by his loyal disciples and devoted to his service. This personal allegiance was almost the only common bond between supporters of diverse social and political origins. Too heterogeneous to enjoy a natural unity of purpose, the movement tried with indifferent success to enforce strict discipline as a substitute.

Power was concentrated in the President of the Rally, General de Gaulle himself, who chose a secretariat and an executive to assist him. The general secretary (at first Jacques Soustelle, later Louis Terrenoire) was named by and took instructions from the President. The secretariat comprised de Gaulle's personal collaborators, working either in Paris or as regional delegates in the field but all meeting weekly in the capital. The executive originally had twelve members, who could not have seats in Parliament (Diethelm, a Gaullist leader from the earliest days, had to resign in 1948 on being elected a senator). In the constituencies power was in the hands of a departmental delegate, selected by and responsible to the centre, which also chose his chief subordinates on his recommendation. The elected departmental council was purely consultative and could communicate with headquarters only through the delegate. The twenty-two regional delegates were members of the secretariat, and checked any tendency by departmental delegates to support their local councils against the centre.[13]

General de Gaulle originally conceived RPF as a broad non-partisan movement appealing to all classes and especially the workers. In the early days the Gaullists gave much attention to organizing workshop cells, and they always retained some influence on the margin of the trade union movement.[14] There was a corporative structure of youth, family and ex-service organizations, and large fractions of the departmental councils, national council (*conseil national*) and annual conference (*assises*) were chosen on a non-territorial basis. The conference selected the national council, on which the departmental councils and national headquarters were represented as well as the social groups (though parliamentarians were at first excluded). It was the national council which in the early days worked out two of the most original

13. Late in 1951 the delegate for Meurthe-et-Moselle resigned in sympathy with the departmental council; it promptly made him its chairman, and was as promptly disaffiliated: *Monde*, 8 and 9 January, 18–19 May 1952; *Figaro*, 17–18 May 1952; cf. n. 16. RPF's formal organization is described more fully in Williams, pp. 123–9.

14. Particularly through the small *Confédération générale des syndicats indépendants*, whose secretary (a former Communist deputy) enjoyed Gaullist support against a rival faction led by the former Vichy minister of labour, René Belin. See references in *ibid.*, p. 124n.; Lorwin, pp. 131, 298–9; Rioux, pp. 104–5; Lefranc, pp. 207–8; Guéry, *Les maîtres de l'UNR*, pp. 130–50 – hostile but informative. In 1948 RPF claimed 145,000 members organized in workplace cells (*groupes d'entreprise*): R. Barrillon in *Partis et Classes*, p. 279.

items of the party programme, educational allowances and the 'association' of labour and capital.[15]

This structure ensured close control from Paris. Local tactics were nationally determined, and parliamentary candidates were personally chosen by the General himself. But control from the centre led to friction at the periphery; at every election RPF suffered a crop of resignations of local leaders affronted by the peremptory instructions from above.[16] The subordination of members of parliament was no less deeply resented. For the deputies who rallied to de Gaulle in 1947 had all been elected without his sponsorship, and after rejecting the discipline of a party few of them were now ready to submit to that of a military leader. The decision to organize 'inter-groups' instead of a separate parliamentary party suited the politicians better than the General: they acquired an electorally profitable label without undertaking any clear commitment, he mobilized an impressive paper following on which he could not rely. Attempts to impose discipline simply provoked resignations.[17] So at the end of 1948 distinct groups of faithful Gaullists were set up in both houses; each was joined by about a third of the inter-group.[18] After the 1951 election the inter-group and its equivocations disappeared from the Assembly.

The parliamentarians gradually obtained a voice in policy-making. In 1949 they were permitted to attend their local departmental council and the national council, and a liaison committee was set up; the General also nominated four deputies and three senators to an enlarged executive of twenty (renamed *conseil de direction* instead of *comité exécutif*). In 1951 the national council was in turn enlarged to give them a quarter of the seats.[19] But at that year's general election most members of the executive won seats in the Assembly, and they soon came to resent the control of tactics by a leader and advisers outside Parliament.[20]

In July 1952 an attempt was made to reimpose the discipline which Pinay had broken. The parliamentarians were given a somewhat greater voice, but

15. See below, p. 143. Fractions: half of each departmental council; nearly a third of the national council; at first a majority, later a large minority of the conference.

16. Thus in 1951 the departmental delegate for Morbihan, the three RPF senators and two RPF candidates came out for the rival Conservative-MRP list with which headquarters had forbidden them to ally. For other examples see Williams, p. 129n., and below, p. 143. For bitter criticism of headquarters for its over-confidence and ignorance of the provinces by an ARS deputy (a former Free French officer) see J. Halleguen, *Aux quatre vents du Gaullisme* (1953), pp. 218–26; for the author's own dictatorial methods as a departmental delegate, *Monde*, 17 May 1950.

17. See above, n. 7, and below, p. 143 and n.

18. The group in the Council of the Republic was called *Action démocratique et républicaine*, and had 58 members. Until 1951 there were two groups in the Assembly, *Action démocratique et sociale* (with 18 members at the end) and *Républicains populaires indépendants* (half a dozen ex-members of MRP, affiliated to the larger group).

19. It was increased from 140 to 233 of whom 40 were deputies and 20 senators; *AP* 1951, p. 294. Fauvet, *Forces*, pp. 242–3nn., names the executive (omitting Diethelm) and some prominent members of the council.

20. Though most members of the executive were now in Parliament (16 out of 29 by 1952), the General still controlled it; after the 1952 pro-Pinay revolt he omitted to convoke it for weeks and then did not invite the chief rebel. At an earlier executive meeting two future rebel leaders had bitterly opposed supporting any cabinet not led by the General (for that policy would not have brought them office, while a revolt might): Noël, p. 46. The deputies themselves had never been allowed to discuss such a policy: Halleguen, pp. 231, 237; on pp. 234–6 he quotes the General's haughty letter to the rebellious deputies.

in return were required to observe discipline on all votes affecting the life of a government and all other major questions where the parliamentary party so decided. These rules were voted by 478 to 56 at a national council meeting at St. Maur;[21] thirty deputies resigned and even the loyalists attacked the new rules. In November General de Gaulle consented to reduce his personal authority and allow more representation to both parliamentary and rank and file opinion. But the damage had been done and six months later, after a heavy electoral defeat, the disillusioned leader withdrew from politics. When most of his parliamentary followers regrouped as the Social Republicans they adopted a title and form of organization borrowed from the Conservatives, founded on departmental autonomy and control by members of parliament.[22]

This choice of organizational form showed that by 1953 Gaullism was no longer a mass movement. Yet at one time it had attracted the largest membership ever attained by a French party. From a million early in 1948 it dropped to 350,000 two years later, recovering by the end of 1950 to 500,000.[23] Its mass support was essentially urban. In the countryside RPF was always a party of notables, familiar figures with a following only in old Conservative or Bonapartist strongholds. But in the cities it appealed successfully to supporters of the Left. At the 1947 municipal elections RPF's own lists (as distinct from coalition ones) obtained under 10% of the vote in the small rural communes but nearly 30% in the towns; in Paris RPF gained 137,000 Socialist and Communist votes, which stayed Gaullist in 1951 but then reverted (usually) to SFIO.[24] Both in 1951 and afterwards the proletarian quarters remained more faithful to the Gaullists than the respectable bourgeois districts.[25]

With their coalition allies the Gaullists had won 38% of the poll in 1947. In 1951 they had 21% (17% of the electorate) and 4½ million votes. This left RPF well behind the Communists but far ahead of the other parties (none of which reached 3 million). And since the electoral law harmed Thorez's followers far more than de Gaulle's, RPF jumped from two dozen seats in the Assembly to first place with 120.[26]

21. On it, Halleguen, pp. 239–42; Noël, pp. 49–51.
22. Goguel, *Le régime politique français*, p. 92.
23. Fauvet, *Forces*, p. 227 and n. Soustelle claimed 800,000 in May 1947 and 1,500,000 requests to join in April 1948; in 1949 only 450,000 asked to renew membership; in 1955 RPF was under 100,000 and the Social Republicans (in 65 departmental federations) only 25–30,000: Barrillon in *Partis et Classes*, pp. 280–4. Coston, p. 291, and Malterre and Benoist, *Les partis politiques français* (n.d., ?1956), pp. 130–1, give only 500,000 in October 1947.
24. Communes over 9,000 inhabitants, 28%; all communes over 2,500, 21%; all under 2,500, 9%: *AP* 1947, pp. 363–4, Fauvet, *Forces*, p. 224. Paris: see Williams, p. 131n. Cf. *Inégalités*, p. 121; *Élections 1956*, pp. 315 (Lyons), 410 (Aisne); and Olivesi, pp. 176–7 (Marseilles). In 1951 RPF's support was much less clerical and more urban than that of the right-wing parties: MacRae, no. 148, p. 295. A 1952 poll (above, p. 125n.) found that 24% of RPF voters were not practising Catholics.
25. Goguel, no. 108, pp. 330, 333; cf. Barrillon, *loc. cit.*, p. 283. In 1951 RPF lost over half its 1947 votes in Paris (and even more in the rich west end) but under a quarter in the working-class *banlieue*. However, Professor N. Wahl kindly informs me that RPF's strongest supporters were non-proletarians obliged by the housing shortage to live in working-class districts (cf. Wylie. p. 218, on village Gaullists).
26. *Apparentés*, here as elsewhere, are counted with the group.

Gaullists of the Left complained of under-representation in the parliamentary party, but did not deny that they were a minority.[27] Almost all the twenty-three departments where RPF polled 20% of the electorate had been right-wing strongholds twenty years before.[28] But outside the Conservative west Gaullist strength lay in the dynamic industrial regions, and south of the Loire it reached 20% only in three west-coast departments – so that it was weak in the old unoccupied zone which Vichy controlled from 1940 to 1942.[29] This strong conservative element reflected the lack of self-confidence which had led so many notables to creep under the General's banner when it was unfurled in 1947. By 1951 many of them – especially Radicals – felt strong enough to confront the electorate without sheltering beneath that long shadow. A year later the right-wing fellow-travellers also defected; the ARS seceders of 1952 were men from a Conservative background or Conservative constituencies, particularly those low on their lists whose seats were unsafe.[30] Their departure left RPF with 74 metropolitan deputies, 53 of them from north of the Loire.

However, as a dynamic modernizing movement Gaullism attracted a following unlike that of the older conservative parties. RPF had a higher proportion of young voters than any rival but the Communists, and even the decaying Social Republicans in 1955 drew 31% of their membership from the under-thirties.[31] Only one metropolitan Gaullist member of the 1946 Assembly was over fifty when elected, though in its heyday RPF attracted senior and successful men; the average age of its group in 1951 was fifty. Only one of its 107 metropolitan deputies had been a wage-earner. The technocratic element was strong; industrialists and engineers were the largest group on the 1950 national council and numerous in the 1951 Parliament. There were few lawyers, and half of these seceded with ARS, leaving the traditional political profession weaker than in any party except the Communist.[32]

The leadership was not very typical of the rank and file. Polls suggested that both in 1951 and 1958 the Gaullists won about 17% of the manual workers' vote and drew about 23% of their support from this class. In 1949 RPF sources claimed a membership of 450,000, of whom 40% were manual or white-collar workers, 20% shopkeepers or *classes moyennes*, 15% peasants and 10% professional men. At RPF's annual conferences the two or three thousand delegates were not drawn from the intellectual or political governing

27. Vallon, pp. 33–4, claims that at least a quarter of RPF's votes but only a tenth of its deputies came from the Left.

28. In 1932 the Right had polled 30% of the electorate in 21 of them, the Radicals in seven and the Socialists and Communists together in only one, Gironde: Goguel, *Géographie*, maps on pp. 49, 77, 107; for Radicals, Pickles, no. 177, p. 178.

29. Morazé, p. 130. Cf. Map 12.

30. See pp. 135n., 153n., and for the electoral system, p. 388. In 16 constituencies the RPF deputies were divided between rebels and loyalists; only in 4 did the man with the best chance of re-election go over to ARS.

31. Votes: 38% according to the 1952 poll as against Communists 42%, Radicals 11%, others 30–31%. Members (18,000 analysed): Barrillon, *loc. cit.*, p. 284.

32. Council: Fauvet, *Forces*, p. 239n. Deputies: Dogan in *Partis et Classes*, p. 298 (there were 49 professional men, 40 businessmen and engineers and 16 agriculturalists); and Barrillon in *ibid.*, p. 282.

classes. André Malraux once referred to the Gaullist clientele as 'the rush-hour crowd'.[33]

3. CHARACTERISTICS

General de Gaulle was no Napoleon. But in the French political tradition RPF was a branch of the Bonapartist stream, which in some regions flows underground for generations, then bursts forth with explosive suddenness.[34] The demand for a government with authority, the passionate nationalism and the determined attempt to woo the Left were hallmarks of its character. But these characteristics, which enabled RPF to penetrate circles which conventional Conservatives could not reach, also made the latter shun such agitations as dangerous adventures into which only the direst necessity could lure prudent men.

Some of the old Conservatives found RPF's nationalist outlook on foreign and imperial questions congenial, though they might feel it was expressed with excessive bluntness. They were willing to accept de Gaulle's emergency leadership even though they distrusted his views on economic and constitutional matters. But they had no real confidence in him, and were profoundly suspicious of some of his associates. They detested the policies of his government at the Liberation – the purge, the nationalization of industry, the admission of Communists to office. Almost all of them had followed Pétain in 1940, and the leading Vichy apologists remained bitterly hostile to RPF. However, in their fear of Communism the Conservative voters turned *en masse* to the new Gaullist movement, and many parliamentary Conservatives thought it wise to follow the trend.

The pressure of these Vichyite votes affected RPF in its turn. The General and the movement gradually shifted their ground on treatment of the imprisoned Marshal, amnesty for the purge victims, and the return of former pro-Pétain politicians to political life. In April 1950 Colonel Rémy, a prominent Resistance and RPF leader, advocated rehabilitation for the Marshal; he declared not only that the Vichy shield had been as necessary to the country in 1940 as the Gaullist sword, but that General de Gaulle had himself spoken of the need for two strings to France's bow. The article was disavowed and

33. Malraux: *ibid.*, p. 277. Members: *ibid.*, pp. 281 and 284; in 1955 RS claimed 21 % manual and 20 % white-collar workers, 18 % professional, 17 % farmers, 14 % shopkeepers, 9 % civil servants. Polls: cf. above, p. 109 n. 14.

34. 'Bonapartism ... aims at establishing an autocratic government within the framework of the democracy. According to this vigorous conception, we should have a national leader chosen by a popular plebiscite, who would curb anarchy and silence the chatterboxes in Parliament. Equality would still exist, but order would prove more excellent than liberty, while the material conquests of 1789 would be guaranteed against not only a return of the *ancien régime* but also against any threat of social revolution ... Bonapartism continues as a latent tendency even outside of any political system. From time to time, it comes to the surface, and its expressions even remind one of the eruptions of a volcano.' Siegfried, *France*, pp. 98–100; *Tableau*, pp. 203–6.

'Springing from all classes, Boulangism cut clean across the parties. They came together, no longer to defend social interests, but for or against the new movement according to their temperaments. ... In our democracy there is always an underlying Boulangism': Dansette, *Le Boulangisme*, pp. 369, 371. In 1947 the Gaullists won a clear majority in the same Paris districts that Boulanger had carried sixty years before: Barrillon, *loc. cit.*, p. 281. And de Gaulle's first appeal to workers was directed to the areas where they had most favoured Napoleon III: Ehrmann, no. 82, p. 166, cf. p. 164.

Rémy had to resign from the Gaullist executive, but the phrase itself was never denied; plainly the General's views had changed since his denunciation of *Père la Défaite*. But de Gaulle had no intention of disavowing the past.[35]

The wartime record which divided de Gaulle from the Right should have brought him closer to MRP. But though millions of its voters transferred their support, these were mainly disillusioned Conservatives who soon found themselves as unhappy with the new movement as with the old. The MRP leaders who went over were very few (though some who did not were friendly to RPF). The rank and file of the party was anxious to establish its republican *bona fides* in Socialist and Radical eyes, and would not tolerate even short-term and tactical alliances with the Gaullists.[36]

The Radicals, considering themselves the incarnation of the Republic, had no such inhibitions. They flocked to de Gaulle's banner in 1947, only to desert it in 1949. A few went over permanently, notably two old Gaullists and spokesmen of 'proconsular' Radicalism:[37] Jacques Chaban-Delmas, who took his local party with him, and Michel Debré, who lost the support of his only at the moment of rupture. But RPF attracted far more short-service recruits from the 'committee Radicals' – typical adherents of France's most temperamentally conservative party, with its anxiety for a quiet life, its distrust of new solutions, its philosophy (so far as it had one) of defending the citizen and weakening the government, and its suspicion of strong leaders, especially generals. The reasons for this remarkable alliance were temporary: men of property looked for immediate protection against Communism, politicians hoped to repair the disaster which had struck their party, Gaullists and Radicals alike detested *tripartisme*. But the alliance also was temporary, and it collapsed as soon as the political situation made dangerous roads to salvation less attractive – especially since the Radicals soon came back to power, and RPF was beginning to display clerical sympathies over that traditional republican touchstone, the church schools problem. The episode again illustrated Radical willingness to associate with any partner in the hope of electoral profit and Radical skill at getting the better of the bargain.

It also illustrated the problem which faced RPF once its initial impetus had declined. The *raison d'être* of the movement was constitutional reform: the Rally was to mobilize members of all parties for this essential but limited objective.[38] Instead, frustrated of early success, it soon developed into a new party in everything but name – a disciplined and autonomous movement seeking power and obliged to take a line of its own on all major issues. Consequently the educational and social questions, over which the other parties fought, faced RPF with an acute internal problem.

At first the movement seemed likely to split from top to bottom over the treatment of the church schools. Like other Resisters, many active Gaullists felt that this was an out-of-date and regrettable dispute. Most of them sent

35. See Williams, p. 134. For his mature view of Pétain, *Le Salut*, pp. 248–50. For the Rémy affair, *AP* 1950, pp. 78–9; Rémy's article in *Carrefour*, 11 April 1950, was reprinted together with some of the replies it evoked in Rémy (G. Renault), *La justice et l'opprobre* (Ed. du Rocher, Monaco, 1950).

36. See above, p. 105, and below, p. 402.

37. See above, p. 116.

38. Its constitutional solution is discussed below, pp. 191–2.

their own children to the state schools, and the RPF leadership (like that of the left-wing parties) included many Protestants and Jews.[39] The general secretary (Soustelle) and propaganda organizer (Malraux) were opposed to the General's own pro-clerical tendencies. But the Catholics pressed their claims hard. At RPF's first conference the education committee failed to reach agreement.

Friction spread to the constituencies, and came to a head at the Melun local by-election of June 1949. Henri Lespès, an MRP deputy turned Gaullist, was nominated by national headquarters to stand for the departmental council. The local RPF members of parliament disliked intervention from Paris, especially on behalf of a clerical candidate; they put up a nominee of their own and he was elected. Three senators were censured by headquarters, and a deputy expelled. The Radical chairman of the Assembly inter-group then resigned in protest, and was supported by his colleagues.[40] The incident accelerated Radical defections from RPF, which was soon left with a following sympathetic to the Church. In 1949 the Gaullists adopted an ingenious solution, the *allocation-éducation* (a subsidy to the parents of school children instead of to the schools themselves), which gave partial satisfaction to Catholics and minimum provocation to anticlericals. And in September 1951 all but five of the 120 RPF deputies voted for the Barangé bill.

In the end it was on social questions that unity proved unattainable. Early in 1950 RPF was still voting with the Radicals and Conservatives to amend, in ways disliked by the trade unions, a bill restoring collective bargaining. But they were also supporting a wage bonus which Conservatives opposed, and violently denouncing the government as a puppet of American trusts. By the 1951 election RPF had lost its politically Radical but socially conservative fellow-travellers. Business money (which had once flowed freely) was diverted to CNIP, a less adventurous party immune from such dangerous if imprecise ideas as the 'association' of labour and capital. General de Gaulle retaliated by bitterly attacking the electoral activities of the *patronat*.[41] In September 1951 RPF joined the Socialists, the Communists and most of MRP in carrying through the Assembly (against the government, Radicals and Conservatives) a bill tying minimum wage rates to the cost of living. In March

39. Barrillon in *Partis et Classes*, p. 279; cf. Coston, pp. 501n., 504, 513. Soustelle, Vallon, Baumel and Schmittlein (president of the parliamentary group first of RS, later of UNR) were among the Protestants; Henry Torrès, Raymond Aron and the Palewski brothers were among the Jews; Michel Debré was half-Jewish. In 1951 and even 1956 the many Protestants of Alsace voted heavily Gaullist: *Paysans*, pp. 380–3, cf. Schram, pp. 136, 148, 167–71, 192; Dreyfus in *Élections 1956*, pp. 414–17.

40. The four members of parliament protested to General de Gaulle: 'We have fought too hard against the feudal power of party executive committees to tolerate it in RPF, whose methods and ukases are transforming it from a national rally into a political party . . .': *AP* 1949, p. 123. At Melun MRP, angry at Lespès' defection, had supported the dissident Gaullists against him despite their anticlerical attitude. But six months later another local by-election in the department was won by a Conservative supported by both RPF and MRP, against a Radical backed by PRL and the Gaullist dissidents. And in the 1951 general election Bégouin, the deputy whom RPF had expelled, was elected as a Radical with a prominent local Catholic as his second – and was opposed by the candidate he had sponsored at Melun.

41. Trusts: Fauvet in *Monde*, 15–16 January 1950. Funds: Barrillon, *loc. cit.*, pp. 277–8; cf. Nicolet, *Cassandre*, p. 102; Ehrmann, *Business*, pp. 230–1. Association: *ibid.*, pp. 359–61. De Gaulle: *Monde*, 24–25 June 1951.

1952 its leaders announced that they would enter no cabinet which excluded either MRP or SFIO.[42] This was the context in which the conservative Gaullists rebelled against the leadership to put and keep Pinay in office. Thereby they further displaced the movement's centre of gravity.

The evolution to the Left was not confined to domestic affairs. Purged of its most opportunist elements RPF lost in weight but gained in *élan*, recovering some of the *mystique* of the past and reverting to a kind of Jacobin revolutionary nationalism.[43] Soon the fight against EDC brought the Gaullists into alliance with neutralists of the Left and made them increasingly tolerant of Russian policies and critical of American. In 1954 Soustelle violently condemned the conduct of the United States in Guatemala. Whereas in 1952 *Le Rassemblement* had treated American suspicions of Gaullist anti-Americanism as a 'fable', two years later it claimed that these suspicions proved that de Gaulle really spoke for France. 'From nationalism to opposition to EDC... to opposition to American policy ... to the assertion that the US and the USSR were equal dangers to peace ... [and] that France must act as a bridge between the two blocs, such was the long road travelled by the General and his companions.'[44]

Gaullist imperial policies evolved equally rapidly. The Indo-China war came to seem a humiliating counterpart of American aid, and a burdensome diversion of French forces from Europe; Christian Fouchet, chairman of the Gaullist deputies, called it the Fourth Republic's Mexican expedition.[45] Over North Africa a similar shift occurred. In 1947 de Gaulle had championed the Algerian settlers and opposed political concessions.[46] But by 1951 the North African election funds were already flowing to apparently safer parties. Liberal Gaullists became increasingly vocal. The Sultan of Morocco, deposed in 1953, was befriended by de Gaulle and chose as his spokesman in Paris the Gaullist deputy and air ace Pierre Clostermann. In the Assembly most Gaullists supported Mendès-France, the General commended him publicly, and when in 1955 he and his successor needed strong proconsuls for North African danger-spots, each sent a Gaullist of liberal reputation: Jacques Soustelle to Algiers, and Gilbert Grandval to Rabat.

In the 1956 election several Gaullists were active on the Left. Clostermann was returned as a Radical and Jean de Lipkowski (Grandval's assistant) as an independent Mendesist; Capitant and Vallon were prominent in various 'new

42. *Ibid.*, 2–3 March 1952.

43. Marcus, *Neutralism and Nationalism in France*, Chapter 3. At the 1952 conference Capitant claimed that RPF would restore to the people the rights of which capitalism and parliamentarianism had robbed them: *Monde*, 12 November 1952, *Rassemblement*, 13 November. Cf. MacRae, no. 149, p. 184.

44. Marcus, pp. 97–105; cf. Morazé, p. 166.

45. *JO* 20 October 1953, p. 4396; *AP* 1953, p. 293. Cf. Marcus, p. 101.

46. To the press, 18 August 1947: '... we must not allow the fact that Algeria is part of our land (*est de notre domaine*) to be called into question in any form, either at home or abroad.' At Algiers, 12 October 1947: 'Any policy which would lead either to a reduction of the rights and duties of France here, *or to the discouragement of the inhabitants of metropolitan origin* ... or, finally, to a belief among Moslem Frenchmen that they might be allowed to separate their lot from that of France, would in truth only open the gates to decadence' (my italics): *La France sera la France*, pp. 178, 181; Grosser, p. 138. On RPF in Algeria see S. Wisner, *L'Algérie dans l'impasse* (1948), pp. 96–8.

Left' groups.[47] But the coming nationalist upsurge soon showed itself in the Gaullist movement. Already most (not all) of the Social Republicans had opposed Edgar Faure's liberal policy in Morocco. After the election Algeria alienated them from Mendès-France, then turned them against the feeble cabinets of 1957–58, and finally enabled them to destroy the Fourth Republic itself.

The Gaullists had always predicted and sometimes promoted the decay of a regime which had never found means of appealing to anyone's imagination, and in its decline provoked increasing impatience and frustration. Administrative scandal, parliamentary intrigue and governmental impotence offered easy scope to its enemies, and the young and enthusiastic found the Fourth Republic as drab or even as sordid as the Third. To his critics, de Gaulle's programme was best summed up by the *Canard Enchaîné*: 'La France manque de pain? Moi, je serai le Boulanger.' The Gaullists of 1947, dynamic, determined and justly proud of their record in the war and Resistance, were convinced that they could rally the people and that the feeble regime would crumble the moment it was challenged.

They had underestimated their opponents, for the Republic, as Anatole France once said, was bad at governing but good at self-defence. On finding themselves condemned to years of unexpected opposition the Gaullists – like so many parties of the Right which pride themselves on their superior patriotism – lapsed into strident and shameless irresponsibility. They charged the parties in power with playing politics at the expense of the national interest – yet they voted with the Communists to destroy the regime in the hope of winning a battle among the ruins. With shrill indignation they exploited the 'affair of the generals' to accuse the governing parties of betraying the soldiers fighting in Indo-China – yet they raised their own party funds from the lucrative traffic in Indo-Chinese piastres. They condemned the System because of its divided cabinets without authority – yet once in office Gaullist ministers busily sabotaged the policies of the premiers who appointed them. They insisted demagogically that the country's disputes and difficulties arose not from her weakened situation or her divided people but from the deliberate choice of the selfish politicians, and that these evils could be simply cured by a new structure of government ensuring determination and authority among the rulers and evoking discipline and sacrifice among the citizens.

Naturally this appeal was stigmatized as fascist. RPF shared some features of fascist movements: the simultaneous demand for national revival and social change, the call for strong government superseding futile party bickering, the evocation of the dignity and power of the state against the rampant demands of pressure-groups and sectional interests. Gaullist psychology was marked by the cult of authority and of the infallible leader. RPF was led by prosperous men but supported by a section of the poor, especially by economic proletarians who resented and repudiated that social classification.

Yet de Gaulle's own record – whether in 1940, in 1944–46 or after 1958 – was poles removed from fascism. The French social structure has little in common with that of the countries which succumbed to fascism between the

47. See below, p. 173.

wars. RPF was based on the dynamic and not the declining regions of France. It was nationalist – but no more so than the German Socialists at the same date. It had neither the extensive capitalist support nor the purely demagogic programme of other fascist movements, and it was never tainted by any breath of anti-semitism. De Gaulle was never prepared to seize power illegally. The movement's propaganda never glorified violence, and its 'shock troops' were kept firmly subordinate. And in demanding 'the balancing, the reconciliation of great pressure-groups by a strong executive' it was putting forward a potentially dangerous remedy – for a potentially fatal disease.[48]

Many RPF supporters who detested fascism would have been content to turn the movement into a respectable parliamentary Conservative party. Rather than permit such a frustration of his purpose General de Gaulle preferred division in the Assembly, disaster in the constituencies, and withdrawal from the political arena. By 1956 his disciples, having lost both their leader and their following, had degenerated into a turbulent and aggressive parliamentary splinter group. But because of the many military and administrative contacts of their leaders, because of their past experience of clandestine political activity, and above all because of the General's own character and reputation, they were well placed to take advantage of the crisis which – as de Gaulle had always expected – eventually shattered the fragile structure of the Fourth Republic.

In 1958 subversion, riot and overt military pressure at last brought Gaullism to power in circumstances which gave maximum scope to whatever fascist tendencies were latent in the movement. Moreover UNR, the dominant party of the Fifth Republic, seemed more prone to right-wing authoritarian temptations than RPF as long as the Left Gaullists were outside the fold. Yet despite the defections of Soustelle and Delbecque an overwhelming majority loyally supported the President's progressive Algerian policies. In power they appeared not as fascists but as middle-class reformers: not sentimental, not particularly humanitarian and not at all liberal-minded, but concerned to create a prosperous and thus strong and united nation.[49]

Like Theodore Roosevelt's American Progressives early in the century, the Gaullists recruited among a younger generation and a different social milieu from the established parties.[50] Again like the Progressives the Gaullist leaders were disagreeably self-righteous; this made them sometimes unscrupulous, frequently heavy-handed, perpetually impatient, and too often grossly ungenerous to opponents (also, at times, ludicrously bombastic). But like the Progressives, too, at their best they remained devoted to an ideal of the public

48. Shock troops: Fauvet, *Forces*, p. 237; Guéry, pp. 24–5. (One of their organizers was Jean Dides, on whom pp. 46n., 52, 348.) 'Balancing': H. S. Hughes in Earle, p. 259 (he argues that RPF was, on the whole, fascist); for the other view see Aron, *Schisme*, pp. 225–6, and no. 5, p. 81 ('neither the strength nor the vices of fascist parties').

49. Far more often than others Gaullist voters said they supported their party 'to shape France's future', and far less often 'to defend my legitimate interests' (11 % of RPF voters, 22 % or more for every other party; they rated leadership much higher and doctrine much lower than anyone else: *Sondages*, 1952, no. 3). But some Gaullist politicians were to display a keen appetite for spoils.

50. This comparison was suggested to me by Professor N. Wahl.

good, contemptuous of private intrigues and social pressures, eager for constructive reform and willing to take personal risks for their conception of public duty – as in 1940, when they threw up their careers and prospects to follow an obscure brigadier-general who knew that he could save his country and that no one else could.

Chapter 11

THE CONSERVATIVE GROUPS

1. HISTORY

Until 1939 an amorphous set of shifting, ill-organized groups stood to the Right of the Radical party in the political spectrum. Although all were broadly Conservative, there were many differences between them which often cut across the nominal lines of political division.

The Right had opposed the Third Republic until, towards the end of the nineteenth century, it became plain that the traditional royalist cause was lost. Among the *laïque* section of the bourgeoisie there then emerged a Centre which took up the defence of social and economic conservatism within the framework of the Republic; it was mainly embodied in a loose organization, *Alliance démocratique*, which often co-operated with the moderate Radicals. But ardent Catholics or nationalists found it hard to accept the regime that had humiliated the army in the Dreyfus affair and imposed the separation of Church and State. Republicans therefore remained suspicious of these openly right-wing elements, and before 1914 governments rarely risked the cohesion of the majority by accepting support from them.

As militant anticlericalism declined and a revolutionary working-class movement arose, the political centre of gravity gradually shifted. Increasingly frequently the dominant Radicals had to rely on support from the Right as well as the Centre at the polls or in Parliament. Such combinations remained unpopular with the militants. But the embarrassment they caused the party was much less acute after the first world war, when hardly any open enemies of the Republic sat in the Chamber of Deputies. For fourteen of the twenty inter-war years the Conservative groups held or shared power.

Yet these groups were never effective in parliamentary action. The Third Republic itself had been established by a monarchist Assembly which could not agree whom to place on the throne. New organizations were set up early in the new century, but they eschewed the name of party, did not impose discipline on their members of parliament, and corresponded only very approximately to the different tendencies of Conservative opinion: *Alliance démocratique* stood for social conservatism but was indifferent to the Church; *Fédération républicaine* had most appeal to nationalists; *Action libérale populaire* attracted devout Catholics, and its successor, the *Parti démocrate populaire*, was so progressive socially that many observers refused to regard it as conservative at all.[1]

Nor were such distinctions of outlook and ideology the only obstacle to strong organization on the Right. With the exception of the extreme nationalists most Conservatives were suspicious of mass movements, which they

1. I use conservative with a small 'c' to denote supporters of a social and economic outlook, and with a capital 'C' to distinguish those who also (whatever their private religious views) supported the claims of the Church in politics. The Conservatives who accepted the Republic usually referred to themselves as *Modérés*.

thought distasteful, demagogic and dangerous. They preferred to base their electoral support upon the local influence of individual notables in areas where the old ruling class retained its traditional ascendancy. But these independent political feudatories, wary of the masses and jealous of their own power and status, found discipline and organization repugnant. No Conservative party ever attained genuine cohesion, exercised real authority over its parliamentary representatives, or attracted a large popular following. Mass movements of the Right always took the form of frankly anti-parliamentary leagues such as *Action française*.

This loose structure gave full scope for the personal rivalries which bedevilled the Right throughout the Third Republic as much as the broader conflicts between groups, policies and ideologies. In the last years of the regime there were several leaders each with a distinct outlook and separate following: among the anti-Germans Louis Marin, the ultra-nationalist president of *Fédération républicaine*, and Paul Reynaud, an unruly individualist from *Alliance démocratique*; on the side of appeasement its president P. E. Flandin, and Pierre Laval, a refugee from the Left who had committed himself to no organization. Outside Parliament Colonel de la Rocque built up *Croix de feu*, an ex-servicemen's association, into a powerful anti-parliamentary league; when it was dissolved in 1936 by the Popular Front government, he transformed it into the *Parti social français* with active constituency committees and a large bourgeois following. Although its supporters in the Chamber were a mere handful, competent observers expected them to number a hundred after the general election of 1940.[2]

In 1940, however, not a new Chamber but a new regime was installed. At first the Vichy government corresponded to the real desires of the great majority of the Right. Admiration for fascism – though for Mussolini rather than Hitler – had been steadily growing among French Conservatives terrified by the Popular Front. Although some prominent individuals like Marin were opposed to Vichy, the majority accepted this authoritarian and traditionalist regime as their own.

At the Liberation, therefore, most right-wing politicians were discredited. Those who remained set about organizing what they hoped would become the great Conservative party of the Fourth Republic, the *Parti républicain de la Liberté*. But the Right still did not take kindly to discipline, and several prominent leaders stayed out, dropped out or were driven out. PRL neither built up an effective local organization nor acquired a popular following. During the 1946–51 Parliament it had nearly thirty deputies (many of whom also followed de Gaulle). But it disappeared as a separate group in the 1951 Assembly.

Two other groups existed in the first Assembly of the Fourth Republic. The Independent Republicans attracted nearly all the Conservatives who stayed out of PRL in 1945–46. They were rather more willing than their rivals to support and join Third Force governments. The Peasant party was the postwar successor of a small and demagogic *Parti agraire*, founded in 1928 by Fleurant-Agricola (M. Fleurant as he then was) and based on the poor

2. Duverger, *Parties*, p. 320; Fauvet, *Forces*, p. 134.

Catholic departments of the Massif Central. Just after the war this area was the seat of four of the six Peasant party federations and returned the half-dozen Peasant deputies, who originally were affiliated to MRP. The party expanded rapidly and by 1950 claimed federations active in forty-five departments, provisional committees in another seventeen, and a total membership of 20,000. At the dissolution in 1951 it had attracted nearly twenty deputies from other Conservative groups. They were more governmental than PRL but less so than the Independents.[3]

These separate groups came together in the *Centre national des indépendants et paysans* (CNIP), which grew out of CNI – a committee set up in July 1948 to co-ordinate the activities of those PRL and Independent members of parliament who rejected the leadership of de Gaulle. Early in 1951 CNI extended its scope and title to embrace the Peasants. In the general election of that year Conservatives sponsored by it ran on common lists, each deputy deciding after his election whether to join the Peasant group or the Independents (who absorbed the remains of PRL). As men elected on the same list usually adhered to the same group, the division was broadly by departments; but colleagues occasionally chose differently, as in Meuse and Aveyron, while conversely Conservatives elected on different lists might find themselves associated for parliamentary purposes, as in Haute-Saône or Basses-Pyrénées. The fifty-three Independents tended to represent northern and industrial Conservatism, while the forty-three Peasants were mainly drawn from the more backward regions.[4]

From opposition to *tripartisme* the various Conservative groups gradually drifted into association with the majority as the political centre of gravity shifted towards the Right. In 1951, out of eighty-seven metropolitan Conservative deputies only twenty-one were elected in alliance with Gaullists; thirty-three formed part of combinations in which Socialists also participated and the rest won their seats in opposition to both. The intransigence of General de Gaulle was mainly responsible for this result, for many Conservatives would have allied with the Gaullists in preference to the government parties if only the former had been willing. But in the new Assembly it was the Conservatives and not RPF who seduced the other's following. Pinay was elected premier in May 1952 with the support of twenty-seven dissident Gaullists, who broke with their party in July and formed a new group, *Action républicaine et sociale*. ARS co-operated closely with CNIP and finally joined it in 1954. And after the 1956 election the Independents, ARS and most of the Peasants formed a single Conservative group in the Assembly (entitled

3. On its membership see Fauvet, *Forces*, p. 114; on its post-war history and outlook, R. Barrillon in *Paysans*, pp. 131–47; on the *Parti agraire*, J. M. Royer in *ibid.*, pp. 154–5. A fourth small Conservative group was the *Union démocratique des indépendants* (UDI) who mostly came from MRP by way of RPF and adhered to CNI (see below) in 1951. On Conservatism in the early years see Marabuto, *Partis politiques et mouvements sociaux*, pp. 47–61.

4. The Independents attracted three-quarters of the Conservative deputies from north of the Loire, the Peasants two-thirds of those from departments along or south of the river. They had respectively 18 and 3 deputies from the advanced departments (index of production per head 110, national average 100); 2 and 15 from the backward departments (index under 70); 27 and 22 from the rest. Later ARS brought in ten more members from the advanced, one from the backward and twenty from the intermediate category (see Goguel, *Géographie*, p. 140, for the departments in each).

Indépendants et paysans d'action sociale). Led by Pinay, this new combination represented the greatest unity the parliamentary Right had ever achieved.

2. ORGANIZATION AND FOLLOWING

This success was primarily due to Roger Duchet, Independent senator for Côte d'Or, the founder of CNIP and its general secretary throughout the Fourth Republic. Understanding the limits of the possible among politicians notorious for their ferocious individualism, he began the *Centre* as a modest clearing-house for co-ordinating Conservative electoral activity. In its early years it concentrated on helping re-elect sitting members rather than stimulating contests throughout the country or proselytizing the electorate. CNIP's executive at first contained only members of parliament, though in time they agreed to co-opt a few outsiders, who often represented sympathetic pressure-groups.[5] The departmental centres (of which seventy-five were represented at the conference of November 1956) were simply committees of notables – local councillors and leaders of the district's business and peasant associations. Active supporters numbered some 20,000 (mostly councillors) during elections and under a thousand between them; the party did not even pretend to seek a rank and file membership.[6] To do so might have its dangers, as was shown when the CNIP conference of December 1954 was swamped by a mass of Poujadist and ultra-royalist activists about whom there was nothing Conservative at all. But not to do so had disadvantages too: lacking voluntary workers and propagandists CNIP members were particularly likely to become mere spokesmen for the local pressure-groups on whose political and financial support they sometimes became wholly dependent.[7]

At first CNIP repudiated any intention of putting pressure on parliamentarians who joined; its first communiqué described them as 'those who mean to preserve their freedom of voting and do not wish to submit to party discipline'. But it was not long before the Independents adopted a party outlook and vocabulary. In the Paris senatorial elections of 1952 they announced that 'All other lists of "Independents" or "French Independents" are regarded by the *Centre* as splitters (*listes de division*)'. At the 1954 conference it was decided to expel members of parliament who joined a cabinet in which the party had by a two-thirds majority resolved not to participate.[8]

The extent to which a party organization can impose discipline on its members of parliament depends largely on the loyalty it can command from its

5. In 1960 the executive included 21 deputies and 17 senators among its 48 members: Laponce, p. 116.

6. Figures from *ibid.* An official circular stated that the national *Centre* 'ne réunit pas de militants politiques'; the model constitution for departmental centres specified that the 'centre est composé d'élus locaux et de personnalités'; ARS announced that its parliamentary founders 'se refusent par avance à instituer une organisation démagogique tendant à tromper les masses en leur laissant croire notamment qu'on sollicite leur avis ...': quoted by M. Merle in *Partis et Classes*, pp. 257–9.

7. *Ibid.*, p. 257 n. 32; M. Dogan in *Paysans*, p. 214.

8. CNIP members of the existing Mendès-France cabinet were not, however, required to resign. In May 1958 Pflimlin's opponents were at first one vote short of a two-thirds majority; later they succeeded in voting the withdrawal of the CNIP ministers, and the premier resigned. First communiqué: *Monde*, 25–26 July 1948. 'Splitters': quoted *Forces nouvelles* (MRP), no. 14, 17 May 1952. Cf. Williams, p. 111n.; Merle, *loc. cit.*, pp. 243–6.

electorate. The allegiance of Conservative voters, which had always been loose, improved markedly during the Fourth Republic.[9] After the 1954 conference CNIP began to undertake propaganda in the country. Its endorsement proved valuable when rival Conservative candidates were in the field, especially in by-elections;[10] and at the 1956 general election, although there were more dissident lists than in 1951, they won less support.[11] But CNIP was not strong enough to make or break a deputy, and while its leaders might try (often in vain) to influence the behaviour of Conservative politicians in a given department they made no attempt to impose a uniform policy throughout the country. Duchet found it easier to increase the number of Conservative deputies than to strengthen their cohesion, and flexibility rather than discipline had to remain his watchword.[12]

The particularism of local magnates was not the only problem, for internecine rivalry among Conservatives was as frequent at the top as in the contituencies. Any attempt at coherent organization had to allow for a tradition so personal independence cherished by men who differed in political outlook, ceonomic interest and constituency background; whose individual ambitions were better served by the continuation of several small parliamentary groups fand leaders); and who reserved the right to give political, personal or group (ealousies priority over the rather nebulous 'general interest' of an inchoate Conservative party.[13] Thus the story of Duchet's achievement is largely that of the changing but ceaseless disputes among his colleagues.

For years the most conspicuous of these was the bitter feud between Pinay and Laniel – protégés respectively of two old enemies from the Third Republic, Flandin the appeaser and Reynaud the opponent of Nazi Germany. Duchet himself was a Pinay man, and in 1950 Reynaud attempted to oust him from the secretaryship of his own organization. Pinay's cabinet in 1952 and Laniel's in 1954 included between them eight members of CNIP's executive – but only one man sat in both. Duchet and Pinay blocked Laniel's stubborn bid for the Presidency of the Republic. But this prolonged quarrel was eventually overshadowed by the struggle over North African policy, and in 1955 the rival Independent leaders stood together in defence of Edgar Faure's Moroccan policy against a right-wing offensive by their ex-Gaullist colleagues of ARS.[14]

9. Merle, nn. 38 and 85; in 1955 a poll found 82% of former Conservative voters meant to vote the same again, the highest percentage of any non-Communist party. Formerly they had been the least stable of all: cf. *Sondages*, 1952, no. 3, p. 43.

10. The right-wing vote was split in 18 of the 29 metropolitan by-elections between 1952 and 1958. All the CNIP candidates ran ahead of their rivals, except for two who fought former local deputies. Thirteen won, seven of them despite split votes, which deprived five others of possible victory. Of course CNIP often endorsed a candidate who could have won without its aid.

11. Lists neither endorsed by CNIP nor *apparentées* with its lists had 20% of the Right vote in 1951 and 15% in 1956; 17% and 9% outside Seine and Seine-et-Oise, the scene of the extreme Right's main effort. In Eure the CNIP nominee defeated a challenger backed by Pinay himself; at Bordeaux a deputy endorsed by CNIP ran far ahead of another with strong local support, though the split cost them both their seats.

12. In 1958 the CNIP group admitted Jean Fraissinet of Marseilles, who at a by-election early that year had defied Duchet by refusing to withdraw, and so had given the seat to a Communist. See also below, p. 154.

13. On these parliamentary disputes cf. MacRae, no. 149, pp. 171–87; and below, pp. 432–3.

14. Duchet later separated from Pinay and became an *Algérie française* extremist; his sympathy

[over

The ARS group brought into the fold about thirty Conservatives who had been Gaullist fellow-travellers. Most were deputies who had sat as Conservatives before 1951, whose seats depended on Conservative votes or who represented the Conservative west; ARS attracted few city members despite its large vote in Paris.[15] Several of its deputies had belonged to PRL, and like PRL members they tended to be further to the Right than the Independents, more sympathetic to urban business than the Peasants, and – as befitted ex-Gaullists – more nationalist than most of their new allies. In 1954 the EDC treaty was opposed by half the ARS members, but only by a fifth of the Independents and a third of the Peasants. The governments of 1956–58 faced more consistent hostility (mainly over Algeria) from ex-ARS members than from former Independents.[16]

The third component of the united Conservative group of 1956 came from one wing of the Peasants. Paul Antier, the ambitious leader of that party, had been the first deputy to join de Gaulle in 1940, and after the 1951 election he favoured a government under Gaullist leadership. While holding office as Pleven's minister of agriculture he worked hard to organize a new majority and install a new cabinet. He was therefore dismissed and replaced by his own under-secretary (a former official of Vichy's Peasant Corporation, Camille Laurens) and the party split. Laurens and most of the 'lawyer-peasant' members of parliament continued to support governments, while Antier, the 'peasant-peasant' deputies and the party executive preferred to oppose them.[17]

The split was healed in June 1952 but reopened within eighteen months. In 1954 Antier's friends left CNIP, though it still endorsed his candidates in the 1956 election. The united Conservative party in the new Assembly absorbed the Laurens faction; Antier's depleted followers formed a separate group which affiliated to it. But in May 1957 that restless leader launched a new alliance with Poujade and Dorgères (a pre-war peasant agitator who had just been elected as an extreme-Right deputy). Again the party executive approved Antier's course, but most of his surviving parliamentary supporters defected and he was left with a tiny splinter group.[18]

Antier's chequered career showed that among peasant politicians the line

for the generals' revolt of April 1961 lost him the secretaryship of CNIP and gave Reynaud a belated revenge.

15. Of 28 RPF members from the previous Assembly 13 joined the rebels (including 8 of the 11 who had been PRL candidates in 1946). So did 8 of the 11 deputies who owed their election to Conservative support; 8 of the 16 members from the west (nine departments from Calvados to Vendée omitting the Breton peninsula); 8 of the 15 Gaullist lawyers; but only 3 out of 22 from the three Parisian departments and only 2 out of 14 from the constituencies including Lyons, Marseilles, Lille, Bordeaux, Strasbourg and St. Etienne.

16. Of 20 ex-ARS deputies 16 voted against all or all but one of these four governments at their fall. Of 29 ex-Independents only 11 did so. Cf. MacRae, no. 149, pp. 180–3; and below, pp. 158–9.

17. When Mendès-France came to power these roles were reversed for a time. On the split see Barrillon in *Paysans*, pp. 135–9. Laurens eventually replaced Duchet as secretary of CNIP in 1961.

18. On Dorgères see below, p. 161n., and on *Rassemblement paysan*, below, p. 166 n. 25. In 1956, out of 32 Peasant deputies standing only 19 were re-elected, compared with 22 out of 26 ARS and 33 out of 40 Independents; Poujadist gains in the countryside had thus changed the composition of the Conservative party as well as reducing its members: Pierce, no. 180, p. 418 and n.

between parliamentary Conservatism and anti-democratic reaction might be imprecise. When Pétain's lawyer Isorni was elected for Paris in 1951 the Independent group would not admit him to membership, and he became a parliamentary Peasant. But the Independents' scruples were short-lived, especially in the capital where the extreme Right was strongest. As the 1953 municipal elections approached the lure of Vichyite votes proved irresistible to Conservatives, neo-Radicals and ex-Gaullists alike. Prominent among the ARS recruits to Conservatism was Frédéric-Dupont, former leader of the riot of 6 February 1934, already boss of the left bank, and henceforth a perpetual thorn in CNIP's side. In the 1958 election he endorsed several dissident candidates of whom one was elected: J. M. Le Pen, a young ex-Poujadist deputy of fascist tendencies. Both men were nevertheless admitted to the Conservative group (which also included all but one of the fourteen unrepentant Vichyite officials who sat in that Assembly, and a far smaller proportion of Resisters than any other party). For CNIP valued numbers more than unity and welcomed any recruit who could carry a constituency – even if he had defied party discipline or bore dubious democratic credentials. As Siegfried had said, 'It is difficult to classify them [right-wingers] all as hostile to the Republic, but she cannot count on them.'[19]

In numbers the Conservative groups increased gradually during the Fourth Republic. At each of the three elections of 1945–46 they polled 2½ million votes; but as they contested fewer departments in the last election, the apparent stability conceals a small advance.[20] In 1951 they faced RPF competition but still held just under 2,300,000 votes, or 9% of the total electorate.[21] In 1956 they won more from the Gaullists than they lost to the Poujadists, and increased their total vote to nearly 3,200,000.

In parliamentary strength they grew steadily: from 62 (metropolitan) deputies in each of the two Constituent Assemblies to 70 in November 1946, 87 in 1951, and 95 in 1956. Including overseas members they had 74 deputies at the beginning of the first legislature of the Fourth Republic and over 80 at the end, in spite of defections to de Gaulle; the 1951 election brought them up to 96, and the RPF split to 135. But at the 1956 election, though their vote increased by nearly a million, the electoral law did not help the Conservatives as it had in 1951.[22] They had expected to gain seats but lost them instead, falling back to 97.

Both the voters and the representatives of the Right were older than their rivals. In the three National Assemblies of the Fourth Republic their deputies had the highest average age of any group (except the Radicals in 1946) and the lowest proportion of young members (except the Socialists in 1946 and 1956);

19. *De la III*e, p. 198; cf. pp. 206, 259. See also below, p. 160 (Isorni); Harrison, no. 123, pp. 147–56 (Dupont); above, nn. 12 (discipline) and 14 (Duchet). Of Conservative deputies in 1958, 25% were Resisters, of MRP members 47%, and in all other groups over 50%: M. Dogan in *Élections 1958*, p. 257. This was partly because Conservatives were old, and young Resisters of the Right had joined other parties: Grosser, p. 133.

20. Husson, i. xxxiii–iv and ii. xxxii gives them 2,546,000 in October 1945, 2,540,000 in June 1946 and 2,466,000 in November 1946 (when by including Gaullist votes Goguel brings them up to three million: *Fourth Republic*, p. 90).

21. Goguel, *loc. cit.* 22. See above, pp. 39–40, 48–9 and below, pp. 313–16.

and 45% of their voters were over fifty (a percentage exceeded only by the Radicals).[23]

Before 1939 the strongholds of Conservatism had been the Catholic west, the eastern frontier departments as far as Champagne, the Massif Central, and a few scattered mountainous areas in the south. In 1951 RPF, MRP and CNIP together dominated the same regions.[24] By 1956 RPF was in decline; MRP was still a vigorous competitor among the devout; and CNIP's support tended to be drawn from provinces where religion was either dead, as in Champagne, weak, as in parts of Normandy, or traditional and respectable rather than a passionately held belief.[25] One poll in 1952 found that 85% of Conservative voters were practising Catholics, but that the devout were much fewer than in MRP. Four years later another poll showed a third of all practising Catholics voting for each of these parties and less than a third for all others combined – but negligent Catholics were four times as likely to choose CNIP as MRP.[26]

Conservative voters included more property-owners than any others and were more prone to justify their party preference as 'defending my legitimate interests'.[27] Polls showed CNIP obtaining at most 7% of the manual and 11% of the white-collar workers' vote, winning a steady 21% of the businessmen and attracting more peasant support than any rival.[28] Electoral analysis confirmed these conclusions. In 1956 20% of agricultural voters supported the Conservatives, but only 14% of others; and in the cities they were strong only in bourgeois districts.[29] Like the Radicals, though less strikingly, they were weak in the industrial areas. The 17 most industrial departments included only two of the fifteen where CNIP's vote reached 20% of the electorate in 1951 and only three of the fifteen where it did so in 1956. In the rest of France their percentage vote in 1951 was well above that in the 17 departments, and even within a region their strength often lay in the backward rural areas.[30]

The same rural bias was reflected in their leadership. Local departmental centres were often dominated by peasant spokesmen.[31] In the National

23. *Sondages*, 1952, no. 3; Duverger, *Parties*, p. 167, for 1946; my calculations for 1951 and 1956.

24. In 1932 there were fifteen departments – of which nine were western and four eastern – in which 45% of the electorate voted for the Right. In 1951 RPF, MRP and Conservatives together reached 45% in twelve of these departments and missed it by less than a hundred votes in two more. Cf. Maps 6, 15, 16.

25. Suffert, pp. 36–7; Fauvet in *Partis et Classes*, pp. 171–2; Merle in *ibid.*, p. 251; *Paysans*, pp. 332–3 (but contrast pp. 502–3). See Maps 5, 14, 20.

26. For 1952 sources see p. 125n.: 73% of MRP and 56% of CNIP voters were devout, 25 and 38% were Catholics (23 and 29% practising) but not devout. For 1956 see Lipset, p. 245. Cf. below, p. 158.

27. *Sondages*, 1952, no. 3, pp. 40–1 (quoted Merle, *loc. cit.*, p. 252); and Appendix VII.

28. Among businessmen it ran well behind the Gaullists in 1951 and 1958, barely ahead of the Poujadists in 1956. Among peasants the detailed figures show highly unlikely variations: 25% in 1951, 45% in 1956, 35% in 1958. For sources see p. 109 n. 14.

29. J. Klatzmann in *Paysans*, p. 50 (agricultural); for cities, Goguel, no. 108, pp. 326–33 for Paris 1951 (for 1946 cf. George in Morazé *et al.*); Merle, *loc. cit.*, p. 251n. for Bordeaux 1951; *Élections 1956*, pp. 320–1 for Lyons; Olivesi, p. 177 for Marseilles 1956 (cf. p. 271).

30. Goguel, *Fourth Republic*, pp. 104, 113 (1951 totals 10·2% in the 17 departments, 7·8% in the rest); *Élections 1956*, p. 485; cf. *ibid.*, p. 390, on Isère. See Maps 14, 20, and 21.

31. Over half the members in Somme, three-fifths in Hautes-Pyrénées – the rest being business or professional men, and few of the peasants being 'large proprietors' (over 250 acres): Merle, *loc. cit.*, p. 255n. On CNIP candidates, *ibid.* pp. 253–4.

Assembly they always had a higher proportion of peasants than any other group.[32] This reflected the influence of the Peasant party, for only five Independents gave agriculture as their profession while half the Peasants did so.[33] But half the Conservatives as against only a fifth of the Gaullists had strong rural links; Dogan calls them the 'country Right' and the 'city Right'.[34] CNIP aspired to be the party of all the well-off, but it was still heavily dependent upon the traditional bulwarks of Conservatism, the rural notables.

3. CHARACTERISTICS

In 1930, at a moment when the entire Right seemed to accept the parliamentary regime, André Siegfried located its base in those classes which mistrusted universal suffrage and claimed (or at least felt) that their birth or fortunes entitled them to rule the country. The battle between Right and Left, he argued, was a contest between the political claims of social hierarchy and those of democratic equality. Around the bishops, landowners and capitalists gravitated larger groups which were socially dependent upon them. French politics 'would be incomprehensible if we lost sight of the fact that the counter-revolutionary party keeps constantly rebuilding itself as its spirit crystallizes into new forms'.[35]

The taint of counter-revolution sometimes made Conservative support an embarrassment rather than an asset to governments. This handicap was reinforced when the most anti-parliamentary Conservatives turned to Vichy and even to fascism, and found themselves discredited by the outcome of the war. Yet the Liberation saw a weakening even of that section of the Right which had defended the Republic and participated in the Resistance. For the rise of MRP deprived many old-style Conservatives of the support of the Church, on which they had hitherto been able to count; and the Gaullist movement won away from them many of their most alert, modern-minded and patriotic (or nationalist) adherents. Like the Radicals, the remnants of the old-fashioned Right suffered from seeming, and being, survivals from the past rather than parties adapted to the post-war world. But the Conservatives had less influence (and the Radicals more) than their numbers would suggest.[36] Much of their energy was dissipated by individualism and diverted into factionalism. A narrow devotion to the interests and prejudices of the

32. A quarter in 1951 and a fifth in 1956; only RPF (till ARS seceded) and the Communists (in 1956) exceeded 10%. CNIP also had most lawyers (over a quarter) and in 1946 most business men, but not later (a fifth in 1951 and a quarter in 1956, the same proportions as for RGR and MRP). See Dogan's tables, p. 68n. above.

33. Among the other half were Pétain's defence counsel, the mayor of Biarritz, and the presidents of the road hauliers' and house-property owners' associations. A 'Peasant' senator, M. Boutemy, distributed the political funds of the employers' federation. Even among the self-styled professional agriculturalists many had rather tenuous connections with the soil.

34. *Partis et Classes*, p. 325. Contrast Barrillon in *Paysans*, pp. 145–6.

35. *France*, pp. 28, 32–4; *Tableau*, pp. 59–60, 68–72. Their outlook had changed little by 1954: see comments and quotations in Merle, *loc. cit.*, pp. 262–3. But see below, n. 49.

36. 'Theoretically a vote of the Right is as good as a vote of the Left, but in practice this is not so. The member of the Left enjoys special privileges owing to the prestige of his party, for . . . the Republic instinctively refuses to allow the nation to be governed by men who are not at bottom inspired by its spirit.' Siegfried, *France*, p. 93, *Tableau*, p. 191. In the Fourth Republic RPF suffered more from these suspicions than the orthodox Conservatives.

better-off hampered their quest for votes. In 1951 Siegfried was still preaching the need for a modern and intelligent Conservatism.[37]

In the Fourth Republic the Conservatives made remarkable progress in overcoming these weaknesses. They consolidated their influence with the peasantry and small businessmen (big business at first usually preferred RPF, and later favoured the right-wing Radicals as well as CNIP). They substantially increased their popular vote and became for a time the largest party in the Assembly. They set up an effective headquarters which brought five-sixths of the Conservative voters and nine-tenths of their deputies under its rather loose control. Tainted at first by their Vichy associations, they were by the end of the regime accepted as good republicans (though many of them proved unwilling to run any political risk in the defence of democracy).

They directed the government only between 1952 and 1954, but their power was greater than the composition of ministries indicated. From 1954 the President of the Republic was a Conservative, Coty. They enjoyed the sympathies of many senior officials, and the newly strengthened employers' organization wielded considerable influence on the administration.[38] The details of economic policy were often repugnant to business or the peasantry, but its general lines were much more satisfactory to these groups than to the industrial workers. More surprisingly, CNIP produced in Antoine Pinay the Fourth Republican leader who won most general and lasting esteem from his countrymen; for Guy Mollet's popularity was less general, Mendès-France's less permanent, and Pinay aroused far less bitter hostility than either – while no one else drew any public following at all. So rapid was the Conservative recovery from the demoralization and discredit of the Liberation that while the Third Republic had begun with MacMahon and ended with Blum, the Fourth – it was said – began with Blum and reverted to MacMahon.[39]

The revival of right-wing strength was accompanied by no great renewal of right-wing ideas.[40] Not all Conservatives were unprogressive. The *classes moyennes* from whom they drew much of their strength were a conglomeration of disparate groups. Dynamic employers, managers in large businesses, and many professional men had as much to gain from economic expansion and modernization as *rentiers*, retired people, small farmers and shopkeepers had to lose.[41] The attempt to appeal to both at once was one reason for CNIP's disunity; while most Conservatives opposed Mendès-France bitterly, eight of them served in his ministry and twenty-two voted for him to the very end. Even among more orthodox party members there were men like Paul Reynaud whom no one could accuse of being out of touch with reality. Nevertheless it was precisely the Conservatives of this type, the least hidebound, the

37. *De la IVe à la Ve République*, p. 176.
38. Ehrmann, *Business*, pp. 257–71 and references there.
39. Duverger, quoted Wright, no. 226, p. 3.
40. One Gaullist wrote bitterly: 'One of the peculiar characteristics of our Conservatives is their refusal to see and accept facts . . . [and] realities. . . . When in the end they give way to them, it is almost always too late. . . . In so far as they recognize change in the world, they prefer to convince themselves that it can continue without Frenchmen having to accept the innovations and sacrifices necessary for coming to terms with it. They mistake stagnation for prudence, passivity for wisdom, apathy for social stability': Noël, pp. 73–4.
41. Merle, *loc. cit.*, p. 273; Wright, no. 227, pp. 10–11.

most capable of adjusting their ideas, the representatives of modern and industrial constituencies rather than backward rural ones, who were most likely to go over to MRP or Gaullism.[42] And with one of these rival movements more attractive to ardent Catholics and the other to passionate nationalists, the orthodox Right found its following severely reduced and its recovery confined within narrow limits.

Attempts were made to regain the lost audience. In 1951 the Conservatives tried both in the election and in Parliament to outbid MRP as defenders of the church schools. But all sections of CNIP suffered serious handicaps in a competition for the allegiance of devout Catholics. Among the Independents one faction was led by Reynaud, who came from the rather *laïque Alliance démocratique*, the other by Duchet, who had once stood for Parliament as an anticlerical Radical. PRL, though more right-wing in its economic policy than MRP, was so little influenced by the Church that in 1946 it had made an electoral pact with the Radical party. And the Peasants were far too regionalized, too reactionary and too exclusively a pressure-group for a single economic interest to attract support away from MRP. Even when in 1954 the orthodox Conservatives began for the first time officially to call themselves an essentially Christian party they (like earlier right-wing leaders such as Maurras) gave mainly secular reasons for their faith: 'mobilizing the divine' as Barrès had once put it.[43]

Nor could the Gaullists easily be overmatched in nationalist fervour by a party among whose leaders 'ex-Vichyites outnumber the ex-Resisters, but both categories are far outstripped by the ex-straddlers'.[44] The task proved still harder after the principal CNIP leaders became ardent defenders of European integration (including EDC) and in Morocco belatedly accepted an imperial retreat more far-reaching than that for which they had destroyed Mendès-France over Tunisia.[45] Nevertheless they did their best. Once the 1956 election was over most of the party, under Duchet's leadership, attempted (in common with many Radicals and some Socialists) to wash away these sins by swimming with the nationalist tide.[46] And in 1958 the majority of CNIP members turned to de Gaulle, despite their deep distrust of him, as the one man who could save the army's unity and *Algérie française*.

42. This remained true in the Fifth Republic, where the conflict over financial policy between Pinay and Albin Chalandon of UNR was largely a battle between stabilizers and expansionists. (Reynaud, like many Gaullists but few Conservatives, was a carpet-bagger with no deep roots in his constituency.)

43. Merle, *loc. cit.*, pp. 265–7; Suffert, pp. 42–3; Sérant, *Où va la Droite*, pp. 33–4. Merle cites from official publications such phrases as 'Religion has provided society with the framework of lasting institutions, and this framework has given to successive generations an impression of security without which no enterprise would have been possible' and '... legislative measures extending the economic functions of the State are opposed to the very spirit of the Encyclicals.' On Catholic attitudes to the parties see above, pp. 109, 155 and notes.

44. Wright, no. 227, p. 5. Cf. n. 19 above.

45. Two-thirds of their deputies voted for EDC; MRP was the only other party to show a majority for the treaty. Pinay and Pierre July of ARS were the ministers directly responsible for the return of the Sultan of Morocco, and they were supported by Laniel, Reynaud and Duchet. On Conservative external policies see Grosser, pp. 132–6.

46. See Bodin and Touchard, no. 21, pp. 277–82; Weber, no. 215, pp. 560–78. As Noël wrote earlier, in North Africa 'When. . . calm prevailed they opposed reforms, calling them useless or premature since the population remained peaceful. When blood has flowed, they have found in that another motive for deciding nothing' (p. 75).

Yet nationalist agitation was not a role in which they were particularly effective. For although their ranks included bitter demagogues like Jean Legendre, accomplished time-servers like Frédéric-Dupont and ambitious factional leaders like Barrachin and Antier, there were also among them many realistic and responsible men.[47] In private though not in public all sections of Conservative opinion doubted the wisdom of the Suez expedition.[48] Pinay himself (not to speak of the Mendesist minority) recognized the inevitability of decolonization in Algeria. Increasingly the party gave its support to European integration. Consequently, while the excesses of CNIP's reactionary wing kept alive all the suspicions of the centre groups, the prudence of its moderate section restrained it from exploiting effectively the nationalist and anti-parliamentary moods of French public opinion.

In the Fourth Republic as in the Third there were always Conservatives who, in the traditional phrase, were republican moderates but not moderately republican, and represented the liberal and parliamentary (though not democratic) strand in the old monarchist tradition.[49] As the Vichy regime evolved towards fascism many more men of the Right came to conclude like Thiers before them that the Republic served Conservative interests best. At the Liberation, therefore, there was a 'new Ralliement'.[50] Many Conservatives suspected the 'Bonapartist' movements of the Fourth Republic, and remained faithful to the centre governments which Gaullists and Poujadists assailed so furiously. Such men were torn between their specific preferences in foreign or social policy and their overriding desire to defend the existing political regime. Like all centre groups they were under constant strain, their loyalty to their party leaders in office constantly eroded by their resentment at the concessions which had to be made to keep cabinets together. Coalition politics accentuated all the differences that separated factions and all the uncertainties that harassed individuals. Ambivalent and divided, the Conservatives were therefore vulnerable to the unscrupulous demagogy of an increasingly vocal and violent extreme Right.[51]

47. 'The moderation of the "Moderates" [Conservatives] does not exclude a marked propensity for the use of vindictive and slanderous behaviour. Under the Mendès-France government we were able to observe . . . the snarling virulence of the traditional Right . . .': *ibid.*, p. 79. Legendre, the ARS 'member for beet-growing' (Priouret, *Députés*, p. 234), was the leader of this attack. Barrachin, once prominent in *Croix de feu*, led the ARS revolt; when de Gaulle reproached him, 'But for me you wouldn't be in Parliament' he is said to have replied 'But for you I would be in the cabinet'. For Antier and Dupont see above, pp. 153–4. For an example of both demagogy and time-serving see CNIP's response to Poujade: Hoffmann, pp. 356–63, Guy, pp. 128–43.

48. See p. 50 n. 12.

49. See Rémond, *La Droite en France*, pp. 25, 31, 84–6, etc.

50. Hoffmann in *Change*, p. 45; no. 126, p. 51. But Siegfried warned that 'On the Right the Republic does not and doubtless never will create unanimity: for even when it seems to have overcome the ancient enmities, they never die': *De la IIIe*, p. 206.

51. For CNIP's eagerness to repudiate the charge of being right-wing, reactionary or even conservative see Merle, *loc. cit.*, pp. 261–2; he also quotes the retort of Abel Bonnard, later a collaborationist minister, in *Les Modérés* (1936): '. . . they are simply property-owners without a doctrine, men who share the same social habits but have no bond of faith to unite them, uneasy egotists, not quite believing in the legitimacy of their own advantages, who merely hope to make sure of enjoying their own life-interest in them . . .'

Chapter 12

THE EXTREME RIGHT

1. VICHYITES AND CRYPTO-FASCISTS

During most of the twentieth century the right-wing enemies of democracy were weak in numbers, though Maurras's *Action française* always enjoyed a good deal of influence among intellectuals, particularly students. The rise of fascism abroad and the fear of the Popular Front at home brought them wider sympathies in conservative and bourgeois quarters, and the defeat of 1940 thrust power into their hands. But there were bitter divisions within their ranks. Marshal Pétain's government and entourage included many followers of Maurras; these reactionary men of Vichy were bitterly attacked by the national-socialist collaborators in Paris (led by the ex-Socialist Déat and the ex-Communist Doriot). The collapse of Germany discredited all the different factions and it was some years before the extreme Right attempted to resume political activity.

Their weakness was not only in numbers. Their 'mania for division' revealed a 'reactionary sectarianism' which closely resembled revolutionary sectarianism in its demand for orthodox purity.[1] This tendency was aggravated by the cult of personality so common on the Right; where the left-winger favours teamwork, 'the man of the Right' (as one of them put it) 'demands the leader and rejects the team'.[2] In the Fourth Republic Gaullists and Poujadists built major parties around the personality of a leader, while the small groups of the far Right, whether formed for electoral battles or for street fighting, were rarely more than the organized clientele of a particular minor chieftain.

The first electoral effort came in 1951. One of the few prominent Pétainists eligible for Parliament, Maître Jacques Isorni, was persuaded by P. E. Flandin to stand in the election. Though his *ad hoc* group UNIR (*Union des nationaux et des indépendants républicains*) ran too few lists to qualify as a 'national party' under the electoral law, it elected three champions of the Marshal: his former defence counsel – Isorni – in north-west Paris, his ex-secretary at Oran (Algeria) and one of his ministers of agriculture for Calvados (Normandy). After some hesitation they were allowed to join the Peasant parliamentary group and became absorbed as active and useful if rather right-wing Conservative members.[3]

This was not the only sign of a change of climate. In 1951 the bitterest enemies of the regime founded *Rivarol*, a weekly organ which except in circulation, proved a worthy successor to the pre-war *Gringoire*. Next year the Gaullists of the capital split over whether to collaborate with Vichyites in

1. Sérant, p. 157.
2. Coston, p. 24. This is both the fullest and the most friendly source for most of these groups. See also R. Barrillon in *Monde*, 14, 15 and 16 February 1958; Weber, no. 216.
3. For 'national parties' and the electoral law see below, pp. 506–7; for 1951, Isorni, *Ainsi*, pp. 8–19; UNIR also won 5% of the vote in a fourth district, Tarn. Some other Conservative deputies had Pétainist sympathies: below, pp. 177, 179n.

the coming municipal elections. In 1953 Parliament, which was soon to elect as President of the Republic a respected politician who had voted for Pétain in 1940, passed an amnesty law allowing others who had done so to resume their parliamentary careers.[4] Several tried; very few succeeded.

Although on the French Right there was little enthusiasm for democracy, its violent enemies were always very few.[5] Most of them were concentrated in the big towns and especially in Paris. In 1954 they formed a short-lived *Rassemblement national*, which began fighting by-elections the following year and in the 1956 general election, allied to other right-wingers under the title *Réforme de l'État*, ran enough lists to qualify as a 'national party'. Its leader Me Tixier-Vignancour was returned as its only deputy in his pre-war constituency of Basses-Pyrénées.[6] In Parliament he became the temporary manager of the inexperienced Poujadists; outside it he was the ardent defender of every fascist conspirator against a regime which he skilfully and unscrupulously undermined, especially in the notorious leakages case of 1956.[7]

A robust and ruthless revolutionary, Tixier hated the Fifth Republic no less than previous numerical variants of the regime. His attitude to them all was one of destructive opposition, more nihilist than conservative. There had always been such right-wing extremists who were delighted to practise the *politique du pire* by encouraging rival extremists of the Left – with whom indeed they shared a common contempt for the feeble creatures who occupied the middle ground. But this attitude did not extend to another sector of extreme-Right opinion, less noisy but perhaps more influential, which drew its inspiration from a crusading wing of the Catholic Church that had more importance at Rome than in France itself. The Catholic extreme Right concerned itself with mobilizing anti-democratic opinion through 'education' and psychological warfare, not with electioneering or revolutionary activity. Its influence on army officers, particularly in the Fifth Republic, shows that the distinction can be exaggerated.[8]

Other movements of the far Right had direct action as their sole aim: the

4. See below, p. 210 n. 9.

5. 'The political dinosaur (*la réaction*) is a species (or specimen) peculiar to France ... hostile, at first actively but later passively, to a political regime which originated much less in the general will than in the bankruptcy, absence and misfortunes of the regimes which preceded it. The Third Republic did not appear in France as a *de jure* but as a *de facto* form of government, in a country which was not and never had been republican but gradually became so ... out of fear of militant clericalism': Thibaudet, *Idées*, pp. 33–4.

6. RN fought every Paris seat in 1956; and though Tixier was elected in the provinces, his votes were urban: *Paysans*, pp. 123–4. However, one peasant extremist – Henri Dorgères, pre-war 'Green Shirt' leader and later active in Vichy's Peasant Corporation – was elected in Ille-et-Vilaine as a champion of the *bouilleurs de cru* (home distillers) against Mendès-France's anti-alcoholism measures: J. M. Royer in *ibid.*, pp. 149–81, cf. Guy, pp. 180–92, Coston, pp. 161–5. His vote was negligible in the towns but reached 30% and even 42% in the poorer rural cantons: *Paysans*, p. 178.

7. On Tixier and the Poujadists cf. below, p. 168; for the leakages trial see above, pp. 46n., 49. Grandson of a Republican deputy of the 1870's, he won a seat in 1936, was unseated for electoral fraud but re-elected. In 1940, as head of Vichy's radio, he was said by Maurras to favour the pro-German Déat: L. de Gérin-Ricard and L. Truc, *Histoire de l'Action française* (1949), p. 240. He was later disgraced by Vichy (not on political grounds). In 1961 he declared in court: 'I will never use the word legitimacy, for I know it has not existed in France since 21 January 1793': *Monde*, 21 July 1961.

8. On it see Bosworth, pp. 183–5, 199–200, 224–8, 334–6; Coston, pp. 509–12; Rémond, nos. 187–8. On the sympathies between extreme Right and extreme Left see Weber, no. 216.

Indo-China ex-servicemen's association which rioted at the time of Dien-Bien-Phu; *Jeune Nation*, later the *Parti nationaliste*, a small but noisy fascist movement started in 1954 by four sons of a leading Vichy *milicien* executed at the Liberation, which joined the *Anciens d'Indochine* in attacking Communist headquarters after Budapest in 1956; the *Parti patriote révolutionnaire*, set up in 1957 by the Gaullist lawyer-adventurer Me Biaggi, which specialized in wrecking opponents' meetings. Many of their adherents found in *Algérie française* the opportunity that some German-Americans saw in McCarthyism: a chance to retaliate against those who had questioned their patriotism. The *presse de la trahison*, once a Resistance name for collaborationist journals, became a term of abuse flung by some of its former victims against left-wing papers sympathetic to Algerian nationalism. These extreme-Right groups kept closely in touch with their fellows in Algeria (Biaggi was the main organizer of the riot of 6 February 1956). And there their allies, constantly plotting against both Fourth and Fifth Republics, acquired at times a substantial following.[9]

The advent of de Gaulle embarrassed both Vichyites and crypto-Fascists. Dorgères supported his election to the premiership; Isorni was the only orthodox Conservative to oppose it (since 'the defender of Louis XVI cannot vote for Robespierre'); Tixier voted for the General's candidature but against giving him full powers (explaining that for casting a similar vote eighteen years before he had been declared unworthy to sit in Parliament by the very man who was now asking him to repeat the performance). All three men were opposed by Gaullists in the 1958 election and all lost their seats. Biaggi in contrast was elected on a UNR (Gaullist) ticket in Paris, but left UNR over Algeria a year later. By this time the government had dissolved most of the direct-action groups and all of them had gone into bitter opposition to the regime. Here they rejoined an old ally of the far Right, to whom Tixier had once paid the richly – if temporarily – merited tribute: 'Thanks to Pierre Poujade we have found our way back to the masses.'

2. POUJADISM: HISTORY AND FOLLOWING

Pierre Poujade, the son of an *Action française* architect at St. Céré in Lot, had belonged to the youth movement of Doriot's PPF before the war and to that of Vichy during it. Escaping to North Africa, he married a *colon*'s daughter and served in the Royal Air Force. After the war he became a commercial traveller, used his savings to buy a small stationer's shop in his home town, and in 1952 was elected to the municipal council as a Gaullist candidate on a Radical list. His movement appealed to the fears of the petty-bourgeois who was determined not to sink into the ranks of the proletariat, and to the antagonism towards the politicians of the System felt by many men of the traditional Left in the poorer parts of the south.

France had a million small shops, far more than other European countries (one for every 54 inhabitants in 1956, compared with a European average of one for every 71), and their number increased by 40,000 between 1950 and 1953. At St. Céré itself the population had been halved during the last century

9. See Williams and Harrison, pp. 45–6, 51–63, 226–7. For their extreme weakness in France see above, p. 54n. For the riots over Indo-China see above, p. 45, and below, p. 167.

while the number of shopkeepers and artisans remained unchanged. With the end of inflation and the rapid growth of competition from co-operatives and multiple stores, the small man could no longer pay his debts and taxes in depreciated francs. The inefficient and bureaucratic fiscal system came to seem oppressive as well when his ex-hero Pinay introduced severe penalties for future tax evasion in return for an amnesty for past frauds. These tighter controls were bitterly resented by those innumerable small shopkeepers – four-fifths of the total – who declared an income lower than the working-class average while remaining grimly determined to differentiate themselves from the despised proletariat.[10] When Poujade organized forcible opposition to a tax inspector's scrutiny of a neighbour's accounts, he began a revolt which spread like wildfire through the south.

The first Poujadist organization, UDCA (*Union de défense des commerçants et des artisans*), was formed in 1953. At the outset the movement was not obviously right-wing. Laniel's Conservative government was then facing the first major strikes for five years and the first widespread blocking of roads by peasant carts. Poujadist propaganda was directed against the rich and powerful, the technocrats and officials, and the recognized spokesmen of the small businessmen like Léon Gingembre; Poujadist influence was concentrated in the traditionally left-wing south and centre; and the Communists, seeing an opportunity to extend their influence and perhaps sympathizing with another revolutionary sprung from the people, gave UDCA full support and in many areas came close to controlling it.[11]

UDCA's change of direction began at its first conference, at Algiers in November 1954. The annual subscription was trebled (to 1,000 francs) and a new weekly, *Fraternité française*, was founded under the editorship of an Algiers extremist, Paul Chevallet. Mendès-France was now in office, and Poujadist attacks were increasingly directed against the Left in general and Jews in particular; they enthusiastically denounced economic progress and the campaign against alcoholism.[12] In January 1955 a monster rally in Paris opened a campaign of pressure on the parties: the Communists reacted with shameless demagogy, the Socialists with equally shameless cowardice and the Conservatives with both – MRP alone retaining some sense of dignity and responsibility. In March the Assembly debated tax controls with a shirt-sleeved Poujade in the public galleries directing the tactics of those sympathetic members (mostly Conservatives) whom he was later to describe as

10. Lipsedge, no. 146, points out that French fiscal administration employed as many civil servants (80,000) as that of the United States and that cafés were subjected to 24 different taxes, garages to 25. Siegfried calls the movement 'a product of deflation'; *De la IIIe*, p. 203.

11. For the economic background see Hoffmann, pp. 14–22; for Communist influence, pp. 38–40; for the changes in Communist policy, pp. 348–56; for Communist support in the early days, *L'Humanite* 6 July 1954, quoted pp. 378–9: 'Union is strength; the Eight of St Céré have kept the faith. Today they are tens and scores of thousands . . .', etc. It was a Communist who first stimulated Poujade to action; not till late 1955 did *L'Humanité* begin calling him 'Poujadolf'. On the movement's leftish tone in the early days and the later change see also J. Touchard's excellent article, no. 210, pp. 30–43; on early Communist influence also p. 83., and Guy, pp. 40–3; on Gingembre, below, pp. 361, 379–80.

12. Hoffmann, pp. 57 (alcohol), 252–3: 'We will defend the traditional structure of the French economy . . . we are against reconversion.' Peasant demonstrators' banners at Chartres in February 1955 proclaimed, 'Milk = Misery, Productivity = Ruin': De Tarr, p. 206.

'grovelling at my feet'.[13] The Poujadists set up 'parallel unions' of peasants, students and workers, and made ostentatious contributions to a number of strike funds.[14] When the local councils were renewed in April they tried – in vain – to unseat their most prominent enemies. Evidently by the middle of 1955 the decision to fight the parliamentary election had been taken, though it was not yet avowed.

They began their electioneering, therefore, long before the other parties. Their candidate in Isère held 51 meetings after the dissolution – but 183 earlier in the year, which had earned him seven appearances in court. Everywhere the Poujadist campaign was slanderous, violent and utterly negative, except over North Africa where the movement expressed the most extreme colonialist views. A favourite technique was bar-to-bar canvassing, and 'non-political' shopkeepers, barmen and commercial travellers made ideal propagandists.[15] Opponents' meetings were broken up, usually by rowdyism and obstruction; juvenile student 'ragging' rather than fascist thuggery was the general tone; and all parties except the Communists suffered from these tactics. Electoral violence is unusual and unpopular in France, and almost everywhere the Poujadists soon abandoned it.[16] But their catchy slogan *Sortez les Sortants!* and their verbal extravagance appealed to the ordinary Frenchman's boundless contempt for all politicians – except, sometimes, for his own deputy.[17] Even the Poujadists underestimated their own success, while the predictions of journalists, prefects and politicians were made derisory by the event.[18] The newcomers won 2,600,000 votes and elected 53 members to form the UFF group: *Union et fraternité française*. The new Assembly, with much legal warrant and no political sense, unseated eleven of them.[19]

Hoping to put his new parliamentary strength to use, Poujade now turned on his extreme fascist associates as he had previously ousted the Communists. Enforcing his demands by a threat of resignation, he moved party headquarters back from Paris to St. Céré, sent Chevallet home to Algiers (where he became an intermediary between the local fascists and the ex-Cagoulard conspirators in Paris), and expelled the extremist leaders of the peasants' and workers' 'parallel unions'.[20] But though he dominated the

13. See Hoffmann, pp. 76–81, 356–63, 368–71; Guy, pp. 99–101, 113–8, 128–43 (party replies); Lavau in *Partis et Classes*, p. 83.

14. Hoffmann, pp. 111–16, and (for the peasants) Royer in *Paysans*, pp. 182–206.

15. Hoffmann, pp. 190–1; *Élections 1956*, pp. 29 (Fauvet), 480 (Goguel); Olivesi, p. 77; *Le Poujadisme* (by Maurice Bardèche *et al.*), p. 6.

16. Their chief victim (Mitterrand) unexpectedly gained votes; the Poujadists did worse in his department than in any of its neighbours. Cf. Hoffmann, pp. 164–5; *Élections 1956*, p. 421; Touchard, no. 210, p. 38 ('success in inverse ratio to violence used').

17. For samples see Hoffmann, Chapter 6; also Williams, no. 168, pp. 156n., 161; Thomas, no. 170, pp. 278–80; *Élections 1956*, pp. 61–4.

18. These authorities relied on traditional opinion-makers such as local councillors, whom the Poujadists by-passed. The Communists were sometimes better prophets: Thomas, no. 170, p. 265. The French Institute of Public Opinion twice concealed the Poujadists under 'others', and in a third poll credited them with 1 % of the votes of youth.

19. The Poujadist success wrecked all the calculations which had led Faure to dissolve: see above, p. 48. The 53 include Jean Dides, who affiliated to the group.

20. For the organization (democratic locally but highly authoritarian at and above the departmental level) see Hoffmann, pp. 262–303. For the peasant union, Royer in *Paysans*, pp. 192–8; Coston, pp. 267–71. The constitutions of both unions, and of UDCA, are published in *Le Poujadisme*, pp. 129–33.

organization, he could not solve the problems that had baffled de Gaulle: retaining the momentum of an anti-parliamentary army with a foothold in the enemy fortress – the National Assembly – and preserving the disciplinary subordination of the invading deputies to a commander who himself still stood outside the abhorred System.

The stationer from St. Céré should have found his troops more manageable than those of his illustrious predecessor. For the RPF deputies in 1951 had been three times as numerous – and so had more to gain by standing together. Without help from them there was no stable majority – and so the System could not survive without splitting or assimilating them. Men of personal distinction were as common in their ranks as they were rare among the Poujadists – few of whom had any political experience and fewer still any political talent.[21] Collectively less indispensable and individually less capable, they – unlike the Gaullists – were rarely courted by and never made any impression upon their colleagues.[22] 'Moved by the one virtue of indignation', wrote a sympathetic Conservative, 'they were, however, incapable of drafting a bill or delivering a speech. They produced no reform, even on fiscal questions. They could never express their wishes and the cries which they conscientiously uttered at regular intervals provoked countercries without ever awakening an echo.'[23]

They might have seemed a sufficiently malleable group (especially as all their members had sworn to maintain discipline under penalty of being hanged). Moreover, taking a leaf from the Communist book, Poujade insisted that the party draw their parliamentary salaries and withhold a levy before paying the balance to the member. But over the 'Euratom' treaty in June the group kept its unity only by abstaining – and allowing three dissidents to vote for the government. In October some Poujadists seem (in a secret ballot) to have disobeyed the order to keep a Socialist out of the chair by voting instead for an MRP leader whom they had bitterly denounced in the election campaign. In November, Poujade amazed his followers by instructing them to vote against 'fighting for the Queen of England' at Suez; a third of them defied him and the articulate few, who were all ultra-nationalists, broke with him for good.[24] Even their loyalist colleagues almost elected a rebel to chair the depleted group.

Disarray in Parliament reflected decline in the country. At a by-election in

21. For thirty of the fifty UFF members this was their first political venture; of the rest only two had stood for Parliament. Ex-Socialists, ex-Radicals and ex-Conservatives each numbered two or three; one had been MRP, four PSF (before the war) and eight RPF like their leader: Hoffmann, p. 162; *Le Poujadisme*, pp. 126–7; Coston, pp. 235–6; cf. Dogan in *Élections 1956*, p. 449.

22. Dr. M. Harrison tells me that committees rarely asked them to report on bills other than their own (and for some time not even these). De Gaulle was the only prospective premier ever to promise (though he did not give) office to any of them: Isorni, *Ainsi*, p. 77.

23. *Ibid.*, p. 75; in *Silence*, p. 57, he adds that their speeches were often written by others. For the extraordinary bills they sponsored see *Le Poujadisme*, pp. 68–70.

24. Among the defectors were two who were in the army, Le Pen (above, p. 154) and Demarquet (below, p. 167); and the three Euratom rebels led by Dides. The last three and two others voted for the government; the party conference expelled Dides from the movement and the other four from the parliamentary group. Seven members who abstained were censured and lost half their salary for three months. Three of the dissidents had already protested in September when the levy on salaries was raised from £20 to £50 a month.

south Paris early in 1957 Poujade himself won less than half the vote obtained by Le Pen a year before. Turning from the fickle townsmen to the perennially discontented peasants, he negotiated an uneasy alliance with two rival rural demagogues, Dorgères and Antier (even lending Antier enough Poujadist deputies to enable him still to lead a parliamentary group when his former followers revolted).[25] This new combination perhaps dissuaded the orthodox Conservatives from making concessions at the peasants' expense. But it failed to restore the waning fortunes of Poujadism in the country, and in Parliament even a vote for Pinay's abortive government in October 1957 brought the party no greater influence. At the end of the Fourth Republic Poujade suffered the humiliation of seeing first his thirty remaining deputies and then his voters repudiate his leadership for that of a more formidable enemy of the System. The deputies defied their leader both in electing General de Gaulle premier and in approving his constitution; but having now themselves become *sortants*, in November they too went down to a defeat as crushing as Poujade's own.[26]

The political Poujadism of UFF was based on the shopkeepers, café and bar proprietors and artisans who adhered to the commercial Poujadism of UDCA; 95% of the UFF candidates and all but five of the deputies were drawn from these occupations. The 1956 election showed that the areas of strength of the two organizations generally coincided closely, and local surveys suggest that the party drew from half to two-thirds of its votes from its professional clients.[27] Those who were on the economic margin were naturally the most tempted by Poujadism; the Poujadist social security administrators elected in 1955 were often declared ineligible for failure to pay their own social security contributions.[28]

Not all the Poujadists were small shopkeepers. Wealthier traders hoped to profit from concessions to their weaker brethren; of 33 Poujadist leaders in Paris, 17 had large cars and 7 had two houses.[29] Many more recruits came from another discontented class, the peasants – particularly the *bouilleurs de cru* and the producers of wine.[30] But large towns and industrial areas gave a

25. On the Paris election see Bodin and Touchard, no. 21; on Dorgères, above, n. 6; on Antier, above, p. 153; on *Rassemblement paysan*, Royer in *Paysans*, pp. 179–81, *AP* 1957, p. 87 – it split in 1959 over Poujade's hostility to de Gaulle.

26. On post-1956 Poujadism see Coston, pp. 237–40; in June 1958 a conference condemned the deputies by 83 votes to 2. Only two of them were re-elected, Luciani as a Gaullist and Le Pen as CNIP. Poujade himself did well at Saumur-Sud (Maine-et-Loire), with 7,000 votes out of 40,000. But the combined national vote of the extreme Right, 'orthodox' Poujadists and ex-Poujadist deputies was under 700,000, less than a quarter of the 1956 figure.

27. For candidates and deputies see Dogan in *Élections 1956*, pp. 433, 456; for local estimates, *ibid.*, pp. 206–7 (south Paris, nearly 60%), 348 (Aveyron, 65%), 401–4 (Aisne, almost 50%), cf. 315–16 (Lyons), 420 (Bordeaux); also Olivesi, pp. 178–80 (Marseilles); and above, p. 68n. In one small Somme village UFF drew 90% of its votes and in another 60% from shopkeepers, artisans or their families: J. Bugnicourt in *Paysans*, p. 484. A national poll found that about half the Poujadist voters were self-employed: Lipset, p. 154 (cf. pp. 163, 225). For a general discussion see Hoffmann, pp. 190–2. For UFF and UDCA, below, p. 167 and n. 37.

28. Hoffmann, pp. 13–14, 150. Poujade's own shop is said to have sold about ten postcards a day.

29. Ministry of finance figures quoted Lipsedge, no. 146; cf. Touchard, no. 210, p. 21; also n. 30 below.

30. Agriculturalist votes for the Poujadists averaged 15%, rarely fell below 10% and sometimes reached 25%: J. Klatzmann in *Paysans*, pp. 48, 50, 59; cf. Royer in *ibid.*, pp. 200–3; Olivesi,

[*over*

poor welcome to Poujadism, except for the declining textile centres.[31] In regions of expansion the movement failed – though in a fast-growing department like Isère a vigorous protest vote for Poujade might come from districts which were losing population to the booming towns.[32] And in the countryside it tended to be strongest in areas where owner-occupied farms were too small to be viable, or where the poverty of the small shopkeeper reflected that of his customers; for, curiously enough, the movement was born and flourished precisely where least taxes were paid.[33] Over great tracts of the impoverished south Poujade ravaged the followings of every party, including the Communists.[34]

But in the west and around Paris he attracted predominantly those right-wing voters who felt betrayed both by RPF, which had become absorbed in the System, and by CNIP leaders who had supported EDC, restored the Sultan of Morocco and voted for higher taxes. Rich and aristocratic 'parlour Poujadists' welcomed a 'poor man's de Gaulle' who could attract mass support to the anti-parliamentary, ultra-nationalist cause. Among the Poujadist deputies from Paris were Dides and Le Pen, and from the west J. M. Demarquet – an organizer of riots against Pleven in 1954 and Mollet in 1956. At a by-election in 1957 the party's candidate was General Faure, the first soldier to plot against the regime in Algiers. Poujadists were active conspirators against the Republic, both before and during the reign of de Gaulle.

Individual extremists came from all over France and above all from Algeria. Most Poujadist voters probably came from the Right, and ex-Gaullists were often the largest single group.[35] But in the nationalist but pro-parliamentary north-east they did very badly, and only one old RPF bastion gave a really warm welcome to UFF: the old Chouan stronghold in the west.[36] Here Poujadist campaign violence was most vicious; and here was the only zone of UFF strength where UDCA afforded no solid professional base.[37]

pp. 93, 196. Again they were not always the poorest peasants: *ibid.*, pp. 76–8, 82; Wylie, p. 329; *Élections 1956*, p. 393. Sometimes even agricultural workers voted Poujadist: Olivesi, p. 85.

31. Hoffmann, pp. 36, 196 (general); Dreyfus, no. 79, p. 540 on north-eastern France, and *Élections 1956*, pp. 392, 394 on Isère (general and textiles); *ibid.*, pp. 401, 416 (textiles).

32. For Isère, *Élections 1956*, pp. 391–4; *Paysans*, p. 203; Williams, no. 168, p. 169 n. 2. Generally, *ibid.*, p. 174 n. 2; Hoffmann, p. 197; Pierce, no. 180, pp. 412–13.

33. Hoffmann, pp. 11–13, 194–5; Poujade's own department of Lot with 4% of the nation's population paid barely 1% of all local taxes. Also *Élections 1956*, p. 343; Prost, no. 185, pp. 74–6 and (with C. Brindillac), no. 31, pp. 446–8. However, there was a negative correlation between the most Poujadist and the poorest rural departments: MacRae, no. 148, p. 297. This is perhaps explained by Poujadist weakness in the Left's rural strongholds (cf. nn. 37 and 38). See Maps 3 and 12.

34. In Bugnicourt's two Somme villages a quarter of the UFF votes came from former Communists: *Paysans*, p. 484. Cf. Olivesi, pp. 37–8, 55–6, 80–2, 221 (Bouches-du-Rhône); Wylie, p. 328 (Vaucluse); *Paysans*, p. 439 (Savoie); *Élections 1956*, pp. 381, 393 (Isère), 421 (Vendée), 480–1, 496; Prost, no. 31, p. 452; Williams, no. 168, pp. 169 n. 2 (Isère) and 173 (for national figures cited above, p. 79n).

35. *Élections 1956*, pp. 404–5 (Aisne), 420 (Gard); *Paysans*, p. 484 (Somme).

36. So did 'little Vendée' in Bouches-du-Rhône, which always voted for extreme-Right movements: Olivesi, pp. 78–82, 116, cf. pp. 40, 178, and Wylie, pp. 329–30. On the north-east see Morazé, p. 211; on RPF and UFF, Map 12. Only 21 of the 52 Poujadists were elected north of the Loire, but 53 of 74 RPF (ARS and overseas members omitted).

37. Conversely, in west-central France – an area of Communist and Socialist rather than Radical strength – UDCA was strong and UFF not. Elsewhere, MRP lost less than the Conservatives to Poujade; perhaps organized parties resisted his inroads better than loose ones. It was

[*over*

3. POUJADISM: CHARACTERISTICS

There were thus two Poujadisms. The extreme Right exploited the movement in the north and west and in Algeria. But economic Poujadism appealed to Left as well as Right: to Protestant as well as Catholic in Gard, to the poor of Boulogne as much as to the rich of Neuilly. Concentrated in 'static France', economic Poujadism was the obverse of Mendesism in the expanding north.[38] Backward businessmen and peasants rebelled against the economic progress that threatened them with proletarianization. Poujade's 'eulogy of sclerosis' appealed to all those who feared reform – whether reorganization of the distributive system, modernizing of industry, rearrangement of scattered agricultural holdings or an attack on alcoholism.[39]

The movement was well equipped to exploit every kind of contradictory discontent at the polls, despite its grave organizational weaknesses which provoked more than one split.[40] Yet the elections came almost at the crest of the wave. Negation and cynicism, xenophobia and violence were effective weapons for a lightning campaign but poor foundations for a lasting party.[41] Positive proposals might have alienated support; Poujade said they were 'the specialists' job'. His propaganda had 'as much intellectual content as a scream'.[42]

Vigorous and vulgar irresponsibility gave Poujadism more appeal than RPF in some groups and areas. Despite his endorsement of Dides and Le Pen, the stationer was more successful than the General in resisting conservative take-over bids, and so long as there were left-wing votes to be lost he would allow no compromising electoral alliances with notorious reactionaries like Tixier or Dorgères.[43] The tone of Poujadist propaganda was quite unlike that of the extreme Right. Where Maurras had vilified the Revolution, Poujade invoked 1789, Valmy, Clemenceau, the Resistance and the Republic, condemned the parliamentarians but not Parliament, and professed profound

claimed (but contested) that many former non-voters turned out for him: no. 31, pp. 445–8; no. 185, pp. 73–4; *Paysans*, p. 484; Wylie, pp. 328–9; Olivesi, pp. 37, 77, cf. 119 and 202–3; contrast *ibid.*, p. 178, Hoffmann, pp. 201–2, Goguel in *Élections 1956*, pp. 480–1. Fullest analysis in Hoffmann, pp. 189–208.

38. Discontent took one or the other form according to regional conditions. For the total Radical poll doubled in departments where the Poujadist won less than 10% of the vote; rose by half in those where they won 10 to 15%; and fell by 5% where the Poujadists exceeded 15%. (For a similar comparison between Communists and Poujadists see above, p. 79n.) On Radicals cf. Wylie, pp. 328ff.

39. Hoffmann, pp. 252–3; Siegfried, *De la IIIe*, pp. 203–4. The regions which had done best under the local autarky of the wartime economy were very susceptible to Poujadism: see maps in Morazé, p. 131.

40. Hoffmann, pp. 49–52, 125–31, 283–93. At the great Paris meeting in January 1955 the organizers forgot to have membership forms at the doors: Guy, p. 161.

41. The party did badly in its homeland, the centre, and especially in Poujade's home department, Lot. An early foothold in Paris gave it no advantage: Touchard, no. 210, p. 41 n. Familiarity perhaps bred contempt; as one journalist was told, 'Poujade's fine, naturally, but after all an election is a pretty serious matter'.

42. Quoted Wright, *France in Modern Times*, p. 542; for samples see references above, n. 17. His boundless cynicism was shown on the day after the elections when he spoke twice about Mendès-France – amiably to *L'Express* and nastily to *Le Figaro*.

43. Hoffmann, p. 340; *Paysans*, p. 177. Wisely: for in some southern villages he took more votes from the Radicals (Wylie, p. 328) or even Socialists (Olivesi, p. 119) than from all the Right. Indeed polls suggested that in religion and connected beliefs Poujadist voters resembled Radicals most, Socialists next: Lipset, pp. 161–2, 245. Cf. Siegfried, *De la IIIe*, pp. 204, 260–2

respect for President Coty.[44] The keynote of *Pierrot*'s appeal was his defence of *les braves gens, les petits*, and the political ancestor he caricatured was Maurras's great enemy Alain, the champion of the people against all the elites: the politicians and the technicians, the officials and the academicians and the rich.[45] If there were far fewer Poujadist *ministrables* than Gaullists in 1951, this was a parliamentary handicap but an electoral advantage, for their inexperienced and inarticulate candidates had an authentic common touch.

Unlike the many RPF carpet-baggers who despised constituency chores, most Poujadist candidates had genuine local roots – except, significantly, for the unknowns who contested Parisian seats and apparently appealed largely to newcomers like themselves. Provincial suspicion and dislike of the capital were as important Poujadist themes as the popular suspicion and dislike of the well-off, the well-educated and the well-placed.[46] Indeed they were the same theme: Poujadism – like American Populism – was a protest against metropolitan sophistication, wealth and success in which a deep but confused sense of grievance found expression (often with highly reactionary overtones) in the popular accents of the underprivileged provincial cut off from the seats of power and unable to understand, let alone influence, the forces which were undermining his way of life.[47]

The movement did not survive its sudden electoral triumph. Yet it was a symptom no less important for being transient. It showed that the political consequences of economic modernization were not as exclusively beneficial as many commentators had supposed, since those who suffered from the process reacted 'with the wild gestures of drowning men'. Like other popular authoritarian right-wing movements it was violent, eruptive and short-lived; but the latent discontent with the political system which they so briefly crystallized remained dangerous after they had disappeared. And, if this popular provincial outburst against modernity, centralization and the state differed from fascism in many ways, it was none the less disquieting that 'the revolt was born, not in circles where faith in the regime was always lukewarm, but at the very base of the Jacobin Republic'.[48]

44. *Ibid.*, p. 203; Touchard, no. 210, p. 28; Hoffmann, pp. 136, 214, 229–31, 242. (Later he visited the Pope and saluted Joan of Arc: *ibid.*, p. 410.)

45. Hoffmann, pp. 171, 211–13, 219–20, 228, 246; Touchard, no. 210, p. 27.

46. Hoffmann, pp. 251–2, 411; Touchard, no. 210, p. 42.

47. Hoffmann, p. 254n., citing R. Hofstadter, *The Age of Reform* (New York, 1955), Chapter 2. There is a still closer parallel with *Uomo Qualunque* in post-war Italy.

48. Hoffmann, p. 387; cf. pp. 388–90, 400, and Siegfried, *De la IIIe*, pp. 204 ('drowning'), 262.

Chapter 13

THE MINOR PARTIES

The Fourth Republic produced a rich crop of minor parties, some of them entirely ephemeral. This chapter examines, first the neutralist or 'fellow-travelling' left-wing groups; secondly the friends of Mendès-France and the opponents of the Algerian war; then a single middle-sized party, UDSR, the uneasy ally of the Radicals; next a number of right-wing splinter groups, mostly linked with both Radicals and UDSR in the *Rassemblement des Gauches républicaines* (RGR) – a nebulous body which in 1955 suddenly became the chief focus for right-wing Radical activity; and finally several groups of overseas deputies.

These little groups were electorally negligible but not without interest or importance. The neutralists and Mendesists influenced the outlook of the Left (and others) much more than their derisory showing at the polls suggested – just as after 1900 *Action française*, which could hardly return a single deputy, had exerted a tremendous attraction on the entire Right. For the small extreme groups enjoyed influential support and sympathy in the press; and they appealed to intellectuals who always helped to create the climate of opinion, and sometimes could influence their neighbours' attitudes to specific problems (though never decide their votes).

Other minor parties, lacking the following to constitute a popular movement or the clarity of outlook that gives intellectual influence, were able through their strategic position to play a vital parliamentary role. There was always an important place in French assemblies for a little group of able men without bitter enmities, whose marginal situation entitled them to a large share of ministerial posts but whose entry into a government aroused little jealousy among the big parties. In the Third Republic this part was played by the Republican Socialists, the party of Briand and Painlevé. In the Fourth it fell especially to UDSR.

Yet other organizations had their origins in history. The list of minor groups was littered with relics of the past. Some like the royalists represented an ancient tradition. A few such as *Alliance démocratique* were remnants of once powerful movements, now dead but for the name and a frustrated politician or two clinging to it – like a National Liberal in Great Britain – in the hope of marginal political advantage. Many were mere cliques formed around a particular leader or group – such as Paul Faure's collection of Socialists who had followed Marshal Pétain. But not all the lesser groups looked backward for their inspiration. Many of the colonial parties were soon to be ruling their own countries. And one major French party, MRP, was built from just such petty splinter groups that had flourished in a previous Republic.

1. THE EXTREME LEFT

The groups discussed in this section and the next were divided among themselves between socialists and liberals, neutralists and westerners, revolutionaries and reformists, supporters and opponents of a new Popular Front. These conflicts kept them for years in ceaseless, amoeba-like effervescence, and were submerged only by the Algerian war and its consequence, the collapse of the Fourth Republic. In the end their common opposition to de Gaulle's regime brought most of them into uneasy association in a single *Parti socialiste unifié*; but even PSU excluded the crypto-Communists, most Trotskyists, and all Left Gaullists.[1]

The three main trends on the Left were represented by the 'fellow-travellers', the neutralists, and the Mendesists. Recruits came from all the Third Force formations. There were fellow-travelling Radicals like Pierre Cot, expelled by their party in April 1946 for preferring a Communist to a UDSR alliance; there were the neutralist Socialists of the *Parti socialiste unitaire*, who had been expelled by theirs for opposing the drastic laws passed during the great strikes of late 1947; there were extreme-Left Catholics. In April 1948 the three groups formed a joint committee along with *Jeune République*.[2] Late in 1950 a broadened version of this committee, renamed *Union progressiste*, was set up as an alliance of neutralists and fellow-travellers.

The Progressives maintained their separate identity in the Assembly, but in order to obtain committee representation they normally affiliated to the Communist group.[3] Most of their French members were Left Radicals who (after expulsion from their old party) had been re-elected with Communist support; from overseas came West African nationalists belonging to RDA.[4] The defection of RDA in 1950 was offset by the adherence of three MRP members who in the same year broke with their party over foreign and social policy: the Abbé Pierre, a marquis, and a professor of medicine who sat for a wine-growing area and had led the battle against Coca-Cola.[5] In the 1951 election the fellow-travelling Progressives accepted places on Communist lists, and four out of six held their seats. But the neutralists stood independently and were all beaten, new neutralist candidates also faring very badly. Two Socialist deputies who had gone over to the Progressives in 1948 were defeated, one as a neutralist in Paris, the other on a Communist list in Allier.[6]

1. On the Left Gaullists see the next section. On Trotskyists and other dissident Communists see Williams, pp. 142–3; in 1951 their half-dozen lists won from 1 to 2% of the vote. On the neutralist Left see Marcus, Chapter 2, and Werth, *France 1940–55*, Parts 4 and 5. Coston, pp. 398–426, discusses most of these groups. Their appeal depended largely on friendly journals like *L'Observateur* (later *France-Observateur*), *L'Express*, *Esprit*, *Temps Modernes* and even *Le Monde*. See C. Estier, *La Gauche hebdomadaire 1914–62* (1962).

2. On JR see p. 103; it had lost most of its leaders either to MRP or to UDSR.

3. Only from 1949 to 1951 had they the minimum membership (fourteen) needed for representation in their own right. They were first called *Union des républicains et résistants*, later *Union des républicains progressistes*.

4. On RDA see below, pp. 176, 180–1.

5. They formed their own group, *Gauche indépendante*, and affiliated to the Progressives (whom they soon joined): cf. Einaudi and Goguel, pp. 171–2. For two other ex-MRP members who briefly associated with them see below, p. 398 n. 8. On Catholic fellow-travellers generally see Dansette, *Destin*, Chapter 5; Bosworth, pp. 110, 183, 265.

6. The four fellow-travellers were the ex-Radicals Cot and Meunier and the aristocrats d'Astier de la Vigerie, editor of *Libération*, and Gilbert de Chambrun (the only Left Catholic to survive).

[over

In 1954 co-operation was resumed with the formation of a Paris liaison committee, nucleus of the future *Union de la Gauche socialiste* (UGS). On it were represented the fellow-travelling Progressives, *Jeune République*, the neutralist *Nouvelle Gauche* (including the remnants of *Gauche indépendante*, and with Claude Bourdet of *France-Observateur* as secretary) and the *Mouvement pour la libération du peuple* (MLP), an extreme-Left Catholic working-class group born from a split in the old family-association movement.[7] In the 1956 election one Socialist federation, Vosges, defied party headquarters and with the Communists and MLP ran a joint list which elected a Communist and a Socialist (who was expelled by the party, sat as an independent, but generally voted with his former friends). As the only case for ten years of a Popular Front in a parliamentary election, Vosges attracted much attention: superficial observers noted that the joint list won 8% more votes than the two parties' combined poll in 1951, but not that this limited gain – in a constituency with heavy unemployment – was below the increase in their national vote and far below their regional increase.[8] Plainly the Popular Front alignment still deterred some potential Socialist voters as it had done over the whole country ten years before.

The Progressives benefited from the Communist advance and regained two of the four seats they had lost in 1951.[9] From time to time one or other of their deputies now voted differently from the Communists;[10] three of them condemned the Soviet action in Hungary, and the whole group ostentatiously stayed away when the Assembly debated it; over Suez, while the Communist spokesman denounced the canal company and the American imperialists, Pierre Cot solemnly appealed to the government to stand by President Eisenhower and Mr. Gaitskell; and in May 1958 the Progressives voted for Pflimlin as premier while the Communists abstained. In the general election of November 1958 two Progressive deputies even fought (unsuccessfully) without Communist support.[11] Despite these unprecedented signs of independence the *Union progressiste* refused to merge into the new *Union de la Gauche socialiste* which was formed in December 1957. UGS therefore embraced only individual Progressives along with MLP, Claude Bourdet's *Nouvelle*

The secretary of the *Parti socialiste unitaire*, which had broken with the Communists over Tito, won 3% of the vote in Aisne where he had been Socialist deputy in 1945. One other new neutralist (in Seine-Inférieure) reached 2%.

7. On MLP see Suffert, pp. 99–105; Dansette, *Destin*, pp. 372–8; Bosworth, p. 110 and n. For UGS's 'clerical' reputation see Ligou, pp. 634–5.

8. In the neighbouring departments the total of votes cast for the Communist and Socialist parties together was 35% higher than in 1951, and their combined *share* of the poll was up by 4½% (whereas in Vosges it was down by 1½%).

9. Chambrun was beaten, but a joint Communist-Radical list won two seats in Creuse, apparently on protest votes (no Poujadist fought this constituency, allegedly because the prefect had persuaded them to withdraw in order to defeat the Communists!) The Radical member (Ferrand) affiliated to the Progressives and eventually joined PSU (see below, p. 174.)

10. They had occasionally done so previously in committee: see *AP* 1953, p. 11 for a case.

11. At Belfort Dreyfus-Schmidt ran ahead of the Communist, who stood down in his favour at the second ballot; in Creuse Ferrand ran behind at both ballots. Communist losses of votes in 1958 were exceptionally heavy wherever a party man was standing in a seat formerly represented by a Progressive. (For the 1958 electoral system see below, p. 316, cf. p. 307.)

Gauche, a majority of *Jeune République* and a few provincial socialist groups, notably in Normandy.

2. THE MENDESISTS

The extreme Left groups, whether neutralist or fellow-travelling, had supported Mendès-France for the premiership but turned against him when, after the defeat of EDC, he took up the cause of German rearmament. Other admirers, however, remained devoted to him despite (or more rarely because of) his foreign policy. Often these were former Catholics or Gaullists (or both) who felt out of place with the traditional Left. Malraux and Mauriac inspired a *Nouvelle Gauche* of more intellectual than political significance, and quite different from Bourdet's movement of the same name. Two deputies and a senator took refuge in *Jeune République* after MRP expelled them for opposing EDC and German rearmament; all three stood unsuccessfully in 1956. JR returned one candidate, Constant Lecœur in Seine-Maritime east. He affiliated to the Radical group, like the only other Left Independent to win a seat, Jean de Lipkowski – Grandval's aide during his Moroccan mission and a future Left Gaullist. Lipkowski's mother was a founder of the *Union Gaulliste* in 1946 and an outgoing RPF deputy; mother and son were both candidates of an ephemeral group of 'Gaullists for Mendès', the *Parti républicain pour le redressement économique et social* (she lost). The Mendesist and neutralist groups of Left Independents polled some 300,000 votes, most of which were probably ex-Gaullist and Catholic; the total Catholic vote for the Left in 1956 was estimated at a million.[12] As the Algerian war became more bitter and nationalist feeling grew in France, the anti-colonialist cause and the defence of civil liberties found among the left-wing Catholics some of their most consistent and courageous champions.

Within the Radical party itself Mendès-France's faithful followers numbered only a dozen deputies in 1956, mostly from the Paris area and parliamentary newcomers; several had belonged to the left-wing Jacobin Club within the Radical party, though one, the air ace Pierre Clostermann, had sat in the previous Assembly as a Gaullist. With their failure to impose party discipline on their senior colleagues these young Mendesists grew increasingly dissatisfied with a party to which they felt no spiritual allegiance. Their closest allies were the Left Catholic critics of the war and its abuses, and those dissident Socialists who shared their views about Algeria and their impatience with the traditional political leaders. Just as an unofficial *Algérie française* party grew up which cut across party lines, so the opponents of the war were driven into closer intimacy. The crisis of May 1958 and the collapse of republican opposition to de Gaulle strengthened these bonds – though severing those with the former Gaullists, who returned to their old allegiance.

The decisive step in the new alignment on the Left was delayed until September 1958. When the Socialist party voted to support the constitution of the

12. *Élections 1956*, p. 141; Suffert, p. 39. JR and the 'Gaullists for Mendès' were the only Left Independent groups to run 30 lists and so qualify to make electoral alliances (see below, p. 313) – though MLP and Bourdet's *Nouvelle Gauche* jointly ran 21. Some Catholic or Gaullist Mendesists belonged to a short-lived *Union démocratique du travail*, revived in the Fifth Republic by the same men as a Left Gaullist party; on it see Coston, pp. 302–7.

Fifth Republic, Mollet's opponents at last lost hope of ousting the general secretary and broke with SFIO to set up their own organization, the *Parti socialiste autonome*. Comprising those who had opposed both the war and the new regime, PSA brought together old-fashioned socialists like Édouard Depreux, revisionists like Daniel Mayer and André Philip, and Mendesists like Alain Savary. In the 1958 election its candidates co-operated with Mendesist Radicals and the left-wing UGS in an *ad hoc* alliance, the *Union des forces démocratiques*, UFD.

Between these grouplets there were still political, ideological and personal differences; but their common interests and enmities finally prevailed. After byzantine negotiations Mendès-France and his leading Radical followers in 1959 made their journey to a Socialist Canossa and were admitted to PSA. Next year the reinforced party fused with the much smaller and more Catholic UGS (whose extreme left wing broke away) and with a tiny dissident Communist group to form the *Parti socialiste unifié*, PSU. The UGS minority soon won virtual control of the new organization, which reproduced within its meagre ranks all the contradictions of outlook, policy and temperament which bedevilled the French Left.

3. UDSR

The most important of all the minor parties was the *Union démocratique et socialiste de la Résistance*, whose working life coincided with that of the Fourth Republic. It was the only political group in France which had its roots exclusively in the Resistance, for it was born in June 1945 as a federation of five Resistance movements which rejected the Communist embrace. Most of its members preferred an alliance with SFIO and, but for the suspicious jealousy of the Socialist rank and file, might have fused with and rejuvenated that ageing party. But few of the newcomers were given good electoral opportunities, and their disillusionment changed to exasperation when SFIO joined the Communists in supporting the first draft constitution in April 1946. Shedding a few members, UDSR turned instead to an alliance with the Radicals in a new combination, RGR.[13] In November 1946 it abandoned its federal structure and formally became a new political party.

The liaison between the movement born in the Resistance and the most typical product of the Third Republic was no love-match.[14] UDSR had far closer affinities with other parties. Its first general secretary – Francis Leenhardt, later chairman of the Socialist parliamentary party –, its assistant secretary and several deputies went over to SFIO. It was also a refuge for Gaullists: in 1946 Capitant, Malraux, Soustelle and most of the few *Union Gaulliste* deputies were associated with it and Jacques Baumel was assistant secretary. Claudius Petit led another wing of progressive Catholics from *Jeune République*, who sympathized with MRP. But the leader, René Pleven, had been a conservative finance minister under de Gaulle, and by 1948–49 the party was behaving almost as a Conservative group.[15]

13. For RGR see next section; for UDSR's early days, Williams, pp. 143–4.

14. Fauvet, *Forces*, p. 123; De Tarr, pp. 93–4 – one Radical summoned all republicans to quit 'this monster' which assembled fascists, clericals and socialists.

15. See for example *AP* 1949, pp. 58–9, 127, 131. Pleven was consistently supported by the [*over*

This central position and these multiple links made UDSR a useful indicator. Its birth marked the failure of one Communist bid for power – an attempt to exploit their influence within the Resistance. Its breach with the Socialists helped to frustrate a second bid – the organization of a Marxist coalition which the Communists hoped to dominate; for by repudiating the Socialist alliance UDSR helped to deprive the Marxist combination of an electoral and parliamentary majority. In turning against *tripartisme* (which a Resistance organization might have been expected to support) UDSR pointed the way the electorate was soon to follow. Although a nucleus of Gaullism and the group from which many of RPF's principal leaders came, it was the first of the parties which had permitted double membership to put an end to 'bigamy'. In spring 1948 Pleven tried to reconcile RPF and the government parties;[16] in June 1949 he could no longer retain both Gaullists and non-Gaullists in his own group; and by July 1950 he was leading a government designed, not to strengthen the majority on its Right by an understanding with RPF, but to restore it on the Left by bringing back the Socialists.

UDSR's relations with its Radical allies had been under severe strain during 1949 while UDSR opposed the Radical prime minister, Queuille. The friction was diminished by Pleven's option for the Third Force, but reappeared within RGR. There the anti-governmental forces remained strong enough to elect Daladier, the opposition Radical leader, as RGR president in May 1950.[17] UDSR was now firmly in the majority and considered abandoning RGR altogether; the combination held together for the 1951 election, but over the church schools problem in the following September most Radicals took the anticlerical side while most UDSR members voted for the Barangé bill. This provoked a clash outside Parliament, and at UDSR's Marseilles conference a month later the pro-Socialist wing, led by François Mitterrand, won control of the (rudimentary) organization. But the deputies remained faithful supporters of each ministry in turn, and voted as steadily for Pinay whom the Socialists opposed, as for Faure whom they had favoured.

UDSR's reconciliation with the governmental parties affected its own character as well as its external relations. At the centre of gravity of an Assembly whose majority was always precarious, it was the chief of those marginal formations whose support every ministry needed.[18] Like the pivot-parties of the Third Republic it was too small to be feared and too essential to be ignored. Thus on emerging as a governmental party it became a favoured recipient of ministerial spoils, and so increasingly attractive to deputies dependent on the sympathy of the administration – above all those representing colonial constituencies. In 1945 these, who were mostly settler members of Gaullist sympathies, made a third of UDSR's deputies. When the Gaullists

Conservatives in his department; Petit's candidature in 1946 was opposed by the local Radicals (De Tarr, p. 93) and in 1951 he stood on a joint list with MRP and CNIP.

16. UDSR had played this role before. When General de Gaulle quarrelled with the Communists in November 1945 and the Socialists early in January 1946, temporary compromises were found by UDSR members.

17. See below, pp. 177–8.

18. In February 1948 it had saved Schuman's first cabinet by abstention, and in September it destroyed his second: *AP* 1948, pp. 19, 154.

left UDSR in 1949 its parliamentary group fell from 27 to 14, only 5 from overseas. But a new overseas element was soon to enter and eventually to dominate the party. In 1950 Mitterrand, as minister of colonies, by his sympathetic handling of a crisis in Ivory Coast won the confidence of the *Rassemblement démocratique africain* (RDA), the main West African nationalist party. At the cost of a party split RDA broke its Communist links, began voting with the government, and entered into close relations with UDSR. After the 1951 election the 9 UDSR members returned from metropolitan France were reinforced by 14 overseas colleagues, and in 1956 the party, with a mere 6 French deputies, survived only by its pact with RDA.

UDSR therefore evolved from a predominantly conservative into a distinctly liberal group. Mendès-France chose Mitterrand as his minister of the interior and was supported by most UDSR members – though the conservative, 'European' and pro-clerical minority remained hostile to him, and Pleven was a bitter opponent. Such drastic shifts in policy could occur because the party was a group of leaders – members of parliament, local councillors and journalists – without strength among the electorate except where an individual deputy had built up a personal following. Having no membership, the organization was available for manipulation by rival leaders;[19] having no ideology, it held together – in spite of its divisions – until the end of the Fourth Republic. But Mitterrand's emergence in May 1958 as potential leader of a Popular Front, and his success in September in carrying the party against de Gaulle's proposed constitution, at last provoked Pleven, Claudius Petit and the old minority to secede. In the election two months later these two were the only survivors from UDSR.[20]

4. RGR, DISSIDENT RADICALS AND CONSERVATIVE GROUPS

Like UDSR, the *Rassemblement des Gauches républicaines* (RGR) was a federation of groups which developed into a separate political party – though the former did so very early in its life, the latter very late. RGR was an alliance between a major party (the Radicals), a middle-sized group (UDSR), and four small ghost parties of Third Republican politicians, mostly ineligible for Parliament under the purge legislation passed at the Liberation. It was formed in 1946 to unite all opponents of Marxism, of the Socialist-Communist draft constitution, and of clericalism. In the elections of June and November 1946 and June 1951 RGR served – as intended – as an electoral clearing-house. But it was also frequently used as a weapon in the struggle to control the Radical party, and in the election of January 1956 the defeated Radical faction took it over and turned it into a new party.[21]

The small components of the federal RGR were cliques centred around political leaders of a previous generation – for few French political movements ever completely disappear. *Alliance démocratique* had been one of the chief conservative organizations in the country, and even in 1939 it retained

19. Cf. Williams, p. 144 and n.

20. Mitterrand lost his seat (despite Communist support) but was returned to the Senate in 1959 – and to the Assembly in 1962.

21. On RGR-Radical relations see De Tarr, pp. 86–95, 133–4, and Bardonnet, pp. 156–60; for 1946, *ibid.*, p. 89.

thirty deputies. But at the Liberation its Resistance element went into PRL, leaving only the personal following of Pierre-Étienne Flandin, a former premier – and foreign minister under Vichy – who was ineligible for Parliament. Several of its members sat in the Assembly (as Conservatives, not as RGR representatives), and some held office – notably Pinay. Its general secretary headed the CNIP list in Dordogne in 1951, and in 1954 it left RGR altogether.[22]

A second small party in RGR was *Reconciliation française*, the remnant of Colonel de la Rocque's *Parti social français*. It was represented in the 1946 Assembly by Guy Petit, a parliamentary Peasant and the mayor of Biarritz, and in 1951 also by Pierre de Léotard, who affiliated to the Radical group; it had several sympathizers in the Conservative ranks. The *Parti socialiste démocratique* consisted of the friends of Paul Faure, who had been general secretary of SFIO for twenty years, leader of the pacifist opposition to Blum, and later a supporter of Pétain; one or two PSD members were to attempt a political comeback in the Fifth Republic. Lastly, the *Parti républicain socialiste* included a few politicians, mostly ex-Socialists, whose central position and pro-government voting records had earned them a large share of jobs in nearly every Third Republican ministry.[23]

The primary interest of these little groups was the return of their leaders to politics through the abolition of the ineligibility law (though most beneficiaries of its repeal in 1953 discovered that even their former constituents had entirely forgotten them). Early in 1951 these groups jointly affirmed their solidarity in opposition to the governments supported by their larger partners, Radicals and UDSR.[24] In the general election of 1951 most of their candidates were given places low on the list with no chance of success. But in Paris, where Radicals headed three lists out of six, UDSR, *Reconciliation française* and the Paul Faure Socialists led one each; though the last two lists gained no seat, one Radical (Lafay) pulled in Pierre de Léotard as his second. Over the whole country 17 constituencies out of 103 were fought by two different lists sponsored by RGR parties; however, only six of these involved outgoing RGR deputies – and in eight of the 17 the rival lists belonged to the same *apparentement* (alliance).[25]

The minor parties had some importance within RGR, since they were over-represented in its governing *bureau* and therefore strengthened the hand of those Radicals – like Daladier – who shared their hostility to the Third Force. In November 1949 Daladier was defeated by Herriot for the presidency of his own party; six months later minor-party votes elected him president of RGR.

22. Its political position had always been confusing: see below, p. 215. On Flandin see above, pp. 149, 152, and below, p. 210 n. 9; the ineligibility law was specially drafted to apply to him.

23. At the time of the constitutional referendum in September 1958 this defunct grouplet was suddenly resurrected and given radio and poster facilities to campaign for *OUI*.

24. *AP* 1951, p. 33. Two years later a Radical complained, 'The other little parties have scoffed at us brazenly, carrying their impudence to the point of insisting on our running candidates who represented nothing whatever and then using the clerical press (*la presse bien pensante*) to disown RGR': Bardonnet, p. 159n.

25. For the electoral law see below, Chapter 22; it multiplied hopeless contests, since only 'national parties' fighting in at least 30 departments could participate in alliances. Twelve of the 17 conflicts opposed a Radical list to a UDSR one; but seven of these twelve UDSR lists were apparently put forward only to bring UDSR's total up to 30.

Herriot resigned as RGR's honorary president and both UDSR and the pro-government Radicals complained that the election had been rushed and irregular.[26]

Daladier tried to strengthen RGR's power and prestige (and his own influence) by proposing the formation of a single RGR group in the new Assembly elected in 1951. A single group already existed in both the Council of the Republic and the Assembly of the French Union. But the Herriot Radicals promptly pointed to Article 61 of the party constitution which – if anyone remembered to invoke it – forbade Radicals to belong to more than one group. Separate Radical and UDSR groups were therefore retained in the Assembly, and Daladier had to content himself with the presidency of an inter-group embracing both. Shortly afterwards he moved to the Left, and the smaller parties in RGR transferred their support to the new leaders of right-wing Radicalism, René Mayer and Martinaud-Déplat.

These were the defectors who overthrew Mendès-France's government in February 1955. Edgar Faure (hitherto considered a man of the Left Centre) accepted the succession and so alienated his former friends and became the standard-bearer of the Right. After the Radical party came under Mendesist control, RGR ostentatiously elected Faure as its president. In December the Radicals expelled first the prime minister for dissolving Parliament, and then several right-wing leaders who refused to resign their posts as party delegates on the RGR *bureau*.[27] RGR was thus transformed into the organ of those Radicals who, under Faure's leadership, chose to fight the 1956 election in alliance with MRP and CNIP rather than with the Socialists. The new party contested 32 constituencies and won 12 seats.[28] It was soon to be overshadowed by a bigger Radical split, but personal rivalries impeded close co-operation between the various dissidents.[29]

Even before Herriot faced his troubles with RGR nationally he had had to meet a local challenge in his own Lyons fief. There the RGR secretary was a rich businessman, Léon Chambaretaud, who recruited individual members into RGR in opposition to the old leader. Not until May 1951 could Herriot persuade the Radical party to expel Chambaretaud and his friends. They retaliated by setting up the *Rassemblement des groupes républicains et indépendants français* (RGRIF) a sham 'national party' to which isolated candidates could attach themselves so as to form electoral alliances.[30] In some areas dissident Radicals and Socialists joined it, in others extreme right-wingers; some of its lists fought alone, but most were allied either with the Third Force

26. *Monde*, 7–8 and 9 May 1950. And see above, pp. 120–1.
27. De Tarr, pp. 133–4; Bardonnet, pp. 158–9.
28. In two seats sitting Radical and RGR deputies fought one another: in Seine-et-Oise north the former doubled his share of the poll (from $6\frac{1}{2}$ to $13\frac{1}{2}$%) while the latter raised his from $9\frac{1}{2}$ to 10%; in Vienne the former gained 2,000 votes while the latter lost 6,000 (two-fifths of his 1951 poll) and his seat. In Sarthe the 1951 Radical candidate stood as RGR and dropped from 13,000 to under 5,000 votes, while a Mendesist newcomer polled nearly 19,000. Four RGR leaders won a smaller share of the vote than in 1951, while Mendesist rivals almost overtook them. Faure increased his own share from about 25% to 35%; so did Mendès-France. See also Pierce, no. 180, p. 415.
29. See above, pp. 129–30.
30. For the subterfuges it used to claim the required total of 30 lists see below, p. 506–7. On Lyons see De Tarr, p. 94.

or with Conservatives (and one – in Yonne – with the Socialists). RGRIF won 5% of the vote in ten scattered departments and elected one Socialist member and five Conservatives;[31] Chambaretaud in Lyons polled enough votes to prevent the government parties securing an absolute majority and all the seats. RGRIF made a fleeting reappearance in 1956 as a satellite of RGR, and Chambaretaud himself stood as an RGR candidate, saying 'I chose the serious one'.

The 'national party' rule was responsible for the creation of yet another *ad hoc* conservative group in 1951: a Taxpayers' Defence movement (*Défense des contribuables*) based on the small business pressure-group *Petites et moyennes entreprises* (PME).[32] It opposed the government coalition and its lists mostly fought in isolation, but one accepted an alliance with other Conservative groups, two with RPF and four with the government parties; these seven included all the five departments in which its vote was over 5%. Its one deputy (Abel Bessac, of Lot) was an MRP member at odds with his party – but he still fought in alliance with the government coalition. The group disappeared in 1956 as its grievances were expressed by the Poujadists, who seem to have taken over most of its votes.[33]

Of all the oddities of French public life perhaps the most engaging is the royalist movement. During most of the twentieth century the driving force behind what was left of French monarchism came from the passionately nationalist and reactionary *Action française*. But a new pretender, the Comte de Paris, broke with family tradition. In the 1930's he disavowed *Action française*, and though he declared his support for Marshal Pétain in 1940 (and for General de Gaulle in 1958) he always insisted that a restored monarchy must repudiate authoritarianism and social and economic privilege. His political bulletin gave steady support to Third Force governments, called for better treatment of the working class, condemned EDC and favoured decolonization. His moderation and responsibility earned him widespread respect; indeed the pretendership was said to be the most ably filled political post in the Fourth Republic.[34] In 1950 Parliament, against opposition from the Communists and the Socialist senators, repealed the law of 1886 which had forbidden pretenders or their eldest sons to reside in France. Members of former reigning families could now stand for Parliament, but were still ineligible (under Article 44 of the constitution) for the Presidency of the Republic. The hereditary pretender's negligible chances of being called to power legally were improved when in 1958 the French people in fear of civil war turned to their self-made pretender, General de Gaulle. For the ban on Pretender-Presidents, retained in the first draft of the Fifth Republic's constitution, was dropped in the final version – allegedly at de Gaulle's wish.

31. On the Socialist (Arthur Conte of Pyrénées-Orientales), see below, p. 328. Some of the Conservatives (who sat for Aisne, Loire, Basses-Pyrénées, Haute-Saône and Gironde west) were open Pétainists. Another RGRIF candidate was Houdet, the rebel Gaullist in the 1949 Melun by-election (above, p. 143).

32. Goguel, *Fourth Republic*, p. 88; Fauvet, *Monde* 15 June 1951; on PME see below, pp. 361f.

33. *Élections 1956*, p. 404 (on Aisne). Bessac joined CNIP, and did not stand in 1956.

34. S. M. Osgood, *French Royalism under the Third and Fourth Republics* (The Hague, 1960), p. 204. On rival royalists see also Girardet, no. 99a.

5. COLONIAL GROUPS

Although developments in the French Union are not discussed in this work, colonial representation in Parliament had an impact on party politics which requires brief mention. The majority of overseas members joined major French parties; those representing native electorates preferred the Communists, Socialists or MRP, while settler members and pro-administration native deputies usually chose MRP in 1946, RPF in 1951, or the Radical party at any time. Their allegiance to their group was generally less close than that of their metropolitan colleagues. Extreme nationalists from Algeria, Madagascar and West Africa formed parties of their own which usually maintained loose links with the French Communists. During the life of the Fourth Republic moderate nationalists also set up several independent parliamentary groups.

The second Constituent Assembly included a dozen representatives of the *Union démocratique du Manifeste algérien* (UDMA); a decade later their leader Ferhat Abbas became the first prime minister of the provisional government of rebel Algeria. Although still a moderate in 1946, he protested against the colonial provisions of the new constitution and refused to contest the November elections. Most of the Algerian native seats then went to administration puppets or to moderate nationalists – who formed a short-lived separate group but soon drifted away into larger parties. But the extreme *Mouvement pour le triomphe des libertés démocratiques* (MTLD) of Messali Hadj elected half a dozen deputies, who usually voted with the Communists (though in November 1947 they supported Léon Blum for the premiership). They were all eliminated in the notoriously dishonest elections of 1951. The three nationalists from Madagascar also lost their seats at this time; they had been jailed since 1947, after a dubious trial, for instigating the great rebellion of that year.[35]

The chief moderate nationalist groups were the Overseas Independents (*Indépendants d'outre-mer*, IOM) whose leaders had often been trained in Catholic missions, and RDA which had a predominantly Moslem leadership.[36] IOM was formed in 1948, mainly by dissatisfied MRP, Socialist and Progressive deputies; for committee representation it affiliated to MRP. RDA broke its links with the fellow-travelling Progressives in 1950, and its members then affiliated to UDSR which they eventually came to dominate.[37]

In the 1956 elections the colonial administrators no longer tried to obstruct RDA (as they had still done in 1951 in spite of its parliamentary alliance with the colonial minister, Mitterrand).[38] IOM, Socialists and conservatives all lost ground to it, and RDA further strengthened its position in the

35. Tunisia, Morocco and Indo-China were protected states, so their native inhabitants had no parliamentary representation (though Cochin-China was till 1954 a colony and could – but never did – elect a deputy); but see below, pp. 209n., 294. For the French Union in the two 1946 constitutions see below, p. 293.

36. On African representation see Guillemin, no. 114. At RDA's 1957 conference 70% of the delegates were Moslem: A Blanchet, *L'itinéraire des partis africains depuis Bamako* (1958), p. 26.

37. See above, p. 176. Gabriel d'Arboussier, in 1950 secretary of RDA and leader of its pro-Communist minority, changed his mind and rejoined his old comrades seven years later.

38. Blanchet, pp. 18–19.

territorial assemblies elected in 1957 under the new liberal *loi-cadre*. This law, by granting home rule, was to accelerate subsequent political evolution.

RDA's success drew all its opponents together. Early in 1958 a new *Parti du regroupement africain* (PRA) was formed by the fusion of eight parties: IOM, recently renamed *Convention africaine*; the *Mouvement socialiste africain*, which had just formally separated from SFIO; and half-a-dozen parties confined to particular territories, which each faced RDA competition at home. RDA was in office and had to compromise; PRA was not.[39] It could outbid its rival by radical demands – for early independence, and for a Franco-African federation based on big regional units rather than separate territories – which found much favour within RDA itself. In 1958 the differences between the cautious RDA leader Houphouet-Boigny and his impatient rivals in and outside his own party dominated the debates on the Community provisions of the Gaullist constitution.

The overseas deputies naturally took a detached view of much French parliamentary business. They behaved, with growing effect, like territorial spokesmen in a federal senate.[40] Their efforts to influence developments north of the Sahara were unsuccessful; there they could never offset the parliamentary, still less the extra-parliamentary power of the settlers. But in Black Africa the electoral law was modified by their pressure as early as 1951, and from 1956 their views were decisive in policy-making for the tropical territories. Here, therefore, overseas representation in Parliament played an important part in the success of French decolonization. Through it the leaders who took over after independence acquired an invaluable political training, an intimate acquaintance with the political system of the metropolitan power, and an opportunity to work with her leaders and spokesmen as equal colleagues.

Looked at from within that political system, the role of the overseas parties illustrated the activities of minor groups in general. Those that were unwilling to compromise were driven – like the Progressives at home, and MTLD or the early RDA abroad – into accepting the patronage of the great party of all-out opposition, and so became identified in the public mind with Communism. If, however, they were prepared to use their votes for bargaining, they could exploit the advantages that the system conferred on all marginal groups. Because of the antagonism between natives and settlers, the net advantage to be gained from their support was nearer fifteen votes than eighty.[41] But the Constituent Assemblies had shown that fifteen overseas votes could well be decisive when the metropolitan members were evenly

39. Guillemin, no. 114, p. 877; cf. Grosser, p. 352, Blanchet, pp. 75–7, 84, 95–6, 102.

40. Guillemin, *loc. cit.*

41. There were 75 overseas deputies in 1946, 77 in 1949, 83 in 1951; but only 52 in 1956 as Algeria did not vote (see below, p. 209n.). Native voters usually chose native members, but in 1951 the colonial under-secretary Dr. Aujoulat transferred from the white constituency in his colony to the native one, proclaimed 'His face may be white but his heart is as black as a black man's', and was triumphantly elected. In 1956 Roger Duveau successfully followed the same course in Madagascar – though Aujoulat was defeated. Gabriel d'Arboussier (son of a French colonial governor and a Soudanese mother) won seats for RDA in Moyen-Congo, Niger and Ivory Coast and later became a Senegalese minister: Blanchet, p. 5; T. Hodgkin, *African Political Parties* (1961), p. 103.

divided.[42] In the Fourth Republic the moderate nationalists tended steadily to support successive cabinets in return for policy concessions, material advantages for their constituencies, and office for their leaders: IOM held a colonial under-secretaryship in seven cabinets and a full ministry in one, Houphouet-Boigny was a senior minister in the last four administrations of the Fourth Republic. Without the excitement and panache of violent agitation, the uninspiring process of bargaining quietly helped both sides. To their clients in Africa the native deputies brought steady if sometimes slow material and political progress. To French governments in trouble they brought a slight but useful reinforcement of ministerial stability. In these Negro leaders the traditional pivot parties of the Third and Fourth Republics had found apt pupils.

42. See below, p. 191.

PART III

THE INSTITUTIONS

Chapter 14

THE CONSTITUTIONAL PROBLEM

1. THE THIRD REPUBLIC

Political and institutional factors acted on one another to produce the governmental instability which characterized the Third Republic. But among its complex causes the most fundamental was the structure of political opinion in the country. For the politics of most Frenchmen were negative. They feared the revival of the reactionaries, the return to power of the groups which stood for a hierarchical society: the landlord, the Church, the great capitalist. They feared that a strong centralized administration would corrupt those who wielded power; ministers of the Left were as distrusted as those of the Right. They supported the Left politically, yet many of them feared social and economic experiment and opposed positive government.

Shaped to serve the purposes of this negative majority, the political institutions of the country had in turn increased its influence. Together the suspicion of governmental power and the fear of social change worked against strong parties and in favour of an electoral system which encouraged negative and individualist politics.[1] The single-member constituency allowed the deputy to entrench himself through local services in a stronghold from which he was hard to dislodge. The double ballot permitted every individualist politician and splinter group to gain publicity by contesting the first round without much risk of presenting the seat to the other side, and at the second it helped the negative voter to block the most dangerous candidate, whether he were a political reactionary or a social revolutionary. The Chamber therefore usually contained a chaotic welter of small groups. While most members came from the political centre, after 1918 they generally needed either clerical or socialist votes at the second ballot against a candidate of the other extreme. Consequently every centre group was internally divided according to the electoral situation of its individual members.

The immediate cause of governmental weakness in France was the artificiality and instability of parliamentary majorities composed from this unpromising material. The moderate supporters of every government feared that their more extreme associates would go too far in policy and so compromise their own electoral prospects; every majority therefore contained a minority awaiting the moment to change partners and enter a new majority. These divisions were counteracted by none of the factors of cohesion which reinforce British party discipline. In Britain a general election imposes a substantial fine on members of parliament, even when they run little risk of losing their seats; and the prime minister's right to dissolve if he is beaten gives him both a weapon against rebels in the house, who are rarely ready to risk a party defeat at an election, and a chance to appeal to the country on a clear-cut issue which divides his own party from its rival. But in France the deputy's re-election depended much more on his personal reputation; expulsion from the party

1. See below, pp. 307–8.

and competition from an official candidate held few terrors for a member whose following was so largely personal that he could distance the intruder on the first ballot and regain the lost votes on the second. The clash of opposing groups was never clear-cut. The head of the government was prevented from dissolving Parliament, not by constitutional law but by political convention.

The convention grew up early in the Third Republic, whose royalist founders had set up a regime designed to be transformed later into a monarchy. They gave the President of the Republic the right to dissolve the Chamber before its legal term was up, provided he obtained the consent of the Senate. Presidency and Senate would, it was hoped, be strongholds of conservatism against the assaults of a Chamber based on universal suffrage, and the dissolution would be their joint weapon for keeping the deputies in check. However, the first President, the monarchist Marshal MacMahon, dissolved the Chamber in 1877 for partisan purposes, tried unsuccessfully to use the administrative machine to secure a conservative majority in the new house, and so discredited the power of dissolution for eighty years. By 1879 the victorious Republicans controlled both houses and the presidency. Before the constitution was five years old the assumptions of its makers had broken down.

After 1879 Parliament would normally elect as President only a safe and mediocre man who would not challenge the authority of the elected house. The Senate passed gradually into the hands of the parties which already dominated the Chamber, and became less and less likely to consent to a dissolution directed against them. It was never asked to, partly because it was sure to refuse but even more because of the popular reaction to the crisis of 1877: thereafter dissolution was associated with an attempted *coup d'état*. Nor were a timid President, a hostile Senate and a suspicious public the only obstacles. French governments were too weak to pass the budget on time, and lived on appropriations voted monthly, so that a ministry wishing to dissolve the Chamber would probably have needed parliamentary consent to an unusually large credit. In 1934, when Doumergue's government seriously contemplated dissolution, its demand for a grant alarmed the Radical party into bringing it down.[2]

Members were therefore secure for four years. The overthrow of a cabinet did not threaten their seats and might indeed open the way to promotion, especially among the pivotal centre groups whose marginal position enabled them to raise 'a record crop of ministerial portfolios to the acre'. So the slight shifts of public or parliamentary opinion, which in Britain cause a trimming of policy or a government reshuffle, in France led always to a change of cabinet. But the practical effect was much the same, for as a rule most members of the old ministry passed straight into the new one.[3]

Besides the electoral system and the deputies' security of tenure, there were less important institutional causes for the weakness of French governments. The standing orders of the Chamber handicapped the administration: control of parliamentary time was jealously preserved by the house itself, and the

2. Soulier, pp. 559–60.
3. See below, p. 206. 'Record crop': Siegfried, *Tableau*, p. 169 (cf. *France*, p. 83).

right of interpellation allowed members to raise a short debate and enforce a vote on any subject. These procedures reflected a conception of politics which preferred a ministry safely subordinate to the representatives of the peoople to one strong and independent enough to govern effectively. So did the committees, which gave Parliament an alternative leadership to that of the cabinet. Each specialized in a sphere corresponding roughly to that of a government cepartment, and they developed a certain corporate sense. Their rapporteurs had opportunities for informed criticism of administration; their chairmen were *ex officio* potential ministers; both enjoyed personal influence and procedural advantages in the discussion of bills. In theory the government should not have suffered, since (from 1910) each committee was based on proportional representation and should have reflected the majority in the house. But that majority was shaky and heterogeneous, and accident might easily concentrate unreliable members in particular committees or positions of influence.

Yet a further obstacle to the power of the cabinet lay in the influential upper house.[4] To the maker of the Third Republic the Senate was the essential bulwark of conserative principles and interests against the danger of universal suffrage. As it was chosen by the local notables under an electoral system under-representing the cities, its composition was weighted heavily against the Left; and though the Radicals overcame these handicaps by ceasing to be radical, the proletarian parties never secured a real foothold in a second chamber far more powerful than the British House of Lords. Unlike a British peer, a senator was not removed from the main political battle, and if he became a minister he was entitled to speak in either house. The two houses had equal rights in legislation and finance (except that the Senate had no power of financial initiative). Senators formed about one-third and deputies two-thirds of the National Assembly of the Third Republic, which elected the President and could amend the constitution. And, since a senatorial seat was influential, sheltered, and tenable for nine years, it often attracted the ablest of the lifelong politicians from whose ranks the senators – again unlike the peers – were entirely drawn. Skilfully and patiently they built up their strength over half a century, never challenging the Chamber unless they were sure of victory. They hampered unpopular governments by blocking legislation, and in the last decade of the Third Republic began to encroach on the executive sphere: the Senate forced three ministries out of office between 1875 and 1929, four between 1930 and 1940.

Yet it was the political situation which made these institutional barriers serious obstacles to governmental authority. Early in the twentieth century the separation of Church and State had provided a real programme attracting a genuine majority. Under the Combes ministry the Chamber was managed by the *Délégation des Gauches*, a steering committee of the majority parties which dealt without difficulty with the interpellation nuisance and the committee danger. Interpellations which might threaten the government were adjourned *sine die*; the majority had a motive for unity and therefore held together to vote for the delay proposed by its leaders. Effective discipline was

4. See below, pp. 276–7.

applied in committees. The ministry, responsive to the wishes of its followers, fell only when its programme had been put into force and their loyalty had weakened.

The powers of the finance committee and Senate were also largely a function of a particular political situation. Since electoral necessity attracted the men of the Centre towards the Left, almost every Chamber opened with an apparent left-wing majority. But this disintegrated once economic and social questions came to the fore, and the search for a new combination began. The Senate and the finance committee owed much of their influence to their key roles in this recurrent struggle. Moderate Radicals, republican and anticlerical but terrified of social experiment, occupied a predominant position in the Senate and a pivotal one in the Chamber. Since the upper house was too cautious to risk its prestige by unsuccessful aggression, it moved against a government only when this crucial group of deputies was wavering. Apparently a rival institution, it behaved in fact as a reinforcement to its political friends in the Chamber. But the finance committee often acted in the opposite direction, focusing the opposition of those Centre deputies who still preferred the left-wing connection and disliked association with the Conservatives. In the recurrent manœuvre by which the Radicals and their friends reversed their alliances, the finance committee acted as a brake and the Senate as a goad.

This did not mean that the Senate was always on the Right. It expressed those negative views, hostile both to clerical reaction and to social change, which predominated in the country. In the 1880's it led the resistance to Boulangism; and of the four governments it destroyed in the 1930's two were of the Right, led by Tardieu and Laval, and two of the Left, under Blum. As the balance-wheel (or millstone) of the system, the Senate prevented policies or governments moving too far from the political centre of gravity. It could fulfil this traditional – but rarely achieved – function of a second chamber because it was so composed that its majority was in accord with the dominant section of the electorate. The roots of its power were more political than institutional. Governments were weak and programmes hard to carry, not because of the provisions of the constitution but because public opinion – or its principal elements – preferred weak government and inaction. That pressure determined the working of the institutions and dictated the character of the system.

The Third Republic was criticized by the Left because the popular house was too weak, by the Right because it was too strong. Socialists wished to abolish the Senate, conservatives to multiply restraints on the power of the Chamber. The Left looked back to the 'Convention government' (*régime d'assemblée*) of the revolutionary period with its omnipotent single chamber. The Right demanded a 'parliamentary government' of checks and balances based on the British constitution. Yet through stressing legal principles and ignoring political realities they had wholly misunderstood the institutions they so ardently admired. 'Parliamentary government' at Westminster in 1850 curiously resembled the Third Republic; and as over the next century its bulwarks were shorn away, the executive emerged far stronger than before.[5]

In Britain between the reform acts of 1832 and 1867 there were always more than two parties, weak, loose and inchoate. At general elections many contests turned on personal and local differences rather than political principles, and the majorities that emerged were highly unstable; only one of the nine Parliaments sustained a single premier throughout. Leaders had to rely on personal followings and skill in manœuvre in default of authority over an organized party. Every ministry, in name or in fact, was a coalition of diverse groups. Important political issues remained open questions on which ministers publicly disagreed. Cabinets survived or succumbed by tiny majorities, and a marginal group like the Peelites enjoyed preferential treatment in the distribution of offices. Occasionally, as in the Crimean war, a surge of revolt would sweep the benches and unite all elements against the administration. Despite the Lords, the Crown and the dissolution prerogative, the House of Commons was at the height of its power.

That power declined as the nominal authority of the House grew. The advance of democracy concentrated in the House more power than it could use effectively, and obliged it to impose tight discipline, organize into rigid blocks, and transfer its newly-extended authority to the government in order to get its business done. Approximating in theory to the omnipotence of an assembly without a rival, it fell in practice to the dependent status of a body which ratifies the decisions of the executive, and from which the parties appeal to the people and test their reactions. Today it only rarely behaves as an independent institution, almost always as a necessary link between cabinet and electorate. The distinction between 'Convention government' and 'parliamentary government' was therefore largely a legal fiction. Based on constitutional forms divorced from political realities, the concepts ignored the crucial factor: the rise of organized parties.[6]

2. THE DEBATE AT THE LIBERATION

The makers of the Fourth Republic gave themselves the impossible task of solving by constitutional arrangements a problem set, not by the forms of the law, but by the divisions of the people. French Republics had always lived dangerously. Since 1871 the regime had been threatened first by a counter-revolutionary Right, then by a revolutionary Left and finally by both. Because of the country's turbulent history and the power of the administration, republican tradition subordinated the executive to the legislature and accepted the high price of this settlement in governmental weakness and instability. Other democratic great powers have tried to avoid these disabilities. The

5. See the lament in *Economist*, 23 April 1853 (quoted *Economist*, 25 April 1953) and Disraeli's speech of 30 August 1848 (*Hansard* ci, col. 705–6). In French discussion 'Convention government' concentrates all power, judicial as well as executive, in a single chamber; 'parliamentary government' has an irresponsible chief of state, ministers responsible to a legislature which can be dissolved by the executive, and (normally) a second chamber and an independent judiciary.

6. Realistic French critics themselves found the concepts inapplicable: see quotations in Williams, p. 167n. For useful discussions see Théry, *Le Gouvernement de la IVe République* (1949), Chapter 5; Duverger, *Demain*, pp. 27–31, 59–61, 102–3, and *VIe*, pp. 42–4.

British solution uses strict party discipline to transform the nominal authority of the House of Commons over the government into the practical control of the government over the Commons; the American solution separates executive and legislature constitutionally, leaving each as master within a sphere which the other cannot conquer. But in France neither the strong, disciplined party nor the strong, independent executive was acceptable, for each aroused disquieting historical memories, and each was sponsored by a group whose democratic good faith was contested by its opponents.

General de Gaulle was alone in advocating a solution restricting parliamentary control over the executive.[7] The Left demanded the omnipotent assembly of revolutionary tradition; the Right and Centre feared that it would be abused by the parties which sponsored it – at worst by the Communists to impose their own dictatorship, at best by the Socialists to keep the executive in intolerable subjection. With the moderate parties insisting on checks and balances and the Left fearing that any prolonged dispute would play into de Gaulle's hands, the Fourth Republic finally came into being as a patchwork compromise, based on Socialist conceptions but tempered by concessions to the supporters of 'parliamentary government'. By 1947 its Socialist and MRP creators had to rely on the friends of the Third Republic for support against the Communist and Gaullist assaults, and the men of the old order, as they gradually regained influence and courage, attempted to adjust the system to their own purposes.

The Communist constitutional solution derived from the Convention of 1793 and the Paris Commune of 1871. It concentrated power in a single Assembly unchecked by any rival authority, electing the President, controlling the government, dominating executive, legislature and judiciary alike. This arrangement gave legal authority to the Assembly but effective power to the government. For a legislature bearing such responsibility would have to discipline itself, and amid several loose and conflicting parties a single coherent group, following a deliberate strategy and recognized leaders, would soon establish its preponderance.

If the Communist party accepted the rules of democracy, this solution would have many advantages. To compete with its power and numbers its opponents would have to coalesce into an equally powerful block, endowing France at last with a two-party system. For the Communist constitutional answer (taken at face value) was very much the same as the British: a legally omnipotent elected house which made its theoretical powers effective by handing them over to a committee of the majority. As in Britain, party discipline was the essential element in this arrangement, without which its advantages and drawbacks cannot be understood.

Such a system is tolerable only when there is confidence that the party in power will not subvert the democratic system; and Frenchmen feared that a two-party system with the Communists as one contestant would soon lead to civil war. Yet many good democrats were attracted to a similar constitutional solution – with safeguards against Communist predominance. In particular the Socialist party, which also accepted the revolutionary tradition and the

7. On it see below, pp. 191–2. He did not campaign for it until 1946.

single Assembly, joined the Communists in supporting the first draft constitution in April 1946. When that draft was rejected at the May referendum the parties of the Left had to compromise with MRP; but the October constitution was nevertheless based on Socialist ideas. Many of its principles and details could be found in Léon Blum's early work on governmental reform and Vincent Auriol's proposals for post-war reconstruction.[8]

The Socialists condemned the Third Republic for buttressing the power of conservative interests and encouraging a politics centred on personal and parochial squabbles rather than on a fundamental clash of policies. To meet the first fault they wanted to abolish the checks to the lower house by destroying the Senate's power and eliminating the Presidency of the Republic. To meet the second they advocated proportional representation in order to extend the politician's horizon, weaken local ties, end the demoralizing alliances of the second ballot, and elevate the tone of public life. They hoped to replace the old shifting, incoherent groups by powerful parties, each with its distinctive outlook and its disciplined following in and out of Parliament.[9] Elections would be fought on clear issues, so a definite majority would emerge and solve the problem of governmental stability. The Assembly would elect a prime minister whose government would represent the majority that had chosen him. This community of outlook would guarantee the security of the government, and it would no longer need means of pressure on the Assembly such as the vote of confidence so prodigally employed in the Third Republic. The executive being a projection of the legislature, the two would normally be in harmony and the stability of the former would be happily combined with the final authority of the latter.

In case of a clash the Assembly was to be able to turn the government out by a vote of no confidence; but to restrain the irresponsibility which had sometimes marred the Third Republic, a government defeat would lead automatically to the dissolution of the Assembly. In minor matters the deputies could instruct the government to change its policy, and the cabinet, unable to call for a vote of confidence, would be obliged to give way. This system would have secured the executive's stability at the price of its authority, for a government would have been subject to the pressure of its followers without effective counter-pressures against them. The plan, reflecting the traditional French democratic distrust of power and its holders, formed a natural basis for compromise in 1946 when government through a strong party seemed to imply Communist domination and a strong presidency meant power for de Gaulle.

Among the other democratic parties, the Radicals simply wished to retain as much as possible of the Third Republic. All Conservatives wanted to strengthen the executive and to impose barriers against the principal Assembly. MRP favoured constitutional provisions reflecting its Catholic and corporative outlook: one characteristic suggestion was to give extra votes to parents

8. Blum, *La Réforme gouvernementale*, especially pp. 39, 62–3, 150–3, 163, 167–9, 175–9, 218, 222–7; Auriol, *Hier ... Demain*, ii. 21, 23, 31, 33, 38, 51, 142, 197–8, 208, 223, 239–40, 249, 261, 273, 285.

9. See below, pp. 387–8. Like the founders of the United Nations they built a constitutional structure on political sand, wrongly postulating that the 'great powers' of the moment would continue in alliance. (I owe this point to Professor Wahl.)

according to the number of their (legitimate) children. Like the Conservatives and Radicals it waged its main constitutional fight to preserve checks and balances and allow the executive some independence.

The debate took place under a provisional regime planned by de Gaulle before the Liberation. Both he and the politicians had known that its structure might well influence the shape of the final constitution, and as the parties were unanimous in demanding that the provisional government must be responsible to the Constituent Assembly (if in nothing else), the General gave way to their insistence.[10] In the first Assembly the Left parties had a majority, and after de Gaulle's resignation they carried their draft constitution; it was rejected at the referendum of May 1946. In the second, the struggle turned on the selection and powers of the President and second chamber, the electoral law, the machinery for constitutional amendment, and the independence of the judiciary. As MRP generally sided with the Right, the balance was very even and several major issues were decided by tiny majorities; the votes of a few colonial members were crucial, and disgruntled conservatives bitterly attacked the 'Madagascar constitution'.

Paul Coste-Floret, the MRP rapporteur of the second constitutional draft, warned that in France presidential government would mean dictatorship (*pouvoir personnel*) and Convention government like that of 1793 would lead to revolution; democracy would work only in a compromise system where Parliament and executive were balanced.[11] The constitution-makers were thus neither able nor willing to erect a new structure, and tried only to repair the faults that the old one had revealed in its years of decline. Article 13 was supposed to prevent the Assembly delegating its legislative power, since timid Chambers in the 1930's had often abdicated and left the government free from parliamentary control. Article 94 forbade constitutional amendment when part of France was under enemy occupation; it belatedly denied validity to the vote of 10 July 1940 conferring full powers on Marshal Pétain, but did not prevent another Republic committing suicide quite constitutionally, in 1958, under threat of 'military usurpation'.[12]

3. THE FOURTH REPUBLIC AND AFTER

The campaign to amend the new constitution began before it was adopted. At Bayeux in June 1946 de Gaulle warned his countrymen that the new institutions were wholly misconceived. In French conditions an executive dependent on Parliament could not be stable; therefore the executive must be independent of Parliament. In normal times this was the only way to remove power from the feeble and factious parties, and in a crisis like that of 1940 it would permit a President to go into exile as a National Assembly of nine hundred men could not.[13] The President would be chosen by an electoral college

10. Théry, pp. 15–16; Wright, *Reshaping*, pp. 82–4; and cf. below, p. 200 and n.

11. *JO* 20 August 1946, p. 3185. He summed up: '. . . if we condemn presidential government and rule out Convention government, we are obliged to revert to . . . parliamentary government'.

12. 'Usurpation': de Gaulle's broadcast of 8 June 1962. On Arts. 13 and 94 see below, pp. 270–275, 302.

13. *AP* 1946, p. 163. Under Article 45 of the 1946 constitution ministers could be appointed only after the election of the premier, 'except when a case of *force majeure* prevents the meeting

[*over*

comprising the two houses of Parliament supplemented – or swamped – by representatives of various aspects of the national life. Rooted in French history, this was a presidential conception resembling George Washington's and not Franklin Roosevelt's. The Founding Fathers of the United States, who had wished to shelter the President from popular pressures and 'factions', were frustrated by the rise of parties. Now de Gaulle was determined to weaken the parties by instituting an electoral college which they could not control.[14]

While the proposed President would choose and dismiss his ministers, they would also be responsible to Parliament – a contradiction resolved neither in the General's sketchy statements nor later in the Fifth Republic (where peace in Algeria was promptly followed by a trial of strength). He could submit to a referendum a bill on which the government suffered parliamentary defeat, and in case of political deadlock he could, with his ministers' consent, dissolve the Assembly.[15] But the deputies would be unable to rid themselves of a chief executive enjoying both the American President's security of tenure and the British premier's power to coerce Parliament. Where the first is weak in dealing with Congress and the second must watch for shifts in the floating vote, he would enjoy the advantages of both offices without suffering the checks imposed upon either.

Such a regime had many precedents in French history. In its theoretical structure it had affinities with both the Second and Third Republics. In its popular support it reflected that Bonapartist demand for a republic with real authority which, as Siegfried remarked seventeen years before the sudden ascent of RPF, was a latent force always liable to explode with eruptive violence.[16] But the General failed to impose his constitution as the Communists failed to introduce theirs, since until 1958 most Frenchmen feared an overweening President no less than a preponderant party.

Although the Gaullist campaign for major reconstruction failed, the constitution of the Fourth Republic was nevertheless amended, like that of the Third, before it was ten years old. The underlying reason in both cases was a shift of power away from the groups which had held it in the aftermath of war: royalist advocates of immediate peace in 1871, disciplined parties of the Left in 1946. Each of these had enjoyed an artificial parliamentary majority and shaped a constitution to fit its own purposes; when the excluded groups returned in force they set about changing the new institutions to suit themselves. The National Assembly of the Fourth Republic resolved on

of the National Assembly'; the proviso was introduced in answer to de Gaulle's criticisms: Théry, p. 117n. (see *La France sera la France*, p. 41, for de Gaulle's statement of 27 August 1946, and cf. above, p. 132n.).

14. In the constitution of the Fifth Republic the electors were parliamentarians, members or delegates of local authorities, and overseas representatives. In 1962 de Gaulle, by referendum, introduced direct election of the President.

15. Asked what would happen if President and ministers disagreed, he replied that in his system this could not happen: *La France sera la France*, p. 49, quoted Williams, p. 162n. In the Fifth Republic the President could dissolve without ministers' consent, and the referendum provisions were also slightly different.

16. See above, p. 141n. For the Gaullist constitution in practice see Williams and Harrison, Part III; D. Pickles, *The Fifth French Republic* (2nd. ed., 1962).

30 November 1950 to amend eleven articles of the constitution; four years later to the day, after elaborate negotiations to assemble an adequate majority, it finally passed the specific amendments.[17] Following the post-war trend, these changes marked a partial return to the constitutional practice of the Third Republic, particularly over the choice of a premier and the powers of the second chamber.[18]

They did not satisfy the revisionists, and within eight months both houses called for further amendments to 28 articles: 23 affecting the French Union and 5 others, notably those regulating the election or ejection of a prime minister by the Assembly. Nothing effective was done for two years, although in the last weeks of the Fourth Republic frantic but ineffective efforts were made to amend these five articles. But members of parliament were prepared to consider only marginal adjustments to the details of the existing system, while opinion in the country was growing increasingly critical of the structure itself. Domestic reformers feared that without a major institutional change, ingenious schemes to prevent the deputies overthrowing a cabinet every six months would merely lead them to install as prime minister a man who would offend nobody – and therefore achieve nothing – even if he survived for five years.[19] Nationalists were convinced that the overseas empire was doomed unless the central power in Paris could be greatly strengthened. Critics on all sides denounced 'the System' by which a Parliament of multiple parties and shifting coalitions excluded strong personalities from power, and deprived the ordinary citizen of any sense of participation in the government of his country.

Although presidential government had long been anathema to good republicans, it attracted some support during the second world war, notably from Léon Blum. In 1956 the cause was revived by Professors Vedel and Duverger, who pointed to significant similarities between the structure of French and American opinion and argued that the people could regain a sense of political participation only if they directly elected the chief executive. Gaullist critics contended more bitterly that the self-seeking parliamentarians had filched sovereignty from the people in whose name they claimed to exercise it. René Capitant pointed to their aversion, not only to the referendum, but to any electoral law which might allow the voters to designate a government or express a clear political demand. Michel Debré, de Gaulle's chief constitutional adviser, accused the politicians of the System of deliberately dividing the nation, raising false controversies and obstructing reforms: he threatened them with imminent revolution unless they promptly mended their ways.[20]

Within months the regime had collapsed under the strain of the Algerian

17. See below, pp. 302–3.

18. On the trend see above, p. 35. On the reform, Campbell, no. 46, Goguel, no. 110, Macridis, no. 151, Pickles, no. 175, Pierce, no. 179, Williams, no. 221; Poutier, *La Réforme de la Constitution*; Drevet, *La procédure de révision de la Constitution du 27-10-1946*; and below, pp. 210, 212, 216–17, 226–9, 237, 239–40, 283–5.

19. See below, p. 241.

20. See Goguel, no. 111; Capitant, preface to Hamon, *De Gaulle dans la République*, pp. iii–vi; Debré, *Ces princes qui nous gouvernent*; Lavau, no. 140; Duverger, *Demain, passim.* Most of these critics were more 'presidential' than de Gaulle himself.

war. The Gaullists came to power and Debré became the main architect of the new hybrid system, the only variant of presidential government to enjoy organized political backing. The parties which had hesitated to make constitutional amendment too easy were now coerced into letting the ministry draft its own proposed constitution; and after refusing to consider a normal presidential system with an independent legislature, they had now to accept a deviant form overwhelmingly dominated by the executive. In September 1958 four-fifths of the voters, disillusioned with the parliamentary republic which had twice failed within twenty years, yet still opposed to the Communists, turned to de Gaulle and accepted the constitutional solution which he had vainly proposed in 1946.

As general staffs are sometimes said to prepare for the last war, the politicians who made the Fourth Republic in 1946 had prepared for the last constitutional crisis. Later parliamentarians who tried to reform the system did so within the same narrow limits, and as early as 1948 the results of their efforts were summed up in the phrase, 'The Fourth Republic is dead, it has been succeeded by the Third'. In terms of constitutional practice Part III of this book is a commentary on that contemptuous verdict. Nevertheless historical experience – and indeed the sequel – give little ground for believing that a stronger regime would have survived without disruption and disaster the tremendous shock of decolonization and the diminution of French power in the world.

Chapter 15

THE PRESIDENT AND THE CABINET

The makers of the Fourth Republic were anxious to diminish the importance of the President of the Republic who was not responsible to Parliament, and increase that of the prime minister who was. In this aim they failed completely. Although the President's powers were strictly limited by the constitution, Vincent Auriol became more influential than any of his predecessors and René Coty, though less active, intervened spectacularly in the crisis of 1958. But while the presidency proved stronger than had ever been intended, the premiership never became the driving force for which the constitution-makers had hoped. The political foundations on which they relied proved shifting and unstable, and instead of the leader of a united team, almost every premier had to be a broker between rivals over whom he had little control.

1. THE PRESIDENCY

The royalists who created the Third Republic had designed it to be transformed into a monarchy as soon as they could agree on a king. Prominent among the bulwarks which they established against the menace of democracy was the Presidency of the Republic. But because of its imposing nominal powers, it was feared and restrained in a number of ways. There was legal restriction: every official act of the President except his resignation required the countersignature of a minister. There was political convention: after 1877 no President ventured to ask the Senate to approve a dissolution of the Chamber. There was also the silent but effective method of keeping dangerous men out of the office. Professor Brogan observed of the first four incumbents that

> Thiers had been chosen as the greatest living French statesman, MacMahon as the most honourable French soldier: Grévy had been elected in 1879 because of what he had said in 1848, Carnot was elected in 1887 because of what his grandfather had done in 1793.[1]

In the Second Republic direct election by the people had made Louis Bonaparte President and then Emperor. In the Third such dangers were avoided; the President was elected for seven years by the two houses of Parliament sitting together as a National Assembly. Its members sometimes made a mistake and chose an assertive man who had to be removed, like Casimir-Périer in 1895 and Millerand in 1924; even Poincaré might not have survived without the first world war. More commonly 'a deep instinct' led Parliament to cast its secret ballot against any strong leader, and Gambetta was beaten by Grévy, Ferry by Carnot, Waldeck-Rousseau by Félix Faure, Clemenceau by Deschanel and Briand by Doumer. As J. J. Weiss remarked in 1885, 'The fundamental principle of the constitution is or ought to be that the President hunts rabbits and does not govern'.[2]

1. *The Development of Modern France*, p. 198.
2. Quoted Théry, p. 29, and Dansette, *Histoire des Présidents*, p. 353. 'Deep instinct': Siegfried, *De la IIIe*, p. 36.

In this tradition the Left in 1945–46 regarded his office as either useless or dangerous. The first draft constitution reflected its desire for a puppet President, who was to be elected by an open ballot of the National Assembly. When this draft was rejected at the referendum of May 1946 the Left made concessions, agreeing to election by a clear majority in a secret ballot of members of both houses, as in the Third Republic.[3] This seemed unimportant politically, for although the senators had enabled the Right to dominate the presidential electorate in the past, the new Council of the Republic was to be so chosen that its political composition would reflect that of the Assembly. But in 1948, when the conservative parties had grown stronger, they adopted a method of electing the upper house more advantageous to themselves. Their victory over the presidential electoral college thus acquired new importance.[4]

There was another struggle over the President's powers. The Third Republic had made him both formal chief of the state and nominal head of the executive, but had robbed him of prestige by subjecting him to nomination by Parliament, and of power by requiring a ministerial countersignature for everything he did. An adroit President could affect domestic affairs by skill in picking prime ministers, and foreign policy by advice to which his status, experience and long tenure gave weight. But his paper authority far exceeded his real influence. The makers of the Fourth Republic set out to correct this discrepancy.

The President was still to sign treaties, receive ambassadors, remain nominal commander-in-chief and preside over the National Defence Council. He took the chair in the cabinet, and was to keep its minutes (a politically crucial innovation in France as in Britain).[5] High officers and officials were appointed by him in a cabinet meeting. He kept some prerogatives which had lain dormant in the Third Republic: the right to address messages to Parliament, which was to prove unexpectedly important in 1958, and to refer bills back for a second deliberation, which was soon found very useful. No bill was ever referred back in the Third Republic, but a dozen were under the provisional government (where there was no revising chamber, and no risk of friction when the premier was himself acting head of the state), and a dozen more in the Fourth Republic.[6]

The President granted pardons in the High Council of the Judiciary, a new body over which he presided and of which he chose two members out of

3. The Left had feared that a secret ballot would help de Gaulle to win by allowing their members to break party discipline, as they had done in the past. They wanted to require a two-thirds majority (or three-fifths from the fourth ballot). The Right would have liked half, and the Gaullists a large majority, of the electoral college to be non-parliamentary.

4. See below, p. 277 (and cf. n. 29). Even without the change the two houses would have differed politically once they were elected at different times; but it was the first election which might have installed de Gaulle.

5. He presided at the *conseil des ministres* but not the *conseil de cabinet*, at which the premier took the chair and junior ministers attended; it met rarely in the Fourth Republic, except under Mendès-France. See F. de Baecque (who was on Coty's staff) in *Les Institutions politiques de la France* (henceforth cited as *Institutions*), i. 201, 234–8, 264–5; Arné, *Le Président du conseil*, pp. 77–9, 90–1; Drago, no. 76; on minutes also Dansette, *Présidents*, p. 324, Siegfried, *De la IIIe*, p. 229.

6. See below, pp. 198 (appointments), 203 (messages), 200 (bills referred back); on the provisional government, Théry, p. 66.

fourteen. Together with the President of the Council of the Republic he could initiate the procedure for deciding whether a new law was in conformity with the constitution.[7] Above all he could nominate candidates for the premiership, and not merely (as in the first draft constitution) transmit possible names to the President of the Assembly. But since almost all his other acts needed a ministerial countersignature, he seemed to have gained more in formal status than in real power.[8]

2. VINCENT AURIOL

The constitution-makers failed to weaken the Presidency; instead its influence increased, thanks to the vigour and determination of the first incumbent – who had once advocated abolishing the office he was to fill so successfully.[9] Vincent Auriol, the first Socialist President, had entered the Chamber in 1910, served under Blum as minister of finance in 1936, and voted against Marshal Pétain in 1940. While interned by Vichy he sketched proposals for constitutional reform which 'the constitution of the Fourth Republic followed more closely than any French constitution had ever followed a theoretical work'.[10] At Algiers in 1943 he became the chief mediator between General de Gaulle and the politicians, and after the return to France he was President of both Constituent Assemblies and acted as unofficial President of the Republic in ministerial crises. In the interminable conflicts of constitution-making he was a tireless producer of compromise solutions.[11] It was appropriate that the man most responsible for the conception and delivery of the new Republic's constitution should become its first official head.

More unexpected was the position he built up, unlike any previous President, as the most influential personality in France. An astute and gregarious southerner, Auriol was at his best in managing the parliamentarians, whom he understood and esteemed. The multiplicity and weakness of the parties and the inexperience of the new leaders gave him advantages which he neither abused nor neglected. Disliking some of the policies and personalities of his old party, he developed into a 'governmental Radical'; and without flouting the proprieties he emerged as a vigorous public defender of French interests abroad and the Fourth Republic at home:

Above the ministers, urging one on and blocking another, having his favourites and often choosing them badly, advancing easily through the parliamentary jungle, striving as if he revelled in the task to find a compromise between men, parties, bills or programmes; involving himself in public affairs beyond his constitutional powers, creating a presidency to his own measure, on occasion relieving a minister of a

7. See below, pp. 299, 305. *Le droit de grâce* covers reprieves and commutations as well as pardons *stricto sensu*.

8. No countersignature was needed for these nominations, which were not effective until approved by the Assembly: Théry, p. 111, Fabre, no. 88, p. 197n., Arné, p. 44; nor for some of his acts as chairman of the High Council of the Judiciary and Constitutional Committee and as President of the French Union: see p. 199 below and nn. 15, 17, 19.

9. Auriol, ii. 234ff. Similarly Jules Grévy, twice President of the Third Republic, had in 1848 proposed a republic without a president. For Auriol's term see Dansette, *Présidents*, Chapter 16; Arné, pp. 67–8, 76–7, 81–2; Pickles, no. 176; Merle, no. 158.

10. Priouret, *Partis*, p. 45; and see above, p. 109n.

11. Wright, *Reshaping*, pp. 151–216 *passim*.

difficult file or bombarding him with a technical note, bullying officials, presiding, travelling, proclaiming, talking a great deal, listening less often, the chief of state: M. Auriol.[12]

As a chairman who was more informed and experienced than the ministers, he could play a major part in cabinet debate. One observer records a foreign policy discussion which President Auriol concluded by turning to the silent prime minister to ask his views; another says it was occasionally hard to tell where presidential advice ended and ministerial decision began. A minister notes, 'his natural dynamism sometimes overcame his perfect courtesy'. In January 1950 it was the President who insisted that the government must act against Communist sabotage of national defence and the Indo-China war. On all major appointments his advice had to be heard, and in practice he generally enjoyed a veto. Outside the cabinet room he had ample opportunity to influence individuals, delegations and audiences.[13]

His views carried most weight in the traditionally presidential fields of foreign affairs and defence. In the Fourth Republic, unlike the Third at times, the President had full access to all diplomatic documents. He was chairman of the National Defence Council, a consultative body which met rarely, and of the defence committee of ministers and soldiers; and he gained unexpected influence simply by continuing in office through the frequent changes in the premiership and defence ministry and the many reorganizations of the defence departments. Auriol used foreign visits, like that to the United States in April 1951, for a vigorous public and private presentation of the French case. He did not conceal his opposition to German rearmament and his irritation with America for supporting it. And he was violently attacked by Communists for denouncing the Cominform's subversive activities, defending the Atlantic pact, condemning the 'iron curtain' and advocating effectively controlled disarmament. In a vigorous defence of his conception of the office, Auriol refused to become a silent figurehead and argued for a 'moral magistracy' entitled to advise, warn and conciliate; impartiality was not indifference. 'Never', a perspicacious observer of his conduct had written early in his term, 'would the Third Republic have tolerated a First Magistrate departing so far from his position of arbiter.'[14]

Auriol was particularly active in two fields where he enjoyed specific constitutional authority: the imperial and the judicial. 'Beyond the vicissitudes of ministries,' wrote Dansette, there was 'an Élysée policy of the French Union'. Though Auriol was a Socialist, and was later to oppose Guy Mollet over Algeria, this policy was not always particularly liberal. Nor was it

12. Fauvet, *IVe*, p. 130. See also Dumaine, pp. 190, 515; Merle, no. 158, p. 295; Dansette, *Présidents*, pp. 267–8 ('most influential'), 325 ('Radical').

13. *Ibid.*, pp. 267–8 (silent premier); Bertrand, *Les techniques du travail gouvernemental*, p. 37 (advice and decision); *AP* 1950, p. 9 (Indo-China); Siegfried, *De la IIIe*, p. 230, Goguel, *Régime*, p. 52, and Georgel, i. 91–2 (appointments); Dumaine, p. 157 (delegations); Arné, pp. 71, 74–7, 81–3, 137. Auriol failed in an epic struggle with Robert Schuman over one appointment (of a cultural director at the Quai d'Orsay): Grosser, pp. 44–5. 'Dynamism': Buron, p. 223.

14. Dumaine, p. 190. See also Suel, no. 206; Grosser, pp. 44–6; Arné, pp. 68, 84–2; Baecque in *Institutions*, i. 196–8; Goguel, *Régime*, p. 51; Merle, no. 158, pp. 300–1; *AP* 1951, pp. 291–2, 669. 'Moral magistracy': Dansette, *Présidents*, p. 270; Georgel, i. 88–9; Pickles, no. 176, p. 111; Arné, p. 68; Drago, no. 76, p. 167.

invariably decisive, but it was actively pursued, especially in his later years. Auriol's talks with the ex-emperor Bao Dai over Vietnamese independence in 1949 were described as the most personal presidential conduct of a negotiation for decades, and three years later he received the same sovereign alone in the absence of the responsible minister, Jean Letourneau. He dispensed with ministerial countersignature for his later letters to other heads of state, including the monarchs of the protectorates; and in the Tunisian crisis of March 1952 he both proposed and drafted an important letter to the Bey.[15]

His second special interest was the administration of justice. The committee on the first draft constitution had reached unwonted unanimity in assigning to the head of the state the presidency of the new High Council of the Judiciary. Within it, he had a casting vote on disciplinary matters and a virtual veto on judicial appointments and promotions. President Auriol watched carefully over the High Council's development, which was difficult both because the ministry of justice resented being partly superseded by the Council, and because some governments brought pressure on it over specific cases. His support was indispensable to its independence. In April 1950, for example, when the cabinet wished to discuss the acquittals of accused Communists, the President insisted that these were matters for the High Council alone. Occasionally he took bolder action, as in October 1948 when he intervened both with the High Council and the senior judges to urge rigour in applying the laws against speculation in foodstuffs.[16]

In 1946 the Communists had tried unsuccessfully to deprive the President of the right of pardon, which at that time (as later in the Fifth Republic) had great political importance. The first draft constitution transferred this right to the High Council; the second provided that the President should exercise it in that body. In practice he was bound neither by the ministerial countersignature, which was automatic, nor by the High Council's views. While he always followed these in lesser cases, reprieve from a death sentence was recognized as his personal prerogative; he commuted two-thirds of those passed between 1948 and 1953. Auriol was to use the right of pardon very liberally in amnestying minor offenders from the occupation period and correcting the sharp discrepancies in sentences awarded by different courts and at different dates. He used it also in one major political case to reprieve the Malagasy deputies implicated in the rising of 1947. Like de Gaulle he took these duties very seriously; they were estimated to occupy a third of his time, and he called them 'my most onerous responsibility'.[17]

15. 'Élysée policy': Dansette, *Présidents*, pp. 325–6; qualifications in Grosser, p. 47. Bao Dai: *ibid.*, p. 46, for 1952 and Berlia, no. 13b, pp. 910–1, for 1949. Countersignature: *ibid.*; *Institutions*, i. 205, 210; Merle, no. 158, p. 301; but cf. Arné, pp. 72, 73n. It was clearly not required for appointments to his own *cabinet* or to the new French Union secretariat, headed by a Moslem Algerian prefect, which he set up in March 1952. On Auriol's Indo-China policy see Fauvet, *IV*[e], pp. 253, 255.

16. On the High Council see below, pp. 293–4; also *Institutions*, i. 206 (discipline and appointments), 210 (countersignature); Arné, pp. 76–7; *AP* 1950, p. 76, and *Monde*, 24 April 1950 (Communists); *ibid.*, 16 October 1948 (speculation).

17. Personal prerogative: see Berlia, no. 13b, pp. 912–4 for fullest discussion, also *Institutions*, i. 196, 210; Arné, pp. 72–3; Dansette, *Présidents*, pp. 270–1, 326; Siegfried, *De la IV*[e], p. 208; Théry, p. 42. 'Pardon': see n. 7. Communists: Fajon in *Séances de la Commission de la Constitution* (first Constituent Assembly, cited as *SCC* I), p. 124. Malagasies: see below, p. 211 (but even

[*over*

These functions were conferred on the President because he was supposed to stand above party quarrels and watch over the permanent interests of the state. Similarly he was the natural spokesman in a national emergency, and in 1947 he presided over a committee, representing every party and religious denomination, which appealed to the peasants to send wheat quickly to the hungry towns.[18] His services could be called upon in a constitutional deadlock, and he was chairman of the new Constitutional Committee which decided whether a newly-voted law infringed the constitution.[19] Paul Coste-Floret, rapporteur of the second Constituent Assembly, described him as 'guardian of the constitution'.[20]

In this unwritten role Auriol always acted circumspectly. He never used his right to send special messages to Parliament.[21] He refused to intervene during the 1947 strikes, when CGT asked him to refer back to Parliament the drastic public order bill which had just been voted against furious Communist obstruction; in January 1948, when the Communists objected to the allocation of vice-presidencies in the Assembly; and in July 1949, when Herriot as its President protested against alleged unconstitutional behaviour by the second chamber.[22] Although Coste-Floret had spoken of his right to refer bills back for a second deliberation as 'fundamental', Auriol knew that its abuse might merely provoke the Assembly to reassert its own view and so damage the prestige of the presidency. He found it a useful way out of political difficulties, notably to resolve two conflicts between the houses (once at the request of the Constitutional Committee and once as an alternative to it). But both he and his successor were wary of using it on matters of political controversy.[23]

While Auriol did not try to extend his powers for the benefit of his office or his party, he did employ all his personal and constitutional influence on behalf of the parliamentary Republic which he believed he had been elected to defend. In 1947 he encouraged (if he did not suggest) Ramadier's dismissal of his Communist ministers. At the height of the Gaullist challenge he emerged both publicly and privately as the leader of the Third Force, denouncing RPF's agitation for new elections as fatal to political stability, insisting that in a republican constitution ministers must be responsible to Parliament, and encouraging conservative politicians to split the attacking forces.[24] Whenever

Auriol could not overcome proconsular arrogance, and the leading witness was deliberately executed before the reprieve could arrive: Grosser, p. 47). Two-thirds: Pickles, no. 176, p. 112 (624 out of 988). 'Most onerous': Auriol to *Figaro*, 9 December 1953, quoted *ibid.*

18. *AP* 1947, p. 104; Arné, p. 81.

19. See below, pp. 305–6. He needed no countersignature to summon it or sign its minutes, but did to inform the Assembly of its decision: Soulier, no. 203, p. 213.

20. *JO* 20 August 1946, pp. 3187–8 (quoted Arné, pp. 57, 66).

21. Below, p. 203. All Presidents sent an inaugural message.

22. Pickles, no. 176, p. 109; also *AP* 1947, p. 243 and Arné, p. 80 (CGT; the non-Communists supported the appeal); below, pp. 237 (Communists), 281 (Herriot).

23. It was proposed by the government (Baecque in *Institutions*, i. 207) and ministers had to countersign: Soulier, no. 203, p. 213, and Drago, no. 75, p. 405. Coste-Floret: *JO* 13 September 1946, p. 3701. For the conflicts between the houses below, pp. 305–6. Eight bills were referred back in the first Parliament, three in the second and one in the third: Baecque, *loc. cit.* Only one was important; it was not discussed again for four years (Arné, p. 71, and below, p. 211n.) and some never were: see Williams, p. 177 and n.

24. Communists: Dumaine, p. 170; Siegfried, *De la IIIe*, p. 155, *De la IVe*, p. 208. Gaullists: at Quimper on 31 May and at Bordeaux on 14 June: *AP* 1948, pp. 332–3; Arné, pp. 67, 81–2; below, p. 433.

a government fell it was his duty to find a new premier who could command a majority; and Auriol probably had more success in getting the man he wanted than any other President. In November 1947 he chose a leader of MRP, which had just suffered a catastrophic electoral defeat; in July 1948 he announced the designation of André Marie in a statement which committed the nominee to a specific political programme, and he persuaded SFIO to reverse its decision not to join the government. Repeatedly he protected 'his' majority by refusing the resignation of a cabinet or putting pressure on the parties, especially his own. In 1952 he put forward Pinay, who split RPF; and in his last long crisis, in 1953, he incurred severe criticism both by his choice of candidates and by his unprecedented communiqués urging Socialists and Gaullists to refrain from wrecking tactics: 'veritable appeals to public opinion' over the heads of the angry and resentful parties.[25]

Communists and – ironically – Gaullists accused him of breaking the tradition of a non-controversial presidency, condemned him for behaving as the leader of the System and not of the nation, and vented their resentment by a disreputable slander campaign against his family and associates. The other parties, including his own, attacked him for interventions which they found inconvenient. But admirers could claim that 'Auriol was a great President of the Republic; no President of the Third Republic participated so directly and so effectively in the life of the state' [26]

3. RENÉ COTY

Vincent Auriol's tenure of the Presidency won him great popularity in the country, raised the status of the office, led to an unprecedented struggle for an unexpectedly desirable succession – and damaged his own hopes of winning a second term from politicians suspicious of men with extra-parliamentary reputations. Moreover, his handling of his last ministerial crisis had offended MRP, Gaullists, Mendesists and SFIO; the Socialists did propose his re-election to break a deadlock, but they found no support at all.[27]

The 'parliamentary congress' which elected Auriol in 1946 had been governed by conventional rules: personal voting without proxies, secret ballot, an absolute majority required for victory. Two weeks before the new election these arrangements were passed into law, notwithstanding warnings that an absolute majority might prove hard to find. It did. Thirteen of the seventeen previous contests had been settled on the first round and four on the second; that of December 1953 took 13 ballots. The successful candidate was in the Third Republican tradition, unknown to the public but esteemed in Parliament; many of his predecessors had presided over the upper house, of which he was senior vice-president. He was personally so modest that he brought no tail-coat to Versailles on the day of his election, and politically

25. Fabre, no. 88, p. 211 ('more success'); Dansette, *Présidents*, pp. 269 ('appeals'), 324; Merle, no. 158, pp. 296–9; Georgel, i. 94–6; Arné, pp. 45–6, 98–9; Fauvet, pp. 236f., Williams, p. 413 (1953); below, pp. 416–17.

26. Duverger, *French Political System*, p. 42; cf. Roche, no. 193a, p. 4; Pickles, no. 176, p. 108: 'one of the greatest Presidents France has ever had'. Auriol was to justify some of the criticisms by his attack on the Fifth Republic ('where there are no ministerial crises there is no liberty'): *AP* 1959, p. 137.

27. See below, p. 416, and Williams, p. 413 (crisis); Melnik and Leites, pp. 177–9 (re-election).

inoffensive, since he had never been a controversial figure and had been ill during the bitter EDC debates.[28] Once again the senators seemed to have swayed the decision in favour of a moderate conservative from their own ranks.[29]

As an unobtrusive conservative in the old tradition, René Coty's conception of his office differed from his predecessor's. He considered he had a duty to express the feelings of the great majority of Frenchmen, but had no right to speak publicly on questions within the province of Parliament. Enunciating only governmental policies, he put forward no personal views except to demand constitutional reform which was (in theory) common ground among supporters of the regime. In cabinet he appears to have participated actively, speaking less briefly and forcefully than Auriol. In ministerial crises he did not fight for his own preferences. The pro-European Conservative President resumed consultations with the Communist leaders whom his Socialist predecessor had recently refused to see; and instead of indulging his personal preference for cautious and comfortable senior politicians, he had instead to bring to the front a new political generation.[30]

He was also less active in the imperial and judicial fields that had attracted Auriol. In 1949 negotiations with Bao Dai were conducted by the President, in 1954 by the government. In accord with successive ministries Coty spoke out repeatedly against 'sacrificing a new Alsace-Lorraine across the Mediterranean'; and throughout the Algerian war notorious judicial abuses met from an Élysée preoccupied with the immediate problem of the army's loyalty only a 'heavy and oppressive silence [which] has contributed to the dissolution of the state'. Yet it was under this conscientious, conventional, self-effacing President that the first dissolution for nearly eighty years took place, and in his final crisis he was to display a more audacious and controversial initiative than any of his predecessors.[31]

In his inaugural message President Coty had paid a warm tribute to Charles de Gaulle. As early as 1954 he made contact privately with the General, and as the Fourth Republic's crisis developed he came increasingly to believe that the way out lay through Colombey-les-Deux-Églises. Early in May 1958 he secretly approached de Gaulle, who refused to appear before the Assembly as a candidate for the premiership. But the circumstances soon changed dramatically. On 14 May the President vainly ordered the army in Algeria to obey the legal government; on the 29th, believing that an airborne invasion from Algiers was imminent and that only one man could avert civil war, he informed Parliament by message that he was sending for de Gaulle, and that if the

28. For Coty's personality, R. Triboulet, *Monde*, 28 November 1962; and Melnik and Leites, pp. 251, 262, 272–3, 277, 280 (no tail-coat). Though his name was never canvassed publicly, he was so classic a candidate that M. Goguel had privately predicted his success: *ibid.*, p. 283.

29. Radical deputies preferred a Socialist, Radical senators a right-wing colleague: *ibid.*, p. 175; cf. *Institutions*, i. 214. Auriol, the only left-wing President, had been chosen at the one moment when the upper house was not biased against the Left by its electoral system: Duverger, *VIe*, p. 101 (cf. above, p. 196; below, pp. 277, 289). On the politics of Coty's election see above, pp. 41–2.

30. Dansette, *Présidents*, pp. 335–40, *AP* 1955, pp. 598, 600 (presidential statements); Arné, pp. 45–6, 55–6, 76n. ('forcefully'), 236 and n.; above, p. 13 and below, p. 416.

31. Bao Dai: see n. 15. 'Silence': Duverger, *Demain*, p. 117. Algeria: *AP* 1957, pp. 544–5, cf. 1955, pp. 598–9, 1956, p. 480, and Arné, p. 83. Dissolution: below, pp. 238–9.

deputies rejected his nomination he would resign. André Le Troquer, President of the Assembly, would then become acting President of the Republic and presumably send for an anti-Gaullist leader to form a Popular Front government.[32]

The presidential right of message, authorized by Article 36 of the constitution, had seemed such a dead letter that only two years earlier André Siegfried had thought it unlikely to be invoked even in the gravest of crises.[33] Only Millerand in 1924 had ever used it for a political purpose, and he was to resign within forty-eight hours. But now a President, though not responsible to Parliament, was threatening resignation as a political weapon. He could justly claim that by doing so he was offering the Assembly a choice of alternative policies. But constitutionally his action (like the circumstances) was unprecedented; rightly or wrongly it was resented as illegitimate, especially by the Socialists without whose votes de Gaulle could not be elected; and therefore politically it was a blunder which harmed the General's chances. It was only after reading an exchange of letters between Auriol and de Gaulle that many Socialist deputies came round.[34]

After the General's election as premier Coty remained President for seven months, but at the end of 1958 he retired two years before the normal end of his term. Describing himself soon after his election as 'still a counsellor of the Republic', he had exercised less influence than Auriol though more than many of his predecessors before 1940. He preferred instead 'a moral magistracy in which Frenchmen of all views could see themselves', and he was rewarded by unexampled popularity.[35]

4. THE PREMIER AND THE CABINET

The presidency, at least under Auriol, had developed potentialities which the constitution-makers had not expected. The premiership failed to fulfil their hopes of real executive leadership. Following Blum in 1919, they looked forward to stronger parties which would enable a united government to command the support of a coherent parliamentary majority; then the prime minister could lead both executive and legislature in pursuit of common purposes. But they hoped that the prestige and power he would need could be conferred on his office without waiting for the slow growth of an effective party system. Blum wished to bring the French system nearer to the British; and by strengthening the lower house against the upper and the premier against the President, the framers of the constitution were consciously pursuing the same objective.[36]

32. The April 1946 draft constitution would have given Le Troquer a veto, for under it messages needed the prior consent of both the premier and the President of the Assembly: *Institutions*, i. 207, Théry, p. 62. Coty's message was countersigned by Pflimlin and Lecourt, MRP minister of justice, to authenticate the signature: J. R. Tournoux, *Secrets d'État* (1960), p. 388n. For Coty's earlier dealings with de Gaulle see *ibid.*, pp. 85, 242–5; Fauvet, *IV*e, p. 345; Dansette, *Présidents*, pp. 340–1. His inaugural message is in *AP* 1954, pp. 51–8.

33. *De la III*e, pp. 230–1.

34. Text of the letters and of Coty's message in *AP* 1958, pp. 538–40, cf. Arné, pp. 68–9; for the parliamentary reactions see Williams, no. 220, p. 38 and Dansette, *Présidents*, pp. 342–5.

35. *Ibid.*, pp. 330, 357; Grosser, p. 48 ('moral magistracy'); Arné, p. 68, and Berlia, no. 13b, p. 910 ('counsellor'); cf. above, pp. 55–6.

36. 'Our aim has been to create a real head of the government, a prime minister in the English sense of the term': P. Coste-Floret, *JO* 5 September 1946, p. 3552. Cf. Blum, pp. 151–3.

The title of *président du conseil* had never been mentioned in previous constitutions; it appeared fourteen times in that of the Fourth Republic.[37] He alone was chosen by the representatives of the people, and other ministers were appointed by him under Article 46. A series of articles asserted his political, legislative and executive supremacy as Blum had demanded in 1919.[38] In the Third Republic a government could be destroyed by the rashness of a subordinate, since any minister could make a matter a question of confidence; now Article 49 reserved this right to the prime minister alone. Under Article 14 every government bill had to bear his signature. Article 38, enacting past practice, required two ministers to countersign the acts of the President of the Republic; the prime minister had now to be one of them, though this intended source of strength carried an additional responsibility which might prove inconvenient.[39]

Article 47 specified that the prime minister was responsible for ensuring the execution of the laws, which in the Third Republic had been the duty of the President (though he needed a minister's countersignature).[40] Most official appointments, but not the most important ones, were made by the prime minister instead of the President.[41] A third paragraph of Article 47 gave the prime minister specific responsibility for defence, though after 1948 his powers were delegated to the defence minister.[42] But while the premier had far more legal authority than in the Third Republic, his great powers were never exercised alone.[43] For his acts under Articles 38 and 47 he needed the countersignature of another minister, and major decisions under Articles 30, 49 and 51 (senior appointments, seeking the Assembly's confidence, and dissolution) had to be settled in cabinet under the President of the Republic.

Perhaps of more practical importance than the legal changes was the creation of a prime minister's office. Blum had regarded this as crucial, since without it the premier must either overburden himself by holding an extra ministry, or weaken himself by having no departmental staff. After repeated changes, in 1934 Flandin set up an *office du président du conseil* at the Hotel Matignon, and Blum strengthened it in 1936.[44] In the Fourth Republic a far stronger department was given permanent control of the civil service and

37. The council of ministers was mentioned twice in the 1875 constitution and five times in that of 1946, which also spoke at four points of the cabinet: Théry, p. 120.

38. Blum, pp. 62–3.

39. In May 1948 Schuman's cabinet was divided over a decree issued by Mme Poinso-Chapuis, MRP minister of health, which indirectly allowed church schools to be subsidized; as his signature had had to appear on the decree, he was badly placed to mediate. Cf. Théry, p. 59, on past practice.

40. The highway code, instituted in 1899 by the President, was revised in 1954 by the premier: Arné, p. 148 (cf. pp. 143–51).

41. The President in cabinet appointed members of the *Conseil d'État*, ambassadors, university rectors, prefects, generals, colonial governors, and other senior officials (Art. 30); judges were named in the High Council of the Judiciary (Art. 84); the prime minister chose his ministers under Art. 46, and made all other appointments under Art. 47.

42. Ramadier kept close control over his Communist defence minister, but some later ministers (notably Moch) had a very free hand. Cf. Suel, no. 206; *Institutions*, i. 255–8; Arné, pp. 114–15, 136–40. In 1948 large powers for the defence of West Africa were delegated to the High Commissioner, but this was attacked as unconstitutional: *AP* 1948, p. 224.

43. Except (in theory) in introducing government bills under Art. 14: Théry, pp. 87–8, 132. But cf. Arné, pp. 170–2.

44. Théry, pp. 123–4; Arné, pp. 28–30, 130–43. Soulier, p. 567, contests its importance.

temporary responsibility for several vital problems.[45] But many premiers still held a major department also: four took the foreign office, three Finance, two Defence and one (twice) the Interior.[46]

These four departments, together with Justice (traditionally the second post in the government) were recognized informally as the senior ministries. Their holders were potential prime ministers and they could be held by an ex-premier without loss of dignity.[47] But above them in the elaborate ministerial hierarchy stood the two dignified ranks of vice-premier (*vice-président du conseil*) and senior minister without portfolio (*ministre d'État*). A vice-premier was almost always a leading figure in his party and sometimes, especially under *tripartisme*, he acted as an 'overlord' co-ordinating all its ministries; he might serve either without portfolio or in a major office. But a *ministre d'État* had no department, except under Mollet; generally he took responsibilityfor a special problem such as constitutional reform, Council of Europe affairs, Indo-China, or Tunisia and Morocco. Next to these senior ministers stood the heads of ordinary departmental offices, of which some were ancient and powerful, others new but well-established, and a few transient creations, invented for parliamentary rather than administrative advantage.

From 1920 to 1945 the creation or merger of ministries had nominally required legal sanction, but under the Fourth Republic premiers could alter the ministerial structure at will and often did. Usually they merely restored a dormant ministry like Economic Affairs, or created one for a new problem, like the Sahara. Occasionally a once-only office was invented and abolished, like Population in 1946 or Youth, Arts and Letters in 1947. But a few reorganizations were sweeping; in 1956 Guy Mollet suppressed nine departments and grouped six of them under a single minister. Flexibility was increased by the use of ministers of state (*secrétaires d'État*) to assist the premier, replace a full minister whose department had lost political status but not administrative identity, or take responsibility for a group of services within an old ministry; they reduced the need for under-secretaries (*sous-secrétaires d'État*) of whom there were few in the Fourth Republic. These two junior offices provided both opportunities for training and selecting politicians on their way up to full cabinet rank, and patronage to attract marginal votes to buttress a faltering majority.[48]

Despite constant complaints the ministerial inflation was no greater in

45. Including food, broadcasting, information and atomic energy: Arné, pp. 129–32; Bertrand, *Techniques*, and no. 16, pp. 435ff.; Marcel, no. 154, pp. 452–99 (reprinted in *Institutions*, i. 221–59); Macridis, no. 150. The premier also controlled SDECE (see below, p. 348).

46. Foreign office: Bidault (1946), Blum, Schuman (September 1948), Mendès-France. Bidault and Schuman had held it in the preceding government; similarly, Queuille kept the Interior on becoming premier in 1950 and 1951. Defence: de Gaulle (1944, 1945 and 1958) and Gouin. Finance: Queuille (in 1948 only), Faure (1952) and Pinay. Cf. Georgel, i. 260–4; Arné, pp. 89–90.

47. See below, p. 415. One premier came from Transport (Pinay) and one went to Education (Marie).

48. Mollet: see below, p. 378. For the hierarchy and number of ministers of different ranks see G. Galichon in *Institutions*, i. 261–8; Dogan and Campbell, nos. 72 and 73, pp. 313–45 and 793–824; Arné, pp. 90–3, 101, 104–5. *Secrétaires d'État* attended the *conseil du cabinet* (see n. 5) but not the *conseil des ministres* unless specially summoned (except for those attached to the premier). *Sous-secrétaires d'État* normally attended neither. A few premiers appointed a full minister (*ministre délégué à la présidence du conseil*) to assist them.

France than in Britain. In each country only about a quarter of the 600 members seriously aspired to office. Though the velocity of circulation was far greater in France, the 'fiduciary issue' (the number of ministers surplus to those whose intrinsic worth creates public confidence in the government) was so much larger in London that the ministerial *masse monétaire* was about the same on each side of the Channel. British ministries usually have over seventy members, almost all French ones had from twenty to forty varying inversely with the premier's prestige; a full minister of commerce or the merchant marine was a harbinger of political storms.[49] While commentators were often dismayed to find that a third or a quarter of the deputies (excluding the Communist or Poujadist enemies of the regime) had held ministerial office, this proportion was always lower than in Britain. But while most British *ministrables* from the majority held office simultaneously, French ones rotated frequently. The large size of a British ministry helped to keep the majority together, while the smallness of the French one was a liability; for at Westminster a quarter of the majority MP's were in office at any time, at the Palais Bourbon rarely a tenth. Even in the House of Commons the ex-minister is a potential danger, but there he is a rarity, while in the National Assembly ex-ministers always far outnumbered the holders of office. Politically, if not administratively, French governments had far too few members for their own good.[50]

The rotation of ministers did not prevent a surprising degree of continuity. In every French Parliament about twenty senior *ministrables* each served in several governments. They provided the core of every cabinet. Around them clustered the newcomers and the transients who were more numerous (usually about fifty) but often less weighty. The six highest governmental posts were held between 1944 and May 1958 by 48 men in Paris, 27 in London and 30 in Washington. Over a period of years the new men introduced to office by French cabinet crises were no more numerous than those brought in by British government reshuffles, so that from 1945 to 1957 there were over half as many full cabinet ministers in Britain as in France (72 against 122) and far more including juniors (295 against 208). As in a major reshuffle at Westminster, in an average cabinet change in Paris about half the ministers kept their old posts, half the rest moved to new ones, and a quarter were replaced – mostly by promoted ministers of state. When Clemenceau was criticized for overthrowing so many governments he had answered that they were all the same. His successors could echo the complaint.[51]

The difference between the two countries was that the British premier could weather any but the most extraordinary political tempest (if necessary by throwing his colleagues overboard) while in France the captain was more vulnerable than the crew to shifts in the parliamentary wind. Once the brief

49. Ramadier had most full ministers (26) when he formed his cabinet in January 1947, and fewest (12) after reconstructing it in October; in 1952 Edgar Faure had 26 in his government of 40, and in 1957 Bourgès-Maunoury had 46 altogether: 14 full ministers, 25 ministers of state and 7 under-secretaries. Cf. Georgel, i, 265–6; Arné, pp. 101 (full figures), 105; below, pp. 418–9.

50. Below, pp. 426, 432; and Dogan and Campbell, no. 72, especially pp. 325–7.

51. *Ibid.*, especially pp. 318, 340; Campbell, nos. 39–41; cf. Williams, pp. 375–6. Six posts (named p. 205): my calculation.

episode of *tripartisme* was over, the political conditions familiar in the Third Republic reappeared. The premier escaped from bondage to three rigid parties, but could not command loyalty from a majority made up of several loose ones; both his cabinet and his parliamentary support were constantly threatened by disruption through conflicts of personal ambitions, party politics or electoral interests. Almost every premier was worn down in six months by the physical strain of shouldering heavy executive responsibilities while fighting daily for parliamentary survival.[52]

Every possible legal text had been provided to make the prime minister a real leader. But by strengthening his nominal powers the constitution-makers had transferred to him the suspicions which had once been concentrated on the presidency. In the Fourth Republic as in the Third, Parliament chose bargainers and conciliators for the office in which a strong man might have proved dangerous; and a prime minister who wanted to act decisively could be thwarted by the refusal of his divided majority, and deterred by fear of the deputies' hostility to him next time he sought their votes. Weak premiers meant a weak premiership, and strong ones were rare because positive leadership was at a discount.[53] The legal reforms did not lead to the constitutional revolution that Blum had hoped for, since the expected revolution in the party system occurred neither in the country nor in the National Assembly.

52. Siegfried, *De la III*^{e}, pp. 239–40; Georgel, i. 261 and n.; Arné, pp. 112n., 246. Significantly Mollet, with a strong party behind him, was not.

53. Soulier, pp. 565–74, for the Third Republic; below, Chapters 17, 28 and 30, for the Fourth.

Chapter 16

THE NATIONAL ASSEMBLY (1): MACHINERY AND METHODS

Under Article 3 of the constitution the sovereign people delegated power (except in constitutional matters) to the popularly elected house of Parliament, which was renamed National Assembly to denote its superiority over the three advisory bodies, the Council of the Republic, Assembly of the French Union and Economic Council. The Assembly had the final word in passing laws, voting the budget and supervising the government. Under Article 45 it elected the prime minister, and Article 48 made ministers responsible to it individually and collectively; while the formal procedure for expressing confidence or censure was laid down in Articles 49 and 50, the Assembly exercised its day-to-day supervision by questions and interpellations and through its committees, which were also its main instruments in legislation and finance. These primary functions are discussed in the three following chapters.[1]

The Assembly was also an electoral college. Under Article 6 it could choose by proportional representation up to one-sixth of the members of the Council of the Republic; this right was fully exercised under the Council's original electoral law in 1946, but waived when the system was changed in 1948.[2] The six hundred deputies and three hundred councillors of the Republic sat together at Versailles to elect the President of the Republic. The deputies for France proper also chose two-thirds (68) of the metropolitan councillors of the French Union. Under Article 83 the Assembly chose nearly half the High Council of the Judiciary, which advised the President on pardons; under Article 19 an amnesty to a class of convicted persons could be granted only by law. The Assembly could impeach the President or a minister before a High Court of Justice chosen, under Article 58, from its own ranks. Under Article 91 it elected a majority of the Constitutional Committee. Constitutional amendments had to be passed by a special procedure; unless it voted them by a two-thirds majority they required approval by the Council of the Republic (and perhaps by a referendum). It had to ratify many kinds of treaty under Article 27, and under Article 28 to consent to their denunciation.[3] Under Article 7 the Assembly had to vote a declaration of war and the Council of the Republic had to be consulted on it.

These varied tasks were performed by a body which had no coherent political majority. The deputies would accept leadership neither from the government like the House of Commons, nor even from their own officers and committees like the House of Representatives. Jealously preserving their control over the arrangement of business, they used their powers so fitfully and inconsequentially that they often frustrated themselves as well as their

1. On Parliament, especially procedure, see Lidderdale, *The Parliament of France*, and Campbell, no. 45. On prestige and titles see below, pp. 280–1, 286n.
2. See below, p. 279.
3. See below, pp. 225 (treaties), 298–300 (impeachment, Judiciary), 302–6 (constitutional).

natural enemy, the executive. The standing orders of the National Assembly were among the institutional causes for the failings of the regime. But the rules survived because the politicians had no common purpose to induce them to sacrifice their personal freedom and prominence. Fearing that strong authority might reduce their own power or damage causes they believed in, they allowed parliamentary procedure to be used for obstructive rather than constructive purposes. The ordinary Frenchman was disillusioned by the impotence of government, and in the end the parliamentarians who had feared an authority subject to their own control found themselves subordinated to one which they could not influence.

In the Third Republic a Chamber of Deputies had sat for four years; in the Fourth, a National Assembly sat for five. Under Article 6 of the constitution the term was fixed by an ordinary law. It was not clear whether a sitting Assembly could properly extend or shorten its own life, but it could unquestionably dissolve itself by a two-thirds majority, and General de Gaulle urged this course on the deputies in October 1947 when he claimed that they no longer represented the country.[4] They rejected his advice, but on 12 May 1951 the first National Assembly did vote a premature end to its own life. The second was elected five months early, on 17 June 1951, and was dissolved by a defeated premier, Edgar Faure, on 2 December 1955. The third relinquished its power to de Gaulle's government on 1 June 1958.[5]

1. MEMBERSHIP

The National Assembly had 627 members in 1951, of whom 544 represented metropolitan France (including Corsica), 30 sat for Algerian constituencies and 53 for overseas departments and territories.[6] Deputies had to be 23 years old and to have completed military service; they might not be serving officers or have held within the last six months certain appointive positions of authority within their constituency.[7] Bankrupts and felons were ineligible for election;[8] so were members of former reigning families, until 1950, and

4. Constitutional amendment required either a two-thirds majority in the Assembly, three-fifths in both houses, or popular approval in a referendum; see below, p. 302. The April draft constitution had expressly provided for dissolution by a two-thirds majority.

5. See below, pp. 275, 313–14, 315–16. The 1951 bill passed the Assembly by 362 to 219 and the upper house by 278 to 35, sufficient to carry a constitutional amendment without referendum; but that procedure required delay (see below, p. 302) which would have made the bill pointless. It therefore went through as an ordinary law, which terminated the powers of that Assembly on 4 July 1951 and of future ones on 31 May in their fifth year.

6. The two Constituent Assemblies had 586 members: 522 for metropolitan, 26 for Algerian and 33 for overseas constituencies (and 5 others representing Frenchmen in Tunisia and Morocco). In June 1946 these became 544, 30 and 45, a total of 619. Three African members were added in 1947 and six in 1951; one seat was lost in 1949 and another in 1954, by the cession of Cochin-China to Vietnam and French India to India. But the 1956 Assembly had only 596 members, as the war prevented elections in Algeria. Three overseas departments (Guadeloupe, Martinique and Reunion) had three members each and French Guiana had one. Fifteen Algerian and five other African deputies represented French citizens (almost all white settlers).

7. M. Rastel, elected UDSR member for Eure-et-Loir in 1951, was unseated because he had resigned too late as prefect of the department: Campbell, no. 43, p. 70; L. Philip, *Les Contentieux des élections aux Assemblées politiques françaises* (1961), pp. 39–40.

8. The Assembly could expel deputies sentenced after election; but three Malagasy members convicted of sedition, and M. de Récy, convicted of fraud, continued until 1951 to count as members for the purpose of reckoning the absolute majority even though they could not vote.

persons sentenced to 'national disgrace' for their wartime activities, until 1953.[9] If a member of one of the four assemblies was elected to another, he had to choose within a month. Similarly, a parliamentarian in most posts paid by the state (ministers were the chief exception) had to resign one or other position.[10] Each Assembly judged the eligibility and verified the credentials of its own members; the rules were tightened in 1952 when a deputy killed in a car crash was found to have two identity cards and, under his real name, to be due for trial as a collaborationist.

Like most parliaments which settle their own election disputes, the Assembly was accused of misusing its power. In 1951 several seats in two constituencies depended on a difficult point of electoral law, which the majority parties decided in their own favour in Seine-Inférieure but against themselves in Bas-Rhin (where they were reluctant to unseat the Gaullist war hero General Koenig). In another legal dispute in 1956 eleven Poujadists were unseated by the left-wing majority, which gained eight seats, against the votes of the Right which could hope for only two; MRP voted first for invalidation and then against, changing after it had gained its one seat. Public opinion was too shocked by this behaviour to recognize the strong legal case against the Poujadists.[11]

Under Article 21 of the constitution a member enjoyed immunity from prosecution or arrest for his speeches or votes in Parliament. Under Article 22 he could not be arrested at all except with permission of the house or when caught in a criminal act (*en flagrant délit*); before the war, and after the constitutional amendment of 1954, this privilege covered only periods when Parliament was sitting. In 1949 a permanent committee on immunities was set up to deal with the growing number of applications to prosecute deputies, particularly Communists;[12] a bill was introduced obliging newspapers edited by a deputy to name another person to take responsibility in libel cases;[13] and

9. Even those whose *indignité nationale* had been remitted for later services; this clause was directed against P. E. Flandin (but in Yonne in 1952, 307 of the 932 senatorial electors nevertheless voted for him). Before the 1951 general election prefects were told to count votes for ineligibles as spoiled; this discouraged several from standing, though some persuaded relatives to do so instead (cf. n. 37). Despite the 1953 amnesty, in 1956 only fifteen ex-ineligibles stood and only four won: Dogan in *Élections 1956*, p. 445. Among them were Georges Bonnet (the foreign minister at Munich) and Tixier-Vignancour. On reigning families see above, p. 179.

10. On leaving Parliament an official regained his post and pension rights. A deputy might not take directorships in certain types of business. For details see Williams, p. 192n.; Lidderdale, pp. 82–5; Meynaud, pp. 143, 317.

11. See *Institutions*, i. 116–18; Philip, pp. 37–57; Campbell, no.43. In December 1945 the Assembly refused to seat Camille Laurens because of his Vichyite past. But in June 1946 it accepted him, and rejected Communist attempts to unseat Daladier and Reynaud as political undesirables; and in 1951 it seated Jacques Isorni (Pétain's counsel), against the Communists' opposition, and Maurice Thorez against RPF's.

12. Between 1902 and 1940 there were 102, between 1945 and 1951 about 350: see J. Duclos, *JO* 22 June 1949, p. 3639; J. Minjoz, *JO* 8 November 1951, p. 7725; and n. 13. The eleven *bureaux*, between which deputies were divided by lot, had nominated all committees until 1910 and an *ad hoc* committee for each immunity case until 1949; thereafter their only functions were verifying credentials. The Fifth Republic restored *ad hoc* committees for each immunity case.

13. It passed in 1952 after prolonged Communist obstruction and evidence that 90% of immunity cases concerned communist editor-deputies: Minjoz, *loc. cit.* A Communist paper in Dakar had once announced, 'As frequent prosecutions for libel have been causing us serious expense, we have entrusted the management of our newspaper to a member of Parliament. It will no longer be possible to sue us for libel without first obtaining the leave of the house': quoted London

[over

another bill tried to guard against any repetition of the Madagascar affair of 1947, when the Assembly had waived the immunity of three nationalist deputies charged with non-capital offences and the government then prosecuted them for treason.[14]

In interpreting *flagrant délit* the courts favoured the accused. At Brest in 1950 the judges refused to try two Communist deputies arrested for rioting, and in 1952 a Paris court severely criticized the police, who had arrested Jacques Duclos during a riot and charged him with conspiring against the safety of the state; the case collapsed in ridicule when the 'carrier-pigeons' found in his car turned out to be his dinner. Parliament, too, was reluctant to authorize prosecution except for grave crimes; the first Assembly allowed only 15 applications out of 328, and in 1953 the second refused by 11 votes to permit five leading Communists to be prosecuted for the sedition imputed to their party. In May 1958, as the Corsican *coup* sent the Fourth Republic tottering, the Assembly consented to the prosecution of the insurgent deputy Pascal Arrighi – though not to his immediate expulsion as the government wished. Its corporate feeling safeguarded rioters and rebels, but also unpopular minority members.[15]

Article 23 allocated to deputies an 'indemnity' for loss of other earnings, related since 1938 and equal since 1950 to the salary of a *conseiller d'État*. In 1955 it amounted to about £2,500, double the figure four years earlier; rather less than half was taxable. A contributory pension varied with length of service up to three-quarters of the current *indemnité*. A member could frank letters from the house; make free telephone calls within Paris; and travel by rail and in Paris and bring his wife to the capital free or at very low fares.[16] To deal with his fifteen letters a day (but up to three times as many if he was in the public eye) he probably shared a secretary with two or three colleagues; and in preparing his bills, amendments and reports he might get help from the secretary of his official committee or his party group.[17]

Times, 11 July 1949. After one editor escaped prosecution on grounds of insanity, concern was expressed that Communist papers might evade the new law by appointing mad co-editors: see *JO* 13 March 1952, pp. 1274–5 (and cf. *Institutions*, i. 121).

14. The upper house opposed it, the President referred it back, and it was revised, reintroduced and passed only in 1953: see Drago, no. 75; Berlia, no. 12b; M. Lesage, *Les interventions du législateur dans le fonctionnement de la justice* (1960), pp. 152–67; and below, pp. 247 n. 24, 306.

15. Pickles, *French Politics*, pp. 269–70, 293–4; *Institutions*, i. 122; Goguel, *Régime*, p. 40; Drago, nos. 74 and 75. The Brest court claimed that by Third Republican custom *flagrant délit* justified arrest but not prosecution without leave of the house; the Assembly disavowed this: *AP* 1950, pp. 74–7, 285–6. Duclos's birds were solemnly pronounced to be eating-pigeons by a jury consisting of a professor of natural history, a military communications expert and the President of the National Federation of Pigeon-Fanciers; his release showed that at the height of French 'McCarthyism' the courts were not intimidated; cf. *AP* 1952, pp. 50–1, 75–6, 1953, pp. 80–1; but see below, p. 351. The proposed bill to expel Arrighi could have been used against any member advocating the independence of Algeria. He escaped prosecution because the regime fell.

16. After essential expenses were met the deputy had about £1,000 to maintain himself, his family and his home in the constituency: Muselier, *Regards neufs sur le Parlement*, pp. 54–60. See also above, p. 80; and Hamon, no. 121, pp. 553–5.

17. On party groups, below, pp. 214–6. Each day from 8,000 to 15,000 letters were received and rather more sent out from the Palais Bourbon: Muselier, p. 142. *Figaro*, 27 and 28 March 1950, estimated that the average member spent half his working time on his mail of thirty letters a day. Some came of course from epistolary lunatics; in 1953 one Parisian deputy heard weekly from an enthusiastic constituent that national salvation lay in paying half of all wages in national lottery tickets. See also below, pp. 329, 340, 374, 429 n. 5; and Lancelot, no. 136.

Each Friday night he would take the train for his constituency to hold his 'surgeries', visit the prefecture and the local mayors and notables, attend party meetings, agricultural shows, festive or sporting events, and deal with the affairs of the town of which he was often mayor or the *canton* which he represented on the departmental council. On Monday night he returned to Paris. Probably he would attend parliamentary party meetings on Tuesdays, committees on mornings later in the week, and the chamber itself relatively infrequently, for two-thirds of the sittings were detailed and dull and attracted only specialists. At some point in the week he had to find time for his visits to the ministries on his constituents' behalf; his job, if he had one; his contacts, not least with the press; his reading; and his family.[18]

2. THE SITTINGS

Normally the Assembly sat at 3 p.m. on Wednesdays, Thursdays and Fridays, but it often met in the morning and evening and sometimes at the weekend. Up to 1951 it averaged 297 sittings a year, afterwards 219, compared to only about 140 for the pre-war Chamber of Deputies. But then the Chamber had had to sit for no more than five months in the year (though extraordinary sessions were usually needed to vote the budget); and its sessions were closed, in theory by the President of the Republic, and in fact by the government of the day. The deputies' standard outcries when they were 'sent on holiday' were neither meant nor taken very seriously.

In 1946 this *clôture* power was abolished. Under Article 9 of the new constitution Parliament sat permanently in theory and for at least eight months of the year in fact. The session began on the second Tuesday in January and should have finished by 31 December, though the time-honoured practice of prolonging the final sitting into early January still had to be employed when the budget was late.[19] Brief extraordinary sessions were usually held in January, not always for budgetary purposes. The right to adjourn was transferred from the government to the Assembly itself, which found it politically difficult to exercise and rarely began the summer recess on time. The constitutional amendment of 1954 therefore made the session begin in October instead of January (so that the annual re-election of *bureau* and committees should not delay the final voting of the budget) and restored the government's right to close it after seven months.[20]

During the Munich crisis Parliament had been in recess and the government did not recall it. Article 12 of the new constitution entitled the *bureau* to convene the house if it considered this necessary, and obliged it to do so on the demand of either the prime minister or a third of the deputies. In September 1949, when France followed Britain in devaluing the currency, the Communists tried unsuccessfully to have the Assembly recalled; in August 1953 a Socialist and Communist attempt narrowly failed, and Parliament discussed

18. On this paragraph see Hamon, no. 121, pp. 554–63 ('a professional exercising a badly organized profession'); Pineau, *passim*; Muselier, pp. 133–65; Buron, pp. 27–34, 71–90, 114–15, 120–1, 134, 142.

19. But M. Goguel informs me that the clocks in the Chamber were not, as often stated, stopped at five minutes to midnight on 31 December (though the calendar was).

20. Adjournments up to ten days before 1954, and eight afterwards, counted in the session.

neither the great strikes nor the deposition of the Sultan of Morocco. The 1954 constitutional amendment required over half instead of a third of the deputies to make recall obligatory. In 1957 the agricultural pressure-groups, reinforced by the Communist party, seemed likely to rally a majority for recall; the government therefore itself summoned the Assembly to meet early.[21]

When the deputies gathered in their semicircular chamber, the Communist benches were on the President's left while Gaullists and Poujadists were seated (violently protesting) on his right. Committee and government spokesmen had special benches in front. Ministers, whether or not they were members of parliament, could speak when they chose in either house. 'Government commissioners' could advise and even speak for them; in 1956 two high officials put the case for Euratom and one of them enjoyed a parliamentary triumph.[22] The deputies often spoke from their places, but long set speeches were made at the tribune under the President's desk. Voting might be by show of hands, by Ayes and Noes respectively rising in their places, or by recorded ballot; each member had white (Aye) or blue (No) cards with his name on them to place in the urns brought round by the attendants. Proxy voting was usually allowed, and all the cards of each party were kept by its whip (*boîtier*), so that a handful of deputies often recorded several hundred votes.[23] A personal vote (*scrutin public à la tribune*) took an hour and a half and became a dangerous weapon of Communist obstruction. From 1947 successive amendments to standing orders restricted its use until in 1952 it was abolished, except on verification of credentials. But in 1955 there was a reaction against proxies, which were forbidden on votes of confidence and censure, the election of a premier, and (if the house so chose) on a vote to ratify a treaty.[24]

By this revolt against proxies the deputies were breaking with an old-established tradition which had a profound effect on their work and outlook. Without proxies members could not have indulged in the absenteeism of which their constituents so often complained; one critic estimated the average attendance at fifteen in the morning, forty in the afternoon, fifty or sixty for a major foreign policy debate, and a full house only for a question of party or electoral importance. Proxies permitted many deputies and more senators to combine their functions with those of local councillor or mayor, to which they often attached more importance and which inevitably coloured their

21. This enabled the government to decide the agenda for the special session, but failed to prevent its defeat two weeks later: *AP* 1957, pp. 86–9. See also *AP* 1949, p. 159; 1953, pp. 61–3, 67; Arné, p. 245. In 1953 the Left was frustrated by the postal strike and the delaying tactics of the majority of the *bureau*, which gained six weeks by obstruction and finally recalled the house only a week before the normal date.

22. Isorni, *Silence*, pp. 66–7; cf. Arné, p. 185; *AP* 1956, p. 70. Advisers hardly ever spoke, but often attended; one ministry had 23 'administrative prompters' authorized: Boissarie, no. 22, p. 21.

23. For example, on 27 March 1952 two dozen deputies carried one amendment to the new standing orders by 343 to 247, another by 352 to 236, and the proposals as a whole by 378 to 100 with 110 abstentions. To vote against his party a member put in *two* cards of the 'wrong' colour; I have heard an experienced parliamentarian admit that he did not know which colour meant Aye and which No, only whether he was voting with or against his *boîtier*.

24. For methods and rules of voting see Lidderdale, p. 141; Blamont, *Les techniques parlementaires*, pp. 69–75. In the Fifth Republic proxies were restricted severely, though in-altogether effectively, and electronic voting was installed; for the results see *Monde*, 27 November, 1963.

outlook and behaviour. Through proxy voting members were encouraged in their illusion that they could carry out their external duties effectively and still keep Parliament permanently in session to guard against executive abuses.[25] Nor was its effect confined to those who normally stayed away. Lobbying was easier when attendances were small. When specialists cast the votes of their absent colleagues, life was easier for the crank or the pressure-group, the assiduous committeeman or the disinterested expert. It was easier for the party leader to withstand revolts, since the *boîtier* voted on behalf of absentees. Thus the system might distort the result of an individual division, and over a period it inevitably diminished the member's sense of individual responsibility.[26]

3. THE PARTY GROUPS

The parliamentary parties, or groups, were far more important in the National Assembly than in the pre-war Chamber. In well-organized parties like SFIO and MRP, one senior deputy was made responsible for the work of each committee; study groups met with non-parliamentarians to formulate policy; and deputies were not supposed to ask questions, make speeches or bring in bills or resolutions without the group's consent. On the Right and Centre (and in the Council of the Republic) the groups were looser, though in the later years Conservatives voluntarily informed their group of their bills and questions. All groups gave their members moral support and material help, such as secretarial assistance, in return for a monthly levy which varied by party from £3 to £9; at the end of the Fourth Republic each group also received £4 per member per month from the Assembly's own funds.[27] Even an ill-organized party like the Radicals met far more often than before the war. At these private meetings argument could be serious and not demagogic, and party interests could be discussed with a frankness impossible in public debate. Here the deputy had a real opportunity to change votes and perhaps alter the decision of Parliament.[28]

Among the looser political formations, parliamentary groups had never had any necessary link with parties in the country. In the Third Republic there were parties with no group and groups with no party, and except on the Left the groups in the Chamber and Senate were quite different. Radicals had not always formed a single group in the Chamber, and never did so in the Senate.

25. Debré, no. 67. Cf. Georgel, i. 254; Noël, pp. 104–8; Goguel in *Le travail parlementaire* (henceforth cited as *Travail*), p. 853; and below, pp. 331, 428 (local government).

26. When Jules Moch stood for the premiership in October 1949, his majority of one included a member in French Congo (who later wired confirmation), another in New York (whose telephoned instructions were inaudible) and a wholly unexpected Gaullist (who was in his Indian Ocean constituency). In 1955 a *boîtier* cast SFIO's votes for the *bouilleurs de cru*, against a group decision; Mollet did the same for the EDC treaty in 1954, but then 53 Socialists switched their votes. For other examples see Meynaud and Lancelot, no. 161, pp. 849–50, on discount rates for housing loans; *JO* 12 and 18 March 1958, pp. 1552 (Barrachin) and 1616 (Bonnet), on constitutional reform. On lobbying see Brindillac, no. 29, p. 59.

27. J. Waline, no. 213, pp. 1207–11, 1215–22; Muselier, pp. 139–41; Buron, p. 120; on finance also *Figaro*, 28 March 1950, and above, p. 65.

28. Hamon, no, 121, p. 560. Isorni (*Silence*, Chapter 8) discusses relations within 'the closed circle of brotherly enemies' (p. 171) and remarks that often convictions may legitimately differ from attitudes (cf. his account of the Conservative meeting on Suez, pp. 172–6).

On the Right a politician's electoral connections often bore little relation to his parliamentary allegiance. In 1928 the 110 deputies supporting *Alliance démocratique* belonged to six groups ranging from the far Right to the moderate Left.[29] Even after 1945, when the political structure of the groups was more straightforward, and Communist, Socialist or MRP groups were merely the parliamentary expression of their parties, a group like UDSR was still the general staff of an army without troops.

At the beginning of the Third Republic groups were regarded with suspicion, for each deputy was supposed to represent the country as a whole and not a geographical, political or social segment of it. At first they could not announce meetings through the Chamber's services or hold them on its premises, and their members could not speak in their name in the house. But Presidents of the Republic had to consult their chairmen over cabinet-making, and in 1910 they at last acquired formal status when the Chamber decided to choose its committees proportionately from them, and obliged deputies to join one group only. Still they existed only for the committee elections. In 1930 a member whose group did not re-elect him to the finance committee formed a new group solely to regain his place (he did); and a group of deputies who would not join a group ranged from dissident Communists to intransigent royalists.[30] A resolution of the Chamber in 1932 required all members of a group to sign a political declaration, but this failed to enforce unity upon them.[31]

Their powers grew if their cohesion did not. They selected the committees, they arranged seating in the Chamber, and their chairmen sat on the presidents' conference which settled the order of business. After 1945 the rights of groups and chairmen were expanded to the detriment of the individual deputy, especially the independent. The groups were mentioned in eighteen of the Assembly's standing orders and (until 1954) in three articles of the constitution.[32] Many parliamentary initiatives were formally considered as party acts; thus an absent proposer of an interpellation was replaced by a colleague from his group. The presidents' conference was given more authority, debates in the house were more and more often 'organized', and sometimes the only members called to the tribune were those who spoke in the name of the group which once they had been forbidden to mention.[33]

29. Middleton, *French Political System*, p. 128.

30. For years it returned to the foreign affairs committee the distinguished Conservative Georges Mandel, once Clemenceau's associate and later the chief opponent of appeasement: Barthélemy, *Essai sur le travail parlementaire et le système des commissions*, pp. 92, 94, 101.

31. *Ibid.*, p. 93, for an apocryphal (or perhaps typical) declaration: 'Ni Réaction ni Révolution. Ni Rome ni Moscou. Le Progrès dans l'Ordre, la Paix dans la dignité. La Main Tendue, mais la Porte gardée. La déflation budgétaire dans le progrès social. La répression de la fraude fiscale sans inquisition ni vexation. La réduction du nombre des fonctionnaires dans le respect des droits acquis.'

32. The Assembly had to elect its *bureau* (until 1954) and its representatives on the Constitutional Committee by group PR; until 1954 a caretaker cabinet in case of dissolution had to contain representatives of all groups (Articles 11, 91 and 52). See also Waline, no. 213, pp. 1189–91; Lidderdale, pp. 115–16, 141, 144, and 238; and Arrighi, *Le Statut des partis politiques*, pp. 14–19.

33. See below, pp. 219–20 (presidents' conference, organized debate), 223–4 (interpellation). The MRP patriarch Francisque Gay once described a committee rapporteur as 'That colleague who has been given the task, in the name of the MRP parliamentary group, to make a report to the committee, and to defend it, who has expressed the MRP position and who on most points has won the day for the views of our party ...': *JO* 11 August 1947, p. 4233.

The party groups brought some much-needed discipline into the individualist disorder of the old Chamber. But members' allegiance to them was never exclusive and rarely complete. In the Third Republic groups for the defence of private local and professional interests had flourished; in the Fourth they were forbidden (by Standing Order 13) but the ban was easily evaded.[34] Many deputies – especially from the Gaullist, RGR and Conservative benches – joined 'inter-groups' which promoted various causes, afforded presidencies and vice-presidencies to impress constituents, and sometimes cut across party lines by reproducing in Parliament the electoral alliances which members formed in the country. In these loose parties of the Right and Centre, with their divided interests and loyalties, the leaders found it very difficult to impose their views; and in the last months of the regime the engagements they made in the 'round table' meetings of party chairmen were repeatedly broken by their followers.[35]

It was hard to use the whip when a rebellious faction could freely set up its own group, with representation on all committees and in settling the agenda. Late in 1957 the Assembly decided to check this proliferation in the next session by recognizing only groups with 28 members, instead of 14; but in the Fifth Republic the Radicals soon found a way round by adhering to a vague combination for committee elections which split into two wholly autonomous (and undisciplined) sections for all other purposes.[36] Thus, though the groups were far more important in parliamentary life after the war than before, they could not cure the congenital individualism of the French politician. Where the party leaders had failed, the officers of the Assembly had little hope of success.

4. THE CONTROL OF BUSINESS

Unlike the House of Commons or the House of Representatives, the Assembly elected its officers in each annual session. At the first sitting the oldest deputy presided and the six youngest acted as secretaries to supervise the counting of votes and drafting of the official record.[37] The Assembly proceeded at once to choose an executive committee (*bureau*) consisting of a President, six vice-presidents who relieved him in the chair, fourteen secretaries, and three stewards (*questeurs*) who organized the administrative and financial services. Until the 1954 constitutional amendment these 24 members had to represent the parties proportionately, and even afterwards the majority continued to elect Communists to junior posts in the *bureau*. Since 1920 the President and vice-presidents, the party and committee leaders had also sat as a business committee of the house, the presidents' conference.[38]

34. See below, pp. 374–5.
35. Andrews, no. 3; Maurice Deixonne, SFIO chairman, *JO* 18 February 1958, p. 890.
36. Waline, no. 213, p. 1218; and see below, p. 433.
37. When the Communist veteran Marcel Cachin was *doyen d'âge*, standing orders had to be amended to limit his rights. In 1951 he was junior to a new Conservative member, Eugène Pébellier, an octogenarian haberdasher from Le Puy who first left his native town to come to Paris in place of his ineligible son and namesake (a former deputy who had voted for Pétain). The son wrote and the father delivered an inaugural speech, praising the Marshal and condemning ineligibility, which contrasted oddly with Cachin's revolutionary discourses.
38. On it see below, pp. 219–20; on committees, Chapter 18; on the change about the *bureau*, p. 237, and Berlia, no. 12b, pp. 685–6.

The Fourth Republic made the President of the Assembly a vice-president of the Republic in all but name. If the Élysée fell vacant he became acting President and took the chair at the parliamentary congress which met within ten days (but up to six months if Parliament had been dissolved) to elect a successor.[39] He promulgated laws if the President neglected to, sat on the Constitutional Committee, and was consulted before a prospective premier was nominated or Parliament dissolved. A dissolution made him premier automatically before 1954, but afterwards only if the government that dissolved had previously been censured by the Assembly.[40]

The new duties did not prevent a resumption of old traditions. French deputies have always preferred a prominent political leader to preside over their debates, rather than a non-partisan Speaker of the British type. Three Presidents of the Chamber (and five of the Senate) had been elected direct to the Élysée, and several had become prime minister. In 1946 the first President of the Constituent Assembly, Félix Gouin, resigned to replace de Gaulle as head of the provisional government; the second, Vincent Auriol, became President of the Republic; and the National Assembly then chose a party leader, ex-premier and ex-President of the Chamber, Édouard Herriot. When he retired in January 1954 the Communists, seeking allies for the fight against EDC, helped to elect the Socialist André Le Troquer against the strongly 'European' Pierre Pflimlin. Next year German rearmament dislocated this fragile Left majority and Le Troquer was defeated by a new MRP candidate, Pierre Schneiter. After the 1956 election the Republican Front restored him to the post he coveted.[41]

Its potential importance was shown in May 1958, when President Coty's resignation would have brought Le Troquer to the Élysée, a Popular Front premier to the Hotel Matignon – and probably the parachutists to Paris. Even in less dramatic circumstances the President of the Assembly could wield great influence. In a recess he could help or hamper a party which wanted the house recalled. Being in close touch with the deputies he could, if he chose, suggest to the President of the Republic a strong candidate for the premiership (or one of whom he himself approved) and indicate where the marginal votes were and how best to woo them. It has been said that in December 1953 Le Troquer influenced the presidential election by adjourning at a psychological moment; and that two years later Schneiter by his formal advice decided the government to dissolve, and then by delaying tactics prevented the opposition recalling the house, before the dissolution could be pronounced, to vote a new electoral law or motion of censure. The constitution-makers of 1946 had meant to weaken the executive by strengthening the President of the Assembly; but if parliamentary rights are opposition rights,

39. In the Third Republic the President of the Senate had presided. 'Vice-president': see Sauvageot, no. 196, and Soubeyrol, no. 202.

40. Arts. 41, 11, 40, 36, 91, 45 (implied), 51 and 52 respectively. No law ever fell to him to promulgate. The 1954 constitutional revision made him less likely to become a dissolution premier but more powerful if he did, since he would control the police (as minister of the interior) as well as the army (as premier): Soubeyrol, no. 202, p. 555, cf. p. 561. It also gave him in practice more influence on the recall of the Assembly in recesses: *ibid.*, p. 561.

41. Cf. below, p. 433. In the eleven years of the Fourth Republic there was an opposition President of the Assembly for only six months in early 1954 and one month in early 1955.

the way the new powers were used confounded their authors by making him in a crisis almost a President against the Assembly.[42]

In normal times the President was much less partisan than the American Speaker, though more so than the British. By custom he neither spoke nor voted, nor did a vice-president at sittings over which he presided (but Herriot broke tradition twice in the Third Republic and once in the Fourth, on 30 December 1949 when he saved Bidault's budget from defeat by Radical defections). His authority was far weaker than that of his Anglo-Saxon counterparts. The deputies treated him with decent respect but no special deference, often contesting his decisions, continuing to speak when ruled out of order, or ignoring the five-minute time-limit imposed by standing orders on certain speeches.[43] The chair could do little to check the irrelevance which was always the cardinal sin of French parliamentary debate. Like the old Chamber, the Assembly disliked binding precedents; it preferred to take important procedural decisions itself and repudiate them later because, emanating from a transient political majority, they lacked moral authority.[44]

The Assembly would not strengthen its President (especially if he were a prominent party leader) because suspicion of power was inbred in the politicians of a deeply divided country. Yet those divisions confronted him with a problem no British or American Speaker faced. Unlike Congress or the House of Commons, the National Assembly always had many members who would cheerfully destroy the parliamentary system to achieve their political aims. Communists might not filibuster as systematically as Irish nationalists or as freely as southern senators, but they exploited procedural loopholes with persistence and ingenuity. In 1950 they used the quorum rules to delay for a month and finally force the withdrawal of a bill that had been expected to pass in a few hours. In the six months after the 1951 election they spoke on the average half as long again as other deputies, and among the six most loquacious members, four were Communists. At critical moments they went beyond verbal obstruction. During the general strike of November 1947 they fought the government's drastic public order bill for 114 hours, one member – protected by his party colleagues – occupying the tribune all one night. When their campaign against the Indo-China war reached its peak in March 1950, a deputy spoke for five and a half hours on one sub-amendment to a bill against sabotage, quoting Soviet price statistics in minute detail; later fighting broke out and the house was cleared by the guards. (Yet both the disputed bills were speedily passed, though with substantial concessions to those non-Communists who thought them harsh.) The Poujadists also provoked some angry incidents, especially when their colleagues were unseated by the votes of their opponents.[45]

42. Soubeyrol, no. 202, pp. 554–63 *passim*. On recesses see n. 21; and on May 1958, above, pp. 202–3.

43. Once when Jean Dides wanted to speak at length, Le Troquer agreed privately to stretch but not to 'forget' the limit of 5 minutes; reminded him after 15; failed repeatedly to stop him; and suspended the sitting in disorder after 35, with Dides still demanding just 5 more: *JO* 25 February 1958, pp. 997–8.

44. Generally, Blum, pp. 171–2 (see n. 56); Lidderdale, pp. 77, 151, 155–6; Noël, p. 169.

45. Blamont, pp. 63–6; Soubeyrol, no. 202, pp. 533–4; Lidderdale, p. 156n. (1947); R. Lamps, *JO* 3 March 1950, pp. 1859–81; *AP* 1950, pp. 51–3, 1957, pp. 24–6, 38–9, 47–8; G. Loustanau-

[*over*

Obstruction and violence obliged a reluctant Assembly to tighten its rules. Personal voting was first restricted and then (for a time) eliminated. The quorum rule was changed, after some delay owing to the absence of a quorum. Standing orders were amended in 1952 against vigorous Communist opposition. Dilatory motions like the previous question were limited, and only four speakers allowed on them. The President was authorized to subject members who defied his rulings to stiffer penalties, including financial sanctions, without seeking the leave of the house; and if these were rarely imposed in the latter years of the Fourth Republic this was partly because warnings were more effective.[46] Interpellations and urgent discussions were permitted only when proposed by the presidents' conference. More and more major debates were 'organized', as in the United States Congress, with the conference distributing the time available; for instance in a debate on family allowances in May 1951 it allotted one hour for voting and 5½ for discussion: three committees had 20 minutes each, the government 30, the Communists 50, MRP 44, SFIO 29 and eight other groups 15 each.[47] This was an invaluable device for saving time, and indeed for improving discussion.

The deputies accepted procedural changes with reluctance, for they feared discipline more than disorder. Their tradition equated presidential firmness with discourtesy; so no vice-president liked to incur needless odium by his severity, while a weak President was apt to remember that he faced re-election within the year and a strong (or tactless) one easily alienated supporters.[48] In theory a majority could end debate by closure, but this had become a dead letter.[49] Even organized debate was no panacea, for members were not always checked when their party's time was up;[50] and if the total time was inadequate the purpose of the debate might be frustrated, or the whole arrangement might collapse.[51] Above all, no rules of debate could check the most dangerous form of obstruction, which was to attack the order of parliamentary business.

The agenda of the house had at one time been proposed by the *bureau*, but since 1920 by the presidents' conference. This was a business committee

Lacau, *JO* 27 March 1952, p. 1528 (RPF members had spoken 42,000 lines to about 48,000 for each of the other major groups and 75,000 for the Communists). Another noisy debate early in 1950 had turned violent when a member shouted 'le mutin' at André Marty, and the Communists thought he had called Jeannette Vermeersch 'la putain': *JO* 27 January 1950, p. 623. Their violence converted many reluctant members to changing the electoral law.

46. Soubeyrol, no. 202, pp. 536–8, 561. But cf. n. 43.

47. *JO* 9 May 1951, p. 4903. Time was not always distributed in this rough proportion to numbers; the Communist opponents of standing orders reform in March 1952 had much more than their strict share (see Williams, p. 201n.).

48. *Travail*, pp. 699–701 (Goguel), 860, 863. Personal as well as political opposition defeated Le Troquer after his first year: *AP* 1955, p. 5. M. Goguel's proposal to strengthen the President by electing him for a whole Parliament was adopted in the Fifth Republic.

49. Lidderdale, pp. 137–8.

50. As Le Troquer admitted: *JO* 3 December 1954, p. 5747, cf. p. 5757, 'It really is curious that one arouses protests every time the Assembly's decisions have to be applied'. On 11 April 1951 a debate on civil expenditure, planned for 2½ hours, took 12. But members did speak (or read) faster in organized debates: Isorni, *Silence*, pp. 127–8.

51. In the debates on the Schuman Plan, tax reform, and the second economic Plan the industrial production committee had only 15 minutes to put its view: Harrison, *Commissions de l'Assemblée* (unpublished), p. 218.

consisting of the President and vice-presidents, the chairmen of the party groups and of the nineteen standing committees, the *rapporteur-général* of the finance committee, and a government representative. It met weekly to arrange business for two weeks ahead. But its programme was often upset by a vote of confidence (which meant delay), the absence of a committee report, or some other unexpected development. Much time was lost discussing the agenda, which from 1948 was made progressively harder to change. Worse still, the conference – in which each member had one vote – under-represented the opposition, which usually held relatively few committee chairmanships and included few of the smaller party groups; consequently its recommendations were often defeated in the house. In 1955, therefore, conference votes were adjusted to party strengths, ministers forming a little 'party' of their own. After this change its proposals were less likely to be upset in the Assembly (though in 1956 the house twice refused to debate repeal of the Barangé law subsidizing church schools) but more likely to go against a government whose majority was melting away. In November 1955 Edgar Faure was beaten first in the conference and then, when he made rejection of its proposed agenda a matter of confidence, in the Assembly.[52]

A disgruntled party would rebel on a matter of parliamentary priority even more readily than on a question of substance, since an indifferent public was less apt to notice and blame it; and all deputies were tempted to postpone uncomfortable subjects like taxes and debate popular topics like higher pensions. The government could resist only by demanding votes of confidence on priority for its own business, like Queuille in May 1951, Pinay in December 1952, Faure in November 1955 and Gaillard in January 1958. Even a premier who survived this test (and only two of these did) found that the more he used his heavy weapons the faster they wore out. Thus the determination of the Assembly to control its agenda was a godsend to demagogues and obstructionists, and a threat to governmental authority.

Accepting no leadership, the Assembly easily fell into chaos, beginning far too many tasks and then leaving them unfinished. In April 1951 the agenda of the dying Assembly still included a constitutional amendment proposed five months before; two major bills of which half had been voted, and four which had been abandoned – one of them back in December 1949; and 140 bills adopted in committee but not yet discussed by the Assembly, three-quarters of them opposed measures. The budget was three months late, and the credits for twelve government departments still had to be voted. The contentious electoral law for metropolitan France was due to return from the Council of the Republic, and that for the overseas territories had not been begun. But the Assembly was most unwilling to give priority to the budget and electoral

52. *Travail*, pp. 819–22 (Galichon), 859; Georgel, i. 234, 241–2; Arné, pp. 180–2; Cotteret, no. 63, pp. 819–20, 824–5; *AP* 1955, pp. 88–9, 1956, pp. 27, 89. Till 1948 any 50 members could move to change the conference's proposals. Afterwards, to hamper the Communists, only the government or a committee or 30 members from three different parties could move a change and only an absolute majority of the house could carry it; and from 1950 it was out of order to propose to change an agenda accepted by the Assembly, or to add an interpellation, an urgent discussion, or a bill on which there was no committee report. Before 1955 PR in the conference had been rejected as making it too powerful: Georgel, i. 241n., Williams, p. 207. The conference 'was an infernal nuisance to governments': Buron, p. 113.

law, which had to be passed if a general election were to take place before the summer holidays.[53]

Yet in refusing a minimum of discipline the deputies stultified themselves, for their attention was distracted to minor matters and major policy frequently escaped their control. When the Assembly recessed in July 1953 it had not debated European, North African, or Indo-Chinese affairs for over a year (not that debates would necessarily have given much guidance to the government).[54] In domestic policy parliamentary and administrative responsibilities were confused, and while the legislature had to decide the number of donkeys in the national stud, the currency could be devalued or the national economic Plan adopted without reference to Parliament. But these absurdities were unlikely to be remedied while the deputies insisted on managing their affairs so badly. 'What a fatal contradiction for the regime: all power in the hands of a powerless Assembly, powerless by its nature, powerless by its rules, powerless by its composition.'[55]

Back in 1919 Blum had denounced the Chamber's habits in an attack which had lost none of its force in the next Republic.[56] All parties agreed that drastic changes were required, and many felt that standing orders stood more in need of reform than the constitution itself. Measures were indeed taken to meet Communist obstruction (inevitably restricting the rights of the individual deputy) but they could not deal with the root of the trouble while the members cared less for the rational conduct of public business than for their private right to change their minds and repudiate their leaders at will. Government supporters were less concerned to get business through than to protect their personal freedom to dissent whenever they chose, and to prevent stricter regulations which might be used against them when they were next in opposition. Fearing leadership, they tolerated anarchy; impeding governmental action, they also crippled effective parliamentary criticism.[57] The real deficiency was one of will, not of technical devices, and it was the division of purpose within the majority that gave the obstructionists the opportunities they exploited so skilfully.

53. *Monde*, 1 April 1951. For the subjects the deputies preferred see below, p. 249.

54. The deputies had considered the main lines of policy in five recent investiture debates, in which the prospective premier appeared without colleagues or staff to answer a confused succession of questions great and trivial; these were a poor substitute for orderly parliamentary discussion. On Tunisia in June 1952, they had found no majority and rejected six successive *ordres du jour*: *AP* 1952, pp. 228–9. (M. Mitterrand pointed out that in 1881 the Chamber had rejected 23 *ordres du jour* on the same subject: *JO* 4 June 1953, p. 1952.)

55. Isorni, *Ainsi*, p. 53. For criticisms by senior parliamentary officials see Goguel, *Fourth Republic*, pp. 167–9, and no. 107, pp. 853–61; Blamont, no. 18, pp. 393–7.

56. '... permanent vices of organization and method. Two or three questions, discussed together, alternate from one sitting to the next. On each, numberless amendments, endless speakers dragging out their interminable remarks amidst universal apathy . . . [at] the slightest incident the Assembly moves abruptly from indifference to rowdy excitement . . . [The President] has nothing to say when four different discussions are begun at once, when the day's business is upset at the last minute, when the same speech is begun again for the tenth time, when a question that had been settled is reopened on a new pretext, when a debate wanders into the most futile digression. . . . All that is needed is a break with tradition. That is essential, but it would be enough.' Blum, pp. 158–9, 171–2 (fuller in Williams, pp. 207n., 209n.). Cf. R. Lecourt, *JO* 25 March 1952, pp. 1461–2.

57. But the government was not blameless and the deputies had some grounds for mistrusting it. Gaillard tried in 1957 to use procedural devices to stifle debate on his Algerian reforms; but the Communists, with support from the rest of the opposition, warned that 'if you play that game all 150 of us will make speeches "explaining our votes"': *JO* 28 November 1957, pp. 5026–7.

Chapter 17

THE NATIONAL ASSEMBLY
(2): GOVERNMENT AND PARLIAMENT

The Fourth Republic proved no more successful than the Third in solving the essential problem in working a democratic constitution: the relationship between legislature and executive. Before 1940 French cabinets had little control over the shifting moods of a Chamber which by constitutional convention they could not dissolve. But the Socialist leaders who largely inspired the new constitution wanted to break with the traditions of the Third Republic. They hoped and believed that the political system would be transformed by the rise of a few strong and disciplined parties. Chamber and government would cease to be rival powers and become complementary instruments of a common purpose: the executive would not need to coerce a majority which shared its objectives, nor the majority wish to upset its own leaders on trivial points of difference. Both would normally survive, as in Britain, throughout the life of a Parliament. A prime minister would be elected individually, to enhance his authority, and by an absolute majority, to ensure that he had solid support.[1] He could be removed only by an absolute majority of the deputies in a formal and deliberate decision sanctioned, if it was repeated, by the automatic dissolution of the Assembly. Irresponsible voting would thus be checked, and the stability of government which France needed would be reconciled with the tradition of parliamentary supremacy which she cherished.[2]

These rules failed to achieve their objects, largely because the constitutional doctrine was applied before its political foundation had been laid. Weak and loose parties soon regained influence in Parliament. Men and measures were found to be inseparable; the leader could not be distinguished so sharply from his team. An absolute majority was assembled more easily for mutual obstruction than for any common constructive aim. Dissolution was made subject to strict conditions, and the deputies tried hard to see that these were never fulfilled. Governments, though as precarious as ever, rarely fell in the manner prescribed in the constitution. A return to the pre-war methods was begun in practice in 1948 and extended by constitutional amendment in 1954, but it solved nothing.

1. PARLIAMENTARY SCRUTINY

The National Assembly spent much more time and energy than most Parliaments on making and unmaking governments, but it also needed milder

1. In reckoning the absolute majority seats legally vacant like the unfilled Cochin-China seat did not count; but three Malagasy deputies did, who were in prison after the 1947 rising and could not vote. See *JO* 21 November 1947, pp. 5113–4, and Drevet, pp. 44–5. The absolute majority was about 294 in the two Constituent Assemblies, 311 in the first National Assembly, 314 in the second and 299 in the third.

2. Blum, especially pp. 150–3, 219–23; Auriol, ii. 50, 244, 249; Théry, pp. 188–92; Wright, *Reshaping*, pp. 85–9. Article 45 of the constitution had a premier chosen for each Parliament in paragraph 1, ignoring other occasions (resignations, etc.) until paragraph 4: Sauvageot, no. 195, p. 242.

procedures for influencing their day-to-day activities. It could express views through its committees, by questions and motions, and in foreign affairs it had to ratify many treaties.

The committees were the most effective instrument of scrutiny. Ministers were often asked to appear, especially before those like Foreign Affairs and Defence which were more concerned with checking administration than with legislating. Others, like Finance, were active in both. The government gradually gained new powers to issue decrees applying budgetary bills, but Parliament required consultation with the finance committees of both houses and sometimes the consent of the Assembly's committee; after 1956 a new budgetary procedure and the use of the *loi-cadre* extended and formalized this practice.[3] Some aspects of administration were supervised by statutory sub-committees representing several standing committees. One on defence expenditure had existed since the early Third Republic; another on public enterprises proved an effective and acceptable instrument of general oversight without vexatious interference.[4] Special committees of inquiry might be useful on administrative questions, but not for probing political scandals.[5]

In the chamber itself members could ask questions or introduce motions, called interpellations, seeking an explanation of ministerial acts or policies. Written questions were very numerous but unimportant, 'free legal advice for the citizen rather than close control of the civil service'. Oral questions were really short debates limited to five-minute speeches by the minister and then the questioner. They never enjoyed the esteem and importance they have in Britain, for there were no supplementaries to give opportunities to the deputy; yet ministers disliked them because the attacker had the last word.[6]

The traditional weapon of the house against the executive was the interpellation, which could make the reputation of a politician who used it skilfully: Clemenceau in the Third Republic, Debré in the Fourth. Unlike a debate on the adjournment in the House of Commons, it ended with a vote – either of a simple resolution, 'The House, having heard the minister's explanation, passes to the order of the day' or of a motion qualified (*motivé*) by

3. See below, pp. 242–3, 268–9, 272–3.

4. On it see Ridley, no. 189; Lewis, no. 145; Lescuyer, no. 143 (cf. below, p. 374n.); and his *Le contrôle de l'État sur les entreprises nationalisées*, Chapters 6, 7 and 11. In 1953 two ex-chairmen of the sub-committee, René Mayer as premier and J. M. Louvel as minister of industry, issued decrees ending the autonomy of the nationalized industries, but in 1955 Parliament reversed these by law. In the third Assembly another sub-committee was set up on *parafiscalité* (compulsory levies, such as social security contributions, which are not part of the state revenue).

5. The Council of the Republic's sub-committee on nationalized industries had one set up, successfully, when Jules Ramarony, minister of state for merchant shipping, tried to obstruct its inquiry into the faulty construction of two liners: Georgel, i. 84–5. But political inquiries usually led nowhere after much acrimony. For instance, on the committee investigating the 'scandal of the generals', the Communist member released confidential documents to *L'Humanité*, the Gaullist chairman and two friendly colleagues interviewed an important witness privately, several members resigned, and the MRP and SFIO survivors disputed bitterly: see Williams, no. 218. A later committee on exchange dealings with Indo-China had little more success. A law in 1953 made their proceedings secret. Generally, see Biays, no. 17; Pactet, no. 171, pp. 165–71.

6. Blamont, *Techniques*, p. 109, and no. 18, p. 391: supplementaries would inevitably have led to impromptu debates and upset business. In the first Assembly about 140 oral questions a year were asked and in the second 200, but only about half were answered. Nearly all the 4,000 written questions asked annually were answered: Campbell, no. 45, p. 361; Noël, p. 9. 'Free advice': M. Prélot in *Travail*, pp. 863–4. Also see Buron, p. 205.

expressions of confidence in or disapproval of the government's attitude. Nearly half the governments overthrown by the Chamber of Deputies were beaten on interpellations, and some members and even ministers subordinated their loyalty to the old cabinet to their hopes of promotion in the new. Often governments were upset by an accidental aggregation of opposites, incapable of sustaining a successor. Yet the procedure was not a cause but an expression (at most an aggravation) of ministerial instability. A disciplined majority could always refuse to debate dangerous motions, as the anticlericals early in the century obediently did at the behest of their steering committee, the *Délégation des Gauches*.[7]

Increasingly, after 1918, the growing number and triviality of interpellations impaired their effectiveness. Members used them to force a debate on a cherished subject, rather than to attack the government. After 1946 legislation took more and more time, and the presidents' conference accepted fewer interpellation debates, usually grouping several motions together.[8] The second National Assembly held full debates on 316 out of 1,549, mostly grouped, and brief ones on 220 more in which a speaker from each party had, in theory, five minutes to discuss the date for the main debate.[9] In February 1953 René Mayer was interpellated on his choice as minister of health of Senator André Boutemy, a former Vichy prefect and the current distributor of the employers' political funds: when the Assembly voted for a debate at an early date, the minister resigned. Laniel's defeat was clearly imminent when five of the six interpellations on the fall of Dien-Bien-Phu came from deputies belonging to the majority. But if crises occurred during a recess, Parliament might well be confronted with a *fait accompli*, as it was when the Sultan of Morocco was deposed in the summer of 1953 and when his successor abdicated in 1955. When the house reconvened in October 1955 Faure faced eighteen interpellations on Morocco.[10]

Foreign policy was a special case. It aroused little attention among voters or members of parliament unless the question was exceptionally controversial. In the first and second Assemblies only a fifth of the votes of confidence related to any external question (even including military expenditure). The few interpellations on foreign affairs usually came from a handful of Communists, 'fellow-travellers', or extremists of the Right.[11] But Parliament's potential power was great, since it had to ratify many treaties – for instance, all those

7. Soulier, pp. 332, 342, 345 (no solidarity); 227–8, 244 (discipline); 237 (opposition); 119 and Prélot's preface (fall of cabinets). In the Fourth Republic 5 governments were defeated on interpellations, 6 on financial and 2 on other bills. On Debré cf. below, p. 281 and n.

8. Blamont, *Techniques*, pp. 103–6: 'in practice the Assembly no longer discusses interpellations unless it wants to satisfy public opinion by holding a debate on a subject of general interest and concern'; cf. no. 18, pp. 390, 393; Georgel, i. 232; Goguel in *Travail*, pp. 705, 863.

9. Of course, little was heard of the date: cf. Le Troquer, *JO* 10 March 1955, p. 1274. On numbers see Noël, pp. 18–19; cf. Campbell, *loc. cit.* At first about 200 a year were put down, but by 1952 there were almost twice as many.

10. Boutemy: Muselier, pp. 95–6. Laniel: *AP* 1954, p. 28. Recesses: cf. Georgel, i. 232, and Grosser, pp. 87–8; before Dien-Bien-Phu fell the chairman of the foreign affairs committee, Daniel Mayer, flew to Geneva to warn the foreign minister (Bidault) against asking for American nuclear intervention, and in 1955 the chairman of the defence committee, Pierre Montel, went to Morocco to urge Ben Arafa not to abdicate. Faure: Arné, p. 252n.

11. Grosser, pp. 79–83. Cf. Blamont, no. 18, p. 390; Georgel, i. 232. On votes of confidence, below, pp. 234–5.

dealing with European union needed ratification, though not those granting independence to Morocco or Tunisia, or treaties of alliance.[12]

On the most controversial treaties the government consulted Parliament before signature. In 1948 the deputies imposed impossible conditions for the setting up of a central German government; they did not have to ratify the treaty, and Schuman's cabinet ignored them, so next year Parliament insisted that it and not the government must give the French consent required by the Atlantic pact before a new partner (i.e. Germany) could join. Before the EDC negotiations began in 1952, Edgar Faure consulted the Assembly; his successors vainly pressed its terms on France's partners, who were misled into overconfidence by the French 'Europeans' and were amazed when the deputies rejected the treaty in 1954. Mendès-France, under allied pressure to admit Germany into NATO instead, also consulted the Assembly first; ninety 'European' MRP and CNIP deputies first consented to the policy, then voted against the treaty; it passed on a second vote, but to get it through the upper house Edgar Faure had to promise to work for the aims sought in the senators' proposed amendments. In 1957 the Assembly easily accepted the Common Market, both before the treaty was signed and when it needed to be ratified. In general foreign policy was imposed on an occasionally indignant Parliament, rather than made by it or even with it.[13] The real influence of the deputies was felt less on the conduct of policy than in the frequent ministerial crises when they could select the men who made it, altering the balance of power in a cabinet, blackballing a foreign minister, and above all choosing a premier.

2. THE INVESTITURE OF THE PREMIER

When a government fell in the Third Republic, the President named a new prime minister who appointed his colleagues and then came before the Chamber of Deputies for its approval. The President could do something to help candidates he favoured and much to hinder those he disliked, for timing was vital and he need not propose his enemies unless they were sure to fail. Critics argued that if his choice coincided with the Chamber's it was superfluous; if not it was undemocratic. The provisional regime of 1945–46 therefore provided that while the new constitution was being drafted, prospective prime ministers were to be designated by the Assembly itself (as in 1848 and 1871).[14] There were two votes, one on the man and another on his team. The Left's first draft constitution kept this system, in the hope that future Presidents of the Assembly would take the initiative in crises, as Vincent Auriol had in the provisional regime; that ministries so chosen would be in harmony with Parliament; and that premiers would thus be better able to resist the mistrusted President, whose name might be Charles de Gaulle. But this constitutional

12. See Arts. 27 and 28 of the constitution. Treaties adding, abandoning or exchanging territory also required the consent of the peoples concerned; but French India was ceded in 1954 with no plebiscite (only a vote by local councillors) and the treaty, signed in 1956, was not ratified until 1962: cf. Georgel, i. 248 and n. Parliament ratified the NATO but not the SEATO pact.

13. Grosser, pp. 88–101; Corail, no. 60, especially pp. 780–816, 837–53.

14. Théry, pp. 90–111; cf. Soulier, pp. 496–7. *Ibid.*, pp. 275–302, on pre-war Presidents; for their critics, P. Cot, *JO* 17 April 1946, p. 1968.

draft was defeated at the referendum of May 1946, and MRP then urged that the Assembly should, like the old Chamber, vote only after the government had been formed.[15]

The final compromise form of Article 45 satisfied the Left by keeping the 'investiture' vote on the leader alone, and MRP by allowing the President to propose candidates. With Auriol and not de Gaulle at the Élysée the premier, working in harmony instead of conflict with the head of the state, could wield his new authority against recalcitrant ministerial colleagues. The Communist ministers who joined their followers against the government on a vote of confidence, in May 1947, would have brought down a Third Republican premier. But Ramadier, supported or instigated by the President, maintained that the Assembly had chosen him and not the cabinet, and that its vote confirmed its confidence in him; when the Communist ministers would not resign, Auriol signed a decree stating that their 'duties . . . had terminated as a consequence of their vote'.[16] In October Ramadier called for the resignation of all his ministers (and halved their number) without himself vacating office.[17] In February 1950 the Socialists left Bidault's government and were replaced. In 1954 Mendès-France twice lost three colleagues, and in 1955 Edgar Faure dismissed his RS (Gaullist) ministers; both premiers filled the vacant posts and stayed in office.[18]

Although the prime minister's right to reconstruct his cabinet became accepted, the Assembly was uneasy when it had to choose a captain without knowing his team. The early premiers accepted interpellations on the composition and policy of their cabinets ending with informal votes of confidence; and in September 1948 Robert Schuman was defeated by six votes because he had appointed a Socialist minister of finance.[19] The Radical premiers of 1948 informally revived the old procedure; André Marie made known the main lines of his cabinet in advance, and Henri Queuille formed his before the investiture debate. In October 1949 first Jules Moch and then René Mayer was elected premier but failed to form a ministry, while Georges Bidault went to the investiture debate with a cabinet in his pocket and was safely elected.[20] On his fall, Queuille was invested as premier by 363 votes to 208, but chose a cabinet too conservative for the Socialists or MRP's left wing; the Assembly

15. They threatened to oppose the second draft constitution unless satisfied on this point and on the secret ballot for presidential elections (above, p. 196 and n.)

16. See above, p. 200. Georges Marrane, the Communist minister of health, had not voted (being a member of the upper house) and was not dismissed, but he resigned at once.

17. Since the new status belonged to the premiership and not to its holder, the minister of state (*secrétaire d'État*) attached to the prime minister's office did not resign either: Sauvageot, no. 195, p. 245.

18. Contrast Third Republican doctrine: Soulier, p. 79n., But in 1950 Blum said it was Bidault's republican duty as well as his constitutional right to stay in office: *Populaire*, 4–5 February 1950. (Pflimlin resigned in May 1958 when his Conservative ministers left him, but this was a pretext.)

19. This was cited as a weakness of the new procedure, but the same had often happened under the old: see Soulier, pp. 119–21.

20. Both Marie and Queuille refused a debate on composition and policy (but allowed a short discussion and vote on their refusal). Bidault refused any debate or vote and the house upheld him by a show of hands; but when the Socialists resigned in February 1950 he accepted a debate and narrowly survived it (they abstained). The rapporteur of the constitution, Paul Coste-Floret, had anticipated both the formation of cabinets before investiture and the later debate: *JO* 28 September 1946, p. 4200, quoted Théry, p. 111, and Williams, p. 181n.

insisted on a debate and overthrew him by 334 to 221. The Radicals now announced that they would vote for no premier without knowing his cabinet; Pleven was elected after conforming to their demand; and a constitutional amendment initiated in November 1950 proposed to revert to the Third Republic's rules. To reinforce the lesson, Guy Mollet in March 1951, René Mayer in July and Maurice Petsche in August all stood without first forming governments – and all lost.[21]

Yet in the new Parliament the constitutional procedure returned to favour; the first six cabinets after the 1951 general election were all formed after the investiture of the premier. René Pleven in 1951 might have lost the Socialist vote by naming his government, which had to follow the election returns in shifting to the Right. In 1952 Edgar Faure was hardly thought a serious candidate until his investiture speech, or Antoine Pinay until the vote was announced. In January 1953 Georges Bidault tried – as in 1949 – to form a cabinet before the vote but this time had to abandon the attempt, while René Mayer again refused to look beyond the investiture debate and at last was successful. In the next crisis, shock treatment from the early candidates failed but the parties took it from Laniel because of the long interregnum; and in 1954, after the fall of Dien-Bien-Phu, Mendès-France disdained to negotiate with them at all.[22] But by the constitutional amendment passed at last in 1954, the Assembly was not to vote on a premier until he had formed his government, and he would no longer need an absolute majority of the Assembly.

Of the first five prime ministers elected after the Liberation, four had had 200 votes more than the absolute majority, and even Bidault, with no Communist support, polled 90 more than he needed. But in December 1946 neither 'Bidault without Thorez' nor 'Thorez without Bidault' won an absolute majority, and after Communists and Gaullists went into opposition the rule became an obstacle. Two more candidates failed to clear it in the first Assembly and six in the second. Of sixteen premiers elected before the constitutional reform, seven had fewer than 50 votes to spare and only Schuman (in 1947) and Mendès-France had over 100.[23]

The proposers of the 1954 constitutional amendment believed that the Third Republic's procedure would shorten crises and make them easier to solve. But Gaullists and MRP warned that more governments would fall if successors were easier to find; they favoured the absolute majority rule because, if a smaller majority sufficed, a government might be formed without them and decide against them on the all-important question of EDC. The rule made them both indispensable (and so, as their views were fundamentally opposed, ensured that nothing whatever could be decided).[24] But the Socialists

21. See Arné, pp. 189–208; also Fabre, no. 88 (only up to 1950). Queuille was elected in March 1951 after telling the Assembly he would keep the old cabinet, but offered Bidault a vice-premiership; the Socialists then insisted that Ramadier must have one too, and only Ramadier himself made them give way.

22. Only he and Faure accepted debates on the composition and policy of their cabinets; see Arné, pp. 197–200. 'Shock treatment': above, p. 40.

23. Details in Arné, pp. 45, 198, 207.

24. MRP senators favoured the change of rule; their spokesman on the constitution (who opposed his party over EDC) argued that narrower majorities would be more coherent and less subject to mutual obstruction than broader ones: L. Hamon, *JO (CR)* 10 March 1954, p. 365,

[*over*

were now adamant that it must go. The Assembly suppressed it only by 309 to 300, MRP and Gaullist ministers voting against their parties; but when SFIO threatened to oppose the whole amendment bill if this vote were reversed, the suppression was confirmed by 321 to 237. In the upper house the Gaullists restored the absolute majority and the Socialist senators duly voted against the bill; the Assembly removed it again (by 412 to 207) and seventy MRP deputies failed to vote for the bill's final reading.[25]

Neither the hopes nor the fears were fulfilled. The prospective premier was handicapped by having to form a cabinet before the vote, for expectant deputies produced about forty more favourable votes than disappointed ones.[26] In the first crisis under the new system Pflimlin failed to form a cabinet, Pineau's attempt to do so contributed to his defeat, and Edgar Faure succeeded only by evading the new rules: he duly chose his senior ministers who could bring him votes, but made no appointments to the junior posts to which wavering 'back-benchers' might aspire until he was safely installed.

The absolute majority rule had been a scapegoat and not a cause. While abstentions blocked a candidate's election, hostile votes were cast only by parties keeping their distance from the majority (as the Communists voted against every prospective premier from 1947 to 1953 and the Socialists against six in 1952–53) or from some particular bugbear (as right-wingers voted against Socialists and Mendès-France, and Gaullists against Queuille). Ordinary opponents abstained, as the Socialists did on one investiture vote in the second Assembly, the Conservatives on two, MRP on three, and the Gaullists on six. 'Investiture courtesy' might even lead members who had an eye to future reciprocity to vote for a candidate they hoped and believed would fail; and Pinay owed his unexpected success as much to his 'courtesy majority' of MRP and Radical enemies as to the 27 defecting Gaullists – who confounded the prophets by turning it into a real one.

The new rules brought new habits, and courtesy disappeared as soon as it might cost something. The first nominee who could have been elected by a relative majority was also the first not to be given one. When Christian Pineau stood in February 1955, after the reform, there were fewer abstentions than on any previous unsuccessful aspirant (except Blum in 1947); fewer favourable votes than for any candidate since 1946 (except Mayer in 1951); and a record hostile vote of 312. In all, nine nominees stood from 1955 to 1958; the new rule did not save the three who were in a minority, or help the four who had an absolute majority. It elected two men who (given identical voting) would have failed under the old rule: Bourgès-Maunoury, one of the weakest premiers of the Fourth Republic, and Pierre Pflimlin who presided over its collapse. It still permitted divided cabinets like Faure's in 1955 and

and *Problèmes constitutionnels et réalités politiques*, pp. 19, 28–30. Others feared that only colourless premiers would win absolute majorities: Goguel, *Régime*, p. 55 (cf. Arné, p. 194).

25. The senators also wanted ministers to appear with the premier when the Assembly voted; the deputies overruled them.

26. Berlia, no. 12a, p. 440n. In the first Assembly the average premier lost 41 supporters, and in the second 11, between the two debates. Only Queuille (in 1951) and Mendès-France gained, and only Bidault avoided a second vote. Schuman was beaten on it in 1948 and Queuille in 1950. Most cabinets also had more opponents than the premier alone. See Arné, pp. 197–8.

Gaillard's in 1957, whose members were mainly concerned to prevent their colleagues taking action. It did not even shorten ministerial crises: before the reform three crises out of twelve lasted longer than three weeks, after it three out of five did so.[27]

The investiture experiment had at least strengthened determined prime ministers, enabling several to dismiss dissentient colleagues and one, Mendès-France, to pick a united team independent of party control. But the professors of law who invented it had unhappily combined proportional representation in the election of deputies with an absolute majority rule for the choice of premiers.[28] This curious conjunction might not have mattered if a few disciplined parties had continued to dominate the Assembly as in 1945–47; but once the looser groups regained their influence it provoked difficulties, and before long the old arrangements were restored. This reversion to the Third Republic did not remedy the weaknesses, which had been political and not procedural. Crises were not solved faster, stronger men were not elected premier, and majorities were no more coherent. The frequency with which governments called on their doubting followers to reaffirm their confidence showed once again that they knew it to be precarious.

3. VOTES OF CONFIDENCE

Third Republican governments could usually get their way in the Chamber only by seeking numerous votes of confidence even on trivial matters. A prudent leader might even resign as soon as his majority dropped and before it disappeared – for he would need the deputies' goodwill in his future career, and must not seem to cling to office against their wishes.[29] These traditions of a Parliament of individualists were always deplored by the Socialists, who condemned both the governments for coercing the Chamber by votes of confidence on minor questions and the deputies for upsetting cabinets on them. In the new regime, with real parties and a real majority, they hoped that new constitutional rules could change the old habits. Their remedy, however, rested both on an insecure and temporary political foundation and on a basic misunderstanding of the British example that inspired it: for Blum imagined that a British government could not seek a vote of confidence from the House of Commons.[30] A French cabinet without this weapon – and lacking any coherent majority, any common purpose shared with its following, or any tradition of parliamentary acceptance of cabinet leadership – would be helpless against the pressure of the deputies and obliged to trim before every breeze of parliamentary feeling. Few premiers would hold office at the price of sacrificing all authority and all consistency of policy.

While the new constitution was being drafted the provisional regime was established by an ordinance of 2 November 1945, which reflected the Socialist

27. Arné, pp. 201–8, 303–5; Georgel, i. 105. Five crises before but only one after 1954 were settled in less than a fortnight. For the votes. see Arné, p. 207.

28. Hamon, *Problèmes*, p. 23.

29. Soulier, pp. 239, 248. *Ibid.*, pp. 114, 233, etc. for complaints of too many confidence votes in the Third Republic; cf. Lidderdale, p. 37; J. Meyer, *La question de confiance* (1948), pp. 17–19; Williams, p. 212. Tardieu asked for 60 in eight sitting months in 1929–30, but this was exceptional: A. Tardieu, *Le Souverain captif* (1936), p. 49.

30. Blum, p. 222 (cf. Williams, p. 214n.).

conception. The government had to resign on defeat on a motion of censure, but not on losing a bill or an estimate, and it was not expected to stake its own existence on a vote of confidence. Within two months these rules led to a direct clash, for when the Socialists proposed to reduce military credits, General de Gaulle unconstitutionally (in their view) treated the vote as one of confidence. The quarrel, briefly patched up, led to his resignation three weeks later.[31] In the new constitution the Socialists had to compromise, and both the April and the October drafts allowed governments to seek a vote of confidence. But for use in ministerial self-defence the weapon was blunted by the conditions SFIO imposed.

Installed by an absolute majority of the Assembly, a prime minister was to be removed only in the same way. This caused no problem if he won a vote of confidence, or if he lost by an absolute majority. But he might be defeated by less. Then, by the Assembly's standing orders, the government was beaten on the point at issue but had not lost the confidence of the house. But whatever the rules no leader, after declining responsibility for governing unless the deputies accepted his policy, was likely to stay in office when they refused him satisfaction.[32]

Articles 49 and 50 endeavoured to make procedure reinforce the position of the ministry. The occasions on which its life was at stake were to be limited, defined, and proclaimed to Parliament and the country. The government need resign only if defeated on a vote of confidence sought by the prime minister (Article 49) or of censure tabled by the opposition (Article 50). The government's decision must be deliberate: the prime minister must consult the cabinet before demanding a vote of confidence. The deputies' vote must be deliberate also: one clear day must elapse between the demand for confidence or censure and the vote upon it.[33] The ballot must be public, and a government need resign only if an absolute majority of the Assembly voted against it. It was therefore expected that ministers would wield votes of confidence less prodigally, and deputies treat them less lightly, than in the Third Republic.

These hopes rested on an unreal political foundation. The Socialists expected politics to be dominated by three great parties and majorities to be formed by their own choice of an ally. But *tripartisme* collapsed in France when co-operation broke down between the international great powers. With a majority as heterogeneous, divided and undisciplined as in the Third Republic, there was no clear clash between loyal supporters and firm opponents of the government. As before, the marginal members of the majority

31. Théry, pp. 188–92; Arné, pp. 268–9; Solal-Celigny, no. 200, pp. 732–3.

32. The second Constituent Assembly, unlike the first, recognized that a defeated government might resign instead: Théry, p. 193, Georgel, i. 55–7. But if it did, it nullified other constitutional provisions (below, pp. 237–8). That governments should not use votes of confidence to coerce the Assembly was held by all parties when they were in opposition: *JO* 16 May 1947, pp. 1656–7 (Giacobbi, Gaullist); 24 June 1950, p. 5263 (Lussy, SFIO); 18 February 1958, p. 844 (Triboulet, RS); *AP* 1956, pp. 51 and 113 (Boisdé, CNI, Viatte, MRP, and Bégouin, Radical); Arné, pp. 257 (MRP), 273 (Pleven and Mendès-France). Cf. Meyer, pp. 119, 127; and *JO* 12 March 1958, pp. 1551–2, for Triboulet's attempt to ban votes of confidence on bills.

33. On the origins of the delay period (which was two days in the provisional regime) see Soulier, pp. 245–6; Georgel, i. 61–2 and n.; cf. Meyer, p. 114.

prized their freedom to switch their votes and allegiance when they chose. Commanding the political decision, they transformed the procedural problem. For they neither needed nor desired the opposition to determine by a vote of censure the moment for their defection from the majority: that procedure therefore became superfluous and inoperative. They did not have to be coerced into supporting the government on great clashes of principle with the opposition; on these their allegiance was safe. But the vote of confidence was often needed to keep individual waverers and hesitant parties loyal to unpopular decisions or unpalatable compromises without which the majority would crack and the government fall. It thus became a common event instead of a rare and solemn one. When the formalities were a nuisance they were evaded or disregarded entirely; when they were convenient the vote of confidence was used as a procedural device. As the politics came to resemble those of the Third Republic, the procedure did so too.

The hopes of the constitution-makers broke down as soon as the majority proved unstable. The first vote of confidence was asked in March 1947 to compel the Communists to observe ministerial solidarity or else resign. The second, in May, put pressure on the Socialists who had said they would not stay in office without the Communists; after voting with the government it was harder for them to leave it. MRP then urged Ramadier to ask for votes of confidence against Socialist demands on civil service wages in July, and on an Algerian government bill in August; meanwhile the other parties persuaded him to seek one against MRP over the municipal election law. In September MRP, having got satisfaction over Algeria, voted confidence in the government over a coal subsidy which they opposed, while the Communists (who approved of it) voted against it to show no confidence in the cabinet.[34]

If friction was too serious, a vote of confidence might so strain relations between parties as to shatter the majority instead of consolidating it. In February 1951 Pleven's compromise electoral reform instituted a double ballot which MRP detested. The prime minister sought a vote of confidence on the bill, but appeased MRP by agreeing to accept the house's decision on a private member's amendment for a single ballot. On 28 February the Assembly voted confidence with most MRP members abstaining; next day it rejected the single ballot, ministers not voting. Now the Radicals demanded that Pleven ask a vote of confidence on the double ballot clause in the bill; he would lose their ministers if he refused and MRP's if he agreed, and to avoid bitterness which would make the next government harder to form, he himself resigned.[35]

When major parties clashed the vote of confidence might fix (or shift) responsibilities, or even postpone the fall of a cabinet. Its everyday use was less dramatic. Free of pressure from the government, the Assembly would often overwhelmingly reject its measures or carry popular proposals which it

34. Meyer, pp. 152, 158, 161, 165, 175; cf. Colliard, no. 58, pp. 222, 225–6; and Arné, pp. 275–6, for similar cases later.

35. He had already done so on 28 February when he won the vote of confidence by only 27; the President refused his resignation then, but accepted Pleven's arguments for it on 1 March.

considered impracticable.[36] A vote of confidence protected not only the ministers but also the deputy, who could tell his critical constituents that he had opposed their favourite demand, or accepted the government's utterly inadequate compromise, only to avoid a cabinet crisis. The less certain the majority, the more votes of confidence were needed: 46 in the first Parliament, 73 in the second and 45 in the short life of the third.

When the formal safeguards were inconvenient they were evaded or laxly interpreted. A premier wanting to use this procedural weapon against obstruction might not have cabinet authorization; he was likely to protect himself for the future by securing it in advance, which eliminated both its inconvenience and its advantages.[37] He might find the day's delay helpful – or a nuisance.[38] In January 1948 Schuman faced forty amendments to unpopular tax proposals; he grouped them by article and subject and held five votes of confidence after one day's delay. This practice permitted unlimited inflation, and on 27 February 1952 Edgar Faure asked for twenty votes of confidence. Yet even a laxly interpreted delay clause slowed the passage of bills – notably the old age pension fund bill of 1956.[39]

The constitutional safeguards were wholly abandoned when a premier informed the Assembly that he would not formally seek a vote of confidence but meant to resign unless he got his way. This practice put less strain on relations between government parties when the demand for confidence was really directed against one of them. Ramadier used it to bring pressure on the Socialists over civil service pay in July 1947, and over the Algerian government bill in August (the SFIO conference had insisted that the formal confidence vote should not be used). Schuman employed it frequently, for instance in March 1948 to evade the delay rule when he feared that after a weekend in their constituencies deputies would be likelier to vote against him.[40] In June 1948 his cabinet decided to use it on the ratification of the London agreements

36. The government lost in December 1949 on ex-service pensions by a unanimous vote; in May 1950 on a bonus for railwaymen by 541 to 27, and on teachers' salaries by 540 to 27; in April 1951 on a 30 % increase in family allowances by 551 to 34. (The minorities were the ministers.)

37. As Queuille did in December 1948 and in May 1951, and Pleven in December 1951: Colliard, no. 58, pp. 222–3; *JO* 24 April 1951; *Monde*, 2 May and 9–10 December 1951; *AP* 1952, p. 19; Georgel, i. 108–9; Arné, pp. 262–6, 270–1, 276; Solal-Celigny, no. 200, pp. 722–3, 735–6. So Queuille could call for a vote of confidence (with proxies) later in May 1951 when the Communist benches began filling up at 5 a.m. in an empty house. Pleven had no authorization in December, so when the Conservatives called a snap vote on the Schuman Plan late at night, President Auriol had to be roused and driven forty miles into Paris to preside at the cabinet which gave it. Snap votes of confidence, censure or investiture were impossible as they all required notice, so the Assembly could safely ban proxies on these in 1955: see Solal-Céligny, no. 201, pp. 305–9, and above, p. 213.

38. It helped to save governments in December 1949 and December 1950, and to gain a majority for the European army in February 1952: *Figaro*, 24–25 December 1949; *AP* 1950, pp. 232–3; no. 200, p. 729, cf. p. 737, and no. 201, pp. 314, 320. But sometimes it strengthened the hostile majority: Blamont, p. 118.

39. *Ibid.*; and Solal-Celigny, no. 200, pp. 724–7 (cf. no. 201, pp. 301–4). On 1948, Colliard, no. 58, p. 230. See also Georgel, i. 109, and Arné, pp. 264–6. Many of Faure's 20 votes were on clauses which had not been discussed – for midnight was approaching and he wanted the 'clear day' of reflection to be tomorrow rather than the day after (but he was beaten on an early vote). The 1954 constitutional amendment ended these midnight votes by changing the delay requirement from 'one clear day' to '24 hours'.

40. Most formal votes of confidence (60 %) were held before the weekend, except by Pinay and Mendès-France, who were popular in the country and had 10 of their 13 on a Monday or Tuesday.

on Germany; in August André Marie did so on Paul Reynaud's bill for financial special powers; in December Queuille used it three times in a day, and by the end of his long ministry the constitutional procedure seemed to have fallen into disuse.[41]

Queuille preferred the informal procedure because it interfered less obviously with members' independence of judgment.[42] But this was a sign of strength, for the unofficial demand for confidence was normally less effective as well as less obnoxious, as it attracted little publicity and did little to screen the deputy from his critical constituents. Bidault, who succeeded Queuille, could afford no concessions; he needed every weapon to save his budget. Besides, all his predecessors were old parliamentary hands and two were traditionalist Radicals; Bidault was a parliamentary newcomer and founder of MRP. Determined to force the Assembly to take the responsibility of ejecting him, he remained undeterred when his majority fell to 6, 4 and 0 on formal confidence votes.[43] For if two governments were defeated in this way the second might be able to dissolve the Assembly: a prospect far more distasteful to Radicals who wanted a new electoral law than to MRP who preferred the existing one. The formal vote of confidence, with its contingent threat of dissolution, was thus a handier weapon for an MRP premier harassed by rebellious Radicals or Conservatives than for a Radical premier facing MRP recalcitrance.[44]

In March 1951 Queuille came back to power leading a very weak cabinet. But an election was imminent and the budget months overdue, so that the party responsible for his fall would provoke resentment which could quickly be expressed at the polls. Queuille now needed the formal vote of confidence, and while in 1948–49 he had used it only once in ten sitting months, in 1951 he employed it nine times in only ten weeks. His successor, Pleven, sought no vote of confidence for months. But this denoted weakness: in the new Parliament the cabinet could not take sides on Barangé's bill subsidizing church schools without a split, or stake its existence on the bill tying wages to the cost of living (which it openly opposed) without courting defeat and playing into RPF's hands.

The vote of confidence was thus both a procedural and a political weapon. Procedurally, the formal vote put more pressure on the deputies, gave time for negotiation, and raised the spectre of dissolution. It enabled the government to regain the parliamentary initiative from the committees, the opposition or rebellious back-benchers, and to choose the time and ground for battle.[45]

41. On this paragraph see Georgel, i. 108; Meyer, p. 152 (civil service); Colliard, no. 58, pp. 222, 225–7 (coal, Algeria, Schuman); *AP* 1948, pp. 95 (Germany), 133 (Reynaud), 226 (Queuille), 326 (Schuman), and 1949, pp. 129, 325 (Queuille on a holiday bonus in July and on petrol rationing in May).

42. His cabinet had authorized formal votes on new taxes in September 1948, on the aircraft industry in June 1949, etc.: *AP* 1948, p. 157, 1949, p. 98. (Queuille, Faure and Mollet were formally authorized to ask for informal votes of confidence, and Gaillard demanded one against a proposal to restrict the use of the formal procedure: Arné, p. 270.)

43. On 31 January 1950 Bidault won four such votes on the budget but lost a fifth by 293 to 293 (a tie is negative in French procedure): *AP* 1949, p. 223, and 1950, pp. 2–5.

44. For dissolution see below, pp. 236–8. Bidault asked for eleven votes of confidence to protect his budget from Radical and Conservative attacks, but none (despite cabinet authorization) to prevent Socialists and MRP rewriting his collective bargaining bill: *AP* 1949, p. 203.

45. Cf. Arné, pp. 270–2; and see Solal-Celigny, no. 201, pp. 312–5, 320 (cf. no. 200, p. 737).

Politically, it subordinated the specific question to the fate of the cabinet and so altered votes, rallying waverers to the government but alienating opponents who agreed with the particular policy; consequently Edgar Faure in November 1955 did not use it on his Moroccan policy, with which the Left opposition sympathized, and Guy Mollet similarly refrained after Suez when he wanted an impressive majority for his foreign policy, which the Right approved.[46]

Political behaviour depended on political circumstances. The first four premiers of the regime asked only 15 confidence votes in almost three years. But their successors had difficulty carrying increased taxation against Radical and Conservative opposition; the next three premiers sought 31 votes of confidence (18 of them budgetary) in twenty months, and in the first sixteen months of the new Parliament three prime ministers asked for 53, all but ten on their budgets.[47] In November 1950 René Pleven's first cabinet was severely shaken by a vote on Indo-China in which its majority was 150, because the omission of the word 'confidence' was the price of the victory.[48] A year later Pleven changed an unofficial vote of confidence (on economies) into an official one because President Auriol wanted him to stay until constitutionally ejected. His successor Edgar Faure formally staked the life of his government on a motion on the European army, which he then withdrew to win Socialist support. When Antoine Pinay tried to avoid votes of confidence, he suffered massive defeats; as opposition grew stronger he had to resort to them.[49]

After his fall the decisive issues were those of external policy, which provoked major clashes between parties rather than contests over details with groups of recalcitrant individualists. The vote of confidence was both less essential and less available: no cabinet could agree to stake its life on EDC. In January 1953 René Mayer won the Gaullist vote and the premiership by a pledge not to do so (for which he was scathingly criticized even by Edgar Faure). In June when Paul Reynaud refused to repeat this pledge, Pierre Cot protested amid applause that so grave a decision ought not to be taken under a threat of dissolution. Mendès-France then promised not to dissolve if beaten, but affirmed that no government could retain authority unless it engaged its existence on so vital a question; yet when he became premier a year

46. Similarly, Pleven was reluctant to alienate RPF by using it on the Schuman Plan in December 1951, but he had to do so to avoid a snap vote. Conversely, Pinay was beaten on his amnesty for tax frauds, but reversed the decision by making it one of confidence: *ibid.*, pp. 723, 727, 735. For Faure, *ibid.*, 1956, p. 315; for Mollet, *AP* 1956, p. 118; for Pleven also *AP* 1951, pp. 321–2; cf. Arné, pp. 273, 275–6. In June 1950 Bidault was defeated in the Assembly on a financial point, and made it a matter of confidence: 30 RGR and IOM rebels now voted for him, while 30 PRL and Peasans who had supported him now obstained. (He lost; below, p. 254.)

47. Only 5 of the first 15 confidence votes were budgetary, but 11 of Bidault's 13, 7 of Pleven's 9 in his first cabinet and 9 of 13 in his second, 20 of Faure's 23 and 14 of Pinay's 17. Queuille's 9 were all on priority for government business or electoral reform before the 1951 election. Of the next 53, less than half were voted on, as Pleven, Faure and Pinay all fell with several pending. For details see tables in Arné, p. 274, and in Solal-Celigny, nos. 200–1; both omit the vote of 1 December 1950.

48. *AP* 1950, pp. 229, 233; cf. *AP* 1957, pp. 22–4 for Mollet's similar Pyrrhic victory on agricultural policy shortly before his fall. An interpellation debate often ended with the Assembly 'expressing its confidence in the government'; if it did not, 'suppressing its mistrust of the government' might be the impression conveyed.

49. *AP* 1951, p. 287 (Pleven), 1952, pp. 74, 80, 83 (massive defeats); below, pp. 238 and n. (Auriol); Solal-Celigny, no. 200, pp. 729 (Faure), 727, 736–7 (Pinay).

later he stayed neutral on the treaty for fear of breaking up his cabinet. Germany, Indo-China and North Africa had pushed the budget into the background of politics, and from 1953 to 1955 there were only twenty votes of confidence: twelve on external affairs and only four budgetary.[50]

At the end of that Parliament it was pointed out that the duration of governments seemed to be inversely related to their predilection for votes of confidence.[51] Yet the next premier, whose party doctrine forbade governments to use this weapon, wielded it more vigorously than any predecessor – and lasted longer. For though Guy Mollet had only minority support in Parliament, few of his nominal opponents wanted to bring him down. At first, MRP and the Conservatives feared to leave SFIO dependent on Communist support and perhaps encourage a Popular Front; when the Communists had turned against him, the Right preferred him to take responsibility for waging (and paying for) the Algerian war. This allowed him to use constitutional votes of confidence to force his hesitant critics to turn him out or accept his domestic policy. Algeria was not yet the most controversial parliamentary problem, and of Mollet's 34 formal votes of confidence 15 were on social policy and 11 (plus several unofficial ones) were on finance.

Under his successors liberals and diehards clashed bitterly over North African affairs, while the domestic disputes between Socialists and Conservatives became more envenomed.[52] Struggling for survival, Bourgès-Maunoury and particularly Gaillard expanded the scope of their votes of confidence to paralyse parliamentary debate by asking for a single vote to open and close discussion on the whole text of a bill with all its clauses. Hitherto Presidents of the Assembly had resisted governments which tried to limit their difficulties in this way, but now Le Troquer allowed the dying Fourth Republic to set a dangerous precedent – thoroughly exploited by its successor.[53]

The formal vote of confidence was most freely used by leaders of progressive majorities facing attack from the Right: Bidault in the first Parliament, Mendès-France in the second and Mollet in the third drew the lines of conflict sharply and repeatedly challenged their critics. More conservative leaders preferred to minimize differences and lower the political temperature: a Queuille, Pinay or Laniel used the informal confidence vote whenever he could and the constitutional form only when he had to.[54] Their formal votes were

50. *AP* 1953, p. 4 (Mayer); *Monde*, 27 March 1953 (Faure); *JO* 27 May 1953, pp. 2867 (Cot), 2870 (Reynaud), 3 June 1953, pp. 2910–1 (Mendès-France); Arné, pp. 272–3; Solal-Celigny, no. 201, pp. 310–1.

51. *Ibid.*, p. 311, cf. p. 321.

52. Of the eleven votes of confidence after Mollet's fall, four were on Algeria and six were budgetary.

53. Arné, p. 276; Blamont, pp. 115–17. Without impeding debate, a 'legitimate' vote of confidence might be quite complex. Edgar Faure's on electoral reform on 12 November 1955 was by no means the most elaborate: 'against the discussion of M. Meunier's or any other counter-proposal, for the adoption of the one clause of the bill as reported, and against any motion, amendment or new clause which would reduce its scope or delay its application'. If in the first two Assemblies a premier asked for one vote of confidence on several items, the President would announce it as several distinct votes; only three times did he allow one vote on two or three connected clauses: Solal-Celigny, no. 201, p. 313.

54. *Ibid.* (see n. 45), on their respective advantages; Blamont, p. 119, on the deputies' growing dislike of the unofficial form. But on 3 June 1958 it was used for the last vote of the National Assembly of the Fourth Republic by Charles de Gaulle.

usually concentrated in the last few weeks when the premier was trying to stave off impending disaster. René Pleven and Edgar Faure each led one government which was attacked by the Left and another which was criticized by the Right; each preferred the light artillery in the former and the heavier weapons in the latter. Félix Gaillard's sweeping votes of confidence offended the conservative elements in his divided majority. The marginal members on whom the government most needed to put pressure were also those who most resented it, for they came from the parties of weak discipline and individualist tradition, and with no solid organization behind them they had most to fear from a dissolution.

4. DISSOLUTION, DEFEAT AND CENSURE

To the makers of the constitution dissolution was the ultimate sanction against parliamentary irresponsibility. They hoped by Articles 49 and 50 to discourage unnecessary votes of confidence and restrict cabinet crises to the rare occasions when a majority, drawn from a few disciplined parties, turned decisively against its own leaders. But parliaments with no coherent majority had been common in the past, and Articles 51 and 52 allowed for their reappearance by organizing the dissolution, under strict conditions, as an emergency exit from deadlock. Although the deputies tried hard to prevent the conditions ever being fulfilled, in 1955 a French Parliament was dissolved by the executive for the first time for nearly eighty years.

In the Third Republic the Chamber could be dissolved by the President with the consent of the Senate. But by convention the power was never used after 1877, so that deputies who felt secure for four years had upset governments without fear of electoral penalties. The Right wanted the cabinet to have power to dissolve; the Left would not hear of dissolution as an executive weapon, but only as an escape from parliamentary irresponsibility or incoherence. The Socialist solution was automatic dissolution. It presupposed a coherent majority normally working in harmony with the executive; two clashes would mean the end of both ministry and Assembly. But the constitution-makers were or professed to be more afraid of futile general elections than of frequent changes of government.[55] The first draft constitution compromised on 'a kind of annual ration of crises'.[56] If the Assembly threw out two governments in a session the prime minister could dissolve, after consulting both the President of the Assembly (the best judge of whether another government could find a majority) and his own cabinet (which would hand over to the caretaker ministry described below). But these cautious provisions applied only in the second half of the Assembly's five-year term.

After their referendum defeat the Left made a few concessions: the caretaker rules were modified, the 'close season' was reduced from a Parliament's first thirty months to eighteen, and the two government defeats could occur within eighteen months instead of twelve.[57] Article 51, then, allowed the

55. *JO* 10 April 1946, p. 1679, and 17th, p. 1952 (Cot); 22 August 1946, p. 3246 (Ramadier); 27 May 1953, pp. 2859 (Lecourt), 2868 (Cot); Auriol, ii. 249; Théry, Chapter 4; Georgel, i. 66, 74–7; Arné, pp. 289–91; Williams, p. 227n. In 1931 Blum had urged dissolution of a conservative Chamber.
56. René Coty, *JO* 12 April 1946, p. 1770.
57. Another compromise: MRP wanted two years, the Left six months.

cabinet to dissolve (after consulting the President of the Assembly) when two crises had occurred within eighteen months, provided: first that both governments were constitutionally defeated under Article 49 or 50 by an absolute majority on a vote of confidence or censure; secondly, under Article 45, that they were more than two weeks old; and thirdly that the Assembly that defeated them was over eighteen months old. It was not to be penalized for upsetting ministries early in its own life, before a majority had crystallized, or early in theirs, since it had chosen not a cabinet but a premier alone.

The power of dissolution was thus made hard to use – or misuse. Article 52 ruled out manipulations like MacMahon's in 1877 by laying down a minimum and maximum period (twenty to thirty days) between the dissolution and the election, and a date (the third Tuesday after the poll) for the new house to meet. It also installed a caretaker cabinet to supervise the administration and especially the prefects, who could influence a local contest by urging a politician to stand or withdraw, to make or refuse an alliance, or to support one candidate rather than another.[58] In the first draft constitution the Assembly's President and committee chairmen took over from the ministers who had dissolved. In the final draft the President of the Assembly became caretaker premier, chose a new minister of the interior in consultation with the *bureau* (elected by PR under Article 11), and appointed new ministers without portfolio from all groups unrepresented in the government. By a curious paradox France was to acquire a cabinet of national union at a moment of bitter controversy.

Some consternation was caused by the fear that these arrangements might bring Communists back to power. They provoked an incident in January 1948, when Herriot was due for re-election as President of the Assembly. His health would not stand the strain of an emergency premiership, and if de Gaulle succeeded in forcing a dissolution he might resign. The obvious substitute premier was the senior vice-president of the Assembly, who in a *bureau* elected by PR represented the largest party, the Communists: thus a dissolution might allow Jacques Duclos to become caretaker premier and appoint a minister of the interior controlling the prefects and the police. He was therefore demoted to third vice-president, behind members of SFIO and MRP; the Communists refused to serve on the *bureau* and appealed to President Auriol as guardian of the constitution, but he declined to intervene. Even so, many parliamentarians thought the caretaker arrangements made a dissolution impossible, and the constitutional amendment of 1954 abandoned them. If a dissolution was not the result of a vote of censure the old administration was now to stay in power; if it was, the President of the Assembly would become both premier and minister of the interior.[59]

During the life of the first Assembly ten ministries went out of office, but

58. In 1956 prefects were said to have intervened in half a dozen of the 103 constituencies, not always to help pro-government candidates; in three of these seats an ex-minister of the interior was standing: Williams, no. 168, p. 153; and cf. Pineau, pp. 18–21. On 1877 see Soulier, p. 49.

59. *Institutions*, i. 186–7, Georgel, i. 115–18; on the 1948 incident, Lidderdale, p. 104n. By 1954 the Radicals, back in power, favoured keeping the old government which in 1946 (in opposition) they had wanted to remove. Many people thought the old Art. 52 required a cabinet formed by PR (cf. Georgel, i. 115 and n.); in fact one Communist minister without a department would have been enough. Some criticisms of the constitution could have been met by reading it.

only one crisis qualified under the strict conditions of Article 51. Instead of staying until ousted constitutionally, most cabinets fell apart internally or resigned on defeat by a simple majority. Two cabinets left office on the election of a new President of the Republic (Blum's) and National Assembly (Queuille's third) as tradition and Article 45 respectively required. Two were defeated on first meeting the house, Schuman's second by a simple and Queuille's second by an absolute majority. Ramadier's, Marie's and Queuille's first governments 'rotted from within' with no vote in the Assembly, and Pleven's first after a vote in which it was neutral. Schuman's first ministry fell because SFIO defected; the premier insisted on a vote, but it was not a constitutional vote of confidence and he lost only by a relative majority.[60] President Auriol tried in vain to encourage premiers to stay in office until constitutionally defeated; he dissuaded several from premature resignation, but could not prevail when the prime minister warned that a formal vote would exacerbate the divisions of a majority on which any government must necessarily be based.[61] So of the ten premiers only Bidault was constitutionally overthrown, by an absolute majority on a vote of confidence when the Socialists moved from abstention to opposition.

The seven premiers of the second Parliament proved much more determined to use their constitutional rights, perhaps because they came from a new political generation.[62] Only Pinay resigned without a vote, when MRP's decision to abstain made defeat inevitable. Faure (in 1952) and Laniel were beaten by relative majorities, but Pleven, Mayer, Mendès-France and Faure (in 1955) all had absolute majorities against them on votes of confidence. After Mayer's fall in May 1953 the deputies had to beware of possible dissolution. When they overthrew Laniel by a relative majority, he wanted to await a constitutional defeat and then dissolve, but he was foiled by the defection of the Radicals, led by Edgar Faure and Martinaud-Déplat, who were against dissolution in 1954 though for it in 1955.[63] Until eighteen months after Mayer's fall Mendès-France could have dissolved on defeat; his difficulties with the Assembly therefore began only in November 1954. A few weeks later he was ousted by an absolute majority, so that when Edgar Faure was ejected in the same way ten months afterwards he was entitled to dissolve. The deputies had miscalculated, for the new standing order banning proxies

60. He asked for a formal vote of confidence against a Radical amendment to reduce the army estimates, which was withdrawn; he was beaten on a similar Socialist amendment after an informal threat to resign if defeated (cf. below, p. 254n.). The Socialist ministers moved to their party's benches during the debate; this traditionally indicated resignation.

61. As Queuille did in October 1949 and Pleven in March 1951. Auriol accepted Marie's resignation in 1948, but said later he had been wrong. He dissuaded Ramadier in September 1947 (his majority had fallen below fifty), Pleven in November 1950 (the Assembly had humiliated a leading minister, see p. 299 below), and Queuille in April 1951 (the deputies had failed to carry electoral reform, p. 288n. below); and he kept Pleven's second cabinet in office until its constitutional defeat (cf. above, p. 234). See *AP* 1949, pp. 169–70, 338; 1950, pp. 231–2; 1951, pp. 39–40, 287; *Monde*, 29–30 April 1951 and 18–19 November 1951; Flory, no. 93, pp. 851–9; Drago, no. 76, p. 166; Georgel, i. 93–4; Arné, pp. 57–63. Auriol's views were shared by many of his predecessors (Soulier, pp. 75–6, 98, 131, 171) and by his successor (cf. Georgel, i. 92–4).

62. See above, p. 13. On resignations with or without votes in Parliament see Arné, pp. 279, 317–30.

63. For periods when dissolution threatened, and for Laniel, see *ibid.*, pp. 280–1.

on votes of confidence had made it harder for the tacticians to do their sums.[64]

The decision to dissolve was taken, exceptionally, by a vote of the cabinet.[65] Neither the prime minister nor the President of the Republic originally favoured it, but it was strongly urged by the President of the Assembly, Pierre Schneiter of MRP, whose advice was constitutionally required. Five Radical ministers had their resignations refused as unconstitutional because the old cabinet now had to retain office during a dissolution. Schneiter stopped the opposition parties recalling the Assembly before the decree dissolving it was published – on the anniversary, as they proclaimed, of Napoleon III's *coup d'état*. But their attack on the dissolution failed. The Communists did not join in, and the critics, finding that public opinion welcomed Faure's action, quickly abandoned their campaign.[66]

Unhappily the dissolution proved no more effective as an escape from deadlock than as a means of governmental pressure. It gave neither Faure nor his opponents a secure majority, and the new Assembly, like the old, offered no basis for stable government. Ministries still resigned in disregard of the constitutional forms. Mollet and Bourgès-Maunoury were defeated by relative majorities, and Gaillard by an absolute majority but on an informal vote of confidence. Pflimlin took the defection of three Conservative ministers as a pretext to resign, despite his comfortable majority, because he feared insurrection by the army.

The attempt to regulate the fall of governments therefore failed entirely, although President Auriol and some premiers tried to make it work. At best, the formal rules might have kept a cabinet in office without power: a leader who did not resign on defeat by a simple majority could not get his measures passed, might have humiliating motions carried against him, and risked offending Parliament and harming his future career; 'the problem was not only to attain and retain the premiership, but to become premier again'. Bidault took the absolute majority rule seriously, and Laniel wished to do so; but six premiers resigned after defeat by a simple majority, and none ever kept office after being in a minority on a vote of confidence.[67]

The constitutional amendment proposals of 1950 would have required

64. Solal-Celigny, no. 201, pp. 307–9; surprisingly, the new rule had thus made dissolution more likely. 'Inside dopesters', who often exaggerated the cunning of the wire-pullers, alleged that Faure had told some loyal supporters to vote against him and ensure a constitutional defeat: cf. Georgel, i. 120; *New Statesman*, 3 December 1955. But of the 21 defectors, 12 were staunch Mendesists, 8 were Moroccan diehards, and 1 was a local rival of Faure (who, resenting his vote, refused a profitable electoral alliance with him).

65. P. H. Teitgen, preface to Georgel, i. IV ('the only vote in my experience'); cf. Blamont, no. 19, pp. 113–14. For the political reasons for it see above, p. 47, and below, pp. 315–16.

66. Blamont, no. 19, states that the President could not refuse a dissolution (p. 113), that Schneiter's opinion was personal, written and secret (p. 112), that ministers could not resign (p. 124), and that a censure motion would have been out of order (p. 118). Cf. *Institutions*, i. 184–7; and Arné, pp. 282–9. On Coty's and Faure's hesitation, *AP* 1955, p. 92 (cf. Teitgen, *loc. cit.*, for Faure); on Schneiter, above, p. 217; on the public reaction, *Élections 1956*, pp. 4–5 (Duverger), 122 (Grosser); generally, Pierce, no. 180, pp. 398–401; J. R. Tournoux, *Carnets secrets de la politique* (1958), pp. 41–61; J. Georgel, *La dissolution du 2.12.1955* (1958). Bourgès-Maunoury as unwilling minister of the interior would take no part in organizing the election.

67. Six: Schuman (twice in 1948), Faure (in 1952), Laniel, Mollet and Bourgès-Maunoury. Quotation: from Duverger, *Demain*, p. 46.

governments so defeated to resign. This would have made it easier to remove them but also costlier, for dissolution would have come much nearer. In 1950 this proposal seemed to command general support, but by 1953 MRP and RFP both strongly dissented; both parties were stronger in that house than they were likely to be in the next. They argued that the absolute majority clause checked 'orange-peel crises' (contrived by the parliamentary tacticians rather than willed by most members of the house) and MRP threatened to oppose the whole amendment bill if it were dropped. It was therefore restored (by show of hands) as the bill was going through the Assembly; the Council of the Republic cut it out by 311 to 3, but the deputies finally overruled them by 500 to 117 and easier dissolution again receded. An alternative adumbrated by MRP members in these discussions was proposed in 1957 by the Assembly's franchise committee, taken up in 1958 by Gaillard's government, and adopted in the Fifth Republic: that any proposal which the government made a matter of confidence should pass unless the opposition carried a censure motion by an absolute majority.[68]

The censure motion had been taken seriously only by the constitution-makers, who envisaged it as the opposition's principal weapon. But the 1947 standing orders did not mention it. In 1949 René Capitant, the Gaullist leader and a professor of law, used it to force a debate on his interpellations on Indo-China; as on a vote of confidence, only five-minute 'explanations' were allowed, and he was easily defeated. The Communists seized on the new device, but the house voted to debate a censure motion by Duclos in eight months' time (which meant never) and three later ones were similarly balked. Early in the next Parliament the Gaullists put down three censure motions and the Communists two. One was never discussed, two were defeated, and two were lost with no vote cast against them; they were intended to force a vote on an unpopular increase in the petrol tax, but as only an absolute majority could pass them, the government's supporters abstained.

As a procedural weapon the censure motion therefore failed, though the Communists still tried occasionally to use it. In 1952 the Socialist leaders introduced a motion against Pinay's economic and social policies, which was more in accord with the intentions of the constitution-makers; and in 1957 one was proposed on Tunisia, by Tixier-Vignancour, and three on Bourgès-Maunoury's agricultural policy, by the Communists, the Conservatives and the peasant lobby. Both governments fell before any of the censures could be debated.[69] Thus in eleven years of the Fourth Republic fewer than twenty censure motions were proposed, only five were discussed, and none passed. British governments always find time for a censure debate; but the Assembly allowed ministries to treat them as a tiresome but unimportant kind of interpellation. The marginal deputies wanted to choose their own moment for defection, and had no need to bring dissolution nearer by censuring the

68. See Moisan's amendment in 1953 (Poutier, p. 122) and the report in 1957 by Paul Coste-Floret of MRP; it was dropped from Gaillard's bill (introduced in February 1958 by Robert Lecourt of MRP) owing to strong Conservative opposition.

69. *JO* 1949, p. 1645 (15 March); 1951, pp. 5060 (11 May), 5118–22 (12 May), 6855–68 (4 September), 7854–60 (9 November), 8146–9 and 8163 (16 November); *AP* 1949, pp. 42–3, 1957, pp. 89–90 and 93; Georgel, i. 113–14; Arné, pp. 253–4; details in Williams, pp. 224–5 and n.

government by an absolute majority when they could so easily deny it their confidence by a simple majority.

Experience thus gave no reason for hoping that procedural gadgets could solve political problems. Yet the tireless search for new ones continued. Some of their sponsors wished to prohibit abstention – which was the recourse of cowardly opponents, but also of members unable (from conviction or electoral necessity) to support the government yet unwilling to bring it down. The Socialists Jules Moch and Francis Leenhardt favoured a Swiss-type system by which the house would choose for two years a premier whom it could not remove. At the end Pflimlin's cabinet tried to disallow negative majorities by permitting a premier to remain, as in West Germany, until ousted by a censure motion naming his successor. There were renewed suggestions to make dissolution automatic on a government defeat, as Paul Reynaud had proposed in 1953.

These 'gadgets' attacked the wrong problem. For the need was not just stability but authority; and if premiers were safe for two years or five, only a man guaranteed to offend no one (and therefore do nothing) would ever be elected. By 1958, therefore, the alternative to ministerial instability seemed to be 'Queuilles in perpetuity', and a growing body of press and academic opinion was turning to the presidential system.[70] Authority and democracy seemed incompatible under parliamentary government, where the sovereign and suspicious deputies contested the executive's right to determine policy, and an alternative and sometimes hostile leadership was institutionalized in the committee system.

70. 'Queuilles': Duverger, *VIe*, p. 121. On all these ingenious devices see *ibid.*, pp. 114–24, and his *Demain*, pp. 44–51; Pickles, no. 175; Georgel, i. 147–53, 320–1; Berlia, no. 15; *AP* 1955, pp. 41, 44–6, 62; 1957, p. 27; 1958, pp. 15–16, 20–1, 28–9, 33, 64, 72–4, 543–4.

Chapter 18

THE NATIONAL ASSEMBLY (3): THE COMMITTEE STRUCTURE

The standing committees were the central feature of French parliamentary procedure. All bills, before the house debated them, went to committees which killed the majority and redrafted the remainder. For some committees like Foreign Affairs, legislation was less important than parliamentary control over the executive. One, the finance committee, reviewed every ministry's budget and scrutinized the whole administrative field.

It was through its committees above all that Parliament asserted legislative and encroached on executive power. But committees and cabinets were not autonomous political forces, they were battlefields where the groups which clashed openly in the Assembly fought out their differences away from public view. In the ministerial arena, however, only the moderate parties were present; in Parliament and its committees the extremists could manœuvre to upset the carefully balanced compromises by which coalitions live. Thereby responsibilities, always hard to establish in a multi-party system, were still further obscured; and governments had to wage an endless uphill battle which drained their energies and diminished their authority.

1. ORIGINS AND ORGANIZATION

In 1875 there were only three 'permanent' committees, Finance, Army and Foreign Affairs; the rest were elected by the *bureaux* (themselves chosen by lot) to deal with each bill presented.[1] The Left fought for permanence and proportional representation, while the Right, remembering the revolutionary Committee of Public Safety, feared that 'little parliaments' would undermine executive authority. But the growing mass of bills made *ad hoc* committees impracticable. By 1898 there were eleven permanent committees, which handled most legislation. The Chamber made all committees permanent in 1902 and accepted PR in 1910; the Senate took a decade longer in each case. Although criticisms persisted from conservatives and others, the Fourth Republic's founders and leaders favoured strong committees, to which Article 15 gave constitutional status.[2]

Article 53 formalized the Third Republic's custom that ministers could appear at their request before any committee. More commonly the committees invited them. They came much more frequently in the Fourth Republic than in the Third: often to the finance committee, about once a month to Foreign Affairs and Defence, and perhaps quarterly to most of the others. Officials could represent their minister, and private persons came occasionally

1. On the history and working of the committees see Lidderdale, Chapter 7, and Barthélemy, *Essai*; also for history, R. K. Gooch, *The French Parliamentary Committee System* (New York, 1935), Chapter 3, and Priouret, *Députés*, pp. 153–4; for working, *Travail*, pp. 684–95 (Goguel), 809–17 (Galichon), 850–8; Pactet, no. 171, pp. 127–72. For their legislative role see below, pp. 237–263; for the foreign affairs committee, Grosser, pp. 84–94; for the *bureaux*, above, p. 210 n. 12.
2. Cf. below, pp. 268, 273n. In the Fifth Republic committees were severely restricted.

(for instance, spokesmen of accident victims on a workmen's compensation bill); but the functions of an American committee hearing in preparing legislation were fulfilled (if at all) by the private consultations of the bill's rapporteur. A committee could extend its ordinary scrutiny of governmental activities by seeking special investigatory powers; each year there were about ten such inquiries from committees of one or the other house. It was also the committees which usually chose Parliament's representatives on about fifty consultative bodies.[3]

Wednesdays and Thursday mornings were reserved for committee meetings. Each committee had its room and its secretary from the Assembly's staff.[4] The finance committee met twice a week or more, and divided its work among rapporteurs; the others usually met weekly or less often, and chose a rapporteur for each bill. In the chamber the committee chairman and rapporteur had a privileged position in debate. The chairmen formed about half of the presidents' conference which proposed the Assembly's agenda.

In the Fourth Republic there were normally nineteen standing committees (and also two smaller permanent committees on Accounts and Parliamentary Immunities).[5] No deputy sat on more than two, finance committee members usually on only one, and some party leaders (such as Thorez, Mollet and Queuille) on none. Each had 44 members, one-fourteenth of the whole Assembly; so each party group had a committee place for every fourteen members. Groups of less than fourteen and deputies belonging to no party had to affiliate (*s'apparenter*) to a larger group.[6] After 1952 a member who changed his party automatically lost his committee places. Parties chose their own representatives and could trade seats in different committees, but the main parties were hardly ever more than one seat up or down. Nominations went to the house as a single agreed list, though fifty deputies could challenge it.[7]

3. Bromhead, no. 32, pp. 152–4; Campbell, no. 45, p. 361; Grosser, pp. 85–6; Pactet, no. 171, pp. 160–6, 170–1. In 1947 the labour committee offered to hear strikers' representatives and negotiate with the government: *ibid.*, p. 166. In 1956 the finance committee held American-style 'hearings' on fiscal reform: Meynaud, p. 105. Committees might meet jointly; in 1954 Pierre Mendès-France addressed the defence, foreign affairs and overseas territories committees together on his vain attempt to amend the EDC treaty. On the attention paid to hearings by ministers see Buron, pp. 203–4.

4. But few committees had even a typist of their own; M. Prélot in *Travail*, p. 854 (though see below, p. 251). Cf. Buron, p. 155.

5. Economic Affairs; Foreign Affairs; Agriculture; Alcoholic Beverages; Defence; Education; Family, Population and Health; Finance; Interior; Justice and Legislation; Merchant Marine and Fisheries; Communications and Tourist Industry; Pensions; Press; Industrial Production; Reconstruction and War Damage; Franchise, Standing Orders and Petitions; Overseas Territories; Labour and Social Security (1952 titles). Beverages replaced Food in 1949. The Assembly would never agree to fewer committees or places: cf. Williams, p. 236n. Special co-ordinating committees sometimes dealt with a treaty interesting several standing committees (see Grosser, pp. 88–9, Arné, p. 252) but had not for decades been used for a bill (Goguel in *Travail*, p. 687).

6. In 1951 Pleven's finance minister Maurice Petsche, an independent Conservative, affiliated for a week to UDSR (which had only thirteen members) and then withdrew again. This timely gesture enabled his prime minister's group to keep its representation on every committee.

7. Assignments were usually made by party leaders (but in SFIO by annual election). Members occasionally joined a party to obtain a committee assignment. In 1954 an ex-chairman of the foreign affairs committee, Jacques Bardoux, was dropped from it by the Republican Independents (CNI) but regained his place by becoming a Peasant. Inter-party trading allowed IOM and RDA members to concentrate in the overseas territories committee; this caused a contest over it

[*over*

Committees of 44 were too big for efficiency, but the penalties for absenteeism were not applied and the quorum of 22 was rarely enforced. On most committees a nucleus of a dozen or fifteen members attended regularly, drafted most reports, and spoke often in the house on the committee's subject.[8] In the Fourth Republic absent deputies were allowed to send substitutes, but these could be casually chosen for a single meeting and weakened the expertise and common purpose which the committee system was supposed to foster. On important bills more deputies attended, from interest or at a summons from their party; on others they often stayed away because much activity, especially on minor committees, was futile. Paradoxically, attendance was best at the committees which met most frequently and made most demands on their members.[9]

Each committee elected a chairman and a small *bureau*, limited (except for Finance and Overseas Territories) to two vice-chairmen and two secretaries so as to check the traditional inflation of these sinecure titles.[10] While there was no seniority rule, chairmen of important committees were always men of standing in the house and party. Those who were not already ex-ministers became *ministrables* by virtue of their election; indeed, Poincaré once attacked them as 'would-be ministers setting ambushes for the present ministers'. There was little evidence of this tendency in the Fourth Republic, although twenty-four committee chairmen resigned to take office.[11] Many others preferred to remain as chairmen, several became chairmen because they were ex-ministers, and few used their positions to oppose or embarrass governments.[12] Most chairmen were drawn from the parties of the majority, some from the 'loyal opposition', few if any from the enemies of the regime.[13]

membership in 1950. Some colonial deputies affiliated to a major party solely to get a seat there, while conversely an Algerian member could ensure a place on the interior committee by joining IOM.

8. Prélot in *Travail*, pp. 852–3. In four busy committees in six months of 1952 one-eighth of the members (23) took five or more bills to report and five-eighths (109) took one or none: from Bromhead, no. 32, p. 148. See also 1954 figures in Harrison, *Commissions*, pp. 72–5, 196–7; I am most grateful to Dr. Harrison for allowing me to use this abundant unpublished material.

9. *Ibid.*, pp. 77–82, 93–4, 97–9. During 1956 average attendance varied from 19 (Pensions) to 35 (Agriculture): *ibid.*, p. 72. Foreign Affairs also had good attendances but the substitutes deprived it of cohesion: Grosser, p. 84 (but cf. Noël, pp. 108–9). Unless specially whipped, Communists were no more assiduous than others: *ibid.*, and Harrison, pp. 97–8; but cf. Isorni, *Ainsi*, p. 55.

10. The pre-war beverages committee had a *bureau* of 21: Barthélemy, *Essai*, p. 121.

11. Five in the first Parliament, eighteen in the second and one in the third. Only five stepped straight from a committee chair to the corresponding ministerial post: Louvel (industry) in 1950, Paul Coste-Floret (constitutional reform) in 1953, General Koenig (defence) in 1954, Juglas (colonies) and Badie (pensions) in 1955; only two of them held the new office for three months. A few others made the move after an interval. Poincaré: in 1933, quoted Soulier, p. 194n.

12. Pierre Montel (Defence) was expelled from Morocco in 1955 for intriguing against the prime minister's policy – but he had been sent there for the purpose by the defence minister: *AP* 1955, p. 70.

13. The last Communist elected was Midol (Communications) who resigned in protest against the defeat of his colleagues: *AP* 1949, p. 3. Not until 1951 did the finance committee remove Communists from its sub-committees and posts as rapporteurs of departmental budgets. The foreign affairs committee set up a sub-committee without Communists or Progressives to deal with the EDC treaty (Grosser, p. 88) and in March 1953 non-Communist members of the defence committee formed themselves into a very large sub-committee. (This had also been done before the war.)

There were no Communists after 1949, no Gaullists in 1951 and no Poujadists ever; but two RPF chairmen were elected by important committees in 1952, when still in opposition, and a year later the majority conceded six chairs (including Foreign Affairs, Justice and Interior) to their Socialist opponents. When SFIO returned to power in 1956 they concentrated parliamentary as well as governmental responsibilities in their own hands.[14] But normally few chairmen were opposed and very few defeated when they came up for their annual re-election.[15]

Parties accepted this continuity because the chairman's power was far less than in the United States Congress. He was expected to guide his colleagues (who did not admire ineffectiveness) but not to dominate or thwart them. He had to fight in the presidents' conference for priority for their proposals. During recesses he might urge their views on officials or ministers. Survival increased his influence, for he might outlast many ministers and gain an expert knowledge of his subject. But unless his committee supported him he had little personal opportunity to help or obstruct legislation.[16]

The committee itself, however, had great power. If hostile it could bury a private member's bill altogether; if favourable it could redraft even a government measure and pilot it through the house. Consequently, when a bill overlapped committee boundaries its title might be chosen so as to steer it in the right direction, and indeed the ability to *jouer les commissions* was one of the skills of experienced parliamentarians (not least of ministers). In 1950 the Communists persuaded the press committee, with its large contingent of editors, unanimously to claim jurisdiction over the bill against libel in journals edited by members of parliament, and charged the committee on justice and legislation with 'imperialism' when it resisted the claim; but the Assembly ruled against them. The Left had more success in extending the jurisdiction of the traditionally anticlerical education committee, to which in 1950 they managed to send a school medical service bill which the health committee had unanimously claimed. In the second Parliament, however, they were weaker: Barangé's bill subsidizing church schools was assigned to Finance in 1951, and a contentious bill on agricultural instruction to Agriculture in 1954.[17]

14. Besides half the cabinet they provided the *rapporteur-général* and thirteen committee chairmen, leaving only five chairs for the whole opposition – in accordance with their old doctrine, 'Toutes les places et tout de suite!' But they were indignant when the Gaullists did the same in 1962.

15. Of the 21 chairmen in 1951, six soon became ministers and two soon died. Of the other 13 and the 8 successors, nine were re-elected (generally unopposed) till the end of the Parliament, and five till they became ministers; five were beaten, but two won again later; one retired; one lost his seat on changing his party. Only one committee (Justice) had a contest every year.

16. Bromhead, no. 32, p. 149n.; chairmen rarely reported on bills. But in 1948, when RPF strongly opposed postponing local elections, a bill to do so was sent to the interior committee because Franchise had a Gaullist acting chairman: *AP* 1948, p. 134. On guidance see Prélot in *Travail*, pp. 853–4, and Isorni, *Silence*, p. 135; on influence in recesses, Grosser, pp. 87–8; on powerful pre-war chairmen, Barthélemy, *Essai*, pp. 124–30, 245–5; on the presidents' conference, Buron, p. 113.

17. *JO* 1 March 1950, p. 2126 (press), 22 June 1950, pp. 5130–4, 5143–4 (medical); *BC* no. 81, 23 March 1954, pp. 2091, 2094 (agriculture; on this bill see *Paysans*, pp. 275–80). In 1951 Education proved to have a pro-clerical majority after all, and refused to claim the Barangé bill. On procedure see Galichon in *Travail*, pp. 810–1; and below, pp. 256–9. On ministerial techniques for dealing with committees, Buron, pp. 203–7.

An interested committee which was not given charge of a bill could ask to present an advisory report offering amendments or criticisms.[18] On a major proposal many committees would usually have views, and sponsors – or governments – could sometimes neutralize one by favourable reports from others. Six committees reported on the Coal and Steel Community, nine on the Common Market and Euratom treaties; in each case only the defence committee was opposed. But the defeat of EDC was presaged by six committee reports, all hostile.[19]

A solidly-based government could call party discipline to its aid, though not with equal effect at all times, in all parties or in all committees. After 1902 the whip of the *Délégation des Gauches* was as potent in committee as in the chamber, and even the undisciplined Radical party of the inter-war years occasionally reacted against flagrant individualism in committee. In the Fourth Republic the government had more chance to use pressure because the well-organized parties were more important. Communists never broke discipline in committee, though their Progressive allies occasionally did. Socialist discipline was also good. On the Centre and Right there was less party cross-voting in committee than in the house, for since each party had very few representatives individual defections were less probable (though more damaging).[20]

The effectiveness of discipline varied between committees as well as between parties. It was greatest in those which dealt with matters of major political importance, least in the specialist committees which concentrated on a limited subject. These were more likely to oppose the government, since they tended to attract members with a special interest – personal, professional or constituency. But their opposition was less dangerous, since they enjoyed less parliamentary prestige.

2. 'SPECIALIST' COMMITTEES AND 'POLITICAL' COMMITTEES

In theory the more technical committees offered many advantages as a legislative device. They afforded to all deputies a training which the House of Commons denies to the majority who never obtain office.[21] Members could be re-elected to the same committee and so gain knowledge and experience in their subject. Bills could be carefully examined in a small expert group, rather than rushed through a large assembly incapable of dealing usefully with detail. A non-partisan approach was possible since committee work attracted little publicity (very brief official reports, hardly any newspaper space and, by

18. There were advisory reports on 9 of the 86 government bills and 7 of the 53 private members' bills which became law in 1956.

19. *AP* 1951, p. 319; 1954, pp. 428–9; 1957, pp. 71–2. In the upper house in 1951 the right-wing opposition was stronger and every specialist committee opposed the coal and steel plan, only the foreign affairs committee favouring it.

20. See figures in Bromhead, no. 32, pp. 154–7, for 1952 (Pinay's year, in which MRP were much more and the Radicals much less divided than usual). Harrison, p. 36, analyses 124 divisions in 1954 and shows the Socialists cross-voting in 11, MRP in 15, Gaullists in 16, Peasants in 18, Republican Independents in 28, and Radicals in 30, almost every party having abstentions but no cross-voting in about as many divisions again. On inter-war Radicals see Barthélemy, *Essai*, pp. 107, 145.

21. See Brogan in *Parliament: a Survey*, pp. 80–3. The Communists did most to maintain continuity and train specialists: Harrison, pp. 63–5, cf. Isorni, *Silence*, pp. 132–3.

custom, no discussion on the floor of the house).[22] In practice there were so many bills that they were not always thoroughly scrutinized, and a high turnover of members reduced specialization.[23] Even where the committees worked best technically, there was a high political price to be paid. For the stronger their corporate sense, the more vigorously they challenged the government's leadership.

Proportional representation did not necessarily ensure a government majority in each committee. Even in Britain the whips feel safer on the floor than 'upstairs', where an individual absence is more serious and the strong views of deeply interested members may prevent the committee being a microcosm of the house. In France the majority was probably smaller and certainly less cohesive, party discipline was less effective, and committees were permanent (in Britain most members have long been appointed by the whips for a particular bill). The opposition might hold influential committee posts. Parties often re-elected dissident deputies who had a reputation in their subject. And all 'technical' committees inevitably approached problems differently from the lay majority, as the parliamentary immunities committee showed in 1949 over the Madagascar prosecutions.[24] Some expressed or intensified a general discontent with the government: the perennial demands of Pensions, and Reconstruction's defence of the housing programme, spelt votes for every deputy.[25] Above all, these committees provided an institutional façade for the operation of pressure-groups.

Every committee attracted members with a personal, professional or electoral interest in its subject. In 1952 MRP's trade unionists went to the labour or industry committee, but its extreme Indo-China diehards preferred to sit on Defence together with three Gaullist generals and one admiral, the most nationalist of Socialists (Max Lejeune) and later the crypto-fascist J. M. Le Pen.[26] The education committee, with its majority of teachers, included the most *laïc* Gaullists, the anticlerical zealots of SFIO (Maurice Deixonne and Rachel Lempereur), and both the priests in the Assembly. The medical professions provided half the health committee. Agriculture drew all but six of its 44 members from the land, and no urban deputy ever stayed on it. In 1949 half the members of the overseas territories committee sat for colonial seats, half those on the reconstruction and war damage committee

22. Lidderdale, p. 169; but cf. *Travail*, pp. 855–6, and Grosser, p. 85.

23. Harrison, pp. 55–63, 112–13. In 1956 139 laws were passed. One committee (Labour) dealt with 25; five (Justice, Agriculture, Defence, Overseas Territories, Finance) with 10 or more; three with 8, four with 3 and six with fewer (my calculations).

24. Above, p. 211. P. H. Teitgen of MRP, a former minister of justice, argued that by pronouncing on these deplorable proceedings before the final appeal the Assembly would infringe judicial independence. The immunities committee unanimously disagreed; its chairman and spokesman was Teitgen's father, also of MRP: *AP* 1949, p. 120.

25. In July 1950 Pensions came within one vote of beating the newly-formed Pleven Government, and in January 1953 it defeated the new premier René Mayer by 424 to 142; in November 1956 it led the house to reject its ministry's budget, which was passed next month on a confidence vote by only five; in January 1958 Gaillard carried a vote of confidence against it by twenty: *AP* 1950, p. 154; 1956, pp. 108, 114; 1958, pp. 6–7; cf. Georgel, i. 233, 240, 242. In 1952 the reconstruction committee considered resigning *en bloc* in protest against a housing cut: *Monde*, 29 February 1952. Cf. *AP* 1952, pp. 90, 137 for both pensions and housing.

26. The defence committee demanded very early on that the press be muzzled over Algeria; *AP* 1956, p. 32.

for Normandy and Brittany. In 1956 two-thirds of the labour committee came from industrial areas; Merchant Marine attracted only seaboard members; of 18 representatives of the Midi wine-growers, 13 were on Beverages.[27]

This was not all. Not only did the interior committee have as many members from Algeria as from France itself: the former attended when Algeria was on the agenda and the latter when it was not. Similarly, the working nucleus of a committee tended to be dominated even more completely than the full body by the strongest interest on it. Since the MRP trade unionists gave the labour and industry committees a left-wing majority, conservatives could achieve little there; so they attended rarely, reported on few bills and moved elsewhere as soon as they could. Again, in assigning bills for report each committee's preferences tended to accentuate its peculiar character. Peasant members reported many bills on agriculture, none on labour questions; MRP deputies were favoured in Finance but ignored in Education; Socialists reported three times as many domestic bills as Gaullists, but on defence the proportions were reversed.[28]

This sectional outlook of the committees might sometimes be an advantage. Why were black Africans satisfied by legislation in 1956 and Algerian Moslems disappointed in 1957? The overseas territories had deputies of their own and a committee which they dominated; they could confront their metropolitan colleagues with realities, and substantially modify the application of Defferre's *loi-cadre*. With a similar institutional base the Moslems might not have changed the Assembly's decision, but at least they could have made it face the problem. But as it was, with no Algerian representation at all in the Assembly, ministers and deputies were so busy whittling down Lacoste's *loi-cadre* to beat off right-wing assaults that they almost forgot, and wholly frustrated, the bill's original aim of conciliating Moslem opinion.[29] In less dramatic circumstances, too, the committees sometimes ensured that Parliament saw a controversial problem from different sides. In 1951 rapporteurs from the same party, MRP, spoke for Agriculture which wanted to legalize *pastis* (an *apéritif* popular in the south) and tax it for the benefit of the peasantry; for Health which wanted it to stay banned; and for Finance which would authorize it only if the proceeds of the tax went to the ordinary budget.[30]

27. For details see Williams, p. 240 and n.; Harrison, no. 122, pp. 172–9; Dogan in *Paysans*, p. 221 (agriculture). Blum had pointed out the tendency in 1919 (pp. 188–9).

28. Harrison, *Commissions*, pp. 74–6, 198, 230, and no. 122, pp. 177–8. Bromhead, no. 32, pp. 148–51; opposition deputies in 1952 reported about half the government's as well as the private members' bills. In 1949 the Left on the labour committee (Communists, SFIO, MRP) attended three times as regularly as the Right for routine business and nearly twice as often for a major bill: see Williams, p. 249n. In 1952 these parties introduced nearly 80% of the bills sent to this committee and reported on 90% of them: Bromhead, p. 149. The committee campaigned hard to raise provincial wages, improve the collective bargaining status of the unions, and tie wages by law to the cost of living; three times in 1952 governments defeated it only by formal votes of confidence (details in Williams, p. 241n.). In the third Parliament it concentrated on family allowances and its demands often embarrassed even so sympathetic a minister as Albert Gazier. On the industry committee MRP members were much more intransigent than SFIO: Harrison, p. 230.

29. Defferre: *AP* 1957, pp. 222–3. Lacoste: Fauvet, *IV*[e], p. 334. *Lois-cadres*: pp. 273–4.

30. For *pastis* see *BC*, no. 149, 29 April 1951, pp. 4646–7, 4658; *JO* 9 May 1951, pp. 4905–6; *Monde*, 11 May 1951; and below, p. 357.

The system might sometimes help conflicting interests to be heard. But it also allowed one committee, packed by a few assiduous defenders of a pressure-group, to obstruct a policy desired by the majority; or several, representing different interests, to join in mounting converging assaults on the public till. Since they had most incentive at election time and most opportunity at budget time, the strongest committee pressures occurred when the two coincided in spring 1951. In one week of April the government found the justice and legislation committee attacking requisitioning of buildings, Reconstruction trying to double housing appropriations, Communications unanimously condemning economies on the railways, and half a dozen others protesting against insufficient credits. In one week of May Labour demanded £250,000,000 to raise family allowances and provincial wage-scales, Education advocated an allowance for students, Finance wanted more money for civil servants' salaries, Interior called for more vigorous action against slums, Justice saved 63 under-worked local courts from abolition, Press opposed economies on the national film centre, and Pensions sought to treble certain war pensions.[31]

Budget debates in an election year are dangerous times for parliamentarians, even in a system without committees, to demonstrate their courage or public spirit. The specialist committees were no danger to the government unless its authority had already been undermined. But they played their part in the undermining, they added to the strain which exhausted the physical stamina and political authority of premiers in a few months of office, and they were often, when policies were being determined, a force for demagogy and against responsibility. As a result their reputation suffered. Specialist committees normally gained victories only when they were used by a party which was indispensable to the majority – as the labour committee, expressing the discontent of MRP 'back-benchers', succeeded over the collective bargaining law in January 1950, family allowances early in 1951, and the sliding scale for wages later in the year.[32] A committee like Press or Beverages, which remained the preserve of a group of specialists or the instrument of a narrow interest, found that its high internal unity did not compensate for its low prestige and that the government could easily beat it in the house.[33] It was from the 'political' and not the 'specialist' committees that the greatest danger came.

The defence, foreign affairs, franchise and interior committees were clearly 'political'; so at times were Justice and Education. Having most prestige (apart from Finance) they enjoyed most continuity of membership; for members of lesser committees had no seniority rule to encourage them to stay there, and preferred to graduate into bodies with more reputation and importance. A few specialist committees were coveted, especially Agriculture, but Merchant Marine interested few deputies. Every party sent its best men to Defence,

31. References in Williams, pp. 241–2nn. See below, pp. 353–8, 373–7 for the direct influence of pressure-groups; pp. 261–3 for some important reservations. The 1956 budgetary reform hampered this pressure: Blamont, p. 98, and below, p. 269.

32. A compromise on family allowances in February 1951 failed in the committee where six MRP members rebelled, and almost failed in the Assembly where 32 did so. In September all MRP committeemen and four-fifths of 'back-bench' MRP deputies voted for a sliding-scale bill opposed by a government including MRP ministers.

33. See below, p. 262. Cf. Buron, pp. 206–7.

Foreign Affairs and Finance, to which the ordinary 'back-bencher' could rarely aspire.[34] On the major committees the party leaders sat, party divisions were mirrored and party discipline was best. They were therefore potentially the most dangerous to the government.

These 'political' committees had more status than the specialist ones – but less solidarity. When Interior fought Ramadier's government in August 1947 over the municipal election and Algerian government bills, and Schuman's in 1948 over dismissals from the civil service, there was no agreed committee view on any of these matters: the hostile majorities were made up of Communists reinforced first by MRP, then by Socialists and Algerian Moslems over Algeria, and lastly by everyone but MRP. Franchise, in December 1950, rejected every proposed electoral reform by differing majorities, so that the rapporteur was obliged to invert normal practice and appeal to the Assembly to give the committee a lead, and the crucial compromises had to be made outside the committee in informal negotiations between ministers and majority party leaders. Again in 1957 the government called a 'round table' (excluding Communists and Poujadists) to work out acceptable terms for its Algerian framework-law (*loi-cadre*); the interior committee promptly destroyed the compromise in a series of contradictory votes.[35]

The foreign affairs committee voted rarely, except to express outraged dignity. But when it did it was often less representative of the Assembly than the other major committees. In the first Parliament it was well to the Left, as a Socialist, an MRP, an IOM and even a Conservative member (Marin) often voted with the Communists; later, its Conservative members were unusually liberal. The European army dispute as usual upset all the ordinary conventions: ten SFIO and four MRP members of the foreign and defence committees opposed the treaty to which their parties were pledged. At the 1954 committee elections two MRP rebels were turned off (a third had already been expelled from MRP) but all but one of the Socialists remained to speak and vote against party policy.[36] Yet this division in committee only reflected the situation in the house, for EDC had corroded party discipline.

On these bitterly controversial issues the government itself might be as divided as Parliament. In 1948 the Assembly had an anticlerical majority (reflected in the education committee) which was small enough to be upset if the Radical and Socialist ministers voted against their parties. When the committee won on two problems involving church schools, it did so first

34. In 1952 new members were two or three times fewer in these three committees than in others. On Bromhead's sample committees (which excluded those with least prestige) about a third of the membership changed between 1952 and 1954; but of the 1947 members still in the house seven years later, between half and two-thirds were still in their old committees: no. 32, pp. 142–4. Over three Parliaments Harrison found that half to two-thirds stayed in the major committees (many were leaders with safe seats) but under half in the minor ones (if they remained deputies they moved up to more senior assignments): *Commissions*, pp. 60–3. On Finance there were 9 ex-ministers in 1952 and 15 in 1957, and on Foreign Affairs 11 and 23 respectively: Bromhead, no. 32, p. 145, and Harrison, no. 122, p. 177.

35. Interior: *AP* 1947, pp. 147–51; 1948, pp. 79–80, 91–2; 1957, pp. 90–3. Franchise: *AP* 1950, pp. 256–7; A.S., no. 194, p. 860; but it protested unanimously when its Gaullist chairman was not invited to confer with majority leaders on the bill a week later. Round table: see below, pp. 411–12.

36. See Williams, pp. 239n., 412n.; Grosser, p. 86.

because the Socialist ministers would not let the premier cast their votes, and again next month through Socialist and Radical support and the weakness of a ministry which had just been defeated in six committees in a single week.[37] The 'specialist' committees might sometimes lead strong forces on to the parliamentary battleground; the 'political' committees were battlegrounds themselves.

3. THE FINANCE COMMITTEE

The finance committee was at once highly political, since it expressed the outlook of Parliament against the executive, and technically specialized, though its scope was all-embracing. For while the competence of its rivals was restricted to one sphere of policy, its own jurisdiction extended over all the activities of the state. As the Assembly's watchdog against both the miserly ministry and the extravagant spending committees, it always played a dual role: the scourge of every finance minister when it opposed higher taxes, but his valued ally against the increased expenditure demanded by private members and sometimes by his own colleagues. Permanent and specialized for over a century, it was approved even by critics of the committee system.[38]

In investigating departmental budgets the finance committee never pedantically limited its sphere. In three successive Republics it was assigned bills to re-establish a Vatican embassy (1920), subsidize church schools (1951) and set up a nuclear striking force (1960). Enjoying the same broad view as a government, it attracted rising men of ministerial calibre: more than half its original non-Communist members obtained office by the end of the first Parliament, one (Pleven) as premier, five as finance minister, and four in junior economic posts.[39] Elder statesmen might prefer the foreign affairs committee with its lighter agenda, but ambitious majority 'back-benchers' and able young opposition critics generally made their way to Finance.

On it there were few passengers. In 1952 the 39 estimates on which it reported were assigned to 27 rapporteurs. In half the year it dealt with 285 bills (while four other busy committees together took only 414). It met three times as often as its most assiduous rivals (Defence, Justice and Foreign Affairs) and a very heavy burden fell on its *rapporteur-général*, who alone reported on 115 of the 285 texts, and on its chairman. To cope with the work the finance committee, like Defence and Pensions, had civil servants permanently seconded to it and allowed (against regulations) to attend its meetings. This 'sometimes transformed the dialogue of Government with Parliament into a discussion between two coteries of the administration'.[40]

As the focal point of most parliamentary pressures, the committee's

37. *AP* 1948, pp. 76–83, 92–5, 224. Cf. above, p. 34.
38. Blum, p. 187; Auriol, ii. 214.
39. Every finance minister of that Parliament came from it, except Schuman (an ex-chairman of it) and Queuille.
40. Goguel, no. 107, p. 856. On officials cf. his *Fourth Republic*, pp. 166–7; Pactet, no. 171, p. 170 and n.; *Travail*, pp. 693, 814, 854–5. On meetings, Harrison, *Commissions*, Table 8; on bills and budgets, Bromhead, no. 32, pp. 148, 150. Mendès-France claimed that as chairman he worked a fifteen-hour day and a seven-day week; every day he received 2–300 letters, only half from constituents and three-quarters asking favours; and as up to fifty visitors or deputations tried to see him daily, he was bound to offend most of them: in Schoenbrun, *As France Goes*, p. 148.

cohesion was constantly under strain. Consequently the new rule allowing substitutes to replace absent members at committee meetings harmed it far more than other committees; while their unity was somewhat impaired, its character was wholly transformed. In the past when it had discussed the agriculture or education estimates, the relevant standing committee sent its rapporteur to advise; now, half the specialist committee might sit as substitute members of the finance committee itself. A reform of standing orders in 1952 checked this abuse by requiring each party to present a list of names, not exceeding half its quota of places, from which Finance substitutes had to be drawn. This change enabled the committee to regain some of its old coherence.[41]

Because it dealt with the whole field of politics, the finance committee carried much more weight than the others and acquired many more responsibilities. It enforced the checks set up by standing orders against the deputies' pressure for spending (and they sometimes drafted proposals as resolutions rather than bills so as to escape its scrutiny). At the end of the Fourth Republic, Parliament even agreed to leave detailed examination of government expenditure to the finance committees of the two houses.[42]

Made prudent by its budgetary bias, the finance committee tended to oppose overdue but expensive social reforms; and, like the house as a whole, it was kinder to farms than to factories. In the first Parliament it tried to divert investment credits from coal-mining to agriculture, but the minister of industry resisted successfully with the help of the industry and economic affairs committees, both urban strongholds. In the second Assembly it whittled down and delayed the industry committee's proposals to raise the inadequate miners' pensions, and in the third it reduced the scope of the government's old-age pensions bill, which the labour committee wanted to widen, and rejected the taxes by which it was to be financed. But its caution also made the committee an indispensable barrier against the flood of demagogic proposals. Only when the majority was determined (in a good or bad cause) did the finance committee side with the spenders – as in 1951, when the finance ministry demanded educational economies, the ministry of education publicly appealed for support to the finance committee, it unanimously condemned the cuts, and they were dropped.[43]

The finance committee was therefore a rival centre of leadership to the cabinet: the most 'governmental' committee of all in outlook, but also the most dangerous if it decided to oppose. In the Third Republic it was accused of being a 'committee of successors' with a bias towards criticism. In the Fourth it harassed and hampered most governments, and some of its early querulousness was due to rising young politicians using it as a springboard for

41. Blamont, pp. 49–50, 90.

42. See below, pp. 268–9; and on resolutions, Harrison, p. 41 (they were easier to pass than bills and almost as useful for propaganda, though they had little or no effect).

43. Investments: *JO* 26 April 1950, pp. 2904–8, 2912–15, 2921–2; the minister and all the committee spokesmen were MRP. Miners' pensions: Harrison, pp. 221–31; MRP members voted for the proposal in one committee, against in the other. Old age: Blamont, p. 51. Education: *Monde*, 15 March and 21 April 1951, *BC*, no. 149, 29 April 1951, p. 4650. When the education committee protested against earlier cuts, the minister thanked the Assembly for its valuable support in his departmental battle: *JO* 26 May 1950, pp. 4016–17. See also Williams, p. 246n.; Buron, pp. 208–10; and below, p. 264.

promotion. Edgar Faure and Maurice Petsche were the leading critics of René Mayer, Schuman's finance minister, who suffered four major defeats in the committee in three months (though he usually got his way later in the Assembly). Soon Petsche was finance minister in Bidault's cabinet, Faure was his minister of state for the budget, and their Radical critics were led by Félix Gaillard and Maurice Bourgès-Maunoury; in December 1949 the committee threw out the budget, substituted an unbalanced one of its own, rejected three compromise plans, supported most of the wrecking senatorial amendments and was defeated only by lavish use of votes of confidence in the house. Before long the new rebels were ministers, and under fire in their turn.[44]

Governments generally beat off these 'young Turk' assaults. Sometimes party discipline persuaded the committee to reverse its own decision, as it did over Ramadier's budget in June 1947 and Pleven's rearmament budget in December 1950.[45] If the committee members would not make public confession of error, ministers could usually defeat them in the house where the marginal deputies had no previous vote to live down. In December 1949 Bidault used six votes of confidence to insist that the Assembly consider his original budget instead of the committee's version and to save its essential points – but was beaten four times when he did not bring this weapon into play. When Bourgès-Maunoury and Gaillard became premiers themselves, they to found that only by wielding the whip could they rally a reluctant majority.[46]

Appearances were often misleading. Governments fell when their support was disappearing through the defection of either a major party, or individuals from the loosely-organized groups. Because the finance committee had so wide a sphere of activity it was often the arena in which these weaknesses first became apparent; its members therefore seemed to overthrow governments to which in fact they had no special hostility. This was particularly true of the committee's five leaders: its two *rapporteurs-général*, Charles Barangé of MRP until his retirement and Francis Leenhardt from 1956, and its three chairmen, first J. R. Guyon till 1951, then Paul Reynaud, and Pierre Mendès-France while Reynaud was in Laniel's cabinet. Guyon and Leenhardt belonged to a disciplined party, SFIO, which was in the majority throughout their terms. Reynaud and Mendès-France were conspicuous among French politicians in their contempt for office for its own sake. Barangé repeatedly refused it, and he and Reynaud were the government's best (and sometimes only) friends on the committee.[47] Mendès-France, once a scourge of cabinets, gave Laniel every help on becoming chairman in 1953; and overthrew him next year because of Indo-China, not finance.

Sometimes the committee's assaults helped wear down a government but

44. Details in Williams, pp. 243–4; the committee's resentment had technical reasons as well, for it was belatedly and often inadequately informed by an administration which had acquired bad habits under Vichy. 'The day when detailed estimates of expenditure are laid before Parliament in good time, governments will regain the confidence of the committee which they have obviously lost': Fauvet in *Monde*, 16 December 1949. (Finance committee Radicals had been equally rebellious in the 1930's, when they were on the Left of the party.)

45. *AP* 1947, p. 117; 1950, pp. 258–62. (In 1950 the sub-committee members who had first successfully proposed economies abstained on the second vote, which cancelled them.)

46. *AP* 1949, pp. 214–19, 221–3; 1950, pp. 1–5, 10; 1957, pp. 65–7, 117–18, 140, 161–2.

47. On Pleven's tax increases in December 1951 they were 2 against 37: *AP* 1951, p. 330.

did not directly overthrow it, as in January 1952 when it rejected Pleven's budget and substituted an unbalanced one. The government won this battle in the Assembly, which agreed to discuss its original budget instead of the committee's, but was destroyed in another – over railway reorganization – in which the leaders of the committee were on its side.[48] Again, when party alignments were moving against the government the shift was more often under-represented than exaggerated in the committee. Thus in July 1948 Schuman was defeated on the military budget. The finance committee had rejected it by 13 Communist votes to 0, government supporters abstaining; but next day Conservatives and MRP had changed their minds and passed the budget by 23 to 13. When it was defeated in the house the criticism came from the defence and not the finance committee, and the vote was on strict party lines, the Gaullist and Communist oppositions being joined by SFIO but by no other member of either committee.[49] Bidault was overthrown on a confidence vote in June 1950, when he challenged under Parliament's financial rules a Socialist bill affecting civil service salaries, which both committee and Assembly had passed. But this was a party division in which the chairman (Guyon) spoke for SFIO and not for the committee, and those of its members who defied their groups did so to support the government, not to oppose it.[50] When René Mayer fell in May 1953 its members were again somewhat more favourable to him than their colleagues.

Only twice did the finance committee participate directly in a government's defeat. In rejecting Faure's tax increases in March 1952 the Assembly was following its lead, and its members were disproportionately hostile to the government; yet even on this occasion Barangé voted for the government (Reynaud was abroad). After 1953, when external affairs came to dominate politics, the only premier overthrown on a financial question was Mollet. The finance committee severely mauled the budget in December 1956, but he carried it by six votes of confidence. In March 1957 Reynaud condemned his economic and financial policy, in May the finance committee rejected 98% of Ramadier's proposed new taxes, and a few days later Mollet was beaten on a vote of confidence. The Centre representatives on the finance committee were much less favourable to him (but the Conservatives slightly less hostile) than other members of their parties.[51]

Politically, therefore, although Finance was a more dangerous opponent for the cabinet than any other committee its opposition usually only registered

48. Reynaud and Barangé voted for the government and no committeeman from a government party defected.

49. *AP* 1948, pp. 115–17; four amendments to reduce military credits had been proposed by members of the defence committee, token ones by its Radical chairman and a Conservative deputy and substantial ones by a Communist and a Socialist; the first two were withdrawn and the third defeated, but the government was beaten on the fourth.

50. On the rules see below, pp. 263–5. The three PRL and Peasant members and one Republican Independent voted with the government against their groups. See *AP* 1950, pp. 123–6, and *Monde*, 24 and 27 June 1950.

51. Among Radicals, UDSR, Republican Independents, and moderate Peasants, half the deputies voted for Faure, but only two of their ten finance-committee men; one of the four MRP deputies to oppose the government was on the committee. A majority of Conservatives voted against Mollet but half their committeemen abstained, including Reynaud; two-thirds of the UDSR, RGR and RS deputies voted for him, but only one of their five committeemen.

the disintegration of the majority; it was no longer the 'hotbed of intrigues against the government' it had been in the Third Republic.[52] Technically, it was often a help to the ministry, beating off many specialist committee assaults which might otherwise have strained either the budget or the majority. Its worst offence was to consume far too much of the scarce commodity it existed to save: parliamentary time. Repudiating budget after budget, but in the end repudiated by the house it was supposed to represent, the finance committee rarely overthrew cabinets but often helped to exhaust them in the endless war of attrition between executive and legislature.

It was not committee intransigence but party incoherence that ensured parliamentary preponderance. Committees were strong because majorities were weak, and meddlesome because governments were timid and divided. Their 'mother-in-law' behaviour was an irritant rather than a threat, and a determined cabinet could almost always persuade the house to disavow a recalcitrant committee.[53] This did not justify the system; the cumbrous machinery for examining bills took much of members' time and energy, but often wasted them on measures with no chance of success, or allowed a bill to be discreetly smothered in committee by a pressure-group which might not have dared to oppose it in the house.[54] But, since the deputies would not put up with the crude methods of selection and rigid government control which prevail in the House of Commons, some variant of it was inevitable. The *ad hoc* committees of the early Third Republic could never have dealt with the modern volume of legislation (and those created early in the Fifth were sometimes even more influenced by pressure-groups than the regular standing committees). Moreover, without committees Parliament would have exercised its powers of scrutiny blindly and haphazardly. Short-lived ministers all too easily became spokesmen of the bureaucracy in Parliament, not of the citizen in the administration. Committee supervision allowed the representatives of the ordinary man to criticize and perhaps influence the operations of government. The results of admitting his influence were sometimes bad, but the results of excluding it might well have been worse.[55]

The system also had effects on the deputies themselves. Committee work was less publicized and less partisan than debate in the Assembly, and built up that spirit of camaraderie which is a virtue and not a vice of parliamentary government. The club atmosphere moderated passions and allowed opposition members to work usefully with their colleagues. It was in committee that Gaullists and even Poujadists grew accustomed to bargains and compromises with the System, and the Communists themselves frequently made genuine concessions to achieve unanimity.[56] Any supporter of the majority or 'loyal

52. Duverger, *Institutions financières*, p. 348.
53. Pactet, no. 171, pp. 171–2. Also in the Third Republic: Barthélemy, *Essai*, pp. 53, 233, 334; Soulier, p. 222; Blum, p. 192. 'Mother-in-law': Wright in Cole, *European Political Systems*, p. 625.
54. See below, pp. 262–3, 373.
55. Blamont, no. 18, pp. 388–9. For a more critical view see Goguel, *loc. cit.* (above, n. 40).
56. Isorni, *Silence*, pp. 134–8; Grosser, p. 86; Dogan in *Paysans*, p. 222; Harrison, pp. 182–3, 234–5. (They discuss five different committees.) Cf. Hamon in *Travail*, p. 851, and no. 117, pp. 387, 390, 406.

opposition' could, unlike the frustrated British back-bencher, make a constructive contribution to policy if he chose (not all did). The committee system therefore encouraged able men to enter Parliament and work hard within it, and gave them a better appreciation of the executive's problems. 'To educate our parliamentary masters, as well as the voters, is one of the functions of Parliament which is better done (at high cost) in the American and French systems. Assiduity, application to a special field, mastery of procedure and of subject-matter, all these virtues are more automatically rewarded in Congress or the National Assembly than they are at Westminster.'[57] Yet though the deputies could do so much more than MPs to scrutinize the budget and amend the laws, they were often even more discontented with the working of Parliament and their own part in it than legislators across the Channel.

57. Brogan in *Parliament: a Survey* (1952), p. 82.

Chapter 19

THE NATIONAL ASSEMBLY (4): LEGISLATION AND FINANCE

The French Parliament was never an efficient legislative machine. A flood of private members' bills competed vainly for time and attention with the government's measures. The Assembly spent far too much time on the bills that failed, too little on those that passed. Since deputies could propose to spend public money, cabinets exhausted much of their political credit in resisting assaults on the budget, which absorbed half the house's time and left it unable to fulfil its other tasks. Cumbrous procedure, shortage of time and dispersed leadership meant that controversial measures had little hope of success unless there was exceptional pressure behind them.

Major reforms could pass only in a major crisis. When there was no secure majority, Parliament could palliate the consequences of its own omnipotence only by abandoning its power to the government. Yet the politicians made more effort than in the past both to tackle substantive problems and to improve the machinery for dealing with them. They streamlined budgetary procedure, restricted the deputy's right to propose expenditure and, when obliged to delegate legislative power to the government, exacted far more effective safeguards.[1]

1. LEGISLATIVE METHODS

By common consent Parliament sat too long and legislated too much. The 450 sitting hours of 1902 had doubled by 1954. Fewer than a thousand bills, resolutions and reports were presented annually to the last Chamber before 1914; 1,800 to the one ending in 1936; 2,700 a year to the first National Assembly of the Fourth Republic, 3,000 to the second and 3,600 to the third. Parliament dealt annually with over 1,300 bills; the first Assembly passed 276 a year into law, its successors 199.[2] This was four times as many as in Britain at the same periods, but a single British bill might correspond to many French ones; at one time there were forty bills in a French budget. Private members introduced far more bills in France, and many matters needed legislation which in Britain the executive could settle. All bills were presented to the *bureau* of the Assembly or, after 1954, of the upper house; printed and circulated with an explanatory note (*exposé des motifs*); and at once referred to a committee which had three months to report.[3] This time-limit was a dead

1. Radical reformers proposed to remedy executive weakness by importing such unloved British devices as more delegated legislation, government control of business, and limitation of amendments: *Travail*, pp. 679, 697, 701, 847.

2. Fullest statistics in Cotteret, *Le Pouvoir législatif en France*, pp. 46–9. See also Campbell, no. 45, pp. 352–3; *Travail*, pp. 681–2, 809; Georgel, i. 236, 247; Arné, p. 169.

3. After the 1954 constitutional amendment a member sent bills to his own house, and the government to either house (but all money bills went to the Assembly): see below, p. 283. The Assembly's *bureau* once refused a bill declaring its author's descent from Joan of Arc (Muselier, p. 68), and its President rejected a few for unconstitutionality; Herriot refused one for a referendum on the electoral law, and Le Troquer rejected Poujadist bills to call the States-General: Blamont, pp. 30–1 (cf. *Institutions*, i. 137).

letter, but the government could extract bills from a dilatory committee if it really wanted to – though it might not like the shape in which they emerged.[4]

The author of a private member's bill often sat on the relevant committee and was frequently chosen to report on it; if he did not, he could attend for the discussion, though not for the vote. But on a government bill the minister had to withdraw before the committee deliberated, and it could and usually did rewrite the bill completely – and often badly. The government could not move amendments, and had to find a friendly deputy to act for it; in the Fourth Republic it had the new and rarely exercised right to ask the Assembly to reject the report and discuss its own original draft – though the committee could then re-examine the text and move amendments. The bill was taken clause by clause, and committee members, being specialists in the subject, usually dominated the debate. The President, unlike the British Speaker, had no right to select amendments (except to stop duplication). On each, in principle, only a proposer, an opponent, a minister and a committee spokesman could speak and the proposer reply; other deputies (unlike senators) could not 'explain their votes'. There was no equivalent of the British 'guillotine', for time-limits were not always respected, even in an 'organized debate', and did not require a vote on a named clause at a fixed time. Deliberate obstruction by a flood of amendments could be met only by rejecting them *en bloc*, which was occasionally done.[5]

The decision on the whole bill was preceded by members' short 'explanations of their vote'. The measure, if passed, was sent to the Council of the Republic; once the two houses had agreed or the lower had overruled the upper, it went to the President of the Republic to be promulgated within ten days (or, very rarely, referred back for a second deliberation). This procedure could be delayed or accelerated. A motion for the previous question (*question préalable*) meant rejection of the proposal before any debate; this was how the Assembly defeated the European army treaty on 30 August 1954, and the repeal of Barangé's law subsidizing church schools (after debating the previous question itself) on 8 November 1956. The *motion préjudicielle*, which delayed discussion until some prior condition had been fulfilled, was used by the Communists to obstruct bills they disliked by demanding priority for popular proposals of their own.[6] A bill could be referred back (*renvoyé*) to the

4. Blamont, p. 50; Galichon in *Travail*, p. 822; Harrison, pp. 107–8: after the three months the government or 50 members could demand an urgent debate on an unreported bill, though this was very rare (but CNIP tried it in June 1957 on their bill to ban the Communist party). Goguel in *Travail*, pp. 695–6, 858–9 thinks the committees had more power to obstruct, and cites three bills of 1948 against alcoholism in the colonies which were never reported. Cf. Malignac and Colin, *L'alcoolisme*, p. 88; Arné, pp. 179–80; and below, pp. 262, 373.

5. For instance at the peak of Poujadist pressure in 1955: H. George, *Le droit d'initiative parlementaire en matière financière depuis . . . 1946* (1956), pp. 153–4. Later, amendments to money bills were normally required four days in advance: *ibid.*, and Blamont, p. 69. On bad amendments in committee, *Travail*, pp. 857–8, and in the house, n. 12 below; on time limits and organized debate, above, pp. 218, 219. See also Blamont, pp. 31–2, 53, 66–9; Campbell, no. 45, pp. 829–30; Arné, pp. 184–5.

6. Lidderdale, p. 186; Blamont, pp. 62–3. The bill against libels by editor-deputies (above, p. 210n.) was obstructed to the limit of the rules by the Communists, who delayed it for 18 months in committee, tried to stop debate with a *motion préjudicielle* (on the unpopular increase in the price of petrol), and extorted much extra speaking time by threatening a flood of amendments: *JO* 8 November 1951, pp. 7702–36.

committee, which itself could insist on a reference-back at any time. Parts of the bill could be separated (*disjoint*) to form a new measure. On dilatory and procedural motions, as on amendments, only four speakers were allowed.

The procedure for urgent discussion was intended to speed up the process, but was so abused by the deputies that it had to be restricted out of existence. In the National Assembly's next session a majority of the bills passed went through under it, and in its second session nearly a third did. In 1948 urgency procedure provoked a protest by the Council of the Republic, whose meagre rights were seriously infringed by it. After this, it had to be asked for by either the government or the relevant committee; but the Assembly wasted so much time deciding between them that in 1950 the rules were tightened until 'urgent' bills were often dealt with more slowly than others.[7]

Minor and uncontentious measures could be dealt with by an unopposed bills procedure, *vote sans débat*, by which after the committee report the Assembly passed each clause and then the whole bill without any discussion. It was used extensively: in 1947 two-fifths of the bills passed, and in 1956 over half, went through in this way.[8] It was proposed by either the government or the committee to the presidents' conference; the government could stop it there, and any deputy before it came to a vote in the house; three-quarters of the objections came from the government.[9] If the committee again asked for a *vote sans débat*, only the government or fifty members could object; if either did, the committee could by an absolute majority apply for a 'restricted debate' (*débat restreint*). But the debates on which that procedure could be used would never have been long ones, and it was not allowed on major bills. On these debate was normally 'organized'.[10]

The first Assembly passed about three-fifths, the second over half of the government bills introduced (compared to 98% in Britain). More than 70% of the bills they passed were of governmental origin, though in the third Parliament the percentage fell to 62.[11] The failure rate was largely due to the

7. In 1947 (January–August) 88 'urgent' and 73 normal bills passed; in the rest of 1947, 42 and 64; in 1948 (January–August), 59 and 178; in the rest of that Parliament, 19 and 495. After 1950 urgency had to be voted by an absolute majority of the committee, which was hard to get, and approved by the presidents' conference; urgent bills were debated on Fridays (a bad day) and one even came up on successive Fridays for six months. So the procedure virtually lapsed except for government bills. In 1956 (my calculations) one private member's bill out of 53, 2 treaty ratification bills out of 14 and 6 other government bills out of 72 went through under it, including longer paid holidays, old age pensions, and special powers in Algeria. See also F.G., no. 105, pp. 345–6; Bruyas, no. 36, p. 549; Galichon in *Travail*, pp. 823–4; Lidderdale, pp. 192–200, 272–3; Harrison, p. 83; Williams, pp. 208–9.

8. Government bills: in 1947, 81 of 207; in 1956, 10 of 14 treaties and 40 of 72 bills. Private members' bills: in 1947, 33 of 66; in 1956, 27 of 53. Ten of the 53, and 4 government bills, needed more than one reading in the Assembly. For 1947 figures see Lidderdale, pp. 201–2.

9. André Mercier, *JO* 25 March 1952, p. 1464 (cf. Raymond Triboulet, *JO* 12 March 1958, p. 1551).

10. On organized debate see above, p. 219. Restricted debate allowed no general discussion, no amendments except ones already rejected in committee, no speech longer than five minutes, and only one speaker per party on the final vote. It could not be used on constitutional, electoral, financial or some judicial matters, amnesties, treaties, bills referred back by the President or Constitutional Committee, or amendments to standing orders. On it see Blamont, p. 40; Noël, p. 191; *Travail*, pp. 702 (Goguel), 824 (Galichon). Eight bills passed in 1956 had had only restricted debate; only one was a government bill.

11. Cotteret, pp. 47–9; Campbell, no. 46, pp. 352–3. Fewer government bills were defeated than the figures suggest, as a later government often abandoned them, or reintroduced them in a new form.

parliamentary log-jam, for which ministers themselves had some responsibility. Since 1930 the administration had grown contemptuous of Parliament; it laid its bills at the last moment, and under urgency procedure which impeded their examination. The government also encouraged Parliament to act, and later acted itself under special powers, on matters which did not need legislative authority. Although it had advice from consultative committees and the *Conseil d'État*, its bills were sometimes so badly drafted by harassed and transient ministers that Pinay in 1952 reproached the departments with relying on Parliament to make them workable. In fact the amendments often made them worse, though they usually improved private members' bills.[12]

Above all Parliament dealt with too many bills in too little time, since it spent half its sittings on the budget and perhaps a quarter on general political debates. Even an uncontentious measure, passed *sans débat* but amended in the upper house, might take a year from introduction to promulgation.[13] Bills referred back by the President of the Republic for correction of technical deficiencies sometimes disappeared for years or for ever. It took seven years to pass a minor measure against socially dangerous alcoholics, four for the overseas labour code, two for penal law reform. A really controversial proposal could be imposed only by a determined government with a loyal majority (and these were rare), an exceptionally powerful interest-group (a weak minority could obstruct but only a majority could legislate), or an external crisis that made Parliament and public conscious of the need for action. The constitution foreshadowed organic laws on the presentation of the budget (Article 16) and on local government (Article 89); Parliament remitted the first to the government in 1955, and never attempted the second. Successive governments vainly strove to carry legislation reforming education, co-ordinating transport, remodelling the fiscal system. Procedure, wrote an expert in 1953, gave no encouragement to efficiency or to making bills coherent, either internally or with other legislation; everything in it tended to slowness of action, narrowness of view, dilution of responsibility and frittering away of authority.[14]

Major reforms required a real majority. The Constituent Assemblies, with their rigid parties, could nationalize industries and institute social security; the second National Assembly voted subsidies to church schools; the third passed major social and colonial measures, but relapsed into impotence or arbitrariness when it turned to finance or Algerian reform. When there was no majority the deficiencies of procedure accentuated parliamentary chaos and irresponsibility. During the Fourth Republic some of these faults were remedied

12. On Pinay, *ibid.* On consultation see *Travail*, pp. 849–50; on the *Conseil d'État*, also Bertrand, pp. 81–8; on the legislative work of the cabinet secretariat, *ibid.*, pp. 62–9; *Institutions*, i. 242–3; Arné, pp. 170–2. On governmental misdeeds, Marcel Prelot in *Travail*, p. 859; F.G., no. 105; Soubeyrol, *Les décrets-lois sous la IVe République*, p. 201; Blamont, no. 18, pp. 395–7, who cites the bill making 1 May a public holiday: it was laid on 29 April 1947 as 'urgent', then amended by a bill laid on 20 April 1948. On bad amendments, Noël, p. 190, Bertrand, pp. 87–8, Isorni, *Ainsi*, p. 58. On private members' bills, Goguel, *Fourth Republic*, p. 168; Buron, pp. 104–5. If seriously intended, these were often drafted with civil service help.

13. Muselier, pp. 65, 81–2 (details on Jean Minjoz's bill to stop the photographing or broadcasting of court proceedings).

14. Goguel, no. 107, p. 856. Cf. Georgel, i. 247, 251–4. For bills referred back, see above, p. 200; and for non-political laws, Isorni, *Ainsi*, Chapter 2; Muselier, p. 65; and J. Charpentier, no. 54, p. 259. (But has the House of Commons a better reforming record on transport, etc?)

by stricter rules, especially financial. Rules were no substitute for political driving force and could make little difference on major matters. But in the absence of a majority they did limit the cost and consequences of political disorder.

2. PRIVATE MEMBERS' PROPOSALS

For 250 years the British MP has been unable to make any proposal costing money. Although in the last century his bills were often important (the first factory acts were among them), there are today few major topics open to private members. MPs who do well in the ballot for places often take an innocuous measure from a colleague, party or government department, or fall back on an animal welfare bill. But the French member in the Third and Fourth Republics (though not the Fifth) could propose expenditure of public funds: a remarkable stimulus to his own imagination, to his constituents, and to the pressure-groups which wrote so many of his bills. In the first Parliament 4,800 private members' bills were introduced (900 by senators) and in the second, 4,000. They accounted for a quarter of the acts passed by those two Parliaments, and for over a third of those voted in 1956–58. Much government legislation was stimulated by their pressure.[15]

Their number was misleading. A topical grievance might evoke a separate bill from each party if it were national, or from each local member if it were not. Communist bills on war damage compensation or hydro-electric development differed only in the name of the department to which they were to apply. Most such bills were short (only a third had more than one clause) and they were often assigned in batches to a single rapporteur.[16] But they were a growing threat to the budget, for when the elector voted for a list in a large constituency instead of a man in a small one, the deputy's fate depended far more on his party and far less on his local services. 'Rivers and harbours' expenditure was therefore outstripped by the competitive pressure of the parties, and the sums demanded by deputies in a pre-war session might now be proposed in a week or two.[17]

The flood was barely retained by a number of dykes – procedural checks applying to all bills, and financial rules protecting the budget against members'

15. Buron, p. 104. Statistical sources: n. 11. Pressure-groups: below, pp. 373–5. In the first session of the second Assembly the most popular subjects of private members' proposals were, in order: budgetary matters; prosecutions of deputies; protection of local products from wickerwork to seaweed and from cauliflowers to sandals; the wine industry; compensation for storm or flood; tax exemptions; keeping open local railway lines; housing. There were bills for a campaign against porpoises, a higher clothing allowance for customs officials, regulating the profession of ju-jitsu instructor, and reorganizing the band of the *Garde républicaine*: *Monde*, 4 October 1952, quoted London *Times*, same date. On the third Parliament see Cotteret, pp. 50–3, and De Tarr, p. 28. In 1958 one of the few proposals not involving expenditure authorized *juges de paix* to try persons prosecuted for not destroying thistles: Yves Peron, *JO* 20 February 1958, p. 919.

16. Harrison, pp. 100–1, 199 (21 identical hydro-electric bills were presented together; none was ever reported). Cf. Buron, p. 155.

17. Private members demanded 15 milliard francs (£1,800 million) of expenditure in 1930: A. Tardieu, *La Profession parlementaire* (1937), pp. 194, 199. In May 1951 the Communist bills alone would have cost £2,000 million: Queuille, *JO* 11 May 1951, p. 5079; and Pickles, *French Politics*, p. 96n. On the budget for 1953, £1,200 million was demanded within a week: Duchet, minister of posts, quoted *Monde*, 5–6 April 1953. On the new electoral law see below, pp. 307–9. On the comparatively responsible handling of 'rivers and harbours' pressures, Buron, pp. 77–8.

bills or amendments. Of the 2,000 or so private members' bills introduced each year, the committees reported only about 700; of the 700 reports only about 250 were submitted for discussion in the Assembly by the presidents' conference; these 250 had still to face the finance committee and the government.[18] This preliminary slaughter, which killed seven bills out of eight without debate, was carried out with the knowledge or even complicity of sponsors who had often meant them for the local newspaper or election address rather than the statute book: M. Henri Thébault, Peasant deputy and mayor of Angoulème, probably expected no action on his resolution to ban tourist cars from by-passes during shopping hours. Rural members and Communists were particularly prone to demagogy. Of seven hundred agriculturalists' bills and resolutions on marketing, wine legislation and compensation for natural disasters in the second Assembly, only a hundred were adopted (and those usually the least important). But the authors of the others spread them over columns and pages at election time to lend credibility to their familiar but still serviceable promises. For this purpose a bill had only to be published, not pressed, and even Communist rapporteurs often killed off their colleagues' measures once they had been safely recorded in *L'Humanité*.[19]

A first and sometimes feeble barrier was the specialist committee. The alcoholic beverages committee might water down an outrageous proposal but hardly ever rejected one, since all its members sat for the wine and cider districts and none could openly oppose a popular proposal. The house therefore treated this institutionalized raiding party with a contempt which safeguarded the members' time and taxpayers' money. Government bills were drafted to avoid it, and its private members' bills were kept off the agenda by the presidents' conference.[20] If ever the committee wanted to legislate rather than make propaganda, it needed a vote *sans débat*; this meant prior appeasement of any opponents and above all of the government, for an opposed bill might get no second chance from the presidents' conference even if the committee later satisfied the objectors.[21]

The real dykes against the flood were thus the rapporteurs and the presidents' conference, who each stopped far more bills than the committees and the Assembly put together. The presidents' conference was at once a 'barometer' for political pressure, a 'market' for deals between parties or committees and the government, and a 'lightning conductor' against the wrath of

18. In the second Parliament nearly 3,000 reports were never debated: E. Moisan, quoted Georgel, i. 243n. The only analysis of the filtering process is unpublished: Harrison, pp. 100–13.

19. *Ibid.*, p. 180: in five years the beverages committee assigned 49 proposals to Communists but received only 22 reports from them; it rejected only one. Most of the unreported 27 were Communist bills. On rural members see Dogan in *Paysans*, pp. 233–7, with edifying quotations from election addresses. M. Thébault's resolution was no. 5,197 of 20 June 1957.

20. Harrison, pp. 152–3 (presidents' conference), 172–6 (the Coca-Cola struggle, cf. below, p. 330), 177–82 (Communist pressure and means of parrying it), 186–9 (low prestige). Of 230 proposals sent to the committee in 1949–55, 7 were rejected and 94 reported; but 59 never reached the Assembly and only 20 passed into law.

21. *Ibid.*, pp. 154–5. Its bills had 49 readings in the house; one went to restricted debate and one came back to committee, and 27 ended in a *vote sans débat*. Of five bills opposed after the committee had refused to compromise, not one got a second chance in the house. (Similarly the funeral trade once got a committee to put up a bad bill for *vote sans débat*; a deputy was found to object and the bill was never heard of again: Hamon in *Travail*, p. 861.)

pressure-groups. It checked undue generosity by members and committees without making electoral disaster the reward for political responsibility. It distinguished serious bills, intended either to pass or to provoke the government to act, from crankish, irresponsible or purely propagandist proposals. But the system obliged conscientious rapporteurs to spend time, goodwill and hard work on measures that were doomed to disappear instead of those that had a chance of passing.[22]

The financial barriers were the strongest of all, and each rampart depended on the ones behind it. The presidents' conference would turn down bills that flouted the financial rules (unless the pressure was very strong and it wanted to give the government a sharp warning: for the same reasons it occasionally put forward a Communist proposal for debate). It was thus really these rules which gave the government the last word: Articles 16 and 17 of the constitution, the Assembly's standing orders 48 and 68, and the so-called *loi des maxima* (first voted in the budget for 1949 and thereafter repeated each year as clause 1 of the finance act). Article 16 confined the budget to financial matters, but it was constantly broken because the government as well as the deputies found that a budgetary clause or amendment always passed more quickly and often more easily than a separate bill; however, the finance committee maintained some check, and after 1955 standing orders were changed to make this 'tacking' more difficult. SO 68, reinforcing Article 16, banned any proposed new clause in budget bills unless it created or released new resources or enforced parliamentary control.[23]

Paul Reynaud complained that Article 17, which forbade any proposal to spend money during debates on the budget or supplementary estimates, still allowed members to play the fool eleven months out of twelve.[24] It did help to check log-rolling – deputies voting constituency favours to one another – which was much harder when proposals came as separate bills, reported at intervals, instead of all together as amendments to the budget. But its main object was to save time rather than money, and it did not rule out moves to reduce taxes.[25] These were barred by SO 48, which was strictly enforced by the finance committee; any amendment increasing expenditure or reducing revenue was *disjoint* to become a separate bill (and no such bill was ever reported on). This rule was wider than Article 17 in including tax reductions and applying at all times, but narrower in checking only 'back-bench' amendments in the house, not those moved in committee or reported by a committee. More general still, the *loi des maxima* disallowed proposals from any quarter which raised expenditure or lowered revenue without creating additional resources to cover the gap.[26]

22. Harrison, pp. 111–13. Cf. Buron, pp. 104–5, 109–10, 112–13.

23. H. George, pp. 42–5 (on Art. 16), 175–80 (on SO 68), 226–7 and *passim* on the origins, scope, advantages and drawbacks of each rule. See also Louis-Lucas, no. 147.

24. *JO* 11 September 1946, p. 3652.

25. George, pp. 49–50 on its purpose, 51–71 on its application. It may even have lost time, for an amendment was less profitable electorally than a bill, and one bill less than two: cf. L. de Tinguy, no. 209, pp. 491–2. As long as any fifty members could have a bill discussed as 'urgent', the Communists had evaded Article 17 by interrupting budget debates with popular proposals; this was stopped by restricting urgency procedure.

26. George, pp. 157–75 (SO 48); 180–217 (*loi des maxima*); 159, 166, 172, 174, 212 (no proposal

[*over*

These ramparts sometimes reinforced one another but often protected different sectors of the front. All were in constant use. In two days in December 1949 seven popular proposals from different parties and committees were checked under Article 17 and six more under SO 48; and on that year's budget the newly-invented *loi des maxima* stopped proposals (mostly Communist) to spend £775 million and reduce taxes by £200 million. In May 1951, a month before the general election, half the 200 amendments to the *loi de finances* and 34 of 36 new clauses were disallowed. In December 1952 the Communists tried successively but vainly to exclude from the scope of the *loi des maxima* social security, war-damage credits, low-cost housing, education, war pensions, and unemployment pay.[27]

The rules did not have to be invoked by a minister. Exceptionally, in 1951, the Assembly's presiding officer used Article 17 against a proposal accepted by both committee and government (the spending minister was present, the finance minister not); in 1955, the MRP chairman of the health committee appealed (in vain) to the *loi des maxima* against a finance committee proposal to prolong the full tax exemption of the *bouilleurs de cru*.[28] But almost invariably it was the ministry which called them into play. Their enforcement then depended on the finance committee, and they were effective only because it showed 'much wisdom and courage [and] a rigour which the Third Republic never knew'.[29] Usually it was an invaluable buffer for the government, but when the pressure was so strong that its members shared the feelings of the house, a wise minister knew it was time to compromise. Thus in April 1949 the cabinet proposed a 14% increase in war pensions; the pensions and finance committees both voted unanimously for 16½%; the government first invoked Article 17, then accepted 15%. In April 1951 the pent-up pressure for higher family allowances became irresistible as the general election drew close. The government offered a 15% increase; the labour committee demanded 40, but dropped to 30 to win the finance committee's support; a Communist proposal for 50 was *disjoint*; the government raised its bid to 20%, was beaten by 551 to 34, invoked the *loi des maxima* against the two committees, but finally agreed to the finance committee's offer of 25%.[30]

In such cases the premier had either to accept the finance committee's terms for compromise or spend some of his political credit by demanding a vote of confidence. A strong leader might prefer the riskier course, but Georges Bidault was overthrown in June 1950 when he appealed to the *loi des maxima* (which the finance committee had refused to apply) against a Socialist

disallowed under either was ever revived, except with the government's consent). Cf. Lidderdale, pp. 221–4; Duverger, *Institutions financières*, p. 352; Galichon in *Travail*, p. 825 on its progressively tighter drafting.

27. *JO* 26, 27 and 28 December 1949, pp. 7241, 7261, 7298, 7493; *Monde*, 20–21 May 1951; *JO* 9 December 1952, pp. 6086–90, and George, pp. 189–90.

28. *JO* 25 October 1955, pp. 5261–2; he sat for Paris and had no *bouilleur* constituents. Art. 17: George, pp. 72–3.

29. *Ibid.*, p. 221; on earlier failures to enforce, pp. 72, 157–8, 184–7, and Théry, pp. 150–3.

30. References in Williams, p. 260nn.; also for the government using Article 17 and the *loi des maxima* against the committee; and for the finance minister giving way over compensation for German requisitioning, despite the *loi des maxima*, after bitter protest from MRP, SFIO, RPF, Communists, and a unanimous reconstruction committee.

proposal concerning civil service salaries. On 20 December 1952, with several votes of confidence pending, Pinay warned the Assembly that its 356 amendments would add £190 million to expenses while taking £200 million off taxes; next day SO 48 was invoked sixty-eight times and SO 68 twenty-three times; the following night he was out of office. For all their procedural defences, as long as home affairs were the main political battleground it was on the budget that ministers faced the hardest fight, had most need to call upon their followers to show confidence, and were likeliest to be disappointed. Up to 1953 financial questions were fatal to all the six governments turned out by the Assembly (though after 1954 they caused the defeat of only one out of six).[31]

There was nothing sacrosanct about the financial rules. Their force depended on political circumstances. In 1946 Pierre Cot insisted both that members of the Assembly must have the right to propose expenditure and, for fear of demagogy, that members of the upper house must not. In 1950 the deputies overrode the senators and decided that Article 17 applied to the 'special treasury accounts'; in 1951 they reversed their own ruling when the Left invoked it against Barangé's bill to subsidize church schools. In 1953 RPF voted for the *loi des maxima* after opposing it in the past, while SFIO, having supported it when in the majority, was now in opposition and voted against it.[32]

The rules could not be divorced from their political context, for expenditure was not always a vice or parsimony a virtue. Some conservative economy campaigns were quite as demagogic as the pressure for spending which they helped governments to resist. Many deputies who favoured reducing state expenditure were against any specific economies, so that ministers found it even harder to cut expenses than to raise taxes.[33] Some demands for spending, such as the Mendesist insistence on developing research and scientific facilities, were of no electoral profit to their sponsors. The Communists attacked the *loi des maxima* for allowing government supporters to make demagogic promises that they knew were out of order, and warned that an administration freed of parliamentary pressure would never undertake social legislation.[34] Even politicians trying to protect their electoral rear against the demagogues often acted more responsibly than they spoke, and a manœuvre staged for the voter's benefit did not always develop into a real assault on the treasury. After all, the *loi des maxima* could at any time have been superseded by a new law if Parliament had not tacitly accepted its superior authority.[35]

After 1953 ministries were less vulnerable on financial questions because, when financial prudence clashed with electoral necessity, the deputies often

31. *AP* 1950, p. 125, 1952, p. 92; *JO* 22 June 1950, p. 5161, 20–21 December 1952, pp. 6690, 6692, 6851; George, pp. 175, 179n. (SOs), 81 (votes of confidence; cf. above, pp. 234–5, 252–5).

32. George, pp. 46 and 89 (Cot), 57 (Barangé), 189 (*maxima*). On 'special treasury accounts' see below, p. 343 and n.

33. Fauvet in *Monde*, 28 December 1949; Edgar Faure in *ibid.*, 25 April 1950, and in *Figaro*, 15 December 1950; Duverger, *op. cit.*, pp. 27, 346, 371–2. Cf. George, pp. 78, 106.

34. *JO* 14 February 1958, p. 785 (Ballanger), 19th, p. 909 (Duclos), 20th, pp. 918–19 (Peron), cf. 913–14 (Pleven and Cot), 924 (Edgar Faure); also 28 December 1949, p. 7493 (Pronteau). And see Goguel, *Régime*, p. 59; Buron, p. 104.

35. To emphasize its importance, Vincent Auriol referred back a bill in 1949: George, pp. 195–6.

gave the government special powers to take action they could not face, or to undo harm they had already done. In March 1958 they accepted the logic of their own restraint and agreed, with little opposition, to renounce by constitutional amendment their right to propose higher expenditure or lower taxation. Few deputies of the Fourth Republic were political heroes, but most cared for the public interest as well, and some even as much, as for their own electoral survival.

3. BUDGETARY PROCEDURE

It was in the budget debates that members had been most prone to generosity at the taxpayer's expense, and that the restrictions therefore bore most heavily. The Assembly's ingenuity in evading the rules was a perverse tribute to the new determination with which they were enforced, and good evidence that they were effectively impeding traditional demagogy. Their gradual reinforcement throughout the Fourth Republic culminated in 1956 in the belated adoption of a new budgetary procedure which left Parliament free to criticize and reject the budget, but sharply reduced its capacity for irresponsible mischief.

French Parliaments always considered the budget both as the most controversial kind of legislation and as their own best weapon for controlling governmental policy. In theory all expenditure and all taxation had to be passed in a single bill by 31 December; expenditure was voted in detailed 'chapters' between which transfers of credits (virements) were forbidden; revenues were not earmarked for particular expenses. Under the new constitution the budget was to include only financial matter, and its presentation was to be regulated by an organic law. These aims were rarely achieved. The regulation took ten years and was the work of the government, not Parliament. Budgets were presented in many bills, discussed in a disorderly way and (at first) voted very late.

To allow the upper house to deal with the budget in better time, it was split up into an appropriation bill for each major service; a *loi de finances* imposing taxes (and sometimes amending the expenditure already voted); monthly credits, known as 'provisional twelfths', for departments whose expenditure was voted late; supplementaries; and special treasury accounts.[36] After inordinate delays on the budgets for 1947 and 1948, expenditure for 1949 was authorized *en bloc* for each ministry; with fifteen items to vote instead of 5,000, the main credits were voted on 3 January.[37] But Parliament resented seeing no detailed appropriations until the money had been spent. Eleven votes of confidence were needed to force through the next budget in February 1950, and the later detailed bills took longer than before the war. The *Cour des Comptes* warned that administrative efficiency and parliamentary control

36. In 1951 the Assembly voted 76 budget bills – 41 for the current year and 35 for the next: Campbell, no. 45, p. 357. There were 33 bills in the budget for 1953 and 31 for 1955: Muselier, p. 89, Blamont, p. 88; cf. his no. 18, p. 401, quoted Williams, p. 255n.

37. For precedents in the Third Republic see Lidderdale, p. 212n.; cf. Duverger, *op. cit.*, pp. 333-334; a similar procedure was followed in 1946. Later budgets facilitated parliamentary control by simpler presentation. The civil budget for 1953 had only 1,200 chapters and 8,000 pages (against 18,000 two years earlier); in 1955 the whole budget had 4,000 pages: see George, p. 31.

both suffered when budgetary bills were spread over the whole year and well over half the expenditure was authorized by provisional credits. 'France', complained Edgar Faure, 'is the only democratic country where the budget is discussed at such time-consuming length that it prevents Parliament voting substantial and indispensable bills.'[38]

Simplified procedure soon became a liability. In the Korean crisis of late 1950 René Pleven passed his new taxes in a separate rearmament budget in January, while the rest of the budget was voted only just before the June general election. Next year he carried all the civil credits before the end of 1951, an unprecedented achievement; but the deputies then baulked at both the economies demanded by his cabinet and the taxes proposed by his successor. For two months the deficit mounted until Pinay became prime minister, pronounced it over-estimated, raised a loan (on outrageously generous terms) instead of new taxes, and obtained powers to cancel by decree expenditure already authorized by the Assembly.[39] His successors were given even greater discretionary powers, as described in the next section.

These powers were in part the executive's answer to a spendthrift Parliament. For the deputies found ingenious ways round the rules against proposing expenditure during the budget debates. The oldest, commonest but weakest was to move token reductions. Poor party discipline made these easier to carry than in the House of Commons, but they had little effect on the government. To evade the *loi des maxima*, which forbade new spending in the current year, in 1951 a proposal was made to take effect a year later; it was accepted by the finance committee and the government, and was at once imitated for other popular causes. This technique was revived in the next Parliament and led Paul Reynaud to complain that every budget had a hidden time-bomb with a twelve-month fuse. Pinay and Mayer then sought and Laniel obtained powers to limit next year's expenditure to the current year's level.[40] The deputies promptly found a new manœuvre: they refused to discuss chapters they thought inadequate until the government made a better offer, or they adjourned consideration of an entire departmental estimate until it was 'rectified'. In December 1951 the government vainly tried to invoke Article 17 against this procedure, which soon became very popular. Four estimates for 1953 were adjourned, and seven for 1954. Mendès-France met a proposal to

38. *AP* 1950, pp. 133–4 (*Cour*); *JO* 18 May 1951, p. 5499 (Faure). The Assembly spent 112 sittings and 383 hours on the budget in 1950, against a pre-war record of 28 sittings and 93 hours; later the total number of sittings dropped (above, p. 212), so the proportion taken by the budget rose from a third to nearly half; cf. also Williams, pp. 254–5, and n. 47 below. On the *Cour des Comptes* see below, p. 338.

39. Cf. Goguel, no. 107, p. 858n. The Third Force governments had faced severe political unpopularity to maintain high investment for reconstruction. Between 1938 and 1951 state expenditure rose by less than half but taxes by 80%; in 1938 40% of expenditure had been met by borrowing or inflation, in 1951 22% was covered by loans, American aid and 'other resources': Edgar Faure, quoted *Monde*, 17 May 1951, cf. *JO* 18 May, p. 5498; Wilson, p. 353n. It was the Conservative champions of sound finance who reduced investments, increased borrowings – and gained votes.

40. See references in Williams, p. 259n.; cf. George, pp. 71, 204. For Reynaud, *JO* 27 May 1953, p. 2847, cf. 2871 (contrast Mitterrand, p. 2866); also P. Courant, *JO* 14 February 1958, p. 782. For Pinay, etc., cf. Chapus, no. 52, pp. 978–9; George, pp. 192–4; Galichon in *Travail*, pp. 826–7.

adjourn the first estimate presented for 1955 (the post office) by a successful confidence vote against this breach of 'the letter as well as the spirit of the constitution'. Three months later it became clear that he had lost his majority when two estimates were adjourned (one, pensions, by a unanimous vote).[41]

The new rules protected governments against direct pressure for expenditure. The presidents' conference effectively discouraged dilatoriness: after 1952, in any week when the house fell behind on the budget it had to meet at midnight on Friday to catch up. The premier could usually rely on the deputies' *esprit de corps* to overcome senatorial obstruction, and on party discipline to defeat opposition from the finance committee (though this used up some of his political authority). But in adjourning estimates the Assembly had found a dangerous loophole. To close it was one aim of the new budgetary procedure instituted in 1956.[42]

Parliament had delegated to Edgar Faure's government its constitutional task of regulating the presentation of the budget; and Faure's ideas, formulated in 1951 and based on earlier procedural experiments, inspired the 'organic decree' of 19 June 1956 which Guy Mollet's cabinet enacted with the approval of the finance committees of both houses.[43] A single budget bill was to be laid by 1 November, accompanied by economic and financial reports, and arranged in economic rather than administrative categories. No amendment was allowed unless it reduced expenditure, increased revenue or enforced parliamentary control. Unless the whole bill passed the Assembly by 10 December, Part 1 (which authorized taxes and loans and classified total expenditure into civil and military, capital and current) was to go by the 15th to the upper house under urgency procedure. Part 2, which could not be begun till Part 1 was voted, divided expenditure first into broad types (*titres*, such as ordinary expenses, investments, subsidies, or war-damage reconstruction) and then by ministry. The Assembly, like the House of Commons, had about 150 items to vote. If these were not passed by the new year the government could make appropriations for continuing services (*services votés*, rather like the British consolidated fund), taking account of changes already approved by Parliament. This meant no more provisional twelfths, and far fewer supplementary estimates. As the new credits were voted the government allocated them to chapters by decree. Unless either of the two finance committees declared its opposition, the money could be spent after two weeks and the decrees were approved after two months.[44] Only if the Assembly's finance committee rejected the decrees (the Council's committee gave only an advisory opinion)

41. *Ibid.*, pp. 827–8 (on 1951), and p. 706 (Goguel); Blamont, pp. 93–4; George, pp. 62–7; Duverger, *op. cit.*, pp. 353–4; Arné, pp. 175–6; Georgel, i. 293–5; *AP* 1954, pp. 89–90. 'Rectifications' in the Third Republic had corrected printing and drafting errors, but in the Fourth they made changes of substance; Laniel needed five to carry the education estimates.

42. Blamont, p. 94, on 1956; George, pp. 152–3 (Fridays), 222–3 on the breaches of classical budgetary rules which were the price of the procedural improvements. See above, pp. 252–3, on the finance committee, and below, pp. 286–7, on the upper house.

43. On it, Blamont, pp. 95–8; *Institutions*, i. 393–441; Duverger, *op. cit.*, pp. 301, 303, 332–40, 352–4, 358–9, 361–3, 370; George, pp. 230–44; Cartou, no. 48. On Faure's ideas, *JO* 18 May 1951, pp. 5498–9.

44. For precedents over military virements and war damage reconstruction see Blamont, p. 60, and over budgetary adjustments see below, nn. 62 and 65. The ministry of finance was allowed, under strict conditions, to authorize virement between chapters.

was Parliament called upon to allocate the new credits by a bill discussed, if the government wished, under urgency procedure.[45]

The organic decree did not guarantee an easy passage for the budget. Mollet needed six votes of confidence for his, and both he and Gaillard were nearly beaten on pensions.[46] But the deputies now had to take responsibility for accepting or rejecting estimates without procedural manœuvres. The specialist committees lost influence, since each ministry's estimate was dispersed over several *titres* and the debate was therefore directed to problems of finance rather than general policy; their rapporteurs might still influence the finance committee, but their weight in the whole house was so reduced that the chairman of the defence committee (Pierre Montel) protested that the finance minister was already the government of France and now the finance committee was to become its Parliament. For while the Assembly could no longer examine expenditure in detail, the finance committee could still do so. It had no less opportunity to oppose the budget, but much less to obstruct it.

The decree saved much time at its first trial, when the *loi de finances* for 1957 passed its first reading on 10 December and its last on the 29th; there were 104 amendments instead of 994, and 29 sittings of the Assembly instead of 122. The administration benefited, for the new rule about 'continuing services' protected it against political disturbance: although the long ministerial crisis of autumn 1957 prevented the budget for 1958 being laid on time, Part 1 was duly voted before the end of the year. In the past, very detailed parliamentary examination had often hampered governmental responsibility and coherence of policy. The new procedure, without depriving Parliament of its authority, gave the administration more chance to function and the government more chance to govern.[47]

4. DECREE-LAWS AND FRAMEWORK-LAWS

The new budgetary procedure was only an exceptionally important instance of Parliament's growing tendency to abandon legislative authority to the government. It could do this either by distinguishing major spheres of policy, with which only Parliament could deal, from minor ones which might be left to governmental regulation; or else by authorizing the executive to act on matters which Parliament specified. The first alternative had support among some Resistance jurists, whose constitutional plans were to be realized in the Fifth Republic. The second had been used extensively between the wars, when Parliament repeatedly abdicated its powers to the executive.[48]

Between 1919 and 1939 eleven governments had obtained special powers to

45. The Council was dissatisfied, for its committee had only ten days on the first reading and five on the sceond; the Assembly's committee had a month, then ten days, then five days to decide finally on third reading. If either acted faster it had more time on the next round, if slower it had less (and if the Assembly took over a month on the first reading its consent was presumed).

46. See above, p. 247n.

47. On its working see Blamont, pp. 98–101, *AP* 1956, pp. 89, 107–8, 120; for Montel, *JO* 20 November 1956, p. 4941. In the Fifth Republic the time spent soon increased again, to 43 sittings and 162 hours on the first reading of the budget for 1962 (cf. n. 38).

48. On the whole problem see Soubeyrol, *passim*; Cotteret, pp. 36–45, 65–83; Galichon in *Travail*, pp. 793–809; Goguel, no. 107, pp. 853–5; Georgel, i. 297–305; Arné, pp. 152–60; Freedeman, *Conseil d'État*, pp. 84–91; Buron, pp. 117–19.

override existing legislation by 'decree-laws'. These theoretically needed eventual parliamentary approval, but they could operate without it and, as their purpose was often to transfer the blame for unpopular decisions from Parliament to the government, members were not always eager to approve them. While decree-laws enabled the executive to act where the legislature would not, they encouraged evasion of responsibility by the deputies and of parliamentary control by the administration. After the early years the authority given was very widely drawn and still more widely interpreted: Laval prohibited foreigners keeping carrier-pigeons under powers given him to defend the franc. Daladier's special powers enabled him to go through the Munich crisis without summoning Parliament and, a year later, to ban the Communist party by decree-law. After the defeat Parliament abdicated all its powers, including that of drafting a new constitution, to Marshal Pétain.[49]

The Resistance movement reacted against these abuses, and in the two Constituent Assemblies only Paul Reynaud defended decree-laws. Article 13 of the constitution enshrined this hostility: 'The National Assembly shall vote the law. It cannot delegate this right.' But jurists held that these words did not prevent ministers being authorized to alter existing legislation by decree, and the constitutional drafting committees seem to have known this.[50] Indeed, René Capitant warned them that unless the new Parliament was capable of acting rapidly, decree-laws would soon revive. But the new Assembly dealt no better than the old Chamber with matters requiring speed or technical expertise or secrecy (such as tax changes). Deputies still feared the electoral consequences of many measures they knew to be necessary, and procedure still hampered leadership and facilitated obstruction. Supporters of Third Republican institutions, including decree-laws, regained influence after 1948. So, 'torn by its double complex of powerlessness and sovereignty', Parliament alternated between delegating its powers to the government and throwing out cabinets which tried to use them. Three distinct techniques were used: first the separation of spheres, as in Reynaud's law of 17 August 1948; secondly, in 1953–55, special powers like those of the inter-war years, but with stricter limits of time, authority and subject-matter; thirdly the framework-laws (*lois-cadres*) by which Parliament after 1956, instead of transferring a specified subject to governmental regulation, passed legislation laying down principles and invited the executive to fill in the details.[51]

The Reynaud law conferred both temporary and permanent powers.[52] 'To make [the administration] more efficient and less costly' (Art. 1) and to

49. Werth, *The Destiny of France*, p. 152 (pigeons); M. Sieghart, *Government by Decree* (1950), pp. 273–304; Soulier, pp. 162–5, 184–9; Galichon in *Travail*, pp. 800–2; Soubeyrol, pp. 21–7.

50. *Ibid.*, pp. 60–1, 64, 70, cf. 56–71, 74, 183–4; Arné, pp. 154–5; Pinto, no. 181; but cf. Georgel, i. 298. Article 13 was meant to exclude from legislative power the Council of the Republic and the Assembly's own committees as well as the government.

51. *SCC* I, p. 102-3 (Capitant); J. Donnedieu de Vabres, quoted *Institutions*, i. 140 ('double complex'); *Travail*, p. 804 (Galichon), cf. p. 847 (Hamon); Cotteret, pp. 40–2, 66–8, 78–9; Soubeyrol, pp. 4–6, 15, 37.

52. Text of the law in *ibid.*, pp. 215–18, and in *AP* 1948, p. 363 (of the original bill, *ibid.*, p. 339). Cf. Pickles, *French Politics*, p. 275n. It is fully discussed by Pinto, no. 181, and by Soubeyrol, pp. 77–90. Marie sent his ministers a circular (printed in Cotteret, pp. 70–1), asking them not to introduce bills where regulations would now suffice.

ensure profitability and encourage individual responsibility in the nationalized industries (Art. 2), the government was instructed to reorganize them; for equally vague objectives it was to reform the social security system and fiscal structure. These powers were subject to time-limits; many decrees under them needed parliamentary approval; and they could not be used to denationalize an industry, give up the state's controlling interest in a mixed company, or reform the army or judiciary. Reynaud's proposed use of them broke up one government (Marie's), and the next (Schuman's second) was slaughtered at birth by the Right because they would have been wielded by a Socialist finance minister. Queuille then took office and used them little, though he did invoke them to introduce an unpopular fiscal reform.[53]

Other powers under this law were unlimited in time, but restricted in scope to matters, enumerated in detail, 'of a nature to be dealt with by regulations'. On these, which covered much the same fields but excluded taxation, broadcasting and the press, governments could override existing (but not future) legislation by decrees which needed no parliamentary approval, though Parliament could always regain its authority by passing a new law. By the end of 1954, 350 decrees had been issued. These permanent powers were used by Pleven in October 1950 to remove the social services of the gas and electricity industries from Communist control, and by René Mayer in 1953 to abolish – temporarily – the autonomy of the nationalized industries.[54]

Reynaud's bill was attacked as unconstitutional by the opposition, René Capitant arguing strongly for the *loi-cadre* against the *décret-loi*.[55] Over the next five years governments frequently obtained powers to carry out economies, or reduce or even increase taxes by decree. But Parliament would not repeat the 1948 precedent on a large scale. Queuille in April 1951 and Pleven in January 1952 sought powers to reorganize the nationalized railways: the former was unanimously opposed by the Assembly's communications committee and the latter (who had also wanted to reform the social services) was overthrown on a vote of confidence. Pinay was driven to resign when in the budget for 1953 he too sought powers to reform the fiscal and social security systems. But six weeks later René Mayer was authorized to do so unless Parliament dealt with them by bill within three months.[56]

Asked by Mayer's government for an advisory opinion on the scope of Article 13, the *Conseil d'État* on 7 February 1953 enunciated 'a solution of compromise and expediency'. It approved the conception (which it had itself invented) of matters 'of a nature to be dealt with by regulations'. But it condemned as unconstitutional any delegation of power, either on the 'essential rules' governing matters reserved to the law by the constitution itself or by the republican tradition expressed in its preamble, or so general

53. This went into force unless modified by Parliament within twenty days; of 962 clauses one was abrogated and one amended: Soubeyrol, pp. 88, 141, cf. 126.

54. The spheres of law and regulations are conveniently summarized in *Travail*, pp. 797–9. See also Cotteret, pp. 41–4; Soubeyrol, pp. 89 and n., 131, 171; Lescuyer, pp. 115–16, 142–70.

55. In 1946 Capitant had argued as a jurist that Article 13 would not prevent decree-laws (cf. n. 51). But in 1948, as RPF leader, he maintained impressively that it did: *JO* 9 August 1948, pp. 5566–70.

56. Soubeyrol, pp. 91–105, 141–3; *Travail*, p. 804; Cotteret, p. 41; *BC* no. 148, 23 April 1951, p. 4634; *AP* 1952, pp. 7–9; below, nn. 62, 65, and pp. 343–4.

or imprecise as to amount to an abdication of parliamentary sovereignty.[57] Later governments tried not to flout these limits too blatantly, and after one more revolt Parliament accepted the inevitable. In May 1953 Mayer was refused powers to impose by decree economies and higher taxes, which offended in particular the powerful alcohol interest. But Laniel, coming to office after a seven-week ministerial crisis, won a striking revenge for the executive. His law of 11 July 1953 temporarily included military and judicial administration and civil service promotions and retirements within Reynaud's matters for regulation. It allowed his own government powers to promote productivity, exports and full employment, and also to defer the operation of any bill costing money (refused to Mayer) and to co-ordinate the transport system (refused to Pleven).[58] After 1953 decrees submitted to the *Conseil d'État* under special powers quadrupled in number.[59]

Under the next premier, Mendès-France, the Left abandoned its opposition to decree-laws. The Socialists voted for his law of 14 August 1954, the Communists abstained, and (despite some criticism from MRP members who had voted for the earlier bills) Article 13 of the constitution was 'formally laid to rest in an atmosphere of good humour and opportunism'. Though his powers were confined to his own government, Parliament renewed them to his successor Edgar Faure – for longer than Faure had asked, and without even a vote of confidence – and indeed extended them widely. There was no more opposition on constitutional grounds. Laniel, Mendès-France and Faure issued over 450 decrees in less than two years.[60]

Up to 1955, 31 bills delegated power to the government, in terms less vague than in the Third Republic but really precise in only ten cases. However, there were more genuine safeguards against abuse (though they differed confusingly from law to law). Under three acts, decrees could be issued only by a specific government; under most, they had to be approved by the cabinet; under all the important ones, they went to the *Conseil d'État*, a new and welcome assurance that they were *intra vires*.[61] Usually (unless 'of a nature to be dealt with by regulations') they required eventual parliamentary approval, which was a more real check than before the war – though the decrees Parliament rejected were too often the better ones, especially on the subject of alcohol. Serious parliamentary criticism was frequently appeased by requiring decrees

57. The opinion is translated in Freedeman, pp. 169–70, and the original is in *RDP* 69. 1 (1953), pp. 170–1; for comments see *Monde*, 20 February 1953; *Travail*, pp. 804–5 ('... expediency'). Guy Petit, as minister of state assisting Pinay, had recently drafted a bill defining the 'domain of the law', but the *Conseil* refused to give an opinion on it then, and in 1956 disapproved Petit's private member's bill embodying it: Cotteret, pp. 71–7 (reprints the later bill and opinion). The *Conseil*'s responsibility for the idea of matters 'by nature' not legislative is asserted by Pinto, no. 181, pp. 518, 531, and by Freedeman, p. 87, and hinted by Soubeyrol, p. 166.

58. Soubeyrol, pp. 107–16, 218–20; Chapus, no. 52 (both giving incomplete texts); *Travail*, pp. 805–6. Where the law of 1948 had prudishly authorized the government to modify 'les dispositions en vigueur', that of 1953 frankly specified 'les dispositions législatives'.

59. The annual average was nil up to 1948, 59 in the next five years (with a peak of 100 in 1948–9) and 241 after 1953 (with a peak of 460 in 1954–5); but from 1956 many were applicable in Algeria and the colonies but not in France. See table in Freedeman, p. 90 and n.

60. Soubeyrol, pp. 117–31. The 1954 law dropped all reference to the two spheres (p. 120), and the extension authorized the government to establish taxes, penalties and courts (p. 127).

61. *Ibid.*, pp. 159–61, 166, 181–2 (10 of 31); Blamont, pp. 80–2; *Travail*, p. 804; Cotteret, pp. 43–5.

to be submitted for the advice of the finance committee of each house and sometimes for the consent of the Assembly's; occasionally other committees were added.[62] After 1953 all the major bills followed the *Conseil d'État* by expressly excluding, first matters reserved to Parliament by the constitution or its preamble, and secondly the goods and liberties of the citizen. But this distinction ominously implied that the constitution did not protect civil liberties. It foreshadowed the encroachments which the Algerian war was soon to bring, across the Mediterranean in Mollet's special powers law of March 1956, and in France itself with Bourgès-Maunoury's law of June 1957.[63]

Jurists disliked the special powers bills of 1953–55, despite the new safeguards, and preferred the *lois-cadres* invented by Blum in 1936 and revived – again by Socialists – in 1956.[64] Gaston Defferre's great colonial reform of 23 June 1956 had nine clauses enunciating principles, to be applied by decrees laid before Parliament. Economic and administrative decrees went into force at once, political decrees (unless amended or abrogated) after four months. The two houses agreed on amendments to all the 17 political decrees and to 23 of the 28 others, accepted four unchanged, and let only one go into force by default. This method satisfied the upper house, and it took only four months to pass the bill into law and thirteen to bring all the decrees into force. Thus a determined government and majority could still work the parliamentary machine efficiently.[65]

Unlike ordinary legislative procedure, this method concentrated parliamentary discussion on the principles and not on the details which usually attracted the local pressures. Even when the decrees needed approval the government was protected, for unless both houses agreed in good time it could enforce its own text. Unlike the decree-law, which gave a blank cheque

62. For instance, the consent of the finance committee of the Assembly was required for tax reductions under a law of 8 August 1950, and for budgetary virements between ministries under Laniel's law (there were precedents as early as December 1945). That of the reconstruction and defence committees was also needed for changes in their credits (laws of 31 December 1953 and of 2 April 1954): Soubeyrol, pp. 45ff., 96, 113, 115. Cf. Blamont, pp. 59–60; Williams, p. 237n.

63. Cf. Soubeyrol, pp. 112, 127. The *Conseil d'État* (like Anglo-Saxon courts) interpreted the government's powers more widely during war or grave disorder (pp. 149–53) and the constitution itself extended them overseas, including Algeria (pp. 154–8). The state of urgency, invented by a 1955 law, was invoked only by Pflimlin in 1958: see Arné, p. 158, and Drago, no. 77. The laws of 1956 and 1957 had no legal or political safeguards at all, except that they had to be renewed when a new government took office; on them see Petot, no. 174, and Charpentier, no. 54, p. 259.

64. *Ibid.* (pp. 220–70); Cotteret, pp. 66–8; cf. M. Prélot in *Travail*, p. 846; L. Hamon, *JO* (*CR*), 25 January 1951, p. 236; R. Capitant, *JO* 9 August 1948, p. 5566; G. Liet-Veaux in *Institutions*, i. 140; and the opinion of the *Conseil d'État* (n. 57). On 1953–5, also Blamont, pp. 80–1; Duverger, *System*, p. 58; cf. Goguel, no. 107, p. 854n. On both, Soubeyrol, pp. 180–6.

65. Charpentier, no. 54, pp. 230–5, 251, 253, 255, 260–3; cf. Blamont, pp. 82–3. The bill had seven other clauses on the electoral system: a matter for the law. Decrees accepted unchanged by the overseas territories committees were not debated in the house. The solitary decree put into force by default had been approved by the Assembly, but the Council thought it unfair to property. On Mollet's political strength see above, p. 235. Defferre's 'tacit consent' procedure had precedents (with less generous time-limits) in Queuille's fiscal reform of 9 December 1948 and Mayer's law of 7 February 1953 (above, n. 53 and p. 271); also in the rearmament budget of 8 January 1951, by which Parliament authorized the cabinet to increase existing taxes by £25 million unless within a month it had voted corresponding economies: Soubeyrol, pp. 98–9, 142–3; cf. Louis-Lucas, no. 147, p. 746. Under it the cabinet raised the petrol tax; the finance committee voted against it by 40 to 1: *BC* no. 9, 13 November 1951, p. 142.

to a man, the *loi-cadre* allowed and indeed required the collaboration of government and Parliament on a precise programme. But this closer contact meant greater political risks, which could be run only by a strong cabinet, and once political conditions ceased to favour this co-operation the new procedure worked less well or was abandoned altogether.[66] The housing act of August 1957, for all its 62 clauses, still left the government undue discretion over aims as well as methods; and the Algerian institutions law of February 1958 disappointed the Moslems without conciliating the Right, whose parliamentary assault was only postponed until the decrees were laid before the house. Two more enabling bills on agriculture and the Common Market were never passed.[67] And Mollet's successors preferred Laniel-type decree-laws for their financial legislation, since those deputies who wanted to avoid responsibility for voting on the details of a law had no desire to pronounce on the decrees which followed.[68]

Delegation had great political advantages. First, it limited Parliament's opportunities to wear down governmental authority. If the premiers of 1953–1955 demanded far fewer votes of confidence than their predecessors, this was partly because special powers freed them from the need to whip their supporters into line on every contentious point. But while a ministry with a stable majority could make constructive use of Parliament, a weak and vulnerable one needed special powers to restore the balance of the system.[69] Secondly, on some contentious questions a parliamentary minority had such opportunities to obstruct, or a majority so feared the electoral repercussions of its votes, that special powers gave the only hope of action. But the determination of the executive could not be inferred from the impotence of the legislature. Parliament showed conspicuous cowardice over all aspects of the alcohol problem – beets, bars and *bouilleurs*; yet the reversal of Mayer's proposals under Laniel and of Mendès-France's decrees under Faure showed that ministers, too, might lack political courage. If governments sought special powers to avoid a legislative battle, they often failed to get them like Pleven and Mayer, broke up over them like Marie, or met a violent reaction when they tried to use them, like Laniel.[70]

The parliamentary bottleneck often made delegation necessary even on uncontroversial matters. When the overloaded *Conseil d'État* was breaking down in 1953, Mayer's government introduced a bill to transfer the lesser cases to lower administrative courts; it was so delayed by other measures and a government crisis that only Laniel's special powers brought it into force that year. In the same Assembly the industrial production committee, which was on excellent terms with its ministers, buried 7 of their 19 bills for sheer lack of time. Unfortunately special powers might make the worst of both worlds, for too often the civil service, unprepared with major reforms, used its delegated

66. Charpentier, no. 54, pp. 252–7, 260–70; cf. Capitant, *JO* 9 August 1948, pp. 5566, 5570.
67. The safeguards and time-limits prescribed differed on each bill. See Charpentier, no. 54, pp. 228, 230–1, 256–7; Blamont, pp. 83–6; and on housing, Cotteret, pp. 67–8; no. 161, p. 846.
68. Charpentier, no. 54, pp. 259–60; Cotteret, p. 44; Georgel, i. 300.
69. Galichon in *Travail*, pp. 808–9; Soubeyrol, pp. 15–16; Solal-Celigny, no. 201, p. 311. On votes of confidence, above, p. 235.
70. Soubeyrol, p. 7 (revolts); below, pp. 356–7 (alcohol).

authority for hasty and piecemeal enactment of minor projects which had been on its shelves for years. Ten weeks before the regime collapsed a Socialist complained that 'more and more we tend to administer from the Palais Bourbon, while more and more the departmental bureaucracy spends its time legislating in our place'.[71]

The grievance was genuine but the trend was not, for in the third Parliament real progress was made in tackling the problem. While the flood of bills somewhat abated, a higher proportion of private members' measures was passed. Within metropolitan France even the governments which abdicated to the military in Algeria made less use than their predecessors of their delegated powers to alter the law. The genuine *loi-cadre* was better than either the uncontrolled decree-laws of the thirties or even the improved model of the fifties, and in different political conditions might have increased Parliament's output without diminishing its authority. But no technical reforms could solve the inextricable political deadlock over the Algerian war; and the Fourth Republic ended, like the Third, with the most sweeping delegation of all when Parliament abandoned its authority to change the laws and the constitution into the hands of a national hero.[72] These capitulations were ratified both by the deputies and by their colleagues who manned that last bastion of republican traditionalism, the upper house.

71. René Dejean, *JO* 18 March 1958, p. 1636. On the courts bill, Soubeyrol, p. 114; on the committee, Harrison, pp. 213–14; on *fonds de tiroirs* reforms, Brindillac, no. 29, p. 58.

72. Of the three laws passed on 3 June 1958, one gave de Gaulle the same Algerian special powers as previous governments. Another gave him full powers for six months, except over: matters reserved for the law by the constitutional preamble; civil and trade union liberties; the definition of and penalties for criminal offences; 'the fundamental guarantees accorded to citizens'; and the electoral law. The third (on which see above, p. 56, and below, p. 303) allowed the government to draft a new constitution to be approved by referendum. This, in its last Article (92), empowered the government during the next four months to do anything necessary for the life of the nation, protection of the citizens, or safeguarding of liberties; and also to settle the electoral law. See *AP* 1958, pp. 71–4, 542–4, 561.

Chapter 20

THE COUNCIL OF THE REPUBLIC

The Senate had been a political bastion of the Third Republic, but its social and economic conservatism made it unpopular in 1946. The constitution-makers reduced its powers and changed its method of election; but when the conservative forces revived they restored the old type of electoral system, in 1948, and some of the lost powers, in the constitutional amendment of 1954. That compromise settlement ended the guerrilla warfare between the houses, for while the new second chamber was no more progressive than the old it was weaker and less obstructive.

1. THE BACKGROUND

The Senate of the Third Republic was the chief obstacle placed by the founders in the way of a majority of the Left. They took every precaution to make it safely conservative. It was elected by delegates of the local authorities whose numbers were weighted, against the great cities, to favour the countryside and later the small provincial towns.[1] These local authorities were often less progressive than their constituents, for many villages which voted Left in national elections chose as mayor a Conservative with the time and experience to run local affairs: Aisne, for example, returned seven deputies of the Left and four senators of the Right. Senators were chosen for nine years, a third retiring at a time; as the local councils had themselves been elected earlier, the Senate represented the out-of-date opinions of an excessively conservative constituency. The minimum age was 40 and the average much higher.[2] A quarter of the members were to be chosen for life by the monarchist lower house elected in 1871.

Although the Senate seemed an impregnable bastion of conservatism, the Right soon lost control of it by internecine quarrelling. In 1884 the Republicans forced through a constitutional amendment which abolished life senatorships as the incumbents died off, and altered the electoral colleges to strengthen the small country towns (though not the great cities) at the expense of the rural areas. By 1900 the Senate and Chamber were both passing from the hands of the moderate Republicans into those of the Radicals. Thus the twentieth-century Senate did not stand openly on one side of the party battle like a French House of Lords; it kept squarely in the centre. It consistently opposed proportional representation, which was favoured by both Socialists and Conservatives but disliked by the groups between them. The typical senator was characterized as a professional man from the provinces, 'a moderate and ardently patriotic Radical; against the Left which threatens his savings; yet

1. Marseilles with 900,000 inhabitants elected 24 delegates; the rest of the department with 250,000 had 313: Sharp, p. 67. Lille's 300,000 people had 24 delegates and so did two dozen neighbouring villages with 4,000 inhabitants between them: Cobban, no. 57, p. 324.

2. But as Louis Barthou wrote, 'By definition all senators are old': *Le Politique* (1923), p. 35. Cf. Herriot's advice to a new senator, quoted Middleton, p. 171, and Williams, p. 267n. Aisne: Weill-Raynal, no. 217, p. 471; and cf. *Paysans*, pp. 459–60.

afraid of being governed by "Reaction"; liberal but conservative, anti-socialist but timid; a subscriber to *Le Temps*, an anticlerical ... whose wife attends 7 a.m. mass'.[3] He and his colleagues were decisive in maintaining the negative policy (*ni réaction ni révolution*) to which the majority of the electorate was wedded: and this was the secret of their power.

The Senate differed from the House of Lords in authority as well as in outlook. Because its members sat for a long term and were generally re-elected, it tended to attract the ablest parliamentarians – who in turn reinforced its power and increased its attractiveness. The senators, unlike British peers, had all undergone a regular political apprenticeship and were elected by active local politicians. More skilful than the Lords, they rarely rejected bills outright: those they disliked were buried in committees and never emerged.[4] They never challenged governments fresh from a general election; they did not need to. For majorities of the Left were always unstable, since their marginal members tended to seek a change of allies when the elections were past and the budget had to be dealt with. When the moderate Radicals in the Chamber began to contemplate switching from working with Socialists to working with Conservatives, their friends in the upper house would intervene to hasten their decision.

Instead of defying public opinion, the senators tried to circumvent it or waited for it to change. Before a surge of popular feeling like that of 1936 they would bow gracefully, accepting legislation which they detested in the justifiable confidence that their revenge would not be long delayed. In the later years of the Third Republic they extended their power to government-making, although constitutionally their right to do so was not clear. After ejecting only three ministries in the first 55 years, they overthrew four in the last decade – of which they found two unduly clerical and two dangerously socialist.

The senators exercised a cautious influence on policy by hampering progressive legislation, wearing down and occasionally destroying governments, and keeping the Élysée, through the presidential electoral college, in safe and conservative hands. With so clear a political bias the Senate's status was naturally controversial. The Radicals wanted to abolish it, until it came under their control; Antonin Dubost wrote a book against it, ended life as its president, and was succeeded in the chair by the first premier overthrown by the upper house, Léon Bourgeois. But the demand for its abolition was taken up by the under-represented Socialists, and at the Liberation the end seemed to have come.[5]

With *tripartisme* in the ascendant and Radicals discredited, the old-fashioned anticlerical conservatism of the Senate was thoroughly unpopular in October 1945; and the 25-to-1 referendum vote against a return to the Third Republic was partly a vote of censure on it. Accordingly there was no

3. W. d'Ormesson, *Qu'est-ce qu'un Français? ... Clemenceau, Briand, Poincaré* (1934), pp. 52–3. I owe this and the Barthou reference to Dr. D. B. Goldey.

4. Woman suffrage and real proportional representation were blocked until the end; effective secrecy of the ballot for nine years, income tax for eight, a weekly rest-day in industry for four, pensions for railwaymen for twelve: Sharp, p. 127; Barthèlemy, *Gouvernement*, p. 82. Cf. above, p. 118 (woman suffrage); below, p. 308 (PR).

5. Forms of influence: Duverger, *VIe*, pp. 98–100; cf. above, p. 196. Dubost and Bourgeois: E. M. Sait, *The Government and Politics of France* (New York, 1920), p. 125.

second chamber, but only two advisory bodies not forming part of Parliament, in the draft constitution which was defeated at the second referendum of May 1946. In the new Constituent Assembly three tendencies clashed. The Radicals and their allies favoured a return to the old Senate. MRP (like General de Gaulle) wanted a broadly corporative chamber representing professional interests, colonial territories, and local authorities. The Communists and Socialists recognized that there had to be a second chamber if the new constitution was to be accepted at the polls, but hoped to keep it feeble and submissive; they prevailed at the time, but had to concede that while the powers of the new body were laid down in the constitution, its composition should be left to an organic law and reconsidered two years later.[6] A new electoral law in 1948 and a constitutional amendment in 1954 partially restored the old Senate.

The Council of the Republic passed through three phases. The first Council was similar to the Assembly in party complexion, and stilled some suspicions by its cautious determination not to overstep the bounds. For a time it was disregarded, but within a couple of years it had defended itself successfully against encroachment by the deputies, helped the government resist their demagogic pressure, and acquired a reputation as a genuine 'house of second thoughts'. The second Council, based on a rural and conservative constituency very like that of the old Senate, was elected when Radicals and Conservatives were fellow-travelling with RPF; and by trying to regain the Senate's powers, revive its conservative role and destroy the Third Force majority, it reawakened old suspicions and damaged its cause. But the absorption of the Gaullists into 'the System' reduced party friction, and when procedural concessions were no longer likely to lead to political deadlock it became possible to remedy the technical faults of the 1946 constitution.

2. COMPOSITION AND POWERS

The Council's composition was laid down by Article 6. It was elected by 'universal indirect suffrage' on a territorial basis by local and departmental communities – a vague formula open to many interpretations; it was to have from 250 to 320 members, renewable by halves; and up to a sixth might be elected by the National Assembly by proportional representation. A complicated law of 27 October 1946 fixed its membership at 315, one more than in the old Senate. Most (200) were chosen by electoral colleges in each department of metropolitan France. These included the local deputies and departmental council (very roughly like a county council) and an overwhelming majority of elected delegates.[7] First the citizen cast his vote for a list of 'grand electors' which he could not alter; between lists the seats were distributed by PR. The electoral colleges then chose the Councillors of the Republic: 68 by simple majority vote in departments which had only one councillor apiece; 59 by PR in the 22 larger departments. Another 73 seats were allocated between

6. An organic law was a law on a major matter of governmental organization (e.g. presentation of the budget, the electoral law). In the Fourth Republic (unlike the Fifth) it was passed in exactly the same way as an ordinary law.

7. There was one 'grand elector' for every 300 registered voters, in all 85,000 – with 3,000 departmental councillors and 544 deputies.

parties to achieve PR (based on the first-stage voting) over the whole country, and to the unelected candidates of each party who had the highest proportion of votes polled in their constituencies. The local government bodies of Algeria chose 14 members, and those of French territories overseas, 51. The last 50 councillors were elected by the National Assembly: 3 to represent Frenchmen living abroad and 5 those in Tunisia and Morocco; 7 assigned to ensure still more accurate nation-wide PR; 35 allocated proportionately between parties in the Assembly. These elaborate provisions ensured that party strengths in the first Council almost reproduced those in the first National Assembly.

Article 102 required the whole Council to be renewed within two years, after the election of new local authorities. By that time the Communists were in active opposition to the regime, and Gaullism had attracted a great following. PR had now lost favour with the parliamentary majority, to whom it would give only a minority of seats. Article 6 was therefore reinterpreted, and a different electoral system was introduced. Under the new law of 24 September 1948, the term of membership was six years; half still had to be renewed at a time. As in 1946 there was a minimum age of 35. A candidate might not stand in more than one constituency at a time (as he could for the old Senate). There were 246 metropolitan councillors (four extra) and 74 from overseas (one extra): in all 320, the constitutional maximum.[8] Each department had a seat for its first 154,000 inhabitants and another for each subsequent 250,000 or fraction thereof.[9] Nation-wide PR and partial election by the National Assembly were abandoned.

In the electoral colleges PR was now to operate only in the 11 departments with a population above 654,000 and four or more seats, which elected 72 councillors. The remaining 79 departments, with 174 seats, elected by majority vote and two ballots.[10] The electoral colleges were revolutionized. With the deputies and departmental councillors there now sat, instead of the 85,000 grand electors, 100,000 representatives of the municipal councils according to their size (which rises, not proportionately, with population). The 1,312 councils of communes with over 3,500 inhabitants elected their delegates by PR; the other 37,000 used a majority vote with three ballots. Thus the 1946 system of thinly disguised direct election was replaced by an indirect method which, as in the Third Republic, favoured small communities against large. As Communists and RPF were strongest in the cities, this electoral law helped the parties supporting the regime.[11]

The weighting was slightly less extreme than before. The rural half of the

8. After French India was ceded there were 319. The members were divided alphabetically by constituencies into two equal groups; one, chosen by lot, was renewed in May 1952 and the other in May 1955.

9. The curious limit of 154,000 gave a second member to Lot, the new constituency of the Council's President Gaston Monnerville: *Inégalités*, pp. 216–18, 259–61. The allotment gave Lozère one councillor for 90,000 inhabitants and Seine one for every 240,000: Goguel, *Régime*, p. 35n.

10. As usual with a double ballot system, for election on the first ballot the majority required was more than half the votes cast and more than a quarter of those on the register; on the second ballot it was a simple plurality. The Assembly was still to elect councillors representing Frenchmen abroad (three), in Morocco (three), and (provisionally) in Vietnam (one, a newcomer); the two from Tunisia were now chosen locally.

11. *Inégalités*, pp. 112–34, 334–6, on the motives of the 1946 and 1948 laws and the way they were framed.

population elected two-thirds of the municipal delegates and the urban half (in communes of more than 3,500 inhabitants) chose one-third. Even in a department with no big city like Oise, nearly two-thirds of the delegates were elected by tiny communes with less than 1,000 inhabitants and under half the total population. In Nord, Lille had 180,000 voters and 64 delegates, Lambersart 18,000 and 27, and Arleux 1,800 and 5. Yet the large cities were under-represented rather less than in pre-war senatorial elections; with three-quarters of the population Marseilles elected 7% of the departmental delegates in the Third Republic, 25% in the Fourth. Paris, with a reduced share of the population of Seine, chose more delegates. The eleven next largest towns, with one-sixteenth of the national population, had 264 delegates before and 900 now, out of 100,000.[12]

The new law weakened those parties which were strongest in the great cities and also those with few allies, hampered by the double ballot; the Communists were doubly handicapped, and elected only sixteen metropolitan councillors in the eleven PR departments. MRP lost votes to RPF and seats to Socialists and Radicals, who allied against it. The two defeated parties had had a majority in the old Council (as in the Assembly), but returned only 40 of the 320 new members. The Socialists with 60 held their own, and the rest went to overlapping groups of Radicals, Conservatives and RPF. In later years the Gaullists lost and the Radicals gained slightly, but the party balance changed remarkably little.[13]

The constitution-makers insisted on the subordinate status of the upper house. Its composition was left to be settled by law (and so, in the last resort, by the National Assembly). In 1946 it was organized in the political image of the Assembly so that it would not, and its powers were restricted so that it could not, challenge the sovereign house. The first safeguard was removed after two years, the second after eight. But the 1954 constitutional amendment satisfied both houses and settled their conflict.

Under Article 5 the Council of the Republic was part of Parliament. It had the same immunity, salary and ineligibility rules as the Assembly, judged the validity of its members' election, and chose its *bureau* by PR. Against the wishes of the Left, it was housed (like the old Senate) in the Luxembourg Palace. But precautions were taken to discourage a revival of the senatorial tradition. The National Assembly was given that title, denoting sovereignty, which had formerly belonged to the two houses meeting jointly to elect a President or amend the constitution. Its President became the second person in the state, and under Article 11 its *bureau* acted in a joint session (in the Third Republic the Senate's *bureau* had acted and its President, as in the

12. Nord: Goguel, *Régime*, p. 35n. Pre-war figures from Sharp, p. 67; post-war calculations mine (details in Williams, p. 272n.); cf. Bruyas, no. 36, p. 553; Duverger, *System*, pp. 71–2; and the exhaustive analysis in *Inégalités*, pp. 214–23, 322–51, 383–4. In Haute-Garonne communes with fewer than 2,000 inhabitants had under 40% of the population and nearly 80% of the delegates, ten times more than Toulouse where most people lived: *ibid.*, p. 345. PR gave representation to the rural minority in industrial departments, but majority election denied it to townsmen in the country areas: *ibid.*, pp. 331–4. The system most favoured the peasants in regions where population was either thin, or scattered so that communes were small (e.g. Brittany as against Normandy).

13. *Ibid.*, pp. 335–6, and below, Appendix v.

Fifth, had precedence). Article 37 allowed the President of the Republic to communicate directly with the Assembly but not the Council. Article 9 required the Council's sessions to coincide with those of the Assembly. But despite all precautions the tradition proved too strong, and in December 1948 the new majority of the Council voted themselves the title of 'Senators, members of the Council of the Republic'.

Under Article 29 the new senators, like their predecessors, joined the deputies in electing a President of the Republic; they had about a third of the votes. They also chose a third of the metropolitan members of the Assembly of the French Union, by Article 67, and four out of thirteen members of the Constitutional Committee, by Article 91. But they had no representative on the High Council of the Judiciary or the High Court which tried political cases (a task performed in the Third Republic by the Senate). They could initiate no constitutional amendment; but they could block one unless either a referendum or two-thirds of the Assembly approved it, and if the President of the Republic agreed they could alert the Constitutional Committee to surreptitious amendment.[14] They had to be consulted (but not necessarily to consent) before war was declared, under Article 7, a treaty ratified, under Article 27, or a law passed, under Article 20.

In June 1949 the new majority of the Council argued that their duty to advise on declarations of war or ratifications of treaties implied a right to discuss ministerial policy. They therefore introduced interpellations, in all but name, by modifying their standing orders on 'oral questions with debate'.[15] The Assembly objected that by Article 48 the government was not responsible to the Council, and so should not be interpellated there; Herriot officially protested to the President of the Republic, but Auriol refused to intervene, saying that the Constitutional Committee existed only to protect the upper house against the lower.[16] A few Radical premiers even disregarded Article 48 altogether. In August 1948 André Marie threatened to resign if the Council amended Paul Reynaud's special powers bill; in March 1955 Edgar Faure sought its approval for his foreign policy, including German rearmament; and in June 1957 Maurice Bourgès-Maunoury in effect asked for its confidence over special financial powers. But such cases were very rare.[17]

In legislation the Council's powers were closely restricted until the constitutional amendment of 1954. Although its members might introduce bills of their own, under Article 14 these had to go to the National Assembly before being debated in the Council. But in June 1949 the upper house decided in its

14. On these institutions and functions see Chapter 21.

15. Previously only a committee, a party leader or 30 members could initiate these 'questions', and no vote was taken.

16. Lidderdale, pp. 267–9; Bruyas, no. 36, pp. 568–70; Georgel, i. 85–7; Blamont, p. 107; below, p. 305; cf. n. 23; and for the Herriot and Auriol letters, *AP* 1949, p. 219. From 10 to 25 oral questions with debate were raised in a year: Campbell, no. 45, p. 361. In fact, if not in law, interpellations did threaten the life of the government; and as constitution-drafter and premier of the Fifth Republic Michel Debré carefully ruled out the procedure which he had himself invented and skilfully exploited. On the Council's scrutiny of governmental actions see also Georgel, i. 84–5 (on a committee of inquiry); Grosser, pp. 89–90; Marcel Plaisant, chairman of its foreign affairs committee, no. 182.

17. Bruyas, no. 36, p. 571, *JO(CR)* 13 August 1948, p. 2402, and *AP* 1948, p. 132 (Marie); *AP* 1955, pp. 29, 359, 691 (Faure); cf. Vedel in *Institutions*, i. 180, Arné, pp. 232–4, 256–7, 270–1.

new standing orders that its committees should examine these bills, unless the author objected, before sending them to the Assembly. The Communist, Socialist and MRP deputies promptly revived the old majority of *tripartisme* and voted by 429 to 150 (Radicals, Conservatives and RPF) to receive no bill after its consideration by senators.[18]

Once a bill passed the Assembly it became law, under Article 20, if the Council did not deal with it within two months. But for budget bills the Council could take no more time than the Assembly had taken, and for bills classed as 'urgent', only as much as the Assembly allowed itself by its own standing orders. The deputies were naturally wary of the senators' traditional delaying tactics, but they committed an opposite abuse by applying urgency procedure to half the bills passed in 1947, and so preventing proper examination in the Council's committees.[19] At last, in June 1948, the Assembly left the Council only 33 hours (including two nights) to consider an urgent but difficult bill; the Council decided unanimously, except for the Communists, to overrun its time-limit; the Assembly, with the agreement of all parties in it, demanded that the bill be promulgated under Article 20. The Council protested to the Constitutional Committee and won its point. The rules of urgency procedure were then relaxed to allow the Council at least three days' grace; and the procedure itself gradually fell into disuse.[20]

A bill which passed the Council unchanged was promulgated forthwith as law. If the Council voted amendments, the Assembly might reject them, or accept them in whole or in part.[21] There could be no further amendments aiming at an agreed compromise, as in the Third Republic's 'shuttle' system of several readings (*navette*). But under the last paragraph of Article 20, if the Council rejected a bill or voted an amended version in public ballot by an absolute majority, the Assembly could overrule it only in the same conditions. This 'veto' seemed unimportant until the law of September 1948 created a Council politically very different from the Assembly. In finance there were further restrictions. By Article 17 only the deputies could initiate expenditure. By Article 14 the Assembly could not receive senators' bills increasing expenditure or reducing revenue, so that no one could discuss these. By their own standing orders senators might not move amendments to increase an amount proposed in the Assembly by the government or the finance committee.[22] In 1950 they were prevented from introducing new material into financial bills by way of amendments.[23]

18. Lidderdale, pp. 259–60; *JO* 28 June 1949, pp. 3801–9, 3836–7.

19. In 1947 (January–August) the Council amended only 27 of the 88 'urgent' bills but 39 of the other 73: F.G., no. 105, pp. 345–6. See also Gerber, no. 97, pp. 407–9; above, p. 259 and n.

20. Lidderdale, pp. 263–4; *AP* 1948, pp. 98, 336; Soulier, no. 203, pp. 195ff. The Assembly's time-limit excluded, the Council's included time spent in committee. Only half a dozen bills had been dealt with by the Council within the Assembly's strict interpretation of the rules: S. Grumbach, *JO(CR)* 15 June 1948, p. 1504 (cf. below, n. 29).

21. Interpreted to include a compromise figure between different amounts: see Blamont, no. 20, pp. 305–6.

22. Lidderdale, p. 265; Galichon in *Travail*, p. 833. Unlike pre-war senators they could move to increase revenue.

23. *JO* 25 April 1950, p. 3957. This practice and oral question with debate were both banned by the original draft of the 1954 constitutional amendment: cf. Williams, p. 279n., and the speech and report of Mme Peyroles, rapporteur (*JO* 29 November 1950, p. 8267; *AN* doc. no. 11,431).

Experience revealed serious technical faults in these legislative arrangements. One flaw followed from the constitutional rules: the Council could not deal with bills till they had passed the Assembly, but both houses had to begin, end and interrupt their sessions together. The Council's agenda was therefore empty when it assembled and crowded just before it recessed, and the senators suffered alternately from frustrating idleness and gross overwork.[24] Another flaw was the rigidity of Article 20, under which any compromise between the houses required unsatisfactory subterfuges.[25] Again, after 1948 the new Council often used its 'veto'. Nearly one in ten of the bills voted in the first Parliament was amended or defeated by an absolute majority of the Council. If the Assembly then reaffirmed its own view by a simple majority only, the bill was neither accepted nor rejected. This deadlock occurred on six bills, including major measures like the electoral law and the budget for 1951; they had to be sent back to the Assembly's committee, or withdrawn and a new version substituted, while a compromise was worked out in private negotiations.[26] The old *navette* had been much more convenient.

The constitutional amendment introduced by the centre parties in November 1950 was intended (*inter alia*) to remedy both these weaknesses. But the Council's political attitude delayed its passage. Socialist and MRP deputies were willing to improve the machinery for co-operation between the houses, but not to help the upper house regain its lost political power; they demanded the abolition of the 'veto' as the price of reform. Conversely the conservative senators feared that without that safeguard the deputies would ignore them entirely. It took four years to appease these suspicions, for the technical problem could not be solved while a left-wing Assembly jealous of its prerogatives confronted a conservative Council with which the Gaullists were trying to shatter the Third Force majority. In 1951 the Right won control of the Assembly also, and when RPF disintegrated the Radicals and Conservatives could hope to amend the constitution – provided they conciliated MRP and the Socialists, ensured a three-fifths majority in the Assembly, and so avoided the referendum which all the centre parties regarded as unthinkable. By the final compromise Articles 14 and 20 were completely changed.[27]

The new Article 14 allowed any bill to be introduced in the upper house, by the government or a senator, except for treaty ratification bills under Article 27 and bills entailing lower revenue or higher expenditure (the Council failed

24. *Ibid.* Cf. Edmond Barrachin, minister for constitutional reform, *JO* 21 July 1953, p. 3595.

25. '... you can watch the deputies falling furiously upon the amendment with big scisorrs and a pot of glue, trying to suppress a few words ... without adding a comma or a syllables (of that would be a breach of Article 20) and to reconstruct a draft which still does not violate syntax too outrageously': Waline, *Les Partis contre la République*, p. 156. For the subterfuges see Mme Peyroles' report, pp. 7–8; Bruyas, no. 36, p. 560; Berlia, no. 11, p. 682 n.1.

26. Blamont, no. 20, p. 309; and cf. below, n. 47. The first Assembly passed 1,360 bills; the Council accepted 774, amended or rejected 540 (121 by an absolute majority), and had 46 outstanding in 1951: *ibid.*, pp. 298, 302. By March 1953 the 121 had risen to 168, with no more deadlocks: Berlia, no. 12a, p. 437. The Council altered two-fifths of all bills, and saw all its amendments accepted on about a third of these, some accepted on half, and none on the rest: Campbell, no. 45, p. 356. But cf. n. 41 below.

27. See above, p. 193; and on referendum-phobia, below, p. 302 and n. MRP was more intransigent than SFIO (it was weaker in the upper house). In November 1954, 21 of its deputies voted against the reform and 50 abstained; cf. above, p. 228.

to limit the last restriction to bills 'directly' causing expense). On Article 20 a complicated bargain restored the *navette*, subject to safeguards against obstruction, in return for the abandonment of the 'veto'. An absolute majority of the Assembly was therefore no longer needed to override an absolute majority in the upper house, but bills could now be read repeatedly. An ingenious system of time-limits encouraged both houses to act promptly, and the Assembly kept its right to the last word.[28]

For its first reading the Council had no more time than before for ordinary bills (two months) or finance bills (the time taken in the Assembly), but twice as much for bills under urgency procedure (double the time the Assembly gave itself by its own standing orders) – though these limits were not strictly enforced.[29] The major change came with a bill's second passage through the Assembly, which opened a *navette* period: a hundred sitting days for ordinary bills, a month for budget bills, and two weeks for urgent measures. After this the Assembly could either pass its own version of the bill or add some or all of the Council's amendments. At each reading within these periods, each house had as much time as the other had taken on its last reading (but at least one day for financial or urgent bills, and seven for others). The Council could have extra time if the deputies consented, and automatically did if they overstepped their own time-limits.[30] These complicated arrangements proved far more satisfactory than those of 1875 or 1946. The *navette* restored flexibility without encouraging delay, since the Council wanted several readings and the Assembly feared to extend the time-limit. Impatient deputies could no longer get their way by ignoring the upper house, and stubborn senators could be overruled in the end; for both there was a premium on co-operation. The Council lost its 'veto' on a bill but gained opportunity and time (two months plus 100 days) to publicize its case.[31]

The compromise was an immediate success. Most of the budget for 1955 was passed in 1954 under the newly-voted rules. The Council did not obstruct and the Assembly often allowed it extra time. Old jealousies did not prevent an amicable agreement between the Presidents of the two houses on the interpretation of the new rules, or unofficial contacts on most controversial bills.[32]

No flood of bills swamped the Council when it won the right of first reading. In 1955, when Edgar Faure led a conservative majority, 41 government bills were introduced there but only one passed; in 1956–58 with the Socialists in

28. An earlier version limited not the time but the number of readings to three in the Counci and four in the Assembly: the senators disliked this. The Gaullists tried to save the 'veto', but were beaten in the Council itself by 197 to 98.

29. Where the old draft had said a time-expired bill 'est promulguée', the new one said it 'est en état d'être promulguée'. See also above, n. 20, and below, pp. 305–6.

30. This last provision nearly wrecked the compromise; the deputies accepted it only by 307 to 305 after an appeal by the premier, Mendès-France. They also wanted a right to add new material without allowing the Council a new reading. Conversely the Council failed to secure an 'EDC clause' that no treaty ratification bill could be classed as urgent without its consent.

31. On the discussions see Poutier, pp. 77–102. The right-wing Radical senator Laffargue admitted that the Council had never expected the deputies to concede so much: *JO(CR)* 16 March 1954, p. 422. On the 'premiums' cf. Gilbert Jules, rapporteur: *ibid.*, p. 425.

32. Poutier, pp. 37–8 on the first month; Blamont, *Techniques*, p. 77 on the *protocole d'accord* (there was another on the working of the *lois-cadres*, *ibid.*, p. 78, cf. p. 84); and see *AP* 1957, pp. 7–8.

office, only 37 were laid before the upper house but 25 became law. Once the senators could debate their own measures they brought in fewer, but passed more.[33] Discussion was not dilatory, and the time-limits worked well; only once did the Assembly vote a bill which the Council had failed to consider in time. Out of 500 bills passed only six, none of them politically controversial, were decided by a 'Waterloo' after the hundred days – the Assembly re-affirmed its own text on five of them and accepted the Council's amendments on the sixth.[34] But its right to the last word, though so rarely exercised, was decisive in preventing obstruction. Mollet's old age pension fund set up in 1956, was financed in ways disliked by the Right and many Radicals: the Council twice voted wrecking amendments, but gave way when the Assembly reasserted its view for the third time, and the bill (which was classed as urgent) finally passed on fourth reading 97 days after its introduction.[35] Here was proof that a determined government and majority could overcome senatorial opposition without undue difficulty or delay. The Council's technical grievances had been remedied without the Assembly's political supremacy being impaired.

3. POLICY AND INFLUENCE

'The Right has social preoccupations but pretends to think only of technical considerations, while the Left proclaims its social repugnances and refuses to pay attention to technical considerations.'[36] This double problem bedevilled discussion of the weaknesses of the 1946 arrangements. But the second chamber's case, already endangered by the black social record of the old Senate and the rural and conservative bias of the reconstructed Council, was for years further imperilled by the irresponsible ways in which some opposition senators sought advantage for their party or their house. They provoked the deputies into jealousy of the Council's prestige, suspicion of its intentions and contempt for its proposals, and they frustrated their own colleagues who tried conscientiously to perform a more modest role.

The first Council of the Republic had made no attempt to challenge a National Assembly controlled by the same parties. At first, 'complacently listening to the echo of its own voice', the Assembly often ignored the suggestions of the Council, which was said to have little more political importance than the *Académie française*.[37] But from June 1947 onwards the deputies became more accommodating; the Communists were in opposition, and the Council explained its proposals by personal contacts between committee rapporteurs or through the good offices of the government. Amendments

33. Figures from Cotteret, p. 48. Until 1954, senators introduced 74 bills in an average year and passed 4; afterwards, 46 and 8.

34. Blamont, pp. 77–8, for the Assembly's decisions, with list of bills. Edmond Barrachin said there were eleven 'Waterloos' and not six: *JO* 12 February 1958, p. 743. In 1956 all but 6 of the 86 government bills which passed, and all but 8 of the 53 private members' bills, took two readings or fewer in each house; only 3 and 1 took more than three readings (my calculations).

35. *AP* 1956, pp. 57–8, 63–4, 125.

36. Hamon, *Problèmes*, p. 25 (from *Combat*, 13 March 1954).

37. Duverger, *Manuel de droit constitutionnel*, p. 355 ('echo'); Priouret, *Partis*, p. 263 ('Académie'). In March 1947 the Council unanimously rejected a series of changes in tenancy laws; they were reaffirmed by the Assembly unanimously and without debate: Gerber, no. 97, p. 407.

clarifying the Algerian government bill and modifying the municipal election bill were accepted by the Assembly.[38]

The Council first acted on the political stage in November 1947, when the Communists – though bitter opponents of a strong upper house – used it to obstruct the government's public order bills during the general strike. In December 1947 and August 1948 the Council helped the government by restoring its original drafts of René Mayer's special levy bill and Paul Reynaud's special powers bill (which the deputies, having shifted the responsibility, then accepted). In September the Council was allowed to amend the new law on its own composition. But when the Communist councillors nearly upset the government by carrying a vote for early departmental council elections, they showed the Gaullists how easily the second chamber could be used as a weapon against the first.[39] The entire upper house faced re-election in November 1948; if RPF won an absolute majority it could block all legislation for which an absolute majority of the Assembly could not be found, and might well be able to force an election.

This strategy narrowly failed. Though RPF's inter-group claimed 150 of the 320 senators, only 58 joined the separate RPF group and many 'bigamists' proved unreliable. In the first test, on budgetary procedure, Pierre de Gaulle mustered only 132 votes (including 21 Communists) against 154. The government thus kept a precarious margin against the opponents of the regime in the supposedly sober 'house of second thoughts'. But the success of Gaullists and Radicals, and the defeat of Communists and MRP, meant that on opposition and government benches alike the social and economic conservatives were far stronger in the second chamber than in the first.[40]

The new majority promptly set out to increase the Council's powers, failing over legislation but succeeding over oral question with debate; to exert a conservative pressure on policy; and to embarrass government supporters by taking up questions which divided them. The Third Force and left-wing deputies retreated – predictably – into a watchful and jealous suspicion, and when the Council amended a bill they often reaffirmed their original view with little discussion and by a larger majority. The senators tried to alter the constitution *de facto* and were then aggrieved that the deputies became wary of *de jure* amendment; they mounted a party political assault and then complained that their friendly advice received insufficient attention.[41]

The opposition senators celebrated their election victory by first amending the *loi des maxima* for 1949 and then rejecting it by 105 to 0; the Gaullists voted against the bill they had themselves reshaped, while 207 government

38. Bruyas, no. 36, p. 547.

39. *Ibid.*, pp. 548, 571; *AP* 1947, pp. 247, 250, 1948, pp. 133, 157–60; and on Mayer's levy, Georgel, i. 83; Arné, p. 233; Hamon, *Problèmes*, p. 26.

40. In January 1949 the 'big three' parties formed three-quarters of the Assembly but only a third of the Council.

41. On jealousy see Cadart, no. 38, pp. 149, 156; the deputies overruled the Council's attempts in this codifying law to deal with the two houses of Parliament separately from the lesser assemblies, and to exclude the word 'deputy' (since 'senator' would not be allowed). For their political reactions see, e.g., *AP* 1949, pp. 1, 81, 1950, pp. 3–4. Years later even a left-wing critic of senatorial conservatism still complained that the deputies often rejected the Council's amendments without reading them: Hamon, *Problèmes*, p. 27, cf. Monnerville, *JO(CR)* 16 July 1953, p. 1339. For the setback to constitutional amendment see Bruyas, no. 36, p. 574.

supporters abstained rather than support the mutilated measure; and the Assembly restored the original provisions. On the *loi de finances* RPF changed tactics; the right-wing opposition amended the bill and then carried it by 150 (less than an absolute majority) to 23 (mainly Communists) with the governmental senators again abstaining. The Assembly once more easily restored its own version, and the manœuvres damaged the prestige of both the Council and RPF, which had so self-righteously denounced the parties for their complex and crafty parliamentary intrigues.[42] 'The power of the senators is not so much themselves to reconsider, as to get the deputies to reconsider. The reproach against them is precisely that they act, or at least talk, in a spirit which is likely to lead to exactly the opposite result. Brandishing its standing orders as a weapon against the Assembly, the government and the regime, the Council of the Republic awakens a reflex of self-defence in those it seeks to combat and destroy.'[43]

Many senators learned the lesson. Next year they were indignant that Georges Bidault had included no senator in his ministry, and reluctant to vote his proposed tax increases.[44] Yet 29 Radicals, after unbalancing the *loi de finances*, abstained to let it pass without an absolute majority (its 158 supporters were three too few). Deadlock was avoided, the Assembly's finance committee made compromise proposals, the Council's amendments were duly defeated, and the leader of the Radical senators (Charles Brune) soon entered Bidault's cabinet. The Council again had to be overruled by the Assembly in January 1951, when it unbalanced Pleven's budget, but thereafter it made less difficulty for the government.[45]

After 1948 the Council gave a small majority to the cabinet when its life was threatened, and a much larger one to conservative policies at other times. In January 1950 the senators amended the bill restoring collective bargaining, to the detriment of the trade unions, and in June they tried to switch 30 milliard francs (£30 million) of investment funds from the nationalized to the private sector; in both cases the old majority of Communists, Socialists and MRP revived in the Assembly to restore the original proposals. Even after the 1951 election they were more conservative than the deputies; they helped the government to block the sliding scale for wages, obstructed Pinay's anti-trust bill, and led the way in demagogic attacks on the nationalized industries. In 1956 they tried unsuccessfully to upset the financing of major bills on housing and old age pensions. Socially and economically the upper house was still a bourgeois and peasant weapon against the town workers.[46]

42. *Ibid.*, p. 557; *JO(CR)* 31 December 1948, pp. 3826, 3897–8; *AP* 1948, pp. 227–8; cf. Arné, p. 233.

43. Fauvet in *Monde*, 4 June 1949 (over petrol rationing); cf. *ibid.*, 6 January 1951; *AP* 1949 p. 81 (petrol).

44. Radical deputies feared to vote for higher taxes lest a Radical senator from their department rejected them and so became a more popular and dangerous rival at the next election (whereas in the Third Republic senators had feared competition from deputies): Fauvet, *Monde*, 22 December 1949, 1 February 1950. See also above, pp. 253 and n.

45. Arné, pp. 233–4; *AP* 1950, pp. 3–4, 1951, p. 2. In 1957 it won some concessions from Gaillard, whose majority in the Assembly was unreliable.

46. *AP* 1950, pp. 11, 133; 1951, pp. 121–2, 136, 335; 1956, pp. 57–8, 63–4; 1957, p. 17; Meynaud, p. 266, Arné, p. 234n. (anti-trust); Lescuyer, no. 143, pp. 1181–2 (nationalized industries), though cf. his book, pp. 250–1; Ehrmann, *Business*, pp. 251–2, 352–3, 383, 387–8 (both).

In constitutional matters the senators, elected by the local politicians of the countryside, preferred the institutions of the Third Republic and especially the single-member constituency system favoured by rural France. In April 1951 they nearly killed any electoral reform by voting overwhelmingly (206 to 37) for *scrutin d'arrondissement*.[47] This had no chance in an Assembly dominated by Communists and MRP. In the new house, however, it won Socialist and left-wing Radical support, and in 1955 a strange alliance developed between progressive Mendesists and conservative senators (countered by an even odder combination of Edgar Faure's right-wing followers with the Communist party). The premier, who wanted early elections with no change of electoral system, was nearly frustrated by the Council's new powers – for the senators could now both stop legislation over a limited period, and repeatedly oblige the deputies to go on record against the system which the country was believed to favour. But he was saved by a miscalculation of his adversaries which unexpectedly allowed him to dissolve the Assembly.[48]

On external affairs the Council's reputation was nationalist. The opponents of EDC were confident that the treaty would never pass the upper house (though Edgar Faure unexpectedly induced it to accept the agreement on German rearmament which eventually took EDC's place). The senators, on whose benches sat some of France's richest colonial capitalists, had no liking for emancipation overseas. In May 1951 they were able, because of the imminence of the general election, to prevent a wide extension of the colonial franchise which the Assembly had accepted. They made difficulties over the Tunisian negotiations of 1956 and the mild Algerian reform bill of 1958. But they displayed unwonted liberalism over the *loi-cadre* for the African territories; the colonialist spokesman (Luc Durand-Réville) found himself isolated, the Council's amendments were limited, and the Assembly accepted them in order that the bill should become law before the summer recess.[49]

Being nationalist and conservative the Council was strongly defence-minded.[50] These preoccupations did not foster liberal values. In July 1953 the deputies agreed but the senators refused to extend to conscientious objectors the amnesty they did not hesitate to grant to former collaborators. The Council was more alert to the perils of untimely progress than to the risks of arbitrary repression. In January 1958 it further mutilated the Algerian reform bill which had already been disastrously emasculated to appease the Right in the Assembly. When internment camps for suspected FLN terrorists were set up in France in 1957, the special powers bill authorizing them was fought line by

47. *AP* 1951, pp. 97, 100; the deputies, owing to Socialist defections, mustered only 308 votes to override it – three short of an absolute majority. The government was about to resign when Herriot proposed to refer the bill back to committee; eventually a 'new' but hardly altered bill was brought in, pressure put on the rebels by SFIO (below, p. 400) and an absolute majority found.

48. *AP* 1955, pp. 85–90; above, pp. 238–9, and below, pp. 315–16.

49. *AP* 1951, pp. 121–2, 136, 335; 1956, pp. 64–5, 214; 1957, pp. 16–17; 1958, pp. 7–8. Despite its anti-European reputation the Council accepted the Common Market and Euratom treaties by a three-to-one majority.

50. In March 1949 the senators, though in opposition, voted the defence minister a third provisional twelfth when the deputies had allowed him only two: *AP* 1949, p. 39.

line in the 'hasty and irresponsible' lower house, where the left-wing opposition secured some important concessions; the 'sober and reflective' senators voted it with little discussion and no important amendment by a majority of ten to one.[51] Not until the Fifth Republic used the same powers and the same camps for right-wing Frenchmen suspected of the same crimes did the enthusiasts for severity begin to view with alarm the menace to freedom.

The conservatism of the upper house reflected that of its electorate. Occupationally the Council was drawn from much the same groups as the Assembly, except that as it had few Communists, only five manual workers were elected in 1948. The 56 lawyers equalled the agricultural, industrial and trading interests together, and 60% of the senators were professional men. Like their predecessors they were active in local government; 20 were chairmen and 124 members of departmental councils, and 107 were mayors. They were rather younger, for the Fourth Republic lowered the minimum age from 40 to 35 and the average dropped from 61 in 1939 to 50 in 1948.[52] As in the past they prided themselves on maintaining a higher standard of dignity and courtesy than the deputies. Speeches tended to be shorter and obstruction rarer in the Council. Angry scenes were frowned upon. To a traditionalist of moderate temper like René Coty, the second chamber had less need of powers than of the pomp and precedence which would attract elder statesmen. He told a young colleague in 1948, 'Your house is too noisy for me . . . the other day I caught myself shouting "Go to Moscow!" at the Communists.' It was his apology for his own decision to become a senator.[53]

To anyone but the most ambitious *ministrable* the Council offered many advantages as a political base. A senator's seat in the provinces could not be won without strong roots in local government, but once won it was far safer than the deputy's. Some of the sixty overseas seats (a fifth of the total) were almost rotten boroughs; twelve votes were cast to elect Luc Durand-Réville senator for Gabon in 1948, and fourteen to re-elect him without opposition in 1952. Pierre Bertaux won a seat in Soudan by 13 to 10 in 1953, then lost it by 15 to 5 in 1955. Interest-groups took full advantage of these anomalies. Henri Borgeaud, the leader of the Algerian *colons*, was for years chairman of the Radical senators. His RPF colleague Antoine Colonna represented the French of Tunisia. At home, peasant organizations naturally had many spokesmen in the 'chamber of agriculture'; their leader was René Blondelle. André Boutemy, the employers' political paymaster, was one of several parliamentary friends of business who preferred the upper house. It was also a convenient refuge for senior party officials like Roger Duchet, secretary of CNIP, Pierre Commin, assistant secretary of SFIO, and Vincent Delpuech, the Radical treasurer until 1955. But André Diethelm, who handled RPF's finances, migrated to the Assembly in 1951.

51. *AP* 1949, p. 39; 1953, p. 59; 1957, pp. 78, 131; 1958, pp. 7–8. Isorni, who worked devotedly for a reform disliked by the Church (legitimizing children by the subsequent marriage of their parents) says it could never have passed if the upper house had kept its old powers: *Ainsi*, p. 46.
52. Occupations: *Le Figaro*, 16 November 1948. Local: Monnerville, *JO(CR)* 17 January 1950, p. 20. Age: Hamon, no. 121, p. 553. On the deputies see below, p. 332.
53. Raymond Triboulet in *Monde*, 28 November 1962.

The passage of time made this step less necessary for the career-minded politician. The senator had always enjoyed influence in his constituency and local party, and gradually he acquired it on the national level. Unrestricted access to the Palais Bourbon enabled him to meet and persuade his colleagues there. At first the senators were 'outsiders', and some of them like Michel Debré in RPF and Léo Hamon in MRP always remained intransigent or isolated in their own parties. But not all did. The Socialist senators obeyed the whip over EDC when the deputies would not (and in 1953 SFIO amended its constitution to give them equal status). When Mendès-France tried to turn the Radicals into a party of principle rather than of compromise, the resistance to him centred at the Luxembourg. In CNIP, Roger Duchet was a strong force for moderation as long as he was in office.

Ministerial promotion was indeed a cause as well as a consequence of the armistice between the houses. The senators gave the budget for 1950 a hard passage partly because none of them had office under Georges Bidault; later premiers learned from his mistake. By 1951 a senator was minister of the interior, and Guy Mollet made even socialism palatable by inviting eight to serve under him. Seven years after Bidault the upper house, its appetite whetted, taught Félix Gaillard a similar lesson for appointing only four (in junior posts). In 1958 the premiership itself was offered to a senator, Jean Berthoin. Nor was it only in appointments that their influence was felt. In 1953 the choice of a Conservative rather than a Socialist President seems to have been due to the Radicals of the Luxembourg, and Coty's personal success to the general confidence of his colleagues there. In 1958 it was the senators who carried SFIO in support of de Gaulle when both deputies and executive were still mostly against him, and in that decisive crisis Gaston Monnerville played a crucial part.[54]

The legal and constitutional concessions to the upper house were thus only a recognition of its growing political weight. Early in the Fourth Republic the second-chamber controversy had provided '. . . a good example of our bad methods . . . a brilliant theoretical debate on the advantages of two solutions and a compromise settlement combining the weaknesses of both'.[55] But in time even men of the Left came to see advantages in bicameralism. An upper house which was not distracted by the fascinating game of making and unmaking governments could give more time to legislation. More time should mean not only closer scrutiny, but also less dependence for information on the administration, a party, or private pressure-groups. A constituency of experienced local politicians might predispose its representatives to reasonable compromise rather than ideological intransigence, and encourage them to offer a psychological as well as a technical corrective to the feverish agitation of the deputies.[56]

54. *AP* 1957, p. 131 (Gaillard); Williams, no. 220, pp. 37–40 (Monnerville, SFIO); above, pp. 202n. (Presidency), 287 (Bidault). For senators in office see Georgel, i. 83, and below.

55. Hamon, *Problèmes*, p. 27 (from *Combat*, 15 March 1954).

56. Hamon, pp. 9, 12, 15; in *JO(CR)* 25 January 1951, pp. 236–7, 10 March 1954, p. 363. Brindillac, no. 29, pp. 60–1. Significantly, among 3,500 conscripts polled in 1957 80% knew that a deputy was a politician (or legislator), but only 13% knew that a senator was: Georgel, i. 177n.

The constitution-makers, then, had set out to establish a second chamber which should have neither the first word nor the last, but whose word must always be spoken. It could not initiate and its advice could always be rejected, but the sovereign Assembly must always hear from the 'house of second thoughts' before making up its own mind. But as long as the Council was being used as a weapon against the regime, these aims could not be achieved. When it accepted its role as a *chambre de réflexion*, the technical faults were remedied and a working relationship between the two chambers at last established. The constitution-makers failed to correct the conservative bias of the upper house, but they did undermine its obstructive power and so achieved a major part of their objective. In some of their other experiments even this qualified success was denied them.

Chapter 21

SUBORDINATE INSTITUTIONS AND CONSTITUTIONAL AMENDMENT

The makers of the new constitution tried to improve on the old one by introducing several subsidiary institutions. A new High Court was to dispense political justice, and a new High Council to supervise ordinary justice. The referendum made a timid and ineffectual appearance in the normal process of constitutional amendment, while surreptitious changes were checked by a new Constitutional Committee. There were new subordinate assemblies to advise on colonial problems and on economic and social affairs. The preoccupation of the constitution-makers with these questions was also reflected in a Preamble which set forth the political principles professed, if not always practised, by the regime.

The declaration of rights took up nearly a quarter of the time spent by the first constitutional drafting committee. But in the referendum of May 1946 the product of their labours was denounced by the opposition as a menace to property, the freedom of the press, and the Church's rights in education.[1] The second drafting committee therefore substituted a short declaration, which was also vigorously criticized. It reaffirmed the 1789 declaration of rights which its authors were simultaneously violating.[2] It appealed to 'fundamental principles recognized by the laws of the Republic' – but open to interpretation in precisely opposite ways.[3] It added supplementary principles: equality of women, the right of asylum, the nationalization of public services and *de facto* monopolies, and a workers' share in management (which no attempt was made to realize). It enunciated respectable but vague aspirations such as the nation's solidarity in meeting natural calamities, and hopefully announced controversial legislation for a misty future: 'the right to strike is exercised within the framework of the laws which regulate it'.[4] And it failed – apparently through inadvertence – to promise the freedom of association which had been deliberately omitted in 1789 by men who detested intermediary bodies between the citizen and the state.

The declaration renounced wars of conquest and announced France's willingness, given reciprocity, to limit her sovereignty in the cause of peace.[5] It proclaimed equality of opportunity throughout the French Union and an intention to lead subject peoples towards democratic self-government. These principles commanded no universal assent, and if a new political majority

1. Wright, *Reshaping*, pp. 135, 156–61.
2. The purge legislation violated non-retroactivity, and some nationalization acts conflicted with the principles of compensation: Duverger, *Manuel*, p. 371; Waline, pp. 125–7.
3. *Ibid.* Waline thought this phrase protected lay education, Duverger the church schools; they agreed that it was the most obscure phrase in the constitution.
4. Cf. Pickles, *French Politics*, pp. 233–5; Noël, p. 132n. As the Fourth Republic got no further than banning police strikes, the *Conseil d'État* acted in default of Parliament: Arné, pp. 158–9. The Fifth also showed reluctance to attempt major legislation.
5. In October 1952 Herriot attacked EDC as unconstitutional because there was no reciprocity, Germany not being a sovereign state: *AP* 1952, pp. 66–7, 70.

chose to ignore them, no method of enforcement was provided. The individual citizen could not rely on them in court. Yet there was perhaps a case, in a country where there was bitter dispute over the fundamentals of politics and conspicuous bargaining and manœuvre over detail, for a solemn and formal statement of the ends which democratic political activity is ultimately supposed to serve.

1. THE INSTITUTIONS OF THE FRENCH UNION

Even before the constitution was adopted it became clear that the liberal professions of the Preamble rested on an insecure political foundation. For, in the first draft proposed, native inhabitants were to enjoy full equality with Frenchmen and the French Union was to be founded on free consent. At the referendum of May 1946 this draft was approved in the few 'old colonies' where native voters were in the majority. But wherever citizenship was restricted to white men it was rejected, and settler deputies were sent back to Paris to impose a different arrangement. General de Gaulle in his Bayeux speech helped them by warning against the disintegration of the empire, and MRP, urged on by Radicals and Conservatives, set out to whittle away what the Left had granted. Colonial nationalists and their French sympathizers wanted self-governing local assemblies to precede federal institutions; instead Bidault as prime minister insisted on creating a strong centralized structure, cautiously parcelling out local autonomy from Paris, and giving white settlers separate representation almost everywhere. In the new version of the French Union little was left of the original liberal approach, except for the mildly progressive phrases of the Preamble. Free consent disappeared, and 'the pious gesture [was] replaced by the *fait accompli*'.[6]

The Union was to consist of the French Republic (comprising Algeria and the overseas departments and territories as well as France itself) and those 'associated states' which chose to join; Tunisia, Morocco, Vietnam, Cambodia and Laos, although governed by France, were legally foreign countries. It was to have an assembly of its own (which was approved both by federalists and by conservatives like Herriot, who feared that the traditional assimilation policy would bring more and more overseas deputies until France became 'the colony of her colonies'). The President of the Republic was *ex officio* President of the Union, though the Associated States had no say in his election; and the Union's High Council was to 'assist the government', which was responsible to the French Parliament alone.[7]

These institutions had little life in them. The rulers of Tunisia and Morocco would not join for fear of prejudicing their nominal independence. There was resentment against the centralized constitution, especially at Article 62 by which the Union's resources were pooled for a defence policy controlled exclusively from Paris. When the High Council met after five years' delay, three Indo-Chinese delegations led by their premiers sat for two days with

6. Wright, *Reshaping*, pp. 179–80, 201–5, 213–15. Cf. Grosser, pp. 247–51.

7. For a useful short summary of the large literature see K. Robinson, *The Public Law of Overseas France since the War*. For the overseas departments see *ibid.*, pp. 21–2, and above, p. 209n. Algeria had a separate (settler-dominated) Assembly from 1948 till its dissolution in 1956.

seven French cabinet ministers under Vincent Auriol's presidency to settle procedure and discuss common military, diplomatic and economic problems.[8] But in June 1953 the King of Cambodia fled to Siam and demanded independence, and in October a Vietnam national congress – opposed to the pro-Communist Vietminh – rejected participation in the French Union (adding later 'in its present form'). Although Georges Bidault, now foreign minister, and President Auriol opposed constitutional concessions, France offered on 3 July to negotiate new Indo-Chinese treaties, and promised in January 1954 that the French Union would be based on the liberal Preamble rather than the centralizing text of the constitution. It was too late to undo the harm done in 1946. Soon only Laos remained within the Union; South Vietnam in 1954, Cambodia in 1955, and Morocco and Tunisia in 1956 became fully independent. The old constitutional structure lay in ruins, but it was still hoped that a new one could accommodate the African territories. The Algerian war destroyed the Fourth Republic before this could be built.[9]

Less shadowy than the High Council, the Assembly of the French Union was mainly concerned with tropical Africa, where French colonial policy was most successful. At its first meeting, at Versailles on 10 November 1947, 75 members from metropolitan France sat with 75 from 'overseas France' of whom 40 came from western and equatorial Africa. Cambodia and Laos joined in 1948 and Vietnam in 1950; with their 27 delegates and the 27 balancing Frenchmen there were 204 members (there would have been 250 if Tunisia and Morocco had attended).[10] The Frenchmen were elected by proportional representation of parties, 68 by the metropolitan deputies and 34 by the senators.[11] Among them were a few experts like the colonial historian C. A. Julien, and many former or intending members of parliament, not all of them interested in or qualified for their task.[12] Although the Assembly was not part of Parliament its members enjoyed parliamentary status, under Article 70.

The Assembly of the Union had to be consulted on laws settling the constitution or changing the status of an overseas territory, under Articles 74 and

8. *AP* 1951, pp. 303–5, 391; 1952, pp. 282–3; 1953, pp. 302–3, 307; Robinson, p. 19; Lacharrière, nos. 133–4; G. Peureux, *Le Haut-Conseil de l'Union Française* (1960), pp. 7–9, 36–52, 168–72. The first annual session set up and the second formalized a presidential secretariat drawn from both Associated States and French ministries. On Auriol and Coty as Presidents of the Union above, pp. 198–9, 202; and on the Union up to 1951, Pickles, *French Politics*, Chapters 10 and 11.

9. *AP* 1953, pp. 247–50, 253–8, 272–4, 282–91, 570–93; 1954, pp. 176–7, 189–90, 202–4, 258, 601; 1955, p. 282; 1956, pp. 178–80. Cf. Grosser, pp. 284–90, 300–3.

10. The Indo-Chinese were chosen by their governments, the other 75 from overseas by the local elected assemblies set up throughout the Union under Article 77. Among the 40 tropical Africans were six from the two UN trust territories, Togo and Cameroons. Of the other 35, 18 represented Algeria, 7 Madagascar, 4 the Indian Ocean territories (Reunion, Comores, Somaliland, French India), 4 the American (Guadeloupe, Martinique, Guiana, St Pierre-and-Miquelon) and 2 the Pacific.

11. Overseas parliamentarians voted in some party meetings to choose candidates for formal election later: *Institutions*, i. 152. In several parties counsellors of the Union, like parliamentarians, were represented on their governing bodies.

12. In July 1952 Raymond Dronne (RPF) denounced the 'flotillas of candidates' intriguing in the lobbies and proposed to suppress altogether this 'asylum for defeated parliamentarians, party officials and personal cronies'. A week later the senators elected among their 34 representatives eight colleagues (four of them Gaullists) who had just lost their seats: *Monde*, 6–7 and 12 July 1952; *JO* 4 July 1952, p. 3543; cf. Arné, pp. 231–2 and n.; J. Raphael-Leygues, no. 186a, p. 120. Yet some of the Assembly's best members were recruited in this way, for example Georges Gorse, a Socialist defeated in the 1951 election, who specialized on Moslem questions.

75, and on decrees applying a French law generally overseas or to a specific territory, under Article 72. Before voting a law to apply overseas, the National Assembly was expected – but not obliged – to consult it. It could send resolutions of its own to the French government, the High Council or the National Assembly. Associated States could seek its views, though none ever did; and so could the government in Paris, which sometimes modified decrees in the light of its advice.[13]

Three-quarters of the Assembly's activity was self-generated.[14] Repeatedly it complained of neglect and humiliation: in 1948 because it was kept insufficiently informed, in 1949 because the government stopped its mission of inquiry into social services in the overseas departments, in 1951 because the deputies voted, without debate, that Algeria was outside its competence.[15] In 1951 the disillusioned President of the Versailles Assembly migrated to the Palais Bourbon and his successor Albert Sarraut mourned its 'sumptuous and glacial exile . . . definitely too far from the other assemblies, the government, the press, and the man in the street'.[16] In the Tunisian crisis of 1951–52 its voice was not heard. It discussed the decrees applying the 1956 *loi-cadre* for the overseas territories – but not the Togo statute which became a yardstick for the others. The resolution by which Parliament decided to amend the French Union clauses of the constitution was submitted to it, but no amendment bill followed.[17] It worked or stagnated amid 'the general indifference of public opinion, Parliament and the government', while the Negro leaders preferred the National Assembly where power lay.[18]

2. THE ECONOMIC COUNCIL

As the Assembly of the Union had been intended to give the colonial peoples a louder voice in Paris, the Economic Council was similarly envisaged as a forum for groups – notably the workers' and peasants' organizations – whose views had often had an inadequate hearing. But though it undertook more useful work than the Assembly of the Union, it suffered almost equally from the inattention of Parliament and public.

Under Article 25 of the constitution, the Economic Council was the lowest in status of the four assemblies; its members had no parliamentary advantages except a salary. The government had to consult it on the national economic Plan, and it gave advisory opinions before the Assembly debated bills within its sphere. By an organic law, this included all economic and social bills except the budget, and any bill ratifying an economic or financial treaty. It could examine these bills on its own initiative, and could be sent others by the Assembly or its committees, or by the government. The Council had twenty

13. See Pickles, *French Politics*, pp. 229–31 on its activity and legal competence.
14. Wright, in Cole, p. 651. Even on its best days its atmosphere was that of a powerless debating body like the Paris municipal council: P. Frédérix, *Monde*, 29 August 1951.
15. *Institutions*, i. 157–8; *AP* 1948, p. 100; *JO(AUF)* 7 April 1949, pp. 427–32, and 15 February 1951, pp. 126–39. (But it did discuss a major bill on Saharan administration: *AP* 1956, p. 235.) Cf. Arné, pp. 232, 250–1.
16. *AP* 1951, p. 185; *JO(AUF)* 12 July 1951, p. 665.
17. Togo: *Institutions*, i. 157, and Robinson, no. 192. *Loi-cadre*: *ibid.*; above, pp. 50, 273. Amendment: *AP* 1956, p. 180; Drevet, p. 97; Coret, nos. 61–2.
18. On African deputies see above, pp. 180–2. 'Indifference': Goguel, *Régime*, p. 77.

days (but only two on urgent bills) for its report, which was circulated to all deputies; its rapporteur could speak in committee and, if the minister or committee so requested, in the house. It had to be consulted on decrees and orders applying bills it had dealt with (and could be, on others). From 1951 it had to present a twice-yearly report on the national income and on means of increasing production, consumption and exports. Disputants could seek its arbitration in an economic or social conflict. In general it dealt with special subjects specifically referred to it, major current problems like the Coal and Steel Community or fiscal reform, and broad general inquiries – into the national accounts, or the housing problem.[19]

All sections of Resistance opinion had wanted an Economic Council, though their conceptions of it differed. The new body fell between the consultative committee of trade unionists demanded by the Left, and the corporative sub-parliament, representing professions and regions, which MRP favoured. Its members were chosen by national organizations of workers or employers to represent their side, rather than as technical or industrial specialists, and its committees were proportionate (for example, only a third of the agriculture committee was rural).[20] Although the backward sectors of the economy were denied the inflated representation they enjoyed in Parliament, the weighting of interests was arbitrary, and was not improved by the changes made for political reasons in 1951.[21]

The Council's methods of work were also unsatisfactory. It met fortnightly at the Palais Royal for discussions that were often hurried, especially at first when it had only two days for the many 'urgent' bills. In 1947 no private disputant consulted it; the deputies ignored three-quarters of its reports; the government sent it no decrees, and modified the Monnet Plan without reference to it; and when it was asked to report on wages and prices it succumbed to wrangling between rival experts. 'When the Assembly refers a bill to the Council the explanation is ... lack of interest in it at the Palais Bourbon; or ... a desire to delay a vote, or to be covered by an independent opinion.'[22] Yet even the deputies were less jealous of it than of the Assembly of the Union, since it reported on bills they had not examined and so did not threaten their prestige. And in time the government if not the Assembly began to find the Council mildly useful. In 1952 it submitted 3 statutory reports, 29 on its own initiative, and 5 requested by the government.[23]

19. Cadart, no. 38, for its status; B. Chenot in *Institutions*, i. 164–5; Aubry, no. 8a, for a full formal account, and no. 8b for its procedure.

20. Chavagnes, no. 55; Archambeaud, no. 4; Byé, no. 37. An Economic Council dominated by civil servants had existed from 1925 to 1940.

21. Duverger, *System*, p. 76; Meynaud, p. 218 and n., and no. 161, p. 851. Of its 164 original members 45 represented trade unions (26 workers, 9 black-coated, 10 staff); 40 industry and commerce (6 nationalized industry, 8 large and 6 small private industry, 10 commerce similarly divided, 10 artisans); 35 agriculture, including 5 workers; 10 were government-appointed economists and scientists (*Pensée française*), 9 co-operators of various sorts, 8 spokesmen of the family associations, 2 of war-damage victims, and 15 of overseas territories. The law of 1951 added five members and instituted regional corresponding members; reduced CGT's seats by half, to equal the other unions; gave 27 of CGA's 30 seats to its constituent units, which were more influential and less left-wing; and substituted *classes moyennes* spokesmen for two intellectuals. Half the members changed.

22. Byé, no. 37; quotation from p. 597.

23. Deputies: Goguel, no. 105, p. 349, and *Régime*, p. 50; but cf. Lavau, no. 138a, p. 826. In

[*over*

The Council was a useful sounding-board for an interest without much parliamentary influence. Big business used it to obtain a hearing at a time when its views enjoyed little political sympathy. But when the climate changed after the end of *tripartisme*, employers soon came to regard the Council as an undesirably public forum in which the Left was too well represented.[24] Organizations rarely sent their most influential leaders there, not wishing their votes to commit them too completely; they often preferred abstention to the bad publicity of opposing a popular proposal; on issues of little direct interest they sometimes traded their votes for future favours; and they tried to avoid discussing problems on which a major interest was split. Consequently a proposal strongly disliked by a big group often met almost universal hostility. Thus in 1949 the trade unions wanted a return to free collective bargaining; they got the Council to debate it in April, and in November to reject by 137 to 0 the government proposal for compulsory arbitration (which was later defeated in the National Assembly). In June 1950 another government proposal – for a special court to deal with cartels – was thrown out by 105 to 4. During 1952 unanimity was complete on 5 reports out of 37, almost complete on 3 more, and complete except for the pro-Communist members on another 7.[25]

In Council voting there were three broad coalitions: labour; business and agriculture, which tended to agree; and the smaller intermediary groups – such as family associations, industrial staffs, artisans, nationalized industries and *Pensée française* (government-appointed intellectuals, who wrote many of the major reports). Generally agriculture found it easiest and CGT hardest to make friends and win votes. Thus in 1952 agricultural and nationalized-industry members almost always voted in the majority, while CGT did so only half the time, and in between these extremes business was on the losing side more often than non-Communist labour. The bigger organizations disliked displaying their internal divisions (except at times within agriculture) or their differences with their allies (except between CGT and non-Communist unions). But they needed support from the middle groups, which often split their votes; and some cross-voting did occur at times. In 1950 CGT allied with the employers to defeat a profit-sharing proposal favoured by the middle groups and other unions, and with CGA and some small employers against the Franco-Italian customs treaty (which passed easily). In 1951 CGT and CFTC supported higher family allowances against opposition from agriculture and FO (which feared they would prejudice wage claims). In 1952 labour

1948 the government refused to send Reynaud's special powers bill to either the Council or the Assembly of the Union (Soubeyrol, p. 80); and its creation of a special commission on the national accounts suggested some mistrust of the Council. On the Council's early working see Pickles, *French Politics*, pp. 230–3, and later Meynaud, pp. 217–21, 255–6, 316–17; Arné, p. 232 and n.; Seligson, no. 197; Lewis, no. 144 (p. 167 for reports in 1952).

24. Ehrmann, *Business*, pp. 253–6, and no. 84, pp. 468–9; Duverger, *loc cit.* Léon Jouhaux was the Council's first President, and Émile Roche its second. For the unions' attitude to and use of it see H. Lesire-Ogrel, 'Les syndicats et le Conseil économique', in A. Tiano *et al.*, *Expériences françaises d'action syndicale ouvrière* (1956), pp. 356–428.

25. *AP* 1949, pp. 64, 203; *JO(ACE)* 1949, p. 408, 1950, pp. 236–9; Lewis, no. 144, pp. 167–9. For other massive abstentions see Williams, pp. 299–300 and nn., and cf. Ehrmann, *loc. cit.*

joined either business or agriculture in the minority on 12 of the 37 reports.[26]

Although the Council's reports were often thorough and informative, the public and parliamentary nature of its proceedings diminished its utility either as a technical advisory chamber or as a focus for the pressure-groups themselves.[27] They had to show solidarity because they were open to the public gaze, and were naturally tempted to combine against the consumer for whom, at a generous estimate, not more than a sixth of the councillors spoke. But on major issues the Council behaved responsibly. It passed by 111 to 15 André Philip's report on the Coal and Steel Community, which for once had a great influence in the National Assembly – partly because he was a prominent ex-deputy.[28] It may have played a useful part in improving the economic education of the pressure-groups, whose claims and attitudes in the later years of the Fourth Republic were often less outrageous than in the past.[29] And there was perhaps some advantage in a direct confrontation, without the refracting medium of Parliament, between the spokesmen of workers, peasants and businessmen. But these spokesmen were rarely the most powerful or representative. The Palais Royal quite failed to attract the lobbyists away from the Palais Bourbon. The Council's detractors therefore maintained that its debates were too political, its reports came too late, its views commanded no attention, and it cost more for less benefit than a proper legislative reference service. Yet it had some staunch defenders, even in the National Assembly.[30]

3. POLITICS AND JUSTICE

Impeachments in France are tried before a High Court of Justice. In the Third Republic the Senate sat in this capacity to judge persons impeached by the Chamber of Deputies (and also those indicted for threatening the security of the state). At the Liberation an exceptional High Court was created to try former Vichy ministers and high officials. Consisting of members of the Assembly (chosen originally by lot, later by PR), it sat from 1945 to 1949, heard 108 cases, and pronounced 18 death sentences and 38 of imprisonment or 'national disgrace'. Its prestige was never high.[31]

In the Fourth Republic Article 57 of the constitution regulated impeachments, and Article 58 set up a new High Court including many deputies. Impeachments were preferred by the National Assembly, voting in secret by an absolute majority of its members excluding those who would have to try the case. The new Court was elected by each National Assembly when it first met;

26. On 1950, Ehrmann, *Business*, pp. 357–9, 404, and *JO(ACE)* 1950, pp. 197, 221; and on 1951, *ibid.* 1951, p. 72; on 1952, Lewis, no. 144, pp. 167–71; on a similar voting pattern in 1953–6, Goetz-Girey, no. 101; on the importance of the 'middle groups' cf. Lesire-Ogrel, p. 367.

27. Cf. Lavau, no. 138a, pp. 826–7; Byé, no. 37, pp. 603–4 ('each group brings ... its own files, its own figures, its own desires for light and for shadow'); Meynaud, p. 220; but cf. no. 161, p. 851.

28. *AP* 1951, p. 298; *JO(ACE)* 1951, p. 269.

29. Lavau, 'Political Pressures in France' in Ehrmann, ed., *Interest Groups on Four Continents* (henceforth cited as *Pressures*), pp. 90–1, and in no. 141, pp. 36–7. Cf. Lesire-Ogrel, pp. 424–71.

30. *Travail*, pp. 848–9 (Marcel Prélot against, Édouard Bonnefous for). A prominent deputy once told me how much he regretted having never had time, in his year on the economic affairs committee, to read a single report of the Council.

31. Duverger, *Manuel*, pp. 333–5; Guérin, no. 116. (Only Brinon, Darnand and Laval were executed.)

a detailed law, under Article 59, was passed in October 1946 at the same time as the constitution itself. The deputies chose by a two-thirds majority in a secret ballot: a President, two vice-presidents and 20 judges from their own ranks by proportional representation of parties; 10 more judges who could not be sitting (but were often former) members;[32] 30 alternates in the same conditions; 3 prosecutors who might be members of the Assembly (in 1953 only one was); and 6 deputies who, with a chairman and two members named by the High Council of the Judiciary, formed the committee of preliminary inquiry (*commission d'instruction*). The Court judged impeachments of ministers for offences in office, or of the President of the Republic for high treason.[33] Its deliberations were normally public, its final decision taken in secret and by an absolute majority.

Two motions came before the National Assembly. On 29 March 1950 the Communists failed to impeach three Socialist leaders (Gouin, Moch and Pineau) over the wine import scandals of 1946. On 30 November 1950 they again attacked Moch over the 1949 'scandal of the generals', and obtained 235 votes against 203, many members apparently wishing to strike a safely secret political blow at the minister, his party, or the government. The premier got a vote of confidence from the Assembly in a public ballot; and as the Communist motion was fifty short of an absolute majority the incident had no sequel.[34]

The constitution-makers were agreed on the principle that the judges should no longer be supervised by the ministry of justice, but by a new body independent of the executive. Like so many of the new institutions this was a compromise. Conservatives and Radicals had wanted a Council chosen by and from judges, to avoid political influence; Pierre Cot and the Communists opposed a close, self-administering judicial corporation and favoured a Council elected by (and perhaps from) the deputies; Socialists and MRP shared both fears. The final composition of the High Council of the Judiciary (*Conseil supérieur de la magistrature*) was prescribed in Article 83, and its functions in Articles 35 and 84. The President of the Republic and the minister of justice became *ex officio* chairman and vice-chairman, and of the twelve members, who sat for six years, half were professional and half political representatives. Four grades of judges (*juges de paix* and courts of first instance, appeal and Cassation) chose one each, and two were appointed by the President of the Republic from the other judicial professions; these six were not re-eligible. The other six were chosen by the National Assembly by a two-thirds majority from outside its own ranks. For every full member an alternate was chosen in the same way.[35]

The political representatives had been advocated as an element free from professional cliques and jealousies – and also, as their term was longer than the deputies' own, from their own 'constituents'.[36] At the first election in

32. Five of the ten elected on 28 August 1951 had just lost their seats.
33. Not defined in the penal code, by which the High Court was normally bound.
34. *AP* 1950, pp. 50, 229–31; cf. Williams, no. 218, and above, pp. 37, 238 n. 61.
35. *SCC* I, pp. 127–32, 615; II, pp. 87–92 (principles). Waline, no. 214 (rules).
36. P. Cot, *SCC* I, p. 129 and II, pp. 89 and 91; P. Ramadier, *SCC* II, p. 88.

March 1948 the Assembly's justice committee drew up an agreed list, and all parties picked jurists rather than politicians;[37] in 1950, when the Communist nominee broke with the party and offered to resign, President Auriol refused.[38] A two-thirds majority was preferred to PR as a way to ensure balanced representation;[39] this invited deadlock, and in 1952 a struggle for a vacant seat lasted without a decision over twelve months and thirteen ballots.

Under Article 35 of the constitution the President exercised his right of pardon in the High Council, which met weekly at the Élysée. He had to ask but not to take its advice; in practice he diverged from it only by clemency. In its first three years the Council considered 75,000 cases (often in groups), and by April 1949, 27,000 out of the 38,000 imprisoned under the Liberation purge, and 15,000 of the 40,000 sentenced to 'national disgrace', had benefited from a pardon.[40] In 1952 the butchers' association advised 15,000 of its members sentenced for price-fixing offences to appeal for clemency to the Council; by threatening to paralyse it, they extorted concessions from the government.[41]

The Council also supervised the judges (the *magistrature assise*) though not public prosecutors and State attorneys (the *magistrature debout* or *parquet*). It was responsible both for their discipline, replacing the Court of Cassation (the highest civil court in France, which had performed this function under previous regimes), and for their promotion, taking over from the ministry of justice; so that the semi-political High Council of the Judiciary was substituted for a branch of the judiciary in one sphere and of the executive in another. Disciplinary action was rare, promotion frequent: in 1949 the Council made a thousand appointments.[42] Article 84, which made the judges constitutionally irremovable, required the High Council of the Judiciary to ensure (*assurer*) their discipline and independence.

A bitter struggle developed around this verb between the Council and a ministry of justice unreconciled to losing its powers. The ministry held that it was against French tradition for an irresponsible organization – and President – to control the judiciary; that the minister's countersignature (though never likely to be refused) was therefore necessary before the Council's decisions could be enforced; and that the Council should perform its supervisory activities from a remote and ineffective height. A tiny staff, inadequate accommodation, and dossiers prepared by the ministry circumscribed the independence of the Council.[43] Yet it was determined to administer its allotted

37. Except that SFIO asked Blum, who refused, and then nominated André Hauriou, a professor of law and a senator. In 1952 SFIO proposed a former deputy (a barrister) for the vacant seat (see n. 38).

38. But he lost his seat after all when the party published a confidential Council document he was suspected of having given them earlier: *Monde*, 20 October 1951.

39. P. Coste-Floret, *SCC* I, p. 617.

40. For the meaning of 'pardon' and the President's role see above, pp. 197n., 199; for the 75,000, C. Anbert in *Monde*, 16 June 1950; for the other figures, *ibid.*, 14 April 1949. Numbers tried and punished were relatively much higher in Belgium, Holland and Norway: see Williams, p. 302n.

41. Meynaud, p. 224.

42. Anbert, *loc. cit.* In six years Auriol's candidates were defeated only three times: *Monde*, 9 May 1953 (but cf. p. 199 above). Coty seems to have had less influence: *ibid.*, 24 November 1962.

43. 'Busily the High Council manufactures bills. Methodically the Ministry buries them. Or rather it does not bury them; bureaucratic routine takes care of that. It simply fails to dig them out': Anbert, *loc. cit.* The High Council's committees met in the ministry's library – in overcoats,

[*over*

sphere and indeed extend it to the *parquet*. In April 1948 the cabinet approved a bill giving the upstart body even less scope than the minister had conceded, but this stayed buried in the Assembly's justice committee. A year later President Auriol announced a bill to remove the examining magistrates (*juges d'instruction*) from the *parquet*'s supervision; three days later the minister of justice, Robert Lecourt, retorted that the ministry would deal with the problem itself; the cabinet supported him, the rest of the Council unanimously protested.[44] But the shortage of parliamentary time prevented any far-reaching reform.

The struggle to take judicial administration out of politics was not concluded when the High Council was set up, but an important beginning had been made. The ministry still influenced promotions but could not finally decide them, and the most powerful deputy had little say on them. Overt political interference was publicized and checked as in April 1950 when the Council (supported for once by the minister, René Mayer) protested at the cabinet's threats against judges who had acquitted accused Communists. These advances of the early Fourth Republic were largely due to President Auriol, under whom 'the centre of gravity of the judiciary perhaps moved from the Place Vendôme to the Élysée'.[45]

French judges, though secure in their posts, had hitherto been subject to political influence because their low pay made them too dependent on promotion.[46] The High Council checked the consequence without removing the cause; the standard of judges could not be improved while their salaries remained inadequate. Bias, conformity, mediocrity and pusillanimity caused some shocking abuses during the Algerian war, especially in the military courts (where civilian judges preside).[47] Experience in the Fifth Republic abundantly showed that the courts were not tools of the government, but their other failings denied them that public confidence which has made their American counterparts the accepted protectors of minorities against the misdeeds of men in power.

4. CONSTITUTIONAL AMENDMENT AND THE CONSTITUTIONAL COMMITTEE

France has had many constitutions, and their status is naturally lower than in the United States. Since the Revolution constitutional theory has insisted on

as the radiators did not work: *Figaro*, 28 October 1949. When President Auriol offered a building attached to the Élysée this was stopped on grounds of 'economy' – for if the Council left the ministry's premises the dossiers might go with it: Anbert, *loc. cit.* The Council eventually obtained its own building.

44. *Monde*, 14 April 1949. While judges could be removed only for cause shown after a hearing before the disciplinary authority, the minister could dismiss members of the *parquet* from their posts (though not from the profession). The *parquet* claimed to supervise and promote *juges d'instruction* because of their investigating functions; but their dependence on it encouraged abuses such as keeping untried suspects too long in prison.

45. Siegfried, *De la IIIe*, p. 230; cf. Goguel, *Régime*, pp. 70–1. But the constitution of the Fifth Republic was drafted by a minister of justice, Debré, and restored some of the ministry's powers at the High Council's expense: see Williams and Harrison, p. 256, but cf. pp. 167–8. On 1950, *Monde*, 28 April 1950; Arné, pp. 76–7; and above, p. 211.

46. Cf. R. C. K. Ensor, *Courts and Judges in France, Germany and England* (1933), pp. 40–2, 118–21; and Sharp, pp. 196–7. But cf. above, p. 211n. 15.

47. See below, pp. 348, 351 and n.

the sovereignty of Parliament; courts have never inquired whether a law conformed to the constitution, and there has been no effective restraint on rulers and majorities who sought to infringe or alter inconvenient constitutional provisions. Assuming that partisan behaviour would recur, all the political groups wished to safeguard their own position. In 1946, when the Left was predominant, conservatives tried to erect barriers against the will of the majority. Later the Right demanded an easier amendment procedure and the Left resisted it.

In the Third Republic a constitutional amendment had only two stages: first a resolution passed by an absolute majority in both houses, then a bill voted by an absolute majority of the two houses sitting together at Versailles. In the Fourth, Article 90 laid down three: a resolution stating the object of the amendment and passed twice (with three months' interval) by an absolute majority of the Assembly; a bill voted in the ordinary way; and a referendum. But the resolution need not pass the Assembly twice if the Council of the Republic also voted it by an absolute majority, nor need the bill go to referendum if it had a special majority (three-fifths in both houses, or two-thirds on its final reading in the Assembly).[48] Referendum or special majority were thus alternative safeguards against abuse. As in the lifetime of the Third Republic, the republican form of government could not be changed (Article 95); and because of its death in 1940, no amendment might be initiated or passed while all or part of France was occupied by foreign troops (Article 94).[49]

The procedure proved unexpectedly hard to operate. In 1945 most deputies, apart from Communists and Radicals, had favoured the referendum. But after a few years in Parliament they became as hostile to it as their predecessors, and by 1953 even keen revisionists preferred no amendment at all to one ratified by the electorate. The special majorities therefore became essential. With the Communists opposed, these were hard to attain: a two-thirds majority required 80 or even 90% of the non-Communist deputies, and for three-fifths to suffice, 75 or 80% of them had to agree with a Council where party strengths were different. As there was more dissent from the constitution than assent to any alternative, it proved impossible to make substantial changes through this procedure.[50]

Resolutions for amendment could be introduced only by a deputy, not by a senator or the government. (This restriction, broken by Pflimlin in the last days of the regime, was very easily evaded: the first senatorial motions asking

48. Except that even two-thirds of the deputies could not abolish the upper house without a referendum, an illusory protection which guaranteed neither its powers nor its composition: A. Philip, *JO* 28 September 1946, p. 4219, quoted Drevet, p. 120, cf. p. 111. The fractions were of votes cast, not of total membership; *ibid.*, pp. 115–16; Goguel, no. 110, p. 487; cf. Poutier, p. 30. The initial resolution went to the upper house only if the lower so chose: Drevet, pp. 50–2.

49. But the constitution was amended in June 1958 while Corsica (and Algeria) were occupied by insurgent French troops.

50. As M. Goguel had predicted: *Régime*, p. 47. Communist strength in the Assembly varied from 16 to 30%. On the referendum debate in 1946 see Drevet, pp. 99–114, and on referendum-phobia later also *ibid.*, pp. 133, 136; Poutier, pp. 42–3; Goguel, no. 110, pp. 487–8. In 1946 the Communists wanted to ban the referendum, in 1953 to make it compulsory: Drevet, pp. 107, 109, 112–13, cf. Poutier, pp. 22, 26–8.

the Assembly to introduce a resolution dated from 1949.[51]) The deputies voted three resolutions: one in November 1950, under which the 1954 amendment passed; one in May 1955, which led to an abortive bill in March 1958, and was the enabling authority for transferring the amending power to de Gaulle's government in June; and Pflimlin's, on 27 May 1958.[52] The Council of the Republic, which could not amend the resolutions, voted the first in January 1951 and the second in July 1955 with accompanying motions of its own: for it feared that a resolution which it had passed in order to increase its own powers might be used by the Assembly to reduce them.[53] This was possible because the Assembly decided in 1950 that the 'object' could be specified merely by enumerating the articles to be amended (so that the purpose of the changes had to be inferred from the committee's report).[54] The rapporteur in 1955 disagreed with this interpretation; but his own resolution, which specified one article only, was amended in the house to add 27 others on which the committee had not reported.[55]

The amending bill under the 1950 resolution was passed by the deputies only on 22 July 1953, by the senators (to whom they allowed extra time) on 17 March 1954, and in final form by the Assembly on 30 November by a two-thirds majority, 412 to 141.[56] Its passage was complicated both by differences between the houses and by a problem of procedure. The amending bill could alter no article not specified in the resolution: but must it change all those specified? By 1953 few people still wanted to amend Article 7 (on the state of siege) and the Assembly voted by 500 to 0 not to do so. But the senators feared that they might accept a resolution in order to increase their own powers, then see the Assembly drop the changes they wanted and proceed only with the rest. They decided by 207 to 0 that every article in the resolution must be amended, and so proposed a purely formal change in Article 7. Proclaiming its right to stand firm, the Assembly gave way. But in 1955 it opened the way to similar manœuvres by a resolution authorizing a separate discussion and vote on the different articles. Intended to prevent disputes on the domestic clauses holding up amendment of the overseas ones, that decision allowed General de Gaulle in 1958 to carry the Fourth Republic's second constitutional amendment. This altered one Article (90) so as to permit his government to draft the whole new text.[57]

51. Drevet, pp. 37–42, Poutier, pp. 9–11, Georgel, i. 18. For the articles most deputies wanted to amend see *ibid.*, i. 13–14, 323–5.

52. The last covered Articles 9, 12, 13 and 45 (as the government proposed) and 48, 52 and 92 (added later), which were to be joined to the bill then before the upper house; it passed on a vote of confidence by 408 to 165, but Pflimlin resigned: Drevet, pp. 173–5, Georgel, i. 320–1 (and above, p. 56). The first two are discussed below.

53. Drevet, pp. 55–8. In 1951 the Council demanded a broader reform and no reduction of its own rights (see also *AP* 1951, p. 8; Berlia, no. 13a, pp. 475–6; and Poutier, p. 18); the Assembly's rapporteur said this motion was unconstitutional. But in 1955 the Council passed another urging priority for amendment of Article 90 itself.

54. Drevet, pp. 60–5. Specifying the 'object' was supposed to avoid the kind of sweeping formula used by Laval in 1940; 1958 showed it did not (pp. 60, 178–9).

55. *Ibid.*, pp. 65–8. To Article 90 were added three articles on the rise and fall of ministries (49–51) which the committee had discussed informally, one on money bills (17) and twenty-three on the French Union (60–82) which it had not.

56. On it see Berlia, nos. 12a and 13a.

57. Drevet, pp. 68–77, 118, 175–81 suggests that Parliament could not legally be excluded from

[over

Experience with the first amendment had shown that only ministers could organize agreement between the parties. But their legal right to do so was doubtful. Until 1958 everyone agreed that they could not propose a resolution (and the Communists contended that they should not even speak). When René Mayer's cabinet brought in an amendment bill in 1953, the *Conseil d'État* advised that this was legal but the Assembly's franchise committee voted that it was not. In 1954, however, Mendès-France's government helped to reconcile the views of the two houses on the *navette*, and saved the critical clause by a majority of only two. In the third National Assembly Guy Mollet called strongly for an amending bill, but would not intervene in detail. Félix Gaillard, when his credit was already wearing thin, introduced an amendment bill of his own which he emasculated in hopes of an easier passage: the franchise committee decided that his action was legal (reversing its view of 1953) but threw out his bill. A new measure was reported out, twice referred back to committee (once after a vote of confidence in the government), and after thirteen sittings passed the Assembly on 21 March 1958 by 308 to 206.[58] But it was not to come into force till a new electoral law was voted. There was some reason to claim that de Gaulle's was the only way the constitution could be amended, and some excuse for the attacks to which Article 90 was subjected.[59]

Yet procedure was not mainly to blame. If the first amendment took four years to pass and the second made little progress in three, the delays were due partly to extraneous factors (elections, government crises, EDC, Algeria) and partly to disagreements of substance. When the object was accepted a formula could be found; the French Union clauses, added to the 1955 resolution at the last minute with no prior discussion in the franchise committee, were the only ones on which that querulous body could agree in 1956.[60] Certainly the special majorities meant that the agreement had to extend to every party which supported the regime. But it was illogical of conservatives to suppose that they could remedy this situation by changing Article 90 so as to remove the veto that every 'republican' party enjoyed: for either all these parties agreed on the object of the revision and Article 90 was no obstacle, or some disagreed and clung to their veto. Controlling the upper house, conservatives naturally favoured an easy amendment procedure, which would allow them to carry proposals when they had a majority in the Assembly and block them when the Left had.[61] But a written constitution is pointless if it can be changed

the process unless Article 3 had been amended (but no resolution had authorized its amendment). De Gaulle's bill was voted by 350 to 163 in the Assembly, where some opponents abstained to ensure a special majority and no referendum, and by 256 to 30 in the upper house.

58. Some politicians amended arithmetic and argued that 308 was three-fifths of 514.

59. Drevet, pp. 78–91, 139–40, 154–5, 170–3; cf. Georgel, i. 18–21, Arné, pp. 173–5.

60. Drevet, pp. 135–8 (delays), 139, 154–5; its own rapporteur, Paul Coste-Floret, admitted that except on the Union clauses its conclusions were useless. (In June 1958 the committee's last fling was to insist that Parliament must vote on de Gaulle's draft, and that it should not go to referendum if accepted there. But the General got his way by threatening to resign.)

61. Cf. Poutier, p. 45. For conservative complaints against the need for compromise see Drevet, p. 133, especially Jean Legaret's: 'a special majority cannot be assembled around great ideas and great texts'. But do great ideas and great texts make acceptable constitutions in divided countries?

like any other law, and in Socialist eyes conservatives had no divine right to a privileged position.

Since the demand for constitutional change came from conservatives, the Constitutional Committee had no function. Created in 1946 to check surreptitious violation of the constitution by the Assembly, it was a compromise between the Right who favoured judicial review of the constitutionality of laws, the Radicals who wanted a strong second chamber, MRP and SFIO who preferred control by referendum, and the Communists who opposed any check at all. The Socialists, fearing obstruction of their social security and nationalization policies, had its competence limited to the first 89 articles of the constitution so as to exclude both the amendment procedure and the Preamble, which thus remained an abstract pronouncement with no visible means of support.[62]

Under Article 91 the Committee included the President of the Republic as chairman, the Presidents of both houses of Parliament, seven members elected annually by the Assembly and three by the Council of the Republic by proportional representation of parties. The seven and three, who could not be members of the chamber which elected them, were often professors of law; in 1946 MRP elected Marcel Prélot, once a university rector and later a Gaullist politician, and the RGR deputies chose André Siegfried. Under Article 92 the Committee could consider only a law referred to it by an absolute majority of the senators through the joint agency of their own President and the President of the Republic within the ten days (five where urgency was claimed) allowed for promulgating the law.[63] The Committee either reconciled the two houses (but the constitution made it hard to arrange a compromise) or decided in five days – two in urgent cases – whether the law 'presupposed amendment of the constitution'. If not, it was promulgated; if so, under Article 93 it was sent back for the Assembly to decide whether to begin the amendment procedure.

As the inventor of the compromise later affirmed, the Committee's function was to protect the Council of the Republic.[64] This was both futile, since the constitution guaranteed the Council's existence but not its powers or method of election, and irrelevant, since the upper house soon proved to be more aggressor than victim. The Committee was therefore called on for only one ruling, in June 1948 when the second chamber was still cautious and co-operative. The issue was not the bill but the urgency procedure under which it had been passed; the Communists therefore plausibly claimed that the

62. *SCC* II, pp. 101–5. The first draft constitution included no checking authority, which was why MRP opposed it: Wright, *Reshaping*, pp. 155–6. After its defeat in May 1946 SFIO accepted the Committee to avoid de Gaulle's alternative, a check by the President. Some authorities thought that decree-laws, though not laws, could be challenged in court for infringing constitutional principles: Pinto, no. 181, pp. 526–7; cf. Pickles, pp. 234, 235n.

63. No countersignature was needed: Goguel, *Régime*, pp. 68–9, cf. Soubeyrol, no. 202, p. 560, and above, p. 200 n. 19

64. On 27 July 1949 Auriol wrote to Herriot, '... the Committee has been instituted to protect the Council of the Republic against the encroachments of the Assembly, and not the other way round': *AP* 1949, p. 335; above, pp. 200, 281; Drevet, pp. 19–21. On his role in 1946, *SCC* II, pp. 405–6.

Committee had no jurisdiction. But all the non-Communists in the Council supported the appeal to the Committee, which ruled in their favour; the Assembly accepted the verdict; and the President found a procedural solution by referring the bill back to the Assembly under Article 36.[65] A year later relations between the houses had grown much worse. In July 1949 the Assembly overruled the Council's amendments to a bill on parliamentary immunity, and then adjourned. Under Article 9 the Council had to adjourn also, and was unable to appeal to the Committee. Since an appeal had to come after a bill had passed the Assembly but before it was promulgated, the Assembly could clearly evade Article 92 by adjourning for ten days after voting a bill challenged by the upper house. But the President of the Republic came to the Council's help and again referred the bill back to the Assembly.[66]

Other appeals were occasionally proposed. In August 1948 the opposition challenged Paul Reynaud's special powers bill under Article 13, which forbade the Assembly to delegate legislative power, but the majority senators voted them down. In September 1951 the anticlericals failed to carry an appeal against the Barangé bill subsidizing church schools, as a breach of Article 1 (*La France est une République . . . laïque*).[67] On such controversial legislation a senator's view on the bill would often decide his vote on the need for amending the constitution. Indeed Article 93 itself, with its hint that the voting of an unconstitutional law would very likely be followed by a constitutional amendment, reflected the low status of French constitutions and the presumption that a temporary but determined political majority would not hesitate to override them.

As it was assumed that majorities would misuse their power, minorities wanted to be able to stop them. The special majority rules gave every party but the Communists an effective veto, and therefore prevented the Fourth Republic undertaking any important change by way of constitutional amendment. To enthusiastic revisionists this was another proof of the decadence of the regime; but many of them (most Conservatives and some Gaullists) wanted a stronger state only to entrench *immobilisme* at home and abroad. Had there been a real majority there would have been little demand (or need) for constitutional reform. Without one, reform agitation was 'the constitutional talisman which diverts attention from political impotence'.[68]

65. Soulier, no. 203, and see above, p. 284 and n. The Committee's decision was unanimous apart from one abstention: Prélot, no. 184, p. 727. Cf. Williams, pp. 290–1.

66. An appeal under Article 92 would also have needed his co-operation. See p. 211 n. 14; Drago, no. 75, p. 404; on Art. 9, above, p. 281; on relations between the houses, above, pp. 286–7.

67. On the appeal, the anticlerical senators were 40 fewer than on the bill itself. Cf. *AP* 1951, p. 224; E. Weill-Raynal in *Populaire*, 25, 26 and 27 September 1951; Lemasurier, no. 142; Pernot, no. 173; and on Reynaud's bill, Pinto, no. 181, pp. 519–20, and above, pp. 270–1.

68. Léo Hamon, quoted Georgel, i. 23.

Chapter 22

THE ELECTORAL SYSTEM

Though electoral systems are often defended on high principles, they are usually chosen for party or individual advantage. In France they were classical terrain for partisan manœuvres. Every great political change brought the adoption of a wider franchise, larger or smaller constituencies, or a new method of allocating seats. Manhood suffrage was instituted in 1848. Women were given the vote by General de Gaulle in 1945. Large multi-member constituencies based on the department prevailed from 1848 to 1852, 1871 to 1875, 1885 to 1889, 1919 to 1927, and 1945 to 1958; electors had sometimes to vote for a list, not a person, and seats were attributed in various ways.[1] In between there were small single-member constituencies based on the *arrondissement*; a candidate was elected at once if he had over half the votes cast and a quarter of those on the register; if no one did, there was a second ballot after a week (before 1914 two weeks) at which the man with most votes won. But the simple Anglo-American system with only one ballot was unacceptable to Frenchmen. For with many parties members would often be elected by a small minority of voters; and if the system forced the citizens of a deeply divided nation into two hostile camps, the consequence (especially if one camp were dominated by the Communist party) might be civil war rather than stable democracy.

1. 'SCRUTIN D'ARRONDISSEMENT' AND PROPORTIONAL REPRESENTATION

Thirteen of the Third Republic's sixteen elections were held under *scrutin d'arrondissement* with two ballots. After 1914, few seats were won by an absolute majority at the first ballot;[2] at the second round most constituencies had a straight fight between Right and Left, some had three-cornered contests, and a handful might have four candidates.[3] The system encouraged small, moderate and ill-disciplined parties. They were small because at the first ballot every individualist and splinter group could spread propaganda and solicit votes without risking the triumph of their worst enemy. They were moderate because at the second round, the serious candidate nearest the centre was likely to win the doubtful voters.[4] 'At the first ballot you choose, at the second you eliminate'. Radicals in the left-wing Midi could attract Conservative support against the more dangerous Socialists, while in the Catholic

1. See Campbell, *French Electoral Systems and Elections* (1957). On 1958, see n. 21.
2. To 1881, 80%; to 1914, 60%; in 1932, 40%; in 1928 and 1936, 30%. *Ibid.*, pp. 34–7.
3. Even in 1928 and 1936 only 130 and 59 seats had three second-ballot candidates with over 1,000 votes, and only 9 and 14 had more: Middleton, pp. 95–6; Williams, p. 310n. (1928); *Inégalités*, p. 272 (1936). On the two blocs see Goguel, *La politique des partis sous la Troisième République, passim*; Siegfried, *France*, pp. 51–2, 68–72 (and *Tableau*, pp. 24, 31–4); Soulier, pp. 401–2, 406–8, 448–9; Duverger, *Parties*, p. 216.
4. Under full PR the Communists would have had 54 more seats in 1928, 38 in 1932, and 21 in 1936; Socialists 8 more, 7 fewer and 28 fewer; Radicals and allies 36, 46 and 30 fewer; groups to their Right 34 fewer, 21 more and 37 more: Soulier, p. 516n.; *Systèmes électoraux*, p. 64; Lachapelle, *Les régimes électoraux*, p. 164.

west they gained Socialist votes against the friends of the Church; in 1928 fewer than fifty deputies won without clerical or socialist help.[5] Members of the centre groups therefore rejected party discipline, since their electoral interests differed regionally. While nominally extreme British parties are brought closer by a common magnet, the floating voter, the theoretically moderate French parties were pulled asunder by their members' dependence on extremist second-ballot support.[6]

As the Radicals benefited from the second ballot, the Socialists and Conservatives both demanded proportional representation (PR); occasionally they made 'unnatural' electoral alliances based on this common interest.[7] Even when the PR supporters captured the Chamber they were frustrated by the Radical Senate, which before the 1919 election imposed a hybrid compromise allowing PR only if no list won a clear majority of votes within a department. This law, which rewarded electoral discipline, helped the Right in 1919 and the Left in 1924. *Scrutin d'arrondissement* was restored in 1927, but by 1945 it seemed to everyone but its Radical beneficiaries as discredited as the Third Republic itself. Yet it was not the cause of heterogeneous majorities in Parliament; it was precisely because there was no homogeneous majority among the voters that most Frenchmen preferred an electoral system of this type. It was a consequence of the division of opinion which it helped to perpetuate.

Scrutin d'arrondissement enabled the citizen to choose a deputy to act as his personal spokesman with the authorities, and as an ambassador from his district to Paris. Critics complained that the clash of political ideas was lost amid the confusion of local interests, and that loose parties, shifting majorities and short-lived cabinets never allowed the voter to pronounce on the record of a responsible government. The supporters of PR believed that it would free the deputy from the parish pump, broadening his own horizon and that of his followers. Real parties, bound together by loyalty to a common political ideal, would permit a real majority at last to emerge. And in 1945 a more immediate reason made every party but the Radicals welcome PR: it ensured them all against a Parliament dominated by one rival, particularly the Communists.[8]

PR was a device to make the citizen choose between ideas rather than men by voting for a party list.[9] If the lists were unalterable the deputy would be subjected to the organization which drew them up; and if they had to contain a name for every seat at stake, it might be hard for small parties and impossible for independent candidates to stand at all. The device was less effective if the lists could be left incomplete or altered by the voter. The 'preferential vote'

5. *AP* 1929, p. 419, quoted Siegfried *tableau*, p. 179. Thus the Radicals, unlike the British Liberals, did not lose from the growth of socialism: Duverger, *Parties*, pp. 323–4.

6. Generally, *ibid.*, pp. 240, 318, 324, 331; Middleton, Chapter 4; Campbell, Chapter 4; Goguel in *Systèmes électoraux*. On the Centre, Soulier, p. 528.

7. Cf. Campbell, p. 89. By this *politique du pire* the Right sometimes forced centre politicians to terms: see Long, *Les élections législatives en Côte d'Or*, pp. 105–6, 204.

8. Goguel, *Fourth Republic*, pp. 61–2, and *Régime*, p. 26.

9. Yet Ireland's single transferable vote combines PR with a vote for men not lists, and allows broad justice between parties without impeding coalitions among them. But when M. Duverger proposed it in 1956, an ex-premier told him it was politically impossible because no deputy could tell how it would affect his own re-election: *Demain*, p. 99, also pp. 91–101. Cf. Campbell, p. 45, *Inégalités*, p. 111.

slightly weakened its force by allowing him to cross names off his chosen list or move them up or down; *panachage* undermined it altogether by letting him distribute fractions of his vote over candidates on more than one list.[10] But PR was also a means to ensure that the conflicting ideas were fairly represented. The larger the constituency within which it operated, the better this function was fulfilled. If the whole country was treated as a unit, as in Weimar Germany, each party was represented proportionately to its share of the total vote and even a tiny minority could win a seat.[11] But with smaller constituencies only substantial minorities won representation. It would take over a sixth of the votes to be sure of a seat in a district with five members, over a quarter in one with three.

General de Gaulle acceded to the parties' demand for PR with rigid lists, but he chose small constituencies without national pooling of votes (and with heavy rural over-representation, later corrected).[12] In October 1945 the first Constituent Assembly was elected under this scheme. In its constitutional drafting committee the principle of PR was adopted by 38 votes to 3, and against Radical and Conservative opposition the 'big three' parties agreed to reject *panachage* and the preferential vote, and to allow national pooling by large parties only. But their bill lapsed when the draft constitution was rejected by referendum, and in the second Constituent Assembly the 'big three' disagreed. Both Communists and Socialists favoured national pooling, but not MRP; and some Socialists wanted *panachage*, which the Communists loathed. By threatening to abstain and let *panachage* pass, MRP forced the Communists to drop national pooling and join an unholy alliance against both amendments. This combination imposed the law of 5 October 1946.[13] Most departments formed a single constituency, though seven were split up; most constituencies had three to five members; PR operated only within the constituency; lists had to have as many names as there were seats; there was no *panachage*, and only a bogus form of preferential vote.[14]

Thus de Gaulle's electoral law, almost unchanged, governed three post-war elections. It decisively marked the politics of the period. Its effects on party discipline are discussed in the next chapter. Between parties, it distributed seats more fairly than *scrutin d'arrondissement* but still with a bias; the Centre had gained from the old system, the new one now helped the Left – for it favoured size, and at each of these elections Communists, Socialists and MRP were the three strongest parties with three-quarters of the seats. Large parties gained because the 'highest average' system of allotting seats was preferred to the 'highest remainder' system (see Appendix VI) and because most

10. Either by voting for a list, but striking out some of its candidates and writing in the names of rivals, or else by writing out a list of his own.

11. But special provisions often debarred it, for many PR advocates worried about justice for large minorities only.

12. *Inégalités*, pp. 48–52; and for the maldistribution of seats, pp. 177–213, 231–61. In 1946 the industrial areas had 38 more seats than de Gaulle had intended, but they were still short and by 1956, after shifts of population, were again badly under-represented. Cf. Maps 4 and 21.

13. *Ibid.*, pp. 53–84; Campbell, pp. 103–12; *AP* 1946, pp. 72–5, 226–8. The alliance revived for PR in municipal elections in 1947, and against a double-ballot system in 1951 and 1955.

14. Seine formed six constituencies, Nord three, and 5 departments two each. Of 102 constituencies 4 had two members, 13 had three, 32 had four, 16 had five, 11 had six, 9 had seven, and 17 had more: 3 eight, 7 nine, 5 ten, 2 eleven.

constituencies were small, so that at least one-sixth of the vote was usually needed to ensure election. In October 1945 and June 1946 each of the 'big three' parties could win a seat for 37,000 votes at most, while the Radicals, half their size, needed 60,000. At least 94% of 'big three' supporters cast their votes for a deputy, but half the Radicals 'wasted' theirs on defeated candidates.[15]

Consequently, PR reduced the number of parties represented in Parliament. This is not strange. The second ballot had strongly encouraged multiplicity, and since PR operated only over a small constituency and favoured big parties, electors preferred to 'vote usefully'. More important still, fear of the Communists drove them to seek an electoral rampart. Independently of the law, it reinforced the stronger parties and impelled them to organize. But the stricter discipline operated not on a majority and an opposition party but on several minority groups, each with a sectional base (assured by PR) which it had little incentive to expand; and the law brought about conflict in the country between the parties which were obliged to co-operate in Parliament.[16]

3. BASTARD PROPORTIONAL REPRESENTATION, 1951 AND 1956

The electoral system of 1945–46 lost favour early in the Fourth Republic. But PR with national pooling remained nearly everybody's second preference, since it offered a universal guarantee against electoral catastrophe; and some form of PR was still the first choice of individuals in all parties, and of both Communists and MRP. Both prized unity and discipline; in both active militants were (at least in the early years) more important than prominent local personalities; both feared that alliances would be made more easily against them than with them. The Communists wanted PR to reinforce their internal discipline: to preserve their deputies from dependence on support from outside the party, and to keep their followers from being tempted either to 'vote usefully' for a strong Left candidate, or to discriminate between the leadership's nominees (this was why they so bitterly opposed *panachage*). It also protected them against a majority system, where alliances would harm them, and against small constituencies, whose boundaries would be drawn against them. The moralists of MRP desired electoral justice (though not to excess: it was they who had stopped national pooling). They were afraid of anticlerical alliances against them on the second ballot between the Radicals whom they despised and the Socialists whom they vainly courted; the departmental and senatorial elections of 1948 confirmed and strengthened these fears. The militants disliked almost equally the willing embrace of RPF,

15. In November 1946 Radicals and Conservatives often withdrew in the other's favour, and so narrowed the gap; RGR put up 21 fewer lists than in June: *AP* 1946, p. 580, Priouret, *Partis*, p. 106n. For the figures cited see Campbell, pp. 107–13; Husson, i. xxxiii–v and ii. xxxii–iii, 253; *Inégalités*, pp. 291–2. In November 1946 less than 2% of Communist votes were 'wasted', 3% of MRP, about 10% of Conservatives and Socialists, 27% of RGR and 47% of Gaullists; MRP paid 32,000 votes per seat, Communists 33,000, Conservatives 35,000, SFIO 38,000, and Radicals 43,000.

16. See below, pp. 317–18, 389. Between the September 1945 majority elections to departmental councils and the October general election under PR, Radical and Conservative votes dropped sharply: Goguel, *Fourth Republic*, p. 63. Supporters of the majority system therefore claimed that it let people vote as they chose without fear of wasting their vote (in Britain it is PR supporters who use this argument).

which would prejudice their hopes of proving themselves republicans of the Left, and the bigamous temptations of local combinations which, differing regionally, would wreck the movement's precious unity and blast their hopes of regenerating French public life. For these active Catholics transferred to politics the habits of discipline learned in their religious organizations as naturally as free-thinking Radicals tended to political individualism.[17]

Indifferent to internal unity and with no aim beyond electoral success, the Radicals were the champions of *scrutin d'arrondissement*. Over the years their many well-known personalities had built up strong local positions, and under the old system they could hope to revive the great days of the Third Republic, when they sat in the middle of the political seesaw and gained both ways at the second ballot; when the deputy's personal standing meant more than his policy, and well-repaired local by-roads could become his highways to political success; when Parliament was the rampart of the provincial petty-bourgeoisie and peasantry against all forms of organized power, whether wielded by bishops or trade unionists, generals or dictators. This was among the few subjects on which Radicals of all wings agreed, and they were convinced that the electorate agreed too.[18]

The other parties were more divided. The well-entrenched Conservatives and Socialists, with their strong local roots, were both traditional supporters of PR among whom *scrutin d'arrondissement* was fast gaining ground. The constituency interests of CNIP parliamentarians and SFIO federations differed too widely for either to have a strong common view; but whereas the individualist Conservative deputy voted for his personal preference, the disciplined Socialists – having little to gain or lose over the country as a whole – cast a united vote for every proposed change.[19] For PR had not fulfilled the hopes that it would improve the quality of candidates or the tone of public life. It hampered alliances at the polls between parties which would have to co-operate in Parliament. It grew increasingly unpopular with the electorate, who preferred to vote for a man, not a list. Above all it guaranteed 180 seats to SFIO's Communist arch-enemies; and in 1951 the ministry of the interior estimated that RPF would win 150, since against the divided centre groups the two oppositions would be the largest single parties and gain the advantage of size which in 1945–46 had accrued to the big three.[20] PR would therefore mean either an ungovernable Assembly or one in which General de Gaulle could dictate terms for his co-operation.

17. Goguel in *Encyclopédie*, i. 354, and *Régime*, pp. 85–6.

18. Perhaps wrongly: a poll in October 1950 showed 22% for a two-ballot system, 16% for a one-ballot majority system, 25% for PR and 37% don't knows: Pouillon, no. 183, p. 99 (cf. *Inégalités*, p. 91). By 1955 *scrutin d'arrondissement* does seem to have regained support as list systems lost it: cf. *ibid.*, p. 106. Mendès-France was always one of its strongest supporters, notably at the Radicals' Deauville conference in 1950 (cf. below, pp. 315, 331).

19. On one vital vote 15 deputies defected, which was rare in SFIO: above, p. 288n., and below, p. 400. But even this showed an ideological rather than a constituency preference: MacRae, no. 149, pp. 209, 210. PR was still favoured in regions where the party was weak; its senators came from its strongholds and were for *scrutin d'arrondissement*.

20. The ministry (which predicted the actual results with striking accuracy) expected from metropolitan France under PR: 159 Communists, 146 RPF, 82 SFIO, 68 Conservatives, 64 RGR, 25 MRP: *Carrefour*, 6 February 1951; for details see Williams, p. 317n. And cf. above, p. 66n., on voting for a man not a list.

This prospect made PR increasingly acceptable to Gaullists. Originally RPF was a centralized movement of new men who demanded strong government and hoped to build a real majority party. Despising parish-pump politics and believing in parliamentary discipline, they advocated large constituencies and a majority list system with two ballots, hoping to lead on the first and attract all anti-Communist votes on the second. But as their impetus declined their preferences changed. If rivals led on the first ballot, they risked defections among their own supporters at the polls and perhaps in Parliament. As an important but isolated minority instead of a potential majority they, like Communists and MRP, found in PR their best hope of internal discipline and fair representation; and by maintaining Communist strength PR would ensure their own bargaining position. In September 1948 RPF for the first time demanded immediate dissolution of the Assembly without prior electoral reform, and in 1950 de Gaulle approved two 'honest' electoral systems: the majority list system and PR.[21] Opponents concluded that RPF wanted to keep PR but blame MRP for it.[22]

If so, it failed. Electoral reform had a difficult passage among the reefs of conflicting party interests, second preferences, and minority opinions.[23] But MRP was isolated among the centre parties in its defence of PR, and was eventually driven to compromise in order to escape unpopularity and an ungovernable (or Gaullist-dominated) Assembly. Yet it feared even these prospects less than the second ballot, and its determination finally obliged the reluctant Radicals and the indifferent or divided Socialists and Conservatives to settle for a single-ballot system of 'bastard PR'. The most fervently moralizing of parties had imposed 'the least honest electoral law in French history'.[24]

The centre parties agreed only on the need to weaken the Communists without strengthening RPF. The Assembly's franchise committee was too divided to report, and when it asked the house for instructions no majority could be found to give them. MRP and many Peasants insisted on a single ballot; the Radicals and most Conservatives demanded two; the Socialists voted for each in turn, and the Communists opposed any change. On 21 February 1951 the 180 Communists, with different allies on each vote, rejected eight successive proposals. The battle lasted six months, provoked a conflict between the houses, and destroyed a cabinet. Many African deputies were concerned only to impose a wide overseas franchise on the reluctant Council

21. *AP* 1948, p. 176; 1950, p. 54. But in power, in 1958, he restored *scrutin d'arrondissement.* His advisers, who often lacked local roots but could ensure their places on a party list, were keener on PR than the Gaullist deputies, who had all been elected on another ticket and hoped to renew their old alliances.

22. P. H. Teitgen, *JO* 21 December 1950, p. 9443. But Michel Debré always wanted a single-ballot majority system.

23. Some UDSR and Conservative members feared that with two ballots the extremists would lead on the first and polarize the centre vote on the second. Some MRP 'back-benchers', too low on their lists to be re-elected in a big constituency, had cultivated a small corner of it in hopes that *scrutin d'arrondissement* would be introduced. Failing it, many Radicals preferred PR with national (not departmental) pooling of votes. Anti-Gaullist urban Radicals needed PR to survive. MRP, allied to the Communists in defence of PR, had as its second choice a single ballot with provision for party alliances, which the Communists loathed.

24. As Rémy Roure called it in *Monde*, 26 April 1951.

of the Republic; many French ones were obstructive in order to avoid a summer election. But on 7 May the prime minister's patience was rewarded and the bill passed by a majority sufficient to override the upper house.[25]

The new law was similar in principle though not in method to that of 1919. It amended and did not repeal the PR law of 1946, keeping the same constituences (except that Gironde was divided), the same system of party lists with a candidate for every seat, and the same illusory preferential vote. But *panachage* was now allowed; by-elections, abolished in 1945, were restored; and though in theory seats were still distributed by PR, two new provisions transformed the working of the system: *apparentements* and the absolute majority rule. Everywhere outside the Paris area lists could form an alliance or *apparentement*, and their votes were then counted together as if cast for a single list.[26] Any list or alliance which won an absolute majority of votes took every seat. PR was still used to distribute seats both within an alliance, and generally when no one won an absolute majority of votes. This system enabled the government parties to combine and so gain the advantage of size which in 1945–46 went to the 'big three', and in 1951 would otherwise have gone to the two oppositions. Moreover, the combined Centre might win an absolute majority, and could therefore attract citizens wanting to 'vote usefully'. Government supporters argued that a vote for RPF was a vote for the Communists.

The system was not condemned by its victims alone; Herriot called it inept and monstrous. Those who disliked PR because they had to vote for a list instead of a man found the new law even worse. If PR had made the elector a puppet of the party bosses, *apparentement* encouraged their most dubious manipulations. In Hérault Jules Moch was in alliance with Paul Coste-Floret, whose brother wanted Moch impeached. In Tarn a Catholic might find his vote for MRP returning the anticlerical zealot Maurice Deixonne. Such combinations, it was argued, were ineffective as well as dishonest, since they would deter potential supporters: so government supporters would either form a large *apparentement* which might well lose votes, or fail to unite so that PR would still operate over four-fifths of the country. Even if the system worked, the electorate would certainly regard it as rigged by the *syndicat des sortants*.

Many of these criticisms were borne out. The voters' choice was still fettered to a list, and *panachage* did not really free it.[27] The anomalies appeared early. MRP leaders in industrial areas like Nord counted on SFIO drawing its full vote by intransigent anticlericalism, while the Socialists needed similar extremism from their Catholic partners. Paul Ramadier in Aveyron was left out of the conservative alliance, and could only hope that RPF would poll

25. Above, p. 288n. See Neumann, no. 165; A.S., no. 194; *Inégalités*, pp. 92–101.

26. But only if they were authorized by a 'national party' running lists in 30 departments. Eleven parties qualified in 1951 and eighteen in 1956, but some of them (and many of their lists) were bogus. The Paris area had a form of PR which helped the weaker parties, depriving RPF and Communists of 9 seats in 1951 and Communists alone of 10 in 1956 (7 going to MRP). On technical aspects of the election law see Nicholas, no. 167. Gironde's 10 seats were split into 6 and 4; cf. below, p. 327n.

27. Jules Moch had *panachage* votes from 7,000 admirers in other parties, which he did not need but which raised the average of his list enough to elect a third Socialist; wanting to help the man but not the party, these 7,000 voters had achieved the reverse. See Appendix VI.

well and rob the *apparentement* of an absolute majority. Everywhere Communists and RPF had a stake in the other's success. At the count, some remarkable results showed that it was substantial. In Hérault fewer than 39,000 Socialists elected three members while 69,000 Communists had none.[27] At Lille 107,000 Socialists had five deputies and 106,000 Communists none; 84,000 MRP voters had four and 94,000 Gaullists none. Gains and losses depended more on a party's alliances than on its own performance. In two of the three departments where they did best the Communists lost seats. The two most successful Socialists in the country were both beaten. A Radical minister (André Maroselli) gained 4,000 votes but lost his seat to an independent Conservative, allied to RPF, who polled less than half his total.

The 'thieves' ballot', as the Communists called it, achieved the intended results. Although critics – including de Gaulle – had warned that disgusted voters would stay at home, there was no evidence that they did.[28] In the 103 constituencies there were 53 alliances of SFIO, MRP and Radicals, 36 of which included Conservatives also. In 31 constituencies the governmental parties won an absolute majority of votes and all the seats.[29] Throughout France the Communists won 71 fewer seats and RPF 26 fewer than the 1946 law would have given them. SFIO profited least, being kept out of the centre alliance in many departments, especially in the west: there were only 16 extra Socialist seats to 30 for MRP, 27 for RGR and 24 for the Conservatives. But arithmetical computations underestimate the Centre's real gains, for 'vote usefully' was a potent slogan and the new law helped its inventors in the polling-booths as well as at the count. Nor was it so exceptionally unjust. In June 1946 PR had given the Communists a member for every 26,000 votes, the Radicals one for every 59,000; the new law gave the Radicals a seat for every 28,000 votes and the Communists one for every 52,000. Yet PR had been vaunted as the height of mathematical fairness by those who vilified the *apparentements* law as a monster of political iniquity.[30]

Like the Anglo-American electoral system, the new law sacrificed abstract justice to make a working majority possible. The old system would have returned at least 172 Communists and 143 Gaullists – together 315 members out of 627. With less than half the votes these parties would have held more than half the seats, and the 1946 law would have endangered a regime which for all its faults was preferred by every Frenchman to the dominance of his extreme opponents, and by most to either of the major alternatives.

The new law found only few and shamefaced defenders, yet it was to remain in use for a second election in very different circumstances. The political conflict was less intense than in 1951 but more straightforward (at least in outline

28. There were 2% fewer non-voters than in 1946; and in the dozen constituencies where the old system was in force because no *apparentement* was made, there were as many as elsewhere. Spoiled papers were up from 360,000 to 540,000, probably because *panachage* is complicated.

29. In 40 constituencies a list (1) or alliance (39) won an absolute majority; it included the Socialists in 31, the Gaullists in 7 and neither in 2. In 2, SFIO and MRP were joined by Conservatives but not by Radicals. Of the 31, 25 were in the old republican zone along and south of the Loire. See Maps 15 and 16.

30. Cf. Campbell, pp. 121–2, and in no. 42; *Inégalités*, pp. 304–10. 'Wasted' votes were 24%, double the proportion under PR but half that under pre-war *scrutin d'arrondissement*.

– the details were as confused as ever) when towards the end of its life the Assembly, following an unbroken tradition, began debating the method of electing its successor. The beneficiaries of *apparentement* had quarrelled before they could begin to enjoy the unfamiliar luxury of a secure majority. As the Gaullists were absorbed by the System, Pierre Mendès-France gradually emerged as leader of the opposition to conservative *immobilisme*, and when his government was overthrown by defections among his fellow-Radicals he set about reorganizing his party with a view to a close alliance with SFIO. Always a staunch defender of *scrutin d'arrondissement*, he now urged it more insistently than ever.[31] Under it he could share out seats with the Socialists and other allies, distinguish between friends and enemies in his own party, capitalize on his popularity by endorsing a single candidate in each constituency, and hope that at the second ballot some Communist voters would (as between the wars) rally to the Left candidate with the best hope of victory.

The conservatives frustrated him. Edgar Faure, his successor and rival, proposed that the election which was due in June 1956 be held in 1955. This would minimize 'election fever', enable a fresh Parliament to take major decisions over Algeria – and give the Mendesist and Poujadist forces less time to organize. It also endangered electoral reform. For although the 1951 system had now no public advocates, many politicians privately hoped to put it to use once more; right-wing alliances would win an absolute majority and all the seats in conservative constituencies, while in Left strongholds PR would operate because the clash between Communists and democratic Left would give a clear majority to neither.[32] In 1954 the Right had used fleeting Communist support for Mendès-France to hint that his policy was treasonable, yet in 1955 they deliberately chose to weaken him by strengthening the Communists. Once again they had succumbed to their fatal penchant for the *politique du pire*.[33]

Just as in 1951, the Assembly's franchise committee could reach no agreement; the deputies rejected sixteen proposals by contradictory majorities; and the senators were overwhelmingly for *scrutin d'arrondissement*. But there were several differences. First, in 1951 the existing system (PR) was favoured by only one governmental party, MRP, which held out for compromise but could not stop change. Secondly, the government was then bent on reform, whereas in 1955 its main interest was in the date rather than the rules of the election. Thirdly, conservatives as well as MRP were now in tacit accord with the Communists, who knew that any majority system meant alliances against them and that under the 1951 law they could count on PR operating over most of France. Fourthly, the Socialists and others had joined the Radicals, so that there was now more backing among the deputies for *scrutin d'arrondissement*. Lastly its senatorial supporters, who then had only a single-shot weapon, the absolute majority on their one and only reading of the bill,

31. Cf. n. 18, and below, p. 331.

32. On these hopes see Pierce, no. 180, pp. 395–8, 420–1; Georgel, i. 118, 120; *AP* 1955, p. 82; *Inégalités*, p. 102; Fauvet, *IVe*, pp. 304–7; Berlia, no. 14, p. 131; *Élections 1956*, pp. 7, 20. Some Conservatives also feared that *scrutin d'arrondissement* would weaken their new-found discipline.

33. *Ibid.*, p. 22. By 1956 the same men were clamouring in patriotic indignation to ban the Communist party.

could now by the *navette* force it to repeated votes in the Assembly – where it found a majority on its third reading, though only a tactical one. The struggle was prolonged, but it was broken off when the Communists switched their tactics and their votes, and the opposition, miscalculating, defeated the government by five votes too many and so allowed it to dissolve the Assembly.[34]

Edgar Faure thus got his early election, and the 1951 law remained in force. But its results disappointed the Right as well as the moderate Left.[35] For the conservatives, whose strategy depended on the Right vote being united while the Left vote was split, had underestimated Poujade. Their alliances went according to plan but the voters did not. There were *apparentements* of the moderate Right (Conservatives, right-wing Radicals, MRP, and most ex-Gaullist deputies) over two-thirds of the country and of the Republican Front (SFIO, most Radicals, and a few Gaullist and small-party candidates) over half of it. But only ten of the Right and one of the Left won absolute majorities; 89% of the seats were distributed by PR, and in these the advantage of size was less than usual since alliances were narrower and competing groups more equally matched.[36] Paradoxically, therefore, on its second trial the bastard PR of the 1951 law gave a more proportional result than the strict PR of 1945–46.[37]

4. MYTHS AND MANIPULATIONS

Politically divided on many questions and by many parties, France has electoral systems which are adapted to this situation and help to perpetuate it. A simple majority system is perhaps unworkable and has certainly been unacceptable, since unchecked majority power is tolerable only to those who are confident that their opponents would not abuse it. In France a national majority has normally seemed unattainable, and in abnormal times it has sometimes loomed as a threat rather than a boon. Devices have therefore been found to protect minorities, like PR, to divide majorities, like the second ballot, or to bolster the safe parties against the dangerous ones, like *apparentement*.

Scrutin d'arrondissement had always been opposed by Republicans until they took it up in 1889 to check Boulanger, who seemed on the way to a national majority (as, ironically, de Gaulle restored it in 1958 to check Soustelle). It

34. On the dissolution, above, pp. 238–9. The pre-war distribution of seats had always been inequitable and was now hopelessly out of date, but a new distribution was too controversial to allow *scrutin d'arrondissement* to pass quickly (the same problem had caused similar difficulties in 1927 and 1951): *Inégalités*, pp. 15–16, 32, 98, 105–6, 261.

35. However, the Right would have fared worse under any other system: see Williams, no. 168, p. 170 and n. Cf. Pierce, no. 180, pp. 405–6.

36. SFIO fought alone in 48 constituencies; it was allied to Radicals in 48, Communists in one (Vosges: p. 172 and n.) and Left groups in six. RS joined the Left in 11. MRP joined Conservatives in 51 seats, 22 of them with RS also, and fought alone in 41. The Poujadists illegally used *apparentements* to split their forces into three allied 'national parties', a real one for shopkeepers and bogus ones for peasants and consumers; this was why 11 of their deputies were unseated. See Map 16.

37. The worst-off party (omitting those polling less than 10% of the vote) paid 27,000 votes per seat more than the best-off party in 1945. It paid 24,000 more in June 1946, 13,000 in November, 26,000 in 1951, and 17,000 in 1956. For the worst-off party, the difference between its percentage of seats and of votes was 4·4, 4·0, 3·0, 8·1 and 2·7 respectively; and the average difference for all parties was 2·4, 2·0, 1·8, 3·6 and 1·6 (my calculations from sources given in n. 15).

was less just than PR, but more effective in encouraging alliances between neighbouring parties; and if the alliances were temporary this was part of its attraction for politicians who preferred not to commit themselves to legal rules or political combinations too far in advance. For circumstances might change and tactics and allies with them; because of the multiplicity of divisions no one could be sure where he would find his friends and enemies in the future.

PR was much fairer, but it separated at the polls parties which had to co-operate in Parliament and so made the task of government more difficult. For a politician tended to depend for support on a restricted social and ideological clientele, and if he tried to extend it he found that the floating vote was not a single group in the centre but a series of grouplets in the interstices between the main parties. A Socialist never appealed to the same voters as a Conservative: in the Midi he might woo away Radicals by stressing anticlericalism and playing down collectivism (but then he must beware of seeming lukewarm to his own supporters); in the north he might acquire merit with the militants by outbidding the Communists (but then he would risk losing votes on his right flank). The Conservative in the west had to prove himself a better defender of property than RPF, and of church schools than MRP. Where social issues predominated over religion MRP might compete with Socialists rather than Conservatives, as in Nord, and Radicals clash with the Right rather than SFIO, as in Paris. But nowhere was there a central pool of doubtful votes open to every party: only separate ponds, each fished by one or two rivals. Every party claimed to be the best defender of some group interest or sectional ideology. The political function of the floating voter in Britain – to attract both parties towards a common mean – was not performed in France.

An occasional protest movement at the crest of the wave might, like Gaullism in 1947 and Poujadism in 1956, attract some votes from all sides. No one else could hope for gains at the expense of their distant opponents, and PR made everyone concentrate his fire on political neighbours who were competing for the same clientele. Under *tripartisme* hostilities were most bitter between Communists and Socialists, and between MRP and the Right. RPF at first directed its main attack on MRP. Instead of exchanging mutual support as in a second ballot system, each party fought in isolation from all others and in special hostility to its potential allies. The bitterest blows of a PR campaign were exchanged by parties which would have to co-operate in Parliament if any government was to be formed. And in guaranteeing every party against disaster PR ensured the enemies of the regime the maximum opportunity for obstruction.

The *apparentement* system tried to palliate these consequences by putting co-operativeness at a premium and intransigence at a discount. Consequently many voters complained of being hoodwinked by the party bosses who fixed the alliances; and any arrangement which weakens the sense of civic responsibility should certainly be scrutinized with suspicion in a country where *incivisme* is so widespread. Yet the managers were not as indifferent to their clientele as was sometimes maintained. In fact *apparentements* allowed the elector two separate choices corresponding to his political priorities. Over most of the country the alliances registered the preference of most voters for the parliamentary regime against either 'presidential' or 'people's' democracy. within this framework the moderate voter could then opt for his economic, social or religious tendency. But where politics revolved around a single issue, that question became the basis of alliances; so in the west, preoccupied with its church schools, the Catholic voter could opt first for the clerical *apparentement* of MRP and RPF and secondly, within it, for the parliamentary or the 'Bonapartist' solution to the country's problems.

Nor was the pressure on the voter so clearly destructive of his sense of responsibility. His desire for a party free of trammels was wishful thinking, a utopian demand and not a political preference. To make the parliamentary system work parties had to compromise in the Assembly: was an electoral law that compelled the voter to face the fact really less honest than one encouraging his illusion that his party lived in a political vacuum? The passionate socialist hated having to choose between intransigent Communists who outraged his principles, and a temporizing SFIO which was for ever compromising them. Yet this was his only real choice. If, in his dream world, no consequences followed the fall of a government and no difficulties restrained his party from enacting its programme overnight, there was something to be said for a mechanism to make him look the nasty world in the face.

Indeed the most cogent criticism was that the compulsion was still far too weak. *Apparentements* differed from one constituency to another and so might pull deputies of the same party in opposite directions. They allowed splinter groups to try their luck without risking any penalty – for unless their enemies had an absolute majority, the splinter group's votes would revert to its allies at the count like those of an unsuccessful candidate on the second ballot.[38] They involved no commitment at all to united action by the allies, and in 1951 they actually encouraged each partner to differentiate itself by a sectarian campaign against associates who might otherwise compromise it with its own followers. They thus did nothing to help and perhaps a little to hinder co-operation between the moderate groups whose individual strength they inflated. They were simply a negative mechanism against the advocates of drastic change.[39]

Under the Fourth Republic the voter participated less than ever in choosing his government. *Scrutin d'arrondissement* had returned majorities which were clear, though often loose, unreliable and short-lived. But after a PR election there were no electoral alliances to impose a choice between the many possible combinations. *Apparentement* encouraged partnerships in the distribution of seats, but not in the campaign, so they were too negative and fragile to stand the slightest strain. Policies were therefore still decided and reversed in Parliament and not at the polls. Majorities were even less coherent and fell apart

38. M. Goguel advocated a majority list system with two ballots to force the centre parties into joint lists and a joint campaign, thus laying the foundation in the country for parliamentary co-operation. But alliances that differed regionally would destroy party discipline, and it would be hard to find a legal formula to prohibit this practice or a political majority to enact it if found – as he remarked: no. 113, p. 294.

39. On the splintering effect of *apparentement*, below, pp. 327–8. Generally, Buron, pp. 44–5.

even more rapidly than in the Third Republic, and the voters merely adjusted the bargaining strength of each party by fractional alterations which marginally influenced the balance of parliamentary power – until new alignments among the deputies transformed it. The first National Assembly opened with the Communists in office and the Conservatives in opposition; within two years the former were out and the latter in. In 1951 SFIO joined in centre alliances against RPF; by 1953 Gaullists were part of the majority and Socialists in opposition. At the 1956 election Socialists and Radicals won a common victory, yet the Republican Front of Mollet and Mendès lasted barely a month and the alliance of their parties was in ruins within two years – its normal life-span in a pre-war Chamber.

Both *scrutin d'arrondissement* and *apparentement* were devices to give more freedom of manœuvre to the men of the Centre from whom governments had to be formed, strengthening their numbers against the enemies of the regime and allowing them to choose and change their associates according to the needs of the moment. Both were often abused: for men who begin by accepting compromise as a regrettable necessity easily come to regard it as a virtue, and no group struggling for power keeps its original ideals wholly untarnished. But the new device had two particular drawbacks. First, where *scrutin d'arrondissement* looked fairer than it really was, *apparentement* seemed to produce blatantly unjust results and so helped to discredit its authors and the regime itself. Secondly it gave less flexibility: parties were more rigid, shifts of alignment more abrupt and crises more prolonged. Instead of a brief interregnum while the balance of petty groups was slightly adjusted, there was now a long one in which the big parties sparred for advantage – often ending much as they began, since they had no real alternative. In Queuille's phrase they were 'condemned to live together' by their fear of the untouchables, the opponents of the parliamentary system.

The electoral system, though subject to perpetual tinkering, underwent major reconstruction only when the political regime itself changed. Because the stakes of the game were high the rules were disputed (and the temptation to cheat on the deal was strong). But the devices used were all self-attenuating. PR protected minorities, but only fair-sized ones; *scrutin d'arrondissement* assembled majorities, but only disunited ones;[40] *apparentements* bolstered the safe parties against the menacing ones, but worked only in times of clear and present danger. Politicians were therefore almost always frustrated when they acted on their belief (or assertion) that electoral reform could revolutionize political behaviour. PR did not ensure stable disciplined parties, large constituencies did not abolish the parish pump, *apparentements* did not provide a secure basis for government, the return to *scrutin d'arrondissement* in 1958 did not check (but helped) the sweeping advance of a new party of largely unknown candidates. More humdrum calculations went equally wrong. PR did not stop the decline of MRP from its peak or the recovery of the Radicals from their hollow; *scrutin d'arrondissement* did not ruin the one or rescue the other; *apparentements* in 1956 did little good to the Right or harm to the Communists (or to the Poujadists either). The one certainty was that the

40. Until 1962?

repeated attempts to fabricate in every Parliament a new law tailored to suit the existing majority inevitably contributed to the ordinary citizen's disillusionment with politics.[41]

41. Many deputies 'thought it was premature to discuss ... an electoral law [which] should be devised in accordance with the political situation on the eve of the election': Fauvet in *Monde*, 15 January 1958. Cf. Campbell, pp. 43–5.

PART IV

THE SYSTEM

Chapter 23

VOTERS AND MEMBERS

In the early years after the war the people were screened from their rulers by the overweening organizations of three rigid parties. To the opponents of *tripartisme*, these had 'confiscated the sovereignty of the people' and it had to be restored by reducing their power. But the decline of strong parties only brought back the Third Republican regime of shifting majorities, minority manœuvres and pressure-group obstruction; and though the shifts and intrigues were often designed to exploit or respond to the voter's own changes of mood, this system was as alien to him as *tripartisme* itself. He neither understood nor approved of the politicians' game, and denounced its consequences without ever realizing his own share of responsibility for them. 'The protest movement is both the safety valve of a society divided by deep conflicts and the traditional French form of democracy.'[1]

1. THE MAN AND THE PARTY

At the Liberation all the traditional rules and assumptions were upset by the electoral law and the electorate, which both favoured the large parties of the Left and the Resistance. But when the political trend was reversed the laws were changed too. The first Council of the Republic was elected in 1946 by PR, which strengthened the machines, but the second was chosen in 1948 under a predominantly majority system with individual candidatures. Party lists were kept for the National Assembly in 1951, but *apparentement* removed the incentive to vote for the large groups. The new laws were as much a consequence as a cause of the new outlook.[2]

To a new candidate the endorsement of a party was always important, and in 1945–46 essential. His choice of party was not necessarily ideological: Bourgès-Maunoury became a Radical because Socialist candidates had to be party members for a qualifying period, and Edgar Faure because he thought (wrongly) that as MRP's standard-bearer in Vaucluse he would lose to Daladier.[3] Reputation among the active party members remained the chief qualification for endorsement in SFIO, and useful in MRP. For Communists (and Gaullists in 1951) acceptability to the national leadership was as or more important. But on the Right and Centre, parties were federations of local politicians with few militants and little discipline; and their nomination did not confer electoral potency on a candidate but recognized that he had it already, usually through past services in local government or peasant organizations. Even in 1945–46 the Radicals survived, not in their traditional strongholds, but where a local leader had kept his reputation and his right to stand. UDSR was never more than a coterie of politicians each with his local following. In 1956 its leader René Pleven deterred any potential constituency rival by

1. Hoffmann in *Revolution in World Politics*, p. 79; and cf. below, pp. 334–5, 383, 451.
2. See above, pp., 278–9, 313–14, and below, pp. 388–9.
3. Faure lost in Paris and MRP beat Daladier: Dumaine, pp. 27–8. On Bourgès-Maunoury see Bloch-Morhange, p. 22.

making a corner in endorsements and becoming candidate also of the Radicals, RGR and CNIP.

As most successful candidates were *têtes de liste*, the lower places were usually bestowed to balance the ticket.[4] Even in 1945–46 local feeling had to be respected. The rival towns of Colmar and Mulhouse shared the top two places on the MRP, Socialist and Radical (but not RPF) lists in Haut-Rhin in 1951. In 1956 there were men from Moulins, Montluçon and Vichy on four of the six main lists in Allier, and in Seine-Maritime west no party neglected Le Havre or Dieppe. Protestants expected representation in Alsace and Basques in Béarn. Veterinarians were at a premium in the countryside, and doctors everywhere – even in Paris. Peasant leaders were in universal demand. Women were thought useful, but rarely placed high; conservative parties sometimes demonstrated their egalitarianism by putting in a railway worker (last). A leading local personality might lend his prestige without seeking election; in 1956 seven senators stood in last place on RS lists, and Charles Barangé and another retiring deputy also agreed to help their successors in this way. Candidates were often chosen to appeal to circles not accessible to the *tête de liste*.[5] The Radical member for Seine-et-Marne in 1951 had a prominent local Catholic as his second, a peasant official third, and ex-Gaullist mayors fourth and fifth. Conversely, even SFIO considered it tactically impossible to head a list with two Jews.

Political balance was a delicate matter. A party strongly influenced by its militants or anxious to make a clear impression on the voter usually chose a fairly homogeneous team; MRP candidates were generally progressive in Seine but conservative in Basses-Pyrénées. But a coalition could represent its various components, a divided party could satisfy both its wings, and a politician whose voters were of different views or traditions could offer appropriate homage to both sides.[6] It was harder to face both ways in making alliances, for these might decide not only whether a party won or lost but whether it was Right or Left. In 1951 conservatives in many parties entered centre coalitions only because RPF refused their approaches. In 1956, the one RS deputy who made an *apparentement* with the Republican Front had previously been refused by their opponents; MRP deputies with shaky western seats insisted on an alliance with the Right which the party's urban militants detested; and Socialists everywhere were attacked by the Communists because their party had agreed to a few local coalitions with pro-clerical Gaullists.[7]

In the campaign itself the party organization played a far less important

4. In 1956 390 deputies had been top of their lists, 109 second, 31 third and 14 lower; only 57 % of Communists but 77 % of others were *têtes de liste*: Campbell, p. 118, and *Élections 1956*, pp. 429–430 (Dogan), 505 (Goguel).

5. *Ibid.*, pp. 430–2, 435–6nn.; *Partis et Classes*, pp. 228–30 (Gourdon on Radicals), 254 and n (Merle on CNIP), 292–3, 299–300, 314–15 (Dogan on the 1951 Assembly); Williams, no. 168, p. 152; Rose, no. 169, pp. 254–5; Pierce, no. 180, p. 403n.; Pineau, pp. 15–17; *Paysans*, pp. 510–11; Buron, pp. 35–42.

6. RGR's list in Indre-et-Loire in 1951 had three Radicals, a UDSR and a Paul Faure Socialist. Pinay's secretary stood for Tarn in 1956 with both the Gaullist and the Vichyite candidates of 1951 on his list.

7. See above, pp. 97n., 121n. also Nicholas *et al.*, no. 168, p. 153, no. 169, p. 253.

part than in Britain, as there were fewer problems of getting out the vote: no register to keep, no canvassing, official dispatch of election addresses, and on polling-day (a Sunday) no cars or party workers required. Public meetings were generally held, since the voters expected them (Marseilles had nearly 600 in the 1956 election), although many candidates doubted their utility. Outside the towns it was essential for the member or his *colistiers* to visit the mayors and local notables of as many communes as possible; in Mendès-France's largely rural constituency of Eure, the lists in 1956 averaged 72 'meetings' which were mostly of this kind. The experienced candidate adapted his speech slightly to his audience, arguing in a conservative stronghold for strengthening the moderating influence of the Senate, and in a mining town for 'associating the second chamber with the work of the sovereign National Assembly'. This conventional type of electioneering was common to all the democratic parties. But for the Communists an election was a recruiting campaign, and they occasionally used house-to-house canvassing. The Poujadists profited greatly from the active support of shopkeepers and commercial travellers.[8]

Less dependent on the organization for money and propaganda activity than a British MP, the deputy became increasingly important to it, especially in the countryside and on the political Centre and Right. Campaigns were fought at the constituency level, for there was no nation-wide press and broadcasting facilities were minimal. In the organized parties headquarters might supply literature and perhaps a little money, but candidates from the looser groups often preferred to rely on their personal reputations and to raise their financial backing locally.[9] Though the national prestige of his party affected the member's chances of re-election, among the centre groups it was rarely decisive.

To the party a strong candidate was vital, for in spite of the list system the voter still chose between men. Even in 1951 over two hundred deputies had no colleague elected from their list.[10] Occasionally a newcomer exploited the confusion caused by the vague interchangeable labels of the unorganized groups; but increasingly lists concentrated their publicity on the man and not the party.[11] Even in the well-organized parties a single leader in each constituency came to personify his movement over a wide area. When *panachage* was introduced in 1951 the elector, while still supporting his party, could repudiate one or more of its nominees and transfer a fraction of his vote to candidates on a rival list; some leaders like Jules Moch and René Pleven attracted thousands of admirers, while others were crossed off their own lists (particularly if they were in coalition with another party).[12] Five years later, when resentment against the *sortants* expressed itself in the Mendesist and

8. *Ibid.*, pp. 152–61, 250–63, 265–80; *Élections 1956*, pp. 322–52 (C. Prieur on Aveyron, p. 325 on the Senate), 353–68 (F. Essig on Eure, p. 354 on meetings), 422 (Goguel); Buron, pp. 48–61.

9. See Williams, no. 168, pp. 153–4; Buron, pp. 68–9; above, pp. 65–6, below, pp. 371–2.

10. In 1951, 209; in 1956, 281: *Élections 1956*, pp. 429–30, 505.

11. *Ibid.*, pp. 422, 504–5; also p. 418 (on confusion among independents in Haut-Rhin) and Y. Lévy, *Le problème des modes de scrutin* (1956), p. 32 (for Communists voting Trotskyist by mistake in 1951, and Mendesists misled in 1956). And see above, p. 66 n. 9.

12. Among leaders who ran behind their lists in 1951 were Georges Bidault, Pierre de Gaulle (both allied to Conservatives) and Maurice Thorez.

Poujadist revolts, some voters loyal to their old party nevertheless deleted the sitting member's name.[13]

The familiar candidate was an asset far more often than a liability, and even organized parties were reluctant to lose him. In 1946 it had cost nothing to discipline a deputy who had held his seat for only a year, but by 1951 he had sat for five and the risks of displacing him were far greater. In some areas and sectors of politics voters and even militants preferred the man to the organization, which indeed he sometimes dominated. Jacques Chaban-Delmas took the Bordeaux Radical party over to de Gaulle; the MRP federation of Charente also followed its member into RPF; its neighbour in Dordogne approved the local deputy (André Denis) in his repeated revolts and final defection to the Left. In 1946 Charles d'Aragon, another MRP left-winger (and a marquis) had headed the poll in Hautes-Pyrénées; five years later he went off to Paris to stand as a neutralist, and the party lost seven-eighths of its votes to the profit of a strong new Conservative, Jacques Fourcade, the President of the Assembly of the French Union. In Somme, where the MRP deputy turned Conservative and the Radical joined RPF, each was re-elected by his own former voters.[14]

When a party was doing well in the country it had little need to worry about discipline; once it began to do badly it could ill afford to apply it. For a recalcitrant deputy could often ensure his own political future by going over to a rising party, which could clinch its prospective victory by adopting the defector as its own candidate. Eight members stood for their old constituencies under RPF's banner in 1951, and six were successful; thirteen fought with the endorsement of another party, and seven won; and in 1956, of 32 Gaullists who had gone over to the Conservatives or RGR, 26 saved their seats. The deputy who stood as an independent had less prospect of success. In 1951 one Conservative dissident, the aged but formidable Canon Kir in Côte d'Or, acquired so much Radical, MRP and even Socialist support that he was triumphantly re-elected; in 1956 his chastened party restored him to the head of its list at the expense of a sitting member, who was beaten.[15] But this was exceptional. Of ten other deputies who stood as independents in 1951 only one was re-elected.[16] In 1956 all five lost.

However, the organization could not lay down the law to a wayward parliamentarian, for a quarrel usually hurt them both. A rebel who could not hold his seat might still deprive the party of it.[17] After 1946 only the Com-

13. Examples in Williams, no. 168, p. 172n. In 1956 Radical sitting members put their vote up 30%, new Radical candidates 80%. CNIP and MRP *sortants* also did much worse than newcomers, but Socialists and Communists did much better and Gaullists a trifle less badly; the electorate discriminated against outgoing deputies from the old majority (notwithstanding Dogan in *Élections 1956*, pp. 442–3). On conditions favouring new men or old see Buron, p. 36.

14. For the villages of Somme see J. Bugnicourt in *Paysans*, pp. 476–7, 480, cf. 471; also Professor J. Blondel kindly showed me his unpublished study of Amiens. On rebellious local parties, *AP* 1947, p. 215, 1950, p. 153; *Monde*, 26 June 1953.

15. Long, pp. 155–64 (for other examples of CNIP flexibility, above, pp. 152,154). Two other Conservatives quarrelled with their local parties and lost; so did three Socialists. In all 31 members stood for a new cause in their old seat; 17 had been MRP, and so had 5 who stood elsewhere; of these 22 only eight won (four RPF and four Conservatives).

16. M. Bessac; see above, p. 179.

17. In 1956 three ex-MRP independents lost, only one to MRP. Three Conservatives without CNIP endorsement lost; one, supported by the Bordeaux party, cost CNIP the seat.

munists dared wield the whip freely. Very few members had to retire from Parliament because of political disputes: perhaps half a dozen MRP deputies in 1951 and three in 1956, and two or three Socialists on each occasion. It became rare in the towns and almost unknown in the countryside for a deputy to be re-adopted in a lower place on the list. Against 35 non-Communists downgraded in 1946, in 1951 there were only ten (of whom three were beaten) and in 1956 eleven (five lost).[18] Laxer discipline gave the member little incentive to break with his party, unless it was on the wane (of 36 deputies who fought under a new banner in 1951, 22 were ex-MRP, and of 43 in 1956, 37 were ex-Gaullists). The public reaction against monolithic parties and the stronger position of the sitting member had swung the balance of power in his favour and given him greater freedom of action. The local organization was unlikely to cause him difficulty unless he neglected the constituency, and national headquarters would do so only against isolated individuals who flagrantly violated a cherished party principle: an MRP rebel could afford to abstain on the Japanese peace treaty, but not to campaign against the European army.

More serious problems arose when the national party clashed with a local branch. Regional differences of outlook and interest often obliged a candidate to adapt his party's appeal and policy to local needs. This bothered neither the undisciplined Right and Centre nor the opportunists of the far Left: the Communists cheerfully attacked the high cost of living in the towns and the low level of food prices in the country, and Radicals had flourished for years by suiting their views and alliances to regional circumstances. But MRP candidates were sometimes embarrassed by the conduct of colleagues from another wing of the party. SFIO was especially vulnerable; its local alliances with pro-clerical candidates in 1951 and 1956 were exploited against it elsewhere, while party headquarters had always to resist the desire of a few branches for a pact with the Communists.[19]

The Communists themselves were concerned to weaken their rivals' discipline and reinforce their own. At the Liberation they had sought immediate electoral influence and parliamentary strength, and therefore preferred well-known candidates. But in later years the leadership valued reliability more than numbers and eliminated doubtful members, notably critics of Stalin's pact with Hitler. Even in 1945 the Lot-et-Garonne branch was forbidden to renominate its hero Renaud Jean, the pre-war peasant leader and chairman of the parliamentary group, who had openly condemned the pact; and the veto was repeated in 1951. Perhaps twenty members at that election and fifteen at the next were removed or downgraded for political reasons.[20] But even the

18. Dogan in *Élections 1956*, pp. 435–8; Pierce, no. 180, pp. 403–4; Williams, no. 168, p. 171. On 1946 see below, p. 388. In urban areas about one member in five and elsewhere about one in eleven was downgraded either in 1946 or 1951. But in 1956 all victims but one were in urban areas (or semi-urban ones where the party was sure of several seats, like MRP in Alsace). The five who lost were 2 SFIO, 2 CNIP and 1 MRP.

19. By law a party's *apparentements* had to be authorized nationally, but only party discipline could stop a federation agreeing to a joint list with another party, as Vosges did in 1956. See above, pp. 97n., 172, 323.

20. In 1951 thirteen Communists were downgraded and in 1956, eight; nine and two were beaten. Politics seems to have caused most of the Communist retirements in both years. See

[*over*

Communists were more ruthless in the towns than in the country, and even their well-disciplined electorate took some account of personality.[21]

One ordinary deputy even defied the party and put it to rout. Louis Prot was a popular veteran, deputy for Somme since 1936; in 1949 a younger colleague tried to force him out. Prot resigned from the party, sent his parliamentary proxy to Thorez to prove his political orthodoxy, and publicly accused the local leaders of organizing an armed robbery at the Liberation and burning down their own headquarters to destroy the evidence. Paris ordered an inquiry, Prot's interesting speeches stopped, and after everyone had been mildly censured he settled down to nine more years of total obscurity as senior Communist deputy for Somme. Other Communist politicians also suffered from bourgeois failings, and Pierre Hervé in Finistère was the victim of a similar campaign by the local leader who had had to make room for him at the top of the list.[22]

Such disputes were more frequent – or more public – in other parties. The Gironde Radicals followed Chaban-Delmas into RPF against opposition from both his predecessor (an ex-senator whom he had displaced from the Assembly in November 1946) and his colleague Marc Dupuy, his senior in age but his junior on the list.[23] Louis Marin, the grand old man of French nationalism, was replaced in 1951 after 46 years as member for Nancy by his second, the steelmasters' spokesman Pierre André, who was barely half his age. Madame Brossolette, a highly respected senator for Seine, was a disciplined Socialist but supported the minority in the party; on this pretext she was downgraded in 1958; Georges Dardel, the local boss who took her seat, turned against Mollet a month later.[24]

It was easier under the 1951 electoral law than under simple PR for candidates to stand as individuals. As between two men of similar views in 1945–1946, either one conceded top place and the seat to the other, or else they ran separately, split their vote, and both failed. In 1951 and 1956 they could present allied lists, combine their forces, and let the voters choose between them. (This partly explains the great proliferation of lists, which averaged five

Williams, p. 353, and sources in n. 18. For Renaud Jean, Rossi, p. 446; Wright in Earle, pp. 224–5, and in no. 228, p. 41.

21. In November 1958 they often polled best, relative to the NON vote at the September referendum, where an outgoing deputy was standing. The fellow-travelling Progressive members proved to have strong personal support not transferable to the Communist party.

22. Hervé: *Dieu et César*, pp. 26–7. Prot: *Monde*, 28 and 29 April, 14 and 21 May, 14 June 1949; *Humanité*, 9 September, *Figaro*, 7 and 11 September. He may have had a still stronger weapon. According to *Histoire*, ii. 27 the decision to approach the Nazi authorities in 1940 was not made, as the official line claims, by local militants who were later disgraced for it, but on direct orders from Thorez and Duclos to a central committee member (later killed by the Germans) who was deputy for Somme; he obeyed but disapproved, and gave the records to 'a comrade from the Somme ... who has already made use of them by way of a shield'. In 1958 Prot fought a hopeless seat 'but this apparently was against the wishes of the Paris headquarters'; his younger rival (René Lamps) was narrowly beaten in the best seat, Amiens: see J. Blondel in *Elections Abroad*, pp. 95, 101–2.

23. Dupuy's strength lay outside Bordeaux, where Chaban-Delmas was mayor. In 1951 he persuaded the Assembly to make Gironde into two constituencies; but a party conference (held in the absence of his supporters) did not renominate him: *Monde*, 22 May and 2 June 1951.

24. See above, pp. 93, 100n.

per seat in 1945–46, seven in 1951, and ten in 1956.[25]) Thus in 1950 the Socialists in Pyrénées-Orientales were split by a quarrel over control of the local newspaper between the veteran deputy and president of the departmental council, Louis Noguères, and the young party secretary, Arthur Conte. The organization supported its secretary and was disaffiliated by Paris. But *apparentement* solved the difficulty; at the 1951 election Conte headed a list of his own in unfriendly alliance with SFIO, Radicals and MRP. He ran well ahead of the official Socialist, affiliated to the SFIO group in the Assembly, and was soon readmitted to the fold.[26]

Relations between competitors did not always permit this happy solution. Some disappointed candidates preferred to fight on their own and so damage (or coerce) those who had repudiated them. In Paris, where the law allowed no alliances, a UDSR candidate in 1956 was accused of splitting the Mendesist vote; he replied that he had accepted second place on the Radical list but then found it had been offered to seventeen others. In Calvados Joseph Laniel belatedly picked as his second a young local councillor who had begun a vigorous campaign against the sitting members in general and his future leader in particular.

If list voting had not eliminated personality from general elections, the individualist had still more scope when by-elections were restored in 1951. In Paris he might reach half a million voters, which was cheap publicity for a politically-minded novelist, a commercially-minded restaurant owner or an earnest-minded crank. In 1952 the founder-president of the International League of Illegitimate Children contested a Paris seat, demanding 23 reforms in the interests of his fellows and the restoration of French as the sole language of diplomacy. Even at a general election independents were not always deterred by the need to form a complete list. Two Paris constituencies had nineteen lists each in 1956. In 1951 6,000 citizens of Allier voted for five members of one family, who appropriately called their list 'Republican Concentration'. A motorists' candidate in Bordeaux urged everyone to strike two names off their own party's list and *panacher* in his favour, which would harm nobody and give him two seats; 1,500 electors (or their equivalent in fractions) responded. In north-eastern Paris there were 4,500 votes for the list of *Mécontents, anti-partis et indépendants nationaux*. Five years later a similar appeal won two and a half million votes and fifty seats.

2. THE CONSTITUENCY REPRESENTATIVE

The function of a party within the regime was to defend the values and interests of a group of prudent and not too discontented voters; its spokesman was normally a local man they knew and trusted. But the protest candidate exploited his fresh appeal and his freedom from sordid parliamentary habits.

25. Campbell, p. 117; Dogan in *Élections 1956*, pp. 426–9 (the proliferation was all on the Right); Goguel in *ibid.*, p. 504; *Inégalités*, p. 319. Pierce, no. 180, p. 402 reckons seven 'genuine' lists per seat in 1951 and eight in 1956. For the Poujadists exploiting this provision, see Appendix VI.

26. He won many non-Socialist votes (and kept them in 1956). But he was far behind the Communist, a champion of private property, dear wine and tomatoes, and no imports from Spain: see Williams, p. 354.

True Gaullists believed with their leader that the 'higher interests of France' were 'quite different from the immediate advantage of Frenchmen'; regarding themselves as representatives of the nation as a whole, they often made it all too plain that the particular territorial base into which the party leaders had 'parachuted' them was fortunate to have the honour of returning them to Paris – an attitude that cost them dear in 1956.[27] The Poujadists, in contrast, were an ostentatiously provincial movement in revolt against the wicked capital. Their candidates combined the appeals of local origins and political novelty – except in Paris itself where they deliberately presented outsiders. The Communists, with their priceless asset of a disciplined following, placed their men and their allies where they could do most good: when Pierre Cot's seat in Savoie was unsafe they moved him to Lyons, Pierre Hervé was sent to head the list in Finistère, and Roger Garaudy and Waldeck-Rochet, as they rose in the party hierarchy, were promoted from provincial constituencies to stand in the capital. But they too presented familiar local figures in the rural departments. In every party discipline was stricter in the towns, where the member's personality counted for less than in the individualist-minded countryside.

The new electoral law did not lighten the member's burden of constituency duties. Indeed it increased the pressure on the government supporter, who heard from his own followers throughout the department, from people with a claim on a ministry held by his party, and from opposition voters who doubted whether their favourite member had influence enough to help them. In return he could write at election time to mayors of his party that their village was at last to have its new school or that the recently abandoned bus service was to be resumed (and sly mayors with more partisan fervour than social conscience were even said to slow up house building till their party came to power in Paris). Moreover, the ministerialist's constituency work not only made friends 'but above all it neutralizes enemies. A Communist mayor devoted to his rural commune has become used to writing to a Conservative when he has need of a deputy; they have come to work together on a non-political basis. It will be hard for the mayor to denounce the member and try to defeat him.'[28]

Even Mendès-France did not disdain to supplement his exposure of conservative follies in Indo-China or North Africa by pointing with pride to the housing achievements of his team of local mayors. A few national figures like Antoine Pinay and Paul Ramadier might say little about constituency problems – but only a long and famous record of local services allowed them to do so. For the deputy who neglected his department was not lightly forgiven, however worthy his reasons. M. E. Naegelen, Governor-General of Algeria for three years before the 1951 election, prudently migrated from his Alsatian seat to the distant Basses-Alpes. André Philip, a devotee of the Council of Europe, was badly beaten at Lyons; his Strasbourg colleague François de

27. Below, p. 429. Quotation: C. de Gaulle, *Le Salut*, p. 28. Types of candidate: Buron, p. 36.

28. *Élections 1956*, pp. 331–2 (C. Prieur on Aveyron). Also Waline, p. 84, quoting Madame Viénot's letter resigning her seat in 1947 because the new system imposed such a physical strain; Wylie, pp. 215–16, 223–7, quoting letters about a village school at the 1951 election; Lavau, no. 141, p. 33, on sly mayors; Dogan in *Paysans*, pp. 225–7; '"subsidyism" is the basis of the electoral life of our countryside', C. d'Aragon in *ibid.*, pp. 512–13; Buron, pp. 24–6.

Menthon profited from the popularity of his second, a local man who answered letters. Ministers were usually safe at the head of their lists – even where *panachage* and preferential voting showed that numbers of their political followers regarded office and fame as no substitute for presence in the district. Lesser figures were in much more danger. An Alsatian MRP member who had repeatedly attacked his party's North African policies was not re-nominated in 1956: Parisians assumed that he was suffering for his liberal views, but he himself explained that his sin was his unwillingness to attend all local ceremonies.[29]

Particularist feeling was strongest among the peripheral groups – Bretons, Basques, Catalans, Alsatians – where a candidate was handicapped if he could not speak dialect. In 1951, when RPF 'parachuted' General Koenig into Strasbourg (the party's birthplace), he had to 'attend his own meetings rather than take part in them' and rarely opened his mouth. Five years later, still a 'foreigner', he was thought to have cost his declining party thousands of votes.[30] A Gaullist in 1951 put out literature in Yiddish in a Jewish quarter of Paris, and in 1956 Socialists had handbills in Arabic for North Africans and in Polish for immigrant miners. Other SFIO leaflets were designed for railwaymen, young people, and Communists; and the Communists organized many of their urban meetings for particular groups – women, youth, teachers, the badly-housed, or transport workers.

Some constituencies or regions depended on a single trade or industry. No special pressure-group was needed to persuade members from the Midi to defend the winegrowers. A doctor-deputy from Hérault, in his concern for hygiene, naturally defended a ban on *apéritifs* based on spirits, like *pastis*, and demanded one on Coca-Cola. In the 1951 election the local Radical member wrote to the Radical premier about the sad state of the wine trade; the Conservative followed suit next day; their MRP rival wrote to the MRP minister of agriculture the day after, and then the Socialist, Jules Moch, trumped them all by taking the matter to the cabinet. In fruit, beet and wine departments in 1956 the prudent candidate tempered his condemnation of alcoholism (women had votes) with a repudiation of any specific measure proposed against it.[31] Coastal members naturally joined to support port improvements and shipbuilding subsidies, but quarrelled over their precise destination. In the regions on which the church schools conflict centred, the activity of APEL and the *Comité de défense laïque* was perhaps as superfluous as it was intense, for even without organized pressure no candidate could win support without committing himself to one side or the other.

29. *Élections 1956*, pp. 335–7 (Ramadier), 362–3 (Mendès-France), 413 (Alsace); Williams, no. 168, pp. 165–6; *Monde*, 16 June 1951 (Menthon); Buron, pp. 81–90.

30. *Monde*, 4 June 1951: the general's predecessor (who changed his constituency at both this election and the next) 'doubtless did not appear sufficiently often in a province ... where people insist on "a flesh-and-blood deputy", "a deputy who is one of us"'. Cf. F. G. Dreyfus in *Élections 1956*, p. 415. In Alpes-Maritimes in 1951 the general who headed the RPF list came from an old local family and it was his second, an aircraft manufacturer who allegedly contributed largely to party funds, who was 'rather out of his element' and had to be kept quiet.

31. *Figaro*, 11 June 1951 (Hérault), cf. *Monde*, 21 May. 'Enfin nous nous attacherons à la formule qui permettra aux petits bouilleurs de cru de concilier leurs revendications bien compréhensibles avec le programme de lutte contre l'alcoolisme': Radical election address in Vienne, 1956, quoted by Thomas, no. 170, p. 270. And see below, p. 357.

Large constituencies made the member's task of reconciling local interests harder, perhaps to the public advantage. Even in mainly agricultural departments candidates were wise to pay attention to minorities of industrial workers, who formerly had often been confined to a single small district. Conversely, outside Paris almost every deputy had some rural voters in his area.[32] To cover his wider parish the member had to spend more time in his department than before the war – yet after all his efforts he knew his constituents far less well than under *scrutin d'arrondissement*. Mendès-France, who had experience of both systems, favoured the small area because the deputy could explain his unpopular votes personally to all the influential men of his district, and so build support which enabled him to resist the pressure-groups.[33]

Even in the cities local services paid impressive parliamentary dividends. Like an American senator with seniority, a French political leader was valued by his constituents for his national reputation which reflected glory on the district, but also because – as he was not slow to remind them – their town or department gained from having its claims pressed by an 'ambassador to Paris' on whom the fate of the minister's bills or the length of his tenure might one day depend. Lyons was a Radical bastion while Herriot lived, though less secure as he grew less efficient as mayor. Rapid Socialist progress in Marseilles owed much to Gaston Defferre's local administration, and at Bordeaux Jacques Chaban-Delmas kept a powerful machine when disaster struck the Gaullist cause elsewhere. Even in the capital the mayor of Vincennes saved his seat in 1956 through the support of his own suburb, which made up only one-twelfth of his electorate but gave him half his votes; and no rising party of the Right could afford (though it might have preferred) to reject the eagerly proffered alliance of the master of the Paris left bank, Édouard Frédéric-Dupont.

The successful politician of the Third or Fourth Republic established his local base among fellow-citizens who judged him on his constructive achievements as well as his ideology; if he had no base he was taken much less seriously by his fellow-practitioners. The Communists were successful municipally because they were efficient and capable administrators; the Poujadists never penetrated local government at all; many Gaullists who swept to the Assembly on a wave of protest in 1958 were surprised to see the 'man of the System' they had expelled from Parliament comfortably returned to his mayoral chair six months later.[34] At a municipal election the voter was electing councillors to support or oppose a mayor whose work he could evaluate

32. 'In my capacity as a rural deputy ... I was often in conflict with my colleagues from the towns. On the other hand, when I was elected on a list system I could reconcile the interests of countryside and town instead of setting one against the other, and thus I could defend the true general interest': V. Auriol, *JO* 2 August 1945, p. 1762 (quoted *Inégalités*, p. 41). But not all members tried. In Eure in 1956 the CNI candidate was a peasant leader who talked of nothing but agriculture; his ARS opponent (the prince de Broglie) concentrated exclusively on the towns: F. Essig in *Élections 1956*, p. 359; cf. Williams, no. 168, p. 170.

33. P. Mendès-France, *La politique et la vérité* (1958), pp. 266–7. But cf. *Paysans*, p. 214.

34. Bloch-Morhange, pp. 175–6; Hoffmann, pp. 405–6 (the Poujadist vote dropped by two-thirds in the municipal elections of early 1956, while it was still rising in parliamentary by-elections); Blondel's study of Amiens (see n. 14); Wylie, p. 238; *Paysans*, pp. 42, 510–13; Williams and Harrison, pp. 112–13; Chapman, *Introduction to French Local Government*, pp. 222–3; Buron, pp. 34, 90–7, 139.

from his own experience. But at a parliamentary election his attitude was quite different. This was an opportunity to send to Paris an envoy either to defend his interests and outlook, or to express his resentments. Both to the prudent majority and to the angry minority the deputy's function was negative: protective obstruction for the one, denunciatory obstruction for the other. In each camp only a few voters imagined that the politician might play a more positive role in supporting a real ministry with a real programme. But this was not because the ordinary Frenchman was incapable of thinking constructively about politics. In local government, for all its limited powers, there was a circuit of confidence between rulers and people. In the National Assembly, for all its omnipotence, there was none.

3. THE MEMBER OF PARLIAMENT

The protest voter in indignant revolt against the political regime was likely to turn to a candidate from his own background, who shared his exasperation and would not be seduced by the wiles of the System. Most Poujadist deputies were small shopkeepers, like the butcher from Haute-Savoie who thought politics a 'métier instable' and kept his shop open at week-ends (wisely: he was unseated). Many Communist members sprang from the working class. But to voters who supported the regime, their deputy was a spokesman for their ideas and an advocate for their interests; it was more important that he should fulfil these roles effectively than that he should himself be one of themselves. Professional men were therefore even more over-represented in the French than in other legislatures. Bodley remarked long ago that half the deputies came from the tiny professional class, and included more lawyers than men engaged – like five-sixths of their countrymen – in industry, commerce or agriculture. In 1946 those three occupations provided 204 deputies out of 544, and the professions 281. Among the 378 non-Communists, lawyers outnumbered workers and peasants by 69 to 62 and teachers businessmen by 57 to 54. Wage-earners were 177 in 1946, 155 ten years later; under half were manual workers, who were nearly all Communists. Middle-class preponderance was still greater in the conservative 1951 Assembly, and in the upper house.[35]

Nevertheless, politics was one of the few ways to rise rapidly in the stratified French social system. Few members had been eminent in another profession before election to Parliament; and indeed, ever since Bodley's day, the old ruling class had lamented its own alienation from the regime and the people by complaining that 'the best men keep out of politics'. In the Assembly there was no social equivalent to the old school tie, and a title did not always win Conservative hearts; one department was represented by the crypto-Communist son of a marquis and a small-town solicitor of Eurasian origin who belonged to the Peasant party. The few women, usually Communist or MRP, dwindled from 32 deputies in 1945 to 19 in 1956, and from 22 senators in 1946 to 9 in 1958.[36] Though there was no locality rule, carpet-baggers were

35. Hamon, no. 121, pp. 548–53; Bodley, ii. 155–63; Husson, ii. xxx; Dogan's tables (see p. 68n.); cf. Williams, p. 206n.; overseas members omitted. On senators see above, p. 289.

36. Hamon, no. 121, p. 549. Women and wage-earners were more numerous among candidates, to balance the ticket, but they usually had low places with no chance of election.

unpopular in the provinces, especially among the traditional parties. Contrary to the popular legend that politicians were excitable men from the Midi, more northerners represented southern seats than *vice versa*; but outside the capital most deputies sat for the department where they had been born.[37] The member's contact with his electors often extended beyond his postbag, his weekly visits and his local government work. Like American congressmen, many deputies had deep roots in their districts and were 'representative' of their people not only in politics.

In Parliament, as in the barrack-room, men from different classes and provinces met and mixed freely. Often the most valuable contacts occurred within the party groups, and as these were sometimes more restricted occupationally than the Assembly as a whole, the geographical melting-pot was more effective than the social. But in so diverse a country the lobby fulfilled an important function as a forum for exchanging experiences, for the prejudiced newcomer soon discovered that 'foreigners' from other regions and 'enemies' with other faiths had personal problems and temptations not unlike his own. He learned the need for compromise between rival groups, opposing interests, even conflicting ideals. Even the famous Gaullist general or Radical lawyer might benefit from meeting less distinguished compatriots on equal terms.[38]

The lobby kept down the temperature of domestic conflict. For Parliament was a club in which success went to the man with many friends and no enemies: the bargainer rather than the fighter. Before the rise of the Communist party, Robert de Jouvenel noted that 'there is more difference between two revolutionaries, one of whom is a deputy, than between two deputies, one of whom is a revolutionary'.[39] Those who suffered from the ingratitude of their 'common enemy, the voter' quite frequently found new public employment from ministers of other parties. Of the leading Socialists defeated in 1951, André Philip was promptly appointed to the Economic Council, Paul Ramadier to the ILO, and J. R. Guyon to the chair of the Alcohol Commission. Even when SFIO was in resolute opposition, Jules Moch represented France in disarmament negotiations for years and M. E. Naegelen was offered the Moroccan residency by Laniel. Though such political appointments were usually criticized, they were often strictly justified by merit; and parliamentary life would not necessarily have been healthier if the livelihood of all the members – and their families – had depended exclusively on their electoral survival.

Members recognized that many opponents were also colleagues. Just as the governmental parties installed political mechanisms that were usually self-attenuating, so they carried on most of their controversies with moderation and rarely exploited their victories to excess. When Frenchmen were needlessly divided the quarrel was often fomented by the enemies of the regime to split and weaken its defenders.[40] Yet even among the protest parties only the Communists resisted (not quite completely) the temptations of the System; the

37. Under half of RPF's deputies but over 60% of CNIP and SFIO were local born. Only one provincial member in ten was born in Paris. (My calculations.)

38. See Hamon, no. 117, pp. 389–90; no. 121, especially pp. 559–60.

39. *La République des camarades* (1914), pp. 16–17.

40. Above, p. 319; below, pp. 315–16, 450–2. Even the insurrectionaries of 1958 chose to show strength rather than use it.

others were absorbed by it within two years of their election. The parliamentary shock-absorber thus cushioned the edifice of French government from the full impact of waves of popular discontent. But the groundswell remained, and exasperation with the politician who talked revolt in his constituency and compromise in Paris contributed to the low repute of his profession in France.

This was undeserved. Most members of the Fourth Republic's Parliaments had been subjected to an unusually severe test of patriotism and courage, for the Resistance and the Free French movement were their principal recruiting grounds. In intellectual capacity the National Assembly certainly stood comparison with the House of Commons. Among leaders and 'back-benchers' alike the great majority were conscientious, well-intentioned and honest men.[41] If the deputy's standing was lower than in the great days of the Third Republic, this was more a result of major social changes breaking the traditional lines of political communication than of any decline in personal quality. Antoine Pinay thought his colleagues in the Fourth Republic better than those of the Third. Another acute observer (with little love for the régime and none for the Resistance) thought that a third of his fellow-members were at once able, disinterested and wholly devoted to their duties; and that as human material the parliamentarians were much superior to their economic, professional or official opposite numbers.[42]

But theirs was a thankless task, for in France more than elsewhere the 'fretful constituent' clamoured for incompatibles and blamed his representative when he did not get them. The cowardly or cynical politician therefore talked one language in his department and another to his colleagues; the conscientious member patiently educated his voters in compromise, explaining the limits of the budget, the price of economic progress, the choice of evils abroad, or the legitimate claims of other classes or regions.[43] But since no party was ever clearly responsible for the government of the country, the most public-spirited member could never be judged on a clear record: only on proposals he and his friends would never have the power to execute, eked out by explanations of the difficulties frustrating them.

This state of affairs exasperated the voters, yet they were themselves largely responsible for it. Choosing deputies to oppose authority, they prevented the emergence of a government effective enough to make contact with the people – who, having no contact with their rulers, chose deputies to oppose, 'using their franchise not to build the State but to protect themselves against it'.[44] That choice, rather than the human frailties of the members, ensured that obstruction always had the advantage over construction in the French Parliament. Yet how could the voter be expected to regard a general election as an opportunity to choose a government, when the deputies cherished their claim to incarnate – and interpret – the will of the people? Before 1940 the majority

41. Noël, pp. 102; Hamon, no. 121, p. 558; Priouret, *Députés*, p. 235; Isorni, *Silence*, pp. 15–16. Senator René Laniel was expelled for business irregularities; the first police action against him had been taken while his brother was premier. Also Buron, p. 107.

42. Isorni, *Silence*, pp. 16–17 and (for Pinay) 36–7. For the social changes see below, pp. 445–7.

43. Cf. accounts of meetings in *Élections 1956* (F. Essig on Eure and C. Prieur on Aveyron, especially p. 340) and in Nicholas *et al.* (Thomas, no. 170, on Vienne, and Rose, no. 169, on Pas-de-Calais).

44. Goguel, no. 113, p. 298.

which the voters thought they had returned never lasted more than two years after the general election. After 1946 its duration was shorter still. In the first National Assembly the 'big three' coalition broke up six months from the election, in the second the Third Force was dislocated within three months and RPF disrupted within nine, and in the third the Republican Front never came to life at all.

The elector therefore felt he had no share in choosing his rulers. So, if he belonged to the large minority of Frenchmen who were exasperated with their own condition or that of their country, he cast a protest vote for a party – Communist or Poujadist, perhaps Gaullist or Mendesist – which could express his resentment loudly enough to be heard in the 'house without windows' where the deputies sat; and unless he was on the extreme Left a new man or movement could always count on a welcome from him. If he belonged to the majority which distrusted sweeping changes, or bitter words, or violent methods, then he cast a defensive vote for a deputy, preferably a familiar and trustworthy figure, from whichever of the safe centre parties would best uphold his personal ideas or interests and oppose 'adventures'.

'It has become conventional to think of human power as a plague to be classed with the plagues of nature: the odious government, the levelling mistral, the flooding Durance.' This was the heritage of intermittent abuse of authority by established governments or their revolutionary enemies, and of continuing arbitrary rule by a remote and centralized bureaucracy which the *ancien régime* had developed and its successors perfected. 'For several decades . . . French voters have chosen their members of parliament with the idea much less of delegating to them the task of government than of acquiring in them intercessors with the mysterious *ils* who represent Power, and gaining protection against the actions of Power.'[45]

45. *Ibid.* 'Plague': Wylie, p. 332.

Chapter 24

POLITICS AND THE STATE MACHINE

Long before she had democratic institutions, France possessed an exceptionally capable, self-confident, powerful and centralized bureaucracy. It recruited many of her ablest men, and French higher education, which was largely geared to its needs, produced a series of tightly specialized professional groups bound together by similar social origins, a common training, and intense *esprit de corps*. This massive machine was not easily controlled by amateur and transient ministers handicapped by unstable parliamentary majorities and divided coalition cabinets. But the politician had some help in penetrating the bureaucratic jungle from his small personal staff or *cabinet* (though in the Fourth Republic this was itself often drawn from the higher civil service). The officials, conversely, found that the diffusion of political responsibility sometimes allowed them to make counter-forays into the parliamentary field.

The bureaucracy adapted itself to weak political leadership by devising procedures and institutions to carry on the nation's government when ministries faltered or fell, and internal controls to investigate and check its own abuses.[1] These tasks of inspection and supervision were performed by the services with most prestige, the *grands corps de l'État*, which attracted the ablest entrants to the civil service and gave them an intimate knowledge of its working. Often their members were promoted to senior departmental posts or seconded to other important public duties. They imposed some unity on a bureaucratic empire made up of many ancient and autonomous baronies.

Some old ministries like Justice, War and Education had for years been the official Parisian bastions of closed and proud professions, which jealously guarded their ramparts against interfering outsiders – such as ministers with minds of their own.[2] History sometimes gave a department a pronounced political character. Education was once a missionary ministry of the anticlericals, and the rural schoolteachers were the 'republican clergy'; Interior was responsible for the defence of the regime and was kept out of Catholic hands; but the foreign office was a stronghold of the old Catholic families who would serve the state only in a military or diplomatic capacity. Under *tripartisme* these departmental differences were accentuated by the parties, which each 'colonized' the ministries it controlled. And for all its great administrative reforms the Fourth Republic never brought under proper control the state machine overseas. Reflecting the outlook and interests of each local European colony, this imperial bureaucracy was protected by political defences in depth as solid as those of the 'corporative' ministries in Paris. Its resistance to reforms helped to provoke the colonial wars which sapped the loyalty of the army and police, and finally undermined the regime itself.

1. Diamant, no. 70, pp. 147–66; and in W. J. Siffin, ed., *Toward the Comparative Study of Public Administration* (Bloomington, Indiana, 1959), pp. 182–218.

2. Cf. Lavau, *Pressures*, pp. 63, 87n.; and below, p. 378. These 'corporative' ministries remained resistant to outside control in the Fifth Republic.

1. THE 'GRANDS CORPS' AND THE 'CABINETS'

After the war a reform inspired by Michel Debré set up an *École nationale d'administration* (ENA) through which all entrants to the higher civil service had to pass. It did not go far to democratize recruitment, since French higher education remained beyond the reach of sons (though not grandsons) of manual workers and peasants. A separate entry competition for lower-grade civil servants went some way to alter the balance, but the *grands corps* of the Fourth Republic continued to be staffed by the sons of the comfortably-off – often, indeed, of higher civil servants. But ENA did break down the co-option which had flourished in certain *grands corps* in the past, when each service controlled its own entry through scores of separate examinations; and perhaps it helped to diminish the conservatism which had made the higher civil service so suspect to the traditional Left. Other factors contributed to the change. The climate of public and especially student opinion had altered greatly, and the conservative *École libre des sciences politiques*, through which almost every high official had passed, was incorporated into the university of Paris and lost its right-wing bias.[3] The higher civil service of the Fourth Republic therefore embraced every shade of political opinion (though Communism was under-represented). The commonest attitudes were a pragmatic zeal for efficiency and modernization, an exasperation with the political defenders of the incapable and the backward, and a sense of duty to uphold the general interest of the community amid the clamour of the pressure-groups and the competitive demagogy of the parties. The high officials 'feel they make history more than the politicians, unstable, incompetent and condemned to superficiality'.[4]

In the absence of effective and respected political controls the bureaucracy had developed powerful institutions to check its own abuses. Legal supervision was exercised by a jurisdiction separate from the ordinary courts, the *Conseil d'État*, which tried cases involving the state. Originally subject to governmental pressure, it became completely independent early in the Third Republic. There were purges in 1879, 1940 and 1945, but otherwise no member was ever removed until 1960. Protected by this independence and fortified by their personal experience of administration, its members made the *Conseil* into a tribunal affording the French citizen better remedies against misuse of power by public authorities than Englishmen enjoyed under Dicey's rule of law. Its jurisprudence frequently made law on highly controversial matters. In the Third Republic a conservative *Conseil*, in tune with prevailing political opinion, for years prevented any development of municipal socialism; and in the Fourth it defined limits on the right to strike of state employees, which according to the Preamble to the constitution should have been laid down by

3. Brindillac, no. 28, pp. 865–7; R. Catherine in *Partis et Classes*, pp. 112–21. Also Bottomore, no. 25; Feyzioglu, nos. 91–2; Diamant (n. 1), pp. 159–62 and 195–7; Bertrand in Robson, ed., *The Civil Service in Britain and France*, pp. 170–84; Chapman, *The Profession of Government*, pp. 80–3, 88–94, 115–24; C. Chavanon in *Aspects*, pp. 161–5; P. Lalumière, *L'Inspection des finances* (1959), pp. 15–21, 28–49.

4. Brindillac, no. 28, pp. 869–77 (quotation, p. 870). Ehrmann is more pessimistic in *Business*, pp. 257–71, a little less so in no. 85, pp. 534–55. Cf. Catherine, *loc. cit.*, pp. 133–6; and below, pp. 343, 345–6.

law.[5] While the *Conseil*, like British and American courts, was willing to allow the government wider freedom of action in war or major civil emergency, it frequently found against the authorities in normal times. It was the recognized protector of the rights of civil servants against the state, and in 1954 it declared illegal the government's attempt to exclude five students suspected of Communism from the entrance examination to ENA. Besides its judicial functions it was often called on to advise the government on the legal aspects of administration, and occasionally on major points such as the extent to which Parliament could constitutionally authorize the government to alter a law. In the Fourth Republic yet another of the *Conseil*'s many tasks, that of advising on the drafting of new government bills and decrees, took on an importance it had rarely enjoyed in the Third.[6]

The bureaucracy also developed checks on its own financial abuses. One of the most powerful and closely-knit of the *grands corps* was the *Inspection des finances*, on whose ability and cohesion the power of the finance ministry largely rested. Its members were in constant demand for key posts elsewhere in the civil service – and in private business, which often tempted them to leave their ill-paid government employment at about forty.[7] Politicians of the Left suspected them of collusion with the 'money power', and in 1946 the Socialist party proposed to abolish the corps altogether. But as SFIO's influence declined the *inspecteurs* soon regained their grip on most of the key economic positions, wrested influence in the nationalized industries from the technicians, and even annexed leading posts in the most exclusive and jealous rival corps, the diplomatic service. 'Under the Fourth Republic as under the Third, we are governed by the *Inspection des finances*.'[8]

Another powerful inspectorate was the *Cour des Comptes*, an ancient administrative tribunal which gained status and influence in the Fourth Republic through the constitution (Article 18 authorized the Assembly to use it for inquiries into public finance) and the Assembly's standing orders (which encouraged direct co-operation between it and the leaders of the finance committee). Expanding its activities and extending its inquiries more widely outside Paris, the *Cour* also audited the public accounts more promptly than it had done before the war. In the early post-war years vigorous reports criticizing extravagance and lax administration gave unprecedented publicity to its work, provided opposition parties with political ammunition, and led to some important improvements. Parliament specifically protected its activities from governmental restriction under the special powers law of August 1948, and

5. The most comprehensive of the many accounts is Freedeman; see also Chapman, *op. cit.*, pp. 229–41, and on the judicial side, C. J. Hamson, *Executive Discretion and Judicial Control* (1954). For municipal socialism see Freedeman, pp. 105–6, 160–1; for the right to strike, *ibid.*, pp. 157–8, Soubeyrol, pp. 152–3, Arné, pp. 158–9, and cf. above, p. 294n.

6. Hamson, pp. 22–41 (ENA); for legislation, *Institutions*, i. 314–24; above, pp. 260, 271–3.

7. Brindillac, no. 128, pp. 863–4, 867–8; Ehrmann, *Business*, pp. 263–4, 267–70; Lalumière, pp. 7, 62–91, 127–75. This *pantouflage* seems to have diminished in the Fourth Republic: see Ehrmann, no. 85, p. 552 and n.; *Entreprise*, no. 384 (19 January 1963), p. 35; Brindillac, no. 28, p. 870. Cf. below, p. 379.

8. M. Waline, 'Les résistances techniques de l'administration au pouvoir politique', in *Politique et Technique*, p. 171. SFIO: Lalumière, pp. 7–8; Catherine, *loc. cit.*, p. 146. Diplomatic; Williams, p. 264, Grosser, pp. 49, 70. And see Buron, pp. 216–7; below, p. 343.

through its subsidiaries they were extended over the social security system and the nationalized industries.[9]

The influence of the *grands corps* was widely felt in the many detached duties to which their members were constantly called, especially in the *cabinet* of a minister. This was a small private office, restricted in 1911 to seven members and in 1948 to ten (these limits, often evaded in the Third Republic, were broadly observed in the Fourth, though not in the post-war interregnum).[10] Few French government departments were subordinated like British ones to a single official head; so, if contacts between the different divisions (*directions*) were not to resemble diplomatic dealings between independent powers, the *cabinet* had to co-ordinate them. It also performed liaison duties with other ministries. But the regular officials often resented its activities. Its members inevitably thought in terms of their minister's plans and career rather than longer-term interests; were properly concerned with parliamentary and tactical considerations, and harassed and hurried a machine that was rarely rapid and sometimes lethargic; insisted on taking over politically difficult questions for which they were not always technically qualified; and frequently proved more sympathetic to pressure-groups than their regular colleagues.[11]

These grievances partly reflected the very variable quality of *cabinets*. A minister could and did choose them from his family, party or home town, especially for liaison tasks with the press, Parliament or constituency for which such political nominees were best qualified.[12] Some politicians were ruined by their bad appointments. Some of Félix Gouin's collaborators, recruited from his Marseilles local base, used his authority to traffic illegally in Algerian wine; and Roger Peyré, the contact-man of the 'scandal of the generals', plied his trade with *cabinets* rather than with ministers themselves.[13] Yet, rightly used, the *cabinet* was a valuable if not indispensable instrument for the politician, who without it would have found it hard to resist the persuasive advice of his 'mandarins'. The system allowed able young men to shake the complacency of their comfortable elders. Some political leaders formed 'brains trusts' of expert advisers, who worked with them out of office, came in with them, and followed them from one post to another. The *directeur* or *chef de cabinet* of a senior minister, like Jacques Duhamel under Edgar Faure or Abel Thomas under Bourgès-Maunoury, could wield much more power at an earlier age than a parliamentarian in junior office.[14] But ministers

9. Details in Duverger, *Institutions financières*, pp. 411–7, 420–2, 429–31; *Institutions*, i. 325–333; Williams, pp. 265–6.

10. *Institutions*, i. 270–4, 277; Seurin, no. 198 (on numbers, pp. 1223–8), and King, no. 131, pp. 436–7; Buron, p. 181.

11. Massigli, *Sur quelques maladies de l'État*, Chapter 3; R. Catherine, *Le fonctionnaire français* (1961), pp. 300–21, 329–31; Seurin, no. 198, pp. 1284–6; Meynaud, pp. 201–2; Lavau, *Pressures*, p. 85; Wahl in Beer and Ulam, pp. 202–3; *Paysans*, p. 249 and n.

12. The surnames of seventeen ministers (nine of them Socialists) occur among the members of *cabinets* between 1945–55 (cf. n. 21); and five Corsicans served in the *cabinet* of one minister from that island: Seurin, no. 198, p. 1234 nn. Young politicians frequently moved from a *cabinet* to Parliament, like Léon Blum, Edgar Faure and Maurice Faure. Cf. Buron, pp. 176–9, 183–4.

13. 'Generals': see below, p. 348. Cf. Brogan, *France*, p. 660.

14. In 1954–55 the *directeurs de cabinet* of Mendès-France and Mitterrand investigated the 'leakages affair' (on which see below, p. 348); Pinay's organized the return of the Sultan of Morocco: and Bourgès-Maunoury's planned the redistribution of constituencies for an (abortive)

[*over*

in the Fourth Republic tended much more than in the past to choose for senior *cabinet* posts high civil servants who combined a modicum of political sympathy with administrative expertise.[15] In some 'technical' ministries an official might make his career in the minister's *cabinet*, passing from one politician to his successor. These trends minimized the risk of corruption and the danger of friction with the permanent staff, but they reduced the advantages as well as the drawbacks of the system.[16]

2. PARTY POLITICS AND DEPARTMENTAL RIVALRIES

Political influence on the administration came through many channels besides the *cabinet*. The tradition of parliamentary intervention to obtain minor favours was long-established. In 1949 a minister of justice received in nine months 11,700 requests from deputies for pardons or promotions for their clients, or one per member per fortnight. In 1957 a minister of the interior found that of 800 candidates for twenty posts as police commissioner, 600 had the support of a member of parliament.[17] Yet this pressure was a nuisance rather than a menace; deputies often forwarded requests which they hardly pretended to support, and officials treated these in the spirit in which they were sent.[18]

Much more serious was the influence of party politics on senior appointments, which became systematic under *tripartisme* when the three government parties parcelled out the administration between them. But the worst of the abuses were caused by the Communists' bid to set up a state within the state, and ended with their departure.[19] Some of their appointees were removed, and many other officials who had been chosen through political influence later allowed their party connections to lapse. Some ministers tried conscientiously to undo the damage. Gradually, as the new institutions were consolidated, the administrative reforms of the Liberation began to improve recruitment to the higher civil service under guarantees of entrance by merit.

The open spoils system was checked, but politics could not be wholly excluded from appointments to policy-making posts. Rigid party spheres of influence disappeared with *tripartisme*, but the Fourth Republic revived the loose allotment of ministries characteristic of the Third. Interior and Education remained Socialist and Radical fiefs, while the foreign office, traditionally a Catholic stronghold, was monopolized by MRP until 1954. The parties generally, and MRP in particular, were charged with trying 'not merely to

electoral reform: Seurin, no. 198, p. 1268n.; cf. Grosser, pp. 57–8. Membership of Chaban-Delmas' *cabinet* gave Léon Delbecque facilities for organizing the 13 May insurrection in Algiers.

15. Between 1945 and 1955 over 85% of *cabinet* members whose professions were published came from the civil service: Seurin, no. 198, pp. 1236–7, cf. pp. 1267–70; King, no. 131, pp. 439–440; Lalumière, pp. 163–4. The main reasons were apparently financial at first, technical later: no. 198, p. 1286; Buron, p. 181, cf. p. 216.

16. No. 198, pp. 1286–93; no. 131, pp. 442–3; Waline (see n. 8), pp. 168–9; cf. Catherine, *op. cit.*, p. 317. On *cabinets* generally see Buron, pp. 176–88.

17. R. Lecourt (Justice), quoted *Figaro*, 27–28 March 1950; G. Jules (Interior), *L'Express*, 1 February 1957. Paul Delouvrier spoke of these personal interventions as 'the immense army of ants': in *Crise*, p. 80. For a defence see Buron, pp. 27–34, cf. p. 87.

18. Massigli, 62–4; Catherine, *op. cit.*, pp. 343–7; cf. Siegfried, *De la IIIe*, p. 219, on the deputy's powerlessness to influence nominations.

19. On these see below, pp. 347, 391–2.

ensure the "loyalty" of the officials who had to work with the minister, but also and perhaps especially to build up gradually a network of judiciously-placed political friends who will remain devoted to the party's policy and to this or that leader for the moment out of office'.[20]

In 1956 more systematic 'colonization' revived when the Socialists, returning to office after five years without influence on appointments, set about making up for lost time. They brought in the largest and most partisan *cabinets* since *tripartisme*; and a long ministry with few coalition partners gave them exceptional opportunities to influence appointments.[21] Yet, as their tenure showed, colonization might defeat its own ends by provoking counter-colonization of the party by the administration itself. If political allegiance affected a civil servant's career he would be tempted to join a party, as in some ministries in the Third Republic he had become a freemason, to improve his chances of promotion. Between 1956 and 1958 there were more signs that SFIO's official and police recruits were influencing the outlook of the party than that they were reinforcing its grip on the state machine.[22]

Ministers often found or felt that officials with a different outlook from their own were a poor instrument for their policies. The ministry of economic affairs so retained the impress of its first incumbents, Pierre Mendès-France and André Philip, that until 1952 only Socialists and MRP left-wingers held the office; conservatives preferred to suppress the department's separate identity rather than fight the views of the civil servants. MRP ministers found some officials and most army officers bitterly hostile to the EDC treaty; conversely Mendès-France and Christian Pineau, taking over a foreign office occupied for ten years by MRP ministers, found little sympathy for their policies among their subordinates. In June 1956 Pineau made sweeping changes which aroused opposition both in the department and among the politicians who counted most friends there. Even so, a few months later he and his colleagues (like their British opposite numbers) conceived and planned the Suez expedition without consulting their civil servants.[23]

If a minister deeply distrusted his staff, he had the last word. After the break-up of *tripartisme* most Communists and some fellow-travellers were removed from sensitive posts (though Bidault was criticized for dismissing Frédéric Joliot-Curie from the atomic energy authority, and the defence leakages of 1953–55 showed that the purge had been limited in scale and effect). Mendès-France's government transferred out of Algeria high police officials who had used the FLN revolt as an excuse to strike at all Moslem nationalists. A determined and politically secure minister would not be deterred from his

20. Catherine in *Partis et Classes*, pp. 127–40; quotation, p. 139. Cf. Buron, pp. 239–40.

21. Previous ministries had had 250–275 members in their *cabinets*, Mollet's had 350 – and more of them were party appointments: King, no. 131, pp. 437, 441n. Officials were fewer than at any time since the previous Socialist-led ministry: table in Lalumière, p. 163. One *directeur de cabinet* was allegedly appointed before his minister: Seurin, no. 198, p. 1235. Colonization was especially active in broadcasting.

22. On SFIO, above, p. 99 and n.; generally, Massigli, pp. 71–3; Noël, p. 135; Meynaud and Lancelot, pp. 54–5. *Cabinet* members in the Cadillac committee might decide Radical policy: Seurin, no. 198, p. 1273.

23. Grosser, pp. 67–8, 72; Massigli, pp. 22–3, 51, 67–71; Planchais, pp. 54–7; for Pineau, Diamant (n. 1), pp. 150n. and 211 n. 14.

policy by official disapproval; the finance ministry could not stop Pinay's amnesty for tax frauds or his cuts in investment. But it might be a different story if the minister suffered from weakness of character or political situation, and a politician whose course was very obnoxious to his advisers sometimes found unexpected difficulties in his way.[24]

The senior civil servants were able, well-informed and tactful men. Unless there were internal conflicts, like that between the road and rail divisions of the ministry of transport, they could generally persuade their ministers to adopt most if not all of the department's attitudes and policies. (There was a striking if trivial instance in February 1950 when a deputy who was demanding cheap fares for students in Paris became minister of transport and rejected his own motion.) But an agreed departmental policy was not enough, for there were always battles with other ministries, even those controlled by the same party. In 1949 the minister of labour clashed with the minister of transport over the dismissal of railwaymen in May, and with his colleague who dealt with the civil service over salaries in September: all three men were Socialists. In the same year Pflimlin resigned the ministry of agriculture after opposing his Economic Affairs colleague, also of MRP, over the guaranteed price of sugar-beet. French administrators, like others, appreciated a docile political master less than one who could win their departmental and parliamentary battles for them.[25]

In the thick of interdepartmental conflict was the ministry of finance, the most powerful department, the most impervious to external pressures, and the focus of most resentment.[26] Every spending department from Education to Defence complained of the miserly treasury which so unjustly rejected its own reasonable demands (and so conveniently refused those of its client pressure-groups which it thus escaped the odium of opposing). For instance, in the third Parliament a Socialist finance minister, Paul Ramadier, was opposed by the Right for overspending and by his own party over his tax policy. His Radical successor Félix Gaillard clashed violently over the defence budget with André Morice, and over social expenditure with Albert Gazier. When Pierre Pflimlin of MRP took over in 1957, his attempt to cut the education estimates was successfully resisted by a minister, René Billères, who (though a Radical) was well known to be a practising Catholic.[27]

To the political parties the finance ministry was a natural target and scape-goat. Socialists and MRP left-wingers saw it as a stronghold of bourgeois reaction, threatening social reform and a controlled economy, needing to be dismantled and subjected to a new ministry of economic affairs; and while

24. Purges: *AP* 1950, pp. 73–4, 286; cf. 1954, p. 290, 1955, p. 179; on leakages see below, p. 348. Brindillac, no. 28, p. 869, suggests that certain high officials brought about Faure's defeat in 1952. (Cf. Chavanon in *Aspects*, p. 176, on Bidault's fall in 1950.) See also nn. 25, 38.

25. On relations between ministers and civil servants generally, see Meynaud, pp. 200–6; Buron, pp. 132, 189–91, 195–9, 205–10; and n. 38.

26. Meynaud, pp. 207–9. 'If you want to act effectively in this field, become a civil servant in the Budget Division and not a deputy': Chavanon in *Aspects*, p. 176. On the ministry see Duverger, *op. cit.*, pp. 317–20, 344; the budget division in Paris had 11 administrative class officials (the budget bureau in Washington has 200). On its reputation, Buron, pp. 72, 208–9, 215–7; *Paysans*, pp. 253–9.

27. *AP* 1957, pp. 39, 80–1, 124.

intransigent Gaullists like Michel Debré accused it of treating France as a business run by the petty-cash clerk, to Peasants and Poujadists it was the bastion of ruthless modernizing technocracy.[28] The fears of the Left seemed to be borne out by de Gaulle's disastrous decision in 1945 to prefer the advice of its minister (Pleven) and the Bank of France to that of the economic affairs minister, Mendès-France. They were reinforced by the policies of most of the Radical and Conservative ministers who held the office from 1947 to 1955. But these politicians were often much more restrictionist than their officials, who unlike their predecessors were 'New Dealers', Keynesian expansionists with no doctrinaire hostility to state intervention in the economy.[29]

With acceptance of an active role for the state went a tendency to extend their own powers. The finance ministry campaigned vigorously against the administrative irregularities which flourished in the upheavals after the Liberation. It sharply curtailed the growth of the 'special treasury accounts', which had proliferated after the war when departments were struggling for autonomy, and were threatening to make coherent financial policy impossible.[30] It also pressed for more influence over the new institutions – the nationalized industries, the Planning Commission and the social security system – which were set up just after the war to fulfil the new economic and social functions of the state. But here it faced opposition from the Left which favoured keeping them autonomous, both on theoretical 'democratic' grounds and because of its fear of the conservatism of the traditional bureaucracy. The social security structure, defended by all the trade unions and their political friends, survived with minor changes; but the nationalized industries, at first a preserve of the engineers and technicians, were gradually subjected to stricter financial control after the political pendulum swung Right in 1947.[31]

Such changes of organization were often a means for the executive to introduce changes of policy without reference to Parliament. But members might revolt. In 1951 Pleven was brought down by the Socialists for seeking special powers to reorganize the railways and social security system; and though in 1953 René Mayer was given them, and tightened ministerial control over the nationalized industries, his principal decrees were reversed by

28. SFIO: above, p. 338. Peasants: *AP* 1952, p. 20. Debré, *La mort de l'État républicain*, p. 19.

29. Lalumière, pp. 179–200, 221; Brindillac, no. 28, pp. 873–5; Ehrmann, *Business*, p. 266. In 1948 Jean Monnet had to mobilize MRP and Socialist support, and to threaten resignation, to prevent Queuille cutting the investments which Marshall Aid had been given to sustain: Fauvet, *IVe*, p. 154. In 1952 the finance ministry vainly opposed Pinay's similar short-sighted policy. (Yet Socialist ministers had few *inspecteurs des finances* in their *cabinets*: Lalumière, p. 165, and cf. above, n. 21.)

30. They covered expenditure ranging from the state lottery to the railway deficit and, from 1951, the subsidies to church schools. Parliament had always fought them, as they frustrated its control; the ministry had once encouraged them (for the same reason) but opposed them after the war. By 1950 the 300 special accounts of 1946 had been reduced to 60 and brought under proper control. See Tinguy, no. 209, p. 495; J. Blocquaux, *JO* 25 April 1950, pp. 2807–8; Duverger, *op. cit.*, pp. 63, 233–4, 330–2; Williams, p. 265; Wilson, p. 340n.

31. On the nationalized industries, see Lalumière, pp. 105–8, 154–8; Ehrmann, *Business*, pp. 264, 349; Lescuyer, Chapters 5–7; B. Chenot, *Les Entreprises nationalisées* (1956), pp. 98, 110–11, and in no. 56, p. 733. The Planning Commission was transferred in 1954 from the prime minister's office to the ministry of finance: *Institutions*, i. 258. Generally, see Brindillac, no. 28, p. 875; Donnedieu de Vabres, no. 78.

Parliament two years later without much opposition.[32] The legislature could thus frustrate attempts at administrative policy-making even when the ministers had special powers; and much more easily when they had not. So when in 1948 Madame Poinso-Chapuis, MRP minister of health, issued a decree indirectly allowing local authorities to subsidize church schools, it caused such a political storm that it was allowed to lapse—though never formally abrogated.[33] In this case the minister first adopted a new policy and then abandoned it under political pressure, all without legislation.

An initiative from the parliamentary side could be met by bureaucratic inertia. Laws could be limited in scope by restrictive drafting of the decrees applying them, as the ministry of education did in 1951 (in opposition to the *Conseil d'État*) with the *loi Barangé* subsidizing church schools. They might even be sabotaged entirely. Two months before the regime fell, René Pleven complained of 'the casual treatment of laws which stipulate that the decrees and regulations applying them must be promulgated within a fixed time-limit'. Sometimes, as with the press law of 1946, the party interests of the minister responsible determined whether the law was carried out to the full or left as a dead letter. Or a new government might dislike its predecessor's policies: Pinay, the hero of small business, passed a mild law against cartels which his successor René Mayer made no attempt to enforce. There might be resistance from a pressure-group which had influence within the administration, or from the ministry of finance. Occasionally Parliament reacted, and in 1957 Bourgès-Maunoury, who had not applied the *loi Laborbe* (a private member's bill on agricultural prices) would have been beaten on this had he not fallen on Algeria first. At least the milk producers waiting for the *loi Laborbe* had more political influence than the civil servants, whose pay was supposed to be governed by a law of 1946 that had never been put into effect.[34]

It was very rare that a united administration found itself ranged in isolation against a hostile citizenry. Much more often there were fierce interdepartmental battles in which both sides enjoyed support outside the governmental machine, and took advantage of the fragmentation of political responsibility to mobilize these external reinforcements. Some departments could always count on widespread parliamentary sympathy: Education on the Left, Defence on the Right, Agriculture everywhere. Just as leading politicians had their brains-trusts of civil servants, so some senior civil servants had their helpful members of parliament whom they could brief to intervene in committee or in the house. The debate on the Sakiet raid, from which the crisis developed that destroyed the regime, was described by one observer as a fight between the army's deputies and those of the foreign office.[35]

32. Above, p. 271; below, p. 361. The powers were usually exercised by the officials: Chavanon in *Aspects*, pp. 173–4.

33. Above, p. 34; and Rémond in *La Laïcité*, pp. 393–4.

34. Barangé, Laborbe: Arné, pp. 149–52. Pleven: *JO* 20 February 1958, p. 913. Cartels: Ehrmann, *Business*, p. 387. Civil servants: Meynaud, p. 229, Duverger in *Monde*, 12 September 1957. See also below, n. 48 (Algeria), pp. 378–9 (pressure-groups), 392 (press law).

35. Faucher, p. 221; cf. Lavau, *Pressures*, p. 88. An important tax reform 'was carried through singlehandedly by a civil servant who mobilized some sectors of the business community against others and finally used the lobbyists of his allies when the bill seemed to falter in parliament. Similar tactics permitted beating back the alcohol lobby with the aid of the oil interests': Ehrmann,

Administrators who had developed the habit of political manipulation were likely, when overruled by their official rivals (or even by their own minister), to reopen the debate elsewhere. Plans and projects could sometimes be killed before birth by the 'national industry or even institution' of well-timed leakages, which allowed ministries to carry on 'private wars . . . torpedoing each other's plans prematurely brought to light'; permitted the civil service unions to launch the great strikes of 1953 against decrees not yet published; and encouraged officials who detested governmental policies to supply ammunition to opposition parties and politicians. The extravagant precautions sometimes taken to avoid publicity were a reaction against a real danger.[36] But conflict within the official world was more memorable than co-operation to those engaged in it, and more interesting to those outside. Public attention was directed to the occasional spectacular clash and not to the normal routine of constructive but unexciting co-operation between officials and departments. In fact it was this regular bureaucratic activity which kept the machinery of French government working without disruption in spite of political instability. Indeed, the Liberation and the Fourth Republic saw the accomplishment of a silent administrative revolution which, though it attracted little attention, made the machine far more efficient than before.

The central direction of policy was reinforced by the establishment of a cabinet secretariat and a stronger prime minister's office. Civil service recruitment was reformed by the creation of ENA. Government bills were much improved by being submitted to the *Conseil d'État* for prior technical examination before they went to Parliament. Jean Monnet's Planning Commission and other new agencies gave the French state machinery for effective intervention in the economic field. The *Cour des Comptes* was given new financial scope by the constitution, and gained new prestige by its work. In local government the decentralizing provisions of the constitution proved a dead letter; on the contrary the new 'super-prefects' (IGAMEs) ensured more effective central control in emergency and interdepartmental co-ordination in normal times. The politicians set up in the High Council of the Judiciary an institution which proved its value in taking justice out of politics.[37]

These improvements in the machinery of government only threw into relief the problem of the political authority which was to control them. In the absence of an effective government they merely conferred more policy-making power on the bureaucracy. Its influence went far beyond the task of daily management which any competent civil service will do for a weak or incapable minister. Some constructive policies of the most far-reaching kind were devised by officials, who then took them out of ordinary party warfare by persuading the rival political groups. Monnet's planning objectives and machinery were accepted by all parties including the Communists, though political struggles

no. 85, p. 548; on alcohol cf. below, p. 356. Generally, Meynaud, pp. 205, 309–10; and cf. above, p. 252, and below, pp. 378–9. Also Buron, pp. 74–5, 105, 206–7.

36. Quotation from Delouvrier in *Crise*, p. 83. Cf. Massigli, Chapter 1; Grosser, pp. 60–2, and below, p. 348. Precautions: cf. Planchais, pp. 67–8; above, p. 341 (Suez); below, p. 346 (Schuman plan).

37. Cassin, no. 50, and above, pp. 204–5, 260, 272, 299–301, 338; below, p. 347.

sometimes occurred when his policies were put into practice. In 1952 he went to the Coal and Steel Community to develop another of his major policies which had become common ground among the parties of the regime; for it was he who had devised the 'Schuman Plan' with the help of his own subordinates and without consulting the foreign office, winning over Robert Schuman only a few days and most of the cabinet only a few hours before the decision was announced to the world.[38] Yet the pursuit of European economic union was taken up by all the parties of government, and though they divided and were defeated when they tried to extend it to the military sphere, they soon reunited on their original line of advance.

Long-range policies had been the work of officials rather than politicians in the Third Republic as well as the Fourth. This situation was a by-product of ministerial instability; however undesirable in theory, it was preferable to having no long-range policies at all. Both economic expansionism and European co-operation corresponded to strong and deep desires of most (not all) thinking Frenchmen, and were perhaps made more acceptable to politicians of different views because they were given detailed form by civil servants rather than by one of themselves. But while the economic bureaucracy accepted change, their colonial colleagues clung to routine; and when France faced the challenge of decolonization, the danger of political abdication became evident. 'The French state reveals its true face when it takes off the parliamentary mask: Vichy, the occupation in Germany, colonialism have shown its authoritarian nature.'[39] Overseas, first the administration and then the army successfully imposed policies on governments too weak, divided or precarious to develop or enforce their own. These policies were in the long run neither workable on the spot, nor tolerable internationally, nor acceptable at home. Tension therefore grew steadily between an overseas bureaucracy and army intent on their own purposes, and a Parliament which gradually became alarmed at the wider consequences. By 1958 the contagion of insubordination had spread to the forces of the state at home.

3. THE DEFENCE AND SECURITY SERVICES

In the government's first line of defence against domestic enemies stood the prefects. They were direct agents of the minister of the interior, and their tenure of their posts was at his discretion. Their main functions were to represent the government in each department, co-ordinate the activities of the different ministries, supervise the local authorities, maintain order, and defend the regime. In the nineteenth century they had also acted as the government's election agents, and as late as 1924 there was a 'massacre' of prefects when the opposition won an election. But as the prefectoral corps gradually developed the habits and attitudes of a career service, its members increasingly kept their posts under successive governments – though purges still occurred in great crises like 1940 and 1944.

38. Gerbet, no. 98, pp. 542–53. On planning struggles see n. 29; and on bureaucratic policy-making, Wahl in Beer and Ulam, pp. 326–30. Cf. Buron, p. 132.

39. Brindillac, no. 30, p. 799. Cf. p. 3 n.2; and Hoffmann in *Change*, p. 91. On the army's policy in Algeria see Girardet in *Military Politics*, pp. 134–41.

The Socialists and Communists had always mistrusted the prefectoral system and the men who manned it. In the 1946 constitution five articles, 85 to 89, expressed an intention to weaken the prefects and strengthen the elected municipal and departmental councils. But when the Communists went into opposition and launched the great strikes of 1947 and 1948, their former partners quickly discovered, like so many advocates of decentralization on acceding to power, that Paris had too little rather than too much control. Following Vichy and Liberation precedents, Jules Moch therefore appointed eight 'super-prefects' or IGAMEs (*inspecteurs-généraux de l'administration en mission extraordinaire*) whose task was normally to organize co-operation between neighbouring departments, and in an emergency to co-ordinate under civil control all forces in their areas (which corresponded to the military regions). In 1953 Laniel's government used its special powers to enact administrative reforms restoring to the prefect some of the authority he had gradually been losing to the local agents of other ministries. The constitutional provisions for strengthening the local councils were wholly forgotten.[40]

Yet the local authorities were not as weak as they looked, for many mayors and departmental councillors were also members of parliament. A prudent prefect had to be attentive, not merely to the reigning minister of the interior, but also to the entrenched local *ministrable* whose parliamentary influence might one day dethrone him. Towns therefore preferred as mayors a deputy or senator whose political influence could temper the theoretical rigours of administrative centralization; and a powerful politician friendly to the regime rarely found an unacceptable prefect sent to his department.[41] These factors mitigated the effect of party politics on the appointment and transfer of prefects. Most of the corps leaned towards the Radical party, which until 1936 had almost monopolized the ministry of the interior; pro-clerical politicians never held it, and MRP in 1951 had no prefect and few sub-prefects in its ranks. While open enemies of the regime were not appointed, there was no purge of the Gaullists who came in at the Liberation, and there were even two Communist prefects and one regional commissioner while the party was in office. Because of their activities Jules Moch, when he became minister of the interior, had to dissolve 11 of the 65 companies of riot police (*Compagnies républicaines de sécurité*, CRS) which were over 80% Communist.[42]

In later years the struggle against Communist influence led some high security officials to patronize other enemies of democracy. Two reactionary freemasons co-operated closely in 'McCarthyite' activities between 1952 and 1954: the Radical minister of the interior Léon Martinaud-Déplat and the Socialist Jean Baylot, who occupied the politically vital post of prefect of police in Paris. When Mendès-France came to power Baylot was removed;

40. Chapman in *Local Government*, pp. 95–106, 119–23; *Prefects and Provincial France*, pp. 61–2, 168–9, 174–7; and no. 51. Panter-Brick, no. 172; Abbott and Sicard, no. 1.

41. Chapman, *Prefects*, pp. 157–61, 200–6. Isorni quotes as a sample of lobby conversation 'Get rid of this idiot of a prefect for me and I'll see if I can change my vote': *Silence*, p. 184. Many prefects and parliamentarians worked closely together on behalf of the constituency: Buron, pp. 25–6, 83–4.

42. MRP: Neumann, no. 165, p. 744n.; cf. Catherine in *Partis et Classes*, pp. 134–5. Mendès-France in 1954 and Mollet in 1957 offered MRP the Interior · Moch: in *Bulletin intérieur SFIO* no. 39 (February 1949), p. 67. Cf. Buron, pp. 213, 240.

within an hour forty members of parliament (including Le Troquer, the Socialist President of the Assembly) had telephoned the premier to protest. Baylot and his collaborator Superintendent Dides later became extreme-Right deputies. The consequences of their control of the Paris police became fully apparent first in the spring of 1958, and then under the Fifth Republic.[43]

Political interference was particularly damaging in the intelligence services. As well as the old rivals, the *Sûreté nationale* and the Paris prefecture of police, there were now several small intelligence organizations attached to different ministries, and one major one directly under the premier: SDECE (*Service de documentation extérieure et de contre-espionnage*), which was once called in court 'the *really* secret secret service'. Constantly at cross-purposes, these agencies arrested and intimidated one another's informers in a struggle which often seemed more concerned with party politics than with national security. Repeated reorganizations failed to cure them. In wartime London SDECE (then called *Bureau central de renseignements et d'action*) was headed by Colonel Passy, who departed with de Gaulle in 1946. The Socialist politician who took it over was utterly isolated in his own agency. When the scandal of the generals revealed that defence information had leaked to the Indo-Chinese nationalists, his Gaullist second-in-command, Colonel Fourcaud, allegedly bribed and intimidated witnesses to support charges of treason against two leading Socialist ministers.[44] But the counter-espionage service of the ministry of the interior (DST) tried to hush up the scandal, either for fear of American reactions as ministers claimed, or to save the government's reputation as the opposition asserted.

The rival services were amalgamated under a new head. In vain: a new scandal again broke over military leakages in 1953–54. Two senior defence officials who opposed the Indo-China war passed confidential information to papers and politicians of the Left. Superintendent Dides and the prefecture investigators failed to discover that they were both 'fellow-travellers' (though one had even been a Progressive local candidate). Instead the prefecture led opposition politicians, the President of the Republic and France's allies to believe there was a traitor in Mendès-France's cabinet – a task facilitated by Martinaud-Déplat, who did not tell his successor that the leakages had been going on for a year. When the case was at last tried by a military court in 1956, Tixier-Vignancour, who was kept well supplied with confidential documents by his friends in the police and secret service, was allowed by the civilian presiding judge to use it for an outrageous campaign against the Left and the Republic – while the highest security officials in France helped him by denouncing one another as undercover Communists. Credulous, unscrupulous and enmeshed in party intrigue, these services did much to discredit the régime they were supposed to serve before they finally betrayed it in May 1958.[45]

43. Protests: Faucher, p. 115. Also see above, p. 52, and below, p. 351.

44. Cf. Williams, no. 218. A former *cagoulard* and later plotter of May 1958, Fourcaud was described at the inquiry as a 'cloak-and-dagger character' who 'conspired morning, noon and night'. Years later he suggested at a trial of de Gaulle's would-be assassins that the attack had been staged by the government – but denied a suggestion that he had himself known of it in advance: *Monde*, 5 and 7 September 1962. On SDECE also Fauvet, *IVe*, p. 162.

45. See references above, p. 46n.

Those administrators and soldiers who served in French-ruled lands overseas had no need of indirect methods. They simply defied the wishes of Paris. As a senior minister confessed when after four years he relinquished responsibility for the Tunisian and Moroccan protectorates: 'The *fait accompli* is the great and constant temptation which it is to their credit that residents-general resist – in so far as they do not succumb. Moreover they themselves are in a similar situation in regard to some services (police, information, etc.). . . . Above the residents-general the minister for foreign affairs is responsible for their administration which is reputed to be in accordance with his own views. This is one of the fictions on which the democratic regime depends. . . .' In 1955 a normally conciliatory premier exploded in Parliament against the mutinous officials in Morocco: 'It is time this stopped. These resignations cancelled and then repeated – it's finished! . . . No more resignations by officials, obedience! . . . We must put an end to proceedings which lead to the disintegration of the state. It's the government that governs and if this government survives tonight, govern it will!'[46]

But it was hard for ministers, however determined, to impose their wishes when their own representatives abroad quickly became the spokesmen of a local administration which sprang from and sympathized with the local French colony. Several ministers and governments conceived liberal policies in North Africa; very few pressed them hard against the settlers and their military and parliamentary friends, who could so easily bring a cabinet down; those that tried found that the administrative machine would not implement policies which the local Europeans disliked. The Fifth Republic was to show that the weakness of will in Paris had been only part of the problem. Not even a determined French government could make the entrenched local community accept concessions, short of total withdrawal when the price of maintaining France's position became too high.

The local resistance took several forms: lobbying by politicians in Paris, rioting by city mobs on the spot, and the continuous sabotage of the government's policies by its own services. The Indo-China war finally became inevitable when a general ordered the bombardment of Haiphong; and the Saigon administration kept such tight control over what Paris was allowed to know that the censor delayed for ten vital days Ho Chi-Minh's telegram to the prime minister (Léon Blum) appealing for negotiation. In Tunisia it was the resident-general who decided to arrest and deport the Bey's ministers; in Morocco it was the resident who deposed the Sultan against instructions from Georges Bidault, who subsequently defended the act he had originally forbidden; and in Algeria army intelligence seized Ben Bella and his companions from their Moroccan plane with the knowledge of a minister of state, Max Lejeune, but not of any member of the cabinet.[47]

Yet these spectacular acts of insubordination were no more damaging in the long run than the electoral manipulation, administrative obstruction and political intrigue by which the Algerian authorities and European community

46. Robert Schuman in *La Nef*, March 1953, p. 68 (quoted Grosser, p. 52; Fauvet, *IV*^e^, p. 215; *AP* 1953, p. 225). Edgar Faure, *JO* 8 October 1955, p. 4956; cf. below, p. 354.

47. Cf. Fauvet, *IV*^e^, pp. 95, 208, 213–17, 294, 319–21; Grosser, pp. 52–3, 256–7, 267, 275–6, 365–6; above, pp. 41, 50 and n.

prevented the reform bill of 1947 ever going into effect.[48] When these methods seemed likely to fail more extreme ones were used. In Morocco the assassination of nationalists and their French sympathizers (Mendès-France was one intended victim) was organized by the police in justified confidence that no local judge would ever convict a European terrorist.[49] Defeat in Indo-China added to the government's problem a new dimension: the exasperation of the army officers with the futile sacrifice of their comrades and their determination never to allow a repetition. By 1956 hotheads like General Faure were already conspiring against the regime, and in 1958 President Coty was officially warned by the senior commanders four days before 13 May that the army would not tolerate a 'government of scuttle'.[50]

By sabotage, blackmail and insubordination the administrators and soldiers tried to eliminate and succeeded in restricting the freedom of action of their political masters. But these too bore a heavy responsibility. Ministers never told the country the truth about Indo-China; if they had, the army might not have suffered a humiliating defeat, and civil servants would have had less excuse for betraying official secrets to help the anti-war campaign. General Faure's plot was exposed by a high official in the Algiers prefecture, who very soon resigned because his protests against the mass 'disappearances' of suspects arrested by the parachutists were ignored by the Socialist ministers who had ordered the operation but preferred not to know about its consequences.[51]

These were new and sensational developments in French government. Not that the services of the French state had ever been free from political interference. But hitherto the police had been criticized by enemies of the regime as the servile instruments of the men in power; and indeed in the early days of the Fourth Republic they were still loyally unravelling plots against it. The judges were always a conservative body, and in 1940 all but one had sworn allegiance to Pétain. But they had never shown the gross anti-republican bias of their confrères in Weimar Germany, and they too had usually been attacked for subservience towards the authorities of the day – notably during and after the Nazi occupation.[52]

The army was traditionally officered by old Catholic families with no great love for the Republic, but despite occasional aberrations it had loyally accepted for generations that its highest duty was unconditional obedience to any legal government – although in 1940 it was taught a different lesson. In the Fourth Republic, as in the Third, there were complaints of political interference with military promotions. A chief of the general staff used a dubious

48. In 1955 Soustelle as governor recommended that the reform bill be applied; the government found justifications for further delay; and the Socialist spokesman asked whether ministers thought the law was optional: Édouard Depreux, *JO* 29 July 1955, pp. 4539–40.

49. As the police chief sent from Paris to investigate Lemaigre-Dubreuil's murder admitted: *Monde*, 13 December 1962, reporting the trial for another offence of one of the assassins, now repentant. (His unrepentant fellow-murderers were at large 'awaiting trial' – after seven and a half years.)

50. See above, p. 50n, 55.

51. *Monde*, 20 and 29 September, 1 October 1960. Would the same paper have received (or published) a report by the committee for safeguarding human rights in Algeria, in December 1957, if the government had acted on it instead of hushing it up?

52. Plots: at one conspiratorial gathering five of the eight men present were officers: Moch, *JO* 14 June 1949, p. 3361. Courts: cf. above, pp. 211, 301.

contact-man to obtain information about cabinet meetings, promotion for himself, and the appointment as assistant director of military personnel of a general whom he called 'a good republican whom, therefore, MRP want to send out of the way'; his candidate got the job after the MRP premier had been replaced by a Radical and the MRP defence minister by a Socialist – and MRP deputies charged that the new ministers were favouring freemasons.[53] In 1958 similar complaints were raised against a Socialist war minister by a right-wing deputy (who had himself tried twenty times to have an officer protégé promoted). Marshal Juin repeatedly encouraged military opposition to government policy, especially over EDC. But these incidents, however disagreeable or discreditable for a government, were not dangerous for the regime.[54]

The Indo-China disaster and the Algerian war, following on earlier humiliations, changed the climate and falsified the old certainties. Judges began to show a conspicuous bias against the anti-war Left which in the Fifth Republic was found – to the dismay of Gaullist leaders and Socialist ex-ministers who had once warmly approved of it – to conceal open sympathy for the OAS.[55] In the police force, many in the lower ranks and some in the higher always remained reliable. But after years of combating the Communists, followed by a bitter fight against the FLN in which many policemen lost their lives, it became clear early in 1958 that some branches were tolerant of or even allied to the fascists. The loyalty of the army had been shaken by military defeat, German occupation and bitter internal division. Indo-China taught the leaders of military opinion that warfare could not be divorced from political direction either in the field or in the capital, and made them contemptuous of politicians who would neither fight the war seriously nor end it honourably. Algeria taught them to act as a pressure-group, urging and bullying the politicians to muzzle the press, chastise the Arabs, and defy the allies. At last the soldiers preferred like Georges Bidault 'to mourn the Fourth Republic rather than *Algérie française*'. By 1958 the regime commanded little loyalty from the people, and still less from the state machine.

53. See Williams, no. 218, p. 475n.; *JO* 3 March 1949, pp. 1204 (Monteil), 1214 (Ramadier), and *Monde*, 18 February 1950.

54. *JO* 4 February 1958, pp. 494–510; also Planchais, pp. 33–4, Faucher, pp. 222–4. Juin: Fauvet, *IV*^{e}, pp. 263–4.

55. As in the Morice libel case: an ex-minister was accused in the press of profiting from building the Germans' Atlantic Wall; the journals were forbidden to give their evidence, as facts over ten years old are no defence for a libel, but he was permitted to state his case in full: *Monde*, 2–3, 5, 6 and 13 November 1958. And in the leakages case: Williams, no. 222, pp. 398–400.

Chapter 25

INTERESTS AND CAUSES

It was the weakness of governmental authority which allowed sections of the state machine to develop their own policies and impose them on their political masters. Outside government, private pressure-groups found their task facilitated by the indiscipline of parties as well as the weakness of the executive. For it is a common illusion that only the party whip prevents the politician searching his conscience to find and follow that nebulous ideal, the general interest. In reality party discipline is a protection as well as a constraint, screening him from the vociferous groups which try to influence his electoral fate.

A disciplined party can withstand pressure better than an individual politician, but it is more vulnerable and more easily tempted in a multi-party system than in a two-party regime where one rival holds power and responsibility and the other hopes to. A majority party (actual or potential) dare not identify itself exclusively with one interest for fear of losing the floating vote. But in France perpetual coalitions obscured responsibility. No party, hopeful of a clear majority, was competing for the rich prize of a central floating vote which would give or withhold power: for this vote did not exist. Instead multiple cleavages split the nation into several opposing camps: bourgeois against worker, peasant against townsman, Catholic against anticlerical. Between these camps votes shifted rarely, within them frequently, for competition was fiercest between rival parties bidding for the same clientele and every moderate had to fear a more extreme defender of the same cause. At elections, parties in a permanent minority dared not offend the group on which they depended – not for victory, but for survival. In a Parliament with no majority, manœuvre and obstruction could often be practised with success.

The groups which exerted pressure on the politician were very various. The most limited local interests, which had been so potent in the Third Republic, lost much of their power when large constituencies were adopted in 1945. But a body like the winegrowers, on whom the prosperity of a whole region depended, could command the support of every politician in the area. Operating on a national scale were some groups who enjoyed the favours of all parties – ex-servicemen, tenants of houses, the peasantry. Workers and employers had their usual range of political friends and enemies. Long ago Thibaudet had warned, 'No hope for a party which writes on its banner: Interests.'[1] But he also pointed out that some interests, broad and inclusive enough to generate political ideologies, could offer to their electoral defenders not only a core of committed support but the satisfaction of championing immortal principles.

Groups large and small could both profit from the consequences of the multi-party system they did so much to engender. Sometimes they pressed outrageous demands with such arrogance and stridency that complaints echoed all along the political spectrum. Yet too many politicians took these

1. Thibaudet, *Professeurs*, p. 256; cf. *Idées*, pp. 57–8, 181–2.

'feudatories' at their own high valuation. Frequently one group could be played off against another which it existed to fight, or with which its interests conflicted (no other taxpayer wanted the Poujadists to shift their burden on to his shoulders). Even when an organization represented a real common interest its power might be limited: the workers were poorly organized, the middle classes and sometimes the peasants unwilling to use direct action. And where the power was available, it had to be used with discretion, for if they were bullied too humiliatingly the politicians sometimes reacted by defiance instead of concession.

Resistance to the pressure-groups often succeeded – or failed for causes quite unconnected with the organization which trumpeted its victory. The 'technocrats' were so freely abused precisely because they often successfully defended the general interest against particular claims. Money without votes to back it was weaker than in the past, and groups that did carry excessive weight rarely had to thank the occult Parisian interests denounced by demagogues of Left and Right. Usually they won because cabinets were weak in Parliament and members obeyed the injunctions of their constituents, who saw no connection between the sectional demands they pressed so impatiently and the governmental anarchy they condemned so harshly.

1. THE PRESSURE-GROUPS

In eighteenth-century France innumerable narrow corporations combined in fierce defence of their historic privileges. The Revolution swept them away, and from the Jacobins to Clemenceau and de Gaulle it was orthodox republican doctrine to deplore and denounce intermediary bodies which came between the citizen and the state. Freedom of association came later in France than in any other major democracy. But the centralized Republic was weak at the top, and loose parties, unmanageable Parliaments and unstable governments gave pressure-groups every opportunity for influence. The consequences were deplored by public figures of all views from the President of the Republic to the royalist pretender; the Pope himself conceded that Catholic approval for social pluralism might need some qualification.[2]

Among those whose nefarious activities were most frequently exposed and lamented were the 'North African lobby' in external affairs and the 'alcohol lobby' in domestic policy. They shared some common features. In each case a small group of wealthy men, exercising considerable influence on the loose parties of the Right and Centre, provided a natural target for left-wing hostility. Each was screened from this attack by a mass of poorer allies, who were convinced that their interests were interdependent and were prepared to defend them by ballot or by riot. Neither faced a direct antagonist of similar dimensions. Both suffered serious setbacks under the Fourth Republic, precisely on those sectors of the front where the rich men's 'lobby' was most exposed; both resisted most successfully where they could call on the aid of their poorer associates. Each found some support in most parties, and each

2. In his letter to Charles Flory in *Crise*, p. viii. The Comte de Paris attacked the 'economic feudalists' in his monthly bulletin, and President Auriol in his speech at Pau: *Monde*, 27 July 1951 and 30 June 1953. Cf. below, p. 385.

had friends as well as enemies within the administration. But the only protector of the alcohol interests within the government was the ministry of agriculture, which was no match for the ministry of finance; they had to redress the balance by calling in the aid of Parliament. The *colons*, on the contrary, controlled the local administration in North Africa through which Paris had to try to execute its policies; and though their parliamentary influence was skilfully and effectively deployed, it was a secondary (and by itself an inadequate) weapon in a well-stocked armoury.

The failure of French policy in North Africa, so sharply contrasted with its successes south of the Sahara, was plainly due in part to the settlers' influence. Theirs had been the first important 'lobby' in the Third Republic, and half a century later they could still sometimes make policy and often veto it.[3] Paris was distant and preoccupied, for Algeria was controlled by a busy minister of the interior and Morocco and Tunisia by an overworked foreign minister. Residents and governors on the spot had a very free hand unless they offended the settler leaders; the few who did, like Eirik Labonne at Rabat and Yves Chataigneau at Algiers, found their authority undermined by political pressure in Paris and did not long survive the return to office of the Radicals.[4] Whether or not that party was financed by the *colons*, as was widely believed, its leaders certainly worked closely with them. René Mayer was deputy for Constantine and a leading minister. Léon Martinaud-Déplat controlled the party machine. Henri Borgeaud was chairman of the Radical senators, and commanded thirty votes in the Assembly which were often enough to provoke or avert a ministerial crisis; the change from reform to repression in Tunisia at the end of 1951 seems to have been brought about by such parliamentary pressure on the feeble Pleven cabinet. 'Here', wrote a progressive senator in 1953, 'the Algerian Radicals are past masters and the colonial *immobilisme* of the Fourth Republic owes much to their understanding of "the music".'[5]

The lobbying of the settlers certainly played an important part in the hesitations and reversals of policy which caused France to miss so many opportunities in North Africa. Yet a liberal policy faced other and greater difficulties. The power of the *colons* had local rather than Parisian roots; and the obnoxious governors might have defeated their parliamentary critics if their efforts had not been paralysed by subordinates on the spot – prefects, prosecutors, policemen – who were bitter opponents of reform. But a determined government could defeat these forces: Mendès-France reversed the whole course of policy in Tunisia, and the Moroccan diehards, using every weapon of administrative sabotage, military disobedience and political intrigue against Gilbert Grandval in 1955, only accelerated instead of preventing the switch from repression to concession.[6]

Although the struggle was so much more long-drawn-out in Algeria, the *colons*' lobby was not the main reason for this. For all its entrenched local

3. The first: Priouret, *Députés*, p. 172. For an early, typical and informed attack see Bourdet, no. 26; and cf. Werth, *Strange History*.

4. *AP* 1947, pp. 285–8, 1948, pp. 19–20, 57; cf. Bloch-Morhange, Chapter 4 (see above, p. 47n.).

5. Hamon, no. 120, p. 840. On *colon* influence on the Radical party see above, p. 126n. On Pleven see references in Williams, p. 190n.

6. Above, p. 349 (sabotage). Fauvet, *IV*^{e}, pp. 296–300 (Morocco).

influence and its devoted parliamentary friends, the 'lobby' alone could have been defeated in Algeria as it was in the protectorates; indeed many of the richest capitalists (Walter in Morocco and Blachette in Algeria) were in favour of conciliating Moslem nationalism. In 1947 an Algerian reform bill was whittled down by *colon* pressure in Parliament, but it could still have transformed the problem if it had not been wrecked by the authorities on the spot.[7] Ten years later the diehards repeated the operation against another reform bill; the result was a parliamentary reaction against them and, in the next ministerial crisis, every political leader who sympathized with them found himself eliminated in the struggle for power. In Parliament they had lost the game, and Alain de Sérigny's story of his efforts to stop Pflimlin only shows the weakness of their hand.[8]

Among the many obstacles to a liberal policy in Algeria, the interests of the big capitalists loomed large only when the question was a minor and secondary one in French politics. Once the issue was really joined they would soon have been swept away, had they not been protected by the fears of nearly a million poor whites, the mutinous mood of a humiliated and frustrated army, the weakness or indifference of the major parties, and the exasperated nationalism of many French voters at home. The proof came in the Fifth Republic, when the old institutions and most of the old leaders had disappeared. De Gaulle had nothing to fear from the *colons*' parliamentary pressure, but the slow and tortuous way in which his Algerian policy evolved over four years showed the real difficulties he still faced even more than his own preference for taking devious paths to his fixed goal.

The powerful and pernicious alcohol interest owed its influence to the millions of Frenchmen who were concerned with the production or sale of alcohol. Between them they imposed on the state a loss of over £10 million a year through its commitment to purchase at guaranteed prices more than twice as much alcohol as the market could hope to absorb; the enormous quantity drunk damaged the nation's health and caused further burdens on the treasury. The various sections of the alcohol lobby were all concerned to maintain this system and to discredit its critics, though there were minor conflicts of interest between them. Numerically the most important groups were: the three million *bouilleurs de cru*, owners of fruit trees entitled to distil a little alcohol for their own consumption (who in fact sold three times as much to the towns); the million and a half winegrowers; and the half-million who owned or worked in bars. As powerful politically and far stronger financially were the 150,000 beet-producers and the rich distillers who bought their crop.[9]

The state began buying industrial alcohol for munitions in 1916, and after

7. Grosser, pp. 152–3 on capitalist divisions, 251–4 on the Algerian debates. One leading Moroccan capitalist, Lemaigre-Dubreuil, was murdered for his liberal views: cf. above, p. 47.

8. A. de Sérigny, *La révolution du 13 mai* (1958), Part I; J. Touchard's review in no. 211, pp. 922–923. Generally, Priouret, *Députés*, p. 234.

9. Among many accounts see Brown, nos. 33, 35; Warner, *The Winegrowers of France and the Government since 1875*, Chapter 10; J. M. Cotteret in *Paysans*, pp. 293–301; Meynaud, pp. 248–54, 259–60; Malignac and Colin (especially Chapters 9 and 11), and no. 153; Ehrmann, *Business*, pp. 244–5; Schoenbrun, pp. 172–3; newspaper and *JO* references in Williams, pp. 355–6nn.; also below, pp. 375, 379.

the war Parliament prolonged the system 'temporarily'. In 1922 the political alliance of northern beets and southern wines was sealed by the market-sharing agreement of Béziers: wine was protected against competition in the market for alcoholic drinks, while beets for alcohol were sold to an obliging state at the same price as sugar-beets. An outlet for some of the surplus was found by its compulsory use in a motor-fuel mixture. From 1931 the state also relieved the overstocked wine market by buying up the surplus for distilling. Beet production doubled soon after the second war because the Monnet planners wanted a bigger supply of sugar. But since refineries were not as profitable as distilleries, no more sugar was produced. The extra production merely added to the budgetary burden and caused conflict between the ministers of finance and agriculture. After Pflimlin resigned over the beet price in December 1949, the cabinet reduced it in order to force production down; in the ensuing political storm the government was assailed by peasant deputies of every party from Conservatives to Communists.

The alcohol surplus and the budgetary deficit continued to mount. After 1950 the lobby again got alcohol compulsorily mixed in motor-fuel. But this made the fuel both dearer than petrol and worse in quality, and exasperated the petrol companies, motorists and road hauliers, themselves an aggressive pressure-group. The subsidy cost the state in 1952 more than half the sum Pinay saved by slashing the desperately needed housing programme.[10] Next year René Mayer tried to check the abuse; the peasants' leader, Senator René Blondelle, rallied seventy rural deputies against him at a meeting chaired by the minister of agriculture's brother, and the spokesman of the lobby (with some exaggeration) claimed credit for the government's defeat. Laniel came to power and obtained the special powers denied to Mayer, but he used them very differently; Henri Cayre, the beet-growers' secretary, boasted of the major part he himself played in drafting the new decree-laws on alcohol.[11] Mendès-France's efforts were frustrated by Parliament, and it was not until the third Assembly that the finance ministry could first halve and then stop the use of alcohol in motor-fuel.[12]

On the human side, much more alcohol was drunk in France than anywhere else, and doctors claimed that the toll of alcoholic diseases was far worse than in other countries. Administrators warned that its direct cost to the state was at least £150 million a year, perhaps much more. But the producers either stoutly maintained that the problem was an invention of Anglo-Saxon soft-drink and whisky manufacturers, or blamed it on the kind of alcohol they did not themselves sell.[13] Under Vichy the advertising, manufacture and sale

10. J. Cayeux, chairman of the health committee, *JO* 30 October 1952, p. 4587. The *Régie des Alcools* claimed there was no loss, as it valued its stocks at the price it had paid for them (so the more unsaleable alcohol it acquired the better off it claimed to be): Warner, p. 208; J. Callen, 'Les secrets du "lobby" betteravier', *France-Observateur*, 13 May 1954.

11. *Ibid.*; when M. Cayre sued the paper for libel the court found only one statement not proven and awarded him 1 franc (a farthing) damages: *Monde*, 19 and 20 December 1956. Also Meynaud, pp. 163, 165n., 312; Brown, no. 35, pp. 988–9 (for Mayer); Lavau, *Pressures*, pp. 82–3.

12. Below, p. 379; Meynaud, pp. 253–4 (and in his *Nouvelles études sur les groupes de pression en France*, 1962, p. 308); Brown, no. 35, pp. 985–6.

13. *Ibid.*, pp. 983–4; *Le Moniteur Vinicole* of 10 November 1956 solemnly warned, 'To drink water may be dangerous, fight against cancer by drinking alcohol.' Cf. Mendras, no. 157, p. 759; [*over*

of certain alcoholic drinks (particularly *pastis*) was restricted by law; the owners of bars – or lemonade-sellers as they preferred to call themselves – insisted that patriotism required immediate repeal. The ban was defended by urban MRP members who were concerned for health and the family, and relied largely on the women's vote. But their rural colleagues deserted when the Radicals, the main advocates of *pastis*, proposed in an election year (1951) that it be legalized and taxed to pay for such popular agrarian causes as higher family allowances for agricultural workers. The repeal was carried because the Communists, who had hitherto feared that it might injure the winegrowers, decided to change sides and vote for it.[14]

Of all the alcohol groups the *bouilleurs de cru* had the worst press (they did no advertising). They were blamed by both the wine and the beet interests for the problem of alcoholism, so far as it was admitted at all.[15] In the towns, where there were no *bouilleurs* and many women voters, they faced universal reprobation. But in eastern France all politicians agreed that the innocent activities of their constituents had nothing in common with the notorious frauds of the Normans, while in Normandy no candidate (indeed no prudent man) would question an abuse so prized by the voters as the *bouilleurs*' tax exemption. For two generations the *bouilleurs* had met inquiring tax-collectors with physical violence and hostile governments by the ruthless use of their votes. As they numbered half the adult male population of twenty departments, and a quarter in another forty, they were a strong and arrogant force which made deputies tremble (perhaps cravenly, for their leader André Liautey was very lucky to win a seat in the Assembly in 1951 and he was badly beaten in 1956).[16] Mendès-France aroused the fury of all sections of the alcohol interest by a frontal attack in 1954, when he reduced beet purchases, imposed restrictions on bars, and limited the *bouilleurs*' tax exemption to farmers only. Within a year his measures – though approved by public opinion – had all been upset by Parliament or by his successor, Edgar Faure.[17]

The alcohol interest was strong because it allied money and numbers. Through the *Régie des alcools* the precarious survival of poor winegrowers of the Midi became dependent on the comfortable and parasitic prosperity of the beet-producers and the distillers. Protected politically by the northern

Royer in *Paysans*, pp. 168–9, 186–9. Cost in money and disease: Brown, no. 35, pp. 977–80; Malignac and Colin; and S. Ledermann, *Alcool, alcoolisme, alcoolisation* (1956).

14. *AP* 1948, p. 157; 1949, pp. 78, 86; 1950, p. 155. *JO* 2 January 1950, pp. 13–14; 24 and 26 July 1950, pp. 5868ff., 6008ff.; 9 May 1951, p. 4906. Meynaud, p. 259.

15. *Ibid.*, p. 251; Brown, no. 35, p. 984. For the lobby's pressure on newspapers see Malignac and Colin, pp. 83–4.

16. Ledermann, pp. 44–8 (numbers, violence); Brown, no. 35, p. 991; cf. below, p. 375. On the election see Williams, no. 168, p. 165; Claudius Petit, who campaigned hard against alcoholism, also lost his seat (but regained it in 1958); but Edgar Faure, after voting against the *bouilleurs*, was re-elected with a very much larger vote than before. On the *bouilleurs*' campaign see Muselier, pp. 165–77, with many edifying quotations; Royer in *Paysans*, pp. 167–74, on Dorgères; cf. *ibid.*, pp. 297–8.

17. Brown, no. 35, pp. 900, 922; Meynaud, p. 260; Werth, *Strange History*, pp. 142–5; Hoffmann, pp. 16, 57, 62–3 on Poujadist use of the theme. In the vote on 8 November 1955 the *bouilleurs* were supported by fewer than a tenth of the members from Seine and Seine-et-Oise, but by three-quarters of the provincial deputies. In 21 cases back-benchers from the same list voted on opposite sides: in 12 the *bouilleurs*' supporter was the lower on the list, in 4 he was the higher, and in 5 he was not up for re-election. (My calculations.) They won by 407 to 188.

conservatives, including some stern Gaullist critics of intermediary bodies, the system could also mobilize left-wing reinforcements from the south, where every deputy had to defend the trade on which his region depended. The wine-growers did so badly from the alliance that their discontent frequently found expression in direct action – from strikes of mayors to highway barricades – or, in 1956, in a massive vote for Poujade.[18] The beet-producers did well only while they faced no opponents stronger than the medical profession or the unorganized women's vote; the motor trade and the finance ministry together were at last too much for them. The *bouilleurs* were influential because hundreds of thousands of Frenchmen were determined to use their vote first and foremost in this not very lofty cause;[19] if the spectacle was unedifying it was hard to see why politicians or institutions (other than those of democracy itself) should be held responsible for it. Gaullist deputies in the Fifth Republic defended the *bouilleurs* as ardently as their predecessors.[20]

The alcohol interest suffered from a bad public reputation which made it somewhat easier for the administration and even for a determined political leader to resist its pretensions; it had the advantage of enjoying support in all parties and organized opposition from none. The ideal situation for a pressure-group was to muster equally widespread support for a cause that public opinion found respectable. It was for this reason that every government found the ministry of pensions budget the hardest to pass, for none could offer enough to satisfy a Parliament in which opposition to the claims of ex-servicemen was unthinkable.[21] Rather similarly, from 1919 onwards, the tenants' organizations were strong enough to maintain rent controls which in the long run stopped the repair of old houses and the building of new ones (though they were unable or unconcerned to press the state or local authorities to provide enough accommodation for the homeless). In the Fourth Republic, where housing had become a desperate problem, the property-owners were still politically weak, but the main tenants' league had come under strong Communist influence and carried less weight than in the past.[22]

The sinister interests manipulated the politicians more successfully in popular demonology than in reality. At worst, like the *colons*, they might help to veto reforms when these could still have achieved a useful purpose. If, like the alcohol interests, they had the backing of several million voters and no organized opposition, they might even be able to impose bad policies on timid ministers. But wealth alone was not enough; when business mounted its major parliamentary operation against ratification of the European Coal and Steel Community, it suffered such a total defeat that it never tried again.[23] And it was rare for any of the lesser groups to have the numbers, or any of the larger

18. For the winegrowers see Warner; Ledermann; and J. Callen in *France-Observateur*, 27 May 1954. (Being poor and on the Left they were attacked less often than their allies by 'men of good-will'.) For their contribution to Poujadism see above, p. 166, Hoffmann, pp. 335–6, Royer in *Paysans*, pp. 186–9; and for their electoral importance, above, p. 330.

19. Perhaps one in ten or twenty of the 3 million *bouilleurs*: Goguel, no. 113, p. 309.

20. Michel Debré frustrated them, obtaining special powers by threatening to enforce Mendès-France's decree. By 1963 the *bouilleurs* were fighting a losing rearguard action.

21. Cf. Goguel, *Régime*, pp. 97–8, Meynaud, pp. 75–6,1 82, 195–6, 229; and above, p. 247n.

22. Meynaud and Lancelot, no. 161; on Communism, Brayance, pp. 143–4.

23. See below, p. 362.

ones the unity, to wield to the full the power they claimed. Big business had different interests and attitudes from small, industry from commerce, wholesalers from retailers, modern firms from backward ones. Sharecroppers did not always agree with owner-occupiers, lessors with lessees, rich regions with poor, efficient farmers with inefficient, winegrowers with beet-producers. Like the parties, the pressure-groups were riven by internal conflicts and differences, and were more effective for negative than for positive purposes.

2. THE SOCIAL CLASSES

No class suffered more from its internal divisions than industrial labour. The workers were fewer in France than in the other great democracies, and harder to organize because the average plant was much smaller. The trade unions were weaker in numbers and resources, for only in brief moments of excitement in 1919, 1936 and 1945 had they ever succeeded in attracting a majority of the proletariat. Faced with the stubborn and bitter hostility of their employers, the workers grew impatient with the slow task of building up industrial bargaining power, and instead launched sudden and violent attacks on entrenched positions which they had not the strength to capture or hold. Serious effort to improve conditions was therefore directed at the government rather than the employer. But labour's influence had always been gravely impaired by its inability to unite. Historically, political disputes had so harmed the labour movement in its formative years that in the twentieth century abstention from political activity became the first principle of trade union philosophy. This did not prevent the division of the labour movement between the revolutionary syndicalists, who preached the general strike to overthrow the bourgeois state, and the reformists who chose to work within it – but with their effectiveness limited by the traditional inhibitions against political action.

Between the wars the revolutionary wing of the movement fell under Communist control, while the reformist wing found its main base in the relatively powerful unions of state employees. Both had the state as target, but both were hampered by the anti-political tradition. After 1945 the Communists won control of the unions, but their violence and intimidation in the strikes of 1947 provoked most of the non-Communist minority to secede from CGT and, with active encouragement from SFIO, to set up CGT-Force ouvrière.[24] This curious amalgam of Socialist reformists, ultra-cautious moderates and old-style anarcho-syndicalists was soon surpassed in militancy by the Catholic unions of CFTC, traditionally a highly conservative body which by the end of the Fourth Republic had developed a wholly new aggressiveness and self-confidence. New minor groups were the staff union, CGC, which was politically rather conservative, and a small and internally divided union, CGSI, in which Gaullists and Vichy trade unionists competed furiously. But all the unions together probably organized in the 1950's no more than 2,500,000 out of about 12,000,000 employed (6,000,000 in industry, mining and transport).

24. On its initial 'subsidy' from Daniel Mayer as minister of labour see Meynaud, p. 70; Lorwin, p. 174n. (CGT and CFTC had had money also). See above, pp. 19, 34, 96–7 and notes for the split and for sources.

CGT outnumbered all the others together; CFTC was rather stronger than FO. But the non-Communist unions were more important than their numbers suggested, for many workers who stayed in CGT were suspicious of its Communist leadership – as they showed in periodical social security elections and in every political strike.[25]

The industrial power of the unions was reduced because CGT often behaved as, and was always suspected of being a tool of the party: many premiers (including Mollet though not Mendès-France) consequently refused contact with it. The political influence of the industrial workers was sterilized because they gave their votes to the Communist 'untouchables', though the non-Communist unions had much influence in SFIO, some in MRP and at times a little in RPF. Their parliamentary instrument was the labour committee of the Assembly, through which in 1950 they defeated the government's plan for compulsory industrial arbitration.[26] Yet, weak though they were politically, the unions could usually achieve more through a sympathetic government than through direct action.

Just after the war both the government and the political climate were exceptionally favourable to labour. In France, as in Britain, drastic social change seemed both inevitable and desirable. French business had been discredited by its conduct under Vichy, which left the *patronat* politically impotent and convinced that its popularity was irremediable: for years it shunned any publicity, indulging a mania for secrecy which continued to harm its reputation. But Vichy had also endowed business with a new organizational structure and leadership which enabled it to make a rapid recovery from the low point of 1946.[27]

In the past, loose parties of conservative individualists like *Alliance démocratique* had been powerfully influenced by business views and interests, though few businessmen had themselves sought a political career. The new party structure, less easily permeated from outside than the old, gave a new reason for tighter pressure-group organization but did not encourage more employers to take to politics. In the Assemblies of the Fourth Republic only about forty of the 600 deputies were industrialists, and only twenty of the country's 500 most important businessmen themselves chose to enter Parliament.[28] Because of the unpopularity of the great economic interests, even conservative politicians usually avoided too close association with CNPF, and few of its spokesmen in the two houses enjoyed much esteem (though René Mayer and Maurice Petsche, two of the very few deputies with big-business experience, between them held the key finance ministry for nearly four years between late 1947 and early 1952). If economic policy was comparatively satisfactory to industry during most of the period, this was due in part to its

25. Above, pp. 83–4. On numbers in 1953 see Lorwin, p. 177, and later Ross, no. 193b, p. 81.

26. On the collective bargaining bill see *JO* 4 January 1950, especially pp. 120–2; a year later an action committee of the unions and family associations used the labour committee to demand higher family allowances: *Monde*, 8 February and 27 April 1951 (and cf. above, p. 264).

27. For fears of publicity see Ehrmann, *Business*, pp. 207–18, 279–84, etc.; American estimates of French profits in a magazine subsidized by business were carefully blacked out before copies reached the news-stands, p. 216n. For short accounts of CNPF see Meynaud, pp. 45–51; Goguel, *Régime*, pp. 105–6; Brown, no. 33, pp. 703–4.

28. Dogan in *Partis et Classes*, pp. 298, 320, and in *Élections 1956*, p. 456.

success in sheltering behind the smaller and less efficient businessmen, who could count on their countrymen's sympathy for the 'little man', and in part to the affinity between the managers in the larger private enterprises and their brethren in the upper reaches of the administration.

The politicians shunned CNPF but courted PME (*Petites et moyennes entreprises*). Conversely the high civil servants considered the first a serious force and the second a noisy nuisance. Léon Gingembre, PME's active leader, was as loud in his denunciations as CNPF spokesmen were discreet in their suggestions. In the early years PME favoured direct action or the threat of it – in 1947 demonstrations (sometimes violent) against rationing and economic controls, in 1948 closing of shops and threats of tax strikes to protest against increases in taxation. As the balance of power shifted, its attention turned to politics. Since the small shopkeeper vote alone was estimated at 2,500,000, and the small man's survival was considered an important object of policy, Radicals and groups further to the Right were responsive to his demands and even Socialists and Communists bid for his support. In November 1949 PME organized an Economic Front with other middle-class bodies to co-ordinate opposition to Bidault's budget, and in the 1951 election this body tried through Taxpayers' Defence lists to organize an opposition Conservatism untainted by association with the government parties. Although this attempt failed, in the right-wing Assembly returned at this election a majority of the deputies joined a parliamentary inter-group pledged to forward the policies favoured by the Economic Front. When Pinay came to power PME 'greeted the government at first as if it had invented it; but as soon as some of M. Pinay's policies incurred its displeasure, it took even more liberties ... than with any of its predecessors'. Gingembre's activities were frequently an embarrassment to the more sedate employers, and it took the emergence of Pierre Poujade to convert him to statesmanship.[29]

The structural issues between these economic interests were important only in the early years. The nationalized industries, violently attacked at first, were by 1951 accepted by CNPF and its political spokesmen, apart from one or two ideological zealots in the upper house. René Mayer did try in 1953 to bring them under stricter governmental control, but this move probably owed as much to the centralizing tendencies of the *inspecteurs des finances* as to the business connections of the premier and his minister for industry, J. M. Louvel – and in any case it was frustrated by Parliament.[30] The installation of the social security system saw a series of battles over its administrative and financial organization, on which the Left usually got its way. But the Communists had to accept the election of administrators instead of their nomination by the unions, and the government and the parliamentary majority together were defeated by the self-employed; a 'Middle Classes Committee', inspired by Gingembre, led a massive refusal of contributions which made

29. See below, p. 379. On PME see Ehrmann, *Business*, pp. 172–84 ('Pinay', p. 180); Meynaud, pp. 51–5; Lavau, no. 139, and in *Partis et Classes* ('Les classes moyennes'), especially pp. 79–80; Brown, no. 33, pp. 74–5. For the influence of the methods and mentality of the small firm on all French business see D. S. Landes in Earle, Chapter 19 ('French business and the businessman') and J. E. Sawyer in *ibid.*, pp. 306–10.

30. See above, pp. 343–4; Lescuyer, pp. 115–16, 142–70.

Parliament give way and exclude them from the ordinary social security system by an amending law in 1948. Social security remained a major PME target, but Socialists and MRP defeated all the right-wing attempts to 'reorganize' it. In the third Parliament the Socialists, back in office, succeeded in establishing an old age pension fund; but Albert Gazier's efforts to reduce the cost of illness to the sick, though strongly supported by the unions and the social security administrators, came up against the stubborn and high-principled resistance so characteristic of doctors everywhere.[31]

In day-to-day politics the clashes between Right and Left turned on the usual questions: the burden and distribution of taxation, which fell the more heavily on the wage- and salary-earner because the self-employed and the professional man could so easily evade it; the size and objects of government expenditure; economic controls, wage and price policies, industrial relations, and social legislation. Often there was a straightforward clash of interests, ideologies or party loyalties; for instance late in 1956 the FO unions protested bitterly when PME demanded that Parliament reject without discussion all the social reforms then before it.[32] During most of the Fourth Republic's life these matters were the stuff of electoral, parliamentary and cabinet debate. Yet often the divisions were less clear-cut. In the early social security debates the Catholic party and union, MRP and CFTC, insisted against Left opposition on an autonomous family allowances fund; in December 1952 MRP brought down Pinay's Conservative government for attempting to tamper with it. Under Pinay and Laniel, PME and the textile industry fought hard against tax changes proposed by the bureaucracy and supported by most of CNPF.[33]

In 1951 the steel and metallurgical industries launched a campaign against the Coal and Steel Community. Léon Gingembre joined in with his customary violence, and the whole employers' organization followed with more restraint. But the steel cartels had inherited a bad reputation from the *Comité des Forges* of the Third Republic, and their opponents in the Monnet organization exploited it against them with great effect. Coal and railways, their former allies, were now nationalized; agriculture, hoping that the Community would form a precedent for similar arrangements for foodstuffs, was on the other side. The minister, Robert Schuman, stood firm and was supported by all the centre parties, and although CNPF had the support of the business Conservatives, the Gaullist nationalists, and the eager Communist advocates of a united front with 'the patriotic employers', the *patronat* went down to a defeat far heavier than anyone had expected: the treaty was ratified by a majority of 144. Thereafter business became very chary of risking its prestige and its unity in an open political battle.[34]

31. Galant, Chapters 4 and 5; Lavau, no. 139, pp. 380, 383; Meynaud, pp. 92–4, 240–3, 264–5, who quotes the boast of the 'Middle Classes Committee': 'Perhaps for the first time in parliamentary history we have seen a law that was voted, promulgated and in operation reconsidered and entirely modified by the same people who had drawn it up' (p. 264n.).

32. *AP* 1956, p. 174.

33. Ehrmann, *Business*, Chapters 6 to 8, for the employers' attitudes on economic issues (on taxation, pp. 309–20). One poll among them (*ibid.*, p. 299) showed that they thought well over half the budget went on civil service salaries (in fact 15% did).

34. Ehrmann, *Business*, pp. 407–16, and no. 84; summarized in Meynaud, p. 268. Cf. Gerbet, no. 98; and below, p. 379.

Lines were particularly blurred in agricultural matters. Few political groups tried simultaneously to attract both workers and bourgeois, and those that did risked their cohesion in the attempt, as both RPF and MRP found in 1952. But everyone courted the peasant vote, and from extreme Right to extreme Left every bench contained members of agriculture's 'invisible party'.[35] In the later years of the Fourth Republic a lobby of 100 was organized: the *Amicale parlementaire agricole*.[36] Sometimes townsmen of all political views combined to resist the pressure, for extreme conservatives were as critical of rural backwardness and privilege as any trade unionist, and their parliamentary representatives resented the fiscal advantages which the peasantry won through their political strength.[37] Parisian politicians who were notoriously subservient to urban pressure-groups spoke and voted with fine Jacobin determination against the outrageous claims of the *bouilleurs de cru*. On the other hand spokesmen for the farmer exalted the unity of the peasantry, denounced trade unions, middlemen and civil servants alike, and sometimes seemed to identify economic backwardness with a higher moral order.[38]

These conflicts did not always take an economic form. The countryside led the way in pressing for a return to the Third Republic, in which the Senate had been a fortress of agrarian influence and the electoral system had satisfied the peasantry by making the deputy essentially a local ambassador to the Paris bureaucracy rather than a champion of political causes. Rural leaders demanded a restoration of the Senate and the old electoral law for the explicit purpose of increasing the political influence of agriculture.[39] Usually, however, agrarian pressure had more immediate objects such as price supports, subsidies, investments and tax reliefs.

The German occupation and post-war shortages had improved agriculture's bargaining and purchasing power, and the peasants were never reconciled to losing these advantages.[40] In 1948 André Marie's cabinet broke up when it offended the trade unions and forfeited Socialist and MRP support by accepting peasant demands for higher food prices. Agrarian members, particularly but not only in the Peasant party, were always suspicious of the Socialists, and blocked Mollet's election as premier in 1951. They also waged a vendetta against René Mayer, the business Radical who as finance minister in 1948 had struck a blow at peasant hoarding by calling in the 5,000-franc notes. Their suspicions of him almost destroyed Pleven's second cabinet, in which he

35. Fauvet in *Monde*, 1–2 January 1950.
36. On the *Amicale* see *Paysans*, pp. 222, 247–8. Edgar Faure was chairman. It excluded Socialists and Communists – but they too courted rural votes: references in Williams, p. 333n.
37. For instance, *JO* 29 July 1950, pp. 6208–9, and 16 May 1951, pp. 5278–9, for attacks on proposals to make townsmen pay for rural family allowances by Robert Bétolaud, a PRL member for Paris, and Émile Hugues, a Radical from Alpes-Maritimes (the Riviera). On the fiscal privileges of agriculture see above, p. 26 and n.; cf. p. 252.
38. Mendras, no. 157, and in *Paysans*, p. 251; cf. R. Barrillon and J. M. Royer in *ibid.*, pp. 140–143, 197, 206; and Chevallier, pp. 141–79. On the *bouilleurs* see above, p. 357 and n.
39. MM. Lecacheux and Chaumié in the Consultative Assembly: *Inégalités*, pp. 40–1. Senators André Dulin (chairman of the agriculture committee) and René Blondelle (then president of FNSEA), reported in *Monde*, 28 February 1950, 3 March 1951, 13 April 1951 (cf. Williams, p. 334n.). Cf. Duverger, 'Conseil de la République ou Chambre d'agriculture', *Monde*, 22 July 1953; Dogan in *Paysans*, p. 214.
40. Agricultural income fell from 17% of national income in 1949 to 12% in 1958: *RFSP* 12.3 (1962), p. 577. Cf. above, p. 26n. 18.

was finance minister, and helped to bring down his own eighteen months later, in May 1953. That summer the end of inflation and the decrees of Laniel's government provoked the peasant organizations into blocking the country roads as a means of pressure. Their success was not forgotten.

Rural discontent greatly swelled the Poujadist vote in 1956, and in the third Assembly the peasant leaders pressed for 'indexation' of agricultural prices (a sliding scale which, like 'parity' in the United States, meant tying the prices of goods sold by the farmers to those of goods they bought). Their agitation weakened Mollet's government without extracting any serious concessions from it. It forced Bourgès-Maunoury to summon a special session of Parliament and would probably have overthrown him if he had not fallen earlier over his Algerian reform bill. Gaillard's ministry finally acceded to the demand for 'indexation', but de Gaulle's reversed the decision a year later; much of the early domestic history of the Fifth Republic turned on the peasants' struggle to recapture the ground they had so briefly won.

Like business and labour, the peasants formed too heterogeneous an interest to be easily brought within a single organization. They too were an object of political pressure as well as a motive force, and they were divided not only by politics but by clashes of interest and tactics between regions, products and economic groups. Because of these internal disputes it was said in the Third Republic that the clamour of one of the postmen's unions sounded louder to the government than that of the whole agricultural interest.[41] But here as elsewhere the Vichy period saw an organizational advance which was to have permanent consequences. Though the Vichy Peasant Corporation did not survive the Liberation, its conception and many of its leaders exerted a lasting influence in the Fourth Republic.

Until the second world war 'the history of agricultural organization is nothing but a long competition between the château-owner and the Radical deputy... after ten years, the Fourth Republic sees the two protagonists once more alone on the field'.[42] At the Liberation both were ousted for a moment by the *Confédération générale de l'agriculture*, CGA, through which a Socialist minister (Tanguy-Prigent) tried to organize the entire peasantry and attach it to his party. But the experiment was brief, for CGA soon became a shadow organization presiding ineffectively over its less extensive but more cohesive components, especially the Farmers' Federation, FNSEA (*Fédération nationale des syndicats d'exploitants agricoles*).[43]

Some departmental farmers' federations favoured the Left and even the Communists, but FNSEA was dominated by the rich capitalist corn- and beet- growers of northern France, who made large profits when prices were fixed at a level to keep the poor and marginal producer in business. Politically it was on the Right: of eighty officials of peasant organizations returned to the 1951 Parliament, half were Conservatives and only a quarter belonged to the

41. Frédérix, p. 36. For peasant diversity see Fauvet and Mendras in *Paysans*, pp. 1–35, and Fauvet, 'Le monde paysan', in *Partis et Classes*, pp. 155–77.

42. Mendras, no. 157, p. 737, and in *Paysans*, p. 232.

43. 'CGA, where certain vassals were more powerful than the suzerain': P. Delouvrier in *Crise*, p. 78. On it see *Paysans*, pp. 236–7 and 287–91; Brown, no. 33, pp. 706–8; Marabuto, pp. 349–59; G. Wright in Earle, pp. 226–31 (on 'Communists and Peasantry'), and nos. 223, 225.

'big three' parties of the Liberation.[44] In the agrarian crisis of 1953 the left-wing leaders of CGA finally lost all influence in their own organization, and their attempts to build a rival base among the poorer peasants of central France had little success.

The Conservative farmers profited little from their victory. Since their political friends were usually in power in the second Parliament, their leaders were reluctant to embarrass governments with excessive demands. This caution lost them support, and in the three Peasant party splits the extra-parliamentary organization always followed (or preceded) the intransigent counsels of Paul Antier. But in stirring up rural discontent no moderate could compete with Pierre Poujade or Henri Dorgères. At the 1956 election the extremists made alarming inroads into the peasant vote, and a year later an alliance of those three agitators forced the parliamentary leadership into uncompromising positions which divided majorities and disrupted governments.[45] Less spectacular but ultimately more serious was the threat to Conservative dominance from the young Catholics of JAC (*Jeunesse agricole chrétienne*), who in many of the regions away from the Paris basin were taking control of the local farmers' unions. They were reformers in outlook, based on the poorer areas, and more interested in land law reform, cheap credits and organized markets than in pressure on government to fix favourable prices. Early in the Fifth Republic their influence began to be felt in legislation, organization and politics, and in 1961 they took over the secretaryship of FNSEA.[46]

3. THE CHURCH AND ITS OPPONENTS

The transformation of the agricultural organizations and Christian trade unions were aspects of a startling development in French society: the vigour and progressiveness of the Catholic Church, which contrasted sharply with the exhaustion and incapacity to adapt displayed among the freethinkers from freemasons to Communists. But this striking political change was for some time obscured by the persistence of the old quarrel over the church schools.

Traditionally the line between Catholic and anticlerical had coincided with the division between Right and Left. The enemies of the Republic had their political base in the Church, while freemasonry mustered and drilled the opposing camp. The Catholic contribution to the Resistance went far to remove these memories, which MRP fervently hoped to erase. But the conflict, though less intense than in the past, was revived and played an important part in the politics of the Fourth Republic. The exclusion of religious teaching from the state schools, and the right of Catholic parents to send their children to denominational schools were generally admitted; the issue was whether private schools could be subsidized from public funds. Vichy revived the dying quarrel by granting subsidies. But at the Liberation the Communists

44. Wright, no. 223; Goguel, *Régime*, p. 104n.: 41 CNIP, 13 RPF, 8 Radicals, 8 MRP, 7 Communists, 6 SFIO. In 1951 CGA's 30 seats on the Economic Council were reduced to 3, 15 going to FNSEA and 12 to other bodies. On FNSEA see Meynaud, pp. 58–62; Goguel, *op. cit.*, pp. 103–5; and sources for CGA.

45. R. Barrillon in *Paysans*, pp. 131–43 ('Les modérés'); J. M. Royer, *ibid.*, pp. 149–206 ('De Dorgères à Poujade'); and above, pp. 155, 166 and nn., 344.

46. Wright, nos. 226, 228; Tavernier, no. 207; and above, p. 110.

successfully demanded their abolition in order to separate Socialists from MRP.[47]

At the 1951 election RPF used the same issue for the same purpose. No Catholic party could fall behind its rivals on this subject without risking the loss of clerical support and the defection of its voters. Throughout the west (where the Catholic school population was concentrated) the supporters of the cause were organized by the *Association de parents d'élèves de l'enseignement libre* (APEL), which successfully sought binding pledges from candidates and, rather less successfully, tried to prevent electoral alliances between allies and opponents of the Church. An *Association parlementaire pour la liberté de l'enseignement* (APLE) organized its 296 pledged supporters to vote only for governments which accepted their programme. In September 1951, helped by overseas votes, they easily carried Barangé's bill to restore the subsidies, which was the cause (or pretext) for the Socialists to break with the Third Force majority which had ruled the country for the past four years.[48]

The opposition centred on the teachers' unions and parents' associations of the state school system. The teachers, perhaps the only really successful trade union in France, had lost their old intolerant atheism but not their fervour for *laïcité*, which was shared even by the Catholic teachers of the CFTC union. In the countryside the electoral organization of the Socialists and to some extent of the Radicals relied heavily on their services. The anticlerical parties and organizations were grouped in a *Comité national de défense laïque* along with intellectual societies like the *Ligue des droits de l'homme*.[49]

Foreigners and Parisians might think this struggle outmoded, but Michel Debré was doubly unjust when he wrote in 1957 that it was a false conflict artificially kept alive for their own ends by the politicians of the System. For, far from wishing to exacerbate the division, the moderate politicians were forced by pressure from the Communists in 1945 and Debré's Gaullist colleagues in 1951 into a battle they had hoped to avoid.[50] Moreover, the quarrel aroused deep historical echoes in the villages. Debré's own attempt to settle it in 1960 was met by an anticlerical petition with ten million signatures. This had a more solid basis than mere prejudice. For state employment and promotion in it often went by preference to those educated in state schools, while many private employers favoured those with a Catholic upbringing; thus France had had separate ladders of social advancement. As the church schools were very unevenly distributed (predominant in the west, rare in the south) each ladder had its foot firmly embedded in the soil of a particular region.[51]

The struggle was thus waged between parties and provinces, classes and

47. The best short account is Rémond in *Laïcité*, pp. 381–400. And see above, pp. 29, 34.

48. Bosworth, Chapter 8, especially pp. 291–301. APLE included all MRP deputies, all RPF but 6, all Conservatives but 2, and 14 RGR: *AP* 1951, p. 179. See also Brown, no. 34; Goguel, *Régime*, pp. 94–7; below, p. 376n. Even in this election over 200 deputies ignored the problem in their election addresses: Rémond, *Laïcité*, p. 398.

49. On it see Charlot, no. 53; on the teachers, below, p. 446; cf. also p. 98, on freemasonry.

50. Rémond, *Laïcité*, pp. 385, 393, 396. Debré: *Ces princes qui nous gouvernent* (1957), pp. 44–6. Cf. above, pp. 22, 29, 39.

51. M. Crozier in *Partis et Classes*, pp. 88, 95–8; cf. above, p. 68, and Map 5. Villages: C. d'Aragon in *Paysans*, pp. 490–2, 504–6.

ideologies, as well as between organizations. But as the prudence of the politicians of the System indicated, it was far less intense in the Fourth Republic than in the Third. The 1945 and 1951 pattern was not repeated in 1956. By the Barangé law the church schools had been allocated a small subsidy, the state schools a much larger sum; the hierarchy was content with its modest success, and behaved with great discretion at the next election, while many anticlerical mayors demanded only half-heartedly the repeal of a measure which was an offence to their personal convictions but a boon to their communal finances. On both sides other issues, especially North Africa, overshadowed the traditional conflict. Some freemasons abandoned their enmity to the Church and went over to the extreme Right. Conversely, François Mauriac appealed to Catholics to support Mendès-France, and some Catholic trade unionists campaigned for the Socialist party. The Left had no wish to offend these new recruits, and though it won a large majority in the new Assembly repeal of Barangé's law was always blocked by defections, particularly among the young Mendesist deputies.[52]

Even on this question which had so long divided the parties, the two camps were far from united internally. The fissure between Communists and other anticlericals was deeper than that between the two traditional antagonists; the debates on the agricultural instruction bill of 1955 revived the old conflict, but in attenuated form because many rural Radicals now feared the *curé* less than the Communist schoolteacher.[53] In some country areas Socialists still hankered after the traditional alignment, often for electoral rather than ideological reasons (in 1955 the chief advocate of permitting local SFIO-Communist alliances was Robert Lacoste); but the party headquarters successfully forbade any such dealings. Most leaders of anticlerical pressure-groups tried to avoid allowing their activities to be exploited by the Communists against their democratic sympathizers.

On the other side the political influence of the Church was now as diverse as once it had been uniform. The attitude of the hierarchy differed sharply according to the state of peasant society in a region, the outlook of the local population and the personal views of individual prelates: even in a conservative diocese where Catholicism was strong, the bishop of Saint-Dié explicitly warned his flock not to forget the need for social justice and peace in the colonies and the world in their zeal for the church schools.[54] Outside the hierarchy political opinions were still more diverse. Those Catholics who refused to break with the Communist party were indeed sharply disciplined (though even here Rome seems to have been much more severe than the French church authorities). But with this exception the spectrum of Catholic opinion remained complete, from the neutralist Left by way of the centre parties and the Gaullists to a clerical-fascist extreme Right. Some Catholics were

52. *Élections 1956*, pp. 131–41 (J. Charlot on the Church), 158–61 (J. M. Royer on the anticlericals), 328 (C. Prieur on state schools), 422 (F. Goguel); Fauvet *IVe*, p. 186; *Paysans*, p. 334. Among right-wing freemasons, Martinaud-Déplat relied on conservative votes in 1956 (Olivesi, pp. 46, 52, 60) and Baylot left SFIO to become a Conservative deputy in 1958: cf. above, pp. 98, 130n., 347–8.

53. R. Leveau in *Paysans*, pp. 269–80; on Radical fears, p. 277.

54. J. Labbens in *ibid.*, pp. 327–43, especially 331–3, 336; Charlot in *Élections 1956*, pp. 132–5 (Saint-Dié).

the most resolute defenders of the rights of man in Algeria; others were crusaders for French sovereignty at any price. The battles within the ranks of the Church, wrote a sympathizer, sometimes seemed 'the only really pitiless struggle being fought out in France'.[55]

Here lay the political weakness, not only of the Church but of all the greatest corporations. Business and labour, agriculture and anticlericalism suffered from it equally. Different from one another in so many respects, they were all broad enough in appeal to form the basis for a political ideology which often had a stronger hold on men's minds than party loyalty. But by the same token they were so heterogeneous that there were few matters on which they could muster their full forces for united action. Occasionally a major common interest would arise: free collective bargaining for the unions, price 'indexation' for agriculture, subsidies for the church schools. But even on these there were often tactical differences which reflected differences of political outlook. On the major disputes of Fourth Republican politics – decolonization, or European union – each of the great corporations was split between the rival camps. And on the lesser matters that directly concerned them there were usually such divisions of interest within their own ranks that common action was impossible. Most of the day-to-day battles were therefore fought out between groups which were smaller but more homogeneous and so more easily mobilized than the great representative organizations. 'States within the State . . . the great confederations often suffer from the same weaknesses as the State.'[56]

55. Grosser, pp. 179–85 ('pitiless', p. 180). References above, pp. 103n., 114n., 161 n. 8, 172 n. 7.
56. Delouvrier in *Crise*, p. 78; cf. Meynaud, pp. 48, 58–9, etc.

Chapter 26

PRESSURE POLITICS

French republican tradition mistrusted intermediary bodies between the state and the citizen. In the Third Republic this disapproval deterred pressure-groups from acting as openly as in other countries. Their distaste for publicity contributed to the widely accepted belief that the country was clandestinely governed by occult forces – trusts or freemasons, oil companies or cardinals, Jews, bolsheviks or bankers – who dominated the politicians, fleeced the people, and stood revealed only when the conspiratorial warfare of rival feudatories broke out in an interminable and incomprehensible political scandal.

Vichy, with its corporative outlook, gave a fillip to organization in sectors of the economy where it had been weak. Post-war governments extended and strengthened this trend. For in 1945–46 the dominant political forces were opposed to individualism, and the overwhelming role of government in economic life obliged every interest to organize. Taxes and subsidies, managed imports and restrictive controls, fixed prices and allocated investments, rationing and nationalization made every trade and union strive to become an arbiter and not merely an object of policy.[1] In the Fourth Republic these activities continued more openly than before, but the traditional suspicion and mistrust persisted undiminished.

The strength of the pressure-groups reflected the weaknesses of the French political structure: sectional parties dependent on a narrow electoral base, a Parliament with no coherent majority offering every facility for obstruction, precarious and divided coalition governments. The groups themselves were often feeble in number, wealth and organization, racked by internal disputes, and unable to mobilize their paper forces. One interest often found another obstructing its demands; and excessive pressure on the politicians sometimes drove them to an indignant and negative response. The pressure-groups were therefore far stronger in defending old positions than in attacking new ones, and their influence contributed to *immobilisme* at home and abroad.

1. PLEDGES AND SUBSIDIES

Different pressure-groups employed varying tactics. The beet-growers shunned publicity as much as the Abbé Pierre's league to aid the homeless welcomed it.[2] The ex-servicemen or the *bouilleurs de cru* wielded electoral power that guaranteed them wide parliamentary support; other groups owed their influence to money rather than numbers. The unions and employers, anti-clericals and the Church each found some parties more favourable than others – but the peasantry despaired of no one. While influence in Parliament had its

1. Hamon, no. 120, p. 844; Priouret, *Députés*, pp. 232–4; Goguel in *Aspects*, pp. 263–5; and above, p. 25–8.

2. Homeless: Meynaud, pp. 224–5, and in no. 161, p. 827. In 1950 the alcohol interests strongly opposed a bill limiting the 'non-repayable advances' the state could make in a year, lest it meant publicity for their subsidy and led to a cut: Warner, p. 276, n. 77; Malignac, no. 153, pp. 906–7.

uses, especially for obstruction, the administration had great power and unpopular groups like big business concentrated their efforts on it. An interest excluded from other channels of communication occasionally gained a hearing through direct action.

This was a last resort, for there were many legitimate opportunities to influence politicians. A general election was one of the main ones. There is no evidence of pressure-groups trying to influence a party's choice of candidate, but once he was chosen they were active in seeking pledges at both national and local level. Some demands conflicted: the friends and enemies of church school subsidies, or of football pools, strove only to frustrate their rivals. Some, like the blind or the ex-servicemen, appealed to every group. Party headquarters made some effort to help their men; in 1956 the Socialists circulated official replies to 29 groups ranging from the students' union to PME, the small businessmen.[3] But the French candidate could not shelter as safely beneath this umbrella as his British counterpart. The Labour or Conservative politician in 1950 had little to gain by pledging support to the Catholic Church over payments to church schools; first the party loyalty of voters was high, secondly he would find it hard to fulfil his pledge if he were elected and everyone knew it, and thirdly his only serious competitor was as likely to resist the demand as himself. The Frenchman calculated very differently. His voters were more easily alienated, he was freer to defend personal views, and a united front of his competitors against the pressure-groups was inconceivable.

Yet, surprisingly often, candidates were not intimidated. In 1956 in Puy-de-Dôme the Conservative and independent Peasant candidates refused any answers at all until after the poll. In Isère even the ex-servicemen had favourable replies only from the Left, and the other parties were silent or noncommittal. At Nancy seven organizations published voting recommendations in the local press; only two had had a reply (even an unsatisfactory one) from more than half the lists, and the Conservatives, who won three seats, gave a favourable answer only to the supporters of church schools.[4] However, many sitting members (especially men of the Right and especially in rural areas) for the first time systematically used letters from local professional groups thanking them for their services, which they hoped would provide a useful shield against the Poujadist assault. Nationally the Conservatives and the Peasant party, faced with the same threat, gave pledges of full support to small business and shopkeeper interests and were often rewarded by praise in the professional press. But 'the discretion of these journals seems to be exactly proportional to the power of the groups whose views they express'.[5]

It did not follow that strong silent groups like the beet-growers, the road

3. J. M. Royer in *Élections 1956*, pp. 154, 155, 162–3; Rose, no. 169, p. 262.

4. Williams, no. 168, p. 167 and n.; the seven were APEL, the CFTC railwaymen, the CGT technical-school teachers, the European Movement (cf. Meynaud, p. 145n.), the tourist trade, the Abbé Pierre's league for the homeless (this was his old constituency), and the pro-Communist tenants' league. In Ille-et-Vilaine two Poujadists sent personal replies to APEL (the party was officially neutral), and eight candidates wrote individually to the victims of war damage: none gained any advantage in votes. Lavau holds that the demands for pledges are ineffective, but distract the candidate from major problems: *Pressures*, pp. 69–70. Cf. Buron, pp. 49–50.

5. Royer in *Élections 1956*, pp. 154–6, 161–2 (quotation from p. 161, cf. pp. 147, 153).

hauliers or CNPF refrained from playing any role at elections. Expenditure was not legally limited. An adequate campaign cost about £6,000 in Paris and £2,500 in an average provincial seat, though in a small or poor department much less would do; within limits these amounts could usefully be exceeded, but in 1956 only one of the few really lavish spenders was successful.[6] Deputies therefore had good reason to fear a dissolution, for an election meant dependence either on the party (and the best-organized were rarely the wealthiest) or on the pressure-groups. Although some basic costs were paid by the state, fully for lists which won 5% of the vote and partially for others, 'the search for campaign funds . . . poisons the life of democracies and of all parties whatsoever. None has any reason to envy or reproach another'.[7]

In secretive France there was even less reliable information about the sources of funds than in other countries. Now and then a little became known. In 1953, when André Boutemy was driven to resign from the cabinet to which René Mayer had imprudently appointed him, it was affirmed without contradiction that through his office in the rue de Penthièvre CNPF had subsidized every party but the Communists. No promises were exacted in return for these subsidies, but the amount 'varied according to the quality or the utility of the candidatures'. In the 1956 campaign the national president of the wholesale clothiers, on behalf of a unanimous committee, circulated his members with a frank appeal against candidates who opposed 'a free and private economy', adding 'It is vital that we should be able to help those who support us, who may however belong to various parties. For this we need money, and money now.'[8] It was alleged that in the Fourth Republic 'all the previous forms of subsidy were employed together'. Business funds were given not only to party leaders, and to individual members for their election expenses, but even for specific votes on bills, amendments or the election of a premier, though the writer admitted that 'this last method seems at the present moment (1953) relatively little used'.[9] The member's self-respect was safeguarded by another common but indirect procedure: some groups amiably offered him the office space and secretarial help which the American congressman is given but the European legislator lacks.[10]

6. Estimates given me at the time by several parties: fuller in no 168, pp. 159–60. In 1946 a right-wing deputy spent a modest 1,800,000 francs (£3,000) and the Communists 3,000,000 in the nine-member Arras seat: Fusilier, no. 96, with figures on SFIO and Communist spending. The ARS winner in a crucial Paris by-election in 1952 spent £14,000: Faucher, p. 27. Robert Hersant stood in 1956 as a Radical in Oise, which has a tradition of heavy spending, and his lavish publicity, children's holiday camps, club subscriptions and film-star visits were said to have cost £100,000; he won, was unseated (nominally for his war record), but was re-elected with a much bigger vote. See Buron, pp. 65–70; and above, p. 65.

7. Dissolution: Berlia, no. 12a, pp. 431–2; R. Lecourt, *JO* 27 May 1953, pp. 2859–60. 'Poisons': Isorni, *Ainsi*, p. 9. A list with under 3% of the vote in 1945–46 (5% from 1951) lost a deposit of £20 per candidate and had to pay for petrol and billposting; with under 2½% (from 1951) it also had to pay for paper, printing and (in theory) postage of election addresses, unless it won a seat. See Nicholas, no. 167, p. 146; Dogan, no. 71, pp. 88–98. Another expense was the hire of professional boxers, who in 1956 cost £4 to £5 a night in the provinces but £30 in Paris with its greater demand and risks: P. Bouju at International Political Science Association, Paris, 29 September 1961.

8. CNPF: Isorni, *Ainsi*, pp. 9–10; Boutemy was said to have paid out a milliard francs (£1,000,000: Schoenbrun, p. 149; Brown, no. 33, p. 717) to over a hundred deputies. The clothiers' letter is given in full by Royer in *Élections 1956*, p. 164. And see above, p. 65.

9. Fusilier, no. 96, pp. 271–2.

10. Ehrmann, *Business*, p. 233; Muselier, p. 168; Priouret, *Députés*, pp. 233–4.

Being concealed, these activities aroused suspicion and speculation. Yet a senior official well placed to judge maintained that the Parliaments of the Fourth Republic were freer from corruption than those before 1940, or even perhaps before 1914. A leading parliamentary journalist wrote in 1957 that 'most members and parties have a hard time making ends meet'.[11] Often the power of money was overestimated. In 1951 Queuille, the Radical premier, personally solicited business funds for Isorni's Vichyites in order to weaken the Gaullists; the damage to RPF was negligible. Next year CNPF seems to have encouraged deputies it had subsidized to desert de Gaulle for Pinay; but these defectors were Conservatives on an electoral hitch-hike rather than real *compagnons*, the General's tactics were keeping their leaders out of office, and when the split occurred RPF's momentum was already declining in the country. Locally as well as centrally business seems to have spread its manna widely and rarely concentrated on a single candidate, so that electoral chances were less unequal than they sometimes appeared. The most conservative parties were usually the wealthiest, but not always. When the Communists were in office at the Liberation they had no difficulty finding 'angels' to subsidize them (if only to buy immunity for less than angelic wartime conduct). Mendès-France's movement did not seem unduly hampered by financial stringency. If money was often spent in the hope of political influence, influence in fact or in prospect attracted money too.[12]

The electoral power of the interest-groups was equally exaggerated. In 1956 the deputy with most business support was beaten in Paris, the leader of the *bouilleurs de cru* lost his seat, and a Peasant party member was ousted in spite of the support, thoroughly and systematically exploited, of all the local agricultural organizations.[13] As in any Parliament many Right and Centre deputies had close ties to business and farmers' groups, but the members of the disciplined parties were little affected by them. Socialists who rebelled against their party did so over the electoral law or EDC. MRP members defected spectacularly during the business-supported Pinay government, and again to support Mendès-France for premier in 1953 (though not in 1954). In 1955 that leader inspired the greatest of Radical revolts, which was directed against the interests rather than for them. On the union side, the opposition of CFTC's left wing did MRP little harm in 1956. The one conspicuous contribution of a pressure-group to a major change of policy was APEL's campaign for church school subsidies in 1951; yet even with no one drilling the clerical forces the voters would probably, under that electoral law, have returned them in numbers sufficient for victory.[14]

11. Delouvrier in *Crise*, p. 77; Fauvet, *Déchirée*, p. 136 (phrase omitted in *Cockpit*, p. 143). Cf. Meynaud, p. 161; Hamon, *De Gaulle*, p. 34, and no. 120, p. 840; Priouret, *Députés*, p. 233; Buron, p. 107.

12. Queuille: Isorni, *Ainsi*, p. 10. RPF: Ehrmann, *Business*, pp. 225, 230–2; Meynaud, pp. 313–14; above, p. 143. Gaullist 'angels' later financed Mendès-France: Guéry, pp. 19, 29, cf. Bardonnet, p. 268n. Local money flowed to a sitting member: Buron, p. 68; above, p. 324.

13. On M. Denais (Paris) see Royer in *Élections 1956*, pp. 162–3; on M. Raffarin (the Peasant) *ibid.*, and Thomas, no. 170, p. 275; on the *bouilleurs*' leader, above, p. 357.

14. Bosworth, p. 297.

2. PARLIAMENTARY LOBBYING

Some pressure-groups found in Parliament the ideal arena for their activities; others preferred to fight on different terrain; none could afford to leave this sector wholly unguarded. A friendly member could render many services. He could inform the group about party and governmental intentions and the likely reception of a group proposal or strategy. He could introduce acceptable bills and amendments, and indeed many private members' proposals were drafted by the groups. PME inspired 32 in eighteen months of the second Parliament, making no bones about announcing publicly that 'At the Federation's request, MM. Boisdé and Frédéric-Dupont have introduced ...' and even more precise statements. Yet though this 'indirect initiative in legislation' was widely used, the results were disappointing for few private members' proposals ever passed into law. Several housing groups gave up sending prefabricated bills, not because they could find no introducer but because the bills failed; instead they fed members with evidence and argument and left them to draw up their own proposals, which in turn sometimes stimulated government action.[15]

It was far easier to stop obnoxious plans than to carry favourable ones. A few friendly members of the right committee, as assiduous in their attendance at the proper time as others were lax, could often obstruct effectively – and in a Parliament chronically short of time a bill delayed was often a bill deceased. A government proposal was harder to block, but could often be amended.[16] The cabinet that insisted on a thoroughly objectionable measure could sometimes be ousted on a different question; its successor might well be more pliable. Even if the bill went into force Parliament could propose to abrogate the detailed decrees applying it. By such means the alcohol interests undid all Mendès-France's measures within a year – and the Left, at the same period, upset René Mayer's attempt to bring the nationalized industries under strict governmental control.[17] Nor were these pressures confined to legislation. In February 1948 all sections of the Assembly combined against René Mayer's recent austerity budget by 'log-rolling' in favour of different categories of state employees (but with the finance committee's help the cabinet finally beat off the attack). In June 1950 the finance committee itself, only MRP dissenting, supported a Socialist proposal about civil service salaries and the Bidault government was overthrown on it.[18] In February 1954 PME instructed its members to put pressure on MRP and other deputies to oppose any move to raise the general wage level. Nine months earlier, 22 members promised to interpellate the government on the cuts in investments on behalf of small business.[19]

'The circulars and the delegations of unions, federations, confederations,

15. Meynaud, pp. 191–9, and no. 161, pp. 846–7 (housing); Lavau, *Pressures*, pp. 86–7, and no. 139, pp. 371–2, 379. On the bills cf. Dogan in *Paysans*, pp. 223–7; Buron, pp. 104–5, 122, 155.

16. Friends of the building companies amended the *loi-cadre* on housing: *AP* 1956, p. 143. Bills against alcoholism in the colonies were never reported: above, p. 258n. Cf. Lavau, no. 141, pp. 16–18.

17. Cf. above, pp. 272, 357, 361; and below, p. 424.

18. *AP* 1948, p. 18; 1950, p. 123; and above, p. 254.

19. Lavau, no. 139, pp. 378, 383.

leagues and associations of all kinds assail the deputies from beginning to end of their term and more or less daily', wrote a former deputy. In eighteen months in 1953–54 PME sent five letters to every senator and twelve to every deputy or every member of the finance committee, on whom the pressure was heaviest.[20] Some groups needed to go no further. The farmers, the small businessmen or the supporters of church school subsidies could count on an attentive hearing from members anxious for re-election. Groups with money but not numbers made the most of the assets they had, and often supplied deputies and especially members of the committees which concerned them with quantities of well-produced and marshalled information. The committees had neither adequate time nor expert staff; and by a curious quirk of parliamentary psychology, this plausible evidence from men with money at stake was often taken more seriously than the information supplied by a disinterested but suspect executive.[21]

Despite all the opportunities for influencing members by votes or subsidies, hospitality or information, pressure-group leaders found them inadequate, and after 1951 they increasingly sought to get into Parliament themselves (some had doubtless used their organizations merely as political stepping-stones). They were not very numerous: a critical left-wing observer reckoned the known interest-group spokesmen at under 60 out of over 900 parliamentarians. But a spokesman could win over his political friends, and sometimes 'influence the ministers belonging to his party even if they hold him in low esteem'. And through these agents the interests 'instigated, animated and directed groups of sympathetic members to defend their cause'.[22]

In the pre-war Chamber of Deputies there had been an astonishing proliferation of groups for the defence of minor interests, from the concierges of Paris to the commercial travellers. They had only 'an insignificant influence on the life of Parliament'.[23] Some observers criticized them harshly, and though the end of *scrutin d'arrondissement* had weakened their electoral importance, the National Assembly of the Fourth Republic tried to ban them altogether.[24] But the deputies evaded the rule by forming groups to 'study' particular questions: there were fewer than twenty of these early in the second Parliament but a hundred in the third (half as many as in the old Chamber).[25] Among the first were the forestry *groupe d'étude* which campaigned for compensation after the great forest fires in Landes in 1949, and the alcohol 'study

20. *Ibid.*, pp. 377–8 (and cf. above, p. 251n.). Quotation by M. Guérin of MRP in 1953: Georgel, i. 183.

21. On the importance and acceptability of documentation, Goguel, *Régime*, p. 105; Meynaud, p. 159; Ehrmann, *Business*, pp. 235–6; Mendras, no. 157, pp. 747–8; Hamon, no. 121, pp. 557–8. On committees: Brindillac, no. 29, p. 61, and above, p. 246f.; through them the road hauliers' spokesmen could influence the rate structure of the nationalized railways: G. Vedel, quoted Lescuyer, no. 143, pp. 1178–9, cf. Duverger, *System*, p. 118.

22. Lavau, *Pressures*, pp. 67, 84. Hospitality : Buron, pp. 107–9.

23. Barthélemy, *Essai*, p. 83 and ff.; the film group wanted free entry to cinemas for its 180 members. Before 1914 there was said to be a group of deputies dissatisfied with their prefects: Jouvenel, p. 72n.

24. Standing Order 13: 'Est interdite la constitution, au sein de l'Assemblée, de groupes dits "de défense d'intérêts particuliers, locaux ou professionnels".'

25. A hundred: Bardonnet, p. 269. Half: cf. Barthélemy, p. 87. Socialists could not join one without the parliamentary party's consent: Waline, no. 213, p. 1211. The standing order was worded more strictly but taken no more seriously in the Fifth Republic: *ibid.*, p. 1207.

group', set up that December with over a hundred deputies from the Right to the Communists and four committee chairmen (including Finance) as vice-presidents; one of its professed objects was to examine the incidence of taxation on the interests concerned with alcohol.[26] Some of the groups held large annual banquets attended by members of Parliament and often presided over by the minister with whom they dealt. In 1954 PME's *groupe d'étude et d'action de l'économie privée* had its general meeting at the Palais Bourbon, attended by both members and non-members of Parliament and with a non-member in the chair. When the *bouilleurs*' leader André Liautey was elected in 1951 he promptly organized a 'study group' of 24 members which 'constituted the parliamentary base of operations for the *bouilleurs* throughout the life of the Assembly'. The powerful *Amicale agricole* played an active part in overthrowing Mayer's government in 1953 and proposed its own vote of censure against Bourgès-Maunoury in 1957.[27]

The main aim of the groups was to focus parliamentary pressure during the budget debates. 'Many groups (particularly, but not only, the farmers) have got into the habit of regarding the State as a universal insurance fund which operates without collecting premiums.'[28] Even before their parliamentary organization had developed, the small business groups mounted a powerful attack on René Mayer's special austerity levy in early 1948 and obtained substantial modifications. Some groups with a wide base of parliamentary support could make trouble for the strongest government, and every year there was difficulty over the post office, education and above all war pensions estimates.[29] The groups were strong when the government was weak. In 1949–1950 they helped to bring Bidault's majority down to single figures. The well-organized alcohol and tobacco-growing 'study groups' obtained some concessions – with the active aid of the chairman of the finance committee, and of a flood of constituents' letters and telegrams urging members to refuse confidence in the government. But the still more vociferous road hauliers' lobby overreached itself; the government refused any concession and was upheld – by four votes. 'People were arrogant enough to bring collective pressure . . . into this very house. In the galleries of the Assembly there appeared more or less qualified representatives of special interests who . . . in the midst of discussion sent . . . their injunctions to certain members of the Assembly. . . . There are dialogues a regime cannot tolerate unless it is ready to sign its own death warrant.'[30]

26. *Monde*, 23 November 1949 (forestry group), 5 December (alcohol group, cf. above, p. 356). The Assembly spent several sittings on agricultural calamities in the summer of 1950 but never debated Korea: *AP* 1950, p. 155.

27. Ehrmann, *Business*, pp. 244 (for road hauliers' banquets), 246–7 (for the PME group, which included a third of MRP, and four Socialists); Lavau, no. 139, pp. 375–6, 379; Brown, no. 35, for the *bouilleurs* (who had had 150 members in their pre-war group: Barthélemy, p. 84); above, pp. 356, 363 (*Amicale agricole*).

28. Meynaud, p. 275.

29. *Ibid.*, p. 164n., Duverger, *Institutions financières*, pp. 143–4 (Mayer levy); Goguel, *Régime*, pp. 97–8, 102. Also above, pp. 247n., 252.

30. H. Teitgen (MRP), *JO* 3 January 1950, p. 26; cf. *AP* 1949, p. 217, 1950, p. 2; *Monde*, 30 December 1949 (Rémy Roure, quoted Williams, p. 337n.), and 4 January 1950; Ehrmann, *Business*, p. 237; Goguel, *Régime*, p. 106. The pressure was so strong that SFIO authorized a member to abstain – and so outrageous that in the end he did not. On earlier pressure by the

[*over*

In this case a powerful pressure-group was worsted by an exceptionally shaky government. Six years later a rather stronger ministry was assailed by a rising popular movement which had already paralysed the administration and intimidated the parties. Edgar Faure, by so contriving the encounter that the deputies could not vote all Poujade's demands without obviously humiliating themselves, managed to deny the agitator the conspicuous political triumph which he wanted far more than limited practical concessions.[31] But most pressure-groups had no such ulterior political aim, and most parliamentary battles were settled by a compromise. In 1957 the tenants' organizations demanded a 2% cut in the interest rate on loans for house building, and got 1%; and won a year's postponement of rent decontrol for vacant ten-year-old houses, after the justice committee had asked for two. Even when one side won, it was not always the rich, modern and powerful, though the senators – more responsive to economic weight than the deputies and less to numbers – enabled the business lobby to prevent effective anti-trust legislation in 1953. In 1957, when a bank strike won salary increases for the clerks, the finance minister tried to defer payment but interpellations in the Assembly made him give way.[32]

Questions of purely local interest often cut across party or ideological lines. On the Mont Blanc tunnel, or the diversion of Loire water to Paris, constituency interests took precedence over political views. All Corsicans (and there were many in Paris) rallied to the defence of their perpetually discontented fellows at home. Gaston Defferre was a Socialist, but also mayor of Marseilles and an ardent and successful advocate of state subsidies for private shipbuilders. Other regional divisions had more far-reaching implications. In 1950 a bill to permit the teaching of local languages in schools outraged the champions of the Republic one and indivisible and provoked a bitter dispute with the Basque and Breton friends of local autonomy. In 1953 an unhappy clash occurred over the trial of thirteen Alsatians who, as conscripts in the German army, had participated in the SS massacre at Oradour nine years earlier: it caused demonstrations in both Alsace and Limousin and divided even the Communist party.[33] Because of the geographical concentration of wine-growing, war damage or Catholic schools, some long-standing political disputes had an essentially regional character.[34]

A wide variety of cause-groups also operated in Parliament. Some, like the

same lobby see the protest of the premier, Queuille: *AP* 1949, pp. 327–9, *JO* 24 May 1949, p. 2871. In 1951 the hauliers' leader was elected a deputy.

31. Hoffmann, pp. 76–84 (cf. pp. 43–6, 65–70).

32. Meynaud, p. 193n. (banks), and no. 161, pp. 847–50 (housing); Ehrmann, *Business*, pp. 386–8 (cartels); Arné, p. 370 (banks).

33. Local groups: Meynaud, pp. 231–6, and his *Nouvelles études* (above, p. 356n.), pp. 148–57. Defferre: Jarrier, no. 128, pp. 890–1; Ehrmann, *Business*, p. 246. Languages: articles by Dauzat in *Monde*, 15 and 29 March, 26 April, 17 May 1950, and Duhamel in *Figaro*, 29–30 April, 5 and 12 May. Oradour: *JO* 19 February 1953; *AP* 1953, pp. 10–11, 14–16; Chapman, *Prefects*, pp. 221–222; Faucher, pp. 27–8 (on the Communists).

34. 'Every member from Normandy votes for apples, every member for Hérault votes for wine. For eight years I voted for Armagnac wheat and brandy': Barthélemy, *Essai*, p. 86; cf. above, p. 330. Of the 15 departments in which church schools taught 25% of primary schoolchildren, 13 were in the west or in the Massif Central (see Map 5). So were 14 of the 21 in which they taught over half the secondary schoolchildren: *Monde*, 8 August 1951.

Abbé Pierre's league to aid the homeless, obtained a ready hearing even though they had little electoral support behind them: their case was obviously worthy and faced no direct opposition. Others like the anti-alcoholic campaign probably had the public (especially women voters) on their side, but their support was shallow and diffused and their opponents, backed by money and substantial numbers, were far more determined and single-minded. Others again, like opposition to the death penalty, were shunned even by sympathetic members because their cause was considered electorally disastrous.[35]

Some political causes enjoyed organized support in several parties. APLE grouped the parliamentary friends of the Catholic schools; the division between Communists and others prevented any similar organization (though not co-operation) of their opponents. Less formally, in the second Parliament, the leaders of pro-European opinion met to concert tactics, and the non-Communist opponents of EDC formed a 'shadow cabinet' extending from Mitterrand and Lacoste to Chaban-Delmas and André Boutemy; its secretary claimed that it intervened effectively in ministerial crises both before and after the defeat of the treaty.[36] As the Algerian war and its repercussions came to dominate the third Parliament, the diehards and the conciliators each developed habits of co-operation which cut across party lines. A 'quartet' of right-wing leaders (Bidault, Duchet, Morice and Soustelle) gave full support to SFIO ministers like Lacoste and Lejeune, while the minority Socialists found themselves far closer in outlook to the Mendesists than to Guy Mollet and the majority of their own party.

On both sides of this conflict the 'causes' outweighed the 'interests'. The men who on progressive or humanitarian grounds condemned repression and demanded a political solution were a minority in Parliament, but not an impotent one. They were able to focus critical opinion, to modify some repressive legislation, and in April 1958 to rout the diehards in the Assembly and drive them into subversion and mutiny. Many parliamentary voices were raised on behalf of liberal principles or policies, yet none spoke for the 'Cartieriste' businessmen who wanted to save money by evacuating Algeria. Conversely the small North African lobby, whose manœuvres had sometimes intimidated governments when their majorities were already melting away, now became a real parliamentary force because the interests of the wealthy settlers were buttressed by the sentiments of the army and of nationalist opinion in France.

3. BUREAUCRATS AND POLITICIANS

In the early years of the Fourth Republic parliamentary influence was valuable to a pressure-group that wished to obstruct governmental action. But it was already inadequate for positive measures, since even a group enjoying general goodwill found it hard to pass a bill through the overloaded legislative machine. Subsequent grants of special powers to the government still further

35. Meynaud and Lancelot, no. 161, p. 844 (homeless); Brown, no. 35, p. 990 (alcohol); Isorni, *Ainsi*, pp. 65–7 (death penalty – which is rarely carried out in France).

36. Europeans: Faucher, p. 91. 'Shadow cabinet': Bloch-Morhange, p. 101, and Chapters 7–15 *passim*.

reinforced the bureaucracy and reduced the value of Parliament, even as a defensive instrument. Whether to put their positive case or to avert decisions harmful to their interests, groups wishing to influence policy found access to the executive essential. Increasingly they directed their efforts to building up consultative machinery outside Parliament to ensure that their views had a hearing at the time and place where they could do most good.

Even if a group was strong enough to get a satisfactory bill through Parliament, the administration could often restrict its application – or, conversely, help the group by narrowing the scope of a bill it disliked. When Parliament was vigilant the executive's power was limited, but when it was inattentive or indifferent the administration often made the decisions. In 1955 a Conservative minister of agriculture accepted the demands of the large and efficient butter producers and banned the preservative which allowed the small farmer's butter, produced in primitive conditions, to be kept for sale in the towns; in 1956 his Radical successor recommended that the ban be applied 'with the greatest tolerance' and in fact it ceased to operate – though a bill to legalize the new decision received only 160 votes in the Assembly. The administration was particularly well placed when Parliament contented itself with passing a *loi-cadre*, and the final vote of the housing law of 1957 was rather the beginning than the end of the struggle of the opposing pressure-groups to get their respective policies put into effect.[37]

The interest-groups therefore usually tried to establish regular relations with the civil servants dealing with their problems (though in a very few cases open warfare prevailed, and Poujade at the height of his power was appeased by the transfer of two civil servants guilty of devising too-effective checks against tax frauds).[38] But as a rule the views of a branch of the administration tended to reflect those of its regular clients, shorn of their least reasonable demands. For few conflicts of interest simply opposed private greed to a clear common good. More often there was a division of forces in which government departments and private interests were ranged on both sides.[39] Only one department, the ministry of finance, was occupationally bound to oppose the pressure-groups; and to all who wanted money (and few did not) it was the fortress to be stormed. All, therefore, wanted allies within the official world fighting for objectives similar to, even if more limited than their own. They valued the administrative autonomy of these allies, and when Guy Mollet reduced the ministries of health, agriculture and merchant marine to mere ministries of state (*secrétariats d'État*) subject to senior 'overlords', there were outcries from the surgeries, farms and ports.[40]

The interests tried to influence the policies of their bureaucratic mentors through a proliferating network of consultative committees whose advice the administration was often required to ask, though rarely to take. By 1957 over

37. Meynaud, p. 240n. (butter), and no. 161, p. 846 (housing law). Cf. Warner, p. 266 n. 88, for the administration's contradictory rulings about *piquettes* (adulterated wines) in 1947; and see above, pp. 343–4, and below, p. 392.

38. Hoffmann, p. 77; Ehrmann, *Business*, p. 492n.; cf. Meynaud, p. 283n.

39. Meynaud, pp. 206–11, 319–20; Ehrmann, no. 85, p. 548; above, p. 344.

40. Doctors: Meynaud, p. 209n.; no. 160, p. 587n. Agriculture: *Paysans*, pp. 139n., 249, 253–60 C. de Vaugelas); cf. Arné, pp. 346n., 362, 367. On industry, cf. Ehrmann, pp. 261–3. Generally Lavau, *Pressures*, p. 72.

four thousand were operating in Paris, and though their importance varied greatly it was quite sufficient for the interests to try hard to expand the number. Some observers indeed feared that consultation had become a euphemism for the dominance of private interests within the administration itself, and a threat to the official's sense of responsibility. The *Conseil supérieur des alcools* gave some plausibility to this view. It included politicians and a majority of group spokesmen as well as officials, and the beet-growers' secretary Henri Cayre boasted that through it he had personally helped draft the Laniel ministry's decrees dealing with alcohol in 1953. Yet three years later, when its ex-chairman was himself in office as minister of state for the budget, its advice was overridden by the minister of finance (Paul Ramadier) and the lobby was routed.[41] And influence went both ways. A pedestrians' association with its headquarters at the ministry of transport provided some slight counterweight to the motorists and the road hauliers. When the steelmasters were campaigning against the Coal and Steel Community, the Monnet organization encouraged the creation of a new association of users of steel products to show that business was not all on one side.[42]

On the executive battlefield the balance of power between groups differed sharply from that prevailing in the electoral and parliamentary arenas. The large modern firms, on whose behalf some politicians might vote but few would speak in public, enjoyed excellent contacts and sympathies among the senior officials. Many links attached the *inspecteurs des finances*, if not to the capitalist magnates, at least to their salaried staffs who shared their own unsentimental concern for efficiency, productivity and modernization and their distaste for the myth of the 'little man' so dear to voters and politicians. Public and private managers had the same educational background and often similar career prospects, for many rising young officials went into private firms at forty. This *pantouflage* gave big business, unlike its political competitors, an able staff which knew exactly how the official machine worked, where to get information, whom to approach and when. 'The frontier between the public and the private sector has become uncertain. . . . It is becoming more and more important for every firm of any size to have in its employ a manager who can be sure of getting without delay a friendly interview . . . with the right senior civil servant. . . .'[43]

Small business used other methods, for CNPF and PME had distinct constituencies, different leadership, and sharply contrasting styles. Big-business spokesmen preferred quiet negotiation over details with their fellow *inspecteurs des finances* to the angry strikes and demonstrations which PME led in 1947–48. They looked down on M. Gingembre as a demagogue and on his organization as a noisy and tiresome agitation of shopkeepers, while he despised the smooth functionaries of the *patronat* and denounced the trusts no

41. Meynaud, pp. 211–16; on Cayre, above, p. 356. Cf. Galichon in *Institutions*, i. 280–2, and in *Travail*, p. 849; Waline in *Politique et Technique*, p. 169; Lavau, *Pressures*, pp. 82–4, 93–4; Ehrmann, *Business*, p. 260, and no. 85, pp. 541–3; Arné, pp. 367–8.

42. Ehrmann, no. 84, pp. 473–4; *Business*, pp. 171–2. Pedestrians: I owe this example to M. Goguel. cf. above, p. 344n.

43. Siegfried, *De la IIIe*, pp. 246–7. See also Brindillac, no. 28; Ehrmann, *Business*, pp. 257–71 and 488, and no. 85, pp. 550–2; above, p. 338 and n.

less than the unions or the technocrats. Yet in a new political and economic climate even he was to discover the advantages of sobriety. When the Radicals and Conservatives returned to office PME had a better hearing from ministers, and soon Gingembre stopped vituperating the technocrats to complain that they did not consult him enough. But he was not strong enough to prevent the modernizing businesses and bureaucrats squeezing the marginal shops and firms of the declining regions where Poujadism was born. Before long Gingembre in his turn was denounced as a timid tool of the trusts, and took up the mantle of the experienced statesman, less noisy but more effective than the excitable agitator from the south.[44]

Access to power thus transformed the behaviour of the groups. When their friends were in office they tried to get their own men into the *cabinet* of a sympathetic minister and ensure that he took the important decisions; when the department was hostile they transferred their attention to Parliament – as the alcohol interests mobilized opposition votes when Mayer demanded special powers but not when the friendlier Laniel administration obtained them. In 1956 FNSEA held several conversations with the minister of finance and then the premier. When these clearly failed it broke relations, and in 1957 it helped overthrow two governments and threatened a direct-action campaign. At length the weak and divided Gaillard government gave way and accepted 'indexation'.[45]

While ministers from the same party held a connected group of offices, responsibilities were clearly established and the influence of the groups was limited. But when several parties divided up a single sector of governmental activity, the group had a good chance of finding at least one sympathetic ministry to help it block distasteful proposals.[46] For most groups naturally had more influence on some parties than on others, and often access depended on the political situation. *Force Ouvrière* could count on Socialist sympathies so completely that in December 1949, when the union called a general strike and the prime minister appealed to workers to disobey the call, his SFIO ministers attended the party executive meeting which urged Socialists to strike. MRP ministers were naturally favourable to CFTC and the family associations. In the third Parliament the owners of house-property kept in touch with a Radical minister personally, with a Conservative mainly through his *cabinet*, with another Radical in both ways, but only with civil servants when a Socialist minister was in power.[47] The 'liberal professions' relied on the conservative groups, especially in a conflict which mingled ideology and interest like the doctors' opposition to Gazier's bill on reimbursement of medical expenses. In many towns small businessmen dominated the loose local Radical and Conservative parties, whose individual deputies often depended heavily on the local urban or rural pressure-groups.

44. Meynaud, p. 55; Lavau, no. 139, pp. 372, 378; Hoffmann, pp. 310–13.

45. Meynaud, pp. 163 (Mayer and Laniel), 225–6 (FNSEA). Yet FNSEA quite failed to defeat the Common Market in July 1957: Arné, p. 354. On *cabinets* see above, p. 339. Generally, Lavau, *Pressures*, pp. 72–4, 89.

46. *Ibid.*, pp. 84–5. But see below, pp. 390–3, on the drawbacks of party sectors.

47. FO: *AP* 1949, p. 200; Arné, p. 127. Mollet, as premier in May 1957, discussed economy proposals with all the major interest-groups except CGT: *AP* 1957, pp. 42–3; cf. Arné, p. 369. Housing: no. 161, pp. 851–2.

Relations between interests and parties showed immense variety. Many political disputes grew from clashes between interest-groups, but some reacted on the interests themselves. The students' union split in 1957 over attitudes to the Algerian war. The great dividing lines in the ranks of labour were the political, between CGT and FO, and the religious, separating CFTC from both; only the smallest of the four confederations (the staff union, CGC) found its exclusive base in a professional interest. Some bodies that looked like pressure-groups were wholly dominated by a party; the Communists had a whole network of them extending into the ranks of the bourgeoisie. One peasant organization had always been an instrument enabling the aspiring Radical politician to provide local services, attract a rural clientele, and advance his political career through channels different from the usual local government ones; it helped many small-town candidates win peasant support but brought few authentic farmers to Paris. But another, CGA, forbade its officials to sit in Parliament. A third, FNSEA, abandoned a similar rule in 1951 and turned to active political pressure;[48] the Peasant party neither wished nor would have dared to oppose its instructions. However, such a relationship was not always static. When a dynamic group with an ambitious leader penetrated far into a promising political field, as La Rocque's *Croix de feu* (originally a league of ex-servicemen) did in the thirties or Poujade's union of shopkeepers and artisans in the fifties, it sometimes changed its character and transformed itself into a party. In a multi-party system it was not always easy to distinguish between the two.[49]

4. GROUP REVOLT AND PARTY RESISTANCE

Some groups relied on or dominated a political party; others enjoyed close relations with civil servants or ministers; yet others could counter the unfriendly administration by mobilizing irresistible parliamentary support. But those who had too little backing among the voters or deputies to overcome the resistance of officialdom were very likely to threaten direct action, and might even embark on it. For many more Frenchmen than Americans or Englishmen looked on the state as an enemy to be frustrated and resisted.

The stubborn selfishness of the rich had for generations taught the poor to expect no reforms except under pressure of major social upheaval, and the French trade unions had developed a theory of direct action as the prelude to the revolutionary general strike. Yet this conception hopefully relied on the fighting spirit of the troops to compensate for their numerical weakness and poor equipment. Frenchmen paid dues to private organizations as reluctantly as they paid taxes to the state.[50] The unions were weak, poor and divided, and

48. On political divisions, Meynaud, pp. 33–4, 67–74, 80. On Communist satellites, above, p. 82, and Brayance, Chapters 7 to 9; for their shopkeeper groups, Hoffmann, pp. 315–18. On peasants, Mendras, no. 157, p. 746, and in *Paysans*, pp. 246–51; for Radicals, L. Latty and J. M. Royer in *ibid.*, pp. 103–8, 112–13, cf. Bardonnet, pp. 215–23, on a vain attempt to create Radical *amicales*.

49. Meynaud, pp. 38, 185–8; his preface to Hoffmann, pp. xix–xxi; Hamon, no. 120, pp. 848–9; Lavau, *Pressures*, p. 68n. On the propensity of ex-service groups to turn to right-wing politics see Rémond, no. 186; and on their pressure-group activities, Brown, no. 33, pp. 712–13.

50. The few well-off organizations often tapped semi-public subsidies or automatic levies which the members paid without knowing it; see for instance Bosworth, pp. 293–4, on APEL; Mendras

[*over*

labour, never being strong enough to bargain from strength with the employers, preferred to seek better wages and conditions by political pressure on the authorities it theoretically intended to overthrow. The meagre results of these tactics occasionally provoked an explosion of dissatisfaction, sudden, spontaneous and sometimes violent, and the old revolutionary tradition perhaps contributed to these relapses into direct action. But they were essentially an alternative means of extracting aid or concessions from a bourgeois government, not of organizing its violent downfall.[51]

France was peculiar because so many social groups resorted so readily to methods which elsewhere were an exclusive weapon of the industrial workers. They too did so to force concessions from a reluctant state. In the post-war scarcity economy, rival groups jostling for position had found that a harassed government listened only to those it could not ignore, and the lesson that the strike was the best way to attract attention was learned too well and applied too widely. Peasants withheld supplies from the market to force the government to change its policy over taxes, prices or imports. Shopkeepers demonstrated violently against controls, refused to pay taxes, and rioted against proper examination of their books. Customs officials became expert at go-slow tactics. The habits persisted after the scarcities. In a not particularly troubled period in 1951 there were serious or token strikes of butchers and bakers, university students and their examiners, mayors and milk producers and bank clerks. In 1950 the bishop of Luçon, on behalf of other western bishops, publicly urged his flock to 'postpone' tax payments till their grievances over the schools question were remedied (though MRP intervened at Rome and he was disavowed). Winegrowers had been encouraged by two victories over the authorities in 1946–47, won by withholding supplies and threatening to refuse taxes and paralyse local administration; in August 1953, led by their mayors and deputies, they barricaded every road in four departments (but without much success).[52] At the same time the public services were stopped by huge strikes erupting spontaneously throughout the country.

Such mass movements from below were formidable but rare. After 1948 the frequent direct-action threats of the pressure-groups contained a large element of bluff. The troops would not usually follow their commanders in serious or prolonged illegality, and rival pressure-group leaders competing for the same clientele, like Gingembre and Poujade, often led their forces into actions for which there was no enthusiasm, and had to beat a retreat. These bureaucrats of protest lived on discontent, canalizing it when it was spontaneous and stimulating it when it was not, for they needed successes to win members and members to win successes. Such tactics were risky,[53] since a defeat that was

in *Paysans*, pp. 241–2 (and no. 157, p. 742) on agricultural organizations. CGA was strong during the post-war scarcity when it issued rubber boots, etc., and lost its hold with this function.

51. Lorwin, Chapters 3, 12, 13, 16; J. Bowditch, 'The concept of *élan vital*; a rationalization of weakness', in Earle, Chapter 3.

52. Bishop: Rémond in *Laïcité*, p. 395; Bosworth, p. 296; *AP* 1950, p. 78; *Monde*, 25 April, 3 May and 22 July 1950. Wine: Warner, pp. 167–8, 183. Generally, Arné, pp. 371–4.

53. Meynaud, p. 116, cf. pp. 119–21; Lavau, *Pressures*, p. 94, on 'officials of protestation'; cf. *Paysans*, pp. 250–1. On retreats, Hoffmann, pp. 69, 87–90, 135–6; Meynaud, pp. 157–9; and Gingembre's own comments in Guy, pp. 168–70.

too costly in prestige or money might well destroy the less solid organizations. Direct action, therefore, was positively preferred only by those who, like the Communist groups, had a vested interest in revolt, or like the Poujadists feared that they were doomed economically without artificial support which would be forthcoming only under extreme political pressure. (Their followers were often interchangeable.) Organizations more confident of their own viability preferred moderate courses which imposed less strain on their unity, carried less risk in case of failure, and in the long run won a better hearing.[54] They resorted to direct action only in times of acute tension or when all other roads were closed. It was not accidental that the first peasant barricades and the first serious strikes for years occurred in August 1953, when Parliament had recessed after granting Laniel the most sweeping discretionary powers any administration had enjoyed since the war. More often than not, strikes and riots were an avowal of political impotence.

Direct action frequently failed. But if it won any concession from a slow-moving administration, it soon found imitators. The homeless found that only illegal 'squatting' on unoccupied premises drew public attention to their plight. In the Maurienne valley in January 1958 a main Alpine railway line was blocked in protest against long delays over compensation claims – which were discussed in cabinet within a week and settled by law within two months. For not all the protesters were putting forward extravagant demands or, like the *bouilleurs*, defending an established but indefensible privilege. All too frequently these civic rebels expressed an angry sense that their grievances were neither understood nor considered important by the mysterious *They* who decided their fate; that richer or cleverer or more unscrupulous rivals had the ear of the authorities; that Parliament was impotent to protect their interests, and that only outrageous behaviour would make *Them* listen. 'The most important heritage of our political history [is] a permanent tension between governed and governors which has led the former to see in the State only a foreign power – "*ils*" – with which the only possible contacts are relations of force.'[55]

The intransigence of the citizen made many French pressure-groups more demanding, arrogant and irresponsible than their counterparts elsewhere. (Perhaps the intensity and ruthlessness of the pursuit of sectional claims by the *corps intermédiaires* was a function of their reputed illegitimacy.) In the Fourth Republic the problem was the more acute because many more decisions than before were made by government. Dissatisfied groups reacted by denouncing the intrigues of their opponents, the venality of the politicians, or the ill-will of the foreigners: *They* were always a ready scapegoat in misfortune and a safe shield against painful self-examination and adjustment. So cabinets hampered by internal dissensions and unreliable majorities found their freedom of action still further restricted by fear of popular disorders which could be

54. The large representative groups often hinted to the civil servants that they did not expect full satisfaction for the demands pressed on them by their members: Delouvrier in *Crise*, p. 87. On the 'respectable' style of action see Meynaud, pp. 119–21, 128–9, 199. In housing matters, influence went with moderation: no. 161, pp. 859–60.

55. Hoffmann, no. 125, p. 820. Squatting: no. 161, pp. 841, 854–9. Maurienne: Georgel, i. 217. Cf. Buron, pp. 27–34.

contained only at a high political price. Each vehemently defending every particle of its own claims, the pressure-groups contributed to the *immobilisme* which ensured that none of them could be satisfied.

Yet they were flimsy organizations, nearly always smaller, poorer and worse organized than their foreign counterparts. Like the parties they suffered from excessive fragmentation; it was perhaps because there was no really effective authority on either side of the negotiating table that orderly bargaining so often gave way to shrill agitation. The politicians were humiliated and the regime discredited by sound and fury which often far exceeded the results obtained. For in the public forum the agitators often failed. The projected Franco-Italian customs union was successfully fought by the cotton industry led by Marcel Boussac, owner of *L'Aurore*; yet in 1953 a major tax change, opposed by the same industry, was enacted by a premier (Joseph Laniel) who was himself a textile manufacturer. At the peak of their power the Poujadists could neither defeat their chosen enemies at the polls, nor win all the tax concessions they demanded from Parliament, nor check the steady growth of co-operatives and chain stores. The bakers and greengrocers failed completely to break the Mollet government's ban on price increases.[56] Behind the scenes there was no single interest which could destroy governments through its financial power, like the (private) Bank of France before the war, or manipulate opinion through the press as effectively as the steelmasters of the old *Comité des Forges*.[57] 'If every group agreed to publish an honest balance-sheet of its interventions with the authorities, the "failures" column would rarely be empty.'[58]

This did not mean the groups were harmless. The *colons* may only have delayed evolution in North Africa: missed opportunities cannot always be retrieved. The alcohol lobby burdened a budget which could never find enough for genuine and urgent needs. Inarticulate or ill-organized groups suffered: the homeless, the aged, the consumers. The lobbies added yet another obstacle against change to those already embedded at so many levels in French society – for though few were strong enough to impose positive demands, many were able to veto those of others, and protect their own *situations acquises*.[59]

It was the weaknesses of the political system and not their own intrinsic strength that gave most of the groups their opportunities. When a third of the electorate opposed the regime, the basis of government was dangerously

56. Ehrmann, pp. 404–7 on Boussac (cf. Grosser, p. 152, Noël, p. 124); pp. 315–17 on tax reform. Hoffmann, pp. 76–86, Meynaud, pp. 147, 269–70, on Poujadist failures; cf. Lavau, no. 139, p. 376, on PME's lack of electoral success. *AP* 1956, pp. 85, 165–7, on Mollet and prices. And cf. above, pp. 362, 372, 375.

57. Delouvrier, *Crise*, p. 81. On the press, Ehrmann, *Business*, pp. 212–13. On the Bank see E. Moreau, *Souvenirs d'un Gouverneur de la Banque de France* (1954), pp. 34–8; cf. Frédérix, pp. 105–7; and Werth, *Destiny*, p. 343 on its arrogant bullying of Flandin: 'Our reply will depend on whether we are satisfied with the actions of the government during the first respite we have given it as a reward for its present determination.'

58. Meynaud, p. 269.

59. Victims: *ibid.*, pp. 94–8; Lavau, *Pressures*, p. 94; A. Sauvy, 'Lobbys et groupes de pression', in *Politique et Technique*, pp. 323–4. Conservatism: when an official inquiry in 1955 found potential wheat consumption to be a third of existing milling capacity, the millers' lobby carried a bill giving each mill a tonnage quota based on its activity in 1935: Schoenbrun, p. 173, cf. Meynaud, pp. 261–2. Uneconomic firms were subsidized for years to avoid unemployment in areas with little industry: Delouvrier, *Crise*, p. 80. Generally Hamon, no. 120, pp. 841–5.

narrow; every vote was or seemed marginal.[60] Deputies and parties dared not alienate support, and cabinets which resisted pressure were almost sure to disappear within a few months. Political courage was never rewarded, for the government which undertook a long-term policy was unlikely to escape immediate unpopularity but quite certain that any ultimate benefit would accrue to a successor. Parties survived at the polls by defending some sectional interest more effectively than their political competitors, then came to terms with their opponents in Parliament in order to form a cabinet. Electoral sectarianism, contradicted by governmental compromise, helped to disillusion the ordinary Frenchman with politics.

Yet the contradiction was in himself. By asking his party to maintain democracy, yet withholding his support if his full demands were not conceded, the voter forced on the politician the double-faced behaviour from which he inferred the rottenness of his representatives and of the regime. It was less surprising that the politicians sometimes gave way to pressure than that they often resisted it. The man in the street, who compounded for his own failings by damning those of the rulers he chose and influenced, frequently enjoyed better political leadership than he deserved.

In the second Assembly complaints of the power and importunity of the pressure-groups were heard increasingly from all parties. President Auriol spoke of Parliament being subjected to 'pressures as impudent as they are scandalous'. René Mayer as a candidate for the premiership declared that 'CNPF + CGA + CGV + PME' was no more desirable a foundation for a majority than 'FO + CFTC + CGC − CGT'. As prime minister he called the Assembly a 'chamber of corporations', while Paul Reynaud denounced the 'economic congregations' which 'paralyse the State within these very walls'.[61] Yet a few years later the groups seemed less excessive in their demands and more prepared to recognize the limits of the possible: contrast the violent business opposition to the Coal and Steel Community with the moderate and reasonable attitude of even a Gingembre to the Common Market.[62] And as the politicians lost credit with the public, and the divided parties came to seem increasingly artificial, some pressure-groups at least (the students, the young peasant leaders, the Catholic trade unions, the *Jeunes Patrons*, and the non-Communists in CGT) began to develop a feeling of responsibility for the country's affairs which transcended corporate interests and contrasted sharply with the earlier blinkered attitude of the lobbies. In the Fifth Republic it became a commonplace – inconceivable a few years before – that serious political activity and real influence among the people were more likely to be found in the *syndicats* than the political parties.

60. *Ibid.*, p. 838: '. . . every vote is marginal or seems to be; consequently the threat of defection is formidable, and it is the organization of private interests that makes this threat count – by representations, by effective publicity given to the member's votes, and by the cultivation of grievances or gratitudes.'

61. *Monde*, 2 January and 10–11 May 1953 (Mayer), 30 June 1953 (Auriol); *JO* 27 May 1953, p. 2850 (Reynaud). Cf. above, p. 353.

62. Lavau, *Pressures*, pp. 90–1, cf. Meynaud, pp. 268–9.

Chapter 27

PARTIES AND COALITIONS: (1) THE BATTLE OF THE MONOLITHS

The early post-war years impressed on General de Gaulle and many of his countrymen a conception of party politics as a struggle between selfish and irresponsible factions which must divide and damage the state. The electoral, parliamentary and (in 1946) governmental scene was dominated by three large and rigid organizations which seemed to have annexed the public domain and parcelled it out amongst them, and apparently found service in the same government advantageous mainly because it afforded facilities for thwarting one another's policies. Their short reign soon gave way to rather looser parties and more flexible coalitions, which marked a partial return to the political system of the Third Republic. But public attitudes towards politics retained the imprint of the brief post-war experiment.

Tripartisme was partly a product of the reaction against the pre-war economic and political regime. The Resistance had been directed against 'the trusts' as well as the Germans, and at the Liberation the old elites were swept into oblivion or disgrace. Power passed to new men, parties and classes who meant to carry out a sweeping programme of national reconstruction. But their leaders were a turbulent group of wartime and Resistance heroes, revolutionary adventurers and fishers in troubled waters, who were often better endowed with generosity or courage than with political experience; and the need for unity against the enemy had concealed the deep divisions within their ranks.

In their midst one disciplined, aggressive and unscrupulous party was manœuvring single-mindedly for power. In 1944 General de Gaulle won the race to establish the new administration over northern France, and the Communists accepted his authority in the south rather than risk a violent conflict while the European war was still raging. But with a foothold in central and local government, with control of the trade unions without whose co-operation reconstruction must fail, and with the prestige of sacrifice and triumph in a cause both patriotic and revolutionary, they could still entertain high hopes of success by peaceful means.

The Communists faced disunited opponents. Tactically, Gaullists and MRP welcomed their support over foreign policy, and Socialists feared their competition in domestic affairs. More fundamentally, General de Gaulle differed from SFIO and MRP over their conception of France's place in the world and her form of government at home. After eighteen months of office the General found the constraints imposed by three rigid and quarrelsome parties intolerable, while the politicians were equally exasperated with his authoritarian temper. A month after the first Assembly was elected the clash came, nominally over the size of the armed forces but at least equally over the shape of the constitution the parties were preparing.

After de Gaulle's resignation the three monolithic parties monopolized the government for twelve months of economic penury and political strife. *Tripartisme* soon became almost as unpopular with the parties in the government as with those outside it. But the circumstances were exceptionally difficult. By their drive for power the Communists forced their rivals into a discipline as rigid as their own, compelled them to take short views (since elections were never more than a few months away) and diverted their energies from constructive reform into self-defence against the threat of dictatorship. Even so the party politicians, first under de Gaulle and later without him, carried an overdue programme of reforms which a Chamber without a solid majority had never been able to impose on a conservative Senate. And, while avoiding a violent clash, they saved Paris from the fate of Prague. There was a price: the revival of the conservative forces they had hoped to displace. The Fourth Republic was the product of a half-completed revolution, and as the flood-waters receded many submerged political features began slowly to reappear on the electoral, parliamentary and governmental landscapes.

1. THE MEMBER AND THE MACHINE

To both Socialists and MRP strong party organizations were indispensable in an efficient and honest democratic system. Before the war local and personal rivalries had confused political issues, weakened loyalties, and obscured responsibilities; parliamentary chaos and indiscipline had prevented the electorate's wishes from ever being translated into action. But once each important ideology had its own organization political life would be transformed. The electorate would enjoy a clear choice, Parliament would function effectively, and politicians would be held accountable for what they did or failed to do. The Fourth Republic would substitute organized for unorganized, and therefore effective for ineffective democracy.

To prevent these new and rigid organizations abusing their monopoly of political activity, their advocates proposed a basic law regulating their structure and activities, the *statut des partis*. Under it the parties would pledge themselves to maintain fundamental liberties and the rights of man, repudiate the one-party state, adopt a democratic constitution, and allow their organization and finances to be inspected by a new authority representing the parties but independent of the executive. Citizens would have to vote, and candidates on a party's list would have to join its parliamentary group. A party could deprive of his seat a member who left it or broke its discipline.

Although Radicals and Conservatives naturally opposed a measure reinforcing the power and cohesion of the detested machines, it was the Communists who saved the individualist groups. Sure of their own internal discipline, the Communists did not want their rivals artificially strengthened; and they would not tolerate inspection of their funds (which in 1945 were large and sometimes ill-gotten) or of democratic control within their organization. But they prudently left the brunt of opposition to allies like Pierre Cot, who could more convincingly denounce the encroaching state, defend freedom of association, and appeal to western democratic opinion. To appease them the majority dropped the party statute from the committee's constitutional draft, and the Assembly never voted on it.[1]

The failure of legal regulation left the power of the party organizations intact. This power was largely based on the electoral law. Proportional representation triumphed at last, and was applied throughout the new institutions, even to the High Council of the Judiciary. At an election the voter had to choose between lists presented by the parties, with a fixed order of names. Small parties and particularly independents were handicapped – and indeed forbidden in the first Constituent Assembly's draft, which lapsed after the referendum of May 1946. Seats were attributed to a party, not to an individual. A vacancy in the Assembly went (until 1951) to the next person on the former member's list, and in the Council of the Republic, once the list was exhausted, to a party nominee. In May 1947 a defeated MRP candidate for the Assembly in Bas-Rhin was named by his party to the upper house.[2]

In many constituencies the head of a major party's list was sure of election, while his followers had little chance. The ambitious politician had therefore to placate not the party voters, but the relatively few militants who ran the organization and drew up the list. Some even considered the local party secretary as the keeper of the deputy's conscience, and in 1945–46 many departmental secretaries were themselves elected to the Assembly, especially in SFIO where the militants were strongest.[3] The parties wielded their new powers vigorously, and in the two elections of 1946 often penalized a member by not readopting him or by downgrading him on the list and perhaps ensuring his defeat. This was not always discipline for its own sake; like other revolutions the Liberation had thrown up many heroes, some adventurers, and a few scoundrels, and members elected in 1945 were rarely chosen for proven political capacity. During the following months some of them found themselves, and others were found by their parties, to be unsuited to parliamentary life.[4] Again, a member working hard for the party in Paris might find his local position undermined by a rival who spent more time in constituency activities. Deputies readopted in a lower place on the list numbered 31 in June 1946 and 10 in November; 16 of the 41 saved their seats for the moment, but downgrading at one election was often a prelude to disappearance at the next.[5]

Opponents as well as supporters of the regime attached crucial importance

1. On it see *SCC* I, pp. 55–66; Debû-Bridel, pp. 105–7; Wright, *Reshaping*, pp. 120–3; Arrighi, pp. 37–48; Goguel, no. 103.

2. Husson, ii. 164.

3. But their strength was organizational, not electoral. In 1945 the left-wing militants of Marseilles opposed the alliance with UDSR, and SFIO headquarters dissolved the federation. The rebels ran a dissident list which won only 6% of the vote, against 25% for the official list led by Gaston Defferre and Francis Leenhardt.

4. The Assembly elected in June 1946 had a legal life of seven months, that chosen in November one of five years; yet members retiring without a contest were twice as many in June as in November. Of SFIO and MRP members who withdrew in 1946, a third stood again for Parliament later. Clearly politics rather than age or health caused many of the retirements.

5. In 1946 there were 16 MRP, 9 Socialists, 6 Communists, and 10 others downgraded. The figures omit those (fairly numerous) who changed party or whose party entered a coalition, and those (generally Communists) who moved up when a leader withdrew, then dropped back later when he returned; but include deputies who were not moved up to fill a vacancy but saw an outsider promoted above their heads. For later figures see above, p. 326 and n.

to the electoral law. It installed for five years deputies subject to an organization which could quickly lose touch with public opinion, as was shown by the two referendums of 1946 and the Gaullist municipal victories of October 1947.[6] But since the new regime ruled out by-elections, referendums or dissolution except in most unlikely circumstances, a divorce between the people and their representatives would rarely become obvious and never influence those in power. The critics hoped by amending the electoral law to shatter the new monoliths and restore political fluidity.

Proportional representation certainly provided a convenient mechanism for the party to exert its power, and contributed to the rise of strong and disciplined groups. But both its friends and its enemies exaggerated its effects, for other factors were also at work. Even under *scrutin d'arrondissement* Communists had enforced strict discipline; even under PR, Radicals were reluctant either to impose it or to abide by it. Even without the legal change the deputy could not have retained his old independence in 1945 and 1946, when the elections brought in new men without the personal following and local influence of their discredited or ineligible predecessors. The approach of these newcomers to politics was set by the voters' fear of the Communists and their own impatience for reform. Together with the electoral law, these produced an Assembly dominated by the three disciplined parties, in which the whole tone of politics was altered.

Parliamentary life was transformed when these great parties together formed a cabinet approved by three-quarters of the deputies. Government policy became the highest common factor of three party programmes, and party discipline carried it through the house as effectively as in Britain. The one political problem was to reach and maintain compromises between the parties, which in agreement could impose their wishes and in discord could paralyse government and Assembly alike. 'The National Assembly of 1947 is much more like a diplomatic congress than like its predecessor the Chamber of Deputies. Parliament is still a theatre and so fulfils its function of publicity; but improvisation on the spot gives way to a script written and rehearsed elsewhere.'[7] Debate atrophied, for members applauded in unison at a signal from their leaders, and votes, rigidly determined beforehand, echoed the decisions of the party executives. If an unexpected development occurred the sitting was suspended to allow the parties to negotiate. The political choices registered in the Assembly were made in party headquarters. 'No longer do any political uncertainties reflect specific moves in Parliament. In committee or in the house each deputy applies the directives of his party. ... Individual crochets, manœuvres, intrigues seem to have disappeared ... we ask ourselves, is this disciplined Assembly really a genuine Parliament? However ... what the new parliamentary practice loses on the side of excitement it gains in productivity.'[8]

Most observers of the House of Commons would find the question more surprising than the description. But to French opinion a bigger legislative

6. Waline, pp. 7–8.
7. Théry, pp. 140–1.
8. Goguel, no. 104, pp. 135–8. Also Hamon, nos. 117–18; Goguel, no. 106; A. Siegfried in *AP* 1946, pp. vii-viii; Waline, pp. 63–7.

output was insufficient to justify the new system, partly because national tradition was different but even more because, while the price paid for political discipline was as high as in Britain, the benefits obtained were far less. Instead of a homogeneous party majority, united by common outlook and interest behind a coherent policy and single leadership, *tripartisme* brought together three suspicious partners who used their power for mutual obstruction as well, or as much, as for construction in common.

2. STATES WITHIN THE STATE

General de Gaulle's premiership imposed limits on the monopoly of the parties and on the extent of their ambitions. With his resignation the year of exclusive party power opened, and a great prize was added to the stakes. The contenders found it wise to regulate their relations and the composition and policy of the next cabinet in an elaborate written treaty.

> The delegates of MRP, the Socialist party, and the Communist party met on 23 January 1946. They proceeded to a broad examination of the situation, and reached agreement in stating that, given the development of the ministerial crisis, the formation of a government with equally shared responsibilities, under the leadership of the President of the National Constituent Assembly, appeared to them as the solution which would best meet their common preoccupations.

The document condemned recriminations between the parties, insisted that they all support the decisions of the new ministry, outlined its programme and 'mandated their representatives in the government to have these proposals included in the ministerial declaration'. But the treaty was a scrap of paper. The signatories disregarded it, not merely as an alliance but even as a non-aggression pact. Before long a Socialist minister was denouncing the Communist leader as a deserter; the Communists were attacking the price policy of the MRP minister of economic affairs; and MRP and SFIO were accusing the Communist minister for industry of incompetence and electoral corruption. 'France . . . had never before seen such flagrant civil war within a government.'[9]

The treaty merely distributed by agreement the spheres of influence in which the parties conducted their distinct policies. Proportional representation was applied within the cabinet by a 'horizontal separation of powers'. Each party bargained with the others to control its own sector of government, staffed it with ministers of its own choice, and co-ordinated their work under its own leader. The cabinet seemed to have sunk into a diet in which the party plenipotentiaries found it convenient to conduct their business, and the prime minister into a mere broker between them. Sometimes he lost even that role: when Ramadier was chosen in January 1947 he found that the offices had already been filled in talks between President Auriol and the secretaries and parliamentary chairmen of the parties.[10]

Once appointed, the antagonists parcelled out the administration among themselves and each exploited his own sector. To preserve party control an

9. Wright, *Reshaping*, p. 222. For the text of the 'treaty' see *AP* 1946, pp. 530–1; and for the disputes, Priouret, *Partis*, p. 225; Debû-Bridel, p. 117; *AP* 1946, p. 214.
10. *AP* 1947, p. 4.

absent minister's duties were usually performed by a party colleague, not by a minister from an allied department. Official appointments were openly made in party interests. This was not wholly surprising. In the past, senior administrative positions had been the preserve of a social class whose political ties were with the very groups most discredited at the Liberation. Few holders of these posts supported either of the two largest parties, Communists and MRP, whose conscious colonization was thus a corrective to the effective monopoly their opponents had enjoyed for years. Then, many officials had to be removed because of their occupation record, and in an emergency period when normal rules for recruiting civil servants could not serve, it was natural to choose active Resisters for these vacancies; but because of their political connections (like those of *Libération-Nord* with SFIO), their entry into the public service automatically contributed to party colonization. 'In 1945 there was a gulf between the new political personnel and the old administrative personnel. ... The injection of new blood into the administration in 1945 was certainly desirable and even necessary; unhappily it was done with too much haste and too little discernment.'[11]

The pace of colonization was set by the Communist attempt to establish a state within the state. In the defence and security services their rivals were wary.[12] But through the elected councils which managed the social security system, the trade unions who were represented on the boards of nationalized industries, and the Communist ministers for the economic and social departments, the party came to dominate the whole public sector from coal to atomic energy.[13] As minister of industry Marcel Paul appointed a *cabinet* of 70 and created 19 divisions in his department where there had been only three. Under Charles Tillon management posts in the aircraft industry were advertised only in pro-Communist papers, and non-Communist officials were purged to make room for party members.[14]

Other parties, particularly the Socialists, competed actively in their own ministries, and in 1948 a very critical but competent observer could write, '... in any given department, if you know the political outlook of the minister who has held office longest since 1944, you almost certainly know also the party loyalty of most senior officials of the ministry – even of the technical services'.[15] But the damage was limited by the mutual suspicions of the parties. Although Maurice Thorez was vice-premier responsible for the civil service,

11. Massigli, pp. 44, 60–1. Cf. Grosser, pp. 68–9.

12. Charles Tillon, de Gaulle's air minister, carried out a thorough purge of the air force; but no other Communist was ever given control over military personnel (François Billoux was defence minister in 1947 but did not decide promotions). On the police cf. above, p. 347. On Communist infiltration generally see Pickles, *French Politics*, pp. 83n., 252; Rieber, pp. 178, 289–92.

13. The coal industry had a board of 18, 6 each for workers, consumers and the state, with a majority of Communists: all six workers, three officials named by Communist ministers, and one 'consumer' – the secretary of the railwaymen's union, improperly chosen by Marcel Paul without consulting either the railway board which the nominee 'represented' or the minister of transport, Jules Moch: Moch, *Confrontations* (1952), p. 240n. Cf. Byé in Einaudi *et al.*, *Nationalization in France and Italy* (Ithaca, NY, 1955), pp. 100–4; and on social security, Galant, pp. 70–5, 123–45.

14. Paul: see *RPP* 594 (January 1950), p. 92. Tillon: Sturmthal, no. 205, p. 374.

15. Waline, p. 69. For rough confirmation compare Catherine's political estimates in *Partis et Classes*, pp. 128 and 131, with his table on p. 138.

he had no control over promotions. The party holding the defence ministry was kept out of the service and supply departments. Ramadier even proposed in 1947 to give every minister an under-secretary from another party (but did not do it). And the worst abuses of colonization disappeared when the Communists left office.[16]

The parties also sought wider opportunities to consolidate their influence. The press law of May 1946 was an extreme case of legislation conceived, opposed, carried, applied and ignored mainly for its impact on party interests. It was drafted by the Socialist minister of information, Gaston Defferre, with the aim of perpetuating the changes made provisionally at the Liberation.[17] The plant and offices of journals which had appeared under the Germans were transferred permanently to a government-controlled holding company for lease to new owners; papers not convicted of collaboration were compensated (inadequately). Radicals and Conservatives fought the law bitterly, but it was carried by the votes of the Communists, Socialists, most of MRP and a few UDSR Resistance leaders. Its effect was limited because, when the Communists went into opposition, the Radicals held the balance in Parliament and demanded the ministries of information and justice, so as to prevent the law being applied. Two Socialist ministers of information, in barely one month of office after the law was passed, transferred over twenty papers convicted of collaboration; under ministers from other parties the rate was under four a month. Of papers not convicted, the Socialists took over nearly one a day; MRP ministers one a month; and Radical and UDSR ministers one in four months.[18]

The parties also used their political monopoly to protect their client pressure-groups and extend their influence. The upheaval of the war had changed the structure of power and brought new organizations to the top. The trade unions had greatly increased their power.[19] Under predominantly Communist leadership they made an essential contribution to reconstruction, and exasperated many of their followers by preaching productivity and wage restraint while the party held office. The unions, in broad agreement with the 'big three' parties and the ministry of labour, shaped the form of the new social security system. The minority views of CFTC and the family associations gained a full hearing and some concessions, since MRP was in power; but those of the artisans and small businessmen were overridden because their political defenders were in opposition, and since electoral pressure was

16. See above, p. 340. Thorez: Rieber, pp. 291–2, and P.C.D., no. 66, p. 270. Ramadier: *AP* 1947, p. 9.

17. See above, p. 61; and on the press law, J. Mottin, *Histoire politique de la presse 1944–1949* (1949).

18. Some local courts also limited the law's scope by restrictive decisions. In all, 136 convicted papers and 60 others were transferred. The ministry of information always went to the premier's party (except under Ramadier when UDSR had it). In October 1949 both SFIO and MRP refused to serve under any premier who gave it and Justice to the same party. Dr. M. Harrison informs me that in the Fifth Republic the application of the law was still discriminatory; the pre-war owners could recover their presses if the post-war paper closed – but only if it had been Communist.

19. But de Gaulle in 1945 refused to receive a CGT delegation to discuss the electoral law, saying unions should be non-political (though in 1958 he asked union leaders to join his cabinet): Arné, p. 358 and n.; *AP* 1944–45, p. 288; *Inégalités*, pp. 45–7.

unavailing the objectors were driven to voice their protests by violent demonstrations.[20]

Business leadership was divided and timid, and the new Conservative party, PRL, was weak and quarrelsome; the *patronat* had to take its place among the many interests which were trying to work through MRP. In the farming community, the old leaders were mostly compromised in Vichy's Peasant Corporation and the Left had high hopes of filling the vacuum. The Socialists used official facilities to build up CGA and looked forward to acquiring a dominating position in the countryside; the Communists also bid for rural votes by strongly opposing Mendès-France's plan to check inflation by currency reform, which the peasants detested. Even the Church hierarchy found MRP's Resistance record a greater asset to the Catholic cause than any political service it could render in return.

3. OVER-MIGHTY SUBJECTS

This defeat or discredit of the old elites created an opportunity for sweeping social change, and the new political leaders thought of themselves more as revolutionaries bent on overturning a narrow and corrupt political class than as ordinary politicians administering or even reforming an established regime. But before their revolution was well under way they were faced by the Communist bid for power, and by de Gaulle's withdrawal into the wilderness to await the call for his return. In the parties' bitter struggle to carry through their reforms, defend the parliamentary system and preserve their own political fortunes, the fraternal feelings of the Resistance movement were soon submerged. The discipline which had been defended as essential for positive reform was used also in frustrating internecine warfare ending, as in Weimar Germany, in stalemate.

Powerful and rigid parties were therefore quickly discredited in France. They outraged the predominant democratic tradition which exalted the Republic one and indivisible and condemned all intermediary bodies. They were denounced for distorting the political process: the voter had a representative foisted on him by the party machines, the deputies voted not as they believed but as they were told, the Assembly merely registered the pressure of irresponsible external organizations, ministries became party fiefs, and the State, like a conquered province, was divided and despoiled. Since the cabinet was a diet where each faction had its veto, the opposition was concealed within the government itself and neither could perform its function properly. Ministerial solidarity and responsibility disappeared together, for the few decisions that were taken derived from the secret battles and bargains of party bosses unknown to the electorate and subject to no public control.[21]

The critics' complaints were excessive. In retrospect it was a considerable success, rivalled only in Italy, for the democratic parties to co-operate with the

20. On unions and Communists see above, p. 24; on social security, Galant, Chapters 3–5, Lavau, *Pressures*, p. 92, and above, pp. 361–2.

21. These criticisms were made not only by de Gaulle and his followers like Debré, Debû-Bridel and Waline. but also by non-Gaullists like Arrighi; Priouret, *Partis*; and Théry, pp. 140–5.

Communists to rebuild the economy without allowing the state to fall completely under their control. But the French politicians did much more, for the reforms of 1945–46, both under de Gaulle and after his departure, were greater than any previous government had attempted (except in 1936, when they did not succeed or did not last). They gave France an improved administrative structure, an overdue but comprehensive social security system, and a foundation on which economic recovery could be built. Admittedly the parties, unable to agree and unwilling to concede, sometimes failed to face a particularly awkward problem. In July 1946 they left employers, farmers and workers to negotiate directly on their differences, and at the Palais Royal conference the interests happily agreed to support both higher wages and higher prices and so displace the economic burden, through inflation, on to the ill-organized and politically weak fixed-income groups. This was a shameful abdication of responsibility, but it could hardly be attributed wholly to the malign influence of organized parties. A year earlier, de Gaulle himself had allowed inflation to take its course when he acceded to the advice of the bankers, the pressure of the peasants, the clamour of the Communists, and the resignation of Pierre Mendès-France.[22]

The opposition was on stronger ground in attacking the political practices of the parties, but its charges were often exaggerated. Some men accused of cynically exploiting their fellow-citizens were in reality courageously accepting a dangerous and distasteful responsibility. Everyone knew that the ministry of food in 1946 was a graveyard of political hopes: this did not stop a Gaullist critic absurdly describing the Socialists as 'comfortably installed' there. For months the Communists courageously risked their popularity in the trade unions by opposing wage demands. The impression of total disintegration of government may indeed have been overdrawn. When men assume heavy responsibilities in common in a situation of extreme difficulty, their mutual hostility usually diminishes. Did the party leaders never dramatize their difficulties with their colleagues in order to ward off impracticable or embarrassing demands from their own followers?[23]

For though discipline was strong and no individual rebel could stand against the parties, coalition imposed a severe strain on their internal unity. The Socialists were the most vulnerable and electorally least successful party of the three, and their leaders, after bravely attempting to educate their rank and file to compromise and to modernize, were overthrown for it by internal revolution in August 1946. In December a quarter of SFIO's deputies defied discipline rather than support Thorez for premier. MRP members were occasionally divided in the Constituent Assemblies, a few of them left to follow de Gaulle, and many more were torn between their loyalties to the man and the party. Even the Communist leaders faced serious criticism from within, which mounted as long as they were in office. The appearance of total

22. Mendès-France: Matthews, pp. 179–94; Fauvet, *IVe*, pp. 37–40. Palais Royal conference: *AP* 1946, pp. 179–89; Meynaud, pp. 247–8; Ehrmann, *Business*, pp. 299–300; Delouvrier in *Crise*, p. 84, and in *Politique économique*, pp. 312–15; cf. C. P. Kindleberger in *Search*, pp. 137–9.

23. Cf. Dumaine, p. 51. Food: Debû-Bridel, p. 115. Communists: above, pp. 24, 74; below, 401. For the Socialist leaders' moderation on *laïcité*, above, p. 97; Matthews, pp. 156–7.

monolithic unity was as misleading as the accusation of unbridled partisan rapacity. The disciplined giants of *tripartisme* were already feeling some of the conflicting pressures of electoral competition, ideological loyalty and governmental necessity, which were to bedevil the precarious coalitions of loose weak parties in the Fourth Republic.

Chapter 28

PARTIES AND COALITIONS: (2) THE WAR OF MANŒUVRE

All politicians are compelled by the nature of their calling to be both fighters and negotiators. But they stress different aspects of their task according to temperament and circumstance, and the intransigent champion of all or nothing is constantly at odds with the shrewd bargainer who prefers a partial and inadequate success to a gallant but unmitigated failure. Usually the two types are in conflict, occasionally each complements the other's efforts. But even when they co-operate for immediate advantage they rarely appreciate one another's outlook.

Most members of parliament, being nearer the seats of power, are readier to compromise than the militants of their own party in the country. But while in a two-party system only one side has direct access to the government, in a multi-party regime every group, apart from self-excluded revolutionaries, can hope to enter a coalition, share power and influence policy. This tends to turn almost all politicians into compromisers, and seems to reduce the parliamentary struggle to a sordid contest for place in which the professionals, within their closed arena, manœuvre unhindered by public pressure or even concern – as in eighteenth- and early nineteenth-century Britain, and in the Third Republic.

But though parliamentarians became imbued with the habit of compromise, many Frenchmen revolted against it – or its results. Parliament often aroused the idealist's contempt, and the hatred of the permanent but not insignificant minority for whom politics were a kind of cold civil war. This minority concentrated its activities, not on elections or the Chamber, but on revolutionary syndicalism, royalist or fascist leagues or conspiracies, and the extremist journalism of *Gringoire* or *Action française*. There was never any lack of contemporary evidence to remind the proponents of bargaining politics that fighting politics had recently been the French style. When the brief reign of the extreme Right ended in 1944, the extreme Left acquired a share in the government and could bid to dominate it.

The collapse of *tripartisme* and General de Gaulle's campaign for power set the characteristic conditions of Fourth Republican government. Under *tripartisme* the three partners had commanded enough votes to carry any policy on which they agreed; effective action when they were united was some compensation for the frequent deadlocks when they quarrelled. But now the majority lacked numbers as well as unity. A precarious coalition, devoted to the parliamentary regime but divided on everything else, was opposed simultaneously by a powerful Communist party and an intransigent nationalist movement. Each of the oppositions could embarrass or seduce one wing of the disparate alliance, or they could combine for its destruction (though for nothing else). Within the majority the parties of policy were rather better disciplined than in the past, and the core of 'king's friends' who supported every cabinet whatever its programme was smaller and steadily diminishing. Negotiation was therefore more open, exchange of concessions more obvious, and responsibility for making, maintaining and breaking a cabinet easier to locate. While the wanton breach of an alliance incurred more discredit, support was given or withheld in larger blocks and so adjustments were less smooth and more sudden. Just because responsibilities were more visible, every cabinet crisis gave rise to elaborate manœuvres to confuse the issue and shift the blame. These might profit an individual party, but always harmed the regime.

From 1947 to 1950 the Fourth Republic seemed perilously vulnerable. SFIO was the most uneasy governmental party, for to compromise with its allies would disrupt its own unity and lose ground to the Communists, and not to do so would wreck the coalition and play into the hands of de Gaulle. When the immediate danger receded the looser parties had gained ground, and soon Parliament again became an arena for factional intrigues and individual ambitions. After 1954 external affairs predominated: first Germany, then Algeria caused splits in most parties. By 1957 every type of disruption threatened the majority at once, and governments found it hard not only to act but even to survive. Sheltered by the 'house without windows', the deputies had not observed that the sky outside was darkening again.

1. WHIPS AND REBELS

The end of *tripartisme* saw a partial and incomplete return to the parliamentary practices of the Third Republic. The centre governments came under fire from two sides. While the Socialists had to fight off Communist raids on their working-class and anticlerical following, their coalition partners were vulnerable to Gaullist attack; differences soon developed between leaders and militants in MRP, and discontent in the country helped Radicals and Conservatives regain their strength. In Parliament the support of small groups and individualists again became necessary, and the precarious majorities and surprise votes of the Third Republic reappeared. René Pleven and his two dozen UDSR followers saved the first Schuman government by their abstention in February 1948 and brought down the second by their hostile vote in September.[1] Decisions such as the comfortable ratification of the Coal and Steel Community, or Pinay's election as premier, confounded the best-informed observers. Life and reality returned to parliamentary sittings, and often the cheers and counter-cheers along the party benches revealed fissures in the ranks which were not recorded in the vote.[2]

Yet formal party discipline was better than was often supposed. Under Pinay's government in 1952 only two groups failed to poll their entire strength, without a single dissenter or even abstainer, in two-thirds of the 672 recorded votes.[3] No group failed to poll 95% of its members in at least seven votes out of eight. These figures conceal great differences between parties, discussed

1. Arné, p. 240, lists five votes in the first Assembly, four in the second, and one in the third where the government survived by a single-figure margin. Cf. above, p. 175n.
2. Hamon, no. 121, p. 563.
3. Radicals in 63%, and MRP, who were exceptionally divided under Pinay, in only 57%: Campbell, no. 44.

below. They slightly overestimate the extent of indiscipline among French politicians, for they include the overseas members who were the most wayward. They somewhat underestimate its importance, for it was worst on major matters when the government's fate was at stake; when no public interest was aroused the deputy might stay away and let the whips cast his proxy for him, defying the party machine only when his constituents were genuinely aroused.[4] Nevertheless the groups played a greater role in the member's life than before the war, and unless the compulsion was very powerful, the deputy who valued his influence with his political friends preferred not to offend their strongly held feelings.

Both the degree of discipline and the attitude to it varied sharply among parties. Under Pinay it was rigid on the Left, good on the Right, and weakest among Radicals, UDSR, dissident and orthodox Gaullists, and MRP. The Communists were always so solid that a vote against the party was unthinkable, though in the later years a fellow-travelling Progressive might occasionally abstain. At the other extreme, the Radicals were normally found on both sides of any question and never imposed *discipline de vote*.[5] A Radical candidate for premier could expect to get the votes of his colleagues – even if they urged members of other parties to withhold theirs – but once elected he could not count on their support. The Conservatives, who had also profited from the popular reaction against rigid parties during and after the period of *tripartisme*, were by 1951 'abandoning the outworn conception of individual independence and gradually substituting that of collective independence'.[6] But they never insisted on disciplined voting, merely trying to persuade minorities to abstain rather than vote against the party. In 1954 resentment against Mendès-France's Conservative ministers led the group to forbid members to take office when a two-thirds majority opposed their doing so – though, characteristically, the rule was not applied to the offenders who had provoked it. Conservatives continued, as in the past, to act without penalty with Gaullists, Mendesists or fascists.[7]

Popular plebiscitary leaders wreaked havoc with discipline, evoking among ordinary Frenchmen strong loyalties which some members of parliament shared and others felt it wise to respond to. General de Gaulle shook the parties in 1947, but the politicians rightly estimated that his impact would not be permanent. He won over a few devoted followers, mostly from MRP, many time-servers who jumped off his bandwagon as soon as it slowed down, and a handful of natural rebels or adventurers seeking a leader against the System – but often no happier with Gaullist discipline than with any other.[8] RPF could

4. Discipline was worse in the upper house where routine votes were fewer; there only 5 groups out of 11 voted solidly in two-thirds, and only 3 polled 95% in seven-eighths of the divisions; and while the Socialist deputies broke unanimity in only 1% of the votes, the senators did in 33%. For votes in the Assembly see the old Chamber, Soulier, pp. 454–76.

5. Once when they did, for postponing Barangé's bill to subsidize church schools, ministers were exempted and seven others voted, unpunished, against the party line: *Monde*, 7 September 1951.

6. Yves Florenne in *ibid.*, 26 May 1951. Radicals: below, n. 9.

7. PRL and the Peasants expelled members in the Fourth Republic, but CNIP never did until 1961: see below, pp. 407, 433. Cf. Waline, no. 213, p. 1220. Two-thirds rule: above, p. 151.

8. Charles Serre of Oran and Albert Lécrivain-Servoz of Rhône were two MRP members recruited by RPF in 1947. The first soon became a Conservative and the second an Overseas

[*over*

insist on strict obedience (though at the cost of defections) so long as it was a large party with hopes of reconstructing the regime. But in 1952 Antoine Pinay captured the sympathies of conservatives both in Parliament and the country, and when de Gaulle's mass support evaporated the RPF parliamentarians were rapidly absorbed by the System.

Pinay attracted conservatives and alienated progressives in other parties too, notably MRP. But under the rule of the Right *immobilisme* soon brought about a revival of discontent in the country, and the new mood was crystallized by Pierre Mendès-France. Learning from RPF's failure the difficulties of launching a new party, he set out at first to mobilize support in all the old ones. In 1953 he aroused a revolt of the rank and file, especially the younger members, against the old leaders.[9] Next year he came to power, but the overthrow of his government by members of his own party convinced him he needed a more secure base, and he sought and won control of the Radical organization. But in 1956 the momentum of Mendesism was halted by Mollet as that of Gaullism had been checked by Pinay; and the Mendesists' attempt to discipline a parliamentary group they did not control merely led to two splits and an even worse dispersion than usual of Radical votes in the Assembly. Pierre Poujade was to suffer a similar disillusionment as a sudden wave of popular discontent apparently bore him forward to power on its crest, then broke and carried his hopes away when the waters ebbed.

In loose parties like the Radicals and Conservatives, members could follow the demands of their constituents or the appeal of a strong leader (often identical) for as long as it was tactically advisable and then return without reproach to the fold. In the better-disciplined organizations they had less freedom of action: the Gaullists in MRP had to change allegiance altogether, and Mendès-France's friends within SFIO could try to influence party policy only by internal pressure. In general MRP applied formal rules much less strictly than the Socialists. After August 1948, when twenty MRP deputies refused to support Paul Reynaud's conservative economic policy, the party often had dissenters of both Right and Left. Usually they were a handful and their lapses were judged more in sorrow than in anger. Occasionally they were more numerous, as in July 1950 when a third of the party rebelled against supporting Queuille's conservative second (and stillborn) cabinet; the militants sympathized with the protest, and the party allowed a free vote. Discipline broke down completely when, to MRP's great embarrassment, the militants and left-wing deputies strongly opposed Pinay who appealed powerfully to the conservative section of the party's electorate. But though by this time *discipline de vote* was only a memory in MRP, its deputies prided themselves on a cohesion based on loyalty to the movement rather than fear of sanctions.[10]

Independent; both then moved through a small pro-Radical group to the *Gauche indépendante* and the fellow-travelling Progressives; both lost in 1951. On ex-Gaullists in 1955 see above, pp. 136, 144, 173.

9. The SFIO group overruled Mollet and its chairman (Lussy) to support him; UDSR was for him but Pleven against; in MRP he had the votes of only 12 of 31 senior men (ex-ministers or committee chairmen) but of 40 of the other 58; on the Radical leaders' intrigues against him see Fauvet, *IVe*, pp. 238–9.

10. Melnik and Leites, p. 82.

They rarely carried their differences with the party beyond abstention to a hostile vote. In June 1953 Mendès-France did provoke a revolt of the 'back-benchers', who mostly voted for him while most of the leaders did not; to avoid another split, *discipline de vote* was restored when Laniel stood for the premiership.[11] But it was not kept up, and no new revolt occurred when Mendès-France came to power a year later, for his Indo-Chinese and European policies aroused general hostility in MRP. Subsequently the main dissenting group was on the Right, and though it centred on Georges Bidault it was tiny and ineffective.

Placing greater emphasis on external observances, and with a constitution giving the militants greater influence, the Socialists had a still more difficult problem. To them a democratic party was one which took decisions by majority vote after a free debate, unlike the totalitarian Communists, and then voted unitedly for them, unlike the careerist Radicals. The *mystique* of discipline was general throughout the party, not least among the men who were to lead the PSA split of 1958.[12] But it broke down on several major votes in the Fourth Republic. In April 1951 15 members rebelled over the electoral law, though all but one came round after a sharp warning. German rearmament caused revolts by 20 deputies in February 1952, 53 in August 1954 (whose votes defeated EDC), and 21 in December; 17 were expelled but readmitted before the next election. In July 1957 26 members (many of whom later joined PSA) refused to vote for the bill allowing internment camps to be set up in France. The Socialists were also divided on the Fourth Republic's first and last candidates for the premiership: in December 1946 25 refused to vote for Maurice Thorez, and on 1 June 1958 42 supported Charles de Gaulle and 49 opposed him.

Indiscipline, then, differed widely between parties both in its extent and in the reactions it provoked. Its causes differed too. Conservative and Radical parliamentarians were individualist notables, whose personal views, ambitions and constituency interests were apparently reflected in a pattern of dissent linked more often to the fate of a particular cabinet, or to personal electoral considerations, than to a general policy alignment. Socialist and MRP indiscipline was associated less with specific ministries and more with problems of principle, often personal and episodic in MRP but grouping relatively substantial and continuing factions in SFIO. (Socialists seem to have judged even the electoral law on general grounds, nearly all the opponents of *apparentements* being on the extreme Left of the party.) But while the timing and motive for dissidence might differ between types of party, neither was likely to make a stable coalition partner.[13]

11. In similar circumstances RPF had restored it in January for Mayer's candidature.

12. As general and assistant secretary until 1946 Daniel Mayer and Robert Verdier were strong disciplinarians, but both rebelled over EDC and Algerian special powers. Édouard Depreux voted for both policies, which he opposed, out of respect for party discipline (as five others did over EDC). Cf. above, p. 93n., 327; and on Socialist alignments above, p. 91n.

13. These conclusions emerge from a thorough statistical analysis of the divisions in each party in Assembly voting throughout the Fourth Republic: MacRae, no. 149. The main splits are also cited in Georgel, i. 202–7. The traditionalist parties were also the most representative of 'backward France' (p. 450n.); and their members had most chance of office (p. 419n., cf. p. 438).

2. MEMBERS AND MILITANTS

Members of parliament in parties where they enjoyed exclusive control behaved differently from colleagues who had to consider the demands and aspirations of party militants in the country. Either would lose his seat if he failed to satisfy his voters, but in a disciplined organization the deputy might get no chance to fight it if he offended the militants.[14] Yet he and they had very different preoccupations. He had to remember that a ministerial crisis might weaken the party's position in the Assembly, alienate the floating voter, or alarm foreign opinion in a critical international situation;[15] it might even threaten the regime itself. To the militants and the party executives these were hypothetical dangers which would be dealt with, if at all, by others. Their concerns were to press the party's demands even at inconvenient moments, prevent unceremonious treatment of its sacred cows, and so protect the enthusiasm and loyalty of the faithful which the compromises of the parliamentarians threatened to dissipate. Living in the closed world of the party and behaving as if it were in a political vacuum, they could play the sea-green incorruptible and win votes and applause at party conferences. The deputies had the less glamorous task of bargaining with other groups to provide France with a government.

Tension existed even in the Communist party, where a member who was assigned to the post of deputy gave it up when he was told to and obeyed orders while he held it: in 1948 Duclos himself read to the Assembly the party secretariat's authorization to the deputies to change tactics and vote for immediate local elections.[16] Yet even Maurice Thorez was criticized by André Marty and the opponents of joining the government, especially when he was defeated for the premiership in December 1946 and the party's hold on the trade unions came increasingly under challenge.[17] Again, when Mollet came to office in 1956 the Communists' support for his government pleased their voters, nostalgic for a Popular Front, but soon offended the militants, who resented appeasement of the ministry that sent conscripts to Algeria; and after their first and last open argument in the Fourth Republic, the Communists decided in June not to vote confidence in Mollet's North African policy. In 1958 de Gaulle's attraction for many Communist voters produced a heresy among younger leaders like Marcel Servin, who wished to minimize the damage by moderating their attacks on the regime.

Nor did the most individualist party escape conflicts between leaders and rank and file. At the Toulouse conference in November 1949 Herriot and the Radical elders were savagely assailed by Daladier, the 'young Turks', and the

14. Party membership and voting strength were almost unrelated: Duverger, *Parties*, pp. 91–101. In 1951 MRP in Haut-Rhin had under a hundred members and 74,000 voters: Fauvet, *Forces*, p. 182.

15. But did he? André Siegfried reproached the deputies for their indifference to foreign reactions both in 1930 (*Tableau*, p. 28, *France*, p. 12), and in 1951 (*AP* 1951, p. xi). And cf. below, p. 423.

16. *AP* 1948, pp. 159 and 347; *JO* 20 September 1948, p. 6737.

17. Priouret, *Partis*, pp. 15, 200–5; Marabuto, p. 170; Rieber, pp. 152, 166–7; Aron, *Schisme*, pp. 191–2; Dumaine, p. 152, writing of January 1947, mentions 'one clear point: the desire of the Communist party to be in the next combination at the price of any concession and of its dignity'. Cf. above, p. 74 and n. 10.

local bosses who saw in outright opposition to the government the short road to electoral triumph. The old 'war of the two Édouards' raged again – so furiously that fear of the party's disintegration shocked the factions into a patched-up truce.[18] But no compromise followed the revolt of 1955, when Mendès-France and his new recruits evicted the old right-wing leaders with the aid of Jean Baylet and his local notables, then lost their allies and their majority by their unpopular stand over the Algerian war. For in 1949 the Radical party had been a loose confederation in which rival bosses struggled to control the machine, a prize that would disappear if the party itself broke up. Seven years later real militants, fighting for policy and not for place, tried to impose discipline from outside on parliamentarians who had always resisted it; as soon as their views began to offend the voters they alienated their fair-weather allies among the traditional Radicals, and so lost the battle.[19]

In RPF a similar conflict was fought between the deputies and the personal advisers of the General. Although a movement founded on de Gaulle's prestige had 'outside dictation' as its very purpose, even RPF parliamentarians resented military discipline in politics. As early as August 1948 the vice-chairman (Pierre Montel) and twelve members resigned from the Gaullist inter-group when ordered to vote against Paul Reynaud's financial policy. A year later the chairman, Paul Giacobbi, resigned over a disciplinary problem: his colleagues gave him a unanimous vote of confidence. In 1952 Antoine Pinay, like Reynaud but on a larger scale, won Conservative RPF members back to the ministerial ranks at the cost of alienating MRP's left wing.[20] For, while the true Gaullist believed that no real reform was possible without constitutional change which compromises and palliatives merely delayed, the ex-Conservative RPF deputy knew that most of his electors supported RPF as an expression of Conservatism. Since the creators of the Rally were not orthodox Conservatives, tension between them and their parliamentary representatives was inevitable.

MRP and Socialist parliamentarians also gave more weight than the outsiders to short-term and tactical considerations. In MRP the party constitution had been designed to strengthen the leadership, though it could not always avoid conflicts or even always win them. In May 1949 Georges Bidault's approaches to RPF were at once disavowed by the party conference, and six months later the national council sided with SFIO against the MRP ministers in insisting (successfully) on a return to free collective bargaining.[21] There was again tension with the militants over support for conservative premiers – Queuille in 1950, Pinay and Laniel. But strong bonds held MRP together: its members shared a common religious faith, a common political experience in the pre-war and Resistance generation, and the sense of a mission to reconcile the Church with the Republic. The rank and file therefore felt a strong sentimental

18. *AP* 1949, p. 198; Fauvet, *Forces*, pp. 105–6.

19. Having no militants CNIP escaped these troubles, but its 1954 conference, and the stormy history of the Peasant party, showed that even the Conservatives were not wholly immune from them: above, pp. 151, 153.

20. Similarly in 1957 he won the Poujadist deputies away from their leader. On Reynaud and Giacobbi see above, pp. 134 n. 7, 143, 399.

21. *AP* 1949, pp. 82–3, 159, and above, pp. 105; 106–7.

veneration and respect for the leaders, which – as in Bidault's case – survived (not always with happy results) long after political sympathy had died. Internal division consequently did less harm to MRP than to other parties. Instead, dissident groups left the movement altogether.

The clash between leaders and followers, parliamentarians and militants was worst in the Socialist party. Spurred by two electoral disappointments, the rank and file rejected Léon Blum's efforts to broaden the party's doctrine and appeal. In August 1946 Daniel Mayer was replaced as general secretary by Guy Mollet, the aggressive prophet of class struggle, who nine months later urged SFIO to bring down Ramadier's government rather than let it continue without the Communist ministers. After winning a large majority in the Assembly Ramadier barely survived the vote in the Socialist national council which, Blum wrote tactlessly, would decide 'in full sovereignty' the strategy of SFIO – and therefore the government of France.

At the next conference Mollet strengthened his hold, and within a year the Socialists had brought down three governments. But each crisis meant a move to the Right, and by 1949 Mollet's friends were advocating participation in government, while ex-ministers like André Philip and Édouard Depreux opposed it. When Daniel Mayer broke up Queuille's cabinet in September, over the return to collective bargaining, the Radicals demanded his exclusion from the next government; after a month without a ministry the Socialist deputies defied the party executive and agreed.[22] In December SFIO assigned tactical decisions in a cabinet crisis to the first policy-making committee it had ever set up with a majority of members of parliament, but this was abolished after only two years. In April 1952 a complicated compromise at last settled the jurisdictional dispute.[23]

Conservative politicians and jurists condemned the Socialist party organization as a menace to parliamentary sovereignty, as in Ramadier's 'vote of confidence' in May 1947, or to governmental stability, as in the long crisis of October 1949. But differences between the deputies and the executive were not fundamental. Often they agreed, and when they did not each side usually had a minority of sympathizers among the others. Over the Poinso-Chapuis decree in 1948 both began intransigently but both ended by compromising. Early in 1951 the executive showed more concern than the parliamentarians for budgetary stability, and a year later it was the deputies who first decided to oppose Pleven's government.[24] The committee twice intervened to save Pleven's

22. Mayer then asked 'to be relieved by SFIO of his mandate as minister of labour': *AP* 1949, p. 180. The party executive picked Dr. Segelle instead, but forgot to tell him – and his cabinet colleagues, when they met at 2 a.m., had to wait for the new minister to be fetched from his bed in the outer suburbs.

23. The executive of 31, of whom 10 were parliamentarians, sat with 9 deputies and 6 senators chosen by their groups to form the 'committee of 46' until December 1951, when a national council restored full powers to the executive. Angry Socialist deputies called the executive 'the politburo' (*AP* 1951, p. 324) and their chairman and vice-chairman resigned in protest. By the final compromise the executive's decision was discussed at a joint meeting with the parliamentary group (at which the deputies had a five-to-one majority) which could either confirm it, reject it by a three-fifths majority, or reject by less and transfer the decision to a special national council. For SFIO's internal evolution see Ligou, pp. 544–53, 557–9, 577–88, 615–25, and references in Williams, p. 372n.

24. *Monde*, 16 February 1951; *AP* 1952, p. 8. The executive also later voted to oppose Pleven

[*over*

successor, Edgar Faure. And although the militants caused no difficulty over the external problems which dominated politics after 1954, the party's life became more turbulent than ever. Over EDC a majority, and over Algeria a large minority of the deputies rebelled against a leadership strongly supported by the executive. When de Gaulle stood for the premiership in May 1958 the executive joined the revolt, and Mollet had to fall back on the support of the Socialist senators and permission for a free vote in the Assembly.

Even when the behaviour of the outside organizations was most unreasonable, it was often understandable. Political compromise is often a necessity, especially in France, but the professional politician too easily came to think of it as a positive virtue. Outside the Communist party few deputies had personal experience of the industrial worker's life (only three Socialists and eight MRP members in the first Assembly, where the problem was most acute). Many French leaders had begun their careers on the extreme Left and gone over to a respectable or disreputable conservatism as their age and fortune grew: Millerand, Briand, Laval, Doriot.[25] Politicians in the disciplined parties sometimes needed reminding that they owed their power to the work and idealism of simple, unsophisticated people, whose hopes might be inconvenient, untimely or impracticable, but could not simply be ignored and derided by their representatives.

Parliamentarians from the looser groups, who did not suffer from this pressure, were freer to pursue personal ambition or factional advantage without risking penalties from their parties. Endangered in the early years by the need of Socialist ministers to satisfy a vigilant executive, governmental stability was more imperilled later by the refusal of Radical and Conservative deputies to honour the commitments made by their leaders. And members from the strictly and the loosely organized groups alike were obliged to listen to the grievances of their voters. If the ordinary citizen took short or partisan views, demanded immediate material concessions or stood firm for a principle, then his representatives were bound to pay attention even at some risk to the stability of government. But the voter also (and not always consistently) put a high value on stability. He set the politician an insoluble problem, and then reproached him for not finding a satisfactory answer.

3. PARTNERS AND RIVALS

In the disciplined parties the parliamentary leaders were under pressure from the membership to carry out the party's policies; in the individualist ones there were always notables seeking more power for themselves or their faction. Coalition governments therefore needed perpetual brokerage to keep them together. The parties composing them were at once partners and rivals, and

by 19 (7 deputies and 12 militants) to 6 for abstention (3 and 3). On five political and two disciplinary decisions in that month, a majority of both deputies and militants defeated a minority of both; they differed only on Pinay's investiture in March, 11 of the 16 militants wanting to oppose him and 7 of the 10 deputies to abstain: *Bulletin intérieur SFIO*, nos. 59 (February 1952), p. 19, and 62 (May), pp. 41–3; fuller in Williams, p. 372n.

25. In Côte d'Or every local leader in the Third and Fourth Republics followed this course: Long, pp. 200–4, 265–72. The Communists' first general secretary, L. O. Frossard, was one of Pétain's ministers in 1940.

the more secure the majority was against opposition attack, the more willing each of its members became to fight for his own hand. Responsibility was hard to define and therefore easy to evade. A party governing alone has to be realistic since its faults may be exposed by the test of practice, but a partner in a coalition had a permanent excuse for every failure to fulfil a promise: that it would have broken up the government. A disunited cabinet lacked authority over its supporters. A heterogeneous majority included unwilling partners who hoped that a change of alliances would bring them more jobs or better policies. An opposition of miscellaneous malcontents, united only in negation, was not made responsible by the prospect of power. Instead of an open clash of political philosophies enabling the electorate to judge, the bargains and manœuvres which go on behind the scenes of other political systems were brought to the centre of the stage.

A party which was asked to join the government often laid down conditions, not always successfully. The Socialists vetoed Paul Reynaud as finance minister in November 1947. By July 1948 the balance of power had shifted against them and they agreed to serve with him, only to resign when he announced his policy. In the following May he launched the Conservatives' ultimatum to Queuille's government to change its economic and social policies.[26] This was resisted by the Socialist ministers, especially Daniel Mayer, who in September broke up the cabinet; SFIO then had to accept a Radical veto on Mayer's reappointment. MRP's power similarly dwindled between March 1952, when the party refused to serve under Pinay unless Robert Schuman kept the foreign office, and January 1953 when it could no longer resist his eviction.

To prevent differences rankling and poisoning the life of cabinets, successive prime ministers strove in vain to establish a 'contract of the majority' committing all the government parties to a common programme. Chained for ten years to the government bench, MRP supported these efforts, but the other parties would never abandon the equivocations by which they tried to combine the advantages of opposition with those of office. When offered the economic ministries by Jules Moch in October 1949, MRP insisted that all government parties accept responsibility for their policies. The Radicals, committed by their votes for Moch to the proposals in his investiture speech, flatly refused any further engagement. Reluctantly MRP gave way, despite protests from the prospective economic ministers who knew what to expect from their colleagues.[27] But when the Radicals demanded the ministry of information too, MRP refused to tolerate other ministers attacking their policies with official resources, and the dispute prevented Moch forming a government. In 1956 Mendès-France, denied the foreign office by the hostility of the 'Europeans', declined the ministry of finance because he had no assurance that his Socialist colleagues would accept his policies. Subsequent quarrels showed he had been prudent.

These manœuvres were inevitable when the reputation of a man or a party

26. *AP* 1949, pp. 78–81, 323–32; Arné, pp. 247, 257, 351.

27. The minority also included Mme Poinso-Chapuis, whose ministerial career terminated with her celebrated decree in 1948; it was not only Socialists who saw the disadvantages of office most clearly when they were personally unlikely to receive it. For the efforts of the premiers and the 'contract of the majority' see Arné, pp. 209–17.

was bound up with the policies and fortunes of a government they did not control. When MRP was driven against the wishes of its militants to join Pinay's government, it refused the economic ministries in order to dissociate itself from the premier's conservative policies, and treated its commitment to its allies as lightly as they had ever done. In the Laniel and Faure cabinets the Gaullists in their turn were to show that ex-critics of the System could outdo its oldest practitioners in their contempt for governmental solidarity. For a group which obtained office because its votes were indispensable to the majority might be unable to dictate policy if rival groups were equally indispensable. Parties entered or supported cabinets because the alternative combination would be worse, or the odium of provoking or prolonging a ministerial crisis greater than that of accepting an unsatisfactory compromise. But such transitory arrangements could evoke no loyalty. No party took risks to defend an unpopular policy which was not its own, or felt any compunction about joining a cabinet and then attacking it.

Battling with the parties for the loyalty of his ministers, a premier had first to struggle for the right to choose them – like a medieval king contesting the investiture of bishops with the Pope. De Gaulle won a tussle with the Communists on this point, and the Socialists refused to serve under Mendès-France when he would not give way on it (though Bidault in 1949 and Pleven in 1950 made personal appointments from SFIO). But this close identification with its chosen representatives made it hard for a party to detach itself from an unsuccessful man or unpopular policy without humiliation for him or embarrassment for them. Jean Letourneau of MRP remained in charge of Indo-Chinese affairs long after his policies had collapsed, and SFIO could oust Robert Lacoste from Algiers in April 1958 only by deciding to stay out of office altogether. On the other hand, since the selection of ministers raised delicate personal problems within a party, MRP sometimes preferred the prime minister to take the invidious responsibility. Any prudent premier naturally tried to choose senior ministers who could bring strength to his government.[28] Some, like Pinay, invited each group to make nominations for minor office.

The individualist groups had more difficulty in influencing their members, among whom the prospect of promotion was a potent lure and the loose party tie a feeble restraint, since the rebel could so easily transfer to another group. Paradoxically, therefore, it was precisely the parties which prided themselves on allowing their members freedom of action which needed the whip to stop individual decisions engaging the group and compromising its reputation. The Radicals warned Mendès-France against becoming Gouin's finance minister in January 1946, UDSR objected to François Mitterrand taking the Interior in September 1948, and in October 1949 when a Peasant deputy accepted junior office from Bidault, his party exacted from him an undated letter of resignation which was sent in two months later.[29] But some groups preferred

28. His 'first concern' from 1875 to 1958: Buron, p. 172. On Mendès-France and SFIO see Fauvet, *IVe*, pp. 283–4.

29. *AP* 1946, pp. 11, 15–16; 1948, p. 152; 1949, pp. 213, 217; 1950, p. 5; Arné, p. 348. The Peasant, M. Ribeyre, emphasized that his resignation was involuntary by voting confidence in the government which his party opposed.

to disavow their ministers without disciplining them; in 1957 Mollet appointed Queuille and another dissident Radical to his abortive government, but none of their fellows voted for him.

Serving ministers often rebelled against discipline. In May 1949 the Peasants and in July PRL expelled members who refused to resign from Queuille's government. In October 1955, when Edgar Faure's Social Republican (Gaullist) ministers called for a new government and were dismissed, one repudiated his party and took the premier's side. Two months later, when Faure himself was expelled from the Radical party for dissolving the Assembly, five of his Radical ministers resigned but three stayed in office. In the new Assembly two Social Republicans joined Mollet 'in a personal capacity' against the party's wish, and in May 1958 one of Pflimlin's four Conservative ministers refused a party summons to resign. Of all premiers, Mendès-France did most damage to party discipline, despite his failure with the Socialists. He gave posts to members of MRP, who were expelled (but readmitted later) and of CNIP, which changed its rules to prevent any repetition of the offence.[30]

Few premiers could count like Mendès-France on the loyalty of personal admirers in many different parties. But all, including him, could expect votes from several quarters, which came from the 'king's friends': the men who systematically supported every government, either in hopes of advantage for themselves or their clients or even on grounds of principle. Dissident Gaullists of 1952 and Radicals of 1955–56 were as reluctant as dissident Socialists before the war to see their careers ruined by a party or leader whose sights seemed set far too high. Other ministerialists traded their votes for concessions to a constituency or a pressure-group. Overseas deputies were divided between those who fought every cabinet (like Irish MP's in the 1880's) and were nearly all eliminated from the Assembly in 1951, and those who preferred (like Scots a century earlier) to support all ministries impartially. The Peasant party was similarly split, either internally or organizationally, between Paul Antier's intransigent wing and the participationist bargainers led by Camille Laurens.[31] But some politicians, who believed that nothing could be done without stability, thought any government better than none and no specific policy worth the disruption of a majority: men like Paul Hutin-Desgrées of MRP, the Breton editor of the largest provincial newspaper, who sought no office, left Parliament disillusioned in 1955, and supported Government as systematically in the Fifth Republic as in the Fourth.

'King's friends' at one time made up a substantial parliamentary force. While SFIO was still in the majority 295 deputies voted successively for a Socialist, a Radical and an MRP leader as premier in October 1949. But with its defection in the next crisis, in summer 1950, only 139 members supported the outgoing and incoming premiers on the four decisive votes. In the second Parliament there was a major change of men and policies when Mendès-France succeeded Laniel, but 102 deputies still voted for both leaders: nearly

30. Arné, pp. 348–9, with other cases. *AP* 1949, pp. 80, 130; 1954, pp. 70, 102; 1955, pp. 7, 72–3, 92; 1956, pp. 18, 27; 1958, p. 63; and above, pp. 151, 398.

31. Above, p. 135. Lawyers, and old parliamentary hands, typically preferred bargaining to intransigent politics: cf. above, pp. 134, 135n., 153 n. 15, 156 n. 32.

all IOM, nearly half the Radicals, and between a fifth and an eighth of every other group except Communists and Socialists; 12% of metropolitan members but 43% of those from overseas.[32] By the third Assembly MRP was less firmly in the majority, the Radical party was in fragments, and the ban on proxies stopped many overseas members from voting. The dwindling band of 'king's friends' could now muster only 40 deputies to vote for both Pinay and Mollet in October 1957. The base of the System was dangerously narrowed by this decline of the 'accommodating and agile men', for whatever their motives they had been 'indispensable to the permanence of public life and the gentleness of transitions'.[33]

4. THE ART OF BROKERAGE

Without the substantial core of support available *ex officio* to his predecessors, a premier of the later Fourth Republic had an even harder task. His resources were few, for once he had formed his cabinet the hope of office was an asset only to his prospective successors. But he could still use the traditional weapons: decorations for the influential constituents of hesitant members – or for the members – and pork-barrel benefits for the districts of deputies from overseas – or from elsewhere. As in the Third Republic, 'a complete day-by-day diplomacy was founded on knowledge of the civil service lists, the art of opportune promotions in the Legion of Honour, a respect for political connections and an adroit use of favouritism'.[34] Now and then major posts outside the government provided more substantial fare: Mendès-France sent Jacques Soustelle to Algeria and Edgar Faure chose Gilbert Grandval for Morocco both as strong administrators with a liberal reputation and as Gaullists whose appointments might rally a wavering party. But often the prime minister could make little use of such patronage, for it was subject to hard bargaining between parties seeking to place their friends, achieve their own policy objectives, or counteract their rivals. On 21 January 1948 the cabinet sent an MRP deputy to govern Madagascar, a Radical official to Equatorial Africa, and a Socialist junior minister to West Africa. A month later the Algerian settlers and their Radical friends, led by René Mayer, demanded the removal of the liberal governor-general Yves Chataigneau; SFIO's opposition was overcome by making him ambassador in Moscow and choosing in his place a Socialist cabinet minister, M. E. Naegelen.[35]

In dividing the spoils it was not easy to satisfy everyone; in deciding controversies over policy it was often impossible. Ministers and party leaders who

32. Almost 200 voted only for Laniel, over 300 only for Mendès-France, and 13 for neither, among them de Gaulle's brother and brother-in-law. SFIO had its 'king's friends' too (notably Paul Ramadier, an old Republican Socialist) but *discipline de vote* made them invisible. A year earlier, the Assembly had overthrown René Mayer and then rejected four premiers-designate before electing Laniel; 35 deputies voted for all six men (of these 35, 7 got office from Laniel and 3 kept it under Mendès-France, who was among the 35). Another 128 voted for five of the six, of whom only 38 did not vote for Mendès-France. (My calculations.)

33. Isorni, *Ainsi*, p. 87 (cf. p. 137). Of the 40, 14 were MRP and 25 from the debris of Radicalism. Of the 29 who later voted for Gaillard and had also voted for Bourgès-Maunoury when he fell, not one was from overseas: proxies might well have saved him.

34. Henri de Jouvenel, *Pourquoi je suis syndicaliste* (1928), p. 21. (I owe this reference to Dr. D. B. Goldey.) For examples under Mendès-France, Faucher, p. 143.

35. *AP* 1948, pp. 8, 19–20; Arné, p. 351; Fauvet, *IVe*, pp. 155–7. But cf. above, p. 333.

had fought hard for the best compromise available often had to settle for much less than their followers demanded. Then, if a well-organized party gave trouble, its leaders could impose party discipline. When the difficulty was with the individualist parties, the cabinet could call for a vote of confidence which helped hesitant deputies to justify an unpopular vote to their constituents.[36] But all such appeals used up part of the government's limited political credit with the discontented groups on the margin of the majority. A prudent premier was therefore sorely tempted to arrange that a dangerous problem should not rise to the surface during his brief incumbency. If his hand were forced he would tend to do a little less of what he was doing before, in compensation making ostentatious gestures elsewhere. When a Socialist-led government repressed an Algerian rising, it was no surprise to find its leaders reassuring their critics (and consciences) that their hearts were still on the Left by speeches criticizing the United States.

A premier could also appeal to the deputies' sense of responsibility by pointing out the catastrophic consequences of a crisis now. But as there was always an international conference, a colonial negotiation or a financial emergency conveniently at hand, this story soon wore thin. Once René Mayer had saved himself by a treasury crisis and a visit to Washington, he could not repeat the performance six weeks later on the eve of the Bermuda conference with Eisenhower and Churchill. Because deputies (like congressmen) resented being defied or constrained, public opinion had to be brought to bear on them by manœuvres, which even the strongest premier did not disdain. Pinay anticipated a coming attack from the Right on his foreign minister by ostentatiously rejecting an 'insulting' American note, a glorious gesture which no Conservative could disavow. Mendès-France, when Gaullists and Socialists were wavering, arranged an interview with a benevolent General de Gaulle and announced a minimum wage increase on the eve of a crucial Socialist caucus.[37]

These devices frequently failed. Then, on a major issue the cabinet fell, on a minor one it accepted defeat. Pinay's ministers were beaten in 102 divisions, out of the 562 in which they voted, and in 41 of these a majority of their nominal supporters voted against them. Sometimes the government avoided defeat by neutrality when it knew its followers would otherwise have rebelled. But in general, though party discipline among deputies was worse on the major questions, the groups of the majority were much more loyal: only once under Pinay did the largest section of any ministerial group vote against the government and it was very rare for them to abstain.[38]

Supporters of the regime recognized the need to sink their differences over policy in order to find a majority and a government. But the differences were genuine and important to both the politicians and their voters. Sometimes a party which would not accept the compromises of office might be ready to keep an unsatisfactory cabinet in power rather than precipitate an insoluble

36. See above, p. 232.
37. Fauvet, *IVe*, p. 235 (Mayer); *AP* 1952, pp. 65, 367–9 (Pinay), and 1954, pp. 79–81 (Mendès-France).
38. Campbell, no. 44, pp. 251–3.

crisis which would endanger the regime. There were recognized gradations of support from marginal parties, ranging from keeping a minority ministry in by not voting against it, through voting for it without joining it, to joining it while criticizing it. Or a government party confronted by an unacceptable policy, and obliged by conviction or electoral necessity to resist all efforts at cajolery or coercion, might still be unwilling to bring the cabinet down. In such cases curious expedients were used to paper over the cracks.[39]

A party might announce that its vote indicated confidence in the government but disapproval of its policy (or *vice versa*).[40] It might authorize ministers to vote with their cabinet colleagues while ordinary deputies abstained, as the Communists did over Indo-China in March 1947, the Socialists over devaluation in January 1948 and an amnesty bill in December 1950, and RPF over the European army in November 1953. Or all ministers might abstain, leaving the 'back-benchers' to decide – the French equivalent of a free vote in the House of Commons. René Pleven's government abstained over electoral reform in February 1951, and Mendès-France's over EDC in August 1954. The perennial disputes over clerical problems were evaded in this way by Schuman in May 1948 over the colliery schools, Pleven in September 1951 over Barangé's bill, and Mollet in February 1956 over its repeal. Pinay's cabinet took no part in 110 divisions, about a sixth of those held in his nine months of office.[41] Much less often ministers voted on both sides, as on a motion to postpone debate on Barangé's bill in September 1951. When Pleven's first cabinet decided to send an ambassador to Madrid, in January 1951, it authorized the Socialist ministers to abstain if an interpellation were moved. Gaillard in February 1958, on MRP's demand, allowed his ministers to vote as they pleased on a motion to restore the pre-war electoral system. Once, in 1948, two ministers voted without authority – or penalty – with their party, UDSR, against Queuille's postponement of local elections.[42]

'Papering over the cracks', strangely enough, was more useful in preserving the edifice than in concealing the gaps in it. For ministers were as unconcerned about attacking their colleagues in speeches as they were reluctant to differ from them in a vote. In 1948 the Socialist minister of education (Édouard Depreux) accused his prime minister (Robert Schuman) of violating the constitution over the Poinso-Chapuis decree, which had not been submitted to him for counter signature. In 1949 a meeting of Conservative deputies criticized new taxes proposed by the independent Conservative finance minister Maurice Petsche; leading the attack were two junior ministers, Antoine Pinay and Jean Moreau. Moreau later expressed sympathy for the parliamentary critics of his own department, the air ministry, whose real target was the Socialist

39. For a full record of party attitudes see the table in Arné, pp. 225–8.

40. Arné, pp. 275–6, and above, p. 231.

41. Arné, pp. 186–8; for Pinay, Campbell, no. 44, p. 251. The executive by convention abstained on strictly parliamentary questions such as waiver of a member's immunity or amendments to standing orders, and had sometimes done so on electoral and constitutional reform.

42. Spain: *Monde*, 11 January 1951. Gaillard: *Inégalités*, p. 108. UDSR: Arné, p. 126n. (with one other case). Also *AP* 1948, p. 160, 1951, p. 220 (Barangé), 1958, p. 22. It was said that some crises were avoided by horse-trading, one party making concessions on church schools and another on naval building: *AP* 1949, pp. 38–9, and *Figaro*, 6 March 1949 (quoted Williams, p. 384n.); cf. Fauvet, *IVe*, p. 157.

minister of defence. At next year's SFIO conference Jules Moch, for once out of office, retaliated by contrasting inadequate governmental provision of schools and houses with wasteful expenditure on an air force with no aircraft (the air ministry was one of the few never held by a Socialist). In 1953 René Pleven, as a senior minister in a conservative government, publicly urged his party to work for a new left-centre majority. Pinay and Mollet denounced one another every week-end under Gaillard's government, in which both their parties served.[43]

Party differences were not the only ones. In this atmosphere of conflict departmental quarrels were magnified too. As Edgar Faure pointed out, ministers who hoped to survive into the next cabinet felt 'more loyal to their respective departments than to the government as a collective entity'.[44] If parties or ministries neutralized each other sufficiently thoroughly, the problem was left to the unregulated clash of group interests, with the usual dangers of inflation or disorder – or overseas repression, continued until a revolutionary crisis became inevitable.[45] After 1953 matters became worse, for the main political conflicts no longer coincided with the lines of party cleavage. First on EDC, then on Algeria, the parties themselves were too divided internally to guarantee that their members would give reliable support to governments in which their leaders served. When Joseph Laniel was accepted as premier by a weary Assembly which had rejected five previous candidates, he formed a broadly-based cabinet which was said to embrace two distinct ministries: Bidault's, which practised a diehard colonial policy, and Reynaud's, which favoured conciliation and retrenchment.[46] The same was true of his successors. Mendès-France's government was divided about EDC until the keen 'Europeans' resigned from it; Edgar Faure's ministers quarrelled openly over Morocco; under Mollet both Socialists and Radicals were split between Lacoste's supporters and opponents. André Morice refused to countersign Bourgès-Maunoury's Algerian reform bill. Félix Gaillard, like Laniel, became premier when, after a long and indecisive crisis, the major government parties stopped obstructing one another in the Assembly – only to project their conflict into the cabinet. As Paul Reynaud put it, 'Bit by bit the cabinet has come to look like a miniature Parliament with its majority, its minority and its manœuvres behind the scenes.'[47]

In the hope of imposing on the parties of his majority a sense of responsibility for governmental policy, Gaillard brought their parliamentary leaders into the discussion of the most controversial problems through 'round-table conferences'. This device had occasionally been used by earlier premiers to settle a difficult problem, prop up a falling cabinet, or overcome the difficulties caused by the exclusion of ministers from the deliberations of parliamentary

43. *AP* 1948, pp. 77–8, 92–3; 1949, pp. 77, 97; 1952, p. 83; 1958, pp. 34–43 *passim*; *Monde*, 29 May 1950, 10 and 11 November 1952, 27 October 1953; Arné, pp. 121n., 126–7, 348; Debû-Bridel, p. 252 (Schuman); Fauvet in *Monde*, 2 May 1958.

44. *Monde*, 27 March 1953; cf. R. Lecourt, *ibid.*, 8 April 1953.

45. See above, pp. 383–4, 394; below, p. 440.

46. Faucher, pp. 64–5; Fauvet, *IVe*, pp. 253–5; Tournoux, pp. 29–31.

47. *JO* 8 October 1955, p. 4960. 'Whoever experienced the old cabinet ... knows it was itself a Parliament where discussions lasted for hours ... often without reaching any conclusion': Conte, p. 10. Morice: Arné, pp. 121n., 368n.

committees on a bill. Bourgès-Maunoury employed it to bring into the discussions of Lacoste's Algerian reform bill the Conservative, MRP and Social Republican groups, which were unrepresented in the cabinet but essential to the majority; it did not save him or the bill from defeat. Undeterred, Gaillard called round tables on the budget, constitutional amendment, electoral reform, and a medical insurance bill. The first two helped the government salvage some of its proposals. The others failed because of the indiscipline rather than the rigidity of the parties. Bargains accepted by their leaders were repeatedly repudiated by the right wing of the Conservatives, whose defection overturned every premier of this Parliament. For neither cabinets nor round tables could conjure up a majority from parties which were aligned one way on the economy and another on the constitution, and from rival camps whose irreconcilable views on Algeria cut sharply across all party lines. At the round table the cabinet abdicated responsibility, but the parties would not assume it.[48]

Just as voters chose their deputy to protect them against the government rather than to uphold it, and members entered Parliament to vote for the claims and interests of their constituents rather than for a policy, so ministers frequently took office to defend their party's supporters against the designs of a rival group with a different clientele to protect. As a Radical deputy once argued, 'But, my dear friends, is it not also true that our presence in the governments has prevented the other parties, too, from applying their programmes?' Even politicians who came hopefully to power with far-reaching aims, and took important decisions in the first honeymoon weeks of office, were soon discouraged or frustrated by the obstacles strewn in their path. Consequently, wrote an excellent critic in 1957, '. . . the reigning ideal is also one of protectionism and security above all – as in so many sectors of the economy, or in the teaching world. French parties do not govern, they occupy power. They do not conceive the need for or the conditions of a genuine executive: they want a right of veto against their allies or rivals . . . all attention is concentrated on the parliamentary game, this system of mutual neutralization . . . in which the players avail themselves of power only to obstruct any effective use of it.'[49]

48. On round tables see Andrews, no. 3. Cf. Arné, pp. 92, 179, 259–60; *AP* 1949, p. 74, 1957, pp. 91–2.

49. Hoffmann, no. 125, p. 816; cf. Hamon, no. 120, pp. 841–8. Radical: Roger Gaborit at a party executive in 1951, cited De Tarr, p. 158. General Koenig in 1955 and André Morice in 1957 conspicuously used their offices to frustrate their colleagues over North Africa and defence expenditure. Honeymoon: Delouvrier in *Crise*, p. 86.

Chapter 29

PARTIES AND COALITIONS: (3) CRISIS AS AN INSTITUTION

The 'system of mutual neutralization' maintained French politics in precarious equilibrium as long as no major decisions had to be taken, but it disintegrated as soon as they could no longer be deferred. The deputies of the majority were not the ideological fanatics foreigners often thought them, tearing the country asunder in their doctrinal zeal; on the contrary, they often seemed to erect compromise into a principle and to prefer office to ideology. But rapid changes in the economy at home and the French position in the world posed problems to which *immobilisme* could not long provide an answer. To the men who had framed the constitution, the prime minister was to become the leader of a coherent majority and the motor of the political system. To those who worked it – mostly the same men – he began as the broker between parties struggling to impose or prevent decisions, and finished as 'the fuse that blows whenever tension rises'.[1] Twelve times in the eleven years of the Fourth Republic's life the fuse blew, and provoked a cabinet crisis.[2]

Most Assemblies contained several alternative majorities, and the more there were the less stable was any one of them. The 'king's friends' were always in them and the enemies of the regime always out, but the 'loyal opposition' could generally count on a 'fifth column' of sympathizers within the majority and even the ministry it was attacking. When enough of the discontented joined the fifth column, the cabinet fell. An effort might then be made to tempt the loyal opposition, or part of it, by offers of jobs or concessions on policy, and if it succeeded some waverers, attached to the discarded men or policies, would retire into the wilderness as the new loyal opposition.

Shifting parliamentary alignments and unstable governments generated new incentives to political fluidity. In Britain almost all governments enjoy a solid party majority which sustains them from one general election to the next. In the United States, a congressional majority which is often negative, undisciplined and incoherent cannot precipitate a vacancy in the executive branch. But in France every change of ministry offered new opportunities for political promotion. A change of government became an end in itself, and after a few months in office most premiers had usually exhausted their political credit and physical health in the endless battle to keep the majority together.

Although the careerist ambitions of groups or men caused a few cabinet crises and contributed to them all, the agents of disruption were generally those who were in the old majority from necessity rather than choice. Sometimes a party, like the Socialists in 1947–50 or Mendès-France's Radical

1. Paul Reynaud, *JO* 27 May 1953, p. 2871.
2. In addition, three premiers were elected at the start of a Parliament, two could not form a cabinet, and five survived less than six weeks (two of whom lasted only two days). Four more had been chosen before the regime was born. See lists in Arné, pp. 305–10, 432.

friends in 1956–57, had to support a government which it could not seriously influence for fear that it would lose votes or credit by provoking a crisis. When democracy was in danger all government parties were inhibited from pressing their full demands for jobs or policies. Yet as the regime grew more secure, the incumbent ministry became weaker. Pressure from the country diminished, making it less necessary for the competing centre groups to behave intransigently. But confidence that the cabinet could now be overthrown without disaster encouraged them to insist on their neglected claims; Mollet met his first parliamentary trouble when by-elections showed a sharp drop in Communist and Poujadist votes. The parliamentary equilibrium was never stable and while short ministries might be a symptom of political malaise, the 'long' cabinet – Queuille's, Laniel's, Mollet's – often survived only because no one wished to confront Parliament and public with dangerous and disruptive problems. 'Those who think only of the general interest, harmed by *immobilisme*, and those who think only of their private interests, harmed by a government that lasts, both want the ministry to fall . . . France governs herself by changing her governments.'[3]

1. THE RULES AND THE REFEREE

Cabinet crises were often turning-points in the shaping of policy and always in the struggle for power. Elaborate rules were therefore devised to ensure a minimum of fair play. The most conspicuous feature of a crisis was the stately ritualism of the public procedure – though it could not always prevent subtle intrigues behind the scenes exerting an influence on the outcome. Some of the conventions (*règles du jeu*) were inherited from the Third Republic; some were modified by the constitution of the Fourth; and others were built up by practice to deal with particular situations as they arose.

When a premier was overthrown it was the task of the President of the Republic, under Article 45 of the constitution, to designate a candidate for the succession 'after the customary consultations'.[4] After René Mayer's defeat on Thursday, 21 May 1953, the following visitors called on President Auriol: Friday morning: the first vice-president of the National Assembly (Herriot was ill) and six of the eleven ex-premiers who sat in it. Friday afternoon: the Presidents of the Council of the Republic, Assembly of the French Union and Economic Council; four more ex-premiers; and delegations from SFIO, RPF and MRP. Saturday morning: five party delegations (Radicals, UDSR and three Conservative groups); the eleventh ex-premier; and Pierre Cot, speaking for the fellow-travelling Progressives. Saturday afternoon: the last party (the Overseas Independents) and the *rapporteurs-généraux* of the two finance committees.

The President could now begin the selection of a candidate. But his hands were still not free, for convention prescribed the order in which each party was given its opportunity, beginning with those who had provoked the crisis and continuing with those who prolonged it. The dangerous opposition was excluded from the list, which opened with the loyal opposition (in 1953 a Socialist and then a Gaullist were asked first, as a matter of form). No one

3. Delouvrier in *Crise*, p. 87.

4. See Arné, p 47 and n.

(least of all themselves) expected them to succeed, since the old government had usually been upset by an alliance of mutually hostile extremes. The waverers who had defected from the defunct majority then had their turn. Sometimes their leader refused; sometimes he would undertake a *mission d'information* before deciding; occasionally he might accept and begin serious conversations. If he made no real effort, other parties with a share of responsibility for the crisis were approached. Once one of them made a genuine effort and failed, the party that stopped him became responsible, and had to try next. But often their victim's group ensured that they should not profit from their obstructiveness, and the advantage went to a third party which stood (or had given the impression of standing) above the battle, wreathed in ostentatious virtue.

The candidate needed personal as well as party qualifications. An opposition leader would normally hold an official post as general secretary of his party or chairman of its deputies. A majority spokesman would have held one of the five highest offices or a senior post without portfolio; only one of the Fourth Republic's fifteen premiers lacked these qualifications.[5] A politician asked to stand for the premiership was called the *président du conseil sollicité* if the approach was very tentative, *pressenti* if it was firm; on acceptance (often preceded by a trial run of consultations, *tour de piste*) he became the *président désigné*. Until 1954 he had to win election by an absolute majority (becoming *investi*), form his cabinet (making him at last *président du conseil*), and even then secure its acceptance by the deputies (which Schuman failed to do in September 1948 and Queuille in July 1950). After 1954 the *président désigné* was elected by a simple majority after first forming his cabinet. To the prudent politician it was dangerous as well as disagreeable to fail at a late stage, for this often caused ill-feeling between parties which had eventually to agree if any majority was to be found. So, of the 59 politicians *sollicités* by Auriol, only 24 agreed to confront the Assembly as candidates, sitting in splendid isolation on the empty government bench to present their prepared speeches, answer the queries of their friends, and evade or fall into the snares laid by their opponents. Only twelve survived the entire ordeal.[6]

The absurd side of these 'rites' needs no emphasis. The gentlemen who paraded before the President of the Republic, each of them entitled to be addressed till his dying day as *Monsieur le Président*, were not necessarily those best able to help him in his task. Presidents of the Assembly of the Union and Economic Council rarely had much political influence, while among the ex-premiers summoned were Édouard Daladier, the man of Munich, Jules Moch, who never actually headed a government, Félix Gouin who had held no office since the wine scandals of 1946 – but not the great critic of the 'rites', General de Gaulle. Usually the largest parties came first, but once alphabetical order was thought more impartial.

5. Cf. above, pp. 205, 206 and Arné, p. 94. In 82 approaches by Presidents Auriol and Coty, only five men not so qualified were asked: four opposition leaders and Antoine Pinay.

6. Under Coty 23 were *sollicités*; three failed in the Assembly and seven succeeded. Lists (of *pressentis*) in Arné, pp. 49–51, 307–10.

Yet the rules were not futile and archaic, as they were often thought. Conventions allowed the responsibilities of causing or continuing a crisis to be fastened on particular groups expert in avoiding them. If a party overthrew a government when it could not impose an alternative, the rules brought home its weakness to its own leaders, and its responsibility to public opinion. They were also useful both to facilitate and to limit the role of the President of the Republic. He needed to be informed of the chances of the candidate he proposed. He could have much influence on the course and terms of party bargaining. Even restrained by the conventions, he could impose serious obstacles to a candidate he disliked; without them he would have had too great opportunities for illicit influence. For the offer of the premiership gave a man or movement a standing and an opportunity others might resent. When Pinay was nominated in 1952 Gaullists were bitter against Auriol for splitting their party (but had he not really meant to show the Right that no defection was to be hoped for?). Only nine months later Radicals attacked him for recognizing RPF as part of the 'loyal opposition' by an approach to Soustelle at a moment when they believed it could have been split again. Conventions both restrained a strong President from abusing his office and encouraged a weak one not to be unduly inhibited by fear of criticism.

The rules left the President a wide discretion – in a grave emergency, even that of settling the crisis quickly without reference to them, as Auriol attempted in July 1948 and when the Korean war began in June 1950. They allowed him to decide which opposition parties were 'loyal' and which were 'dangerous': thus Coty resumed consultations with the Communists, which Auriol had briefly abandoned, and early in May 1958 made a confidential approach to General de Gaulle himself. They left the President to assign the responsibility for overthrowing the late government, which was not always obvious.[7] And they gave him a wide choice of men, for there were usually about twenty political leaders conventionally qualified for the premiership.

This discretion had to be used with care, for the prestige of the presidency was damaged by failures like those of Léon Blum in November 1947 and Guy Mollet in March 1951 (especially as both belonged to Auriol's own party) and by the massacre of five successive candidates in May and June 1953.[8] To avoid such incidents the device of *missions d'information* was developed: the President commissioned a political leader to investigate on his behalf without either man's reputation being formally engaged. Until Auriol's last year only one prospective premier, Bidault in October 1949, accepted nomination without any preliminary inquiry at all. About half the candidates undertook informal missions for the President, and so did three men who were not candidates, Robert Lecourt and André Marie in September 1948, and Guy Mollet in July 1950. But this practice met growing criticism from both Right and extreme Left, and when Mollet was chosen the Radicals refused to discuss the situation with anyone but a premier-designate. *Missions d'information*

7. Arné, pp. 53–4.

8. In 1949 Auriol talked of resigning if Bidault, like Mayer and Moch, failed to form a government: Fauvet in *Monde*, 26 October 1949. On 1947 see Sauvageot, no. 195, pp. 247–8; on 1953, Fauvet, *IV*[e], p. 240.

were less used thereafter, but René Pleven and Robert Schuman undertook them for Coty in 1957.[9]

The politicians had their own tactical problems which were the obverse of the President's. An opposition leader might refuse an offer of the premiership at once, to emphasize his party's detachment from the men in power and to avoid the humiliation of failure. Alternatively he might welcome it – without taking it seriously – because it gave him a chance to prepare the way for a genuine effort later, an opportunity to discredit rival parties for their obstructiveness, a platform to put forward an attractive election programme, or even (to the Gaullists in 1953) a certificate of republican respectability. Within the majority parties, too, different leaders might take different views. Prudent and senior men often preferred not to stand and fail – or succeed, if the new ministry was likely to face very unpopular decisions. Between 1949 and 1953 Bidault and Pleven each declined five separate approaches. Quite frequently a leader would reject an offer early in a crisis, but accept a few days later, when the situation had evolved. (But these calculations might go awry, for the 'snow-plough', called in to clear the way for others, sometimes – like Pinay in 1952 – went ahead and made the journey itself.) Similarly an experienced politician, looking ahead, might decide that the future seemed more propitious than the present and bide his time till the next crisis. In January 1952 it was known that the Socialists would not return to office at once but hoped that they might do so later, so the Radical *caciques* chose to wait (in vain) for the chance of a relatively comfortable spell in office. Then the President would send for a rising young man with his way to make, like Edgar Faure, or for an older leader who after earlier failures dared not refuse a last chance, like René Mayer a year later.

If the shift of policy required to reassemble a majority was expected to be a minor one evoking little friction, a member of the old cabinet was often asked to form the new one, in which he would reserve a place of high dignity for his recent chief. But if relations within the old majority were too strained, the President was more likely to summon a weighty personage who had been out of office long enough for his past mistakes to be overshadowed by the current controversies from which he had prudently kept detached. Whenever an attempt was made to win over a section of the loyal opposition there were always majority leaders who, against that very day, had carefully cultivated friendly relations with the party to be approached. Georges Bidault was, of all leaders of the Centre, the most acceptable to RPF. Antoine Pinay was adept at winning conservatives away from their party allegiance. Pierre Mendès-France appealed to progressives and to admirers of strong leadership. Christian Pineau was MRP's favourite left-winger in 1955. SFIO could be tempted by a sympathetic Radical: Queuille (or Pleven) in the first Parliament, Mendès-France in the second, Bourgès-Maunoury, in very different circumstances, in the third.

Normally, therefore, a politician was made 'available' by his standing with

9. *AP* 1957, pp. 54, 102; the same criticisms were heard. For missions see Arné, p. 48; Georgel, i. 94–5; Dansette, *Présidents*, pp. 269 and 324; Williams, p. 186n. On Auriol and Coty see above, pp. 201, 202. Pleven's mission made him 'available' for the *next* crisis: Fauvet, *IV*^{e}, p. 332.

other parties rather than with his own: for he could almost always count on the votes (if not necessarily the goodwill) of members of his own group.[10] But at times a majority party had to be made to swallow distasteful medicine, which was best prescribed by a doctor in whom the sufferers had confidence. In March 1951 Queuille was chosen to persuade his Radical friends to give way over electoral reform, and in January 1953 Bidault, then still a hero to his party, was the natural first choice to remove Robert Schuman from the Quai d'Orsay.

Here, too, the most valuable qualities were those of the conciliator. When a cabinet broke up through internal dissension, as so many did before 1951, the minister who had tried hardest to hold it together was often invited to lead its successor. A chance to solve a crisis might thus be a reward for efforts to avert it, as with André Marie in 1948 and Jules Moch in 1949, or to settle a previous crisis, as with Guy Mollet in 1951. Moderation, caution and acceptability were the qualities that brought success, and the bold, challenging, uncomfortable leader could rarely hope to secure even a precarious and fleeting grip on power. His opportunity came only when the situation was not merely desperate, but manifestly seen to be desperate by the President, the rival *caciques* and the ordinary deputies alike.[11]

2. THE PLAYERS AND THE MOVES

Once chosen, the premier-designate assumed the immediate responsibility for solving the crisis. He too undertook the 'usual consultations', adding to his list of visitors the specialists on the major problem of the day – treasury and bank officials if it were financial, generals if it were military, leaders of the parliamentary committees in any event. He was subjected to pressures which grew stronger as the crisis approached solution.[12] Men sought office for themselves or their friends; parties struggled to preserve or extend their influence. An interest-group which had fought the last government would naturally work for a friendlier successor; but a group which had no responsibility for the crisis was not debarred from exploiting it, whether its objective was dearer cider or no European army.

Like an American presidential candidate, the nominee had to try not to tie his own hands if he won by the promises made to secure the victory. Jobs had to be allotted to the majority parties in rough proportion to their numbers (Laniel adjusted them to favourable votes), and while the deputies' expectation of office might help a candidate for the premiership, their disappointment with his choice was sure to do him harm.[13] The individualist parties had always thought of political rewards in terms of spoils, and their diverse factions were hard to woo by other means; so governments formed by Radical and Conservative premiers averaged 34 members to 28 in MRP or Socialist-led ministries and 23 in General de Gaulle's. But as majorities grew harder to

10. Exceptionally, in May 1958, MRP openly blocked Georges Bidault. But in 1953 even Mendès-France's bitterest Radical enemies voted for him (though ardently urging others not to: Fauvet, *IVe*, pp. 238–9; cf. above, p. 399 n.).
11. See below, p. 422. On conciliators in the Third Republic see Soulier, pp. 484–5, 488, 494.
12. Arné, pp. 96–8. See below, p. 432.
13. See above, p. 228 and n.

find ministries became steadily larger, averaging 27 in the Constituent Assemblies, 28½ in the first National Assembly, 33 in the second and 35 in the third.[14]

A prospective premier found that since his party ties and personal reputation reassured one section of the potential majority, his policy had to calm the doubts of the others: consequently in October 1949 the social programme of René Mayer, a conservative Radical, was more progressive than that of Jules Moch of SFIO. But any attempt to appease one group of waverers would probably provoke an equal and opposite reaction on the far wing of the majority, as Schuman found in September 1948 and Queuille in July 1950. The easy way out was to evade the awkward problem. Pleven appointed an investigating committee on the Catholic schools question;[15] this prevented it arising throughout his first cabinet, though he returned to office in time to be plagued by it a year later. René Mayer in January 1953 tried by ingenious equivocation to convince MRP that he favoured the European army and the Gaullists that he did not.

Shifts and evasions might discredit those who used them, but a bold move was unlikely to meet with success, at least at the start of a crisis. In the summer of 1953 Reynaud, Mendès-France and Bidault all flatly refused to negotiate with the parties.[16] After they had failed, André Marie reverted to cautious conciliation rather than harsh instransigence, appealed to tried experience instead of youthful vigour, and evaded commitments as blatantly as his predecessors had welcomed them: the performance shamed the deputies into giving him the lowest vote of all, and in the end success went to Joseph Laniel, whose haughty attitude proved the unexpected prelude to a year of *immobilisme* ending at Dien-Bien-Phu. By then the Assembly was so hungry for leadership that it chose Mendès-France. Yet even he could not avoid concessions. He made no promises to the parties, chose his own ministers, ignored the customary *dosage* – but appointed 'Europeans' and 'anti-Europeans' in equal numbers to office; and having proclaimed a year before that no self-respecting government could fail to stake its existence on the EDC treaty, he proceeded to resort to cabinet neutrality on the question like any Pleven or Queuille.

By allowing the European army to be defeated, Mendès-France earned the bitter hostility of MRP; by agreeing to German rearmament through NATO instead, he made enemies of the Communists. These two groups, supporters of his liberal policy in North Africa, joined hands with its opponents among the Conservatives and right-wing Radicals to overthrow him on it in February 1955. His fall led to a typical ministerial crisis.[17] Its course was

14. My calculations from Arné, p. 101; before 1951 no ministry had more than 35 members, later over half did. By party: Campbell, no. 41, p. 33. In 1945–57, 324 appointments were given to 78 MRP or SFIO members, but 335 were shared between 119 Radicals, Conservatives and RS: my calculations from Dogan and Campbell, no. 72, p. 327. Spoils: cf. pp. 400, 438.

15. A device also used in the Fifth Republic (and in Britain).

16. The Assembly did not maintain the tone of the candidates; questions to Mendès-France, for instance, came from deputies representing the neglected overseas departments and the prosperous but greedy cider lobby. Laniel refused to answer questions (a precedent cited and followed by de Gaulle in June 1958). *JO* 3 and 4 June 1953, pp. 2913, 2958.

17. Except that his government had included much of the normal opposition in its majority, while most of the normal majority opposed it.

decided by MRP which, having served in three cabinets of the Right and opposed one of the Left, was now determined to repudiate the welcoming conservative embrace and reaffirm its allegiance to the cause of progress.

President Coty's first nominee was Antoine Pinay, since Laniel's fall the recognized leader of the Conservatives, the strongest section of the loyal opposition and indeed of the Assembly. He had been out of office for two years and three ministries. His popularity with the Right in Parliament and the country made him the best man to persuade his followers to accept inevitable concessions in North Africa, and later he did so – with little difficulty over Tunisia and much over Morocco. While he could count on the Right, he needed reinforcement on the Left, and therefore presented a very progressive economic, social and colonial programme. But for MRP to support a Conservative would have printed even deeper the right-wing brand they were determined to erase; and, faced with their firm opposition, Pinay withdrew without seriously trying to form a cabinet.

The crisis thus became the responsibility of MRP, who had both fought Mendès-France and checked Pinay. Neither the Radicals nor the Conservatives, therefore, had reason to wish them well; nor had either the Socialist supporters of Mendès-France or the 'anti-European' Gaullists. So the prospect for an MRP candidate was poor, and the choice consequently fell on a newcomer to the front rank, Pierre Pflimlin. His special qualification was his responsible attitude over German rearmament; when nearly all the MRP leaders vented their rancour at the defeat of EDC by voting against the treaties which replaced it, and even Robert Schuman abstained for the sake of party unity, Pflimlin had become the leading supporter of the agreements in the party. This was enough to win him the nomination, but not the premiership. Radical friends of Mendès-France did not intend MRP to profit from its opposition to their leader; and the Radical minority opposed to him claimed a disproportionate share of cabinet posts in order to strengthen their influence. So Pflimlin, too, abandoned his task.

The third man came from SFIO. Christian Pineau, whose parliamentary prestige was rising, had strongly advocated the European army. Among those who had supported Mendès-France, he had the best chance of winning over MRP – overjoyed to proclaim its left-wing loyalties by voting for a Socialist. But few others wished to abet what they saw as MRP's manœuvre to escape the consequence of its past actions, and even Socialists showed little enthusiasm for their champion's candidature. Pineau's ministerial appointments did him harm, driving even the Overseas Independents into opposition. His speech to the Assembly sounded like a bid for votes in the country rather than in Parliament (and before long the Socialist election campaign was making copious reference to his proposals). So the Assembly defeated him.

As Conservatives, MRP and SFIO had all tried and failed, it was the Radicals' turn. Their obvious candidate was Edgar Faure, an arch-conciliator who had served as minister of finance under both the Conservative Laniel and the 'New Dealer' Mendès-France. As a man with friends in all parties he was eminently 'available'; as a colleague who had shared responsibility for

Mendesist policies, he would blunt his late leader's formidable attack; and as an astute politician he turned into an asset the cabinet-making problem which had damaged his predecessors, giving the foreign ministry to Pinay and the finance ministry to Pflimlin – but withholding until after the vote the junior posts to which wavering deputies might still aspire.[18]

These proceedings took four nominees and eighteen days to arrive at an obvious outcome, widely canvassed before the crisis began. But the delay was necessary, for the solution of a crisis always took time. At first the parties bargained hard over the distribution of offices and the direction of policy. But their intransigence diminished as the crisis went on: for, if it was usually unpopular to overthrow a government, it was almost always thought discreditable to prevent one being formed. So the mere passage of time brought pressure on a party which was being 'difficult' because it feared that concessions might cost it votes. When public exasperation mounted so high that stubbornness would forfeit more support than conciliation, the crisis was ripe for solution.

Before Edgar Faure could emerge in February 1955, his rivals had to be chastened. The Conservatives had to be shown that they could not themselves prevail, and must accept a premier more liberal than they would have liked. MRP had to face its extreme unpopularity and moderate its terms. The *opération Pineau*, long canvassed in the lobbies, was needed to prove to its advocates that a pro-European combination of the Left did not have the votes. Wearing down resistance and 'clearing off the mortgage' were necessary preliminaries to a solution, and in twelve of the Fourth Republic's eighteen elections of a premier, three candidates had to be discarded before a winner emerged.[19]

These prolonged negotiations offered every opportunity for manœuvres by parties or pressure-groups to obscure and shift the responsibility for their actions. In July 1950, Georges Bidault decided not to stand for election because SFIO was plainly against him; a successor was picked, for whom the Socialists at once virtuously announced that they would of course vote – as for any other republican candidate who might be proposed. In June 1957, when Pierre Pflimlin was a candidate, SFIO put forward impossible conditions for its support; when Bourgès-Maunoury was nominated instead, the conditions were forgotten. The polite gesture was popular only when it cost nothing (though occasionally by miscalculation it returned a Pinay, who won such support in the country that his many enemies preferred not to risk the odium of removing him from office).[20]

The President's craft therefore lay in his timing. If he put forward his favourite's name too soon, the candidate would fail and his own prestige might suffer. But if he misjudged the proper moment and waited too long, a nominee might succeed who had been expected – or intended – to fail. He could not hurry, for skimped bargaining meant a precarious settlement, and

18. Gossip said he had promised sixty-two. Cf. below, p. 432.

19. List in Arné, pp. 307–10. Of 23 premiers elected in 1947–58, 3 were chosen after an election; 12 settled a crisis; 3 lasted less than six weeks, and so merely interrupted one; 4 were 'stillborn' counted in the text as unsuccessful candidates) : the last was de Gaulle. Cf. n. 2.

(20. SFIO: *AP* 1950, p. 128, 1957, pp. 58–60. Pinay: above, p. 228.

cabinets put together within two weeks generally fell apart within six.[21] He had to try to avoid that acute temptation in a long crisis, a patched-up truce which decided none of the problems at stake. For cabinets where advocates of contradictory policies sat side by side either broke up as soon as a choice had to be made, like Marie's in 1948, or survived by postponing decisions, like Mayer's and Laniel's in 1953–54. Such impotent combinations did even more harm to the political system than prolonged crises.

But here the President of the Republic could play a decisive if only a negative role. Though he could not impose a candidate he could, and in the Third Republic often did, systematically exclude the strong (or dangerous) leader from power. Mendès-France had his opportunities in 1953 and 1954 only because Vincent Auriol and René Coty so chose. He was denied a third in 1956 because Coty sent for the other leader of the Republican Front, Guy Mollet (who was the chief of its largest party; more acceptable to the MRP waverers without whose votes the new ministry would depend on Communist support; and less hated by the Algerian settlers and their friends in Parliament). Again, in 1957 and 1958 Coty gave no nomination to the rising leader of the Left opposition, François Mitterrand, for fear of the probable settler and army reaction in North Africa.[22] The strong leader was dependent for an opening on the President's goodwill and judgment (or perhaps misjudgment); and it was the President's task to choose when to confront politicians and parties – and voters – with the consequences of their own decisions and policies. In a particular crisis he had to find the man and the moment for a solution; in a whole term of office, to pick the crisis at which a necessary psychological shock could most effectively be administered to Parliament and the country – as Auriol did in May and June 1953, and Coty had planned to do, even before the riots, in May 1958.[23]

3. LOSSES AND GAINS

These ministerial crises fulfilled an essential function. Given the system, they were not the futile aberrations they were generally supposed to be (by Frenchmen even more than foreigners), but met a need: 'to use new combinations of men, and the restlessness which a vacuum of power creates, to restore a new inspiration to the government of the Republic . . .'[24] Naturally some politicians saw – or made – in them opportunities to advance their careers. But in doing so they had to attach their fortunes to a problem of public policy, and might even contribute to its solution.

None the less the drawbacks were grave. The game of making and unmaking cabinets so absorbed and fascinated the players that sometimes they forgot the outside world altogether. In 1949 the King of Cambodia spent three

21. From 1948 the only exceptions were the cabinets of Pinay and Mendès-France, who won by surprise and then enlisted public opinion to overawe the deputies, and Mollet, the first premier after an election. On the length of crises see Arné, pp. 199–200, 208, 303, 305–10; Georgel, i. 105, 107; above, p. 229.

22. But the press suggestions that he might were perhaps intended to produce the army reactions that deterred him: see Arné, p. 56n. Mollet: Fauvet, *IVe*, p. 308.

23. See above, pp. 40, 55. For some presidential misjudgements see Fauvet, *IVe*, pp. 164, 249.

24. Isorni, *Silence*, p. 99. Cf. Arné, pp. 302–4, 320–4; Georgel, i. 131–8.

weeks in France waiting for a government with which to negotiate a treaty. In December 1951 the Assembly voted the expenditure for 1952, then overthrew two cabinets on their proposals for meeting it – and the deficit mounted daily as the crisis continued. In 1957 a parliamentary delegation was in Peru when Mollet fell, and another in Japan when his successor was defeated; every deputy at once flew home, leaving the senators to represent France. Edgar Faure deplored the 'psychological perversion which makes us live here in a pre-crisis atmosphere ... of perpetual tension'.[25]

For the fact of instability created an expectation of instability. 'In the houses of Parliament and in the local parties the frequent crises keep hope and excitement alive.' The prospect of office was not the only stimulus to speculation on the succession. A parliamentarian might hope to sell his ideas and policies, as well as his services, to an incoming premier. A high civil servant, discontented with his political master, could play for time until the next arrived. A pressure-group, offended by the decision of a minister or cabinet, had only to await – or provoke – the next crisis and then use its influence on marginal deputies to demand better treatment. 'Parties, groups and members set conditions for voting investiture or confidence. Many decisions take root at these times. Instability weakens the administration's power of resistance ... the pressure-group leaders are themselves subject to their members' vote. What one minister has refused the next may grant. So they must ceaselessly renew the attack ...'[26] The alcohol interest recouped under Laniel what it had lost under Mayer, and many of Mendès-France's measures against it were reversed under Faure. Like the North African settlers, the trade unions and the peasant organizations, the alcohol lobby had a hand in causing several crises (although the parties might in any case have provoked some of them of their own accord).[27]

Ministers were always tempted to postpone necessary but unpopular decisions of which they could not hope to reap the fruits – and then 'freely to discourse on how they would have managed the situation they bequeathed to their successors'. The fact of instability might enable them to escape from their rasher promises: and the prospect of it encourage them to make more.[28] Parties were unwilling to offend a rival or an interest whose support they might need in the next crisis, and had no incentive to exchange the major mutual concessions which alone could have turned a temporary alliance into a lasting majority. When the loyal opposition found its road to office (if not power) through the ministerial crisis rather than the general election, it had no need to mobilize the support or indignation of public opinion outside.[29]

25. *JO* 23 February 1958, p. 923. M. Goguel drew my attention to the 1957 incidents.
26. Delouvrier, *Crise*, pp. 86–7 (from start of paragraph). Cf. Buron, p. 132.
27. Settlers: against Mendès-France, Bourgès-Maunoury, Gaillard and Pflimlin. Unions: Marie, Queuille (1949), Pleven (1952). Peasants: Mayer, Mollet (both in 1951, when he was not elected premier, and in 1957), and Bourgès-Maunoury. Alcohol: Pinay, Mayer and Mendès-France. Also above, pp. 356–7 (alcohol); for warnings against pressure-group activities in the 1953 crisis, Ehrmann, *Business*, pp. 238–9, and above, p. 385; generally, Arné, p. 364; Meynaud, pp. 311–13; Lavau, no. 139, p. 375; Hamon, no. 120, pp. 838–43.
28. Quotation from L. B. Namier, *Europe in Decay* (1950), p. 22 – on Flandin in 1936. I owe it to Dr. D. B. Goldey and the next point to Dr. M. Harrison. On promises, cf. Buron, p. 209.
29. Brindillac, no. 29, pp. 55–7.

Responsibility was diffused over men and parties which were all partly in power and partly out, never holding it long enough or clearly enough for any credit to accrue to them from a success or for any blame to be fastened on them for a failure. 'When the general election comes the voter finds that for five years the government has consisted of everybody and nobody.'[30]

As no one could be judged on their record over a period, a general election was not an occasion for the voter to reward or punish his rulers. Between elections, therefore, ministers, majorities and oppositions alike could behave irresponsibly without risking too serious a penalty. But the parliamentarians took pains to reduce the risk still further by minimizing the intervention of public opinion in their affairs, and thereby bought immunity for personal or party misdeeds at the cost of further weakening the hold of the regime on the citizens.

Now and then a crisis broke on an indifferent country solely because of a domestic dispute in the 'house without windows'. Sometimes one party would manœuvre another into upsetting a government which both were determined to destroy: so the Radicals managed to delay their attack on Pinay until after family allowances appeared on the Assembly's agenda – when MRP had to take the responsibility of removing him. Rebellious deputies whose motives were particularly discreditable tried to find a lofty pretext: Mendès-France complained of opponents who talked North Africa while voting alcohol.[31] But at least as frequently the politicians chose to overthrow a cabinet on a relatively trivial matter, for fear that an open clash on a major problem of policy might make it harder than ever to reunite a majority behind the next government. When tension was high a party might be forced to take that risk in order to retain its support in the country, as the Socialists were in 1948 and 1949. But thereafter the crucial disputes were kept in the background, and no government was overthrown on German rearmament, or on Indo-China till after Dien-Bien-Phu. Indeed the emergence of North African problems into the forefront in the later years was a sign that some players were no longer observing the rules of a game in which the stakes had become alarmingly high. The decisive leader who tried to cut through the tangle, impose unwelcome choices, expose clear responsibilities and appeal to public opinion found his one opportunity in such desperate circumstances. But he also committed the supreme affront to his sovereign parliamentary colleagues.[32]

These habits, devices and conventions had a common consequence: *le peuple absent.*[33] Sometimes because they were behaving irresponsibly and knew it, but equally when they felt a deep responsibility not to widen the divisions among Frenchmen, the parliamentarians tried to avoid a clear-cut choice of men or measures being presented to the voter. He did not understand the politicians' game because they were careful he should not. He resented his inability to participate in the decisions of the authorities – and by voting

30. Grosser, p. 51. Cf. Edgar Faure, *JO* 2 November 1955, p. 5490. For the parties' efforts to shift the blame for North African repression see Williams, no. 168, p. 167. Cf. below, p. 434.
31. *JO* 3 December 1954, p. 5575.
32. See below, p. 440.
33. Duverger, *Demain*, pp. 21–6.

Communist or Poujadist ensured that the authorities would do their best to keep him from participating. He condemned the regime for its failures (or successes) of policy but most of all for its failure of style. At each crisis the newsreels showed the procession of politicians on the Élysée steps, and the laughter in the cinemas became increasingly tinged with exasperation. A ministry of information film, showing them all in quick succession, was among the most effective devices of Gaullist propaganda for the referendum on the new constitution in 1958.

Yet the people were present more than they realized. Outside forces, ignored or underestimated by the parliamentarians, still set limits to their freedom of action. The deputies, having surprised themselves by electing Pinay and Mendès-France, did not dare to remove them for several months. The tacticians who upset a precarious equilibrium in the hope of improving their position often found instead that they had weakened it. From 1947 to 1951 the Socialists normally provoked crises – but the Right profited from them. In 1952 MRP abandoned Pinay – and Robert Schuman had to leave the foreign office. In 1955 the North African settlers' leaders overthrew Mendès-France for his liberal policies in Tunisia – and found that his successor extended them to Morocco. In 1958 the Algerian diehards brought down Gaillard – and exposed their own weakness in Parliament, which they could redress only by instigating military sedition across the Mediterranean. For all its faults, the System did not enable the inhabitants of the 'house without windows' to defy any real movement of opinion outside.

Adjustments in the political balance occur – or rather show themselves – more frequently in multi-party systems than in two-party politics. But there too alignments and public moods change, and British by-elections or American mid-term elections affect the men in power. Administrations do not resign, but they do change course to respond to new directions of the wind, as Attlee's Labour government found prudent in 1947, Eisenhower's Republicans in 1955, Macmillan's Conservatives in 1962. Despite its reputation the French Assembly was highly sensitive to such movements in the electorate. But in Paris a new policy was less likely than in London or Washington to be carried out by exactly the men responsible for the old one.

Many crises facilitated or followed from such changes of public mood, reflected in shifts in the composition of the majority. Parties moving from opposition to office progressed by stages; the Gaullists were warned in January 1953 that 'it's a long way from purgatory to paradise'. A couple of minor offices were bestowed on the dissidents who had left them nine months earlier to support Pinay, while the main body began to work its passage by voting for Mayer and supporting his government. After the next crisis both wings were represented in the cabinet. Conversely a declining party yielded ground gradually, like SFIO in the first Parliament or MRP in the second.[34]

Other crises were the precise equivalent of a British government reshuffle, except that the prime minister himself changed. They gave an opportunity to bring in new blood, remove unsuccessful ministers, and create an impression

34. See above, p. 405.

(or illusion) of fresh minds at work.[35] When a British or American cabinet minister becomes vulnerable, critics concentrate their assault against the individual; in France they tried to use him to bring the whole government down. But the consequences of their success were not very different, for in most crises the turnover of personnel was small: about half the old ministers kept the same places, half the rest moved to new posts and a quarter went out of office. And of the 23 premiers elected under the Fourth Republic, 16 had belonged to the cabinet which preceded their own and 12 joined the one which followed it.[36] This practice mitigated some consequences of ministerial instability but aggravated others. Continuity was greater than it looked bnt solidarity less, since a minister might further his own career by well-timed disloyalty to his chief, and responsibility was hard to fasten on men who were generally in office but frequently exchanged functions.

Conducting in the open manœuvres which elsewhere are concealed if not always prevented, the System gave wide scope for easy irony against the politician who accepted office (for his greed and impatience) or refused it (for his 'flight from responsibility') or survived in it (for his resigned conviction that delay would dispose of most troublesome problems).[37] It permitted Englishmen or Americans whose decision-making process is paralysed for half a year in every four to view with complacent alarm the interruption of government from which France suffered during one month in every eight. Yet the crisis was also a decision-making device, 'a method of government by shock treatment'.[38]

On a grave problem, leaders or parties who felt strongly – or thought their voters felt strongly – might resist all attempts at decision or concession. Then the sacrifice of a cabinet might be the price of a solution. Responsibility, so hard to fix in a multi-party system, could at last be brought home to the recalcitrant party. The blame for governmental instability was attached to the party leaders, and the cost of insisting on their policies made plain to their voters, so that reasons of electoral prudence were brought into the scales to weigh against intransigence. Obliged to face the facts they hoped to dodge, politicians repeatedly conceded to the new premier the very demands on which they had overthrown his predecessor: electoral reform to Queuille in 1951, special powers to Laniel in 1953, Tunisian autonomy to Faure in 1955, higher taxes to Bourgès-Maunoury in 1957, an Algerian reform bill to Gaillard in 1958 – and appeasement of Bourguiba to de Gaulle later that summer. All too frequently a year with no crisis meant a year with no policy, and the continued presence of a group of ministers distracted attention from the absence of a government.

Every crisis did not produce a political decision. A very difficult problem might bedevil and finally terminate the life of several cabinets. A financial

35. This was especially necessary in France because of the strain on the health of ministers, particularly the premier: Isorni, *Silence*, p. 98; Siegfried, *De la IIIe*, p. 239; Arné, pp. 112n., 246; P. Courant, *JO* 11 March 1958, p. 1523; Andrews, no. 3, p. 497; Edgar Faure, quoted Fauvet, *IVe*, p. 191.

36. See Arné, p. 94; Georgel, i. 135–7, cf. 273n.; and above, p. 206.

37. As throughout Leites, *On the Game of Politics in France*.

38. Edgar Faure in *Monde*, 27 March 1953. Cf. Sirius (Hubert Beuve-Méry) in *ibid.*, 30 April 1958; Fauvet, *Cockpit*, pp. 39–40, *Déchirée*, p. 34; Arné, pp. 302–4 and n.; above, p. 414.

policy to satisfy both Socialists and Conservatives proved as hard to find in the first and third Assemblies of the Fourth Republic as it would have been in the House of Commons if there, too, both parties had been needed to form any majority. In 1948 the impossibility of a frankly Conservative policy was shown by Marie's downfall, and of a Socialist one by Schuman's defeat a week later; the crises of 1949 and 1950 merely indicated that subsequent governments had to keep to the same narrow and treacherous path. In 1957 a long autumn crisis ended in an equally precarious equilibrium, soon upset by the more desperate problems of North Africa. When a major decision was needed, instead of a premier tackling a question, the question might dictate the choice of a premier – as defeat in Indo-China brought Mendès-France to power in 1954.[39]

Governmental instability was not an ideal device for taking major decisions (though the record of the 1950's does not suggest that Britain or the United States have found the best mechanism either). The French method detached political choices too far from public opinion, and encouraged decision-makers to seek power while avoiding responsibility. When parliamentary government was in danger parties made sacrifices to keep cabinets in being, but their ability to compromise was limited by fear of losing support to the enemies of the regime. When it was safe, the risks of a crisis were less and parties could give freer reign to their appetites, electoral interests, and ideological imperatives. But even at best the range of political opinions required to support a ministry was so great that there were always wide and genuine differences of view. If the governmental parties did not succeed in neutralizing one another's pressures, cabinets lost office and politicians generally lost reputation; if they did, choices were deferred until external events imposed a decision. Either the ministerialists were many and deadlocked by disagreement, or they were agreed but too few to win. Three months before the regime collapsed a disillusioned minister remarked sadly that for forty years the opposition had had a majority in Parliament. 'The majority is a *de facto* provisional association with no formal basis, constituted out of weariness after a long interregnum by the temporary aggregation, without the slightest commitment, of the ballot-papers of deputies on their way into opposition.'[40]

39. Morazé, p. 152. Cf. Georgel, i. 131–2.
40. Robert Lecourt (MRP), *JO* 14 February 1958, p. 788 (and *AP* 1958, pp. 20–1).

Chapter 30

THE MEN AND THE SYSTEM

An Assembly with the responsibility for choosing and sustaining a government, yet with a vocation to check its actions and a deep suspicion of its motives, was a novelty to observers from the English-speaking world. Like American senators, French deputies belonged to an Institution.[1] The Third Republic guarded against the dangers of proletarian revolution or backward-looking autocracy or plebiscites manipulated by a popular dictator by requiring legitimate political action to be mediated through a sovereign Parliament: an arrangement which naturally gave political and psychological satisfaction to generations of parliamentarians. Six years after its downfall a Constituent Assembly of new men from the Resistance, nearly all of whom condemned and repudiated the pre-war regime, found the fears that had inspired it and the habits it had created too strong for them. Their new system rapidly came to resemble the old one.

The habits and the fears were both important. The obscure parliamentary game, so suspected and disapproved by the voters, could flourish only in an Assembly with no majority – and there was no majority because the voters chose deputies to restrain and not to maintain a government. The members were proud of their vocation to protect the citizen against the authorities – and gratified by the frequent opportunities they enjoyed to humble the men in power. Parliamentarians mistrusted mass pressure from without, having good historical reason to do so – and disliking interference with their own freedom of action. With authority fragmented, and responsibility diffused, neither the deputy nor the party nor the political leader found it easy to use the parliamentary system to pursue positive policies. But as the greatest of parliamentary managers once boasted, 'An assembly has at least as many weaknesses as qualities. It is most important to know how to use the weaknesses.'[2]

1. TYPES OF ACTIVITY

The outlook, temperament and interests of the members were as diverse in Parliament as in any collection of a thousand people. Many of them never tried to make a reputation. Nearly all overseas deputies concerned themselves exclusively with the problems of their own territories, and most peasant members were equally parochial. The mayor of a large city, whose task was absorbing, time-consuming and almost wholly unpaid, might enter Parliament to earn a living or gain influence with the remote administration in Paris on whom his success so largely depended; once there, he was unlikely to find his parliamentary work so satisfying as to supersede his municipal preoccupations. Some politicians, especially those who had been active before the war, concentrated almost exclusively on building up an impregnable position by favours

1. Cf. W. S. White, *Citadel: The Story of the U.S. Senate* (New York, 1956).
2. Briand, quoted J. Kessel and G. Suarez, *Le onze mai* (1924), p. 42. I owe this quotation to Dr. D. B. Goldey.

to constituents. This kind of activity was commonest among rural deputies but it could be profitable in Paris. Many conscientious members toiled away usefully in silence – like M. Grimaud, the Alpine MRP member who undertook the herculean task of redrafting the tangled rent laws.[3]

More prominent figures also used their energies in very different ways, for not all were absorbed in the struggle for office. There were zealots like the devoted European André Philip, or the old-style 'priest-eating' anticlerical, Maurice Deixonne. Some *grands ténors* among the lawyers regarded Parliament as a minor field of activity; other lawyers were politicians first, like the brilliant 'outsiders', Pierre Cot on the far Left and Tixier-Vignancour on the far Right, who specialized in disrupting the majority's cohesion and peace of mind. Among the Radicals in particular there were local barons like Jean Baylet or André Maroselli, who were potentates in their region and influential in the party but little known elsewhere. Here and in the adjoining Conservative thickets of the political jungle was the habitat of the parliamentary chameleons like Bernard Lafay.[4] Here too were concentrated the lobbyists, the parliamentary defenders of a particular pressure-group such as Henri Borgeaud, leader of the Algerian *colons*, Marcel Anthonioz of the hotel and bar trade, Pierre André who spoke for the steelmasters, and André Liautey, the general secretary of the union of *bouilleurs de cru*.

Among those who rose above their fellows three types stood out: those who concentrated on specialist work on their favourite questions in committee; those who sought office whenever their party was in power (and for some that was almost always); and those who preferred attack to defence, demolition to construction, or principle to place. Charles Barangé on finance, Jacques Isorni on legal matters, Senator René Coty on the constitution, Albert Lalle on agriculture, Albert Gazier on social questions were among the men who made their names as hard workers in committees on their own lines, either as individual specialists or, in MRP or SFIO, as party spokesmen. RPF had many distinguished generals, professors and diplomats who were recognized authorities on their own subjects – and were often shocked by the humble constituency services a deputy was expected to perform (one reason why their reputations were so often higher outside Parliament than in it).[5] Some of its

3. Overseas: Guillemin, no. 114, pp. 846–9, 876–7. Peasants: Dogan in *Paysans*, pp. 217, 220–7. Mayors: Debré, no. 67, pp. 25–8; Siegfried, *De la III*^{e}, pp. 219, 244–5; Buron, pp. 95–7; Isorni, *Ainsi*, pp. 38–40. Grimaud: *ibid.* Harrison, no. 123, on Frédéric-Dupont, champion of the Paris concierges (who once put down a parliamentary question because a constituent, owing to her age, had not been made lavatory attendant at a national theatre: *JO* 19 February 1958, p. 898), Bodin and Touchard, no. 21, pp. 282–3 on the electoral uses of this activity; also above, p. 329ff. On Mendès-France as mayor see Werth, *Strange History*, pp. 314–6; on the deputy's local role, Buron, pp. 23–8, 34, 75–7, 91, 139.

4. He had been a Popular Front supporter before the war, worked with a Communist minister (François Billoux) in 1945, became a Radical municipal councillor in Paris, joined RPF and quickly left it, was both a Radical deputy and vice-president of APLE, voted for Mendès-France, then became RGR, and finally Republican Centre with Conservative support. In 1958 he proclaimed himself France's first Gaullist, for he had been devoted to the General's father who taught him at school. In 1961 he accused President de Gaulle of reducing France to anarchy: 'There is no excuse for his failure and no remedy for his obstinacy': *Monde*, 10 October 1961. Cf. *Elections Abroad*, p. 53.

5. Besides jobs, licences and decorations (above, pp. 340, 408), constituents sought subsidies for local authority projects, answers to political and pressure-group demands and even shopping

[*over*

front-rank leaders always rejected the temptations of the System; Jacques Soustelle was a deadly destroyer of ministries, while Michel Debré failed to match his reputation only because he sat in the wrong house. The Radicals, on the other hand, attracted both the bright young gladiators like Félix Gaillard or Maurice Bourgès-Maunoury, who made their names by attacking successive cabinets until the day they were invited to join one, and the respected elder statesmen without whom no ministry seemed complete.

The fifty or so *ministrables* who were serious candidates for the highest offices had normally to come from a party near the centre of gravity of the majority, and to be personally acceptable to members of other political groups. Some were elder statesmen surviving from the last regime: Blum, Ramadier, Queuille. A few owed their power to the loyalty of a strong party whose support was indispensable to a majority: Georges Bidault in the early years, Guy Mollet and Antoine Pinay in the later. (The mere party manager without a national reputation, like Roger Duchet or Léon Martinaud-Déplat, was unlikely to reach the very top though he might wield great influence behind the scenes.) Many *ministrables* were skilful specialists at reconciling opposites, among them René Pleven of UDSR, André Marie the old Radical, and Jacques Chaban-Delmas the Radical in Gaullist clothing. Others, like Jules Moch or René Mayer, had a 'no nonsense' reputation.

Individuals sometimes changed roles. The whole aim of the 'gladiator' was to graduate quickly into a *ministrable*. A specialist minister like Robert Lacoste of SFIO (industry) or Pierre Pflimlin of MRP (agriculture), or a local magnate like Gaston Defferre of Marseilles, could rise over the years to the front rank. More rarely a leading *ministrable* like Robert Schuman or Jules Moch would withdraw to the background as a foreign-affairs specialist, or like Claudius Petit retire from the race for office to become a voice of conscience, respected if rarely heeded. François Mitterrand, once a plain *ministrable* of the Centre, became a spokesman of colonial reform and ended as the potential leader of a Popular Front. Pierre Mendès-France was until 1950 the most distinguished financial technician in the Assembly; then by establishing a new reputation as the intransigent Cassandra critic of successive governments he made himself for a time the champion of all who demanded a change of policy, like SFIO, of style, like the stern unbending Gaullists – or indeed of men, for among both the rebellious *piétaille* (back-benchers) and the leaders most hostile to the System he won sympathies denied him by *ministrables* of the same parties.[6] But by the vigour of his attacks, and by giving the dismaying impression that he meant every word of them, he cut himself off from the parliamentary fraternity.

Those who accepted the rules of the System were bound together by a strong club sense, in which political opponents recognized their common function of absorbing and moderating the clash of hostile forces in the country. The

services for their wives: Muselier, p. 143. For a Gaullist's indignant reaction see Noël, pp. 115–18; cf. above, p. 329, and Sir P. J. Grigg, *Prejudice and Judgment* (1948), for the similar view of a brilliant British administrator turned unsuccessful politician; contrast Buron, pp. 27–34.

6. See above, p. 399 and n.

bargaining politician flourished in this atmosphere, and the intransigent fighter was a little suspect even to his own party colleagues. Members were willing to strike but reluctant to wound, and really bitter criticism of another member of the club was widely resented as bad form. Politicians of the System had seen the consequences of unrestrained political passion too often in their country's history, and felt the need to practise mutual self-restraint. They had learned the lesson so well that at times mutual restraint seemed not far short of reciprocal complicity.

Open enemies of the regime were kept out of the fraternity and prided themselves on having no part in its bargains and manœuvres. Their opposition could be a positive asset to a premier, actual or prospective, who would reject their occasional overtures, as Mendès-France in 1954 and Pflimlin in 1958 refused proffered Communist votes, and would treat their normal enmity as proof of his own virtue, as Guy Mollet in 1956 and 1957 stressed Communist and Poujadist hostility to his leadership from the Centre. Yet time and good behaviour might allay this ostracism, and parties did not remain long in the wilderness unless they chose to; few did. Tainted Socialist and right-wing votes, which governments incurred criticism for accepting before 1914, became respectable between the wars. The Gaullists were feared as a threat to the regime when they entered Parliament in force in 1951; within nine months they had split and after two years they were in office. The Poujadists also defied their leader's instructions after nine months; a year later they supported Pinay for the premiership. Even the Communists at times became tainted with compromise, for motives not easily distinguished from those of the respectable party leaders. While in the United States extreme groups cannot hope for electoral success unless they come to terms with moderate opinion, in France they found it was easy enough to enter Parliament – but that if they hoped for office it was then necessary to work their passage to respectability.

Office itself could be as educative as the struggle for it. Men who came to power with limited ideas and a narrow clientele sometimes learned from experience and began to govern; before long they were using their authority to impose on their own following concessions to the general interest.[7] Pinay, at first a hero to small businessmen, was soon warning them against endangering the policies they favoured by their short-sighted greed. A right-wing diehard who was given responsibility for Tunisia and Morocco soon discovered the need for liberal policies. With less happy results Socialist leaders learned in February 1956 that the Algerian problem was much less simple than it had seemed in the election campaign six weeks before.

These advantages of the system were more than offset by its growing drawbacks. At first, under *tripartisme*, disciplined parties discouraged political individualism, and members with objectives beyond their own career and re-election were willing to perform useful but inconspicuous service to their cause. There were complaints of the absence of striking personalities, and in his valedictory article on 'the faceless Assembly' of 1946–51 François Mauriac even lamented that the scandals of those years had been so insignificant, and

7. Brindillac, no. 29, p. 56.

hoped that future leaders would wage alongside the party struggle 'a hidden contest of private passions'.[8] He was to get his wish.

As the individualist parties recovered and majorities became precarious, the System again proved fertile soil for ambition, jealousy and intrigue. Once more the Institution displayed both the assertive pride of the United States Congress (uninhibited by any separation of powers) and the feverish excitement of a party convention in permanent session. The 'hunt for portfolios' was resumed with new zest as everyone again speculated on the fall of the government. Edgar Faure, in a rare spell out of office, remarked on the resentment of 'back-benchers' against a minister of the same party who stayed in too long and blocked the way for others. The Radicals, who had been eager to remove Pinay as soon as others could be manœuvred into taking the responsibility, hampered his successor (René Mayer, one of their own leaders) by demanding and getting far more than their share of the spoils. In 1953 Conservatives who followed Pinay feared that his chances of the premiership would be less with Coty as President. In 1956 moderate Conservatives were keener to oust Mollet than reactionary ones, for they were likelier to get office.[9]

In the individualist groups this hunger was expressed increasingly crudely.[10] But while they contained the most active seekers after office, the disciplined parties afforded better protection to any of their members who obtained it. This was an important asset, for men and parties tried to deny office to their enemies as well as to obtain it for themselves or their friends. Sometimes the enmities were over policy. The Right overthrew Schuman for appointing a left-wing minister of finance in September 1948, and the Left Queuille for choosing a conservative cabinet two years later. In 1957 SFIO would not serve with Soustelle because of his commitment to the Algerian settlers – or Mitterrand with Lacoste, for the same reason. But political and personal resentment might be hard to distinguish. In 1948 René Mayer refused to join a government which included Jules Moch; in 1953 RPF tried to stop the ARS leaders benefiting from their recent desertion; the Radicals vetoed Daniel Mayer in October 1949 for breaking up Queuille's cabinet, and André Morice in April 1958 for his obstruction under Bourgès-Maunoury and for splitting their party in 1956. Power positions, too, might be at stake. In February 1955 Mendès-France's Radical enemies (among whom were two bosses from the Paris region, Bernard Lafay and J. P. David) demanded half the jobs offered to the party so as to strengthen their influence. Having lost the party battle they were expelled in December; before long Lafay and David had ideologically indistinguishable but bitterly antagonistic organizations of their own.[11]

8. *Figaro*, 24 April 1951. Cf. Priouret, *Partis*, pp. 81–3.

9. Faure: *Monde*, 27 May 1953. Radicals: *AP* 1953, p. 7; Georgel, i. 208. Pinay: Noël, p. 98. Mollet: *Monde*, 18 and 22 December 1956. 'Permanent party convention': T. White, *The Making of the President 1960* (1962), p. 189. Generally, see Noël, pp. 94–8; Buron, pp. 133–5 on ex-ministers (also above, p. 206).

10. Faure in A. Stibio, *Antoine Pinay* (n.d., ?1955), p. 107, and Arné, p. 97. Cf. above, pp. p. 400, 418–19; below, p. 438; and for the next point, above, p. 406.

11. For Lafay's invasion of Frédéric-Dupont's fief, see Bodin and Touchard, no. 21, p. 277; *AP* 1957, p. 4. See also *AP* 1949, pp. 175, 178–9; 1953, p. 6; 1955, p. 17; 1957, pp. 60–1, 96; 1958, pp. 50–1; Georgel, i. 208–9, and Fauvet, *IVe*, pp. 154 (Mayer), 232n. (ARS).

Some feuds were exclusively personal. Joseph Laniel was defeated for the Presidency thanks to Roger Duchet whom he had recently evicted from the cabinet. The Radicals were said to have 'sentenced' the Conservative Jacques Fourcade to five years without office for his *lèse-majesté* in standing against Herriot for the Presidency of the Assembly – and running him close. Herriot's successor, André Le Troquer of SFIO, displayed in his 1957 inaugural his resentment against Pierre Schneiter, who had committed the same offence against himself; and in 1958 he pronounced unconstitutional the 'Algerian charter' that Pleven as prospective premier had omitted to submit to him before consulting the parties. CNIP, which had tolerated both Mendesist and fascist deputies in its ranks, expelled its first member in 1961 on the insistence of Frédéric-Dupont, whom the victim had kept out of the chair of the defence committee.[12]

This political climate, in which lofty sentiments often covered sordid objectives, favoured a lush growth of political hypocrisy. Individual deputies brought in demagogic bills, not to pass them but to quote them in their election addresses. Opposition parties – RPF in the second Parliament and CNIP in the third – imputed treason to any premier who accepted the Communist votes with which his accusers cheerfully overthrew him.[13] To weaken the Gaullist challenge a Socialist President encouraged the creation of a Conservative central organization, and a Radical premier induced business to finance Vichyite candidates in the 1951 election. Edmond Barrachin, proposing to amend standing orders to disallow very small groups in the Assembly, asked why there should be fifteen of them when there were only six major tendencies in the country: he should have known, having rebelled against de Gaulle to form the ARS group six years before. André Morice, who led the Radical revolt against Mendès-France's 'totalitarian' conception of a disciplined party with a policy, was soon deploring the indiscipline of all French parties. Certain political chameleons voted for Mendès-France's Indo-China settlement in 1954 and denounced it at the next election; but *L'Express* in its Mendesist crusade for political decency was hardly more scrupulous about the means it used to discredit the unrighteous.[14]

Irresponsibility flourished along with cynicism. Respectable MRP and CNIP leaders like Maurice Schumann and Paul Reynaud, who knew that rejection of the agreements rearming Germany would destroy France's alliances, nevertheless voted against them because they blamed Mendès-France for the defeat of EDC – on the open assumption that they would be relieved of a distasteful responsibility by the premier's supporters, whom they

12. Duchet: *ibid.*, pp. 241–3; Faucher, pp. 63–4. Fourcade: Faucher, p. 39. Le Troquer: *JO* 3 October 1957, p. 4487; *AP* 1958, p. 47; Fauvet, *IVe*, p. 343n.; cf. above, p. 217. CNIP: cf. above, pp. 151, 154. On the Assembly's hierarchical structure see Buron, p. 170.

13. Except when a conservative majority survived, as in 1955, with the help of these 'votes that are found unhealthy and void when they are for and perfectly valid and undoubtedly patriotic when they are against': Edgar Faure, *JO* 2 November 1955, p. 5490. Cf. Duverger's 'unwritten article of the constitution' that Communist votes counted to defeat a premier but not to elect him: *Monde*, 6–7 October 1957. On demagogic bills see above, p. 262.

14. Auriol: Wahl in Beer and Ulam, p. 280. Vichyites: Isorni, *Ainsi*, p. 9. Morice: *JO* 30 September 1957, p. 4451. Barrachin: *JO* 10 February 1958, p. 743. *L'Express*: Grosser in *Élections 1956*, pp. 115, 126; De Tarr, p. 183; Williams, no. 168, p. 167. On the consequences of a political vocabulary unrelated to reality see Lavau, *Partis politiques et réalités sociales*, pp. 135–62.

were simultaneously accusing of collusion with the Communists. P. H. Teitgen led the attack for the 'Europeans', and Gaston Palewski headed the Gaullist opponents of any German rearmament; both then joined Edgar Faure's cabinet which carried the agreements through the upper house, but thought it unnecessary to explain their conversion in public.[15] While domestic affairs dominated politics, ministers who disapproved of government policy either sacrificed their views to preserving the majority – or their careers – or else fought for them from within to the great detriment of cabinet coherence. Between Mendès-France's resignation over economic policy in 1945 and François Mitterrand's over North Africa in 1953, the only minister to give up office over a policy dispute when his party did not was Pierre Pflimlin, who resigned in 1949 on the guaranteed price of sugar-beet. But the great crises after 1953 brought more resignations. The 'Europeans' who left Mendès-France's cabinet over EDC were followed under Mollet by Mendès-France himself, over Algerian policy, and by Alain Savary on the arrest of Ben Bella.[16]

With few individual resignations and perpetual coalition governments, responsibility could rarely be clearly assigned and authority was always diffused. No leader or party could ever wield full power with its attendant dangers and benefits; but each had plenty of scope for manœuvres to claim the credit for success and avoid the blame for failure or unpopularity. The balance-sheet submitted to the public's judgment was not that of a government enjoying power to act and time to await the results, but the blurred record of a Parliament where everyone had been in power, but also in opposition.

2. CONCEPTIONS OF PURPOSE

Men and groups with no aim but office, or with unrealistic objectives that practice never clearly showed to be impossible, could survive far longer when they were not exposed to the glare of responsibility. The Fourth Republic allowed diehards to fight battles long since out of date; it drove visionaries to escape the constraints of the ugly present by setting splendidly remote targets for the far future; it frustrated reformers who tried on the margin of the System to work for realistic and progressive policies without becoming absorbed by it; and it bred many compromisers who made the best of it, and not a few profiteers who made the most out of it.

It was not always easy to tell the unscrupulous politician whose lofty verbiage camouflaged a precise financial or careerist interest from the honest diehard who, from misplaced but disinterested conviction, ignored the problems, dangers and opportunities of the moment and spent his energies fighting battles of an earlier day. By no means all of these were on the Right. For instance, there were two conflicts centred around the ancient clerical problem. One was a difference of opinion over the genuine but limited problem of the church schools and the Barangé law which gave them a small grant (and the state schools a much bigger sum). This was disputed with reasonable moderation on both sides. But there was also a furious symbolic battle in which one small group of fanatics seemed to fear the imminent return of the *loi Falloux*

15. Cf. *Monde*, 25 December 1954; M. Pellenc, *JO*(*CR*) 26 March 1955, pp. 1090–1.
16. See above, pp. 46, 49, 50n.

and a clerical monopoly in education, while another ardently resisted, if not the Jacobin cult of Reason, at least the crudely militant atheism of the free-masons of 1910.

Another potent source of honest but irrelevant emotion was old-fashioned nationalism, especially concerning Germany (it was not always disinterested over North Africa). In every party some men were understandably cautious towards their neighbours across the Rhine; but others, from the fossil Conservative General Aumeran to the republican sage Édouard Herriot, appeared to think they were still at war with the Kaiser (and perhaps even in alliance with the Tsar). Confronting dead dangers as resolutely as any right-winger, some Radicals and Socialists sought Communist help in 1946 against the fascist leagues of 1934; many fought hard and successfully against the strong executive power which Marshal MacMahon had abused in 1877; and others like Édouard Daladier (as anticlerical as ever but more anti-German than in 1938) seemed to suspect Schuman and Adenauer of trying to resuscitate Charlemagne's holy Roman empire.

At the other extreme, the visionaries were concerned with real problems but their solutions distracted attention from immediate tasks. Most of them were outside the System in the rank and file (not the leadership) of the Communist party or even the extreme Right, or among Catholics with a social conscience like MLP.[17] There were few among the Socialists, Radicals or Conservatives, though MRP at first had many. Europe was among their favourite causes. Some practical politicians, despairing of structural reforms through the existing political machinery, hoped in a united Europe to break the *liberum veto* of the pressure-groups and open up the protectionist French economy. Some progressive 'Europeans' in SFIO and MRP saw in Europe an agency for social reforms blocked at home; to planners like Jean Monnet it was an essential condition of modernization; men like Robert Schuman hoped at last to end the ancient quarrel with Germany. Once under way, however, the idealistic European movement soon attracted most of the least progressive and least visionary elements in French public life.

There were visionary anti-Europeans too, and patriotic passion, as the Resistance had shown, was not always backward-looking or irrelevant. Many Frenchmen could not conceive of any revival of the nation's influence without driving force at home, and feared that a diversion of effort to Europe might well postpone reform instead of promoting it. Men as different as Pierre Mendès-France and Michel Debré feared that without a modernized state and a real political will in Paris, economic progress would be hampered and social reform blocked. To Gaullists these changes were an indispensable prelude to any concession to colonial nationalism; for a strong state could safely grant reforms which, extorted from a weak one, would rapidly lead to a total collapse of all French authority overseas. One of them, Jacques Soustelle (who was thought dangerously left-wing when Mendès-France sent him to Algiers in 1955), reacted to French retreats elsewhere by championing the thoroughly visionary demand for the total integration of Algeria into France; it won some genuine support in the army and a great deal of lip-service from settlers and

17. On MLP see above, p. 172.

right-wing politicians. But the nationalists came into increasingly bitter conflict with another visionary group, drawn mainly from progressive Catholics and Socialists in Léon Blum's revisionist tradition, who recognized that the old ideal of assimilating the colonies was impracticable and accepted their coming independence (not always with a very accurate appreciation of the real aims and outlook of the overseas nationalists whose cause they defended).

Alike among nationalists and emancipators, 'Europeans' and social progressives, the visionary fighting passionately for a cause found at his side less emotional, more hard-headed exponents of similar policies: men like Pierre Mendès-France, Jules Moch, perhaps François Mitterrand and even Paul Reynaud: the reformers. They were not numerous, since for historical reasons the formal demand for more effective government machinery came from the old Right who wanted it the better to resist change, while men of the traditional Left rejected the political instruments needed to carry the social and colonial policies they favoured. They were not necessarily distinguished by moral superiority, for some reformers were as concerned for their careers as any compromiser. But they shared a willingness to promote or at least accept adjustments in the political system to meet the sweeping transformation of France's situation and the world around her.

The Resistance had brought a new crop of ardent young reformers into politics. But in SFIO (and sometimes in MRP) they were broken by party discipline, like Alain Savary, or escaped from this fate into constructive local work, like Gaston Defferre.[18] Those Gaullist reformers who resisted the wiles of the System often became obsessed with the struggle against it, discredited themselves by plotting with its most disreputably reactionary enemies, and sometimes – like Jacques Soustelle – forgot their original objectives in the process. Some reformers from RPF, many from MRP, and most from UDSR and the Radical party were absorbed by the regime and transformed into compromisers – who might retain reforming ideas without reforming zeal, like Edgar Faure, or not, like Bourgès-Maunoury. When Mendès-France won an opportunity for the lonely band of reforming democrats in 1954, it was lost by the quarrel over Europe with MRP, the friction over domestic methods and priorities with SFIO, and above all the Algerian war. The reformers' stand over that conflict was soon to alienate some of their own number, all their potential allies, and the mass of their misled and misinformed countrymen.

Some progressive-minded politicians were unwilling to risk their careers and reputations and stultify their activities for years, perhaps for ever, in any unpopular cause. Such a man might co-operate and even sympathize with the reformers, but their style of action was quite alien to him and in a major crisis he always preferred the company of the compromisers who kept the system going. These were of many different types, and no party was wholly without them. Neither Gaullists nor Poujadists maintained disciplined opposition for long after they entered the Palais Bourbon in force. Many Conservatives on the floor of the house and Socialists in party meetings urged their more

18. But Defferre was responsible for one of the Fourth Republic's major reforms, the colonial *loi-cadre* of 1956.

intransigent colleagues to join the cabinet and press their policies from within, rather than preach the party's pure (if nebulous) doctrine in the wilderness. But above all the compromisers were concentrated in the two great pivot parties which were enabled or constrained by parliamentary arithmetic to participate in almost every majority and cabinet.[19]

The Radical Socialists had taken over this role from the better-named Opportunists at the turn of the century, and retained it into the Fourth Republic. Electorally they had pacts with the Communists in 1945, with the right-wing opposition in 1946, with the Centre in 1951 and with the Socialists in 1956. They provided many members (and opponents) of Third Force cabinets from 1948 to 1951, right-wing governments in 1952 and 1953, Mendès-France's left-wing ministry in 1954, Edgar Faure's conservative administration in 1955, and Guy Mollet's Socialist-led cabinet in 1956. When Mendès-France tried to transform this old electoral co-operative society into a party with a policy, he alienated four-fifths of its deputies and all the potential leaders with whom it was so well endowed, and made majority-building and cabinet-making even harder than before.

But in the Fourth Republic these problems had already been complicated by the emergence of a second pivot party, MRP, which proved as indispensable to every majority as the Radicals (it opposed no premier except Mendès-France himself). For MRP members differed from their permanent partners both on every major problem of policy – from colonialism to education and from foreign policy to the electoral system – and in their basic outlook as Catholics and not free-thinkers; moralists and not men of the world; Resisters and not *attentistes*; men aware of the social problem of the working class which the Radicals had neglected, hostile to the Third Republic for which they longed, and favourable to the party discipline which they detested. MRP also was compelled by the situation to participate in every combination – with Communists against Conservatives in the Constituent Assemblies, with the Third Force against the Communists in the first Parliament, with the Right against the Socialists in the second, and with a Socialist-led majority in the third. It too had to make repeated concessions to its partners and abandon most of its crusading zeal. Its members who were least willing to compromise went over to RPF, the Catholic Left, or, like Georges Bidault in 1958, the extreme Right. As its fervour for improving working-class conditions cooled and its ministers became committed to repressive colonial policies, MRP broke first with the Socialist party and then with the Catholic trade unions. But the progressive hopes the movement renounced elsewhere were all invested in Europe, a cause for which MRP displayed a willingness to lead public opinion and to renounce governmental office which the Radicals had rarely shown.

Instead of a single pivot party bent on power and relatively unconcerned with policy, there were now two with conflicting views and attitudes. MRP, being the more compact, was potentially a strong hinge for a coalition, but it was too heavily encumbered with principles and sometimes lacked flexibility. The Radical party resisted the new vocation to which Mendès-France

19. From 1945 to 1957 56% of all governmental appointments went to MRP, Radicals and allies: my calculation from Dogan and Campbell, no. 72, p. 327.

summoned it, but the battle destroyed its capacity to fulfil its traditional role. When it disintegrated, the dwindling band of individual 'king's friends' was left without a focus, and in the third Assembly no leader emerged to fill the place once occupied by Queuille, Pleven and Faure. UDSR, RGR, ARS, the 'lawyer-peasants' and overseas members engendered even more cynicism than the Radicals themselves about their character and motives by their search for jobs and favours for client and constituency. By the end of the second Parliament almost half the Radical and allied deputies had held office, and of the fourteen who revolted against Mendès-France in 1956, seven were offered posts within a year.[20]

The politicians of the System were not the only profiteers from it. Weak ministers became dependent on or ineffective against their official subordinates and their personal assistants. Interest-groups benefited: wealthy ones with direct influence in cabinets, like the North African settlers through their Radical friends, or in the Assembly and the ministries, like the beet-growers; poorer ones with political protection, like the railwaymen with their early retiring age, or the tax-defrauding small businessmen, or the *bouilleurs de cru*; powerful social forces to which competing parties looked for support, like the Catholic Church with its claims for its schools. Generally it was 'Gingembre's France', the interests opposed to modernization, which concentrated on political manipulation: the others did not need to. Yet riots against tax controls and barricades on rural highways and European economic treaties showed that the backward forces, though they might delay progress, often failed to get their way.

Protests and delays alike afforded opportunities for another body of profiteers: the opposition parties, which could be extravagant in their criticisms when they ran little risk of responsibility. Many Radicals and Conservatives behaved like demagogues over economic policy in 1949; so did MRP over foreign policy in 1954, and Socialists over Algeria in 1955: but even the least scrupulous men of the System rarely matched the uninhibited licence which its enemies allowed themselves. If Gaullists (until 1951), Poujadists and Communists were unable to extract other advantages from it, they made up for that by vigorously profiteering in votes, multiplying their numbers and exaggerating their power by exploiting the discontent of Frenchmen who were not extremists but merely protesters. Finally there were secondary profiteers who fed on these (often inflated) threats to democracy: Conservative deputies who used the Poujadist danger to demand lower taxes for their clients; Socialist ministers who warned of riots in Algiers or mutiny in the army so as to forestall concessions to the Moslems or to muzzle the French press; above all the anti-Communist demagogues – bad employers, blind settlers, McCarthyite politicians like Léon Martinaud-Déplat, right-wing Catholics and nationalist Gaullists who tried to mesmerize their opponents into accepting another 'unwritten constitutional law ... that Communist votes do not count to adopt a reform but only to oppose one'.[21]

20. Half: *ibid.*, p. 323. Some said Pascal Arrighi, the neo-Radical who led the Corsican insurrection in May 1958, was discontented at not having been a minister like his fellows (and like all the other representatives of those well-connected islanders).

21. Duverger (n. 13); cf. Arné, p. 239 and n.

The line between compromisers and profiteers was hard to draw, and the same man might adopt the two attitudes at different times (or indeed both at the same time, for men's motives are often mixed). Some supported governments out of belief in their policies, desire for stability, or a resigned recognition that there was no alternative: others welcomed a situation which they believed could be turned to their own advantage. The list system at general elections may have been advocated on genuine grounds of principle: it proved highly advantageous to party leaders whose seats remained impregnable even when their personal popularity had waned.[22] The *apparentements* of 1951 were perhaps necessary to produce a manageable Assembly: they were also a device enabling outgoing members to save their seats (and incidentally to give the supporters of the church schools an inflated majority). The absence of any clear demarcation line between majority and opposition helped to temper the jejune indignation (or enthusiasm) of the political newcomer or extremist: and conveniently enabled the careerist without convictions to repudiate responsibility for a policy that had failed. The repeated ministerial crises were a device for taking difficult decisions: and also an opportunity for ambitious men to hasten the day of their admission to the cabinet. The stability of ministers offset the instability of governments: and ensured office in perpetuity for any prominent member of the individualist parties who was prepared to temper the rigour of his principles by a statesmanlike indifference to their actual application. The System gave every facility to the political opportunist; and he fulfilled a necessary role in it. Whenever the compromisers of the Centre were polarized between more fervent, principled, and intransigent forces, the democratic regime was threatened with collapse and France confronted the spectre of civil war.

French parties, therefore, were ill-adapted to their century.[23] Ideologies that had become increasingly irrelevant were still professed, in the organized parties because the militants insisted on keeping verbal faith with the past, in the individualist groups because politicians with few principles found it convenient to utter sentiments of impeccable respectability which committed them to no precise course of action. Would-be modernizers were broken like Daniel Mayer in 1946 or Pierre Mendès-France ten years later. Any party of the regime that made an attempt to bury the past and face the future could be sure that Communists or Gaullists or fascists would revive the dead issue – the clerical quarrel, or the German menace, or the imperial dream – to defeat a government, shatter a coalition, or undermine a Republic. Every party, including those in opposition, came more and more to represent a clientele – naturally conservative – rather than profess a faith or promote a general political objective. This gave them strong defensive positions against intruders like de Gaulle or Mendès-France, but inhibited all constructive action. For the real issues divided each group internally.

22. Such as Christian Pineau in 1946, and P. H. Teitgen in 1956: cf. Williams, no. 168, p. 172n., and *Elections Abroad*, p. 85n.

23. Lavau, *loc. cit.*; Hoffmann, no. 125, pp. 814–18; Hamon, *De Gaulle*, Chapter 2; and above, pp. 411, 412.

Within the Assembly as well as the government there was a stalemate which rarely allowed any forceful course to gain a majority. In the first Parliament cabinets were paralysed over economic policy, in the second over international policy, in the third over colonial policy. In 1957 a ministry had to emasculate both its repressive measures against Algerians in France, to get Socialist support, and its reforms in Algeria, to win Conservative votes.[24] The decline of the 'king's friends' had made both indispensable.[25] But while any majority based on a deal between parties was hopelessly divided on policy, any majority based on policy outraged the entrenched organizations and the politicians who depended on them or simply were loyal to them.

3. STYLES OF LEADERSHIP

In these conditions it was an uphill task to achieve any positive objective. Some men succumbed to the System as their will to act was exhausted by the effort to surmount the innumerable obstacles. Others defied it and were broken by it. If a leader tried to govern by using the whip of public opinion, his premiership was likely to be spectacular, brief – and singular. Another type, whose ministries were less impressive but plural, accepted the limits on his freedom of action and worked within them, earning the scorn of ordinary Frenchmen by conforming to the System even while deploring its effects. Even Mendès-France, after insisting in 1953 that his ministers would have to promise not to serve under his successor, omitted this demand in 1954 when it might have lost him his next opportunity to govern.[26]

Only a very bold and self-confident leader dared bring direct pressure on the deputies by going over their heads to public opinion, for members detested and resented the threat to their freedom of action, their reputations and their careers. Broadcast talks to the nation by its chief executive, so commonplace in the United States or Britain, aroused the direst parliamentary suspicions against Gaston Doumergue in the Third Republic, Pierre Mendès-France in the Fourth and Charles de Gaulle in the Fifth.[27] The offence was more unforgivable still if a leader emphasized his scorn and dislike for his colleagues by stressing the contrast between an upright and far-sighted ministry and petty and self-seeking legislators. Members then bitterly resented his lack of club spirit and suspected him of exploiting latent anti-parliamentary feelings. Mendès-France, who first stood aloof from the System and then denounced it, was shunned until a major crisis arose, then tolerated reluctantly while he assumed responsibilities that others were delighted to escape, and removed as soon as possible – and permanently, for the public which had acclaimed his decisiveness and foresight in 1954 abandoned him in 1956 to the isolation of a virtual exile in his own country.

The problem for the politician who wanted either to keep his influence on his country's future, or to enjoy a successful career, was thus 'not merely to

24. *AP* 1957, pp. 74–7, 84–93; Isorni, *Ainsi*, pp. 113, 129; Fauvet, *IVe*, p. 334.
25. Cf. above, pp. 407–8.
26. The omission allowed the one ex-premier in his cabinet of newcomers to succeed him.
27. I owe this point to Dr. N. Wahl. (The French opposition had no recognized leader, and no right of reply.) On premiers and public opinion see Arné, pp. 375–93.

become premier but to do so again'.[28] This meant that he had to allow for and appease the feelings of his parliamentary colleagues. When René Mayer stood for the premiership in 1949 he refused any dealings with the parties, won his vote, but then failed to form a cabinet. In 1951 he tried again and was beaten. In 1953 he succeeded at last, by masterly equivocation, in leading a cabinet (it was weak as well as short). After Georges Bidault brandished the vote of confidence to impose his policies on the reluctant Socialists in 1950, they never let him form another cabinet. Antoine Pinay kept MRP in his majority by the pressure of public opinion, and they blocked him whenever he stood for the premiership again.

Party leaders like Bidault or Pinay, so long as they kept their organizations behind them, could never suffer a catastrophe like that which befell Mendès-France. Guy Mollet, at the head of a highly disciplined party whose votes were essential to the majority, could remain the dominating figure in a Parliament even when he had lost the premiership. Yet these magnates, though secure against political storms, were too dependent on their organizations to shake off a taint of partisanship, and too committed to them to make wholly acceptable brokers. That essential function of French parliamentary leadership was better performed by a politician from a very loose or tiny group, the typical premier of the Fourth Republic as of the Third. A Pleven, a Faure or a Gaillard built up his reputation over the years in debate or in office until he attained the premiership, where he was almost sure to damage it – either by decisions which made him enemies or by indecision which gave him a longer life but a worse name. He would then rebuild his credit by a discreet withdrawal from active parliamentary life, followed in a year or two by a well-timed *rentrée*: normal and sometimes very convenient stages in the career of a successful *ministrable*.

Some premiers, like René Pleven, were skilled at evacuating office in time to avoid dangerous decisions and returning to it at a calmer moment, thus preserving a high reputation for statesmanship. A few like Bourgès-Maunoury were dominated by more forceful men;[29] but this formula was so unsatisfactory that Laniel, who reigned for the year before Dien-Bien-Phu by refusing to choose between the policies of Reynaud and Bidault, was the only Fourth Republican premier never to hold any office again. One or two like Edgar Faure, beneath an appearance of mental agility unembarrassed by any convictions, skilfully manipulated the System to achieve positive objectives. In a conservative Assembly, wedded to economic backwardness at home and reaction in North Africa, he pursued a successful policy of economic expansion and carried by twelve to one the Tunisian agreements on which Mendès-France fell; in a nationalist upper house he put through the unpopular treaties rearming Germany; against determined obstruction from many of his own ministers he repaired the follies of his predecessors in Morocco; and when the Assembly finally brought him down he belied his reputation for malleability by promptly dissolving it.[30]

28. See above, p. 239.
29. Arné, pp. 109, 350; Fauvet, *IVe*, p. 332.
30. See Arné, pp. 395–426 for sketches of each of the premiers; De Tarr, Chapters 7 and 8, for Queuille, Faure and Mendès-France.

All these practices led to the same result: the System devoured its children. Some men were feared for showing too much forcefulness, others discredited for too little, yet others stayed 'available' for the future by long spells of unavailability in the present. The later years of the Fourth Republic therefore saw several exceptionally young premiers: four were under fifty and one of them under forty. As Pierre Cot reproached Félix Gaillard, some men of this new generation still followed the old men's policies. But, as Gaillard replied, a minister soon found that his margin for manœuvre was far smaller than the critics supposed.[31] A leader with a great party behind him was unacceptable to the rival powers; a leader without one was acceptable precisely because of the weakness of his personal situation. 'An ephemeral monarch among the barons who enthrone or dethrone him, he can preserve his equilibrium in his high position only by giving way to the most demanding, and otherwise trying to neutralize them by playing one against the other. Nine-tenths of his time are taken up by this task, as futile as it is exhausting. In it he ruins his health, and loses his integrity.'[32]

The contrast between the leaders who accepted these limits and those who rebelled against them was one of style more than policy. Gaullists admired, supported and served under Mendès-France because of his methods as much or more than his objectives; and Mendès-France was only one of many left-wing critics of the System who were turning to de Gaulle in the last months of the regime.[33] But there were other leaders who tried to struggle on within the rules, seeking to achieve their ends by guile, deviousness, skilful timing, and immense pertinacity and patience. The regime bred in these men a professional pride in their obscure art; and in some MRP and Gaullist leaders who had once rebelled against it, a masochistic pleasure in displaying the skills they had first condemned and then acquired. De Gaulle had grounds for his warning against 'the games, the poisons and the delights of the System'.[34]

Yet the limits were set by the situation, quite as much as the character of the politicians. Throughout the Fourth Republic any drastic change of government and policy would have entailed an alliance with opponents of the regime, whose price its supporters feared to pay – whether because it would have weakened their power, injured their interests, or imperilled democracy itself. Under the Fifth the private pressure-groups and the public services did not abandon their anarchical habits merely because a strong executive had been installed. In both regimes ministers pursued in office policies they had denounced in opposition; juggled with the price index to hold off wage increases; and arbitrarily confiscated whole issues of opposition journals (though whereas during 1957 left-wing papers were seized for what they themselves had

31. Above, p. 13. On premiers' ages see Arné, pp. 51–2.

32. Sirius (Hubert Beuve-Méry) in *Monde*, 30 April 1958. Cf. Aron, no. 7, pp. 263–4.

33. See above, p. 54.

34. On 6 May 1953: *AP* 1953, p. 476. To conclude his first investiture speech Faure quoted Montesquieu: 'It is not the means that should be splendid but the end. True politics means reaching it by obscure paths': *JO* 17 January 1952, p. 276 (and cf. *AP* 1952, p. 13; De Tarr, p. 176). Lecourt said of the 1953 presidential election, 'Since Bidault withdrew our role consists of counting corpses': Faucher, p. 82. Cf. Diethelm (above, p. 136) and Chaban-Delmas (*JO* 20 November 1953, p. 5635). Leites (p. 426n.) dissects scientifically all the acts and attitudes of this kind committed by parliamentarians or alleged by their enemies; and discusses nothing else.

written, after 1958 they were often punished for the offences of others, so as to make the seizure of a right-wing journal more palatable to the army). No political manœuvre of the Fourth Republic did more by its conduct to discredit the regime (and its author) than the equivocation, prevarication and slow elimination of every alternative by which Edgar Faure, at some cost in human lives, brought a suspicious right-wing majority and an indignant army to accept the virtual independence of Morocco. Yet the President of the Fifth Republic with his unexampled prestige and authority found very similar tactics necessary to arrive at the same result in Algeria.

The System was often criticized for infirmity of purpose, 'a daily nibbling by which the policy the government has adopted is gradually emptied of its substance'; inconsequence, 'a policy which drifts with the stream, with no aim but to pass round obstacles as they arise, hoping for the best without knowing how or why'; disingenuous conservatism, 'easily agreeing to grant bogus nominal satisfactions in the hope of averting real reforms'; and the sham solidarity of *immobilisme*, 'believing union in doing nothing is better than the united action of a homogeneous power'. The reproaches were justified. Yet all these comments were directed against the first government of General de Gaulle, before there was any Parliament to obstruct him.[35] The men and institutions of the Fourth Republic had many faults, but new men and institutions proved as inadequate in 1958 as in 1945 to install at last the long-promised *République pure et dure*.

35. Three in Mendès-France's letter of resignation written on 18 January 1945, printed in his book (see p. 331n.), pp. 334, 338, 340; the last by Jules Moch in *Populaire*, 6 January 1945 (I owe this one to Dr. B. D. Graham).

Chapter 31

SOCIETY AND THE STATE

The Fourth Republic lasted less than a dozen years, but during that brief period French economy and society changed more quickly than it ever had in the preceding century. Economic modernization and new means of mass communication reduced the old differences between regions and classes, but brought new tensions between those who gained and those who lost. In so conservative a country, this pace of progress imposed severe strains – greatly accentuated by the external crisis which began before the Fourth Republic but reached a climax under it. For men humiliated in 1940, who had rapidly rebuilt and increased the absolute strength of their country, were called on to adjust to a sharp decline in its power relative to its rivals and former subjects. Within Europe, France made her adjustment to the new conditions more readily than Britain; outside Europe, far less readily. The tensions born of simultaneous progress at home and retreat abroad came to a head over the Algerian problem, which first paralysed the working of government and then threatened political liberties.

These problems were dealt with by new men working a new constitution. The parliamentary personnel of the Fourth Republic was largely recruited through the Resistance and the Free French movement, and inspired by outraged patriotism and impatient exasperation with the manœuvres, compromises and evasions of the pre-war politicians. Yet the new men quickly resumed the practices they had once roundly condemned. The regime was remade in 1946 in order to destroy the bad old ways; but before long the System reappeared. This return (not persistence) of traditional attitudes and methods suggests that the problem of adapting the political mechanism to social change lay not in the faults of character of two very different sets of men, or the institutional weaknesses of two constitutions devised for quite different ends, but deep in the history and social structure of France.

In twentieth-century French politics the cleavages of the past remained as wide as those of the present day. France had her incomplete industrial revolution before the political victory against authoritarianism had been won. No consensus had been found about the objectives of political action, and no rules agreed for the tenure and transfer of power, when industrial civilization raised the stakes of the political game by provoking demands for governmental protection of the producer against domestic or foreign competition, the capitalist against the claims of labour, the worker against the pressure of his employer.

The French industrial revolution was itself localized, incomplete and stunted. Over most of the country the old order of self-sufficient peasants and artisans survived, and they used their disproportionate political influence to protect their own interests and those of their rich allies at the expense of the industrial workers. An overcrowded tertiary sector, above all in commerce, offered the traditional outlet for the many who sought a precarious and unreal economic independence. A majority of voters wanted the diffusion of wealth and power, and resisted speed and standardization, mass production and large-scale organization, plenty and instability – in a word, Americanization. Through her thwarted economic development, France acquired the social problems of industrialism without its material benefits. Two distinct types of politics coexisted there: a revolutionary class struggle, dominant in most industrial areas, a traditional ideological conflict which prevailed mainly in backward regions. Politicians had to shape their attitudes to the needs and demands of both, and the diversity of issues and alignments created many parties and factions: the reflection, not the cause, of the absence of an electoral majority.

The old political fabric was torn asunder by the sweeping social changes of the post-war years and the governmental policies which encouraged them. For the first time for over a century the birth-rate rose. The traditional domination of the family by the older generations was upset. New age-groups pressed impatiently on the heels of their elders, acceding to responsibility – in business, politics, agriculture, the civil service – far younger than in the past. They called for expansion to accommodate the growing numbers of Frenchmen, invented new voluntary associations for common purposes, and insisted on a wider conception of governmental activity than the mere preservation of *situations acquises*. A new attitude to risk-taking and modernization soon spread from industry to agriculture. The industrial structure was transformed by the growth of large plants and of specialized skills, which broke up the old uniformity of the working class and created in the newer industries a common interest in stability between management and worker. Under the impact of material prosperity, labour shortage, and the reforms of 1936–37 and 1945–46, labour relations and even class divisions gradually began to lose some of their old bitterness. The rapid growth of towns upset the country's social and geographical balance, until one Frenchman in four lived in an urban area of over 100,000 inhabitants. The old self-sufficiency of the village disappeared; prosperity and paid holidays brought townsmen to the countryside, while agricultural mechanization and the decline of the artisan reduced employment in the rural areas.

New social conditions broke the old lines of political communication. The small-town newspaper declined as a political force, but neither the regional nor the Paris press took its place – except for *Le Monde*, which soon acquired the status of a republican institution. Even broadcasting had far less political importance than in Britain or the United States, and television arrived too late to play a significant role in Fourth Republican politics – though within its narrow geographical range it contributed to a growing uniformity of tastes and interests.

As urbanization spread and regional differences waned, the ancient quarrel between Church and *Université* lost its former virulence. The *curé* was withdrawn from some parishes, and where he remained he might well champion progress, not conservatism. The new and radical grass-roots organizations were often founded and manned by young Catholic laymen, products of the flourishing Church youth movements. On social and especially colonial questions many Catholics were active reformers – and some anticlericals from the traditional Left took up conservative or reactionary stands. When the Algerian war revived the passions of the Dreyfus case, the alignment was new and unexpected: in 1900 Church and army had stood together against the indignant protests of the teachers and intellectuals, but now the angry officers found many of their former allies in the opposite camp, along with the *Université*. As the clergy withdrew from militant opposition to the regime, and as political power shifted from the countryside to the towns, fewer village schoolteachers regarded themselves as the embattled missionaries of the Republic. Every year diminished the large fund of accumulated mistrust which still remained for political exploitation, and with its decline the two great corporations lost their central place in political organization and conflict.

Other factors helped to promote the nationalization and modernization of political life. With the abolition of small single-member districts and the growth of official and semi-official regional institutions, the prefect became less of a focus for political activity and the deputy lost some of the social standing he had formerly enjoyed in his constituency (if not in Paris). Wider horizons and stronger parties weakened the authority of the individual politician, though less than was expected in the first post-war years. The traditional notables, the professional and business class of the small town, lost their dominating influence over their fellows as education became more general, modern communications made the country more uniform, and the tiny autonomous unit, after falling behind its big competitors in industry and then in agriculture, began to lose ground even in its last strongholds: commerce and politics. The state, traditionally feared and restricted, exercised so powerful and pervasive an influence throughout the economy that the old contrast between the *pays légal* and the *pays réel* came to seem meaningless even to extreme conservatives.[1] The new professional organizations – of labour, business, the peasantry and various middle-class groups – rapidly acquired an altogether new solidity and influence during or just after the war. While after 1948 the trade unions lost most of the ground they had gained, the other confederations survived to play a growing role in politics. But since they usually acted by pressure from without, rather than directly in the electoral or parliamentary struggle, these new corporations did not replace the old decaying political mechanisms.

Indeed, in the short run better organization merely allowed the conflicting groups to express more vigorously their unanimous conviction that others were being favoured at their expense. The hungry occupation years had been a godsend to the peasantry, and the black market and inflation were the shopkeeper's golden age; both resented the return to normality which cost them their privileged positions. The social reforms of the Popular Front and the governments issuing from the Resistance did not wholly reconcile the industrial workers to the regime, but they did alarm employers whose power was challenged. Yet the state on which all these pressures converged was

1. Isorni, *Ainsi*, p. 53. (I owe many ideas in this chapter to the authors named on p. 465.)

poorly armed to resist them, for the politicians who were eager to expand its functions economically were afraid of strengthening the executive politically. Historic fears of reaction and revolution imposed 'the paradox of a weak government with a strong state';[2] and the administration's Maginot line against the invading pressure-groups could often be turned by an attack on its unfortified parliamentary flank.

Some groups fought for their interests in the old ways; and any effort to impose taxes on peasants or collect them from small businessmen, cut the alcohol subsidy or make railwaymen work beyond the age of 55, would cause a political storm and provoke the party whose clients were threatened to overturn the government. Some sections of the new middle class, concerned for modernization and efficiency and dissatisfied with the traditional parties, contributed to a floating vote far larger than before the war and gave emphasis to the fluctuations of public opinion. Other victims, finding the old lines of communication inadequate, resorted to disorderly and extravagant forms of protest. Some felt wholly cut off from their political representatives. Suspicious of a government whose processes they could not understand and whose policies they abhorred, and convinced that occult forces had captured the state for their own nefarious ends, they inspired outbursts as furious and irrational, though not as dangerous, as those of the Third and Fifth Republics.

At home the growth of the economy aroused resentment among those who lost by it or who benefited little; identifying the misfortunes of their class with those of their country, they clamoured for diehard resistance to change both abroad and at home. Poujadism, the rebellion of static France against the economic ascendancy and progress of the advanced regions, was also a protest against any concession in the empire. But the new psychology which underlay the expansion in 'modern France' was partly a product of revolt against the collapse of 1940, and for many modernizers the very purpose of this economic progress was to rebuild the power of the French state even more than the prosperity of individual Frenchmen. The crucial decisions on atomic development were taken by Fourth Republican premiers, including Mendès-France – whose eloquent appeals for national resurgence made him for a time a hero of the Gaullists. Men from the Resistance and Fighting France, who against all prudent calculation had entered upon a struggle against overwhelming odds in 1940, were often unimpressed by appeals to historical inevitability or demonstrations that France had not the strength to hold her place in the new world. Thus economic progress gave rise to exasperation as well as satisfaction when the country, feeling a new internal strength and vigour, found itself faced with a steady decline in its external power.

It was therefore not surprising that the familiar problem of reconciling France's ends and her means was not always discussed in purely rational terms. In 1945 only the Socialists stood out against the policy of crushing Germany on which nationalists and Christian Democrats, Gaullists and Communists agreed; and many Frenchmen seemed to find Soviet Russia a more congenial diplomatic partner than democratic America. But within five years

2. Siegfried, *De la IIIe*, p. 251, cf. *ibid.*, p. 51; Hoffmann in *Change*, pp. 73–4; Hamon, no. 120; Priouret, *Députés*, Chapters 11–12.

France was committed, despite violent opposition, to the Atlantic alliance; and many Resisters, whose proven patriotism under Nazi occupation gave them a clear conscience, had taken up the old themes of intelligent defeatists like Caillaux and Laval and were preaching Franco-German reconciliation. In 1954 a revolt of neutralists and nationalists defeated the European army plan after a furious battle which divided Resisters as well as Vichyites, and Left as well as Right. But the new perspective of European unity had caught the imagination of many able and idealistic young Frenchmen, and after the EDC struggle which seemed to purge the old hatred of Germany, the adjustment to a new constellation of forces in Europe was accepted without friction – even by its former opponents when they came to power in 1958.

Elsewhere the change was harder to tolerate. Progressive internationalists in France had always fought for equal rights for the colonial peoples, not for independence. Nationalist conservatives who had painfully accepted reality in one sphere found it all the harder to abandon their remaining illusions. So the business defeatists like Raymond Cartier, who attacked the Algerian commitment as too expensive, found no hearing in the Fourth Republic. Instead, on Left and Right alike, old conservatives and new nationalists combined to silence the liberals and the realists until it was almost too late in Tunisia and Morocco, much too late in Indo-China and Algeria. Their task was the easier because the colonial bureaucracy was as conservative as the economic bureaucracy was progressive; and above all because France, alone among colonial powers, had a mass Communist party. Neither politicians nor voters were prepared to pay the price for its support; and while without it the decolonizers were outnumbered, with it they were discredited. Social reformers at home faced the same dilemma, and the housing and educational opportunities of the poor remained shamefully inadequate. But there desirable measures could be deferred without immediate disaster. Overseas, time was fast running out.

Despite the obstacles, parties and people slowly accepted the need for change, and by 1958 the diehards commanded only a quarter of the National Assembly and a minority of the public. At this point the struggle moved to a new plane, for the humiliations and retreats of twenty years had had their deepest effect on the men who had borne the brunt of them, the army officers. More democratically recruited and less traditionalist in outlook than ever in the past, they had been taught in 1940 that there were higher duties than obedience to the legal government. One defeat in Indo-China reinforced their determination not to tolerate a second in Algeria. For two years fear of military insubordination helped to paralyse ministers, who abdicated to the army while publicly proclaiming confidence in its fidelity. So the Fourth Republic was destroyed at last, like most previous French regimes, by a foreign failure; its own servants repudiated it, and an indifferent people no longer felt sufficient loyalty to come to its defence. Unhappily, the circumstances of the collapse made the twin problems of legitimacy and authority more acute than ever. For if the Fourth Republic had shown the perils of weak political authority in its lifetime, its death reminded Frenchmen that revolutionary violence still seethed not far below the political surface, and that dangerous hands were waiting to grasp the levers of a strong governmental machine.

'All government ... is founded on compromise and barter. We balance inconveniences; we give and take; we remit some rights that we may enjoy others ... Man acts from adequate motives relative to his interests; and not on metaphysical speculations.' In the shadow of Bonapartism and the Commune John Morley suggested that in France these words of Burke 'ought to be printed in capitals on the front of every newspaper, and written up in letters of burnished gold over each faction of the Assembly, and on the door of every bureau in the Administration'. At the end of the century, Bodley remarked: 'There is a nation to the members of which Frenchmen are more revengeful than to Germans, more irascible than to Italians, more unjust than to English. It is to the French that Frenchmen display animosity more savage, more incessant and more inequitable than to people of any other race.' Half-way through the next century Raymond Aron observed that republicans and Resisters, royalists and reactionaries had one common characteristic at least: their relish for proscribing one another.[3]

The politicians of the regime learned the lesson and accepted the reproach. The institutions of the Third Republic were soon warped into the system of 'stable instability', by which conflicts were absorbed and compromises arranged by frequently changing combinations of the same ministers, closely supervised by a vigilant Parliament. In the Fourth Republic men and institutions were shaped by this old mould instead of breaking it. Yet the post-war reforms were by no means a total failure. The silent administrative revolution undertaken by de Gaulle and his immediate successors, and the new financial and legislative procedures gradually hammered out over the next decade, might have helped the Third Republic tackle many of the domestic problems with which it had failed to deal.[4] They were inadequate for the violent storms of the post-war world; but would a different regime have averted or weathered the tornado from Algiers?

The new institutions enabled some dangers to be avoided, decisions taken and policies pursued without parliamentary obstruction. They could not solve a problem arising out of the party system, not the formal rules. Under *tripartisme*, three strong parties provided a majority without coherence or durability. But when faced with Communist opposition, Socialists and MRP had to call in the old political world to redress the balance of the new, so that governments depended simultaneously on the traditional and ill-organized groups and on the newer and better-disciplined parties. Whereas in the Third Republic a prominent non-partisan figure had often been able to exploit parliamentary fragmentation to assemble a majority, the better-organized groups now resented his influence on their members. Whereas under *tripartisme* the party leaders had been able to trade concessions and enforce their bargains, the chieftains of the looser groups could never commit their troops, and on major issues every party of government was now

3. Morley, *On Compromise* (1874), p. 136; Bodley, i. 215; Aron, no. 7, p. 262.
4. Above, pp. 263ff., 268–9, 272–5, 284–5, 343, 345; cf. Williams, pp. 403–4.

vulnerable to indiscipline. Mendès-France had to work with less malleable material than Poincaré; MRP operated less smoothly as a pivot party than the Radicals; round-table decisions were repeatedly upset in the Assembly; over EDC and Algeria the divisions were within parties rather than between them.

The traditional parliamentary game complicated still further an already confused situation. Its skilful and single-minded practitioners in the old ill-organized groups were enabled to resume the game by the deliberate choice of their newer and more solid rivals. For these feared the extremists who wanted a strong state under their own control; lest they should either capture and abuse power, or precipitate civil war in the attempt, the cautious politicians took measures to reduce the political weight of 'modern France' whence the dangers mostly came. 'Static France' was favoured by the electoral laws of 1948 for the upper house and 1951 for the lower, and as in the Third Republic the second chamber and the electoral system became devices buttressing the backward areas, the individualist parties, and the traditional style of politics.[5] So the compromisers and careerists still had a necessary role to play – and the system rewarded them well for it. The National Assembly continued to breed political opportunists (as the House of Commons breeds yes-men, and the Senate of the United States exhibitionists). Critics accused the men of the System of raising artificial disputes in order to divide the people; their real fault was that they concealed genuine divergences in order not to.

If the weak parties quickly resumed the bad habits of the past, the stronger ones quite failed to fulfil their hopes of transforming political behaviour. Having no prospect of winning independent power, each of them adopted sectional policies expressing the outlook or interests of the limited clientele on which it depended for its very existence. These policies could rarely be applied, for the parliamentary situation usually gave several parties a veto on action; and as they were not implemented, they were regarded with cynicism by politicians and voters alike. Either to make a career or to influence policy, the parliamentarian's road to power led not through the patient mobilizing of electoral support but through the subtle and absorbing parliamentary game; and the struggle for power, which occurs every four years in other great democracies, never ceased in France. 'Among Western legislators, only the French deputy took part in an execution (the overthrowing of a Cabinet), in a festivity (ministerial crisis), and in a prize-giving ceremony (the formation of a Cabinet), every three, six or twelve months.'[6] True, the instability was less damaging than it seemed, since the ministers so often kept or exchanged their places. True, the crises fulfilled a function, since they enabled difficult decisions to be reached. But the system exasperated the voter, who soon

5. Just half the metropolitan deputies sat for the 30 most industrial departments. In 1946 these returned half the Radicals and Conservatives, 55% of the Communists and Gaullists, and 47% of SFIO and MRP; in 1951, 37%, 65% and 45% respectively; in 1956, 42% of the traditionalist members, 55% of the Communists, and 54% of the Socialists, MRP and strict Mendesists. The Radicals and Conservatives made 50 net gains in 1951, 45 of them in the less industrial half of France. (My calculations.) Cf. above, pp. 400, 418–9 and nn.; but cf. Aron, no. 6, pp. 12–13.

6. Aron, *Steadfast*, p. 24.

became indifferent to or contemptuous of 'the shuffling of a greasy and well-marked parliamentary pack'. With no circuit of confidence between rulers and people there could be no majority to take responsibility; and with no majority, there could be no clear allocation of responsibility, and therefore no circuit of confidence.

The Fourth Republic, like the Third, proved successful in absorbing the dangerous movements in the country, only to succumb beneath an external shock because it had failed to convince the ordinary Frenchman that it was really *his* government. Yet many of the manœuvres he so despised were promoted by hope of gaining votes, and more by fear of losing them. Few crises originated exclusively with the players of the game. Much more frequently 'the professionals ... [gave] expression to them; perhaps they aggravated them; all too often they could not resolve them; but they did not create them'.[7] It was natural for the citizen to blame the mirror rather than the original for the ugly figure his representatives often cut. 'Very often the Palais Bourbon has been described as a house without windows, blind, shut off from the realities of life and the world. Nothing is falser. It should rather be reproached with being too open to the thousand changing humours of opinion, too accessible to every demand from outside, too close to a whole people, the most ungovernable in the world, of whom, whatever they think, it is the all too faithful image ...'[8]

Some of the outsiders who denounced the parliamentarians' obsession with their private game were equally obsessed by it themselves. For in attributing all the faults of the System to the legislature or its members, they convinced themselves that the problem could be simply solved by a constitution which kept the deputies subordinate. Yet, as French history had amply shown, ministerial instability characterized authoritarian no less than liberal regimes; private interests were not less influential or rapacious when they operated secretly on the executive rather than openly on the legislature; and if popular resentment was deprived of its normal channels of expression it would burst violently through some irregular outlet. Conflicts are not settled by being hidden from view, and it is a function of the politician to draw attention to grievances before they fester and become dangerous. In a regime which scorns him, this function is not always performed. As an American conservative warned long ago, 'Monarchy is like a splendid ship, with all sails set; it moves majestically on, then it hits a rock and sinks for ever. Democracy is like a raft. It never sinks, but, damn it, your feet are always in the water.'[9]

Right-wing critics of the System could claim that conservatives of the Left exploited the fear of strong government to preserve the political System, and so they did: but there were real dangers of abuse if the centralized administration were freed from democratic control. Left-wing critics complained that fear of Communism was exploited by conservatives of the Right to entrench the existing social order, and so it was: but a Communist party, once installed,

7. *Ibid.*, p. 28, cf. p. 34.
8. Isorni, *Silence*, pp. 14–15. 'The faults of the Fourth Republic arose from its being too responsive ... [its] weaknesses ... were the weaknesses of the nation it represented too well': W. G. Andrews, *French Policy and Algeria* (New York, 1962), p. 163.
9. Fisher Ames, cited Brogan, *The Free State*, p. 7.

rarely recognizes electoral defeat as a reason for relinquishing power. So moderate politicians, who feared their countrymen's propensity for political extremism, were accustomed not to exploit their victories to the full; to ensure through self-attenuating devices that minorities were not reduced to total powerlessness; and to avoid open clashes on major issues before the public. They abhorred the referendum, stigmatized the dissolution as a *coup d'état*, shunned any electoral law which might help to assemble a coherent parliamentary majority, ostracized any member of the club who looked for support outside the walls of Parliament, and even tried to avoid by-elections. Repeatedly a party was offered office or power when it was declining in the country and no longer dangerous or demanding – SFIO in 1946, MRP in 1947, RPF in 1953, Radicals in 1957. The narrowly parliamentary outlook of the political class conveniently helped to maintain their own exclusive power; it arose none the less from French historical experience.

In the abstract it may well be absurd to identify a presidential constitution with authoritarian rule, and 'direct democracy' with Bonapartist plebiscites. But if enough people behave as if a referendum were a plebiscite, it will become one. If the advocates of a reinforced and independent executive depend upon the groups which have always loathed democracy, then the political system which they favour will be warped unrecognizably by the forces which sustain it. Indeed, the presumed advantage of the presidential system is that an electoral majority is believed to be more easily assembled than a parliamentary one. But to obtain the electoral majority, the voter's whole political approach must be changed; and the inevitable tendency will be to seek this result by employing the one active tradition available for the purpose, the plebiscitary appeal on behalf of a strong national leader.[10]

Where its predecessors had excluded the 'unformed' opinion of the masses and confined political activity to the 'informed' and sophisticated elites, the Fifth Republic took the opposite course; exploiting 'unformed' against 'informed' opinion, it attracted the unpolitical majority while alienating almost all the politically conscious.[11] 'Both maintain the traditional distance between the leader and the led which protects them all from "*l'horreur du face à face*". Both excuse the leaders from having to mobilize the led and preserve the happy irresponsibility of the led.... Inevitably, these patterns result in arbitrariness, and then provoke protest and revolt.' Unable to participate in their government, Frenchmen united in their private corporations and agitated for their claims like 'angry creditors of a bureaucratic state'; their clamour confirmed their masters' fear of participation and determination to treat the citizen as an *administré*.[12] But men rarely behave responsibly before they are given responsibility.

The evil had ancient roots. 'The division of classes was the crime of the old monarchy, and later became its excuse; for when all those who make up the rich and enlightened part of the nation can no longer understand and

10. Written in 1953: Williams, p. 403. The objections are somewhat less applicable to proposals for simultaneous direct election of Parliament and chief executive, such as those of M. Duverger in *Demain* and *VIe*.

11. G. Tillion, *Les ennemis complémentaires* (1960), pp. 96–7.

12. Hoffmann in *Change*, pp. 105, 115 (cf. p. 222).

help one another in the government, the self-administration of the country is virtually impossible, and a master has to intervene. . . . It is no small task to bring together again citizens who have thus lived for centuries as strangers or enemies, and to teach them to conduct their own affairs in common. It was much easier to divide them than it is now to reunite them. . . . Even in our own day their jealousies and hatreds survive them.'[13] In times of crisis the fear or the experience of revolution and dictatorship kept open the wounds between Catholic and anticlerical, proletarian and bourgeois, Communist and non-Communist. Even in periods of normality, the arbitrary arrogance of a centralized bureaucracy busily manufactured the 'angry subjects' of whose conduct it complained; and the educational system which was the pride of the Republic was geared to the production of 'critical and autonomous individuals rather than responsible and participating citizens'.[14] A tradition of opposition and defiance of authority produced Resisters and Poujadists, men who rebelled to keep Algeria French and others who protested at the odious methods used to do so – but no model bureaucrat of the gas-chambers like Eichmann.

'The most fickle and unmanageable people on earth' could not for long be ruled by force. In normal times it could be managed by a patient and unglamorous process of endless compromise between the conflicting groups; but then the intermediaries monopolized power, the people felt no sense of participation, and when the stalemate so impeded decision that the national community was threatened in power or status, it was the regime that paid the penalty. In a great crisis a rare charismatic leader might identify his cause and his person with the latent general will which the parliamentary system had failed to crystallize; but then he might admit no intermediaries between the people and the remote (even if benevolent) power that determined their destinies. In either case democratic government, if it survived, was warped and stunted. The historic dilemma remains unresolved: to find a regime under which governments would be strong enough to act, yet not overweening and oppressive; secure enough to think ahead, yet not so secure as to ignore criticism; receptive to the voter's claims and grievances, but not so obsessed with them as to be incapable of leadership; concerned for the needs of ordinary people, but aware that their deepest discontents may not have material causes; neither obliviously neglectful of that splendid abstraction, 'the higher interest of France', nor loftily contemptuous of 'the immediate advantage of Frenchmen'.[15]

13. A. de Tocqueville, *L'ancien régime et la révolution* (1952 ed.), pp. 166–7.
14. Crozier, no. 65, p. 210.
15. Quotations from de Gaulle, *Le Salut*, pp. 28, 43.

MAPS

The main influences on French political geography are economic and historical. The pattern of prosperity and decline is shown in Maps 1, 3, 4 *and* 21.

1. Income per head 1951

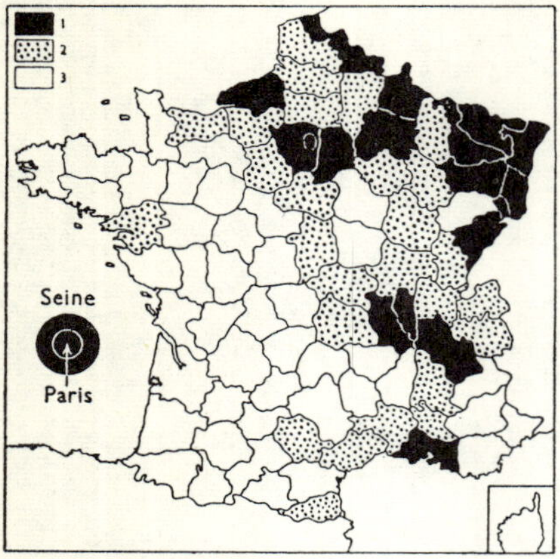

1. Above national average
2. Above 85% of national average
3. Below 85% of national average

Source: INSEE

2. The Left in the 3rd Republic

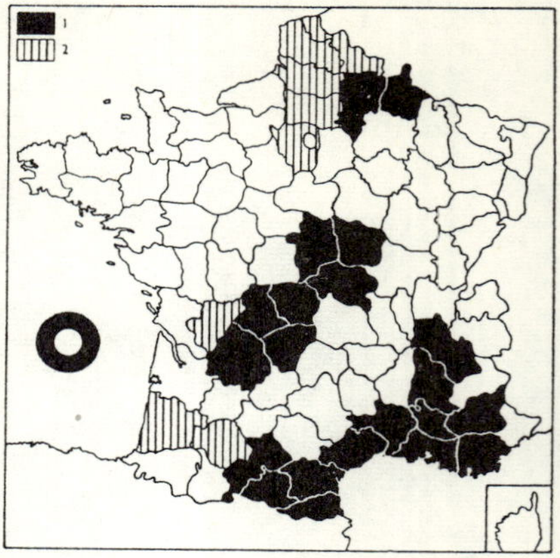

1. On Left since before 1900
2. ,, ,, 1940

From Goguel, *Géographie*, p. 105 (adapted)

3. Agriculture and poverty 1954

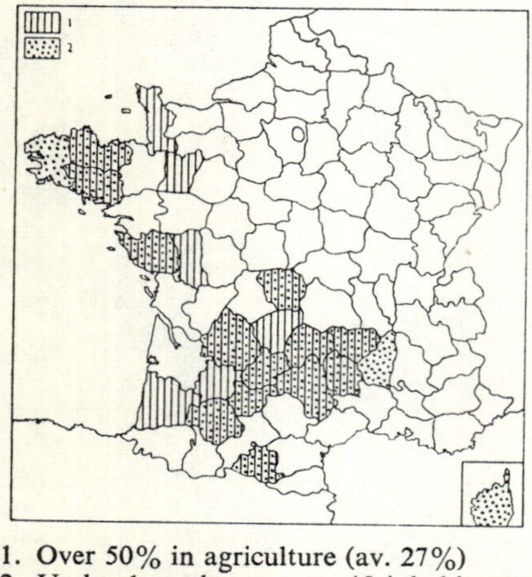

1. Over 50% in agriculture (av. 27%)
2. Under 1 modern car to 45 inhabitants (national average 1 to 30)

Source: J. F. Gravier, *Paris et le désert français*, pp. 189–90

4. Population increase 1946–54

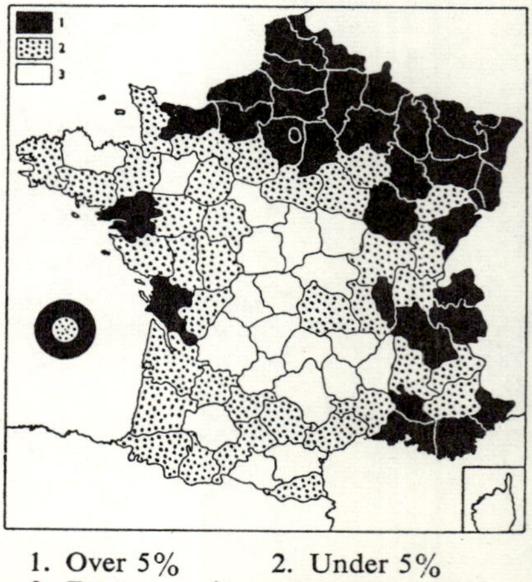

1. Over 5% 2. Under 5%
3. Decrease (nat. average +5·6%)

Source: INSEE

The traditional French political pattern based on regional attitudes to religion appears in Maps 2, 5 and 6.

5. Catholic areas

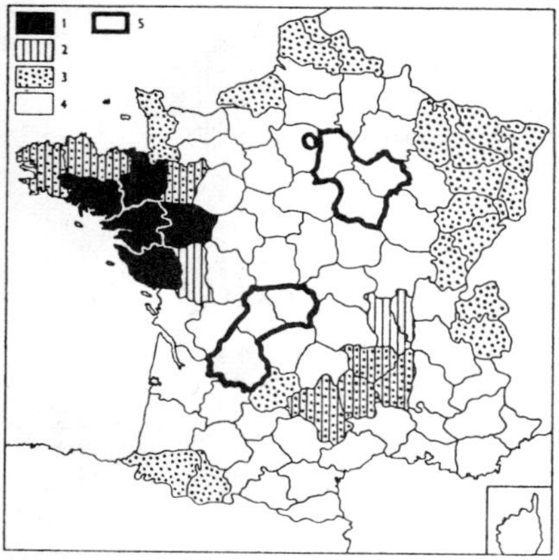

1. 50% } children in private
2. 25% } primary schools
3. Most
4. Minority of } adults attend Mass
5. Very few

Sources: Bosworth, p. 347 and *Sondages*, 1952, no. 4, p. 31

6. The Right in the 3rd Republic

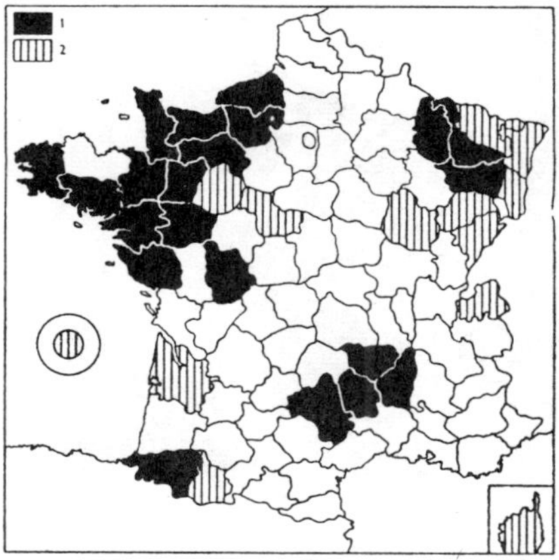

1. On Right since before 1900
2. ,, ,, ,, ,, 1940

From Goguel, *Géographie*, p. 103 (adapted)

7. Electoral turnout 1946–51–56

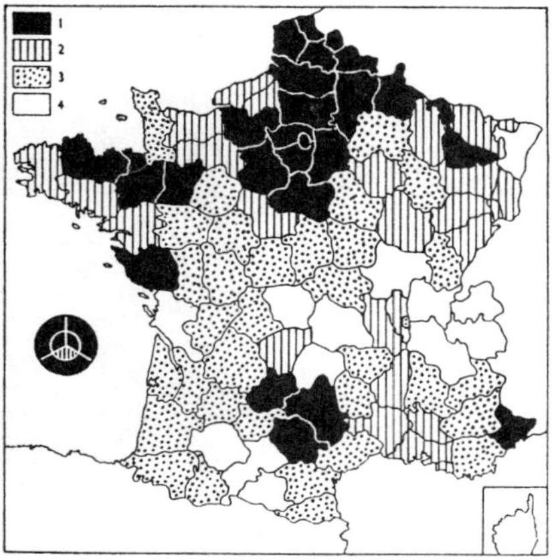

1. Always above national average
2. Sometimes ,, ,, ,,
3. Never ,, ,, ,,
4. Never within 3% of national average

Both economic and religious influences: workers vote most, Catholics next, mountaineers least.

8. Electoral evolution 1946–56

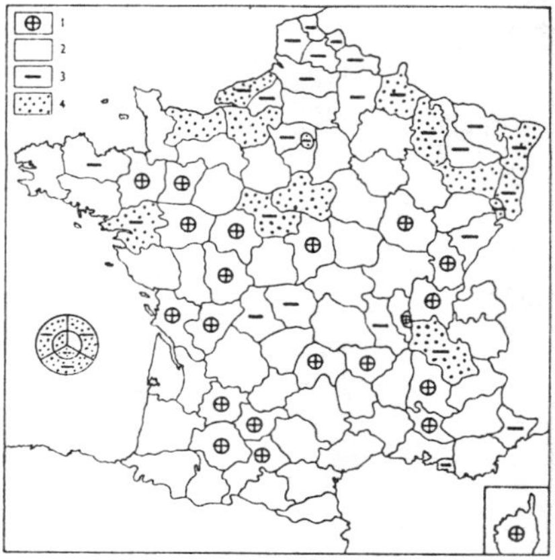

1. Right gains 10%
2. Right gains less
3. Left gains
4. Right gains 4% '51; Left 4% '56

(% of the *vote*; Left includes Com., Soc., Left Ind., and Rad. where they were Mendesist '56.)

Compare Map 4. Left gains in the expanding regions.

The Communist, Socialist and RPF vote (and the Radicals in 1956) show the economic pattern modifying the historical.

9. Communists 1946–51–56

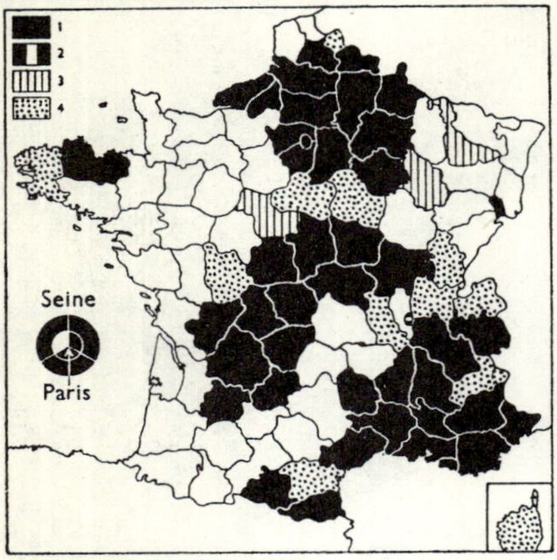

1. Safe: 20% '46, '51, '56
2. 20% except '51
3. Gain: 20% '56 but not '46
4. Loss: 20% '46 but not '56

10. Socialists 1946–51–56

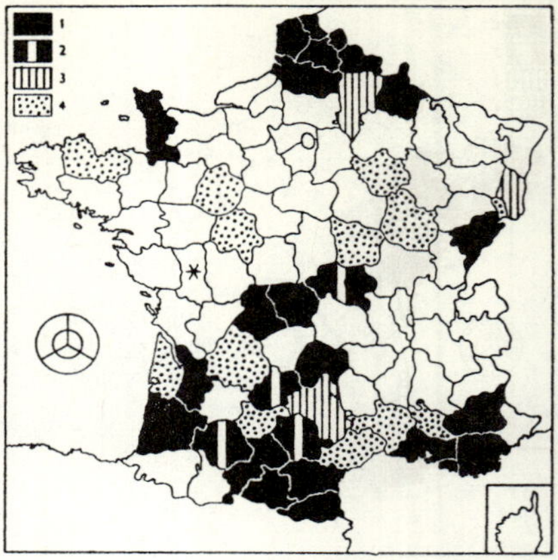

1. Safe: 15% '46, '51, '56
2. 15% except '51
3. Gain: 15% '56 but not '46
4. Loss: 15% '46 but not '56

* 15% '51 only

11. Radicals 1946–51–56

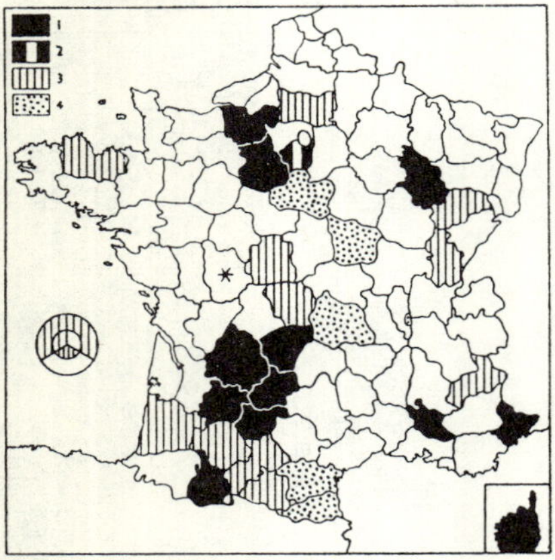

1. Safe: 15% '46, '51, '56
2. 15% except '51
3. Gain: 15% '56 but not '46
4. Loss: 15% '46 but not '56

Includes all factions and allies.
*15% 1951 only.

12. RPF 1951: Poujadists 1956

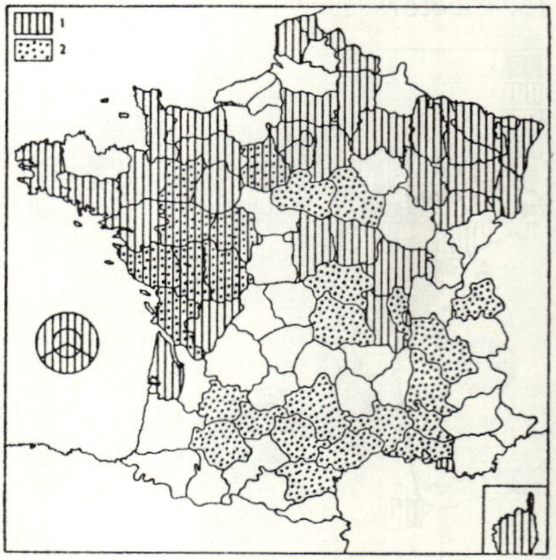

1. RPF 15% 1951
2. Pouj. $12\frac{1}{2}$% 1956

Note small overlap.

Radicals and Poujadists confined to the backward areas. Cf. Maps 3 and 4.
ALL PERCENTAGES OF ELECTORATE

Catholicism (Map 5) influences the MRP vote more than the Conservative.

13. MRP 1946–51–56

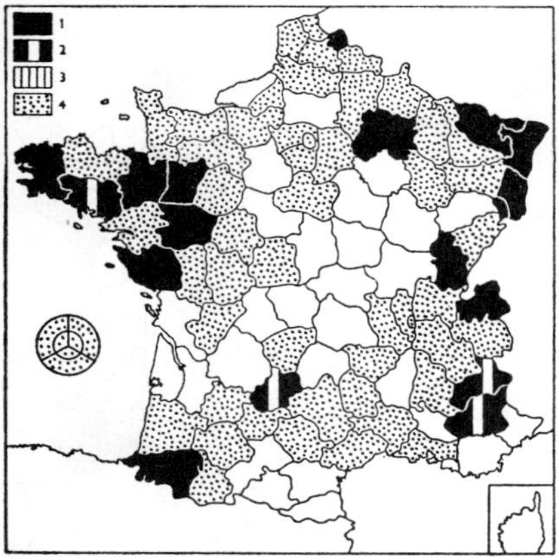

1. Safe: 15% '46, '51, '56
2. 15% except '51
3. Gain: 15% '56 but not '46
4. Loss: 15% '46 but not '56

* 15% '51 only

14. Conservatives 1946–51–56

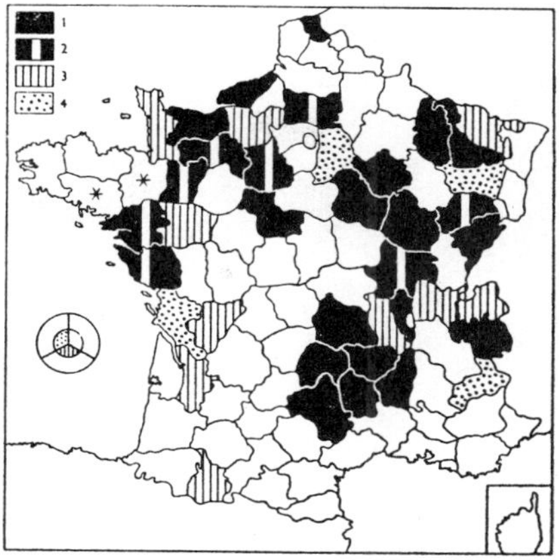

1. Safe: 15% '46, '51, '56
2. 15% except '51
3. Gain: 15% '56 but not '46
4. Loss: 15% '46 but not '56

* 15% '51 only

PERCENTAGES OF ELECTORATE

15. Electoral alliances 1951

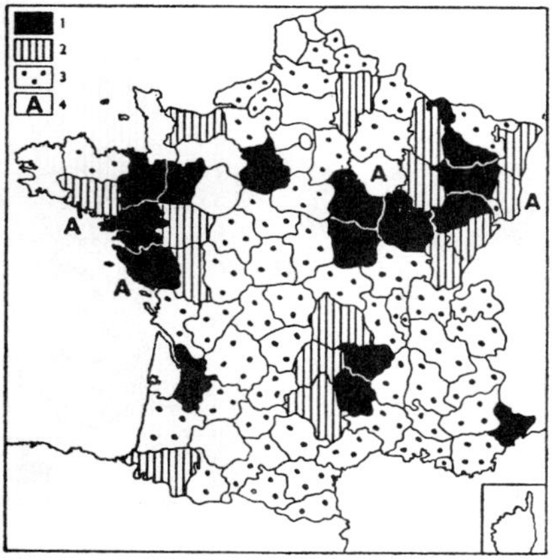

1. Alliance *in*cluding RPF
2. ,, *ex*cluding Socs. *or* RPF
3. ,, *in*cluding Socs. and clericals
4. ,, of anticlericals (Soc., Rad.)

1: also P-O
3: also E-et-L, M-et-M

16. Absolute majorities 1951, 1956

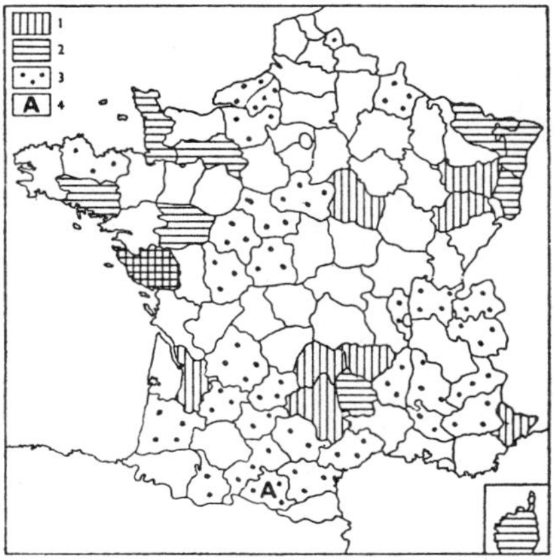

All seats to alliance:
of anti-Socs.: (1) 1951, (2) 1956
including Socs. and MRP: 1951 (3)
of anti-clericals (Soc., Rad.): 1956 (4)

Catholicism prevents any alliance between clericals and Socialists.

The historical pattern reappears strongly in the three referenda for or against de Gaulle. The broad division between Left and Right still follows it (Map 20).

17. Referendum 21-10-45
Oui à de Gaulle

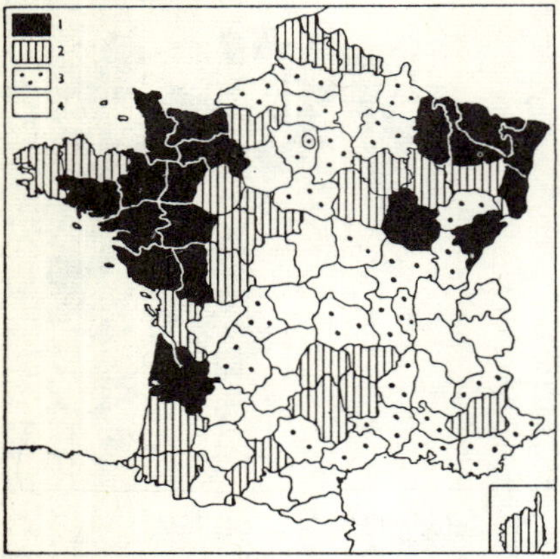

Limiting the Constituent Assembly's powers; opposed by Coms. and Rads.
OUI: 1. 70% 2. 60% 3. 55% 4. Less

18. Referendum 13-10-46
Constitution of the 4th Republic

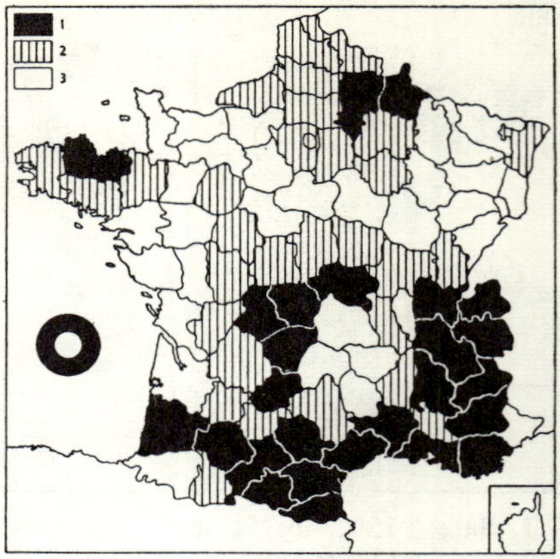

Opposed by de Gaulle, Right, Rads.
1. OUI 60% 2. OUI 50% 3. NON

19. Referendum 28-9-58
Oui à de Gaulle

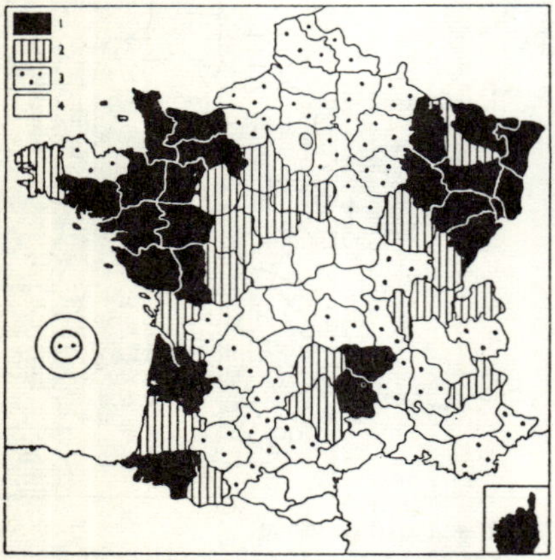

Constitution of the 5th Republic: opposed by Coms., many Rads., etc.
OUI: 1. 85% 2. 80% 3. 70% 4. Less

20. The Right 1936 – and 1956
1956: *Cons., MRP, RS, RGR; not Poujadists*

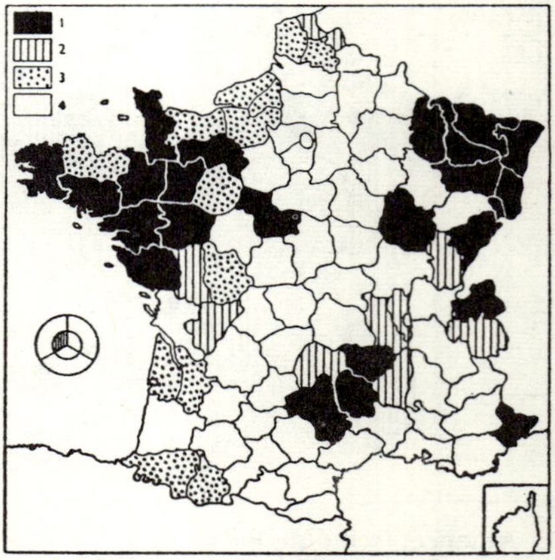

'Strong': '36 37½%, '56 30%
1. Strong both '36 and '56
2. Strong only '56
3. Strong only '36

17, 18, 19: % of the *vote*. 20: % of the *electorate*.

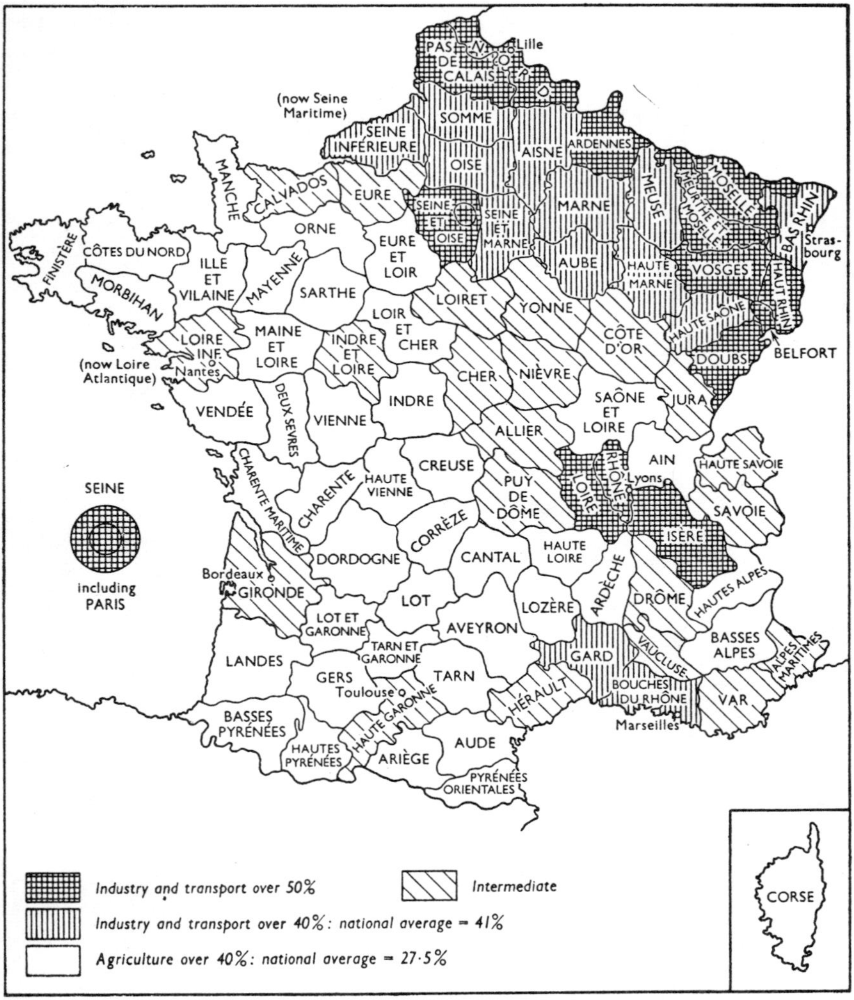

21. Distribution of Industry 1954 (working population)

BIBLIOGRAPHICAL NOTE

This brief selection, which does not aim at comprehensiveness, indicates sources (particularly in English) that I have found useful. It includes a few books not cited in the text, and a very few authors cited in one chapter only. Otherwise such authors are not listed; for their works the reader should consult the index and the first footnote reference. Where more than one book by an author is listed, an identifying letter distinguishes them. Collective works appear, where only one contributor has been cited, under his name; otherwise under the key word of their titles, as in the footnotes. Books are published in London (if in English) or Paris (if in French) unless otherwise stated. All articles are cited throughout by number from the alphabetical list on p. 470.

Part I

BODLEY'S substantial, discursive and opinionated volumes give invaluable background on French society and politics in 1900. SIEGFRIED (*a*) gives the best short account of political attitudes and views between the wars, MIDDLETON and SOULIER of political institutions, and SHARP of administration. MAILLAUD is a brilliant short explanation of French problems to the wartime English reader. A. COBBAN gives an excellent brief description of France's wartime history in the *Survey of International Affairs 1939–46*; HOFFMANN (nos. 126–7), makes an exceptionally interesting attempt to set Vichy briefly in perspective. DE GAULLE's war memoirs (*b*) are splendid works of literature with long documentary appendices. The struggles of the parties against de Gaulle and against one another, from which the Constitution of the Fourth Republic emerged, are described in perceptive and lively fashion by WRIGHT (*a*). WERTH (*c*) gives a useful summary of wartime developments; after 1945 his account is coloured by his strong neutralist sympathies.

Among general works on the Fourth Republic, PICKLES (*c*) and GOGUEL (*f*) are good brief introductions for the reader without previous knowledge. Books on social changes are discussed at the end of this note. The comprehensive narrative by FAUVET (*d*), with character-sketches of leading personalities, is complex, but excellent for the informed reader. The first part of the period is well covered by PICKLES (*b*), who concentrates on problems of policy, and GOGUEL (*d*) who traces party and parliamentary developments. The journalistic comments by SIEGFRIED (*b* and *c*) contain less malice and more reflection than those by BLOCH-MORHANGE and FAUCHER. GROSSER is admirably clear and balanced, if rather condensed, on the controversial problems of external policy. PLANCHAIS gave in February 1958 a prophetic account of the army's mood, on which GIRARDET is highly intelligent and informative. T. OPPERMANN's solid *Le problème algérien* (1961) is such a rarity amid the ephemera that its left-wing publisher feels it necessary to apologize for its impartiality; E. BEHR's *The Algerian Problem* (1961) is a very good book in English. For a brief account of the collapse of the regime and the beginnings of its successor, see WILLIAMS AND HARRISON and other works mentioned on pp. 57, 192n.

Part II

The electoral geography of France has been subjected to minute scrutiny, but the practical functioning of French parties has had little attention. Most of them must be studied in general and collective works. PRIOURET (*a*) is a useful journalistic description of them in the early days; the contributions in EARLE are spotty, and the best general accounts of the early years are FAUVET (*b*) and GOGUEL (*b*). Later, their social composition is analysed with varying degrees of thoroughness in *Partis et Classes*, their rural influence in *Paysans*, and their external policies by GROSSER. WAHL (*b*) gives a good general account from a point of view different from mine. COSTON, though strongly marked by extreme right-wing sympathies, is full of information on papers and personalities. Some facts and many stimulating ideas can be found in DUVERGER (*b*).

Strangely, the only full account of a party is HOFFMANN's monograph on Poujadism. The Radicals are well covered by BARDONNET for their organization, and DE TARR for their ideological divisions. GOGUEL (*e*) on MRP is also largely ideological, and now somewhat dated. On the Communist party WALTER's informative apologia ends in 1940; ROSSI's bitter but documented exposures deal with the early war years; RIEBER analyses the party's tactics while Russia was allied to the West; DOMENACH's sympathetic account dates from 1951. For later years we have only articles (GODFREY, no. 100; MACRIDIS, no. 152) and the tediously theological works of ex-Communists. On the Socialist party there are polemics, and an enormous and pedestrian history by LIGOU. RÉMOND's admirable work on the Right has little after 1945, and the gap is filled only by the excellent but brief and unfriendly chapters in *Partis et Classes*, by MERLE, and in *Paysans*, by BARRILLON and ROYER. On RPF the reader must await the forthcoming study edited by WAHL.

Part III

Almost all French textbooks on political institutions have a strong juridical bias, least marked in DUVERGER (*a*). Among the more politically conscious general works are THÉRY, now dated, and ARNÉ, a mine of well-organized information; GEORGEL is also full of material, presented in an assured and aggressive preaching style. WAHL (*b*) offers a suggestive presentation of the Fourth Republic's institutions in terms of the clash between the representative and administrative traditions of politics. *Institutions* is informative, and more politically sophisticated than most official productions. By far the best analysis of the factors and forces governing French policy-making is in GROSSER.

LIDDERDALE, a House of Commons Clerk, described parliamentary procedure with professional thoroughness, clarity and political virginity; CAMPBELL, no. 45, brings him up to 1953. The preparation of governmental legislation and work of the cabinet secretariat are concisely set out and compared with British and American practice by BERTRAND. Many aspects of the legislative process are well analysed, also comparatively, in *Travail*; others emerge more fully from HARRISON (unpublished). Other sources on committees are BARTHÉLEMY (*a*: pre-war but still well worth reading) and BROMHEAD, no. 32. SOLAL-CELIGNY's articles (nos. 200–201) and the law theses by H. GEORGE, SOUBEYROL and DREVET deal competently and thoroughly with their respective subjects. There is no single good and up-to-date source on the upper house. A succinct little book by the secretary-general of the Assembly, M. BLAMONT, gives a specialist's description and critique of parliamentary methods on the eve of the collapse; the all too brief observations of his colleague in the Council of the Republic must be collated from the end of GOGUEL (*d*), from his articles (nos. 107, 111–13), and from *Travail*.

Part IV

The electoral system and elections are most competently and concisely analysed by CAMPBELL. From 1956 every election and referendum has been very fully dissected, but earlier ones had less thorough treatment. On 1951 see GOGUEL (*d*), and on 1956, see *Élections 1956* and, more briefly, NICHOLAS *et al.* (nos. 167–70) and PIERCE (no. 180). Most French works on administration are legalistic: LALUMIÈRE on the *Inspection des Finances* is an exception. FREEDEMAN on the *Conseil d'État*, CHAPMAN (*a*, *b*) on local government, and the articles by BRINDILLAC, no. 28, DIAMANT, no. 70, and EHRMANN, no. 85 deserve special mention. On their respective spheres of policy, EHRMANN (*b*) and GROSSER are also most illuminating. A general account by BLONDEL AND RIDLEY is to appear shortly.

Our knowledge of French pressure-groups has greatly expanded in recent years. We owe a most stimulating analytical introduction to LAVAU (*b*), a thorough inventory and methodological critique to MEYNAUD, and several major contributions to American scholars: a very careful and critical study of the *patronat* to EHRMANN (*b*); an admirably perceptive and balanced historical account of the labour movement to LORWIN; some excellent essays on rural politics and organization to WRIGHT, nos. 223–9 (and to the French writers in *Paysans*); case-studies of two major measures to GALANT, on social security, and to ARON AND LERNER on EDC; and a careful examination of Catholic organizations and attitudes to BOSWORTH. A special number of *Esprit* in 1953 has many good and relevant articles (nos. 28, 107, 120, 128, 138a, 153). Other useful studies on individual groups are LAVAU, no. 139; BROWN, no. 35; EHRMANN, no. 84; MEYNAUD AND LANCELOT, no. 161. HOFFMANN is most informative on Poujade and his small-business rivals.

Parliamentary life under *tripartisme* was excellently described by HAMON in nos. 117–18; and later on by the same author, no. 121, by DEBRÉ, no. 67, by ISORNI (*a*, *b*) and, from outside, in a popular, lively and informative little book by MUSELIER. ARNÉ and GEORGEL both deal with some aspects of coalition politics and the party system. LEITES concentrates exclusively on its seamy side, analysing dubious evidence with subtlety and malice. Some shrewd observations are buried in his huge joint work with MELNIK, but the urbane JOUVENEL is still a better guide to the peculiarities of parliamentary psychology. BURON, a minister in two Republics, published his frank, informative and unpretentious description and defence of the political profession after this manuscript was completed.

Of general books on French life, MORAZÉ's brilliant intuitions dazzle as much as they illuminate. Continuity and resistance to change are stressed in EARLE (especially by the economic and sociological writers); by LÜTHY in scintillating overstatements, offset by unmemorable qualifications; by WYLIE in his attractive account of southern village life; and by FAUVET's intelligent and balanced anatomy of French divisions (*c*). More recent works emphasize change; notably TANNENBAUM on the cultural side, and the Harvard volume *Change* on the political, social and economic. The relationship between politics and society is discussed by ARON, nos. 6 and 7, a vigorous challenge to GOGUEL (*d*); and in a special number of *Esprit* in 1957, notably in the articles by BRINDILLAC, CROZIER and HOFFMANN (nos. 30, 64, 125). The latter extends his analysis in no. 126, and in *Change* he carries it into the Fifth Republic. ARON's lectures (*b*) give an excellent and balanced summary of France's failures, successes and problems in 1959; the summing-up observations of an American economic historian (LANDES, no. 135) and political scientist (EHRMANN, no. 86) are penetrating and suggestive. Much of the vast literature on institutional reform is out of date in the Fifth Republic, but DUVERGER (*e*, *f*) remains a brief but powerful critique of both the old regime and the new.

LIST OF BOOKS

ARNÉ, S. *Le Président du Conseil des Ministres sous la IVe République*, 1962.
ARON, RAYMOND. (*a*) *Le Grand Schisme*, 1948;
(*b*) *France Steadfast and Changing*, Cambridge, Mass., 1960;
(*c*) — and D. LERNER, *France Defeats EDC*, 1957;
and nos. 5–7.
ARRIGHI, P. *Le Statut des partis politiques*, 1948.
ASPECTS: Aspects de la société française by A. SIEGFRIED *et al.*, 1954.
AURIOL, V. *Hier . . . demain*, 1945. 2 vols.
BARDONNET, D. *L'évolution de la structure du Parti radical*, 1960.
BARRILLON, R. in *PARTIS ET CLASSES*; *PAYSANS.*
BARTHÉLEMY, J. (*a*) *Essai sur le travail parlementaire et le système des commissions*, 1934;
(*b*) *Le Gouvernement de la France*, 1939 ed.; first pub. 1919.
BEER and ULAM, see WAHL.
BERTRAND, A. (*a*) *Les techniques du travail gouvernemental dans l'État moderne* Brussels, 1954;
(*b*) in *The Civil Service in Britain and France*, ed. W. A. Robson, 1956;
and no. 16.

BLAMONT, E. *Les techniques parlementaires*, 1958; and nos. 18–20.
BLOCH-MORHANGE, J. *Les Politiciens*, 1961.
BLONDEL, J. in *ÉLECTIONS 1956*; *ELECTIONS ABROAD*.
BLUM, L. *La Réforme gouvernementale*, 1936; first pub. anonymously, 1918.
BODLEY, J. E. C. *France*. 1st ed., 1898. 2 vols.
BOSWORTH, W. *Catholicism and Crisis in Modern France*, Princeton, N. J., 1962; and no. 24.
BRAYANCE, A. *Anatomie du Parti communiste français*, 1952.
BROGAN, D. W. (*a*) *The Development of Modern France 1870–1939*, 1940.
(*b*) *The Free State*, 1945;
(*c*) in *Parliament: a Survey*, ed. Lord Campion, 1952;
and see WERTH.
BURON, R. *Le plus beau des métiers*, 1963.
BYÉ, M. in EINAUDI, M. *et al. Nationalization in France and Italy*, Ithaca, N.Y., 1955; and no. 37.
CAMPBELL, P., *French Electoral Systems and Elections 1789–1957*, 1957; and nos. 39–47.
CAPITANT, R., see HAMON; VALLON.
CHANGE: France: Change and Tradition, by S. Hoffmann *et al.*, 1963; also pub. as *In Search of France*, Cambridge, Mass., 1963.
CHAPMAN, B. (*a*) *Introduction to French Local Government*, 1953;
(*b*) *The Prefects and Provincial France*, 1955;
(*c*) *The Profession of Government*, 1959;
and no. 51.
CHEVALLIER, L. *Les Paysans*, 1947.
COLE: see WRIGHT.
CONTE, A. *La Succession*, 1963.
COSTON, H. *Partis, journaux et hommes politiques d'hier et d'aujourd'hui*, 1960.
COTTERET, J. M. *Le Pouvoir législatif en France*, 1962;
and in *INÉGALITÉS*; *PAYSANS*; and no. 63.
CRISE: Crise du pouvoir et crise du civisme, Lyons, 1954. (Semaines sociales.)
DANSETTE, A. (*a*) *Le Boulangisme*, 16th ed., 1946;
(*b*) *Destin du Catholicisme français 1926–1956*, 1957;
(*c*) *Histoire des Présidents de la République*, 2nd ed., 1960.
DEBRÉ, M. (*a*) *La mort de l'État républicain*, 1947;
(*b*) *Ces princes qui nous gouvernent*, 1957;
and no. 67.
DEBÛ-BRIDEL, J. *Les Partis contre de Gaulle*, 1948.
DELOUVRIER, P. (*a*) in *CRISE*;
(*b*) — and NATHAN, R., *Politique économique de la France* (Lectures at Institut d'Études Politiques 1955–56).
DE TARR, F. *The French Radical Party from Herriot to Mendès-France*, 1961.
DOGAN, M, in *Les nouveaux comportements politiques de la classe ouvrière*, ed. L. Hamon, 1962;
in *ÉLECTIONS 1956*; *ÉLECTIONS 1958*; *PARTIS ET CLASSES*; *PAYSANS*; and nos. 71–3.
DOMENACH, J. M. in EINAUDI, M. *et al. Communism in Western Europe*, Ithaca, N.Y., 1952.
DREVET, P. *La procédure de révision de la Constitution du 27.10.1946*, 1959.
DUMAINE, J. *Quai d'Orsay*, 1955.
DUVERGER, M. (*a*) *Manuel de droit constitutionnel et de science politique*, 5th ed., 1958; first pub. 1948;
(*b*) *Political Parties*, 1st Eng. ed., 1954; pub. in French, 1951;
(*c*) *Institutions financières*, 2nd ed., 1957;
(*d*) *The French Political System*, Chicago, 1958;
(*e*) *Demain la République*, 1958;
(*f*) *La VIe République et le Régime Présidentiel*, 1961;

and in *ÉLECTIONS 1956*; *PARTIS ET CLASSES*; *SYSTÈMES ÉLECTORAUX*; and no. 81.

EARLE, E. M. *et al. Modern France: Problems of the Third and Fourth Republics*, Princeton, N.J., 1951.

EHRMANN, H. W. (*a*) *French Labor from Popular Front to Liberation*, New York, 1947;
(*b*) *Organized Business in France*, Princeton, N.J., 1957;
see LAVAU; and nos. 82–6.

EINAUDI, M. *et al.*, see BYÉ; DOMENACH; GOGUEL.

ELECTIONS ABROAD, ed. D. E. Butler, 1959.

ÉLECTIONS 1956: Les élections du 2 janvier 1956, 1957, ed. M. Duverger, F. Goguel and J. Touchard. (Association Française de Science Politique.)

ÉLECTIONS 1958: Le référendum de septembre et les élections de novembre 1958 by J. TOUCHARD *et al.*, 1960. (Association Française de Science Politique.)

FAUCHER, J. A. *L'agonie d'un régime*, 1959.

FAUVET, J. (*a*) *Les Partis politiques dans la France actuelle*, 1947;
(*b*) *De Thorez à de Gaulle: Les Forces politiques en France*, 1951;
(*c*) *La France déchirée*, 1957, translated as *The Cockpit of France*, 1960;
(*d*) *La IVe République*, 1959;
and in *PARTIS ET CLASSES*; *PAYSANS*; and nos. 89–90.

FOGARTY, M. P. *Christian Democracy in Western Europe 1820–1953*, 1957.

FRANCE, see GAULLE, C. DE.

FRÉDÉRIX, P. *État des Forces en France*, 1935.

FREEDEMAN, C. E. *The Conseil d'État in Modern France*, New York, 1961.

GALANT, H. *Histoire politique de la Sécurité Sociale*, 1955.

GAULLE, C. DE. (*a*) *La France sera la France: Ce que veut Charles de Gaulle*, 1951;
(*b*) *Le Salut: Mémoires de Guerre*, vol. 3, 1959.

GEORGE, H. *Le droit d'initiative parlementaire en matière financière depuis la Constitution de 1946*, Bordeaux, 1956.

GEORGE, P. *et al. Études sur la Banlieue de Paris*, 1950.

GEORGEL, J. *Critiques et réforme des Constitutions de la République*, 2 vols., 1959.

GIRARDET, R. in *Changing Patterns of Military Politics*, ed. S. P. Huntington, Glencoe, Ill., 1961.

GODFREY, E. D. jr. *The Fate of the French Non-communist Left*, New York, 1955; and no. 100.

GOGUEL, F. (*a*) *La politique des partis sous la Troisième République*, 1946;
(*b*) in *Encyclopédie politique de la France et du monde*, 1950;
(*c*) *Géographie des elections françaises*, 1951;
(*d*) *France under the Fourth Republic*, Ithaca, N.Y., 1952;
(*e*) in EINAUDI, M. and GOGUEL, F. *Christian Democracy in Italy and France*, Notre Dame, Ind., 1952;
(*f*) *Le régime politique français*, 1955;
(*g*) — *et al. Nouvelles études de sociologie électorale*, 1954;
and in *ASPECTS*; *ÉLECTIONS 1956*; *CHANGE*; *SYSTÈMES ÉLECTORAUX*; *TRAVAIL*;
and nos. 102–13.

GROSSER, A. *La IVe République et sa politique extérieure*, 1961;
and in *ÉLECTIONS 1956*.

GUERY, L. *et al. Les Maîtres de l'UNR*, 1959.

GUY, C. *Le Cas Poujade*, Givors, 1955.

HAMON, L. (*a*) *Problèmes constitutionnels et réalités politiques*, pamphlet, 1954;
(*b*) *De Gaulle dans la République*, 1958, preface by R. Capitant;
see also DOGAN; and nos. 117–21.

HARRISON, M. 'Regards sur les Commissions de l'Assemblée Nationale', unpublished thesis, Institut d'Etudes politiques, Paris, 1958;
see also WILLIAMS; and nos. 122–3.

HERVÉ, P. (*a*) *Dieu et César sont-ils communistes?*, 1956;

(*b*) *Lettre à Sartre et a quelques autres par la même occasion*, 1956; and no. 124.
HISTOIRE: Histoire du Parti communiste français, n.d., published anonymously 1962 by an opposition group of party members. 2 vols., incomplete.
HOFFMANN, S. (*a*) *Le mouvement Poujade*, 1956;
(*b*) 'Protest in Modern France' in *The Revolution in World Politics*, ed. M. A. Kaplan, 1962;
in *CHANGE*; and nos. 125–7.
HUSSON, R. (i) *Les élections et le référendum des 21 octobre 1945, 5 mai 1946 et 2 juin 1946*, 1946;
(ii) *Les élections et le référendum des 13 octobre, 10 novembre, 24 novembre et 8 decembre 1946*, 1947.
INÉGALITÉS: Lois électorales et inégalités de représentation en France 1936–60 by J. M. COTTERET, C. ÉMERI and P. LALUMIÈRE, 1960.
INSTITUTIONS: Les Institutions politiques de la France by F. DE BAECQUE *et al.*, 1959.
ISORNI, J. (*a*) *Le silence est d'or*, 1957;
(*b*) *Ainsi passent les Républiques*, 1959.
JOUVENEL, R. DE, *La République des camarades*, 1914.
KAYSER, J. *Les Grandes Batailles du Radicalisme 1820–1901*, 1962; and in *ÉLECTIONS 1956*; *ÉLECTIONS 1958*.
LACHAPELLE, G. *Les régimes électoraux*, 1934.
LAICITÉ, see REMOND (*b*).
LALUMIÈRE, P. *L'Inspection des Finances*, 1959; and in *INÉGALITÉS*.
LANCELOT, A., see MEYNAUD.
LAPONCE, J. A. *The Government of the Fifth Republic*, Berkeley and Los Angeles, Calif., 1961; and no. 137.
LAVAU, G. E. (*a*) *Partis politiques et réalités sociales*, 1953;
(*b*) 'Political pressures in France' in *Interest Groups on Four Continents*, ed. H. W. Ehrmann, Pittsburgh, 1958; more fully as no. 141;
in *PARTIS ET CLASSES*; and nos. 138–41.
LEFRANC, G. *Les expériences syndicales en France de 1939 à 1950*, 1950.
LEITES, N. *On the Game of Politics in France*, Stanford, Calif., 1959; and see MELNIK.
LERNER, see ARON.
LESCUYER, G. *Le contrôle de l'État sur les entreprises nationalisées*, 1959.
LIDDERDALE, D. W. S. *The Parliament of France*, 1951.
LIGOU, D. *Histoire du Socialisme en France 1871–1961*, 1962.
LIPSET, S. M. *Political Man*, 1960.
LONG, R. *Les élections législatives en Côte d'Or depuis 1870*, 1958.
LORWIN, V. R. *The French Labor Movement*, Cambridge, Mass., 1954; and in EARLE.
LÜTHY, H. *The State of France*, 1955; pub. in French 1955.
MARABUTO, P. *Les Partis politiques et les mouvements sociaux sous la IVe République*, 1948.
MACRIDIS, R. C. and BROWN, B. E. *The De Gaulle Republic: Quest for Unity*, Homewood, Ill., 1960; and nos. 33-5, 150–2.
MAILLAUD, P. *France*, 1942.
MALIGNAC, G. and COLIN, R. *L'alcoolisme*, 2nd ed. 1958; first pub. 1954.
MARCUS, J. T. *Neutralism and Nationalism in France*, New York, 1958.
MASSIGLI, R. *Sur quelques maladies de l'État*, 1958.
MATTHEWS, R. *The Death of the Fourth Republic*, 1954.
MELNIK, C. and LEITES, N. *The House without Windows: France selects a President*, Evanston, Ill., 1958.
MEYNAUD, J. (*a*) *Les groupes de pression en France*, 1958;
(*b*) — and LANCELOT, A. *La participation des Français à la Politique*, 1961; and nos. 160–1.

MIDDLETON, W. L. *The French Political System*, 1932.
MILITARY POLITICS: see GIRARDET.
MORAZÉ, C. (*a*) *Les Français et la République*, 1st ed., 1956;
(*b*) — *et al.*, *Études de sociologie électorale*, 1947.
MUSELIER, F. *Regards neufs sur le Parlement*, 1956.
NICOLET, C. (*a*) *Pierre Mendès-France ou le métier de Cassandre*, 1959;
(*b*) *Le Radicalisme*, 1957.
NOËL, L. *Notre Dernière Chance*, 1956.
OLIVESI, A. and RONCAYOLO, M., *Géographie électorale des Bouches-du-Rhône sous la IVe République*, 1961.
PARLIAMENT, A SURYEY: see BROGAN.
PARTIS ET CLASSES: Partis politiques et classes sociales, ed. M. Duverger, 1955.
PAYSANS: Les Paysans et la politique dans la France contemporaine, ed. J. Fauvet and H. Mendras, 1958.
PICKLES, D. (*a*) *France between the Republics*, 1946;
(*b*) *French Politics: the first years of the Fourth Republic*, 1953;
(*c*) *France: the Fourth Republic*, 1955;
and nos. 175–6.
PINEAU, C. *Mon cher député*, 1959.
PLANCHAIS, J. *Le malaise de l'Armée*, 1958.
POLITIQUE ET TECHNIQUE by G. BERGER *et al.*, 1958.
POUJADISME, LE by M. B. (Maurice Bardèche) *et al.*, 1956.
POUTIER, C. *La réforme de la Constitution*, 1955.
PRIOURET, R. A. (*a*) *La République des Partis*, 1947;
(*b*) *La République des Députés*, 1959.
RÉMOND, R. (*a*) *La Droite en France de 1815* à *nos jours*, 1954;
(*b*) 'Laïcité et question scolaire dans la vie politique française sous la IVe République', in *La Laïcité, by* A. AUDIBERT *et al.*, 1960.
and nos. 186–8.
REVOLUTION IN WORLD POLITICS: see HOFFMANN.
RIEBER, A. J. *Stalin and the French Communist Party 1940–47*, New York, 1962.
RIOUX, L. *Où en est le Syndicalisme?*, 1960.
ROBINSON, K. *The Public Law of Overseas France since the war* (pamphlet), revised ed., Oxford, 1954; and no. 192.
RONCAYOLO, M., see OLIVESI.
ROSSI, A. (*a*) *Physiologie du Parti communiste français* (1948) translated, slightly abridged, as *A Communist Party in Action*, New Haven, Conn., 1949;
(*b*) *Les communistes français pendant la 'drôle de guerre'*, 1951.
(*c*) *La Guerre des Papillons*, 1954. [Neither (*b*) nor (*c*) is cited in text.]
ROYER, J. M. in *ÉLECTIONS* 1956; *PAYSANS.*
SCHRAM, S. R. *Protestantism and Politics in France*, Alençon, 1954.
SCHOENBRUN, D. *As France Goes*, New York, 1957.
SÉRANT, P. *Où va la Droite?*, 1958.
SHARP, W. R. *The Government of the French Republic*, New York, 1938.
SIEGFRIED, A. (*a*) *Tableau des Partis en France*, 1930; translated as *France: a Study in Nationality*, New Haven, Conn., 1930;
(*b*) *De la IIIe à la IVe République*, 1956;
(*c*) *De la IVe à la Ve République*, 1958;
see also *ASPECTS;* and no. 194.
SOUBEYROL, J. *Les Décrets-lois sous la IVe République*, Bordeaux, 1955; and no. 202.
SOULIER A. *L'Instabilité ministérielle sous la IIIe République*, 1939, preface by M. Prélot; and no. 203.
SUFFERT, G. *Les Catholiques et la Gauche*, 1960.
SYSTÈMES ÉLECTORAUX: L'influence des systèmes électoraux sur la vie politique, 1950, by M. DUVERGER *et al.*
TANNENBAUM, E. R. *The New France*, Chicago, 1961.

THÉOLLEYRE, J. M. *Le Procés des fuites*, 1956.

THÉRY, J. *Le Gouvernement de la IVe République*, 1949.

THIBAUDET, A. (*a*) *Les Idées politiques de la France*, 1932; (*b*) *La République des professeurs*, 1927.

TOURNOUX, J. R. *Secrets d'État*, 1960.

TRAVAIL: Le Travail parlementaire en France et à l'étranger, by F. GOGUEL *et al.*, 1954. (Special number of *RFSP*.)

VALLON, L. *L'Histoire s'avance masquée*, 1957, preface by R. Capitant.

WAHL, N. (*a*) *The Fifth Republic*, New York, 1959; (*b*) in *Patterns of Government*, ed. S. H. Beer and A. B. Ulam, 1st ed., New York, 1958.

WALINE, M. *Les Partis contre la République*, 1948; in *POLITIQUEET TECHNIQUE*; and no. 214.

WALTER, G., *Histoire du Parti communiste français*, 1948.

WARNER, C. K. *The Winegrowers of France and the Government since 1875*, New York, 1960.

WERTH, A. (*a*) *The Destiny of France*, 1937; (*b*) *The Twilight of France*, 1942, introduction by D. W. Brogan; (*c*) *France 1940–1955*, 1956; (*d*) *The Strange History of Pierre Mendès-France and the Great Conflict over French North Africa*, 1957; (*e*) *The De Gaulle Revolution*, 1960.

WILLIAMS, P. M. (*a*) *Politics in Post-war France*, 2nd ed., 1958; first pub. 1954; (*b*) — and HARRISON, M. *De Gaulle's Republic*, 1960; and in *ELECTIONS ABROAD*; and nos. 218–22.

WILSON, J. S. G. *French Banking Structure and Credit Policy*, 1957.

WRIGHT, G. (*a*) *The Reshaping of French Democracy*, 1950; (*b*) *France in Modern Times*, 1960; (*c*) in *European Political Systems*, ed. T. Cole, New York, 1953; in EARLE; and nos. 223–9.

WYLIE, L. *Village in the Vaucluse*, Cambridge, Mass., 1957; and in *CHANGE*.

LIST OF ARTICLES

1. ABBOTT, R. S. and SICARD, R. ... The Super-Prefect, *APSR* 44.2 (1950), 426–31.

2. ALLEN, L. A. Mendès-France and the Radical Party, *WPQ* 13.2 (1960), 445–65.

3. ANDREWS, W. G. ... The Committees of the Majority, *P. Aff.* 15.4 (1962), 485–99.

4. ARCHAMBEAUD, Y. Conseil économique et régime démocratique, *Politique* 36 (July 1948), 578–91.

5. ARON, RAYMOND. Les contradictions de la démocratie, *La Nef* 75–6 (April-May 1951), 68–87.

6., 7. — Réflexions sur la politique et la science politique française; Électeurs, partis et élus, *RFSP* 5. 1 and 2 (1955), 5–20 and 245–64.

8a., 8b. AUBRY, M. Le Conseil Économique, *RDP* 67.2 (1951), 414–77; 69.3 (1953), 701–18.

9a. BARNES, S. H. The politics of French Christian labor, *JP* 21.1 (1959), 105–22.

9b. BAUCHARD, P. La presse de province, *Esprit* 213 (April 1954), 593–605.

10. BEAULIEU, G. DE. Les résultats des élections aux caisses de Sécurité sociale, *Politique* 25 (July 1947), 557–63.

11. BERLIA, G. Les propositions parlementaires de révision constitutionnelle, *RDP* 66.3 (1950), 676–90.

(*over*)

12a. — Le projet de révision constitutionnelle, *RDP* 69.2 and 3 (1953), 434–47 and 680–96.
12b. — La loi du 31.7.1953 et l'immunité parlementaire, *RDP* 69.3 (1953), 697–700.
13a. — L'avis du Conseil de la République sur le projet de révision, *RDP* 70.2 (1954), 473–97.
13b. — De la Présidence de la République, *RDP* 71.4 (1955), 909–14.
14. — La dissolution et le régime des pouvoirs publics, *RDP* 72.1 (1956), 130–42.
15. — La réforme constitutionnelle devant le Parlement, *RDP* 74–1 (1958), 81–90.
16. BERTRAND, A. La Présidence du Conseil et le secrétariat-général du gouvernement, *RDP* 64.3 (1948), 435ff.
17. BIAYS, P. Les commissions d'enquête parlementaires, *RDP* 68.2 (1952), 443–86.
18. BLAMONT, E. Les conditions du contrôle parlementaire, *RDP* 66.2 (1950), 387–402.
19. — La seconde lecture dans la Constitution de 1946, *RFSP* 1.3 (1951), 298–310.
20. — La mise en oeuvre de la dissolution, *RDP* 72.1 (1956), 105–29.
21. BODIN, L. and TOUCHARD, J. L'élection partielle de la première circonscription de la Seine, *RFSP* 7.2 (1957), 271–312.
22. BOISSARIE, A. Où est la Gauche française?, *La Nef* 75–6 (April-May 1951), 17–24.
23. BOIVIN-CHAMPEAUX, J. Les Indépendants, *RPP* 593 (Dec. 1949), 379–82.
24. BOSWORTH, W. The French Catholic hierarchy and the Algerian question, *WPQ* 15.4 (1962), 667–80.
25. BOTTOMORE, T. La mobilité sociale dans la haute administration française, *Cahiers Internationaux de Sociologie* 13 (1952), 167–78.
26. BOURDET, C. Les maîtres de l'Afrique du Nord, *TM* 80 (June 1952), 2247–64.
27. — La politique intérieure de la Résistance, *TM* 112–13 (1955), 1837–62.
28. BRINDILLAC, C. Les hauts fonctionnaires, *Esprit* 203 (June 1953), 862–77.
29. — La réforme des institutions, *Esprit* 210 (Jan. 1954), 51–62.
30. — Décoloniser la France, *Esprit* 256 (Dec. 1957), 799–812.
31. — and PROST, A. Géographie électorale, *Esprit* 236 (March 1956), 437–61.
32. BROMHEAD, P. Some notes on the standing committees of the French National Assembly, *PS* 5.2 (1957), 140–57.
33. BROWN, B. E. Pressure politics in France, *JP* 18.4 (1956), 702–19.
34. — Religious schools and politics in France, *Midwest Journal of Political Science* 2.2 (1958), 160–78.
35. — Alcohol and politics in France, *APSR* 51.4 (1957), 976–95.
36. BRUYAS, J. L'évolution du Conseil de la République, *RDP* 65.4 (1949), 541–74.
37. BYÉ, M. Le présent et l'avenir du Conseil Économique, *Politique* 36 (July 1948), 592–610.
38. CADART, J. La loi ... du 6 janvier 1950, *RDP* 66.1 (1950), 147–63 .
39–41. CAMPBELL, P. The Cabinet and the Constitution in France, *P. Aff.* 4.3 (1951), 341–51; 9.3 (1956), 296–306; 12.1 (1958–9), 27–36.
42. — ... La loi électorale française du 9 mai 1951, *RFSP* 1.4 (1951), 498–502.
43. — 'Vérification des pouvoirs' in the French National Assembly, *PS* 1.1 (1953), 65–79.
44. — Discipline and loyalty in the French Parliament, *PS* 1.3 (1953), 247–57.
45. — The French Parliament, *P. Adm.* 31.4 (1953), 349–63.
46. — Constitutional reform in France 1950–54, *Political Science* 7.2 (Wellington, N.Z., 1955), 76–100.

(*over*)

47. — French party congresses, *P.Aff.* 10.4 (1957), 412–23; — and see DOGAN.

48. CARTOU, J. ... Le décret du 19. 6. 56, *RDP* 73.2 (1957), 256–95.

49. CASALEGNO, C. Grandezza e decadenza del movimento gollista, *Occidente* 9.6 (1953), 392–410.

50. CASSIN, R. Recent reforms in the government and administration of France, *P.Adm.* 28 (1950), 179–87.

51. CHAPMAN, B. Organization of the French police, *P.Adm.* 29 (1951), 67–75.

52. CHAPUS, R. La loi ... du 11.7.1953 et la question des décrets-lois, *RDP* 69.4 (1953), 954–1006.

53. CHARLOT, J. and M. Un rassemblement d'intellectuels: la Ligue des Droits de l'Homme, *RFSP* 9.4 (1959), 955–1028.

54. CHARPENTIER, J. Les lois-cadres et la fonction gouvernementale, *RDP* 74.2 (1958), 220–70.

55. CHAVAGNES, R. D'un véritable Conseil National Économique, *RPP* 586 (March 1949), 209–24.

56. CHENOT, B. Les paradoxes de l'entreprise publique, *RFSP* 5.4 (1955), 725–35.

57. COBBAN, A. The Second Chamber in France, *Political Quarterly* 19.4 (1948), 323–35.

58. COLLIARD, C. La pratique de la question de confiance sous la IVe République, *RDP* 64.2 (1948), 220–37.

59. CONVERSE, P. E. and DUPEUX, G. Politicization of the electorate in France and the United States, *Public Opinion Quarterly* 26.1 (1962), 1–23.

60. CORAIL, J. L. DE. Le rôle des Chambres en matière de politique étrangère, *RDP* 72.4 (1956), 770–853.

61.–62. CORET, A. ... La révision du Titre VIII de la Constitution ..., *Revue Juridique et Politique de l'Union Française*, 10.1 (1956), 87–142; 12.3 (1958), 452–94.

63. COTTERET, J. M. L'ordre du jour des Assemblées Parlementaires, *RDP* 77.4 (1961), 813–27.

64. CROZIER, M. France, terre de commandement, *Esprit* 256 (Dec. 1957), 779–98.

65. — Le Citoyen, *Esprit* 292 (Feb. 1961), 195–213.

66. P. C. D. Pour un Plan Monnet administratif, *RPP* 579 (June 1948), 267–75.

67. DEBRÉ, M. Trois caractéristiques du régime parlementaire français, *RFSP* 5.1 (1955), 21–48.

68. DERCZANSKY, A. Il y avait des militants socialistes, *Esprit* 238 (May 1956), 674–7.

69. DERRUAU-BONIOL, S. Le département de la Creuse, structure sociale et évolution politique, *RFSP* 7.1 (1957), 38–66.

70. DIAMANT, A. A case study of administrative autonomy: controls and tensions in French administration, *PS* 6.2 (1958), 147–66.

71. DOGAN, M. Quelques aspects du financement des élections de janvier 1956, *RFSP* 7.1 (1957), 88–98.

72.–73. — and CAMPBELL, P. Le personnel ministériel en France et en Grande-Bretagne, *RFSP* 7.2 and 4 (1957), 313–45 and 793–824.

74.–75. DRAGO, R. L'évolution de la notion d'inviolabilité parlementaire, *RDP* 65.2 (1949), 350–70, and 66.2 (1950), 403–17.

76. — L'article 32 de la Constitution du 27.10.1946, *RDP* 69.1 (1953), 157–69.

77. — L'état d'urgence et les libertés publiques, *RDP* 71.3 (1955), 670–708.

78. DONNEDIEU DE VABRES, JACQUES. The formation of economic and financial policy (France), *International Social Science Bulletin* 8.2 (1956), 228–39.

79. DREYFUS, F. G. ... Sociologie politique de la France de l'Est, *RFSP* 10.3 (1960), 527–61.

80. DUPEUX, G. Orientations of French electoral sociology, *British Journal of Sociology* 6.4 (1955), 328–34;
— and see CONVERSE.
81. DUVERGER, M. SFIO, mort ou transfiguration?, *TM* 112–13 (1955), 1863–85.
82. EHRMANN, H. W. Political forces in France, *Social Research* 15.2 (1948), 146–69.
83. — The French peasant and Communism, *APSR* 46.1 (1952), 19–43.
84. — The French trade associations and the ratification of the Schuman Plan, *WP* 6.4 (1954), 453–81.
85. — French bureaucracy and organized interests, *Administrative Science Quarterly* 5.4 (1961), 534–55.
86. — On democracy in France, *The Colorado Quarterly* 9.4 (1961), 5–27.
87. *Esprit* 80 (May 1939) number on 'Le Régime des Partis'; especially 'Le Parti radical-socialiste', by B. S. (pseudonym of F. Goguel)
88. FABRE, M. H. Un échec constitutionnel: l'investiture du Président du Conseil, *RDP* 67.1 (1951), 182–211.
89. FAUVET, J. Les partis de gouvernement, *La Nef* 75–6 (April-May 1951), 9–16.
90. — La démocratie en question, *Terre Humaine* 33–4 (Sept. 1953), 106–13.
91.–92. FEYZIOGLU, T. The reforms of the French higher civil service since 1945, *P.Adm.* 33.1 and 2 (1955), 69–93 and 173–90.
93. FLORY, M. La liberté de démission du Président du Conseil, *RDP* 67.3 (1951), 815–40.
94. FOUGEYROLLAS, P. Polycentrism :France, *Survey* 42 (June 1962), 121–31.
95. FRENAY, H. Le Travaillisme, enfant mort-né de la Résistance, *Preuves* 73 (March 1957), 43–8.
96. FUSILIER, R. Les finances des partis politiques, *RPP* 631–2 (Oct. and Nov. 1953), 146–61, 258–76.
F. G., see GOGUEL, no. 105.
97. GERBER, P. Les attributions législatives du Conseil de la République, *Politique* 34 (May 1948), 404–11.
98. GERBET, P. La genèse du Plan Schuman, *RFSP* 6.3 (1956), 525–53.
99a. GIRARDET, R. L'héritage de l'Action Française, *RFSP* 7.4 (1957), 765–92.
99b. — Pouvoir civil et pouvoir militaire dans la France contemporaine, *RFSP* 10.1 (1960), 5–38.
100. GODFREY, E. D. The communist presence in France, *APSR* 50.2 (1956), 321–38.
101. GOETZ-GIREY, R. La 'distance sociale' et les groupes du Conseil Économique, *Revue Economique* 5 (1957), 890–903.
102a. GOGUEL, F. . . . Programme de travail constituant, *Esprit* 112 (Nov. 1945), 746–51.
102b. — Géographie des élections du 21.10.1945, *Esprit* 113 (Dec. 1945), 935–956.
103. — Le problème du statut des partis, *Esprit* 118 (Jan. 1946), 96–106.
104. — Une nouvelle coûtume parlementaire, *Esprit* 118 (Jan. 1946), 135–7.
105. — Premier bilan de la constitution, *Esprit* 137 (Sept. 1947), 341–53.
106. — Les partis politiques dans la IVe République, *Politique* 27 (Oct. 1947), 685–95.
107. — Déficience du Parlement, *Esprit* 203 (June 1953), 853–61.
108. — Structures sociales et opinions politiques à Paris d'après les élections du 17.6.1951, *RFSP* 1.3 (1951), 326–33.
109. — Élections sociales et élections politiques, *RFSP* 3.2 (1953), 246–71.
— *RFSP* 4.4 (1954), see TRAVAIL in list of books.
110. — La révision constitutionnelle de 1954, *RFSP* 5.3 (1955), 485–502.
111. — Vers une nouvelle orientation de la révision constitutionnelle, *RFSP* 6.3 (1956), 493–507.

(*over*)

112. — L'élaboration des institutions de la République dans la Constitution, *RFSP* 9.1 (1959), 67–86.
113. — Sur le régime présidentiel, *RFSP* 12.2 (1962), 289–311.
— and see no. 87.
114. GUILLEMIN, P. Les élus d'Afrique noire à l'Assemblée Nationale sous la IVe République, *RFSP* 8.4 (1958), 861–77.
115. GRAWITZ, M. Monographie du parti socialiste à Lyon, *RFSP* 9.2 (1959), 454–65.
116. GUÉRIN, M. La réforme de la Haute Cour, *Politique* 35 (June 1948), 554–7.
117. HAMON, L. Le régime parlementaire de la IVe République, *Politique* 24 (June 1947), 385–411.
118. — La fin du régime de quasi-unanimité, *Politique* 25 (July 1947), 523–34.
119. — Origines et chances de la Troisième Force, *Politique* 31 (Feb. 1948), 101–19.
120. — Gouvernement et intérêts particuliers, *Esprit* 203 (June 1953), 831–52.
121. — Members of the French Parliament, *International Social Science Journal* 13.4 (1961), 545–66.
122. HARRISON, M. The composition of the committees of the French National Assembly, *P.Aff.* 11.2 (1958), 172–9.
123. — Paris 5: safe seat, *PS* 7.2 (1959), 147–56.
124. HERVÉ, P. Le parti communiste de 1944 à 1961, *Crapouillot* 55 (Jan. 1962), 54–79.
125. HOFFMANN, S. Politique d'abord!, *Esprit* 256 (Dec. 1957), 813–32.
126. — The effects of World War II on French society and politics, *French Historical Studies* 2.1 (1961), 28–63.
127. — Aspects du régime de Vichy, *RFSP* 6.1 (1956), 44–69.
128. JARRIER, B. L'État investi par les intérêts, *Esprit* 203 (June 1953) 878–902.
129. JEANNEAU, B. Les élections législatives partielles sous la IV République, *RDP* 71.4 (1955), 915–65.
130. JUSSIEU, M. Crise à l'ACJF, *Esprit* 234 (Jan. 1956), 116–25.
131. KING, J. B. Ministerial cabinets of the Fourth Republic, *WPQ* 13 (1960), 433–44.
132. KLATZMANN, J. Comment votent les paysans français, *RFSP* 8.1 (1958), 13–41.
133. LACHARRIÈRE, R. DE. La fonction du Haut Conseil de l'UF, *Revue juridique et politique de l'Union française* 3.1 (1949), 1–25;
134a. } (ANON.) La seconde session ..., *ibid.* 6.4 (1952), 533–47; La troisième
134b. } session ..., *ibid.* 7.4 (1953), 500–6.
135. LANDES, D. S. Observations on France: economy, society, polity, *WP* 9.3 (1957), 329–49.
LANCELOT, A. see MEYNAUD, J.
136. LANCELOT, Mme. M. T. Le courrier d'un parlementaire, *RFSP* 12.2 (1962), 426–32.
137. LAPONCE, J. A. Mendès-France and the Radical Party, *WPQ* 11 (1958), 340–56.
138a. LAVAU, G. La dissociation du pouvoir, *Esprit* 203 (June 1953), 817–30.
138b. — Destin des Radicaux, *TM* 112–13 (1955), 1886–1905.
139. — Notes sur un 'pressure-group' français: la CGPME, *RFSP* 5.2 (1955), 370–83.
140. — La réforme des institutions, *Esprit* 265 (Sept. 1958), 230–57.
141. — Groupes de pression: France, paper to International Political Science Association, 1957 (see LAVAU in list of books).
142. LEMASURIER, J. Difficultés relatives à l'interprétation des Articles 91 et 92 de la Constitution, *RDP* 68.1 (1952), 176–86.
143. LESCUYER, G. Les entreprises nationalisées et le Parlement, *RDP* 76.6 (1960), 1137–87.

144. LEWIS, E. G. The operation of the French Economic Council, *APSR*, 49.1 (1955), 161–72.
145. — Parliamentary control of nationalized industries in France, *APSR* 51.3 (1957), 669–83.
146. LIPSEDGE, M. S. The Poujade movement, *Contemporary Review* (Feb. 1956), 83–8.
147. LOUIS-LUCAS, P. Les pouvoirs propres des commissions des Finances, *RDP* 70.3 (1954), 722–52.
148. MACRAE, D., JR. Religious and socio-economic factors in the French vote 1946–56, *American Journal of Sociology* 64.3 (1958), 290–8.
149. — Intraparty divisions and cabinet coalitions in the Fourth French Republic, *Comparative Studies in Society and History* 5.2 (1963), 164–211.
150. MACRIDIS, R. C. The cabinet secretariat in France, *JP* 13.4 (1951), 589–603.
151. — . . . Revision of the Constitution of the Fourth Republic, *APSR* 50.4 (1956), 1011–22.
152. — The immobility of the French Communist Party, *JP* 20.4 (1958), 613–34.
153. MALIGNAC, G. Le Statut de l'alcool, *Esprit* 203 (June 1953), 903–8.
154. MARCEL, J. La Présidence du Conseil, *RDP* 74.3 (1958), 452–99 (reprinted in *INSTITUTIONS*, see list of books).
155. MARTINET, G. La Gauche non-conformiste, *La Nef* 75–6 (April-May 1951), 46–56.
156. — Traditions révolutionnaires, *Esprit* 256 (Dec. 1957), 772–8.
157. MENDRAS, H. Les organisations agricoles et la politique, *RFSP* 5.4 (1955), 736–60.
158. MERLE, M. The Presidency of the Fourth Republic, *P.Aff.* 7.3 (1954), 287–302.
159. — Les élections législatives partielles sous la 2e législature, *Revue Int. Hist. Pol. et Const.* (1956), 51–66.
160. MEYNAUD, J. Les groupes d'intérêt et l'administration en France, *RFSP* 7.3 (1957), 573–93.
161. — and LANCELOT, A. Groupes de pression et politique du logement, *RFSP* 8.4 (1958), 821–60.
162. MICAUD, C. A. Organization and leadership of the French Communist Party, *WP* 4.3 (1952), 318–55.
163. NATANSON, T. Léon Blum au Congrès de Tours, *La Nef* 65–6 (June-July) 1950, 88–99.
164. NAVILLE, P. Le Parti Communiste et le front uni ouvrier, *TM* 112–13 (1955), 1906–21.
165. NEUMANN, R. G. The struggle for electoral reform in France, *APSR* 45.3 (1951), 741–55.
166. — Formation and transformation of Gaullism in France, *WPQ* 6.1 (1953), 250ff.

NICHOLAS, H. G. *et al.* The French election of 1956, *PS* 4.2 and 3 (1956):
167. NICHOLAS, H. G. Electoral law and machinery, 139–50.
168. WILLIAMS, P. M. The campaign, 151–75.
169. ROSE, S. Guy Mollet's election campaign, 250–63.
170. THOMAS, M. The campaign in the department of Vienne, 265–82.
171. PACTET, P. Les commissions parlementaires, *RDP* 70.1 (1954), 127–72.
172. PANTER-BRICK, K. French regional administration, *P.Adm.* 29 (1951), 245–51.
173. PERNOT, G. Le contrôle de la constitutionnalité des lois, *Revue politique des idées et des institutions* (Oct. 1951), 481–90.
174. PETOT, J. La résistance à l'insurrection, *RDP* 74.1 (1958), 53–80.
175. PICKLES, D. The French Presidency, *Political Quarterly* 25.2 (1954), 105–15.

(*over*)

176. — The reform of French political institutions, *P.Aff.* 10.1 (1956–7), 94–103.
177. PICKLES, W. The geographical distribution of political opinions in France, *Politica* 2.6 (1936), 159–87.
178. PIERCE, R. De Gaulle and the RPF, *JP* 16.1 (1954), 96–119.
179. — Constitutional revision in France, *JP* 17.2 (1955), 221–47.
180. — The French election of January 1956, *JP* 19.3 (1957), 391–422.
181. PINTO, R. La loi du 17.8.1948 . . ., *RDP* 64.4 (1948), 517–48.
182. PLAISANT, M. Le contrôle de la politique étrangère par le Conseil de la République, *RPP* 598 (May 1950), 113–22.
183. POUILLON, J. Les sondages et la science politique, *RFSP* 1.11 (1951), 83–105.
184. PRÉLOT, M. Ministères éphémères, transformations profondes, *Politique* 37 (Sept. 1948), 720–30.
185. PROST, A. Géographie du Poujadisme, *Cahiers de la République* 1.1 (1956), 69–77; and see BRINDILLAC.
186a. RAPHAEL-LEYGUES, J. L'Assemblée de l'Union Française, *RPP* 611 (Oct. 1951), 113–22.
186b. RÉMOND, R. Les anciens combattants et la politique, *RFSP* 5.1 (1955), 267–90.
187., 188. — Droite et Gauche dans le catholicisme français contemporain, *RFSP* 8.3 and 4 (1958), 529–44 and 803–20.
189. RIDLEY, F. Parliamentary control of public enterprise in France, *P.Aff.* 10.3 (1957), 277–87.
190., 191. RIMBERT, P. L'avenir du Parti Socialiste, *Revue Socialiste* 54–5 (Feb. and March 1952), 123–32 and 288–97.
192. ROBINSON, K. Constitutional reform in French tropical Africa, *PS* 6.1 (1958), 45–69.
193a. ROCHE, E. L'élection présidentielle . . ., *RPP* 634 (Jan. 1954), 3–10.
193b. ROSS, A. M. Prosperity and labor relations in Italy and France, *Industrial and Labor Relations Review* 16.1 (Oct. 1962), 63–85.
194. A. S. L'élaboration de la loi électorale du 8 mai 1951, *RDP* 67.3 (1951), 841–88.
195. SAUVAGEOT, A. Le cabinet Ramadier et la pratique constitutionnelle, *RPP* 576 (March 1948), 239–52.
196. — Le Président de l'Assemblée Nationale, *RPP* 581 (Oct. 1948), 122–33.
197. SELIGSON, H. An evaluation of the Economic Council of France, *WPQ* 7 (1954), 36–50.
198. SEURIN, J. L. Les cabinets ministériels, *RDP* 72.6 (1956), 1207–94.
199. SHOUP, C. S. Taxation in France, *National Tax Journal* 8.4 (1955), 325–44.
200., 201. SOLAL-CELIGNY, J. La question de confiance sous la IV République, *RDP* 68.3 (1952), 721–56 and 72.2 (1956), 299–329.
202. SOUBEYROL, J. Le Président de l'Assemblée Nationale, *RDP* 72.3 (1956), 526–63.
203. SOULIER, A. La délibération du Comité Constitutionnel du 18.6.1948, *RDP* 65.2 (1949), 195–216.
204. STOETZEL, J. Voting behaviour in France, *British Journal of Sociology* 6.2 (1955), 104–22.
205. STURMTHAL, A. The structure of nationalized enterprises in France, *Political Science Quarterly* 67.3 (1952), 357–77.
206. SUEL, M. La Défense nationale et la Constitution, *RDP* 66.3 (1950), 649–75.
207. TAVERNIER, Y. Syndicalisme paysan et politique agricole, *RFSP* 12.3 (1962) 599–646.
208. TILLION, G. Démocratie et Colonialisme, *Preuves* 112 (June 1960), 3–16.
209. TINGUY: L. DE TINGUY DU POUËT, Pour un budget clair, complet,

(*over*)

efficace et moderne, *Revue politique des Idèes et des Institutions*, 15 and 30 Oct. 1949, 490–7 and 520–6.

210. TOUCHARD, J. Bibliographie et chronologie du poujadisme, *RFSP* 6.1 (1956), 18–43.

211. — La fin de la IVe République, *RFSP* 8.4 (1958), 917–28.

— and see BODIN.

212. VAN DYKE, V. The position and prospects of the communists in France, *Political Science Quarterly* 63.1 (1948), 45–81.

213. WALINE, J. Les groupes parlementaires en France, *RDP* 77.6 (1961), 1170–1237.

214. WALINE, M. Le contrôle contentieux des élections au Conseil Supérieur de la Magistrature, *RDP* 69.2 (1953), 448–69.

215. WEBER, E. La fièvre de la Raison, *WP* 10.4 (1958), 560–78.

216. — Nationalism, socialism and national-socialism in France, *French Historical Studies* 2.3 (1962), 273–307.

217. WEILL-RAYNAL, E. L'élection du Conseil de la République, *Revue Socialiste* 21 (May 1948), 467–76.

218. WILLIAMS, P. M. L'Affaire des Généraux, *Cambridge Journal* 4.8 (1951), 469–80.

219. — The French elections, *The Fortnightly* (Sept. 1951), 580–9.

220. — How the Fourth Republic died, *French Historical Studies* 3.1 (1963), 1–40.

221. — Constitutional revision in France, *PS* 3.2 (1955), 153–6.

222. — The case of the Leakages in France, *Occidente* 12.5 (1956), 387–414.

— and see NICHOLAS *et al.*

223. WRIGHT, G. French farmers and politics, *South Atlantic Quarterly* 51 (1952), 356–65.

224. — Four Red villages in France, *Yale Review* 41.3 (1952), 361–72.

225. — Agrarian syndicalism in post-war France, *APSR* 47.2 (1953), 402–16.

226. — Catholics and peasantry in France, *Political Science Quarterly* 68.4 (1953), 526–51.

227. — The resurgence of the Right in France, *Yale French Studies* 15 (Winter 1954–55), 3–11.

228. — The Red and the Black in rural France, *Yale Review* 52.1 (1962), 39–54.

229. — The Dreyfus echo: justice and politics in the Fourth Republic, *Yale Review* 48.3 (1959), 354–73.

JP	*Journal of Politics*
P.Adm.	*Public Administration*
P.Aff.	*Parliamentary Affairs*
PS	*Political Studies*
RDP	*Revue du droit public et de la science politique*
RFSP	*Revue française de science politique*
RPP	*Revue politique et parlementaire*
TM	*Temps modernes*
WPQ	*Western Political Quarterly*

APPENDIX I

CONSTITUTION OF THE FOURTH REPUBLIC

Articles 96 to 106, forming Chapter 12 (Transitional Provisions) are omitted. Where articles were amended in 1954 the new version appears beside the old. Page references to the text are given after each chapter heading (in Chapter 2, after each article).

PREAMBLE

(*pp. 292–3, 294*)

On the morrow of the victory gained by the free peoples over the regimes which attempted to enslave and degrade the human person, the French people proclaim anew that every human being, without distinction of race, religion or creed, possesses inalienable and sacred rights. They solemnly reaffirm the rights and liberties of man and the citizen consecrated by the Declaration of Rights of 1789 and the fundamental principles recognized by the laws of the Republic.

They further proclaim as most necessary in our time the following political, economic and social principles:

The law shall guarantee to women rights equal to those of men in all spheres.

Any man persecuted by reason of his activities in the cause of liberty shall have the right of asylum in the territories of the Republic.

It shall be the duty of all to work, and the right of all to obtain employment. None may suffer wrong, in his work or employment, by reason of his origin, opinions or beliefs.

Every man may protect his rights and interests by trade union or professional activity [*l'action syndicale*] and belong to the organization of his choice.

The right to strike shall be exercised within the framework of the laws which govern it.

Every worker shall participate, through his delegates, in collective bargaining on the conditions of labour as well as in the management of the firm.

Any property, or firm, which possesses or acquires the character of a national public service or of a *de facto* monopoly must come under common ownership.

The Nation shall ensure to the individual and family the conditions necessary to their development.

It shall guarantee to all, especially to the child, the mother and aged workers, the protection of their health, material security, rest and leisure. Every human being who is unable to work on account of his age, his physical or mental condition, or the economic situation, shall be entitled to obtain from the community decent means of support.

The Nation proclaims the solidarity and equality of all Frenchmen with respect to burdens imposed by national disasters.

The Nation shall guarantee the equal access of children and adults to education, professional training and culture. It shall be a duty of the State to organize free and secular public education at all levels.

The French Republic, faithful to its traditions, shall abide by the rules of public international law. It will undertake no war for the object of conquest and will never employ its forces against the liberty of any people.

On condition of reciprocity, France will accept the limitations of sovereignty necessary to the organization and defence of peace.

France together with the overseas peoples shall form a Union founded upon equality of rights and duties, without distinction of race or religion.

The French Union shall consist of nations and peoples who pool or co-ordinate their resources and their efforts to develop their respective civilizations, increase their well-being and ensure their security.

Faithful to her traditional mission, France proposes to guide the peoples for whom she has taken responsibility into freedom to administer themselves and conduct their own affairs democratically; rejecting any system of colonial rule based upon arbitrary power, she shall guarantee to all equal access to public office and the individual or collective exercise of the rights and liberties proclaimed or confirmed above.

THE INSTITUTIONS OF THE REPUBLIC

CHAPTER 1. SOVEREIGNTY

(*pp. 208, 280, 303 n. 57, 306*)

1. France shall be an indivisible, secular, democratic and social Republic.

2. (i) The national emblem shall be the tricolour flag, blue, white, red in three vertical bands of equal size. (ii) The national anthem shall be the 'Marseillaise'. (iii) The motto of the Republic shall be: 'Liberty, Equality, Fraternity'. (iv) Its principle shall be: Government of the people, for the people and by the people.

3. (i) National sovereignty belongs to the French people. (ii) No section of the people nor any individual may claim the exercise thereof. (iii) In constitutional matters, the people shall exercise it by the vote of their representatives and by referendum. (iv) In all other matters, they shall exercise it through their deputies in the National Assembly, elected by universal, equal, direct and secret voting.

4. All French nationals and subjects of both sexes, who have attained their majority and enjoy civil and political rights, shall have the vote under the conditions decided by law.

CHAPTER 2. PARLIAMENT

5. Parliament shall consist of the National Assembly and the Council of the Republic.

(*p. 280*)

6. (i) The length of the term of each Assembly, its mode of election, the conditions of eligibility, the rules of ineligibility and incompatibility shall be decided by law. (ii) However, the two Houses shall be elected on a territorial basis, the National Assembly by direct universal suffrage, the Council of the Republic by the communal and departmental collectivities, by indirect universal suffrage. The Council of the Republic shall be renewable by halves. (iii) Nevertheless the National Assembly may itself elect by proportional representation councillors whose number must not exceed a sixth of the total number of the members of the Council of the Republic. (iv) The number of members of the Council of the Republic cannot be less than 250 or greater than 350.

(*pp. 208–9, 278–9*)

7. [1946] (i) War cannot be declared without a vote of the National Assembly and the prior opinion of the Council of the Republic.

[1954] (i) *unchanged.*

(ii) A state of siege shall be proclaimed under the conditions prescribed by law.

(*pp. 208, 281, 303*)

8. Each of the two Houses shall judge the eligibility of its members and the regularity of their election; and alone may accept their resignation. (p. 210)

9. [1946] (i) The National Assembly shall convene automatically [*de plein droit*] for its annual session on the second Tuesday in January.
(ii) The total length of recesses cannot exceed four months. Adjournments of the sitting for more than ten days shall be considered as a recess.

(iii) The Council of the Republic shall sit at the same time as the National Assembly.
(*pp. 212, 281, 303n., 306*)

[1954] (i) The National Assembly shall convene automatically for its ordinary session on the first Tuesday in October.
(ii) When this session shall have lasted at least seven months, the prime minister may pronounce it closed by a decree issued in cabinet. This seven-month period shall not include recesses. Adjournments of the sitting for more than eight full days shall be considered as a recess.
(iii) *unchanged.*

10. (i) The sittings of the two Houses shall be public. Verbatim reports of debates and also parliamentary documents shall be published in the *Journal Officiel.* (ii) Each of the two Houses may go into committee for a secret session.

11. [1946] (i) Each of the two Houses shall elect its bureau every year, at the beginning of its session, by proportional representation of party groups.
(ii) When the two Houses assemble jointly to elect the President of the Republic, their bureau shall be that of the National Assembly.
(*pp. 215n, 217n, 237, 280*)

[1954] (i) Each of the two Houses shall elect its bureau every year at the beginning of its ordinary session and under the conditions provided by its standing orders.
(ii) *unchanged.*

12. [1946] When the National Assembly is not sitting, its bureau, supervising the activities of the cabinet, may convene Parliament; it must do so at the request of a third of the deputies or of the Prime Minister.

[1954] (i) When the National Assembly is not sitting, its bureau may convene Parliament for an extraordinary session; the president of the National Assembly must do so at the request of the prime minister or of the majority of the membership of the National Assembly. (ii) The prime minister shall pronounce the extraordinary session closed under the procedure prescribed in Article 9. (iii) When the extraordinary session is held at the request of the majority of the National Assembly or of its bureau, the closure decree cannot be issued before Parliament has exhausted the specific agenda for which it was convened.

(*p. 212–1, 303n.*)

13. The National Assembly alone shall vote the law. It cannot delegate this right (*pp. 191, 270–5, 303n., 306*)

14. [1946] (i) The Prime Minister and the members of Parliament may propose legislation.
(ii) Government bills and bills proposed by members of the National Assembly shall be registered with the latter's bureau.
(iii) Bills proposed by members of the Council of the Republic shall be registered with its bureau and transferred without debate to the bureau of the National Assembly. They shall be out of order if they would result in a reduction of revenue or a creation of expenditure.

[1954] (i) *unchanged.*
(ii) Government bills shall be registered with the bureau of the National Assembly or the bureau of the Council of the Republic. However, bills to authorize the ratification of the treaties prescribed in Article 27, budgetary or financial bills, and bills involving reduction of revenue or creation of expenditure must be registered with the bureau of the National Assembly.
(iii) Bills introduced by members of Parliament shall be registered with the bureau of the House to which they belong and transferred after adoption to the other House. Bills introduced by members of the Council of the Republic shall be out of order if they would result in a reduction of revenue or a creation of expenditure.

(*pp. 204, 257, 281–5*)

15. The National Assembly shall examine the bills [*projets et propositions de loi*] which are submitted to it, in committees of which it shall settle the number, composition and competence.
(*p. 242*)

16. (i) The budget bill shall be submitted to the National Assembly. (ii) This bill may contain strictly financial provisions only. (iii) An organic law will regulate the mode of presentation of the budget.
(*pp. 260, 263 and n., 268–9*)

17. (i) The Deputies in the National Assembly may propose expenditure. (ii) However, no proposal entailing an increase in the expenditure prescribed or creating new expenditure may be presented during the discussion of the budget, the estimates or supplementary credits.
(*pp. 263–5, 267, 282, 303n.*)

18. (i) The National Assembly shall regulate the nation's accounts. (ii) In this task it shall be assisted by the *Cour des Comptes*. (iii) The National Assembly may entrust to the *Cour des Comptes* any investigation or inquiry relating to the administration of public revenue and expenditure, or to the management of the treasury.
(*p. 338*)

19. Amnesty may be granted only by a law.
(*p. 208*)

20. [1946] (i) The Council of the Republic shall examine, in an advisory capacity, the bills voted by the National Assembly on first reading.
(ii) It shall give its opinion at latest within two months of being sent the bill by the National Assembly. Where the budget bill is concerned, this period may be shortened if necessary so as not to exceed the time used by the National Assembly for its examination and vote. When the National Assembly has determined to adopt an urgency procedure, the Council of the Republic shall give its opinion in the same period as that prescribed for the National Assembly's debates by the latter's standing orders. The periods prescribed in this article shall be suspended during recesses. They may be extended by decision of the National Assembly.
(iii) If the opinion of the Council of the Republic is in agreement or if it has not been given within the periods prescribed in the previous paragraph, the law shall be promulgated in the draft voted by the National Assembly.
(iv) If the opinion is not in agreement, the National Assembly shall examine the bill on second reading. It shall take its final and sovereign decision solely on the amendments proposed by the Council of the Republic, by accepting or rejecting them in whole or in part. Should these amendments be wholly or partially rejected, the vote on second reading of the bill shall take place by public ballot, by an absolute majority of the membership of the National Assembly, whenever the vote on the whole bill was

[1954] (i) Every bill shall be examined successively in the two Houses of Parliament with a view to securing adoption of an identical text.
(ii) Unless it has examined the bill on first reading, the Council of the Republic shall pronounce at latest within two months of being sent the draft adopted on first reading by the National Assembly.
(iii) Where budget bills and the finance bill are concerned, the period allowed the Council of the Republic must not exceed the time previously used by the National Assembly for their examination and vote. When urgency procedure is invoked by the National Assembly, the period shall be double that prescribed for the National Assembly's debates by the latter's standing orders.
(iv) If the Council of the Republic has not pronounced within the periods prescribed in the previous paragraphs, the law shall be ready to be [*en état d'être*] promulgated in the draft voted by the National Assembly.
(v) If no agreement is reached, each of the two Houses shall continue its examination. After two readings by the Council of the Republic, each House shall be allotted, for this purpose, the period taken by the other House over the previous reading, except that this period cannot be less than seven days or one day for the texts covered by the third paragraph.
(vi) Failing agreement within a period of a hundred days counted from the sending of the draft to the Council of the Republic for second reading, but reduced to a month for budgetary bills and for the finance

taken by the Council of the Republic in the same conditions.

bill and to fifteen days under the procedure applicable to urgent matters, the National Assembly may take its final decision either by reaffirming the last draft voted by it, or by modifying it by adopting one or several of the amendments proposed to this draft by the Council of the Republic. (vii) If the National Assembly exceeds or extends the periods of examination allotted to it, the period prescribed for agreement by the two Houses shall be increased by the same amount. (viii) The periods prescribed in this Article shall be suspended during recesses. They may be extended by decision of the National Assembly.

(*pp. 281, 282–5*)

21. No member of Parliament may be prosecuted, sought out, arrested, detained or judged on account of opinions expressed or votes cast by him in the exercise of his functions.
(*p. 210*)

22. [1946] During his term of office, no member of Parliament may be prosecuted or arrested for a crime or misdemeanour without the authorization of the House to which he belongs, except *flagrante delicto*. The detention or prosecution of a member of Parliament shall be suspended if the House to which he belongs so demands.

[1954] During the session no member of Parliament may be prosecuted or arrested for a crime or misdemeanour without the authorization of the House to which he belongs, except *flagrante delicto*. Any member of Parliament arrested out of session may vote by proxy as long as the House to which he belongs has not pronounced on the waiver of his parliamentary immunity. If it has not pronounced within the thirty days following the opening of the session, the arrested member shall be released automatically. Except in cases of *flagrant delicto*, authorized prosecution or final conviction, no member of Parliament may be arrested, out of session, without the authorization of the bureau of the House to which he belongs. The detention or prosecution of a member of Parliament shall be suspended if the House to which he belongs so demands.

(*pp. 210–11*)

23. Members of Parliament shall receive compensation settled in relation to the remuneration of a category of civil servants.
(*p. 211*)

24. (i) No one may belong both to the National Assembly and to the Council of the Republic. (ii) Members of Parliament may not belong to the Economic Council or the Assembly of the French Union.

CHAPTER 3. THE ECONOMIC COUNCIL

(*pp. 295–6*)

25. (i) An economic council, whose constitution shall be regulated by law, shall examine, in an advisory capacity, the bills [*projets et propositions de loi*] within its competence. The National Assembly shall submit these bills [*projets*] to it before debating them. (ii) The Economic Council may also be consulted by the Cabinet. It is necessarily so consulted on the establishment of a national economic plan having for its object the full employment of men and the rational use of material resources.

CHAPTER 4. DIPLOMATIC TREATIES

(*pp. 208, 224–5, 281, 283*)

26. Diplomatic treaties regularly ratified and published shall have force of law, even when they may be contrary to French domestic legislation, without requiring to ensure their enforcement any legislative provisions other than those necessary to ensure their ratification.

27. (i) Treaties relating to international organization, peace and commercial treaties, treaties which commit the finances of the State, those relating to the personal status and property rights of French citizens abroad, those which amend French domestic legislation, as well as those which allow the cession, exchange or acquisition of territory, shall be final only after having been ratified by force of law. (ii) No cession, no exchange and no acquisition of territory shall be valid without the consent of the populations concerned.

28. Since diplomatic treaties regularly ratified and published have authority superior to that of domestic legislation, their provisions may be neither abrogated, amended nor suspended except after a formal denunciation, notified through diplomatic channels. Whenever one of the treaties covered by Article 27 is concerned, the denunciation must be authorized by the National Assembly, except for commercial treaties.

CHAPTER 5. THE PRESIDENT OF THE REPUBLIC

(*pp. 196–7, 203, 204 and n., 208, 217n., 281, 299, 306*)

29. (i) The President of the Republic shall be elected by Parliament. (ii) He shall be elected for seven years. He shall be re-eligible once only.

30. The President of the Republic shall appoint in Cabinet the *Conseillers d'État*, the Grand Chancellor of the Legion of Honour, ambassadors and envoys extraordinary, members of the Higher Council and the Committee of National Defence, University rectors, prefects, directors of the civil service departments, general officers, representatives of the Government in the overseas territories.

31. (i) The President of the Republic shall be kept informed of international negotiations. He shall sign and ratify treaties. (ii) The President of the Republic shall accredit ambassadors and envoys extraordinary to foreign powers; foreign ambassadors and envoys extraordinary shall be accredited to him.

32. (i) The President of the Republic shall preside over the Cabinet. (ii) He shall have minutes of the meetings kept and shall retain them.

33. The President of the Republic shall preside, with the same functions, over the Higher Council and the Committee of National Defence and shall take the title of Commander-in-Chief.

34. The President of the Republic shall preside over the High Council of the Judiciary.

35. The President of the Republic shall exercise the right of reprieve [*le droit de grâce*] in the High Council of the Judiciary.

36. (i) The President of the Republic shall promulgate laws within ten days of the law as finally adopted being sent to the Government. This period shall be reduced to five days in cases of urgency declared by the National Assembly. (ii) Within the period laid down for promulgation, the President of the Republic, in a message stating his grounds, may ask the two Houses for a new deliberation, which cannot be refused. (iii) Failing promulgation by the President of the Republic within the periods laid down by this Constitution, the President of the National Assembly shall see to it.

37. The President of the Republic shall communicate with Parliament by messages addressed to the National Assembly.

38. Every act of the President of the Republic must be countersigned by the Prime Minister and by a Minister.

39. Not more than thirty days and not less than fifteen days before the expiry of the powers of the President of the Republic, Parliament shall proceed to elect a new President.

40. (i) If, in application of the preceding article, the election must take place within a period when the National Assembly is dissolved in conformity with Article 51, the powers of the incumbent President of the Republic shall be prolonged until the election of the new President. Parliament shall proceed to elect this new President within ten days of the election of the new National Assembly. (ii) In this event, the designation of the Prime Minister shall take place within fifteen days following the election of the new President of the Republic.

41. (i) In the event of an impediment duly recognized by a vote of Parliament, in the event of a vacancy due to death, resignation or any other reason, the President of the National Assembly shall temporarily assume the duties of the President of the Republic. He shall be replaced in his own duties by a Vice-President. (ii) The new President of the Republic shall be elected within ten days, except as stated in the preceding article.

42. (i) The President of the Republic shall be accountable only in cases of high treason. (ii) He can be impeached by the National Assembly and arraigned before the High Court of Justice under the conditions prescribed in Article 57 below.

43. The post of President of the Republic shall be incompatible with any other public office.

44. Members of families which once reigned over France shall not be eligible for the Presidency of the Republic.

CHAPTER 6. THE CABINET[1]

(*pp. 191n., 204, 209, 215n., 217n., 230ff, 236–8, 242, 281, 303nn.*)

45. [1946] (i) At the beginning of each legislature the President of the Republic, after the customary consultations, shall designate the Prime Minister.	[1954] (i) *unchanged.*
(ii) The latter shall submit to the National Assembly the programme and policy of the cabinet which he intends to form.	(ii) The latter shall choose the members of his cabinet and shall present the list to the National Assembly, before which he shall appear to obtain its confidence on the programme and policy which he expects to pursue, except when *force majeure* prevents the National Assembly from meeting.
(iii) The Prime Minister and Ministers cannot be appointed until the Prime Minister has been granted the Assembly's confidence in a public ballot and by an absolute majority of the Deputies, except when *force majeure* prevents the National Assembly from meeting.	(iii) The vote shall take place in a public ballot and by an ordinary majority.
(iv) The same procedure shall be followed in the course of a legislature in the event of a vacancy due to death, resignation or any other cause, except as stated in Article 52 below.	(iv) The same procedure shall be followed in the course of a legislature, in case of a vacancy in the premiership, except as stated in Article 52.
(v) No cabinet crisis occurring within a period of fifteen days from the appointment of the ministers shall count for the application of Article 51.	(v) *unchanged.*

46. The Prime Minister and the Ministers chosen by him shall be appointed by a decree of the President of the Republic.

47. (i) The Prime Minister shall ensure the enforcement of the laws. (ii) He shall make all civil and military appointments, except those prescribed in Articles 30, 46 and 84. (iii) The Prime Minister shall supervise the armed forces and co-ordinate preparations for national defence. (iv) The acts of the Prime Minister prescribed in this Article shall be countersigned by the ministers concerned.

48. (i) The Ministers shall be responsible collectively to the National Assembly for the general policy of the Cabinet and individually for their personal actions. (ii) They shall not be responsible to the Council of the Republic.

1. *Conseil des Ministres*, as everywhere except: in the phrase 'cabinet crisis' (*crise ministérielle*) in Arts. 45 (v) and 51 (i); and in Arts. 12, 45 (ii), 48 (i), 49 (iii, iv), 50 (i) and 52 (i) where the text has *Cabinet. Président du Conseil* is translated 'Prime Minister'.

49. [1946] (i) A vote of confidence may be called for only after discussion by the Cabinet; it may be called for only by the Prime Minister.	[1954] (i) *unchanged.*
(ii) A vote of confidence cannot occur until one clear day after it has been called for in the Assembly. It shall take place by a public ballot.	(ii) A vote of confidence cannot occur until twenty-four hours after it has been called for in the Assembly. It shall take place by a public ballot.
(iii) Confidence may be refused to the Cabinet only by an absolute majority of the Deputies in the Assembly.	(iii) Confidence shall be refused to the cabinet by an absolute majority of the deputies in the Assembly.
(iv)[2] This refusal shall entail the collective resignation of the Cabinet.	(iv)[2]

50. [1946] (i) The voting of a censure motion by the National Assembly shall entail the collective resignation of the Cabinet.	[1954] (i) *unchanged.*
(ii) This vote cannot occur until one clear day after the motion was introduced. It shall take place by public ballot.	(ii) The vote on a censure motion shall take place in the same conditions and manner as the vote of confidence.
(iii) A censure motion may be adopted only by an absolute majority of the Deputies in the Assembly.	(iii) *unchanged.*

51. (i) If, within a single period of eighteen months, two cabinet crises occur in the conditions prescribed in Articles 49 and 50, the dissolution of the National Assembly may be determined by the Cabinet, after an opinion from the President of the Assembly. The dissolution will be pronounced in conformity with this decision, by a decree of the President of the Republic. (ii) The provisions of the previous paragraph shall apply only at the expiry of the first eighteen months of the legislature.

52. [1946] (i) In the event of dissolution, the Cabinet, with the exception of the Prime Minister and the Minister of the Interior, shall remain in office to attend to current affairs.	[1954] (i) In the event of dissolution, the cabinet shall remain in office.
(ii) The President of the Republic shall designate the President of the National Assembly as Prime Minister. The latter shall designate the new Minister of the Interior in agreement with the Bureau of the National Assembly. He shall designate as senior Ministers without portfolio [*Ministres d'État*] members of the party groups not represented in the Government.	(ii) However, if the dissolution was preceded by the adoption of a censure motion, the President of the Republic shall appoint the president of the National Assembly as prime minister and minister of the interior.
[*over*	[*over*

2. Inadvertently repealed in 1954 owing to an error in the paragraphing of the constitution as promulgated in 1946, which had to be corrected retrospectively.

(iii) A general election shall take place not less than twenty, nor more than thirty days after the dissolution.	(iii) *unchanged.*
(iv) The National Assembly shall convene automatically on the third Tuesday following its election.	(iv) *unchanged.*

53. (i) Ministers shall have access to the two Houses and to their Committees. They must be heard when they so request. (ii) They may be assisted in debates in either House by commissioners designated by decree.

54. The Prime Minister may delegate his powers to a Minister.

55. In the event of a vacancy due to death or any other cause, the Cabinet shall instruct one of its members to exercise temporarily the functions of Prime Minister.

CHAPTER 7. THE RESPONSIBILITY OF MINISTERS UNDER THE PENAL CODE

(*pp. 298–9*)

56. Ministers shall be legally responsible for crimes and misdemeanours committed in the exercise of their functions.

57. (i) Ministers may be impeached by the National Assembly and arraigned before the High Court of Justice. (ii) The National Assembly shall take its decision by secret ballot and by an absolute majority of its membership, with the exception of those who may be called upon to take part in the prosecution, investigation or judgment of the case.

58. The High Court of Justice shall be elected by the National Assembly at the beginning of each legislature.

59. The organization of the High Court of Justice and the procedure followed before it shall be decided by a special law.

CHAPTER 8. THE FRENCH UNION: I. PRINCIPLES

(*pp. 193, 281, 293–5, 303n., 304*)

60. The French Union shall be composed, on the one hand of the French Republic which comprises metropolitan France, the overseas departments and Territories, and on the other hand of the Associated Territories and States.

61. The position of the Associated States within the French Union shall depend in each case on the act which defines their relationship with France.

62. The members of the French Union shall pool all their resources in order to guarantee the defence of the whole Union. The Government of the Republic shall undertake the co-ordination of these resources and the direction of the policy appropriate to prepare and ensure this defence.

II. ORGANIZATION

63. The central organs of the French Union shall be the Presidency, the High Council and the Assembly.

64. The President of the French Republic shall be president of the French Union, whose permanent interests he shall represent.

65. (i) The High Council of the French Union shall consist of the President of the Union as chairman, a delegation of the French Government, and the representatives that each of the Associated States shall be entitled to accredit to the President of the Union. (ii) Its function shall be to assist the Government in the general direction of the Union.

66. (i) The Assembly of the French Union shall consist, half of members representing metropolitan France, and half of members representing the overseas departments and Territories and the Associated States. (ii) An organic law will decide the conditions under which the different sections of the population may be represented.

67. The members of the Assembly of the Union shall be elected, for the overseas departments and Territories, by the territorial assemblies; they shall be elected, for metropolitan France, in the proportion of two-thirds by the members of the National Assembly representing metropolitan France and one-third by the members of the Council of the Republic representing metropolitan France.

68. The Associated States may designate delegates to the Assembly of the Union within limits and conditions settled by a law and a domestic act of each State.

69. (i) The President of the French Union shall convene the Assembly of the French Union and close its sessions. He must convene it at the request of half its members. (ii) The Assembly of the French Union cannot sit during Parliamentary recesses.

70. The rules of Articles 8, 10, 21, 22 and 23 shall apply to the Assembly of the French Union under the same conditions as to the Council of the Republic.

71. (i) The Assembly of the French Union shall be cognizant of the bills or proposals which are submitted to it for its opinion by the National Assembly or the Government of the French Republic or the Governments of the Associated States. (ii) The Assembly shall be entitled to pronounce on motions presented by one of its members, and, if it decides to consider them, to instruct its Bureau to send them to the National Assembly. It may make proposals to the French Government and to the High Council of the French Union. (iii) To be in order, the motions covered by the preceding paragraph must relate to legislation pertaining to the Overseas Territories.

72. (i) In the Overseas Territories, legislative power shall belong to Parliament in matters of criminal law, the regulation of civil liberties and political and administrative organization. (ii) In all other matters, French laws shall apply in the Overseas Territories only by express provision or if they have been extended by decree to the Overseas Territories after an opinion from the Assembly of the Union. (iii) Further, by derogation from Article 13, special provisions for each territory may be enacted by the President of the Republic in Cabinet after a prior opinion from the Assembly of the Union.

III. OVERSEAS DEPARTMENTS AND TERRITORIES

73. The legislative system of the overseas departments shall be the same as that of the metropolitan departments, unless otherwise determined by law.

74. (i) The Overseas Territories shall be granted a special status which takes into account their particular interests within the framework of the general interests of the Republic. (ii) This status and the internal organization of each Overseas Territory or group of territories shall be settled by law, after an opinion from the Assembly of the French Union and consultation with the Territorial Assemblies.

75. (i) The individual status of a member of the Republic and of the French Union shall be subject to change. (ii) Alterations of status and transfers from one category to another, within the framework settled by Article 60, may follow only from a law voted by Parliament, after consultation with the Territorial Assemblies and the Assembly of the Union.

76. (i) The powers of the Republic shall be vested in the representative of the Government in each territory or group of territories. He shall be the head of the territorial administration. (ii) He shall be responsible to the Government for his actions.

77. An elected Assembly shall be instituted in each territory. The electoral system, composition and competence of this Assembly shall be decided by law.

78. (i) In the groups of territories, the management of common interests shall be entrusted to an Assembly consisting of members elected by the Territorial Assemblies. (ii) Its composition and powers shall be settled by law.

79. The Overseas Territories shall elect representatives to the National Assembly and to the Council of the Republic under the conditions prescribed by law.

80. All subjects of the Overseas Territories shall have the status [*qualité*] of citizen, by the same right as French nationals of metropolitan France or of the Overseas Territories. Special laws will lay down the conditions under which they exercise their rights as citizens.

81. All French nationals and subjects of the French Union shall have the status of citizen of the French Union which shall ensure for them the enjoyment of the rights and liberties guaranteed by the Preamble to the present Constitution.

82. (i) Citizens who are not subject to French civil law shall retain their personal status [*subject to indigenous law*] so long as they do not renounce it. (ii) This status [*statut*] may in no circumstance constitute a ground for refusing or restricting the rights and liberties pertaining to the status [*qualité*] of French citizen.

CHAPTER 9. THE HIGH COUNCIL OF THE JUDICIARY
(*pp. 204n., 208, 299–301*)

83. (i) The High Council of the Judiciary shall consist of fourteen members:
(ii) The President of the Republic, chairman;
(iii) The Keeper of the Seals, Minister of Justice, vice-chairman;
(iv) Six persons elected for six years by the National Assembly, by a two-thirds majority, outside its membership, six alternates being elected under the same conditions;
(v) Six persons designated as follows:
(vi) Four members of the judicial profession elected for six years, representing each branch of the profession, under the conditions prescribed by law, four alternates being elected in the same conditions;
(vii) Two members designated for six years by the President of the Republic outside Parliament and the judiciary, but within the legal professions, two alternates being designated under the same conditions.
(viii) The decisions of the High Council of the Judiciary shall be taken by a majority vote. In the event of a tied vote, that of the chairman shall prevail.

84. (i) The President of the Republic shall appoint, on the proposal of the High Council of the Judiciary, to judicial posts, except for those of public prosecutor.

(ii) The High Council of the Judiciary shall ensure, in conformity with the law, the discipline of these judges, their independence and the administration of the courts. (iii) These judges [*les magistrates de siège*] shall not be removable.

CHAPTER 10. TERRITORIAL COLLECTIVITIES
(*pp. 260, 347*)

85. (i) The French Republic, one and indivisible, shall recognize the existence of territorial collectivities. (ii) These collectivities shall be the communes and departments, and the Overseas Territories.

86. The framework, the extent, the possible regrouping and the organization of the communes and departments, and the Overseas Territories shall be settled by law.

87. (i) The territorial collectivities shall administer themselves freely by councils elected by universal suffrage. (ii) Their mayor or president shall be responsible for carrying out the decisions of these councils.

88. The co-ordination of the activity of civil servants, the representation of the national interest and the administrative supervision of the territorial collectivities shall be ensured, within the departmental framework, by Government delegates designated in Cabinet.

89. (i) Organic laws will extend departmental and communal liberties; they may prescribe for certain large cities, rules of operation and structures different from those of small communes, and may include special provisions for certain departments; they will decide the conditions of implementation of Articles 85 to 88 above. (ii) Laws will also decide the conditions under which the local services of the central administration shall operate, in order to bring the administration closer to those with whom it deals [*les administrés*].

CHAPTER 11. AMENDMENT OF THE CONSTITUTION
(*pp. 191, 193, 208, 209n., 215n., 217n., 281, 301–6*)

90. (i) The amendment procedure shall be as follows: (ii) Amendment must be decided on by a resolution adopted by an absolute majority of the membership of the National Assembly. (iii) The resolution shall specify the object of the amendment. (iv) It shall be submitted, after a minimum period of three months, to a second reading at which proceedings must follow the same conditions as at the first, unless the Council of the Republic, apprised by the National Assembly, shall have adopted the same resolution by an absolute majority. (v) After this second reading, the National Assembly shall draft a bill to amend the Constitution. This bill shall be submitted to Parliament and voted by the same majority and in the same manner prescribed for an ordinary law. (vi) It shall be submitted to a referendum, unless it has been adopted on second reading by the National Assembly by a two-thirds majority or has been voted by a three-fifths majority in each of the two assemblies. (vii) The bill shall be promulgated by the President of the Republic as a constitutional law within eight days of its adoption. (viii) No constitutional amendment concerning the existence of the Council of the Republic may be adopted without the agreement of this Council or recourse to the referendum procedure.

91. (i) The President of the Republic shall be chairman of the Constitutional Committee. (ii) It shall comprise the President of the National Assembly, the President of the Council of the Republic, seven members elected by the National

Assembly at the beginning of each annual session, by proportional representation of party groups, and chosen outside its membership, and three members elected under the same conditions by the Council of the Republic. (iii) The Constitutional Committee shall examine whether the laws voted by the National Assembly presuppose [*supposent*] amendment of the Constitution.

92. (i) Within the period allowed for promulgation of the law, the Committee shall be apprised by a joint reference from the President of the Republic and the President of the Council of the Republic, the Council having taken its decision by an absolute majority of its membership. (ii) The Committee shall examine the law, shall endeavour to promote an agreement between the National Assembly and the Council of the Republic, and if it does not succeed, shall give a ruling within five days of the reference to it. In cases of urgency, this period shall be reduced to two days. (iii) It shall be competent to give a ruling only on the possibility of amending the provisions of Chapters 1 to 10 of the present Constitution.

93. (i) A law which, in the opinion of the Committee, implies amendment of the Constitution, shall be returned to the National Assembly for a new reading. (ii) If Parliament confirms its first vote, the law cannot be promulgated before the Constitution has been amended in the manner prescribed in Article 90. (iii) If the law is held to be in conformity with the provisions of Chapters 1 to 10 of the present Constitution, it shall be promulgated within the period prescribed by Article 36, the latter being extended by the periods prescribed for in Article 92 above.

94. In the event of the occupation by foreign troops of the whole or part of metropolitan French territory, no amendment proceedings may be initiated or continued.

95. The republican form of government cannot be the object of an amendment proposal.

USING THE INDEX

Arrangement

Principal page references are set in **bold** type.

French names are indexed according to French practice, with the article, but not *de* or geographical prefixes, as part of the name: e.g. Bas-Rhin and Haut-Rhin under R, de Gaulle under G, Le Pen under L, de La Rocque under L, Mendès-France under M.

Organizations are indexed under their initials, where these are used in the text, at the beginning of the first letter in the title: e.g. CFTC is the first entry under C. Full titles are in the list of abbreviations on p. ix (and for collective books, indexed by short title, on pp. 465 f.).

Where a source is quoted on three or more pages, the index references are preceded by 'cit. nn.': all subsequent references are to footnotes and not to the text.

Biographical notes (corrected to the end of 1963)

For political careers beginning before 1945, only the date of first election to either house of Parliament (MP) or appointment as prime minister (PM) is normally given. For those extending into the Fifth Republic, only major changes of party are noted. In the Fourth, a few shifts between conservative groups are not recorded. Where a member sat both before and after 1958 for a department which formed more than one constituency in the Fourth Republic, the constituency number is pre-1958. Members of de Gaulle's provisional government at Algiers in 1943–4 (*commissaires*) are referred to as 'Gaull. m.' The June and November elections of 1946 are referred to as '46J and '46N.

Abbreviations

A:	*see* Appendix
admin	-istration, -ive
AFU:	Assembly of French Union
amb	-assador
b:	born
CR:	Council of the Republic
cand	-idate
cap	-ital (of department)
Com	-munist
Cons	-ervative
cons.-gen.:	conseil-général, departmental council
const	-itutional
C'tee:	committee
d.:	deputy
dd.:	died
dir. de cab	directeur de cabinet
diss	-ident
econ	-omic
elec	-toral
gov	-ernment
MP	member of parliament
m:	minister, -ry
NA	National Assembly
org	-anization
P.	Party
PM	Prime minister
Parl	-iament, -ary
Peas	-ant
Pres	-ident
Prog	-ressive (pro-Com.)
Rad	-ical
rapp.-g.:	rapporteur-general of the finance committee
rep	-resentation, -ives
Rep	-ublican
RI	Republican Independent
S:	senator
sec.-g.:	secrétaire-général
Soc	-ialist
TU	trade union, -ist

INDEX